ADVANCED FINANCIAL RISK MANAGEMENT

TOOLS AND TECHNIQUES FOR INTEGRATED CREDIT RISK AND INTEREST RATE RISK MANAGEMENT

ADVANCED FINANCIAL RISK MANAGEMENT

TOOLS AND TECHNIQUES FOR INTEGRATED
CREDIT RISK AND INTEREST RATE RISK
MANAGEMENT

Donald R. van Deventer
Kenji Imai
Mark Mesler

John Wiley & Sons (Asia) Pte Ltd.

Other Wiley Editorial Offices

John Wiley & Sons, Inc., 111 River Street, Hoboken, NJ 07030, USA
John Wiley & Sons Ltd, The Atrium Southern gate, Chichester P019 8SQ, England
John Wiley & Sons (Canada) Ltd, 22Worcester Road, Rexdale, Ontario M9W 1L1, Canada
John Wiley & Sons Australia Ltd, 33 Park Road (PO Box 1226), Milton, Queensland 4064, Australia
Wiley-VCH, Pappelallee 3, 69469Weinheim, Germany

Library of Congress Cataloging-in-Publication Data
0-470-82126-4

Typeset in 10.5/13 points, Times by Cepha Imaging Pvt. Ltd., India
Printed in Singapore by Saik Wah Press Pte Ltd
10 9 8 7 6 5 4 3 2 1

Dedication

For Ella Ke'alohilani Ku van Deventer

One day on Kailua beach with you is one trillion times more important than this book.

D.v.D.

For Yasuko, Tomoki, and Anna.

K.I.

For my parents, Leon Mesler and Patricia Crowell.

M.M.

Contents

Credit Risk Models 257

Interest Rate and Credit Model Testing 347

Risk Management Applications, Instrument by Instrument 393

Introduction

R isk management has changed a lot since the first of the three of us grad-
uated with a newly minted Ph.D. and went to work as a banker in 1977.
We know so much more now than we knew then, and everything we can do
now is so much better than what we could do then. We have all the data on the
balance sheet of a major financial institution at our finger tips, or we should
have. We know the mark-to-market value of every transaction on the balance
sheet as of the end of trading last night, or we should know it. We know the
potential variation in the cash flow or net income of our financial institution,
or at least we should know it. Most importantly, we know the risk that macro-
economic factors like interest rates and the state of the economy mean for every
individual, corporation or government borrower's default probability. Even
more importantly, we know what they mean for the default probability of our
own institution.

The evolution in our views on creation of shareholder value added can be
traced in the books that the three of us have been involved in. Dennis Uyemura
and Don van Deventer focused on the common sense integration of risk management with shareholder value creation in *Financial Risk Management in
Banking* in 1993. Kenji Imai and Don van Deventer discussed the exciting
power of interest rate term structure models as risk management tools in
Financial Risk Analytics (1996), much of which is updated in this book. Kenji
and Don discussed credit risk modeling using the structural and reduced form
models in *Credit Risk Models and the Basel Accords* in 2003.

The three of us have collectively been involved in risk management
practice and implementation for more than 65 years. More than 25 of these
years have been devoted to the Kamakura Risk Manager enterprise-wide risk
management system and its sister products, the default probabilities from
Kamakura Risk Information Services. In this role, we have gone from literally a blank piece of paper to more than 250,000 lines of software code and
risk management technology now used by major financial institutions all
over the world. When it comes to the implementation of the approach to
risk management we outline in this book, we have 'been there and done that'.

1

This book reflects the collective experience of our colleagues at Kamakura, our clients and our friends in the industry who have provided so much valuable advice and counsel.

We would like to thank all of our colleagues at Kamakura who have made this book so much better than it would have been without their thoughts. First and foremost is Professor Robert Jarrow, Kamakura's director of research since 1995. Bob has been a constant source of inspiration and motivation and so much of what we explain in this book is a practical banker's interpretation of Bob's guidance on the risk management issues of the day. Warren Sherman and Leonard Matz, two of the key members of the managing committee at Kamakura, have insured that we remain relentlessly focused on practical solutions to risk management problems for all our clients using the best available computer science and financial theory. Without their help, this book would have never been written.

We would also like to thank many financial market participants around the world for their ideas and encouragement. We can't mention all of them here, but we need to single out a few for special mention: Steve Carritt, Alejandra de Gaustad, Jeong-rim Park, Tim Pickering, Jim Salem, Robert Selvaggio, Rolf Hengsteler, Rich Owens, Brent Smith, Brian Ranson, Cameron Evans, Howie McQuarrie, S. H. Jeon, Anastasia Marina, Junji Hatano, Barbara Zvan, Leo de Bever, and Francois Gingras have all made an enormous contribution to anything you like about the 44 chapters which follow. Anything that you don't like is the sole responsibility of the authors.

The authors would like to thank Nick Wallwork and his colleagues of John Wiley & Sons in Singapore. Nick was the inspiration for this book, and he and his colleagues are a wonderful pleasure to work with.

We would also like to thank our families and friends for their enormous patience while this book was being prepared. We want to assure you that we will now turn our full attention to you and to a thorough enjoyment of the Polynesian kingdom that we call home.

We look forward to our readers' comments and suggestions about what follows.

Donald R. van Deventer
Kenji Imai
Mark Mesler

Kamakura Corporation
Honolulu, Hawaii
September, 2004

Risk Management:
Definitions and Objectives

A Risk Management Synthesis: Market Risk, Credit Risk, Liquidity Risk and Asset and Liability Management

The field of risk management has undergone an enormous change in the last 30 years and the pace of change is accelerating. It hasn't always been this way in the risk management field, as Frederick Macaulay must have realized nearly 40 years after introducing the concept of duration in 1938. The oldest of the three authors entered the banking industry in the aftermath of what seemed at the time to be a major interest rate crisis in 1974–1975 in the United States. Financial institutions were stunned at the heights to which interest rates could rise, and they began looking for ways to manage the risk. Savings and loan associations, whose primary asset classes were 30-year fixed-rate mortgages, hurriedly began offering floating-rate mortgages for the first time. In the midst of this panic by management, where did risk managers turn? To a mark-to-market concept and hedging using Macaulay duration which we discuss in Chapters 4–10? Unfortunately for many of the institutions involved, the answer was no.

During this era in the U.S., a mark-to-market approach came naturally to members of the management team who rose through the ranks on the trading floor. In this era, however, and even today, chief executive officers who passed through the trading floor on their way to the top were rare. Instead, most of the senior management team grew up looking at traditional financial statements and thinking of risk on a net income basis rather than a mark-to-market basis.

As a result, the first tool to which management at the time turned was simulation of net income, normally over a time horizon of one to two years. Given the Wall Street analyst pressures that persist today, it is no surprise that net income simulation was the tool of choice. What is surprising, however, is that it was often the only choice and the results of that decision were fatal to a large number of U.S. financial institutions when interests rates rose to 21% in the late 1970s and early 1980s. One trillion dollars later, U.S. financial institutions regulators had bailed out hundreds of failed financial institutions that disappeared because of the unhedged interest rate risk and the credit risk which was driven by the high interest rate environment.

This must have been only mildly satisfying to the fans of Frederick Macaulay and his analytical, mark-to-market approach to risk management. Even in the mid-1970s when a moderate crisis had just occurred and hints of the crisis to come were getting stronger, resistance to mark-to-market concepts in risk management were strong and the costs to its advocates were high in career terms. The eldest of the three authors, encouraged by the U.S. Comptroller of the Currency, pushed hard for the adoption of mark-to-market-based risk management at the sixth largest bank in the U.S. from 1977 to 1982. The chief financial officer, one of the brightest people in banking at the time, listened carefully but did not accept the concept. He was so programmed by that stage of his career that the mark-to-market approach to risk management was a foreign language that he would never feel comfortable speaking. The advocate of the mark-to-market approach to risk management had to change firms.

While this type of financial accounting-focused executive is still in the majority today, the risk they face from ignoring mark-to-market risk measurement is much larger and more subtle. The National Australia Bank, one of the most sophisticated financial institutions in the Asia-Pacific region, reported a loss on foreign exchange options trading in January 2004 of A$360 million. Mark-to-market technology, and more importantly, how to undertake mark-to-market risk management, was at the heart of this incident. An understanding of mark-to-market risk management is essential to have at both the board of directors level and at the senior management level. The lack of this understanding in the right places can have serious consequences.

Risk Management: Definitions and Objectives

In the last decade, the definition of risk management has changed dramatically for reasons we outline in this chapter. At this point, the best practice definition of risk management can be summarized as follows:

> *Risk management is the discipline that clearly shows management the risks and returns of every major strategic decision at both the institutional level and the transaction level. Moreover, the risk management discipline shows how to change strategy in order to bring the risk return trade-off into line with the best long and short-term interests of the institution.*

This definition has no boundaries in terms of the nature of the institution. It applies to:

- pension funds;
- insurance companies;
- industrial corporations;

- commercial banks;
- cooperative financial institutions, such as savings banks;
- securities firms;
- national government treasuries;
- foundations and charities.

Similarly, this definition has no boundaries like those that have traditionally constrained the discipline of risk management from achieving this integrated approach to risk management. This definition of risk management includes within it the overlapping and inseparable sub-disciplines such as:

- credit risk;
- market risk;
- asset and liability management;
- operational risk;
- performance measurement;
- transfer pricing;

and many other sub-disciplines. The primary focus of this book is to show how to execute the practice of risk management in a way that is fully integrated and makes no distinction between these sub-disciplines. There should be no distinctions between these sub-disciplines of risk management because they are simply different views of the same risk. They share the same mathematical roots, the same data needs, the same management reporting needs, and increasingly, the same information technology infrastructure, which we discuss in detail in Chapter 43.

Even more importantly, as the incident in Australia illustrates, this definition of risk management applies to all layers of management and to all of those in positions of responsibility for the institution, including the board of directors, the company's auditors, and the institution's regulators, if any. All layers of management share a common obligation with respect to the practice of risk management. The Basel Committee on Banking Supervision (see www.bis.org) has recognized this, as have banking regulators all over the world, in their increasingly strict 'separation of duties' requirements because of incidents like this:

Internal auditors at one of the biggest firms on Wall Street, ABC & Co., approached a trader in exotic options and asked how they could come up with an independent estimate of a certain type of volatility. The trader replied "Call Joe at XYZ Brothers at 555-1234." The auditors retired to their offices to dial Joe but before they did the trader had called Joe himself, an old drinking buddy, and told him what answer to give to the auditors' question.[1]

Conflicts of interest become starkly apparent in the execution of best practice risk management. All too often over the last 30 years, the only people expert enough to assess the risk of certain complex transactions have had a vested interest in mis-stating the risk, and often the valuation, of the transactions. For example, early reports on the incident in Australia[2] speculate that the formula used for estimating the volatility of out-of-the-money foreign exchange options gave the traders a mark-to-market value that deviated substantially from true market prices. Traders' mark-to-market gains, using these formulas, were automatic but artificial. The *Australian Financial Review* reported on January 30 2004 that National Australia Bank's senior foreign exchange trader admitted that he took advantage of loopholes in the Bank's back office systems, in-house market risk management system, and the dealing room accounting system in order to create paper profits.

This incident confirms the risk that comes from an expertise differential between trading and risk control. Fortunately, the developments in financial technology over the last 30 years have led to a sharp narrowing of the gap in spite of the National Australia Bank incident. More importantly, the incident at National Australia Bank confirms the need for this progress to continue. We can trace the rapid advance in risk management technology to a number of factors.

Advances in Integrated Risk Management and Institutional Barriers to Progress

For most of the last 30 years, risk management has been compartmentalized in narrowly defined areas. Market risk was focused on a narrowly defined set of instruments accounted for on a market value basis, traded on a trading floor, with prices that were generally observable in the market. Credit risk was split into two sub-disciplines that were often disconnected:

- The decision about whether or not to originate a particular loan or private placement;
- The on-going assessment of portfolio quality on instruments that have already been put on the balance sheet.

The first discipline was largely based on internal and external ratings of riskiness, which we discuss in Chapter 15, and traditional financial analysis. The second discipline was conceptually more difficult but lower quality

---

[1] We wish to thank our colleague Tatsuo Kishi for this story about his former employer, a well-known investment banking firm.

[2] According to a story appearing in January 2004 and posted on www. risklatte.com.

analytics normally prevailed—it consisted mainly of measuring the slowly changing migration of the portfolio from one distribution of ratings in the portfolio to another. Neither discipline led to useful insights on pricing, valuation or hedging of risk.

The asset and liability management risk in major banks and insurance companies was normally confined to very short-term forecasts for financial accounting-based net income. Best practice consisted of using a small number of scenarios for testing net income sensitivity to specific changes in the shape and level of yield curves. In commercial banks, at least, both sides of the balance sheet were included in this exercise. In life insurance companies and pension funds, the analysis of income and cash flow was generally restricted to the investment portfolio—the asset side of the institution only. The actuaries were responsible for the liability side and were not part of the income simulation process.

Performance measurement was another compartment with substantial differences among types of institutions, even though their balance sheets were nearly identical in composition. To a pension plan, performance measurement applied only to the asset side of the organization and it referred solely to whether the investment portfolio, sector by sector, outperformed a specific benchmark index. To a commercial bank, performance measurement meant 'transfer pricing', the assignment of financial accounting profits to each asset and liability on the balance sheet of the bank and the subsequent compilation of financial accounting profits for each business unit. This process was further complicated by 'capital allocation' that assigned capital to business units even if they had no liabilities and could have used the same performance measurement approach as a pension plan.

In Chapters 39–42, we explore these institutional differences in detail and reconcile the differences in implications and management actions, even though the financial institutions and major corporate treasury operations we are discussing are very similar to each other.

A number of key breakthroughs in financial theory, financial instruments and computer science have proven that this 'silo' approach to risk management is no longer tenable. Furthermore, these developments have shown that the differences in risk management approaches by institution type are unnecessary and often counterproductive.

The key events in this realization are summarized as the following:

Black-Scholes options model

The introduction of the options pricing model by Fisher Black and Myron Scholes [1973] showed how to value a financial security that until that point had been considered impossible to value if there was not an observable market price. Just as importantly, Black and Scholes and associates like Robert Merton showed explicitly how to incorporate riskiness into security valuation. This era provided the foundation for modern risk management.

Merton and Vasicek term structure models

In the middle of the 1970s, Robert Merton [1973] and Oldrich Vasicek [1977] introduced models of the yield curve that were consistent with the 'no arbitrage' foundations of Black and Scholes and based on the assumption that the short-term rate of interest varies randomly. From these assumptions, which we address in detail in Chapters 10–12, they were able to derive the entire yield curve and price a wide array of fixed income securities analytically.

Interest rate risk crisis

The interest rate 'spikes' of the late 1970s and early 1980s in the U.S. created a strong need to put the new risk management technologies to work as soon as possible.

Advent of the personal computer

The advent of the personal computer and popular spreadsheet software democratized risk management analysis, bringing to the working level the potential to go far beyond the insights that could be gained by large, old-fashioned mainframe systems then dominating the financial services industry. High quality risk management analysis could be explored and proven on small budgets. Once these 'proof of concept' explorations were accepted by management, enterprise-wide risk management had the political support necessary to commit major resources to a larger, state of the art system.

Expansion of the interest rate derivatives market

The interest rate derivatives market triggered a 'chicken and egg' relationship between financial theory and the exploding market in interest rate swaps, caps, and floors in the middle and late 1980s. New financial analytics for valuing these instruments ensured that popular acceptance of these risk management tools was very rapid.

Rapid declines in the cost of computer storage capacity

Rapid declines in the cost of computer storage capability meant that transaction-level risk management could become a reality in two senses. First, multiple copies of the same data could be used by many analysts, who no longer were blocked from access to the (formerly) single mainframe source of the data. Second, processing speed and level of precision took a great leap forward.

Monte Carlo simulation gains acceptance

Another important development in the mid-1980s was the rapid adoption of monte carlo simulation as a risk management tool, further accelerating the analysis of risk and return by major financial institutions. Faster computer chips were an essential component in making this step forward possible.

Development of quantitative credit models and the introduction of credit derivatives

The next major development that resulted in an acceleration of progress in risk management was the introduction of quantitative models of credit risk and the proliferation of credit derivatives such as credit default swaps, first to default swaps, and collateralized debt obligations. Researchers such as Robert Jarrow [1999, 2001], Jarrow and Turnbull [1995], and Duffie and Singleton [1999] constructed elegant models of credit risk on a random interest rate framework, completing the analytical integration of credit risk and interest rate risk.

Measuring the Trade-Offs between Risk and Return

The implications of these developments for integrated risk management and a more sophisticated trade-off between risk and return were huge. For the first time, risk could be measured instead of just debated. In addition, alternative strategies could be assessed and both risk and return could be estimated using transaction-level detail for the entire institution and any sub portfolio within the institution. Just as importantly, these developments eliminated any rationale for the 'silo' management of risk except that of sheer corporate politics. Market risk, credit risk, and asset and liability management all use the same mathematics. They use the same data, they are caused by the same macro-economic factors and they impact their institutions in the same way. Any argument that they are separate and distinct is a hard one to justify from the perspective of the twenty-first century.

The authors hope that this book will help convince any doubters by the time the last chapter is read.

When Bad Things Happen to Good People

In Chapter 2, we discuss the nature of risk and return measurement and the organizational structure consistent with best practice in risk management. Before dealing with these concepts, however, general discussion about risks taken that turn out badly provides some practical insights into the kinds of analytics we need to undertake in order to assess the likelihood, magnitude, and timing of specific risks.

These three factors are closely linked. The likelihood of a risk occurring depends on the time interval over which we measure the probability of occurrence. A given risk (like an earthquake) can have different magnitudes, and the probability of an event of size X is not the same as the probability of an event of size Y. Finally, timing is everything. An earthquake tomorrow has a greater present value cost than an earthquake in the year 2525.

All of these points are obvious, and yet much of risk management has been slow to progress from simple one-period models that assume many different risks that are homogeneous in nature. For example, a common calculation in the collateralized debt obligation (CDO) market is to assume there is only one period (of perhaps five years in length), that all reference names have the same default probability, and that all pairs of reference names have the same pairwise correlation in their default probability. This simplistic analysis seriously understates the risk of buying a CDO tranche.

We can understand why the likelihood, magnitude and timing of risks have to be analyzed in a more sophisticated manner by discussing how a specific type of institution can fail and what actions would have had to be taken to save the institution.

U.S. Savings and Loan Crisis

The U.S. savings and loan crisis of the 1980s was predominantly due to interest rate risk, together with interest rate-induced credit risk. The savings and loan associations owned huge portfolios of home mortgage loans with fixed-rates for 30 years. Most of the coupons on these loans were in the 8–10% range, although older loans bore much lower coupons. Passbook savings accounts were federally insured and yielded less than half of the mortgage coupons at the beginning of the crisis. Interest rates on the accounts were capped by federal 'Regulation Q'. As short-term rates began to rise, the savings and loan associations were reasonably complacent. They funded a fairly modest portion of their balance sheets with certificates of deposit.

As rates began to rise, two things became increasingly clear to the public, if not to management of the savings and loan associations. The first point was that the value of the mortgages was declining rapidly. The second point was that the savings and loan associations had a very limited ability to hedge the interest rate risk exposure they had, so that things were sure to get worse as interest rates rose. Finally, the public began to realize that the value of the assets of the savings and loan associations was less than the value of the savings and loan associations' obligations to depositors.

What happened next? Interest rates on certificates of deposit of the savings and loan associations, even with U.S. deposit insurance in place, rose to a substantial premium over U.S. Treasury bills, which, in theory, were the same risk. Regular savings depositors withdrew their deposits in droves and savings and loan associations were unable to fund their cash needs in the certificate of deposit market. The 'greater fool theory' (that is, assuming that, although your net worth is negative on a mark-to-market basis, someone else will be silly enough to buy your certificates of deposit') failed as a funding strategy.

Long-Term Capital Management

The collapse of the prominent hedge fund, Long-Term Capital Management (LTCM), in the late 1990s was a similar story. The fund took large positions arbitraging credit spreads using a very high degree of leverage. Credit spreads moved against LTCM in a significant way. As a private institution, it was very difficult for market participants to know what capital remained and so they did the prudent thing—they declined to continue providing funding against LTCM positions, forcing LTCM to dump their large positions at disadvantageous terms. The LTCM partners were too smart to rely on the greater fool theory and sought help to liquidate the firm in a smooth way, but they weren't smart enough to have correctly assessed the likelihood, magnitude, and timing of the risk inherent in their portfolio.

Acquisition of Security Pacific Corporation by Bank of America

In 1992, BankAmerica Corporation acquired Security Pacific Corporation of Los Angeles in one of the largest U.S. bank mergers of the 1985–1995 period. While not well known at the time, the acquisition was in fact triggered by excessive credit risk at Security Pacific National Bank, the principal subsidiary of Security Pacific Corporation. Security Pacific Corporation had significant 'double leverage', the aggressive bank holding company practice of issuing commercial paper or bonds at the parent company level and then using the proceeds to buy the common stock of a subsidiary bank in order to manipulate the bank's capital ratios and capital positions. Security Pacific Corporation needed dividend payments from Security Pacific National Bank in order to firstly pay interest on existing debt obligations at the parent level and secondly to have the financial strength to continue to access the commercial paper market, where Security Pacific Corporation was an aggressive issuer.

Once credit risk hit Security Pacific Bank hard, regulators cut off dividend payments to the parent company. Security Pacific Corporation was quickly shut out of the commercial paper market as a result. BankAmerica Corporation came to the rescue in a merger in which Security Pacific had little bargaining power.

A Thousand Cuts

These three case studies show how the magnitude, likelihood, and timing of risk are intimately linked. They also show that the greater fool theory rarely works for long.

That being said, risk 'gone bad' can still destroy value without leading to the demise of the institution. The National Australia Bank case illustrates how a risk going bad can destroy value and yet leave the institution to go forward, wounded but still alive.

That is why our definition of risk management earlier in this chapter is so important—institutions will sometimes lose their bets, but if management has been careful about analyzing the trade-offs between risk and return, the magnitude of the losses will be small enough to allow the institution to recover and move on. If management has not been careful, 'death from a thousand cuts' can still come about.

With this in mind, we now turn to the nature of the risk/return trade-off.

CHAPTER 2

Risk, Return and Performance

In Chapter 1, we defined risk management as the discipline designed to help management understand the relative risks and returns from different strategies, both at the portfolio level (the perspective of the chief executive officer) and at the transaction level (the perspective of the trader, portfolio strategist, or lending officer). In this chapter, we focus on the nature of risk and return in a practical sense, not a philosophical sense. The practical definition of risk and return reflects the differences in perception of different parts of the financial world. The definitions also introduce a number of biases into perceived risk and return that can be very dangerous. We will point out these dangers in this chapter and then spend the rest of the book talking about how to avoid these pitfalls in the conventional wisdom.

Similarly, there is an on-going debate in the financial services industry as to how risk and return should be measured. Fund managers and the asset side of pension funds are almost always on a mark-to-market basis. Insurance companies and commercial banks use a mix of mark-to-market risk/return management and a variation on financial accounting called 'transfer pricing', which separates the interest rate risk portion of net income from the non-interest rate-related components. We discuss the 'common practice' of transfer pricing and its history in the last half of this chapter. We discuss the 'best practice' of transfer pricing and performance measurement in the remainder of this book.

Practical Quantification of Risk

In December 2002 at a major risk management conference in Geneva, Nobel prize winner Robert Merton told a story about the equity salesman from a major securities firm who was trying to convince a portfolio manager to switch the emphasis of his fund from fixed income securities to equities. Merton quoted the salesman as saying:

'Over the 40-year time horizon that your fund has, you have a 99% probability that an all-equity portfolio will return more than a portfolio of bonds.

There's no way that you'll have less money in 40 years than the current par value of the bonds you own now.'

Merton said the portfolio manager thought for a minute and then said to the salesman:

'Well, if you're right, I'd like to buy a put option from your firm to put the equity portfolio you want me to create back to your firm in 40 years at my current portfolio value. Since your argument is so persuasive, I am sure that put option will be very cheap.' Naturally, he never heard from the salesman again.

The salesman Merton spoke about was using a tried and true technique, talking about expected returns and ignoring risk. The portfolio manager replied, however, in a way that reflects the highest standard of risk management theory and practice: he asked the price of a contract that insures perfectly[1] against the risk that concerns him. This approach is being pursued aggressively by practitioners and academics who believe, like we do, that many traditional measures of risk are much too simple. Robert Jarrow, in a working paper "Put Option Premiums and Coherent Risk Measures," argues the virtues of put premiums like the one requested by the portfolio manager as a particularly high quality measure of risk.[2]

Other measures of risk have understated true risk in a more subtle way. Some of the understatement is an accidental reflection of how much more we understand now about risk than we understood when the risk measure was introduced. Sometimes, risk measures that understate risk have a longer life than they deserve when some parties have a vested interest in perpetuating the understatement.

We turn to various risk measures to point out these potential pitfalls in the next section.

Perils and Pitfalls in the Measurement of Risk: The Impact of Selection Bias

A major bank with a significant portfolio of loans in the Asia Pacific region once retained one of the authors as a consultant in assessing the risk of the portfolio. As part of the assignment, the chief financial officer of the bank requested a historical value-at-risk analysis of the bank's 100 largest counterparties in Asia. We of course did the work he requested but provided the analysis in the context of a letter that explained the nature of the results. The work was done, we explained, using industry standards and 'best practices' of value-at-risk analysis but the 99th percentile 'worst case' we described in the results section was in fact the 'best case worst case' that the bank would experience.

---

[1] Assuming of course that the securities firm providing the insurance is riskless.
[2] Working paper, Cornell University and Kamakura Corporation, February 2001.

'How does that help me with bank regulators?' the chief financial officer asked, not fully appreciating that we were trying to save his job. We explained the bias in value-at-risk patiently to him as follows:

1. You have selected 100 of your current counterparties in Asia.
2. By definition, they are your counterparties now because they have not defaulted.
3. You asked us to do a historical analysis of value-at-risk using the bonds of these counterparties over the last 12 months.
4. We have done that and produced a 99th percentile 'worst case' for you as you requested, however;
5. It is the best case worst case scenario, because we are doing a historical analysis of 100 names over a period in which none of them defaulted. The very nature of the risk measure and the nature of the counterparties guarantee that this seriously underestimates the credit risk in this portfolio. If the chief financial officer wanted a more accurate assessment of the risk, the test should have either been based on 100 counterparties randomly chosen as of a year before (and indeed some of them subsequently defaulted) or we should have done a forward-looking simulation that allows for default on a name by name basis.

He conceded the point and hedged himself with the Board, avoiding the career-ending scenario if a risk turned out to be much worse than the advertised 'worst case'.

We now turn to some of the most common examples of this selection bias in measuring risk.

Biases in Return versus a Relative Benchmark

In the fund management and pension fund business, most portfolio manages are judged by measures of their 'plus alpha' or risk-adjusted return versus a predefined benchmark. An example might be a fund manager who manages a 'large cap' portfolio of common stock who is told he must keep a tracking error of less than x and that he is expected to earn a return in excess of the return on the S&P500. This is a very, very common kind of risk and return measurement system on the 'buy side' of financial markets.

What is wrong with this as a risk and return measurement system? Everything that was wrong in the story in the previous section.[3] We can see this by taking apart this risk management system piece by piece.

---

[3] The authors would like to thank Leo de Bever, Barbara Zvan, Francois Gingras, and Barbara Chun of Ontario Teachers Pension Plan for their insights and inspiration of this section of the book.

First, how is tracking error measured? There are many variations, but in most cases a regression is run on two data series—the stock price of ABC company versus the return on the S&P500 index. By definition, tracking error will only be known for ABC company if that stock price series exists (i.e. if the company has not been delisted from the exchange due to bankruptcy). Our risk measure for ABC company is a 'no credit risk' risk measure. Similarly, what about the credit risk of the S&P500? Generally speaking, as a company's credit quality (and/or market capitalization) declines, they are dropped from the S&P500. This happens after the close of business, and on the subsequent opening, the price of the stock falls considerably in a way that is unhedgable unless one predicts the change in S&P500 composition. The S&P index is not affected by this fall, but the holder of the common stock of the company dropped from the index will suffer a large loss.

Therefore, the most common performance measure used in the equity markets ignores credit risk completely, even though on average between 1.00% and 1.5% of listed American companies have defaulted over the 1963–2004 time period. We are substantially understating the risk component of this traditional performance measure.

How does the risk of bankruptcy affect our fund manager if the risk occurs? It depends on whether or not:

1. ABC company is in the manager's portfolio;
2. ABC company is in the S&P500;
3. ABC goes bankrupt or is dropped from the S&P500 for credit quality reasons.

If ABC company is dropped from the index, the manager will have a decline of as much as 20% or more and yet there will be no corresponding change in the index. The manager will have a big 'negative alpha' because he couldn't get out of ABC company until after the announcement that ABC company is no longer in the index. If ABC does go bankrupt while still in the index, the drop in stock price could be as much as 100%, but at least the index will also be affected.

If the manager owns a stock that goes bankrupt and is not in the index, he has a negative alpha versus the index that tracking error completely ignores. Even if the company is merely dropped from the index, the manager will suffer a negative 20% or so stock price decline that is not offset by the movement of the index and not reflected in 'tracking error'. This same kind of problem affects fixed income performance measurement versus a benchmark like the Lehman Brothers Government Bond Index, but in more subtle ways.

We turn to another common measure of risk with similar pitfalls.

Historical Value-at-Risk: Selection Bias Again

There are as many approaches to value-at-risk as there are risk management analysts, but in general value-at-risk calculations fall into three basic categories:

1. A 'historical' value-at-risk which measures dollar price changes for specific securities over a period in history;
2. A variance/covariance approach which measures the variances and covariances of past returns and implies (from this implicit assumption of normally distributed returns) the Nth percentile worst case;
3. A forward-looking simulation of returns over the desired time horizon.

The comments of this section apply only to methods 1 and 2.

What are the concerns of these calculations that have been much used and much discussed over the past decade?

1. Credit risk is completely ignored. We have discussed the selection bias earlier in this chapter.
2. Since, by definition, current counterparties have not defaulted at any time during the historical period, the measured risk will be smaller than the true credit adjusted risk.

Still, there are two other problems with these two approaches to value-at-risk that are just as serious:

3. They ignore all cash flows between time zero and the value-at-risk horizon (10 days, one month, three months, one year) since these approaches are effectively a single period analysis which implicitly assumes you own the same things at the end of the period that you owned at time zero.
4. They cannot answer the question posed by the portfolio manager in the story by Robert Merton—what is the hedge and how much does it cost?

Both of these drawbacks seriously affect value-at-risk as a risk measure. In the end, on a fully credit-adjusted basis, we need to know what the hedge is and how much it costs as Robert Merton and Robert Jarrow advise.

Monte-Carlo Based Value-at-Risk

Many thoughtful risk managers have sought to bring credit risk into traditional historical or variance-covariance value-at-risk by either simulating default/no default during the VAR time period or by using a 'transition matrix' approach.

As an 'interim fix' this approach is a step forward, but again some key problems remain that understate the risk remaining:

- Common macro-economic factors that drive correlated default are not specified. This will generally result in a significant underestimate of the 'fat tails' from credit losses. Van Deventer and Imai [2003] discuss the impact of macro factors in detail and we analyze these later in this book.
- The default probabilities are implicitly held constant over the time period. In reality, these default probabilities rise and fall through the credit cycle and holding them constant again understates the level of credit risk implicit in the portfolio.
- The timing of defaults during the period is ignored, when in fact the exact timing is very important (see the next section for the reasons).
- Interim cash flows are again ignored (unless it is a multiperiod simulation).
- What's the hedge? Again, we can't answer the portfolio manager's question in the Robert Merton story.

Expected Losses on Tranches of Collateralized Debt Obligations

In the last decade, the market for credit default swaps and collateralized debt obligations has exploded. Ratings have been assigned and CDO tranches have been marketed on the basis of the 'expected loss' on the CDO tranche. These expected losses have been calculated using the approach of the previous section[4] with all of its associated problems plus one more:

The focus is purely on expected losses and ignores the fat tails that are typical of the worst part of the credit cycle.

This explains the horrified reactions of institutional investors to CDO tranche losses as credit losses peaked in 2001–2002.

As always, to fully understand the risk, we need the full probability distribution of the losses and most important, we need to be able to stress test it in order to calculate the hedge.

We turn now to the other side of the risk-return horizon.

Measuring Return: Market versus Accounting Returns

The nature of risk measurement is complex enough, as we have seen in previous sections, but there is more complexity involved—the definition of return. There are a few key determinants of what approach is used to measure return:

---

[4] In a sense, these approaches have at least helped some investors get familiar with limited-use monte carlo simulation. See the Standard & Poor's Corporation *CDO Evaluator* on www.sandp.com for a representative example of this approach to CDO evaluation.

- The nature of the institution involved;
- The nature of the regulatory agencies involved;
- The availability of observable market prices;
- The time horizon of greatest concern.

For managers of common stock portfolios, the decisions are pretty straightforward. The market prices of the common stock are observable, regulation is market-value based,[5] and there is an observable daily benchmark. Moreover, industry expert bodies such as the Association for Investment Management Research (AIMR) have instituted a step-by-step approach to daily performance benchmarking.

In other industries, things are more complex. How do you deal with life insurance policy liabilities and an asset mix of equities, bonds, real estate and commodities? What would you do if your liabilities were pension fund obligations? What if they were passbook savings?

The result is often a system of splitting risk and return using a technique called 'transfer pricing', which in this context has a much different meaning than its meaning to tax experts. We now discuss how commercial banks have established this practice and what the current state of the art is. In the rest of the book, we will strive to show how 'best practice' can be improved.

Introduction to Transfer Pricing: Extracting Interest Rate Risk in a Financial Accounting Context

The subject of transfer pricing represents one of the greatest differences in asset and liability management practice between large banks internationally and between banks and the fund managers mentioned in the previous section. In the U.S. and Australia, the so-called 'matched maturity transfer pricing system' is accepted as an absolute necessity for the successful management of a large financial institution. In Japan, by way of contrast, the first bank to use multiple rate transfer pricing adopted a very simple system more than 20 years after Bank of America initiated a much more sophisticated system in 1973.

The rationale for 'transfer pricing' as an alternative to the investment management business' reliance on a mark-to-market approach is a simple one. With tens of thousands of employees and hundreds of business units that invest in assets with no observable price, it is literally impossible to manage a commercial bank on a mark-to-market basis at the working level. Transfer pricing is the device by which the rules of the game are changed so that actions are consistent with a mark-to-market approach but the vehicle by which the rules of the game are conveyed is in financial accounting terms.

---

[5] Notwithstanding bank regulators in Japan who lag their counterparts overseas by a few decades, even there the pace of progress has been increasing recently.

We start by presenting a selective history of the transfer pricing discipline in the U.S. We follow with a detailed description of the current 'common practice' in transfer pricing, with examples of its practical use, in the remainder of the chapter. We will return to this issue at the end of the book in detail, because the current 'state of the art' leaves much to be done.

Bank of America: 1973–1979

Interest rate risk management has advanced in bursts of energy that usually follows a period of extremely high interest rates in the U.S. market, and this segment of risk management has, until recently, been the main focus of transfer pricing. In the early 1970s, the entire home mortgage market in the U.S. was made up of fixed-rate loans. The floating-rate mortgage had yet to be introduced. Interest rates were beginning to be deregulated, and the first futures contracts (on U.S. Treasury bills) had not yet been launched. In this environment, a rise in market interest rates created a double crisis at banks with a large amount of retail business. Consumer deposits flowed into unregulated instruments like Treasury bills or newly introduced money market funds, and the banks suffered from negative spreads on their large portfolios of fixed-rate loans.

A spike in interest rates beginning in 1969 triggered a serious reexamination of financial management practice at the largest bank in the U.S. (at the time), the Bank of America. A team of executives that included C. Baumhefner, Leland Prussia, and William 'Mack' Terry recognized that changing interest rates were making it impossible for existing management 'accounting' systems to correctly allocate profitability among the bank's business units and to set responsibility for managing interest rate risk. Until that time, the bank had been using a single internal transfer pricing rate that was applied to the difference between assets and liabilities in each business unit to allocate some form of interest expense or interest income in a way that the units' assets and liabilities were equal. This rate, known as the 'pool' rate for transfer pricing, was a short-term interest rate at Bank of America calculated as a weighted average of its issuance costs on certificates of deposit.

The disadvantages of such a single rate 'pool rate' system are outlined in later chapters of this book. Given the sharp changes in rates that were beginning to look normal in the U.S., senior management at the Bank of America came to the conclusion that the existing system at the bank was dangerous from an interest rate risk point of view and made proper strategic decision-making impossible. Strategic decision-making was handicapped because the single rate transfer pricing system made it impossible to know the true risk-adjusted profitability of each business unit and line of business. The numbers reported by the existing system mixed results due to business judgment ('skill') and results due to interest rate mismatches ('luck', which could be either good or bad).

Although the bank had a very sizable accounting function, the responsibility for designing the new transfer pricing system was given to the brilliant young head of the Financial Analysis and Planning Department of the bank, Mack Terry. This division of labor at the bank was the beginning of a trend in U.S. banks that resulted in the total separation of the preparation of official financial reports, a routine and repetitive task that required a high degree of precision and a low level of imagination, from management information (not managerial 'accounting') on how and why the bank was making its money. Mack Terry, who reported directly to chief financial officer Lee Prussia, took on the new task with such vigor that most knowledgeable bankers of that era acknowledge Mack Terry as the father of the new discipline of 'matched maturity transfer pricing'.

Mack Terry and the bank were faced by constraints that continue to plague large banks today:

- The bank was unable to get timely information from loan and deposit mainframe computer application systems regarding the origination, payment schedules, and maturities of existing assets and liabilities.
- The bank had neither the time nor the financial resources to develop a new transfer pricing system on a mainframe computer.

Personal computers, needless to say, were not yet available as management tools.

The danger of future rate changes and incorrect strategic decisions was so great that bank management decided to make a number of crude but relatively accurate assumptions in order to get a 'quick and dirty' answer to the bank's financial information needs. The fundamental principle developed by the Financial Analysis and Planning Department was the 'matched maturity' principle. A three-year fixed-rate loan to finance the purchase of an automobile would be charged a three-year fixed-rate. A 30-year fixed-rate mortgage loan would be charged the cost of fixed-rate 30-year money. At other U.S. banks, it was more common to use the bank's average cost of funds or its marginal cost of new three-month certificates of deposit. The average cost of funds method had obvious flaws, particularly in a rising rate environment, and it ultimately contributed to the effective bankruptcy of Franklin National Bank and many U.S. savings and loan associations. We discuss how these transfer pricing rates are calculated in later chapters.

The Financial Analysis and Planning (FAP) Department team agreed that the bank's 'marginal cost of funds' represented the correct yield curve to use for determining these matched maturity transfer pricing rates. The bankers recognized that the bank had the capability to raise small amounts of money at lower rates but that the true 'marginal' cost of funds to the bank was the rate that would be paid on a large amount, say $100 million, in the open market.

This choice was adopted without much controversy, at least compared to the controversy of the 'matched maturity' concept itself.

One of the first tasks of the FAP team was to estimate how the internal profitability of each unit would change if this new system were adopted. It was quickly determined that there would be massive 'reallocations' of profit and that many line managers would be very upset with the reallocation of profit away from their units. In spite of the controversy that management knew would occur, management decided that better strategic decision making was much more important than avoiding the short-term displeasure of half of the management team (the other half were the ones who received increased profit allocations).

Once a firm decision was made to go ahead with the new system, implementation decisions had to be dealt with in great detail. The systems 'queue' was so long at the bank that it was impossible to keep track of transfer pricing rates on a loan by loan or deposit by deposit basis. The first unit of measurement, then, was to be the 'portfolio' consisting of otherwise identical loans that differed only in maturity and rate, not in credit risk or other terms. In addition, the bank (to its great embarrassment) did not have good enough data on either its own loans or its historical cost of funds to reconstruct what historical transfer pricing rates would have been for the older loans and deposits making up most of the bank's balance sheet. Estimates would have to do.

These estimates were at the heart of the largest of many internal political controversies about the matched maturity transfer pricing system. Much of the fixed-rate real estate portfolio was already 'under water'—losing money— by the time the transfer pricing system was undergoing revision. If the current marginal cost of funds was applied at the start of the transfer pricing system to the mortgage portfolio, the profitability of the portfolio would have been essentially zero or negative. On the other hand, Mack Terry and his team recognized that in reality this interest rate risk had gone unhedged and that the bank had lost its interest rate bet. Someone would have to 'book' the loss on the older mortgage loans.

Ultimately, the bank's asset and liability management committee was assigned a 'funding' book that contained all of the interest rate mismatches at the bank. The funding book was the unit that bought and sold all funds transfer priced to business units. At the initiation of the matched maturity system, this funding book was charged the difference between the historical marginal cost of funds that would have been necessary to fund the mortgage portfolio on a matched maturity basis and the current marginal cost of funds. This 'dead weight loss' of past management actions was appropriately assigned to senior management itself.

Because of the lack of data, the bank's early implementation of the matched maturity system was based on the use of moving average matched maturity cost of funds figures for each portfolio. While this approximation was a crude one, it allowed a speedy implementation that ultimately made the bank's later troubles less severe than they otherwise would have been.

Finally, the system was rolled out for implementation with a major educational campaign aimed at convincing lending officers and branch managers of the now well accepted discipline of 'spread pricing', pricing all new business at a spread above the marginal cost of matched maturity money.[6] Controversy was expected, and expectations were met. A large number of line managers either failed to understand the system or didn't like it because their reported profits declined. Soon after the announcement of the system, Mack Terry began receiving anonymous 'hate mail' in the inter-office mail system from disgruntled line managers.

Nonetheless, senior management fully backed the discipline of the new system, and for that the Bank of America receives full credit as the originator of the matched maturity transfer pricing concept. In an ironic footnote, the bank suffered heavily from an interest rate mismatch as interest rates skyrocketed in the 1979–1980 time period. The transfer pricing system made it clear that senior management was to blame since the asset and liability management committee had consciously decided not to hedge most of the interest rate risk embedded in the bank's portfolio.

First Interstate: 1982–1987

In the years to follow, a number of banks adopted the matched maturity transfer pricing system. The oral history of U.S. banking often ranks Continental Illinois as the second bank to move to a matched maturity transfer pricing system, not long after the Bank of America implemented the idea. At most banks, however, the idea was still quite new and the early 1980s were largely consumed with recovering from the interest rate-related and credit risk-related problems of the 1979–1981 period. By the mid-1980s, however, banks had recovered enough from these crises to turn back to the task of improving management practices in order to face the more competitive environment that full deregulation of interest rates had created. First Interstate Bancorp, which at the time was the 7th or 8th largest bank holding company in the U.S., approached the transfer pricing problem in a manner similar to that of many large banking companies in the mid-1980s.

---

[6] From a 2004 perspective, this emphasis on the marginal cost of funds as a basis for pricing is showing its age. We discuss problems with this concept in later chapters as part of the continual battle between those with a financial accounting basis ('how can we make money if we don't charge at least as much of our cost of funds') and those with a market orientation ('this credit is priced 10 basis points over market for AA-rated companies and the fact that we are a triple BBB bank is irrelevant').

First Interstate's organization was much more complex than Bank of America's since the company operated 13 banks in nine western states, all of which had separate treasury functions, separate management, separate government regulation, and separate systems.[7] In addition, the bank holding company legal entity First Interstate Bancorp had a number of 'non-bank' subsidiaries that required funding at the holding company (parent) level. Most U.S. bank holding companies consisted of a small parent company whose dominant subsidiary was a lead bank that typically made up 90% of the total assets of the company in consolidation. The lead banks were almost always considered a stronger credit risk than the parent companies because of the existence of Federal deposit insurance at the bank level but not the parent level and because of the richness of funding sources available to banks compared to bank holding companies.

In the First Interstate case, things were more complex. The lead bank, First Interstate Bank of California (FICAL), represented only 40% of the assets of the holding company and therefore its credit was generally felt by market participants to be weaker than that of the parent. Moreover, the First Interstate Banks did not compare funding needs, and as a result, it was often said that a New York bank could buy overnight funding from one First Interstate Bank and sell it to another First Interstate Bank at a good profit. The transfer pricing system at First Interstate had to cure this problem as well as address the correct allocation of profits and interest rate risk as in the Bank of America case.

Management took a two-fold approach to the problem. At the holding company level, the corporate treasury unit began 'making markets' to all bank and non-bank units within the company. Because First Interstate was much more decentralized than the Bank of America, funds transfers between the holding company and subsidiaries were voluntary transfers of funds, not mandatory. In addition, since each unit was a separate legal entity, a transfer pricing transaction was accompanied by the actual movement of cash from one bank account to another.

The holding company transfer pricing system began in early 1984 under the auspices of the holding company's funding department. The department agreed to buy or sell funds at its marginal cost at rates that varied by maturity from 30 days to 10 years. No offers to buy or sell funds were to be refused under this system. The transfer pricing system, since it was voluntary, was received without controversy and actually generated a high degree of enthusiasm among line units. For the first time, the units had a firm 'cost of funds' quotation that was guaranteed to be available and which could be used to price new business in line units on a no-interest rate risk basis. Demand from line

---

[7] The multi-state nature of commercial banking is commonplace in the U.S. in 2004 but it was a significant barrier to implementation of comprehensive risk management in the mid-1980s, just as national barriers are today.

units was very strong, and the parent company became an active issuer of bonds and commercial paper to support the strong funding demand from both bank and non-bank subsidiaries.

Among bank subsidiaries, the 'on-demand' transfer pricing system had the effect of equalizing the cost of funds across subsidiary banks. High cost of funds banks immediately found it cheaper to borrow at the lower rates offered by the parent company. Regulatory restrictions kept the parent company from borrowing from subsidiary banks, but there was an equivalent transaction that achieved the same objective. After the transfer pricing system had been in operation for some months, the parent company had acquired a substantial portfolio of certificates of deposit of subsidiary banks. These certificates of deposit could be sold to other banks within the system. By selling individual bank certificates of deposit to other First Interstate banks, the holding company reduced the size of this portfolio and effectively 'borrowed' at its marginal cost of funds, the yield it attached to the certificates that it sold.

The transfer pricing system at the holding company did have implementation problems of a sort. Generally, rates were set at the beginning of a business day and held constant for the entire day. The parent company soon noticed that borrowings from affiliates, and one subsidiary in particular, would increase when open market rates rose late in the day, allowing subsidiaries to 'arbitrage' the parent company treasury staff by borrowing at the lower rate transfer price set earlier in the day. This got to be a big enough problem that rates for all borrowings above $10 million were priced in 'real time'. Most large banks use a similar 'real time' quotation system now for pricing large corporate borrowings. What will surprise many bankers, however, is that 'in-house' transactions ultimately also have to be priced in real time in many cases. This is a variation on the arbitrage of FX options models that plagued National Australia Bank in the incident described in Chapter 1.

At the same time that the parent company was implementing this system, the parent company's asset and liability management department and the financial staff of FICAL began to design a Bank of America-style matched maturity transfer pricing system for FICAL. Personal computer technology at the time did not permit PCs to be used as the platform, so the company undertook a very ambitious mainframe development effort. After a complex design phase and a development effort that cost close to $10 million and two years of effort, the system was successfully put into action with considerably less controversy than in the Bank of America case. Such a system today would cost much less from a third party software vendor.

The biggest practical problem to arise in the FICAL transfer pricing system was a subtle one with significant political and economic implications. During the design phase of the system, the question was raised about how to handle the pre-payment of fixed-rate loans in the transfer pricing system. The financial management team at First Interstate dreaded the thought of explaining 'option-adjusted' transfer pricing rates to line managers and decided to perform internal transfer pricing on a 'non-prepayable' basis. If the underlying asset was prepaid, then the treasury unit at the center of the transfer pricing system would simply charge a 'mark-to-market' prepayment penalty to the line unit, allowing it to extinguish its borrowings at the same time that the asset was prepaid. This simple system is standard practice in many countries, including even the retail mortgage market in Australia.

This decision led to unforeseen consequences. During the latter half of the 1980s and continuing into the 1990s, interest rates declined in the U.S. and were accompanied by massive prepayments of fixed-rate debt of all kinds. As a result, the FICAL transfer pricing system's reported profits for line units were soon dominated by huge mark-to-market penalties that line managers didn't have control over and generally didn't understand.

Bank management quickly moved to a transfer pricing system that allowed for 'costless prepayment' by incorporating the cost of a prepayment option in transfer prices. This trend is firmly established as standard practice in most banks today.

Common Practice in Transfer Pricing Today

The physical process of implementing a transfer pricing system involves two principal activities—storing the transfer price for the life of the loan or deposit, and efficiently making use of the transfer price once it has been stored. From a systems point of view, the transfer price simply becomes one more field in the record of any individual transaction that is (ideally) maintained in an enterprise-wide database. For many years, as the Bank of America example indicates, computer systems technology made it very difficult to perform these two tasks easily. With the advent of parallel processing and more powerful personal computers, this once-daunting task has become a day-to-day reality at almost all large banks in the U.S. over the last 10 years.

Almost every vendor of financial information systems or asset and liability management systems in North America now offers some kind of transfer pricing system for a price so reasonable that no bank would be able to duplicate the cost through the in-house development of a similar system. The very best systems store data on a loan-by-loan, deposit-by-deposit basis and offer the user the choice of a number of methods for establishing transfer prices for both interest rate-related items and non-interest income and expense items.

It's safe to say that no major financial institution can claim to be well-managed without having some kind of multiple rate transfer pricing system in place. The remainder of this section deals with the implementation of such a system.

Major issues

Every institution that seeks to enhance its transfer pricing system has to deal with a number of strategic issues that can be summarized in the following questions:

1. Measurement of risk:
   Should risk be measured in terms of net income volatility or the volatility of the mark-to-market value of the portfolio involved?

2. Risk limits:
   Given the proper risk measure, how big should specific risk limits be for each part of the organization?

3. The transfer pricing book as a separate portfolio:
   Should the transfer pricing book be categorized separately or should it be included in the 'all other' category of risks that haven't been assigned to a specific unit other than the asset and liability management committee?

4. Transfer pricing book profit objectives:
   Should the transfer pricing book be a trading type profit center?

5. Transfer pricing book risk limits:
   How big should the risk limits be on the transfer pricing book?

6. Basis risk:
   Who should bear the risk that a pricing index, like the prime rate, doesn't move with perfect correlation relative to market interest rates? How should this risk be measured, and who should bear the risk?

7. Line units: asset portfolio or asset generator?
   Should line units be given credit for the on-going net interest income from assets generated in the past, or should they only be paid a credit for assets generated in the current period?

8. Credit risk:
   Where should credit risk be housed in the organization?

9. Liquidity risk:
   How do you deal with the situation where line unit demands for short-term interest rate-based pricing create the need for more short-term funding than liquidity considerations will support?

10. Investment securities:
    What should be the transfer pricing rate for investment securities, and what unit should hold the securities?

11. Prepayment and early withdrawal risk:
    Who bears this risk and how is it charged?

We will answer each of these questions, based on examples of leading banks and other financial institutions around the world, after discussing briefly the organizational structure that we assume for these discussions.

In the remainder of this book, we discuss extending the state of the art. What follows in this chapter is restricted to the most common practices of sophisticated financial institutions.

Assumed organizational structure

We assume the formal organizational structure outlined in Appendix 1, which breaks the organizational units into the following seven classes:

Retail lending and insurance businesses
1. Executive vice president level.
2. Individual branch level.

Other wholesale financing units, including leasing
3. Executive vice president level.
4. Individual business unit level.
5. Holding company trading for its own account, if any
6. Transfer pricing book.
7. Asset and liability management committee.

The following discussion assumes that risk and responsibility are divided among some or all of these seven units. Additional units are ignored in order to simplify the explanation below.

Question 1: Measurement of risk

Should risk be measured in terms of net income volatility or the volatility of the mark-to-market value of the portfolio involved? This is one of the most difficult questions in risk management, and it is easier to answer by process of elimination. Before doing so, however, it is useful to characterize the difference in attitudes between how an investment management firm and a bank approach the same risks.

Investment managers and bankers

Many very large investment management firms have large yen and dollar fixed income portfolios. In the dollar portfolios, the managers can and do purchase the following securities:

- U.S. Treasury securities;
- Eurodollar deposits;
- Reverse repos;
- Credit card receivables;
- Mortgage-backed securities;
- Collateralized mortgage obligations, with both fixed and floating-rates tied to LIBOR, 11th District Cost of Funds index, prime rate, one, three and five-year maturity Treasury rate.

In short, there is nothing that a bank has on its balance sheet that cannot be found on the balance sheet of a large fixed income fund manager in the U.S. From the asset side perspective, the fund management firm *is a bank*. On the liability side, the same is true—liabilities are made of a large number of small retail deposits that vary in amount daily at the whim of the depositor. The objective of the fund manager is to invest these deposits in a way most satisfactory to shareholders, which in this case are identical to depositors.

In the investment management world, there are three ways to measure risk:

1. Mark-to-market;
2. Mark-to-market;
3. Mark-to-market.

In short, it is no exaggeration to point out that net income simulation, often considered the core of the risk management tools for the banking industry, is never considered as a risk management tool in the fund management business. The same is true, to only a slightly lesser extent, with gap analysis. Bankers have been prisoners, in a sense, of the accounting profession's dominance of the banking business over the last few centuries. Consider how differently an investment manager without this prejudice operates:

- Risk limit: the fund manager seeks to match the risk of a specific portfolio, often labeled an 'index' like the Lehman Brothers U.S. Treasury index based on all outstanding U.S. Treasury issues
- Communication of risk limit to shareholders: the fund manager clearly communicates the name of the index by which he measures risk to depositor/shareholders
- Performance measurement: good performance is defined as a total return in excess of the base portfolio or index, without taking risk in excess of that embedded in the index[8]

In no case does a measurement of net income come into play. The following is an important observation:

Investment managers are very smart. If the simulation of the net income of their portfolios would improve their risk/return performance, they would use net income simulation. They don't. Therefore, it is the judgment of a very intelligent class of financial experts that net income simulation per se isn't helpful in their management of risk.

---

[8] The pitfalls of this approach were reviewed in previous sections, but at least it is far superior to a net income-based approach.

If this is true, why has the banking industry clung so tightly to net income simulation as a risk management tool? There are a number of reasons:

- Management has historically communicated both risk and return to shareholders (and analysts) in the form of a communication about net income. For the time being, senior management must communicate with shareholders using both the mark-to-market and the net income vocabulary.
- Branch managers are compensated on the basis of financial accounting net income of their branches: it is too complex to judge branch performance on a total return on a given portfolio. Net income is easier to understand and administer.
- Banks have historically had trouble getting market value estimates on large portions of their portfolio, although this is less true with each passing year.

All of these factors mean that net income and financial accounting concepts will continue to supplement market-based risk measures at large banks for decades to come. Nonetheless, the decline in the importance of net income-based risk measures is clear. The Federal Reserve, in its October 1993 interest rate risk and capital ratio proposal, did not even justify its reliance on market-based risk measures; its superiority over a net income standard was judged to be obvious.[9]

Measuring risk
Given this background, it becomes relatively easy to say when mark-to-market risk limits and net income-based financial accounting figures have to be used to measure risk. Almost all financial institutions end up using these tools in the following cases:

Portfolio Being Measured	Use Mark-to-Market Risk Limits?	Use Net Income Risk Limits?
Retail Lending		
Executive vice president level	No	Yes
Individual branch level	No	Yes

---

[9] As the Federal Reserve observed in a recent study, 1,442 banks went bankrupt in the U.S. between 1982 and 1992. Needless to say, almost all of these would have been doing some kind of net income simulation. The fact that such a risk measure didn't prevent bankruptcy speaks for itself.

Other Wholesale Business units		
Executive vice president level	No	Yes
Individual business unit level	No	Yes
Trading activities	Yes	No
Transfer pricing book	Yes	No
Asset and liability management committee 'book'	Yes	Yes
Total Bank Risk	**Yes**	**Yes**

Both financial accounting-based net income risk limits and market risk limits are used for total institution risk management and the asset and liability management committee (ALCO) portfolio. In the case of the transfer pricing book and trading activities, mark-to-market is the consensus standard. At the individual business unit and branch level, financial accounting-based net income measures are the standard.

Transfer pricing is the tool by which a market-based risk management system for the total bank can be translated into practical tools for the management and motivation of a large and diverse organization firmly rooted in financial accounting systems.

Question 2: Risk limits

Given the proper risk measure, how big should specific risk limits be for each part of the organization? This is one of the most difficult questions to answer in risk management, since financial theory provides so little guidance.

Concerning the maximum risk limits for the organization as a whole, risk should not be taken to such a degree that the presence of risk lowers shareholder value. For a broad range of risk levels, shareholders are indifferent to risk. For example, one interest rate risk strategy might be to structure cash flows from the organization in such a way that the bank generates cash for shareholders exactly like a sequential investment in three-month Treasury bills, where the investment is rolled over every three months. In this case, the net income of the bank will rise and fall as rates rise and fall, but the bank's stock price will be very stable, just like the price of a three-month Treasury bill. The bank can never go bankrupt because its stock price will never be zero, just as a Treasury bill's price can never be zero.[10]

---

[10] See *Financial Risk Management in Banking* by Dennis Uyemura and Donald R. van Deventer for more on this concept.

An alternative interest rate risk strategy might lead the bank to lock in a fixed level of net income exactly at the level of the coupon on a 30-year Treasury bond, the bank's stock price will be volatile, just like the price of the 30-year Treasury bond, but net income will be stable. The bank will never go bankrupt, since its stock price cannot reach zero just as the price of a 30-year Treasury bond can never be zero.

In short, shareholders are indifferent between these two strategies for two reasons:

1. The bank can never go bankrupt from an interest rate risk perspective[11] (so there is no chance that bankruptcy costs will be incurred); and
2. If the shareholder doesn't like the bank's target risk level, the shareholder can use futures or swaps to change the level of interest rate risk in a portfolio that includes their investment in the bank's stock and the right hedge to adopt their target risk level.

Once the bank moves outside this 'safety zone', the bank faces a possibility of going bankrupt because of interest rate risk, which would cause it to incur bankruptcy costs that shareholders can't hedge. That leads to a situation where the stock price of a bank declines once it moves outside of the safety zone.

Total bank risk should be set at a level such that the bank will never leave the interest rate risk safety zone. In practice, this means that the bank should set risk limits in such a way that does either of the following:

- The market value of portfolio equity (market value of assets less the market value of liabilities) can never be negative for any level of interest rates; or
- The annual cash flow (for which net income is a proxy) will never be negative for any level of interest rates.

Various tools are used to achieve these objectives. Sensitivity of the market value of portfolio equity and value-at-risk type calculations are used to quantify the first type of risk limit. Net income simulation is usually used as a proxy for the second type of objective.

Setting risk limits for various organizational units

Within an organization, interest rate risk limits must be set in a consistent way that reflects both the experience and seniority of the individual in question.

---

[11] We're temporarily ignoring credit risk but will come back to it in detail in the rest of the book.

While it is impossible to generalize the right approach in just a few words, some basic principals can be stated:

- The individual running the transfer pricing book and a trader on the trading floor should have similar risk limits if they have similar skills and experience.
- Most of the risk in a large institution is of such significant size that it should be explicitly allocated to senior management and explicitly separated to show that allocation of risk.
- Risk limits for the transfer pricing book should be large enough to allow for efficient execution of hedges.

Question 3: The transfer pricing book as a separate portfolio

Should the transfer pricing book be set out separately or should it be included in the 'all other' category of risks that haven't been assigned to a specific unit other than the asset and liability management committee?

Many institutions have an attitude toward transfer pricing that is internally inconsistent. Almost all large banks require loan officers to get real time cost of funds quotes for large fixed-rate loans over a set limit, say US$ 1 million, to allow the transaction to be hedged in real time. At the same time, some institutions do not isolate the transfer pricing portfolio as a separate identifiable portfolio with a specific manager, which means that fixed-rate loans will be made every day that go unhedged because the size of the transaction is less than the US$ 1 million limit. The aggregate amount of these small credits is usually much larger than the amount of fixed-rate corporate credits that exceed the US$ 1 million limit. Why require strict match-funding of some transactions but not others?

We feel strongly that all interest rate risk exposure must be monitored and hedged on a timely basis and that no organization can neglect this task, even with the justification that individual transactions are small—only their aggregate size is relevant. In order to assure this constant monitoring, the transfer pricing book should be managed in the following way:

- A manager of the book should be explicitly identified;
- The hedging of the book should be the manager's primary responsibility;
- The book should be hedged on a mark-to-market basis rather than a net interest simulation basis;
- Risk exposure should be measured daily and reported daily to the relevant senior manager;
- The asset and liability management committee should review the risk of the transfer pricing book at each meeting;
- There should be formal numerical risk limits on the transfer pricing book;

- Any violations of these risk limits should be reported in writing to the Asset and Liability Management Committee and prompt corrective action taken;
- Failure to adhere to risk limits should result in disciplinary action.

Question 4: Transfer pricing book profit objectives

Should the transfer pricing book be a trading type profit center?

Every large bank has a trading floor that acts as a profit center. The question above should really be rephrased as follows: does the bank want to have two different sets of people using two different portfolios to achieve trading profits? The obvious answer is no, but there are many good reasons for this answer that are not that obvious.

Clearly, the transfer pricing book should not be used as a profit center to avoid the obvious duplication of effort. There are more important issues at stake, however. First, the manager of the transfer pricing book is almost always viewed with suspicion by line unit managers. Borrowers from the book feel rates are too high and lenders to the book feel rates are too low. If large interest rate risk positions are taken within the book in an attempt to make profits, any resulting gains or losses will reinforce the suspicions of line units. If there are profits, line units will feel they have been 'ripped off' by the pricing of transactions with the transfer pricing book. If there are losses, the transfer pricing book manager will be regarded as incompetent. This 'all downside risk' scenario is very common at large banks. To insure the political integrity of the transfer pricing system, we feel that modest risk limits and a non-profit objective is essential.

The reason that the transfer pricing book has risk limits that are non-zero is the need for good execution—if risk limits were truly zero, the manager of the book would have to micro-hedge every fixed-rate loan made by the bank individually, even if the principal amount were very small. Clearly, better execution can be obtained by using a temporary, less precise hedge while accumulating a position that can be efficiently hedged. Non-zero risk limits allow this to take place.

Another reason for non-zero risk limits is the reality of early prepayments by bank customers, which in turn leads to automatic prepayment by the bank branches which have borrowed from the transfer pricing book to lend to those customers. This complex option-related type of transfer pricing is difficult to hedge and the manager will need some leeway in their risk limits to do it well.

Finally, the risk of the transfer pricing book may well be in the opposite direction of the interest rate risk in the rest of the bank. In this case, as long as the manager of the book is within their risk limits, there is no reason to hedge from the shareholders' point of view since there is a natural offset within the bank.

For all of these reasons, there will be a gain or a loss in the transfer pricing book. In some organizations, a gain is divided among line units and a loss is carried forward until offset by gains in later years. This reinforces the image of the transfer pricing book as an efficient and skillful unit whose main objective is not trading oriented.

Question 5: Transfer pricing book risk limits

How big should the risk limits be on the transfer pricing book?

As mentioned in the answer to question 2, we feel that the interest rate risk limits imposed on the manager of the transfer pricing book should be explicit numerical limits consistent with the limits that the same individual would have if they were on the trading floor trading swaps or government bonds. Specifically, the transfer pricing book should not be the 'plug' or 'garbage disposal' for all other risks not otherwise assigned, because the mid-level manager of the book does not have the experience or seniority to handle risk of such a large size. All risks not assigned elsewhere should be assigned to the Asset and Liability Management Committee, not the transfer pricing book.

Question 6: Basis risk

Who should bear the risk that a pricing index, like the prime rate, doesn't move with perfect correlation relative to market interest rates? How should this risk be measured, and who should bear the risk?

Basis risk, resulting from the choice of pricing indexes like the prime rate in the U.S. or home lending rates in Japan, Canada, and Australia, should be born by someone with the authority to change the index (normally a very senior line manager), rather than parties without that authority (like branch managers or the manager of the transfer pricing book). If the senior line manager doesn't want to change or can't change the use of the index, they have the option to arrange a hedge of their basis risk exposure with the manager of the transfer pricing book. If unhedgable, basis risk is assigned to the transfer pricing book, the responsibility and the authority of the transfer pricing book are inconsistent and the manager has the responsibility but not the authority to fix the basis risk problem.

Question 7: Line units: asset portfolio or asset generator?

Should line units be given credit for the on-going net interest income from assets generated in the past, or should they only be paid a credit for assets generated in the current period?

Historically, transfer pricing systems have looked at branches as asset portfolios, earning income over the multi-year life of assets generated over past years. The recent trend, however, has been to give branches ('marketing offices') credit for selling, not for retention, of assets. This trend has been accelerated by the huge success of the mortgage banking industry in the U.S. and Australia in taking market share away from commercial banks and savings and loan associations. The offices of a mortgage company are given credit solely for the origination of a loan on a fixed fee per loan generated.

After the origination of the loan, no subsequent credit is given to the originating office. This discipline forces mortgage company offices to grow and shrink costs as business volume grows and shrinks. The bank approach gives managers very little incentive to manage costs closely to changes in business volume, so we expect the view of line units as asset portfolios will be de-emphasized except for those assets (like commercial loans) where on-going credit risk management is required by the branch office or those liabilities (like demand deposits) where a high quality of customer service by the branch is necessary to retain the deposit (and in the latter case 'customer service' increasingly means electronic customer service, not personal service).

Question 8: Credit risk

Where should credit risk be housed in the organization? This is one of the most critical issues we will be dealing with in this book. We summarize current common practice in this chapter and discuss how to modify common practice to achieve best practice in the rest of the book.

Common practice says credit risk should be housed in the unit that makes the 'yes' or 'no' credit decision. If the deciding unit is the branch, then credit risk and credit spread should remain at the branch level. If the credit decision is centralized, then an average credit spread should be given to the decision unit and actual credit losses should be charged to the unit as an expense.

Question 9: Liquidity risk

How do you deal with the situation where line unit demands for short-term interest rate-based pricing create the need for more short-term funding than liquidity considerations will support?

This is one of the most difficult issues in transfer pricing. In general, the transfer pricing unit bears this risk without compensation since there is minimal ability to specifically assign the responsibility for creating the liquidity problem in the first place. Ultimately, someone with higher liquidity risk will face a higher marginal cost of funds that can be charged through the transfer pricing system. We'll revert to an alternative approach to liquidity risk in later chapters.

Question 10: Investment securities

What should be the transfer pricing rate for investment securities (usually 'risk-free' government bonds), and what unit should hold the securities? This is an area we will spend a lot of time on in later chapters because the conventional wisdom is in a considerable state of flux.

It is 'common practice' for securities to be held for three purposes:

- As a source of trading profits;
- As a substitute for loans when lending is not profitable but deposit gathering is; and

- As a reserve of liquid assets that provides a source of liquidity when incremental funding is not readily available.

In the former role, securities have a pure trading floor role and that is where the responsibility should be housed. In the latter two roles, the Asset and Liability Management Committee is ultimately responsible and the securities should be booked into the ALCO portfolio. Securities should earn their true yield, i.e. the risk-free yield, rather than the bank's marginal cost of funds (which is what a rote application of the transfer pricing system would dictate). This is a common conclusion in major banks, which avoids charging a penalty (the difference between the risk-free yield and the bank's marginal cost of funds) to the unit holding the risk-free securities. It is usually justified on the basis that 'it wouldn't be fair'. There are two more significant reasons that we deal with in subsequent chapters—since every bank holds risk-free government securities, the transfer pricing conventional wisdom (transfer price every asset at the marginal cost of funds) must be wrong. There must be shareholder value-added created by holding government securities or banks wouldn't do it. We explore this rationale repeatedly in following chapters.

Question 11: Prepayment and early withdrawal risk
Who bears this risk and how is it charged?

This simple question hides an enormously complex issue. In theory, there are two ways to charge for the possibility of early prepayment on an asset or early withdrawal of a liability:

- Transfer price the asset or liability with funds that assume no early termination, and then charge a mark-to-market penalty upon prepayment or early withdrawal.
- Increase (decrease) the transfer pricing rate to reflect that option value of early prepayment (withdrawal) and extinguish the transfer pricing transaction without penalty when the asset or liability disappears from the line unit's balance.

Both of these approaches are fine in theory but much different in practice. We believe that it is politically impossible to make a mark-to-market penalty approach effective for a simple reason: interest rates in every market move in long trends that can result in many years of steady interest rate rises or declines. Over this period of years, like the decline in interest rates during the Reagan administration in the U.S., there can be a massive amount of prepayments. The mark-to-market penalties associated with these prepayments can be so large that they negate the net interest income from remaining transactions on the books of the line unit. The result of the large size of these penalties is very serious—they are little understood by line units and their presence can cause the entire transfer pricing system's integrity to be called into question. This has been a problem at many institutions and we strongly recommend that transfer pricing:

- recognizes optionality; and
- does not charge prepayment or early withdrawal penalties to line units, but instead embeds an option premium in the rates charged to fund assets subject to early prepayment.

Appendix 1

Examples of Transfer Pricing System in Action

Perhaps the best way to illustrate the general principles listed in this chapter is to go through a fairly realistic development of a bank's full transfer pricing process from the day of its founding. We will reflect the transfer pricing position of each of the seven relevant units after each transaction. We denote the amount of assets by positive numbers and liabilities by negative numbers. This section reflects the common practice rather than the best practice outlined in later chapters.

Transaction 1: Formation of Bank with $100 Capital and $100 in Risk-Free Government Securities Held as Investment Securities

Description of the transaction

The bank is formed with $100 of capital. The ALCO authorizes the purchase of $100 of one-year Treasury bills.

Status of the bank

Branch banking
   Executive vice president level
   Individual branch level

Other business units
   Executive vice president level
   Individual business unit level

Trading activities

Transfer pricing book

Asset and liability management committee
   100   One-year Treasury bills
   −100   Shareholders' equity

Transaction 2: Branch 3 Accepts $50 in Deposits for Three Months

Description of the transaction

Branch 3 accepts $50 in three month deposits, which is invested in overnight federal funds while awaiting loan opportunities. The transfer pricing book borrows the funds for three months from the branch and lends it over night to the trading floor. The trading floor doesn't need the funds to manage its position, so the funds are laid off in overnight federal funds.

Status of the bank

Branch banking

Executive vice president level
Individual branch level
Branch 3

50	Three-month loan to transfer pricing book
−50	Three-month deposit

Other business units

Executive vice president level
Individual business unit level

Trading activities

50	Investment in overnight federal funds
−50	Overnight borrowing from transfer pricing book

Transfer pricing book

50	One-day loan to trading floor
−50	Three-month borrowing from Branch 3

Asset and liability Management Committee

100	One-year Treasury bills
−100	Shareholders' equity

Transaction 3: Branch 5 Makes Three-Year Fixed-Rate Auto Loan for $25

Description of the transaction

Branch 5 makes a three-year fixed-rate auto loan for $25. The transfer pricing book lends $25 fixed-rate for three years to Branch 5. This would violate the transfer pricing book risk limits. The transfer pricing book manager decides to partially hedge by issuing $20 million in two-year fixed-rate liabilities through the trading floor, which passes the funds through to the trading book. The other

$5 is funded by reducing funds sold to the trading floor, which in turn reduces federal funds sold.

Status of the bank

Branch banking
Executive vice president level
Individual branch level
Branch 3
| 50 | Three-month loan to transfer pricing book |
| -50 | Three-month deposit |

Branch 5
| 25 | Three-year fixed-rate auto loan |
| -25 | Three-year fixed-rate borrowing from transfer pricing book |

Other business units
Executive vice president level
Individual business unit level

Trading activities
| 45 | Investment in overnight fed funds |
| -45 | Overnight borrowing from transfer pricing book |

Transfer pricing book
25	Three-year fixed-rate loan to Branch 5
45	One-day loan to trading floor
-50	Three-month borrowing from Branch 3
-20	Two-year fixed-rate borrowing via trading floor

Asset and liability Management Committee
| 100 | One-year Treasury bills |
| -100 | Shareholders' equity |

Transaction 4: Commercial Bank Unit 6 Makes a Prime Rate Loan for $20 to ABC Company

Description of the transaction
Commercial banking unit 6 makes a prime rate loan for $20 to ABC company. The prime rate has historically been 2% over the six-month moving average of the six-month certificate of deposit rate. Commercial banking unit 6 is charged a cost of funds of prime rate—2% by the executive vice president (EVP) in charge. He in turn is charged the six-month moving average CD rate by the transfer pricing unit, which actually issues three-month negotiable CDs through the trading floor to fund the loan.

Status of the bank

Branch banking

Executive vice president level

Individual branch level

Branch 3

50	Three-month loan to transfer pricing book
−50	Three-month deposit

Branch 5

25	Three-year fixed-rate auto loan
−25	Three-year fixed-rate borrowing from transfer pricing book

Other business units

Executive vice president level

20	Loan to unit 6 at prime rate—2%
−20	Borrowing from transfer pricing at average six month CD rate

Individual business unit level

Corporate banking unit 6

20	Prime loan to ABC company
−20	Borrowing from EVP at prime rate—2%

Trading activities

45	Investment in overnight federal funds
20	Loan at three-month CD rate to transfer pricing book
−45	Overnight borrowing from transfer pricing book
−20	Issue of three-month negotiable CD

Transfer pricing book

25	Three-year fixed-rate loan to Branch 5
45	One-day loan to trading floor
20	Loan at average six-month CD rate to EVP, other business units
−50	Three-month borrowing from Branch 3
−20	Two-year fixed-rate borrowing via trading floor
−20	Issued three-month negotiable CD via trading floor

Asset and liability management committee

100	One year Treasury bills
−100	Shareholders' equity

Transaction 5: ALCO Decides Interest Rates are Going Up and Sells Securities and Borrows Long-Term

Description of the transaction

ALCO decides interest rates are going up. It sells $50 million in one-year Treasury bills and lends the money on a floating-rate basis to the transfer pricing book, which in turn passes it through to the trading floor to invest in federal funds.

Status of the bank

Branch banking

    Executive vice president level

    Individual branch level

    Branch 3

        50   Three-month loan to transfer pricing book

      −50   Three-month deposit

    Branch 5

        25   Three-year fixed-rate auto loan

      −25   Three-year fixed-rate borrowing from transfer pricing book

Other business units

    Executive vice president level

        20   Loan to unit 6 at prime rate—2%

      −20   Borrowing from transfer pricing at average six-month CD rate

    Individual business unit level

    Corporate banking unit 6

        20   Prime loan to ABC company

      −20   Borrowing from EVP at prime rate—2%

    Trading activities

        95   Investment in overnight federal funds

        20   Loan at three-month CD rate to transfer pricing book

      −95   Overnight borrowing from transfer pricing book

      −20   Issue of three-month negotiable CD

Transfer pricing book

        25   Three-year fixed-rate loan to Branch 5

        95   One-day loan to trading floor

        20   Loan at average six-month CD rate to EVP, other business units

      −50   Three-month borrowing from Branch 3

      −20   Two-year fixed-rate borrowing via trading floor

      −20   Issued three-month negotiable CD via trading floor

      −50   Overnight borrowing from ALCO committee

Asset and Liability Management Committee

        50   One-year Treasury bills

        50   Overnight loan to transfer pricing book

    −100   Shareholders' equity

Transaction 6: ALCO Wants to Increase Bank's Ability to Benefit from Rising Interest Rates and Borrows $15 Million Fixed-Rate for Four Years from Transfer Pricing Book

Description of the transaction

ALCO gives an order to the transfer pricing book manager to issue $15 million in four-year, fixed-rate money on ALCO's behalf. ALCO sells the money back to the transfer pricing book in the form of federal funds, which are passed through to the trading floor.

Status of the bank

Branch banking
   Executive vice president level
   Individual branch level
   Branch 3
      50   Three-month loan to transfer pricing book
      −50   Three-month deposit
   Branch 5
      25   Three-year fixed-rate auto loan
      −25   Three-year fixed-rate borrowing from transfer pricing book

Other business units
   Executive vice president level
      20   Loan to unit 6 at prime rate—2%
      −20   Borrowing from transfer pricing at average six-month CD rate
   Individual business unit level
   Corporate banking unit 6
      20   Prime loan to ABC company
      −20   Borrowing from EVP at prime rate—2%

Trading activities
      110   Investment in overnight federal funds
      20   Loan at three-month CD rate to transfer pricing book
      −110   Overnight borrowing from transfer pricing book
      −20   Issue of three-month negotiable CD

Transfer pricing book
      25   Three-year fixed-rate loan to Branch 5
      110   One-day loan to trading floor
      20   Loan at average six-month CD rate to EVP, other business units

     15   Loan at four-year fixed-rate to ALCO
    −15   Four-year fixed-rate bond issued by trading floor
    −50   Three-month borrowing from Branch 3
    −20   Two-year fixed-rate borrowing via trading floor
    −20   Issued three-month negotiable CD via trading floor
    −65   Overnight borrowing from ALCO committee

Asset and Liability Management Committee

     50   One-year Treasury bills
     65   Overnight loan to transfer pricing book
    −15   Four-year fixed-rate borrowing from transfer pricing book
   −100   Shareholders' equity

CHAPTER 3

Capital Regulation, Risk Management and Performance

In Chapter 1, we defined the principal purpose for risk management—to clearly define the risks and returns of alternative strategies at both the portfolio and transaction level. In Chapter 2, we introduced some of the tools and techniques that have historically been used to measure and manage risk. We continue this process in this chapter, bringing in capital to the risk management process.

Our primary purpose in this chapter and subsequent chapters is to present 'common practice' in various parts of the financial services business and to contrast the approaches used by different institutions. When we see institution A and institution B managing similar risks but using different approaches to the measurement and management of risk, we will carefully note the differences and seek an explanation. Often, institutional barriers to change delay the synthesis and common practices that we would expect from two different groups of intelligent people managing the same kind of risk.

This difference is particularly evident in the role of capital in risk management and risk measurement. Commercial banks are extensively focused on capital-based risk measures, and almost no other types of financial services businesses are. Why? We begin to answer this question with some additional perspectives on the measurement and management of risk. We then talk about managing risk and strategy in financial institutions, business line by business line, and how capital comes into play in this analysis. We then turn to the history of capital-based risk regulations in the commercial banking business and discuss its pros and cons.

Perspectives on Measuring Risk: One Source of Risk or Many Sources of Risk?

Risk management has been an endless quest for a single number which best quantifies the risk of a financial institution or an individual business unit. In Chapter 1, we discussed how Robert Merton and Robert Jarrow have suggested that the value of a put option that fully insures the risk is the current 'best practice' in this regard. This risk measure also provides a concrete answer to the question that best reveals the strengths or weaknesses of a risk management approach: 'What is the hedge?'

Over the last 50 years, the evolution of risk management technology toward the Merton and Jarrow solution has gone through two basic steps:

1. Assume there is a single source of risk and a risk measurement statistic consistent with that source of risk.
2. Recognize that in reality there are multiple sources of risk and revise the measure so that we have an integrated measure of all risks and sources of risk.

Interest Rate Risk Management Evolution

In Chapters 4–9, we review traditional and more modern tools of interest rate risk management. The first sophisticated interest rate risk management tool was the Macauley [1938] duration concept. In its traditional implementation, managers who own fixed income assets shift a yield curve up or down by a fixed percentage (often 1%) and measure the percentage change in the value of the portfolio. This measure shifts yield curves at all maturities by the same amount, essentially assuming that there is only one type of interest rate risk, parallel movements in the yield curve. Clearly, that is not the case in reality and therefore the duration measures some, but not all, interest rate risks.

The next step forward in sophistication was to recognize that yield curves in fact move in non-parallel ways. The term structure models that we discuss in Chapters 10–13 allow analysts to move one or more key term structure model parameters (typically including the short-term rate of interest) and observe the response of the full yield curve. This provides a more sophisticated measure of duration that allows for non-parallel shifts of the yield curve.

Fixed income managers in both commercial banks and other financial services companies recognize, however, that both of these approaches are abstractions from reality. There are multiple factors driving any yield curve, whether it is a credit risk-free government yield curve or a yield curve that embeds the default risk and potential losses of a defaultable counterparty.

In recognition of these N factors driving the yield curve, fixed income managers have overlaid practical supplements on the theoretical models discussed above:

1. Interest rate sensitivity 'gaps' (see Chapter 6) which show the mismatches between the maturities of assets and liabilities (if any) period by period. These gaps provide visibility to managers that allow them to implicitly reduce the risk that interest rates in gap period K move in a way different from the assumed duration or term structure model specifies.
2. Multi-period simulation of interest rate cash flows using both single scenario interest rate shifts and true monte carlo simulation of interest

rates. Managers can measure the volatility of cash flows and financial accounting income period by period, again to supplement the interest rate models which may understate the true complexity of interest rate risk movements

What is the equivalent of the Merton and Jarrow put option in the interest rate risk context? It is the value of an option to buy the entire portfolio of the financial institution's assets and liabilities at a fixed price at a specific point in time. From a pension fund perspective, a more complex string of options which guarantees the pension fund's ability to provide cash flow of $X(t)$ in each of N periods to meet obligations to pensioners would be necessary.

We return to this discussion in more detail in Chapters 39–44.

Equity Risk Management Evolution

Risk management in the equity markets began in a similar fashion with the powerful and simple insights of the capital asset pricing model. This model initially suggested that all common stocks had their returns driven by a single common factor, the return on the market as a whole, and an idiosyncratic component of risk unique to each stock. By proper diversification, the idiosyncratic component of risk could be diversified away. The single risk factor, the exposure to changes in return on the market, was measured by the beta of both individual common stocks and on the portfolio held by the equity manager.

As in the interest rate case, risk managers quickly seized the insights of the model and then generalized it to recognize there are multiple drivers of risk and the multi-period nature of these risk drivers. In Chapter 2, we introduced the need to add credit risk to the multi-period equity risk models that reflect current 'common practice'.

Option Risk Management Evolution

The Black-Scholes option model brought great hope to options risk managers in much the same way that the capital asset pricing model did. Options portfolio managers (and managers of broader portfolios of instruments with options characteristics) quickly adopted the delta of an options position, the equivalent position in the underlying stock, as an excellent single measure of the risk of an options position.

With experience, however, analysts realized that there was in fact a 'volatility smile'. The volatility smile was the graph that showed that the Black-Scholes options model implied a different level of volatility at different strike prices with the same maturity. Analysts have tended to 'bend' the Black-Scholes options model by using different volatilities at different strike prices rather than looking for a more elegant explanation for the deviation of options prices from the levels predicted by the Black-Scholes model. In effect, analysts are using the Black-Scholes model as an N factor model, not a single factor model with the stock price as the risk driver with a constant volatility.

Credit Risk Management Evolution

The integration of credit risk, market risk, asset and liability management and performance measurement is one of the central themes of this book. Analysts have moved from traditional credit analysis on a company-by-company basis to more modern technology over the last 15 years. The more traditional credit analysis was a single company analysis that involved financial ratios and occasionally simulation to estimate a default probability or rating that summarizes the risk level of each company, one by one.

Now the kind of quantitative credit models that we discuss in Chapters 14–20 allow us to recognize the M common macro-economic risk factors that cause correlated defaults among a portfolio of companies. These insights allow financial institutions to move to a macro-hedging program for a large portfolio of credits for the first time.

It also provides a framework for the quantification of risk as Robert Merton and Robert Jarrow have suggested, with a put option on the credit portfolio.

We now turn to the management process in commercial banks, insurance companies, and pension funds and analyze how and why capital came to play a role in commercial banking risk management and strategy, but not in other institutions.

Managing Risk and Strategy, Business-by-Business

One of the major differences between financial institutions is the number of people who are involved in asset generation. In a life insurance company, a vast majority of the employees are involved in the generation, servicing and pricing of life insurance policies. On the asset side, investment activities are much more 'wholesale' and the number of people involved per one million dollars of assets is much less. In an asset management company, the total staff count is also generally less than 1,000 people. The same is true for pension funds.

For very large commercial banks, the number of people involved is significant because almost all banks these days are heavily involved in the retail generation of assets and liabilities. A bank with 20,000 employees is not considered large. In the U.S., 100,000 or more employees is not rare and in China the numbers are astronomical.

There is another important difference between commercial banks and the rest of the financial community. For asset managers, pension funds, and insurance companies, most of the people managing the assets of the company work in one central location. In a commercial bank, there can be thousands of branches involved in asset generation across a broad swath of geography.

For that reason, in what follows we will largely discuss management of risk and business strategy in a banking context because most of what happens in other financial institutions is a 'special case' of the banking business, including even the actuarial nature of liabilities of all of these types of financial institutions.

Risk and Strategy Management in a Complex Financial Institution

From Chapter 2 and the introduction to this chapter, we know that in the banking business, various parts of the institution are managed by one or more bases from both a risk and return point of view:

- A mark-to-market orientation for the institution as a whole, the trading floor, and the transfer pricing book.
- A financial accounting point of view for both the institution as a whole and almost all non-trading business units.

Moreover, as we say in the introduction to this chapter, multiple risk measures are applied depending on the business unit involved:

- **Complex interest rate risk measures** are applied to the institution as a whole, the trading floor, and the transfer pricing book.
- **Less sophisticated interest rate risk measures** are usually sufficient for most business units because the transfer pricing process in most institutions removes the interest rate risk from line units. Depending on the financial institution, the basis risk (a lack of synchronicity between movements in the interest rate on an asset with a floating-rate pricing index and market rates) usually stays with the business unit and with the head of that business unit, normally the person who has the responsibility for selecting the pricing index for that type of asset.
- **Yes/no credit risk measures** are applied at the 'point of sale' in asset generating locations, often controlled by a central location.
- **Portfolio credit risk measures** are applied by the business unit responsible for maintaining or hedging credit risk quality after the generation of assets.
- **Market risk and credit risk measures** are almost always applied together on the trading floor because so much of the market risk-taking business has taken the form of credit risk arbitrage, even in the interest rate swap market. The percentage of derivatives contracts where at least one side

Figure 3.1   Comparing Risk and Return Profiles

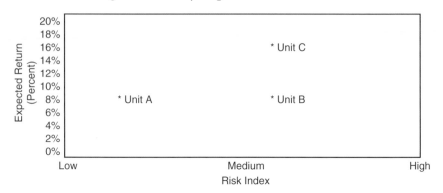

is held by one of the top ten dealers is astronomical, especially as the bank merger trend continues in the U.S.

- **Return measures are stated either on a market-based total return basis or a net income basis,** usually after interest rate risk is removed via the transfer pricing system.

We defined risk management in Chapter 1 as the discipline by which management is made aware of the risk and returns of alternative strategies at both the transaction level and the portfolio level. Once we have coherent measures of risk and return, management often encounters situations such as represented in Figure 3.1, where the risk and returns of three alternative business units A, B, and C are plotted. Unit C is clearly superior to Unit B, because it has a higher expected return than B. Similarly, Unit A is superior to Unit B because Unit A has the same expected return, but less risk than Unit B. It is much harder to compare Units A and C. How do we select business units which are 'over achievers' and those which are 'under achievers'? This is one of the keys to success in financial institutions management.[1] The Sharpe ratio is commonly cited as a tool in this regard, but there is no simple answer to this question. We hope to provide extensive tools to answer this question in the remainder of the book. There are a number of hallmarks to best practice in this regard:

- A tool which cannot provide useful information about which assets are the best to add at the **transaction level** cannot be useful at the portfolio level, since the portfolio is just a sum of individual transactions.

---

[1] See Chapter 1 of *Financial Risk Management in Banking* by Dennis Uyemura and Donald R. van Deventer for more on this chart.

- **Buy low/sell high** contains a lot of valuable wisdom, as simple as it seems. If the financial institution is offered the right to buy asset 1, with a market value of 100, at a price of 98, it should generally say yes.
- **If the bank has to choose** between asset 1 and asset 2, which has a market value of 100 and can be purchased for a price of 96, the bank should buy asset 2. If the bank is solvent and its risk is not adversely affected at the portfolio level, the bank should buy both. The market price summarizes risk and return into one number.
- Risk/return tools should provide value from **both a risk management perspective and the perspective of shareholder value creation**. These tools are not separate and distinct—they are at the heart of good management.

What Causes Financial Institutions to Fail?

In deciding at the transaction and portfolio levels which assets to select for a financial institution as a whole, the criteria for selection are not independent of which assets and liabilities are already on the books of the financial institution.[2]

The dominant reason for financial institutions to fail in the twenty-first century is credit risk, now that the interest rate risk tools and techniques discussed in the next few chapters are used effectively. This has been confirmed by many studies of bank failures in the U.S., most importantly the Financial Institutions Monitoring System implemented by the Board of Governors of the Federal Reserve in the U.S. in the mid-1990s.[3] The effort to better predict financial institutions failure and the subsequent losses to deposit insurance funds gained new momentum with the announcement of its new Loss Distribution Model by the Federal Deposit Insurance Corporation on December 10 2003.[4] We discuss the loss distribution model in detail in later chapters.

Given the importance of credit risk in the failure of financial institutions, an integrated treatment of credit risk, market risk, asset and liability management, and performance measurement is critical from a risk perspective.

In part for this reason, capital has become a critical component of both regulatory and management supervision of the diverse business units involved in a complex financial institution.

---

[2] Donald R. van Deventer and Kenji Imai discuss this issue extensively in *Credit Risk Models and the Basel Accords* [2003] in Chapters 1 and 2.

[3] Ibid, Chapter 9.

[4] A copy of the FDIC Loss Distribution Model is available on the research page on www.kamakuraco.com.

The Role of Capital in Risk Management and Business Strategy

Given the diverse business units in a large, complex financial institution, lots of complexities come into play. First of all, some types of financial institutions have a very large institutional divide between the asset side of the organization and the liability side. Pension funds, life insurance companies, property and casualty insurance companies, and asset management companies are almost always clearly divided between the two halves of this balance sheet. This means that most managers either oversee assets or liabilities but almost never both. The author would argue that this split is unfortunate from a 'best practice' risk management point of view since many risk factors affect both sides of the balance sheet. Nonetheless, this political reality simplifies managerial reporting.

In commercial banks, senior management is faced with three types of business units:

- Those who own only assets (specialized lending offices);
- Those who own only liabilities (the unit issuing wholesale certificates of deposit);
- Those who own both assets and liabilities (retail branches, business banking offices, trading floors doing repurchase agreements, etc).

The largest number of business units falls into the last category, where the business units have both assets and liabilities. Management has two challenges:

1. Put the business units on a common basis;
2. Adjust differences between units so that an 'apples to apples' performance comparison can be made.

Implicit in these two tasks are the assumptions that a common basis is possible and that backwards-looking market data or backwards-looking financial statements are a good indicator of future performance. The latter assumption is more tenuous than the first.[5]

There are two steps in accomplishing these two tasks:

A. Specify the method by which business units with different risks can be compared to each other (especially in the base of a comparison like Unit A and Unit C graphed in Figure 3.1);
B. Do the calculations that make this comparison possible.

The 'common practice' in this regard is what we focus on in this section. In the last section of this chapter, we talk about the pitfalls of the common

---

[5] Ibid., Chapter 9.

practice and spend the last chapters of this book refining these calculations using the tools that we develop in the rest of the book.

- Step 1: **Choose the basis for the calculations** (market value basis or financial accounting basis). As mentioned in Chapter 2, most commercial banks use a mix of these approaches but choose a financial accounting basis for the vast majority of business units. We assume that choice is made here.
- Step 2: **Select the adjustments to nominal net interest income** for the business unit that must be made to allow for units of different risk to be compared.
- Step 3: **Select a common basis for comparing business units** of different levels of net income to better understand relative risk-adjusted performance.

For a pension fund, this process is quite straightforward. The basis is the market value-based return on the asset portfolio being analyzed. There are no adjustments to this basis except to subtract the relative performance of the benchmark index by which performance is judged. A check is also done to ensure that the risk (usually tracking error) of the funds invested was within an acceptable tolerance around the risk of the benchmark.

For a bank, this process is much more convoluted. Some of the complexity is productive and some is done to ensure maximum employment in the performance measurement unit.

Here is a sample of the kinds of calculations (see Table 3.1) usually made on a sample portfolio of external transactions like this:

Assets

Three-year fixed-rate auto loans: 100

Liabilities

90-day certificates of deposit: 120

All assets are funded with matched maturity borrowings from the transfer pricing center as discussed in Chapter 2 using the techniques of the following chapters. All funds from the certificates of deposits gathered are sold to the transfer pricing center. 'Capital' is then assigned depending on the nature of the assets and the nature of liabilities. Proceeds of the capital are sold back to the transfer pricing center with a maturity to match the period over which the amount of capital is held constant. The result is a financial accounting-based management information system that would look something like this:

The portfolio of three-year auto loans yields 6.76%. The exact day-count matched maturity transfer pricing system assigns $100 in borrowings to fund the three-year auto loans on a matched maturity basis. These borrowings have

Table 3.1 Calculating Total Risk-Adjusted Return

	Balance Sheet	**Yield (%)**	**Income**
Assets			
3 year fixed rate auto loans	100	6.76	6.76
90-day loans to the transfer pricing center	120	1.50	1.80
Capital-related loans to the transfer pricing center	7.7	1.50	0.12
Total assets			8.68
Liabilities			
90-day certificates of deposit	120	1.37	1.64
3-year borrowings from the transfer pricing center	100	5.18	5.18
Total Liabilities			6.82
Capital assigned for 90-day certificates of deposit	1.2		
Capital assigned for 3-year auto loans	6.5		
Total Capital Assigned	7.7		
Total Liabilities and Capital			1.86
Risk-Adjusted Return on Auto Loans			24.31%
Risk-Adjusted Return on Deposits			13.00%
Total Risk-Adjusted Return			24.05%

a yield of 5.18%. We discuss how to calculate a transfer price for auto loans like these in Chapters 7 and 8. In a similar way, the 90-day funds raised by the business unit from issuing certificates of deposit are sold on a matched maturity basis to the transfer pricing center at 1.50%, a premium of 0.13% over the 1.37% cost of the certificates of the deposit to the business unit. This premium is a function of the marginal cost of issuing large-lot 90 day certificates of deposit, not an arbitrary premium.

The next step is where there is a considerable lack of consensus among financial institutions for the reasons we outline in the next section. Most leading international banks assign 'risk-adjusted capital' to each asset and each liability. The rationale for this assignment of capital varies widely from bank to bank but they include the following common themes:

1. The total amount of capital assigned, when added across business units, should sum to the total amount of capital in the organization. The total

amount of capital in the organization in some banks means financial accounting capital and in other banks it means the market value of the bank's common stock.

2. The amount of capital assigned to each asset depends on the risk of the asset class. Van Deventer and Imai [2003] show how the Shimko-Tejima-van Deventer [1993] model of risky debt can be used to do this while considering both the interest rate risk and the credit risk of the asset category.

3. The amount of capital assigned to each liability depends on its maturity and the 'liquidity' protection the deposits provide. This is perhaps the most controversial step in the calculation.

4. Risk-adjustments come in two places. Interest rate risk is removed from the business unit by the assignment of matched maturity transfer pricing assets and liabilities to each transaction. Credit risk is reflected in the risk-weighted capital assignment.

5. The result is a risk-adjusted return on capital. For the auto loan portion of the portfolio, the interest rate risk-adjusted net income is the $6.76 in income on the auto loans less the $5.18 cost of matched maturity funding on that portfolio, for an interest rate risk-adjusted net income of $1.58. This is a 24.31% return on the $6.50 in risk-adjusted capital assigned to the auto loan portfolio. Note that the interest rate adjustment comes in the numerator of the return calculation (since net income is net of interest rate risk) and the credit risk adjustment comes in the denominator via the risk-adjusted capital assigned.

6. In a similar way we can calculate a 13% risk-adjusted return on the deposit portfolio and a 24.05% risk-adjusted return for the business unit as a whole.

For a comprehensive survey of this risk-adjusted capital allocation system, interested readers should see Matten [1996].

Common practice in the banking industry says that, armed with these figures, we can do the following:

1. We can clearly judge which business unit creates the most shareholder value;

2. We can rank the business units from best to worst;

3. We can decide which business units should be expanded (receive more capital) and which business units should be discontinued;

4. We can carry this managerial process to the individual transaction level and set correct pricing for every asset and liability for a clear 'accept/ reject' criterion. More generally, this risk-adjusted capital allocation system correctly calculates the true value/market price of each asset and liability and the bank should buy assets that have an offered price

(not yield) below this in the market and issue liabilities that have a market price (not yield) that is above their theoretical price under the capital allocation-based pricing system.

If this is true, we have a powerful tool. If this is more than a touch of over-selling the concept, we need to be careful how we use it. We turn to those issues next.

Capital-Based Risk Management in Banking Today: Pros and Cons

The previous section outlines the common practice for risk-adjusted asset and liability selection in the commercial banking business. We discussed the same process in the pension fund industry in Chapter 2:

1. Select a benchmark index that best matches the nature of the assets being analyzed.
2. This benchmark should be a simplistic strategy that any institution could achieve with a minimum of internal staff and analysis (such as buy every stock in the S&P500 or buy every U.S. Treasury bond outstanding).
3. Measure the tracking error of the asset class being studied to ensure that the asset class is within the limits for tracking error versus the benchmark.
4. A good manager has assets whose total return in excess of the benchmark return is 'plus alpha', a positive risk-adjusted return.

This approach is distinctly different than the approach taken by the banking industry:

- It is based on market returns, not financial accounting returns;
- Risk-adjustment is reflected in the returns of the benchmark and the limits on tracking error;
- There is no transfer pricing of matched maturity funds;
- There is no capital allocation;
- There is no risk-adjusted return on capital calculation;
- There is also no pretence that the methodology provides a tool for pricing the assets in question, only that skill of the manager selecting the assets can be measured.

While we discussed the concerns about this calculation in Chapter 2, it has a simplicity and elegance and lack of arbitrariness that distinguishes it as a managerial tool.

Why did the banking industry turn to such a convoluted calculation instead?

- The banking industry has many more people to manage.
- The banking industry has many classes of assets and liabilities that don't have observable market prices.
- The banking industry feels it cannot manage its huge number of business units on a mark-to-market basis.
- The banking industry has many business units that have both assets and liabilities, so the concept of 'capital' is a natural one.
- In many business units, they originate more liabilities than assets so there has to be some adjustment to a normal basis.
- Many of the regulatory restrictions on banks revolve around capital.

There are a few more important points about the common practice in banking risk-adjusted capital that need to be mentioned. Van Deventer and Imai [2003] in Chapters 9 and 10 go into these points in detail:

- The risk-adjusted return on capital is backward-looking, not forward-looking. It has long been known that past returns on a security are fully reflected in its market price and therefore provide no guidance on the level of future returns.
- The risk-adjusted return on capital assigns capital in a well-intended way unsupported by a sophisticated theory of capital structure (although the approach van Deventer and Imai [2003] recommend is a step in this direction).
- No theory of asset valuation in financial economics yet incorporates the capital of the potential buyer in the valuation formula.

Are these concerns just academic concerns or do they indicate severe problems with the approach taken in the banking industry?

A few examples prove that the problems are severe:

1. The common practice in banking industry, risk-adjusted return on capital, indicates a negative risk-adjusted return on holding government securities because they have a negative spread versus the marginal cost of funds for the bank. This signal says no banks should own risk-free government securities, but in fact almost all banks do. Therefore the decision rule is wrong. Banks seek to overcome this obvious 'miss' in the rule with ad hoc adjustments.
2. Anecdotal evidence from many banks that have carried out this analysis to the transaction level indicates that the prices are consistently 'off the market', which is no surprise, since the transactions are not benchmarked in current market prices.

3. If this method were superior to the approach used by fund managers, then fund managers would use it.

Calculation of 'shareholder value-added', which measures true cash flow rather than financial net income, is a partial step in the right direction. It falls short of the mark in applying a minimum hurdle rate for acceptable return, which is not consistent with actual returns in the market (in contrast to the approach that pension funds take). For more on the conventional implementation of shareholder value-added, see Chapter 2 of Uyemura and van Deventer [1993].

As a result of these concerns about risk-adjusted capital allocation, the authors recommend that the risk-adjusted capital allocation approach be restricted to the largest consolidated business units in the banking business (for example, wholesale corporate lending, investment banking, retail banking, and so on) and not be carried down to the smaller business unit level or the transaction level. They don't work on a micro-level and their errors at the macro level are obvious enough that senior management can bear the problems in mind when making decisions.

The methodology is not sufficiently accurate to provide a high quality guide to asset and liability selection. We discuss advanced methodologies that provide better guidance to asset and liability management selection in Chapters 39–44. We now turn to regulatory views of capital management.

History of Capital-Based Regulations in Commercial Banking

Capital allocation by banks and regulators has had a complex 'chicken and egg' relationship that has obscured bank management's ability to adopt the correct risk-adjusted strategies for asset selection. When regulatory constraints are imposed that are not based on market values and market returns, bank management teams are forced into regulatory 'arbitrage' that stems from their conflicting dual obligation to do what regulators insist they do and at the same time seek to maximize risk-adjusted returns to shareholders in the long-term.

As Uyemura and van Deventer [1993] outline, the regulatory process in the U.S. has historically had a tri-partite structure:

1. System liquidity provided by the Board of Governors of the Federal Reserve System;
2. Interest rate-related regulations, the now defunct Regulation Q;
3. Deposit insurance managed by the Federal Deposit Insurance Corporation.

The role of the Federal Reserve in providing both institution-specific liquidity when necessary (for example in the wake of the September 11 2001 attacks on New York City), and systemic liquidity is well known.

What is less well-known is why the U.S. regulators maintained a limit on the maximum deposit interest rate that any commercial bank could pay, known as Regulation Q. For many years the maximum interest rate that could be paid on savings deposits with balances of $100,000 or less were at levels of 5.00–5.25%. The theory was that this limit would prevent aggressive risk-seeking banks from bidding up deposit rates to expand their activities rapidly.

The emergence of 'money market funds' which pooled the funds of small depositors so they could earn the higher returns paid on deposits of more than $100,000 spelled the end of Regulation Q in the U.S., which required regulators to take a more sophisticated approach to risk management.

In 1980, the passage of the Financial Deregulation and Monetary Control Act ended Regulation Q and led financial regulators in the U.S. to turn to capital-based regulations to insure the safety and soundness of financial institutions.

The regulators' first attempt in this regard was to define the concept of 'primary capital'. The regulatory definition of capital was firmly rooted in financial accounting-based capital, not market values.

They included in 'primary capital' common equity and retained earnings, perpetual preferred stock (an instrument which until then had rarely been issued), the reserve for loan losses (even though this amount was usually set by commercial banks to be consistent with expected losses), and so-called mandatory convertible notes, a specific type of debt instrument which became the primary vehicle for arbitrage of the primary capital concept by commercial banks.

This regulation triggered a number of actions by bank management which led regulators to conclude that the primary capital calculations were misguided and that the actions they engendered increased, rather than decreased, the risk in the banking system:

- Banks reduced their assets subject to the capital regulations by selling their safest, most liquid assets (government securities), increasing liquidity risk at many banks.
- Banks sold their head office buildings to book an accounting 'gain' that increased capital ratios but as a result added to the fixed costs that banks would have to incur on an on-going basis.
- Banks began to engage in an increasing number of 'off-balance sheet transactions', obscuring the accuracy of financial statements on which regulations were based.

Bank failures dramatically increased throughout the 1980s so it is hard to argue that the concept of primary capital was effective in reducing the risk in the banking system. The primary capital concept was ultimately scrapped in favor of a system that was both more international in scope and more sophisticated.

In 1986, the Board of Governors of the Federal Reserve System and the Bank of England announced the concept of risk-based capital. The risk-based capital concept was specifically designed to address some of the major deficiencies of the primary capital concept:

1. Make a distinction among asset classes by riskiness.
2. Incorporate off-balance sheet transactions to reduce regulatory capital arbitrage.
3. Adopt common standards internationally for a fair international competition in financial services.

The risk-based capital regulations had two basic components:

a. A revised definition of regulatory capital.
b. An introduction of the 'risk-weighted asset concept'.

Risk-weighted assets are a variation of the bank risk-adjusted capital concept outlined in the previous section except that the riskiness of an asset class is reflected in risk weighted assets associated with the financial accounting assets for that class, rather than the risk-adjusted capital assigned to the asset class. Low risk assets were assigned risk-weighted assets that were a small fraction of their financial accounting amounts or market values. Higher risk assets were assigned a risk-weighted asset amount closer to or equal to their financial accounting values. This change in capital regulations was designed to encourage banks to retain liquid assets on their balance sheets by reducing the capital ratio penalty of the primary capital concept. These changes were ultimately labeled 'Basel I' after the headquarters city of the Bank for International Settlements, which coordinated the international negotiations for the capital accords.

Bankers and regulators quickly noted that the regulations were too simple (and therefore inaccurate) in two respects. First, they almost completely ignored interest rate risk. Second, the risk-weighting schemes of Basel I were so few in number that finer gradations of credit risk were ignored, again penalizing asset classes with a risk level lower than average in their Basel I risk category.

The Board of Governors of the Federal Reserve in the U.S. moved to address the first point with a proposal that would link interest rate risk to capital levels. This proposal made use of Macaulay's duration concept [1938] that we discussed in Chapter 1 and which we review in detail in later chapters. This proposal was never adopted as the banks in the U.S. were incapable of understanding the basics of duration, or at least they claimed as much. Cynics responded that it was harder to get a driver's license than to be a bank CEO, where no license is required that certifies a basic understanding of how to run a bank. The Federal Reserve, even today, is very nervous about safety and soundness regulations which exceed a minimum level of complexity and that has affected U.S. participation in 'Basel II', to which we now turn.

The Basel Committee on Banking Supervision began its deliberations on how to address the shortcomings of Basel I in the late 1990s, and it has issued a steady stream of pronouncements and proposals beginning in 2001. These are available on the web site of the Bank for International Settlements (www.bis.org). As of this writing, the final regulations have not yet been released but they promise a substantial increase in complexity that is related to credit risk measurement.

Van Deventer and Imai [2003] discuss the outline of the Basel II, as the draft proposals are known, in detail. In Chapter 19–21, we discuss the biggest problems with the Basel II pronouncements—capital ratios, however derived, are weak predictors of the safety and soundness of financial institutions and they significantly underperform models such as the recently announced Loss Distribution Model of the Federal Deposit Insurance Corporation (see the December 10 2003 press release of the FDIC available on www.kamakuraco.com or on the website of the FDIC).

Because of the high cost and low predictive power of the Basel II capital ratios, U.S. regulators currently intend to restrict their applicability to only 10 or 11 of the 8,000 U.S. commercial banks. Regulators in other countries, however, have shown much greater enthusiasm for the Basel II concepts. For the remainder of this book we will draw a steady contrast between 'best practice' risk management and 'common practice risk management' and the Basel II proposals.

We begin that journey with the foundation of financial institutions risk management—interest rate risk.

CHAPTER 4

Interest Rate Risk: Introduction and Overview

Interest rate risk is the essence of all aspects of integrated risk management—credit risk, market risk, asset and liability management (ALM), performance measurement, and even operational risk. Credit risk analysis that is not built on a random interest rate risk framework completely misses one of the key macro-economic factors driving default, as the one trillion dollar bail-out of the U.S. savings and loan industry confirms. Market risk at most institutions involves a large proportion of fixed income instruments, so we have to deal with interest rate risk in a comprehensive way to deal with market risk. Asset and liability management at most institutions involves both sides of the balance sheet and a range of instruments with complexities that go far beyond those found in market risk, such as pension liabilities, insurance policies, non-maturity deposits, credit card advances, and so on. Analysis of each of these instruments must be based on a random interest rate framework as well. In ALM, the complexity of the task is aggravated by the frequent need to do the analysis both on a mark-to-market basis and on a net income simulation basis looking forward.

For this reason, we pay special attention to interest rate risk in this book. In this chapter, we focus on the big picture—is there an optimal interest rate risk position for a financial institution and, if so, what are the determinants of what that position should be?

A Step-by-Step Approach to Analyzing Interest Rate Risk

Our goal in this chapter is to address the big picture of determining the optimal degree of interest rate risk for a major financial institution. In Chapter 5, we discuss the implications of this for total balance sheet management on both a mark-to-market and a net income simulation basis. We discuss in detail the kind of trade-offs involved in a hedging program, for example, and the alternatives that are important from a shareholder value point of view.

In Chapter 6, we introduce the major tools of interest rate risk in a 'plain English' fashion and then plunge into interest rate analytics in a detailed way in Chapters 7–10, revisiting the key interest rate risk issues to show how the new tools shed light on key interest rate risk management strategies.

Analytical techniques for interest rate risk management have generally fallen into two basic approaches:

- Analysis of the current portfolio;
- Analysis of the current portfolio and changes in the portfolio going forward.

Analysis of the Current Portfolio

Analysis of the current portfolio is usually based on a combination of approaches, which we discuss in detail going forward:

- **Gap analysis:** the traditional analysis of the effective interest rate sensitivity of the balance sheet or portfolio by 'time bucket' or maturity interval, based on what we own today. Gap analysis can be done both on a financial accounting basis (common at the total balance sheet level) and a market value basis (standard on a trading floor).
- **Stress testing:** where the financial institution calculates how the market value of its portfolio changes for specific changes in the interest rate environment. This stress testing ranges from the 1938 Macaulay duration approach to more modern stress tests of all ranges of movements in yield curve shapes and relationships between yield curves. They go under the name of concepts such as 'key rate duration' and 'basis risk analysis'.
- **Capital adequacy:** which analyzes the risk of the institution at hand and estimates the amount of capital necessary to bring that risk into line with limits set by management or regulators. This is what was at the heart of the primary capital guidelines, Basel I and Basel II that we introduced in the previous chapter.
- **Limits:** which can be set to control either interest rate risk allowed to one trader or allowed in one segment of the portfolio or to control exposure to one particular counterparty or group of counterparties from a credit risk perspective.

We will devote a lot of attention to these concepts throughout the remainder of the book. For the most part, if the institution is dealing with instruments with an observable market price, this analysis of the current portfolio dominates the analysis of interest rate risk.

Analysis of the Current Portfolio and Changes in the Portfolio Going Forward

While the analysis of the current portfolio dominates most financial institutions' interest rate risk analysis, it is not the only technique used and for many types of institutions it may not be the most important analysis. Thirty years ago, interest rate risk analysis at major banks was done primarily by means of 'net income simulation' which consisted of an analysis of the financial accounting income of the institution modeled going forward, based not only on what the institution has on its balance sheet today but also based on what it expects to have on its balance sheet in the future. Net income simulation isn't fashionable given the current 'high tech' approach to risk management, and its adherents are often described as the dinosaurs of risk management by the rocket scientists of the credit derivatives market, or the market risk-focused analysts of risk.

This criticism of the net income approach has some justification, since the entire savings and loan industry, wiped out by interest rate risk in the 1980s, was relying heavily on net income simulation for risk analysis and either completely failed to perceive the risk (the harshest view) or knew of the risk and couldn't do anything about it given the state of financial markets at the time (a minimal amount of floating-rate mortgages, not much access to long-term finance, and so on). The former view is held by many because most analysts of net income simulation at that time focused on a short-term view of accounting net income one to two years forward. This approach ignores all risks on the balance sheet with a long maturity, and that's why many lack confidence in this type of risk analysis and its practitioners. Even today, one of the U.S.'s three largest banks devotes more than 15 employees primarily to a detailed analysis of net interest income over the last seven days of each month.[1] While this analysis may be useful to the CEO's earnings commentary to Wall Street, it isn't risk analysis.

A revisionist view of this kind of multi-period analysis would describe it as a lost art that is now being revived and on the leading edge of risk analysis for purposes such as:

- Multi-period monte carlo simulation of losses on tranches of a collateralized debt obligation;
- Multi-period simulation of a first to default swap on a basket of five names (say IBM, General Motors, AMR (parent of American Airlines), Republic of Korea, and UBS AG);

---

[1] Presentation by the bank to the North American Asset and Liability Management Association, Tampa Florida, September 2001.

- Multi-period simulation of cash flows and stress testing for an 'own name' liquidity crisis;
- Multi-period simulation of savings deposit and checking account balances to determine credit risk-related run-off of balances;
- Multi-period simulation of pension fund assets and liabilities to determine the most likely timing and probability of a cash flow shortfall for the pension fund.

This kind of multi-period simulation adds to the insights gained from a pure current period mark-to-market and stress testing of the assets and liabilities an institution owns today. In many cases, this kind of forward-looking simulation means we must embed in the analysis rational actions that will be taken by management in the future including both asset selection (in good times) and asset liquidation (in bad times). These management actions by definition need to reflect the environment in a dynamic way, rather than hard coding 'average behavior' into a net income simulation as was common practice 30 years ago.

These two approaches to risk management, the current book versus the simulated future book, can lead to conflicting implications for management. That sometimes obscures the big picture of how much interest rate risk is the right amount.

What Number is Interest Rate Risk Management All About?

In Chapter 1, we noted how Robert Merton and Robert Jarrow have both proposed that a properly described put option is the single number which best describes the integrated risk in most situations. In the previous section, if we are thinking only about our current portfolio, this put option is a European put option exercised only on one specific date. If we are thinking about a multi-period analysis of our balance sheet going forward, this put option can be an American put option exercisable at many dates in the future.

We can describe almost all common risk management risk measures using the Merton and Jarrow analysis of the put option. When we think about it, the put option is a much more precise summary of the risk than other terms which are more commonly used to describe risk.

For example:

- Instead of the 10-day **value-at-risk** of a trading portfolio, what is the value of a 10-day put option on my current portfolio with an exercise price equal to the portfolio's current market value? The price of the put option will increase sharply with the risk of my portfolio, and the put option's price will reflect all possible losses and their probability, not just the 99th percentile loss as is traditional in value-at-risk analysis.

- Instead of **stress testing the 12-month net income** of the financial institution to see if net income will go below $100 million for the year, what is the price of a put option in month 12 which will produce a gain in net income exactly equal to the shortfall of net income versus the $100 million target? The more interest rate risk in the balance sheet of the financial institution, the more expensive this put option will be. The put option will reflect all levels of net income shortfall and their probability, not just the shortfalls detected by specific stress tests.
- Instead of the **Basel II risk-weighted capital ratio** for the bank, what is the price of the put option that insures solvency of the bank in one year's time? This put option measures all potential losses embedded in the financial institution's balance sheet and their probability of occurrence, including both interest rate risk and credit risk, as we discuss at the end of this chapter.
- Instead of **'expected losses' on a collateralized debt obligation tranche's B tranche**, what is the price of a put option on the value of the tranche at par at maturity? This put option reflects all losses on the tranche, not just the average loss, along with their probability of occurrence.
- Instead of **'expected losses on the Bank Insurance Fund'** in the U.S., the Federal Deposit Insurance Corporation has valued the put option of retail bank deposits at their par value as discussed in the FDIC's loss distribution model announced on December 10 2003.

With this key Jarrow-Merton insight in mind, a lot of the debate about the proper focus of interest rate risk management fades away. Three different dimensions of a financial institution's risk have dominated past arguments about how much interest rate risk is the right amount:

- **Net interest income (or net income)**, a measure that by definition is multi-period in nature and includes instruments that the financial institution owns today and those that it will own in the future. Net interest income as the focus of risk analysis is unheard of on the trading floor but is much discussed by senior management of many financial institutions.
- **Market value of portfolio equity**, which is 'bank speak' for the market value of the assets a financial institution owns today less the market value of its liabilities. This is the common trading floor choice, aided by the luxury of having market prices for almost every asset and liability in full view. It is also increasingly popular among sophisticated total balance sheet risk managers even when the balance sheet is dominated by assets and liabilities with no observable market price.

- **Market-based equity ratio**, which is the ratio of the mark-to-market value of the equity of the portfolio ('market value of portfolio equity' in bank speak) divided by the market value of assets. This is most closely related to the capital ratio formulas of the primary capital era, Basel I, and Basel II.
- **Default probability of the institution**, which is another strong candidate as a single measure of risk. The complexity here is over which time period the default probability should be for.

While these measures can move in conflicting directions under specific scenarios, the put option proposed by Merton and Jarrow behaves in a consistent way, which is why Professor Jarrow labels the put option a 'coherent risk measure' as noted in Chapter 1.

For a discussion of the differences between the implications of net income, market value of equity, and the market-based equity ratio, see Chapter 5 of Uyemura and van Deventer [1993].

Trading Assets versus a Bank Balance Sheet

In Chapter 5 of Uyemura and van Deventer [1993], the authors study the simple case of a bank with one asset worth $1,000, one liability in the amount of $800, and newly invested capital of $200. The asset is $1,000 invested in a properly priced loan at the bank's six-month certificate of deposit rate plus 2%. We assume the bank can issue certificates of deposit at 6% at any maturity. This loan's interest rate will be reset every six months depending on current market rates at the time.

The bank has to choose a funding strategy—what maturity (in months, N) of CDs has to be issued to fund this loan for 'optimal interest rate risk'? Once N is chosen, the bank will reissue an N-month CD every time it needs funding.

Uyemura and van Deventer show that the obvious choice (six months) minimizes changes in the market equity ratio. From a mark-to-market hedging point of view, the bank is 'long' a six-month asset worth $1,000, and to protect the current market value of equity of $200, the bank would have to issue a CD with a longer maturity than six months since the par value of the CD is only $800. We show how to do this analysis in detail in later chapters. From a one-year net income point of view, Uyemura and van Deventer show that a CD shorter than six months is necessary to minimize the variation in net income.

For the first six months, the loan of $1,000 earns 8% or $40 in revenue. The expense on the six-month CD is $24 if the CD rate is 6%. The earnings of $16 come from two sources: $8 in spread income of 2% on the $800 in CD money, and $8 from the $200 in equity which earned the loan yield of 8%. If in the second six months the six-month CD rate falls to 4%, revenue on the

Figure 4.1   Why Net Income Varies When a Six-Month CD
Maturity is Chosen

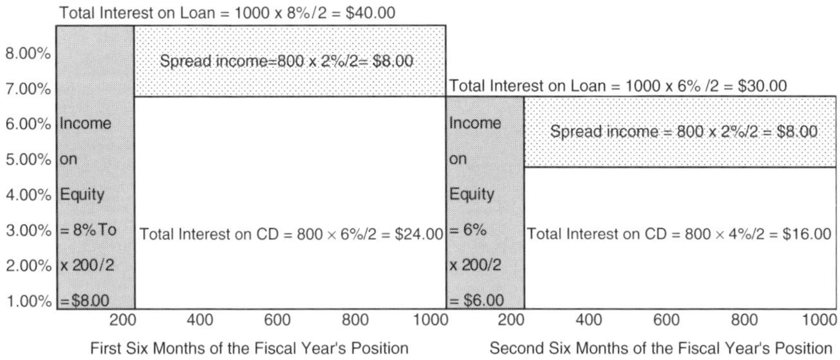

loan falls to $30 and the expense on the CD falls to $16, leaving profits of $14 for the semi-annual period. This $14 in six months income is composed of $8 of spread income on the $800 CD and lower earnings of $6 on the $200 in equity earning the 6% yield on the loan.[2]

This earnings impact of equity in the simplest bank imaginable is very important for a number of reasons and the implications are worth summarizing:

- If the assets of a newly-formed financial institution are all funded on a matched maturity basis, the net income of the bank will rise and fall when interest rates rise and fall.
- This occurs because the income stream of the financial institution has two components—a fixed component consisting of the 'locked in' spread income on the loan, and a floating component consisting of the earnings on equity.
- For transfer pricing purposes as discussed in Chapter 2, we have to clearly identify the net interest income impact of equity so that it does not obscure our perception of the impact of changes in spread on income.
- If we assume the loan will never default (we re-examine this assumption below), we know the market value of equity is the sum of a six-month LIBOR floating-rate security with a perpetual maturity and a perpetual fixed cash flow of $8 every six months (assuming all earnings are paid out semi-annually).

We now turn to the implications of this simple financial institution for risk management.

---

[2] William Mack Terry, developer of the Bank of America transfer pricing system discussed in Chapter 2, devoted a substantial amount of time making this earnings impact of equity clear to senior management.

Credit Risk and Interest Rate Risk are Inseparable

In the example above, we divided the net income of our simple financial institution into pieces on the assumption that the loan borrower cannot default. Based on that overly optimistic assumption, we have three neat pieces of the revenue on the loan to divide:

1. Locked in spread income of $8 every six months;
2. Floating-rate earnings on the equity of the bank;
3. Earnings to exactly cover the cost of the certificate of deposit.

From this simple perspective, we are in the 'safety zone' from an interest rate risk perspective because there is no level of interest rates for which net interest income on this simple financial institution can be negative, so the financial institution can never go bankrupt.

Unfortunately, this simple financial institution is much more complex because these three components are in reality much more like a modern collateralized debt instrument. We now turn to that analogy.

The Simple Financial Institution as a Collateralized Debt Obligation

When we divided the revenue of this simple financial institution into three parts in the previous section, we ignored the possibility that the loan might default. We now restore the possibility of the default and see what we have instead:

1. **Locked in spread income of $8 every six months** is in reality a credit default swap payment which is partial payment for the fact that the bank's shareholders have to absorb the first $200 in losses on the loan. The bank's equity, in this case, is the 'equity tranche' of a collateralized debt obligation with the loan as the only reference credit in the CDO.
2. **Floating-rate earnings on the equity of the bank** are in fact the other compensation to the bank for taking on the role of equity tranche in this simple CDO and being willing to absorb the first $200 in losses. That is why the loan yields in excess of the risk-free rate.
3. **Earnings to exactly cover the cost of the certificate of deposit** obscure the fact that the bank is paying a risk premium on its certificate of deposit over and above the risk-free yield curve. This premium, which is received by the holder of the CD, is the insurance premium to the CD holder for being in the 'senior tranche' of the CDO. If the loan defaults, the bank shareholders absorb the first $200 in losses and the CD holder absorbs the rest, because after $200 in losses the bank is

bankrupt. These losses could be as much as the entire principal amount of the CD, $800.

4. The dividends paid by the bank semi-annually in our assumption actually allow the holders of the equity tranche to get some of the cash flow out of the CDO and move it to a 'bankruptcy remote' location where no one else can get it. This bankruptcy remote location is the pockets of the common stock/equity tranche holders. This is why bank dividend payouts are tightly regulated at troubled institutions.

From this perspective, it is clear that even though we neatly divided up the revenue of the simplest financial institution in the world, there is credit risk in each of the three pieces which is inseparable—we can hedge the interest rate risk on the assumption that there is no credit risk, but we'll be missing the mark and doing something grossly inaccurate.

Measuring the Bank's Risk as a Put Option in the Merton and Jarrow Sense

We can look at the simple financial institution from the perspective of the put option that measures true risk in the sense of the Merton and Jarrow risk measure from Chapter 1. If we choose a one year horizon:

- The value of deposit insurance (the obligation of the Federal Deposit Insurance Corporation in the U.S.) is the value of a put option on the assets of the bank (the loan) at a strike price of $800, because if the loan is worth less than $800 at maturity the FDIC will have to at least partially cover depositors' losses. This put option covers all 'loss given default' amounts and probabilities. If we had more than one loan, it would cover the joint distribution of defaults and default amounts given the amount of correlation among the default probabilities of the borrowers. We will devote a considerable amount of time to that in the credit risk section of the book.
- The risk of loss on the initial equity investment of $200 is the value of a put option on the loan value less the deposit obligation with a strike price of $200. If we chose to mismatch the funding of the loan, this put option would combine the interest rate risk of the funding strategy and the credit risk of the borrower. Again, these two are very strongly linked if the default probability of the borrower is correlated with interest rates.

If we take a longer view, we can see that the FDIC insurance cost is really an American put option with a long maturity, not a short-term European put option. The probability that this put option is exercised is the default probability of the financial institution. We will spend the rest of this book studying the links between these measures.

The Interest Rate Risk Safety Zone

The complex interaction between interest rate risk and credit risk shouldn't be allowed to obscure a key conclusion about interest rate risk.

We could have changed our simple example to make the loan balance $800 and to assume that it was perfectly match-funded with a six-month certificate of deposit. That would leave us with $200 in equity to invest in risk-free government securities.

Assuming away the potential default of the loan borrower:

No matter which maturity of investment we make with the $200 of equity, this bank will never go bankrupt from interest rate risk. This bank is in the 'safety zone' and shareholders are indifferent to the choice of maturity on the investment of these equity funds. The reason they are indifferent is because, even at the retail investor level, the investor can form a model portfolio with the investor's desired risk. For example, what if management invested the equity in 10-year bonds and the retail investor wanted the funds invested in a one-year maturity? The investor achieves that by buying x% of the bank's common stock, selling short x% of the $200 in 10-year bonds,[3] and buying x% of $200 in one-year bonds.

Once the bank begins to mismatch on the loan funding, the probability of bankruptcy increases from zero. For any mismatch, there is an interest rate scenario (often an incredibly unlikely, but theoretically possible scenario), which can cause bankruptcy. Once this bankruptcy probability becomes a significant probability from a practical point of view, shareholders begin to bear the expected cost of bankruptcy, which is the unhedgable loss of the perpetual ability of the financial institution to generate profitable assets that earn an excess above the return on traded securities of equivalent risk available in the market. It is this expected bankruptcy loss which causes the bank stock price to decline when the bank moves out of the safety zone. As long as the bank is within the safety zone, the bank's stock price will be unaffected[4] by the level of interest rate risk, all other things being equal, because the interest rate risk is hedgable even by retail investors for their own account.[5]

As we delve into the interest rate analytics first and the credit risk analytics second, we should not lose sight of this simple truth about interest rate risk.

---

[3] More practically, the investor would 'short' government bond futures.

[4] This doesn't mean that the bank's stock price won't decline if Bank A has taken more risk than Bank B. It means only that Bank A and Bank B, all other things being equal, will have the same initial stock prices if both differ only in the degree of interest rate risk taken in the safety zone.

[5] Lot sizes for financial futures are so small that the argument that this hedging can be done at the retail level is a practical one. At the institutional investor level, of course, this hedging could be much easier.

CHAPTER 5

Interest Rate Risk Mismatching and Hedging

I n Chapter 4, we introduced the concept of the interest rate risk 'safety zone'. We will return to this concept frequently as we discuss interest rate risk and the implications of interest rate risk for the total risk, including credit risk, of the institution. In this chapter, we focus on the strategy and tactics of changing the interest rate risk of a financial institution from both a political and economic point of view. In Chapter 6, we will introduce some of the most traditional interest rate risk management and measurement tools and then follow with a discussion of more modern interest rate risk management tools and techniques in later chapters. It is these more modern techniques that will allow actual implementation of the Merton-Jarrow approach to risk management, using the put option concept as a comprehensive measure of risk for the institution.

We start by reviewing the kinds of analytical issues and political issues that frequently arise when making a decision to change the interest rate risk profile of an institution.

Political Factions in Interest Rate Risk Management

In Chapters 2 and 3, we discussed how performance measurement systems differ by type of institution. These institutional differences have a big impact on the politics of measuring and changing the interest rate risk of a financial institution.

Pension fund considerations

As we discussed in Chapters 2 and 3, a pension fund is typically divided between the asset side of the organization and the liability side of the organization. The liability side of a pension fund has a heavy actuarial component, and expert actuaries calculate the most likely benefits that must be paid to the beneficiaries of the pension fund. The board of directors of the organization then establishes the best mix of various asset classes that the fund will invest in. Typically, the asset classes selected include:

- **Fixed income securities**, which are designed to provide a steady amount of cash flow toward the pension obligations. The manager of this sub-portfolio is typically measured against a naïve benchmark such as the Lehman Brothers Government Bond index.
- **Equity securities**, which are designed to provide a higher long-term expected return than fixed income securities, while at the same time, partially capturing any benefits from an inflationary environment to help offset a rise in pension obligations that inflation would trigger.
- **Commodities and real estate**, which are almost exclusively designed to capture returns from inflation to offset an increase in pension benefits that occur in an inflationary environment.

The amount of risk that the fund has is analyzed on two levels. The first level is at the macro level, where the decision is made about what proportion of the total portfolio should go to these three components. The second level is to analyze the level of risk of the sub-portfolio versus the naïve benchmark that is selected as the performance benchmark for the sub-portfolio. The total amount of risk taken by the organization is largely determined by the first of these two decisions. The Jarrow-Merton 'put option' framework offers considerable benefits in quantifying the many factors that can cause a mismatch in returns on the asset side and obligations on the liability side (inflation, interest rate movements, changes in the life expectancy of the pension beneficiaries, movements in building and commodity prices, and so on). This is an extremely important issue that most sophisticated pension funds are just beginning to quantify. There will be enormous progress on this issue over the next decade that will involve simultaneous analysis of mark-to-market technology and multi-period simulation, techniques that we discuss in the rest of this book.

Things are more manageable at the sub-portfolio level. Consider the fixed income sub-portfolio. The manager of the fixed income sub-portfolio will have tracking error versus the Lehman Government Bond Index in two dimensions. One contribution to tracking error comes from the potential for default if the manager is buying fixed income securities with credit risk. The second contribution to tracking error comes from the mismatch in the maturity structure of cash flows in the actual portfolio versus the cash flow associated with the components of the Lehman Government Bond Index.

The politics of where to fall within the tracking error allowed to the fixed income portfolio are more straightforward in pension funds than they are in most institutions because of the relatively small number of people involved. Normally the board of directors will specify the maximum tracking error versus the benchmark and the head of fixed income (or a small committee) will decide where the portfolio should fall within that tracking error benchmark. This will be determined in many cases by advantages in execution rather than by outright interest rate 'bets'.

How about the risk/return trade-off at other institutions?

Life insurance companies and property and casualty insurance companies

Changes in the level of interest rate risk in a life insurance company have many of the characteristics of the pension fund decision-making process. The liability side is analyzed by actuarial staff and the head of the investment department, supervised by the board of directors, is given specific performance benchmarks that he must exceed while keeping tracking error within pre-set limits. Most of the politics of risk-taking in an insurance company is focused on the credit risk of the benchmark fixed income portfolio and who bears credit losses—if the actuaries ask for a BBB-rated return but the investment department suffers any related credit losses, the incentive system is flawed.

One other complexity is found in the life insurance business, which pension funds don't face so directly. Insurance companies must report earnings quarterly or semi-annually, at least to regulators and often to outside shareholders.

In that sense, the risk/return trade-off involves both a mark-to-market orientation (how does the value of the Jarrow-Merton put option on our portfolio change if we take less risk?) and a net income orientation. We turn to that in our discussion of the banking industry in the next section.

Property and casualty insurance companies have still another added complexity—the payoffs on the liability side are much more volatile from year to year because many important classes of property and casualty insurance losses are much more volatile than payouts on life insurance policies. This brings into play many of the liquidity considerations that we discuss in Chapter 40.

Commercial banks

The politics of interest rate risk/return strategy in commercial banking is the most complex because all of the complications mentioned previously (with the exception of property and casualty insurance losses) are present and the number of players in the decision is very large. A partial list includes the following parties to the interest rate risk and return strategy decision:

- Board of directors of the bank;
- Chief executive officer;
- Managing committee of the bank (asset and liability management committee or ALCO);
- Heads of major business units;
- Day-to-day manager of the transfer pricing book;
- Manager of the trading floor;
- Bank regulators.

The politics is particularly complex because (unlike pension funds, for example) many of the decision-makers are decision-makers not because of their expertise in interest rate risk but because of the size of the businesses they run. Someone who is running a network of 1,000 retail branches is too busy to be an expert in interest rate risk strategy, but they are still a voter in major interest rate risk decisions.

In Chapter 2, we summarized the impact that a common practice transfer pricing system has on bank interest rate risk strategy:

- Day-to-day interest rate risk mismatches are moved via the transfer pricing system to a central 'transfer pricing book' where the manager has interest rate risk limits consistent with their seniority and the limits they would have if they were trading bonds for the bank.
- Huge macro mismatches are the responsibility of the ALCO and must be approved by the board.
- Basis risk from non-market sensitive pricing indexes (such as the average cost of funds of the 11th District savings and loan associations in the U.S., once an extremely important pricing index for home mortgages) is born by the heads of business units.

Within this general structure, there are a number of political games and tactics that exist to advance the career aspirations or personal wealth of one manager instead of the aspirations of the shareholders. These are too numerous (and too humorous) to cover in depth, so we'll just outline the highlights:

- 'I can predict interest rates, why can't you?' This strategy is the oldest in the book. A member of senior management claims he can predict interest rates and urges the transfer pricing book management to take on a huge interest rate risk position. It does. If rates move as predicted, the senior manager takes the credit. If rates move the opposite direction, the transfer pricing book manager takes the blame. This is combatted with the limits structure on the transfer pricing book and a separate 'book' for the ALCO committee where every position is carefully recorded and the advocates noted by name.
- 'My assets are liquid so give me a short-term interest rate.' This is the second oldest ploy in the book, usually argued by the head of the trading floor or the head of a portfolio that can be securitized. In both cases, the advocates of this position want to avoid paying a matching maturity cost of funds and to avoid the liquidity premiums that arise from borrowing too short as we discuss in detail in Chapter 40. This strategy is combatted by saying 'no' and following a more modern approach to transfer pricing, which we discuss in Chapters 39–44. On the argument

that 'my assets are liquid and we can securitize', we note that a sharp risk in interest rates puts the mark-to-market value of a fixed-rate loan portfolio below par value—very few institutions will securitize if it means recognizing this mark-to-market loss.

- 'I want the long-term historical weighted average cost of funds, not the marginal cost of funds.' If rates are rising, this is a common request by the asset side of the organization. If rates are falling, the liability side of the organization wants the long-term weighted average cost of funds. This is why the marginal cost of funds system has to be very comprehensive or this kind of manipulation of the transfer pricing system is endless.

If the performance measurement system is designed correctly, politics (for the most part) falls by the wayside and the relevant decision-makers can focus on the right risk-return trade-offs.

It is to that task we now turn.

Making a Decision on Interest Rate Risk and Return: The Safety Zone

There are two environments in which management has to make a decision about whether to change the interest rate risk of the institution:

- Inside the 'safety zone';
- Outside the 'safety zone'.

If the institution is still inside the safety zone that we discussed in Chapter 4, then shareholders don't care (as a group) what the interest rate risk position is. They don't care because they can form a portfolio of the institution's common stock and fixed income securities for their own account that exactly offsets any decisions made by the management of the financial institution and gets the 'pseudo financial institution' exactly where the individual shareholder would like them to be from an interest rate risk perspective. If the financial institution is inside the safety zone, we can focus on the pure economics of changing the interest rate risk position because it is impossible for the financial institution to go bankrupt while in the safety zone.

If the financial institution is outside the safety zone, shareholders are being forced to suffer some of the expected costs of the potential bankruptcy of the institution. The interest rate risk/return estimation should include the reduction of these expected losses from bankruptcy as part of the calculated benefits of reducing risk.

Obvious Interest Rate Risk Decisions

Some decisions about interest rate risk have obvious 'yes or no' decisions, while others are more complex. Some of the obvious decisions are listed here:

1. Is the put option that eliminates the interest rate risk of the institution in the Jarrow-Merton sense from Chapter 1 so expensive that the financial institution can't afford to buy it? If that is the case, the interest rate risk of the institution is way too large and has to be reduced by other means.
2. If a change in the cash flow structure from an interest rate-related transaction smooths net income but leaves the Jarrow-Merton put option value unchanged, then the transaction is worth doing. This has an 'information' benefit to shareholders who might otherwise misperceive the risk of the institution based on short-term changes in net income.
3. If the change in cash flow structure from an interest rate-related transaction smooths net income but leaves the bank well within the safety zone, then it is probably worth doing.

Assessing the Risk and Return Trade-Offs from a Change in Interest Rate Risk

For all other changes in the financial institution's interest rate risk and return policy, there are a number of tools for quantifying the benefits of a change in the interest rate risk position of the institution. The two most important components of the benefits of a change in the interest rate risk of an institution consist of the following:

- The change in cost of the Jarrow-Merton put option that would be necessary to completely eliminate the financial institution's interest rate risk.
- The change in the expected costs of potential bankruptcy of the institution, which we discussed in Chapter 4.

These two are critical to deciding when to hedge and when not to hedge. If the financial institution is well within the safety zone, we don't need to spend much time on this analysis. If the bank is near the boundaries of the safety zone or outside it, this analysis becomes very important.

In the next chapter, we introduce traditional tools for supplementing the Jarrow-Merton put option analysis and expected costs of bankruptcy. From Chapters 7 onward, we lay the foundation for calculating the Jarrow-Merton put options cost and the changes in the expected costs of bankruptcy.

CHAPTER 6

Traditional Interest Rate Risk Analysis: Gap Analysis and Simulation Models

U yemura and van Deventer [1993] discuss the '80/20 rule' in the context of risk management, and it still applies today to a certain extent. The 80/20 rule is the observation that 80% of the benefits can be achieved with 20% of the effort that would be required to secure 100% of the benefits. This rule of thumb is probably still a good one, except when it involves the computer science aspects of risk management. The state of computer science and risk management software has evolved so far in the last decade that 98% of the benefits can now be achieved with 2% of the effort required for a perfect answer. We'll keep that distinction in mind through this chapter, where we review traditional interest rate risk management tools for two distinct purposes—communication with senior management and day-to-day decision making with respect to interest rate risk.

Measuring Interest Rate Risk: A Review

In Chapters 4 and 5, we discussed how financial institutions can measure risk in a number of ways:

- The **Jarrow-Merton put option**: the value of a put option that would eliminate all of the interest rate risk (the downside risk only) on the financial institution's balance sheet for a specific time horizon.
- The **interest rate sensitivity of the market value of the financial institution's equity**: often proxied by the mark-to-market valuation of the financial institution's assets less the mark-to-market valuation of its liabilities.

- **The interest rate sensitivity of the financial institution's net income** (or Cash Flow) over a specific time horizon.

In Chapters 7–44, we emphasize a modern approach to each of these risk measures with respect to both interest rate risk and credit risk. In this chapter, we summarize the more traditional approach to interest rate risk measurement and management that has prevailed in some form for most of the last 30 years. In each case, we are careful to point out the pitfalls of these early techniques that have led to more sophisticated technology.

Interest rate sensitivity gap analysis

Chapters 4 and 5 discuss the concept of the interest rate risk management 'safety zone' in which it is impossible for the financial institution to go bankrupt from interest rate risk. Every senior officer of a financial institution needs to know the answers to a number of questions related to the safety zone concept:

- How do we know whether the financial institution is in the safety zone or not?
- If we are out of the safety zone, how far out are we?
- How big should our interest rate risk hedge be to get back into the safety zone?
- How much of a move in interest rates would it take to cause bankruptcy from an interest rate risk move?

Interest rate sensitivity 'gap' analysis was the first attempt that most financial institutions made to answer these questions. Today, financial institutions use this expository technique to communicate with senior management. It is not used for decision making because its implications are too crude to be accurate and too subject to arbitrary assumptions that can literally change the measured impact of higher interest rates on the financial institution from positive to negative or viceversa. It does have a 30,000-foot level of usefulness on much more precise risk systems but certainly doesn't do much more than this for most financial institutions.

How does an interest rate sensitivity gap work? We return to the simple example of Chapter 4, in which $1,000 is invested in a floating-rate loan with a floating-rate interest rate that resets semi-annually. We assume the maturity of the loan is three years. The loan is financed with $800 in a matching maturity six-month certificate of deposit and $200 in equity, since we assume the bank was newly formed. We reproduce the change in net income and its composition from Chapter 4 in Figure 6.1.

How this balance sheet would look in a standard interest rate sensitivity gap is shown in Table 6.1.

Table 6.1 Standard Interest Rate Sensitivity Gap Analysis

Balance Sheet Category	1 Day	2–7 Days	8–30 Days	2 Months	3 Months	4 Months	5 Months	6 Months	12 Months	2 Years	3–5 Years	Over 5	Other	Total
Assets														
Commercial Loan								1000						1000
Liabilities								1000						1000
Certificates of Deposit								800						
Interest Rate Sensitivity Gap	0	0	0	0	0	0	0	**200**	0	0	0	0	0	800
Cumulative Rate Sensitivity Gap	0	0	0	0	0	0	0	200	200	200	200	200	200	200

Table 6.2 Standard Interest Rate Sensitivity Gap Analysis: Equity Invested in Overnight Funds

Balance Sheet Category	1 Day	2–7 Days	8–30 Days	2 Months	3 Months	4 Months	5 Months	6 Months	12 Months	2 Years	3–5 Years	Over 5	Other	Total
Assets														
Overnight Funds	200													200
Commercial Loan								800						800
	200	0	0	0	0	0	0	800	0	0	0	0	0	1000
Liabilities														
Certificates of Deposit								800						800
	0	0	0	0	0	0	0	800	0	0	0	0	0	800
Interest Rate Sensitivity Gap	**200**	0	0	0	0	0	0	**0**	0	0	0	0	0	**200**
Cumulative Rate Sensitivity Gap	200	200	200	200	200	200	200	200	200	200	200	200	200	

Table 6.3 Standard Interest Rate Sensitivity Gap Analysis: Long-Term Bonds

Balance Sheet Category	1 Day	2–7 Days	8–30 Days	2 Months	3 Months	4 Months	5 Months	6 Months	12 Months	2 Years	3–5 Years	Over 5	Other	Total
Assets														
Long-Term Bonds												200		200
Commercial Loan								800						800
	0	0	0	0	0	0	0	800	0	0	0	200	0	1000
Liabilities														
Certificates of Deposit								800						800
	0	0	0	0	0	0	0	800	0	0	0	0	0	800
Interest Rate Sensitivity Gap	**0**	0	0	0	0	0	0	**0**	0	0	0	200	0	**200**
Cumulative Rate Sensitivity Gap	0	0	0	0	0	0	0	0	0	0	0	200	200	

We show the $1,000 in loans in the six-month 'time zone', not its actual maturity, because the interest rate resets in approximately six months. The $800 in certificates of deposit goes in the same time bucket.

What about the effective maturity of equity? While some large financial institutions believe they know what the effective maturity of equity is, independent of the actual balance sheet, most sophisticated practitioners and essentially all (if such a thing is possible) academics believe that the effective maturity of the financial institution's capital is derived from the net of the impact of assets less the impact of non-equity liabilities.

Therefore, the mismatch we show in month six of $200 is the effective maturity of the common stock of this financial institution.

If the financial institution had just issued $200 in equity for cash, the financial institution could have made $800 in loans funded with $800 in CDs and then invested the $200 in securities at any maturity. If the proceeds were invested in overnight funds, the interest rate mismatch would be computed as in Table 6.2.

This financial institution is 'asset sensitive' because it has more short-term asset exposure than it does liabilities. Without doing any multi-period simulation, we know from this simple table that net income will rise sharply if interest rates rise.

What if the proceeds of the equity issue instead were invested in long-term securities? Then the interest rate sensitivity gap is as in Table 6.3.

The net income of the financial institution will not change in response to short-term changes in interest rates because the capital of the institution is invested in long-term securities.

The safety zone
All three of the interest rate risk positions of the financial institution we have discussed so far are in the 'safety zone'. The financial institution can never go bankrupt from interest rate risk alone because all short-term liabilities are

Figure 6.1 Interest Rate Sensitivity Gap

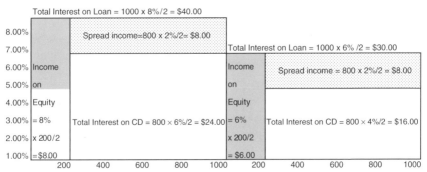

invested in matched maturity assets. The capital of the bank can be invested at any maturity.

What does this imply for the interest rate sensitivity of the financial institution's common stock? As we discussed in Chapter 4, it moves in three different ways for these three balance sheets:

Case 1: The common stock trades like $200 in six-month instruments, since capital is invested in the six-month reset loan, plus the present value of the constant spread on $800 of the loan.

Case 2: The common stock trades like $200 in overnight instruments, since capital is invested in the overnight market, plus the present value of the constant spread on $800 of the loan.

Case 3: The common stock trades like $200 in long-term bonds, since capital is invested in the long-term bond market, plus the present value of the constant spread on $800 of the loan.

Since all of these investments are at market at the time they are done, they neither create nor destroy value. They are all in the safety zone, but the financial institution's common stock will respond differently in the three scenarios to changes in interest rates. In no case, however, can the financial institution go bankrupt from interest rate risk, so no hedge is necessary.

What if the management thinks shareholders want stable net income? Then they should invest in long-term bonds instead of the overnight market, but either position is in the safety zone and shareholders should be indifferent—as discussed in Chapters 4 and 5, the shareholders can convert the $200 from overnight money to long-term bonds or vice-versa, by doing transactions for their own account in combination with their holdings of the financial institution's common stock.

What's wrong with gap analysis?

What's wrong with gap analysis? As an expositional tool for communicating with non-specialists, nothing is wrong with it.

As a decision-making tool, though, it has serious flaws that led to the Office of the Comptroller of the Currency of the United States stopping the requirement for gap analysis to be reported in the Quarterly Report of Condition for commercial banks in the U.S.

We can summarize some of the problems with gap analysis briefly:

- It ignores the coupons and unscheduled cash flows on all assets and liabilities.
- Gap analysis typically uses accounting values of assets and liabilities, not market values. Two bonds with accounting values of $100 but market values of $120 and $80 respectively are both put in the gap chart at $100.
- The time buckets typically used are very focused on short-term maturities and tend to be very crude for the long-term interest rate risk, where the real big risk to the institution lies.

- Gap analysis ignores options—An 8% 30-year mortgage may have an effective interest rate sensitivity of 30 years when market interest rates are 12% but an effective interest rate sensitivity of 30 days when interest rates are at 3% because prepayment is about to occur.
- Gap analysis cannot deal with other instruments where payments are random, such as property and casualty insurance policies, savings deposits, demand deposits, charge cards, and so on.
- Some interest rates have a lagged adjustment to changes in open market rates, such as the prime rate in the U.S. and home mortgage indexes in Japan and Australia. Gap analysis does not capture these lags.
- Many balance sheet items (charge card balances, deposit balances) have a strong seasonal variation—they flow out and flow back in again. Do you classify them by the first outflow date and ignore the seasonal inflow?
- Assets with varying credit risks are mixed and visibility on credit risk is completely blurred across the balance sheet.

Sophisticated risk managers use detailed transaction level, exact day-count interest rate risk analysis such as that detailed in the remainder of this book. They use gap charts to communicate their conclusions to senior management, if the senior managers are non-specialists.

Multi-period simulation

Many senior managers of financial institutions have learned the hard way that interest rate sensitivity gap analysis can be a very crude, and often grossly incorrect, indicator of what happens to net income if interest rates move. It can be even more incorrect if it used as a proxy for changes in the value of the financial institution's common stock as interest rates move.

Simulation analysis was the next tool to which major financial institutions turned. In the 1970s, most of the focus was on net income for a one to two year horizon. This focus was understandable but fatal for thousands of U.S. financial institutions which had interest rate risk in the form of 30-year mortgages which short-term net income simulation does not detect. Fortunately, we now have much more sophisticated tools available, which we outline in the remainder of this book. Nonetheless, it is important to review the kinds of considerations that have played an important role in the simulation exercises of major financial institutions over the last three decades.

Key assumptions in simulation

Simulation can be done in many ways:

1. Simulate N discrete movements in interest rates with the current balance sheet held constant and produce market values and net income.
2. Simulate the current balance sheet held constant and interest rates held at current levels.

3. Move yield curves through multiple specified changes over the forecasting horizon with specific new assets and liabilities added.
4. Randomly move interest rates over the forecast horizon and dynamically simulate which assets and liabilities will be added as interest rates changes.

Most financial institutions employ some combination of these techniques, but in the more modern way that we discuss in later chapters:

- Chapters 7–13 show how to model random movements in interest rates and how to calculate market values based on this random interest rate movement.
- Chapters 14–18 show how to model the credit spread and events of default.
- Chapters 19–21 show how to test the accuracy of these models.
- Chapters 22–38 show at the individual security type level how interest rate and credit risk impact valuation and cash flow for various financial instruments.
- Chapters 39–44 integrate the previous chapters and summarize a more modern approach to risk measurement that integrates credit risk and interest rate risk in the current information technology environment.

Even in the more modern style, however, simulation involves a number of key assumptions:

- **Movements in balance sheet amounts**: How will seasonal variation in deposit balances and commercial loans be modeled? How will cash flow from coupon payments be invested? Will these decisions be independent of interest rate levels or shall they be set as a function of interest rates?
- **Maturity of new assets and liabilities**: What will be the maturity structure and options characteristics of new assets and liabilities? For example, the mix of home mortgage loans between fixed-rate loans and floating-rate loans changes substantially over the interest rate cycle. How should this be modeled?
- **Yield curve movements**: How will movements in yield curves be modeled? This is our principal focus in Chapters 7–13, but in an earlier era this set of assumptions was both very arbitrary and very central to the quality of the analysis.
- **Administered rate analysis**: How should interest rates which respond with a lag to changes in open market rates be modeled?
- **New business:** How should 'new business' (as opposed to cash flow from existing assets rolling over) be modeled?

Data aggregation in simulation modeling

One of the issues in traditional simulation has been the degree to which individual transactions should be aggregated for analysis. Many analysts even today think that aggregation is normally a harmless convenience, but more thoughtful risk managers are horrified at the thought. It is done only as a necessary evil that produces some offsetting benefit, such as allowing a larger number of monte carlo scenarios or faster processing times.

In an earlier era with limited computer speeds and limited memory, data summarization and how to do it was a major issue. In a more modern era, no one would average a $100,000 8% coupon mortgage with a $100,000 10% mortgage and say they were the effective equivalent of $200,000 in a 9% mortgage. The entire discipline of market risk is built around the constant search for more accuracy (and slightly different, higher precision), but in an earlier era in asset and liability management this kind of approximation was necessary under the 80/20 rule that we introduced earlier in this chapter.

Constraining the model

Assets and liabilities of a financial institution can't be modeled independently of each other. If the objective of the modeling exercise is a detailed estimate of net interest income, then of course assets and liabilities have to be equal. This is not a trivial exercise in simulation, as the amount of certificates of deposit that a bank, for example, must issue depends on cash used by every other asset and liability on the balance sheet. This is determined by insuring that cash in equals cash out. The 'plug' item which makes cash in equal to cash out is the amount of new certificates of deposit or some other residual funding source.

Modeling the maturity structure of a class of assets

In the early days of simulation modeling, the maturity structure of a pool of assets (like home mortgages) was not visible to the analyst. The team led by William Mack Terry at Bank of America (see Chapter 2) in the 1970s, for example, was not able to get the exact maturity dates and payment schedules of each mortgage loan at the Bank. They had to estimate a 'tractor' type roll-off of old mortgages and their replacement by new mortgages (see Chapter 7 in Uyemura and van Deventer [1993] for more on this approach).

Fortunately modern financial systems now should be based on exact day-count and exact maturity dates. This is actually less work than summarizing the data in a way that doesn't distort the results.

Periodicity of the analysis

In an earlier era, the periods of the simulation were often hard coded to be of equal length. For example, periods could be monthly, but the differences in lengths of the month (from 28 days to 31 days) were often ignored.

Now analysts specify the exact start date and end date of each period, which can differ in length from month to month. Modern risk analysis is firmly rooted (for the most part) in exact day-count technology.

Exceptions to the exact day-count trend

An exception to the trend toward exact day-count precision of simulation is the brief risk management detour of value at risk analysis, which we discussed in Chapters 1 and 2. This single period analysis effectively ignores all cash flows (and their exact day-count) between the date of the analysis and their horizon. A similar set of assumptions is commonly applied to get quick (and very dirty) answers on instruments like collateralized debt obligations. These simplistic approaches are being rapidly replaced by more sophisticated simulation like that discussed in Chapter 23 on collateralized debt obligations.

Stepping Up to the Plate: Doing It Right

In the first six chapters of this book, we have put the discipline of financial risk management in historical context. We now turn to the current state of the art. In a step-by-step way, we will try to show how the current 'best practice' and 'evolving practice' differs in implications from the more traditional way of looking at risk.

We start with analyzing precise yield curve analytics in Chapter 7.

Fixed Income Mathematics: The Basic Tools[1]

I n the first six chapters of this book, we discussed measures of risk and return in a general way. We discussed the Jarrow-Merton put option as a measure of risk along with more traditional measures of risk such as the sensitivity of net income to changes in risk factors and the sensitivity of the net market value of a portfolio (i.e. the value of equity in the portfolio) to changes in risk factors.

In the following chapters, we discuss the implementation of these concepts in a very detailed and practical way. Implementation requires accurate and efficient modeling of market values of every transaction in the portfolio both at the current time and at any time in the future. Valuation and multi-period simulation also require exact knowledge of cash flow dates and amounts, recognizing that these amounts may be random (like an interest rate on a floating-rate mortgage, early prepayment on a callable bond, or payment on a first to default swap). We turn to that task now.

Modern Implications of Present Value

The concept of present value is at the very heart of finance, and yet it can seem like the most mysterious and difficult element of risk management analytics even seven decades after the introduction of Macaulay's duration in 1938. It is safe to say though, that no self-respecting finance person in a large financial institution should look forward to a pleasant stay in the finance area if they are uncomfortable with the present value concept and the basics of traditional fixed income mathematics. At the same time, the basic principles of present value have so many applications that a good understanding of them would be very beneficial to a wide variety of finance professionals. In this chapter, we present an overview of present value and fixed income mathematics. We will touch on a wide variety of topics and leave a few to be covered in more detail in later chapters. Yield

---

[1] An earlier version of this chapter appeared as Chapter 1 in van Deventer and Imai [1996].

curve 'smoothing' is covered in Chapter 8, duration and related concepts are covered in Chapters 9 and 10, and more sophisticated models of movements in interest rates are explained in detail in Chapters 11 to 13. We integrate this pure interest rate risk-focused section with credit modeling in Chapters 14–18.

The present value concept and related issues such as yield to maturity and forward interest rates provide the building blocks for these more complex issues. These concepts will be familiar to many readers, but they have significant implications for the measurement of risk and return that we discussed in Chapters 1–6.

Price, Accrued Interest, and Value

The accounting profession and the economics profession have engaged in many 'wars' during their history. Occasionally, there have been periods of peaceful coexistence and general agreement on the importance of various concepts. That seems to be happening now with the implementation of the market value-based Financial Accounting Standard 133 and the related International Accounting Standard 39.

However, there was one important battle lost by the economics profession that still causes finance professionals pain. That battle was fought over three concepts—'price', 'accrued interest', and 'value'.

In this chapter, we will focus consistently on the concept of value—what a security is worth in the market place. In a rational world, a security's value and the risk-adjusted present value of future cash flows should be close to the same thing or the reader is wasting a lot of valuable time reading this book when they could be arbitraging the market! For the purposes of this book, when we say value, we really mean present value—what a rational person would pay today for the risk-adjusted cash flows to be received in the future.

Unfortunately, this simple concept has been complicated by the idea that we 'earn' interest on a bond even if we buy it just after the most recent coupon payment was paid and sell it before the next coupon payment is paid. This idea isn't harmful in itself, but, in the form that the idea has been implemented in many markets, nothing could be farther from economic reality. The person who receives the interest on a bond is the person who is the owner of record on the record date that determines who receives the interest. For accounting (not economic) purposes, the accounting profession has decided that the value of a bond has to be split into two pieces: the 'price', which is intended by the accountants to be relatively stable, and 'accrued interest', which is an arbitrary calculation that determines who earned interest on the bond even if they received no cash from the issuer of the bond.

The basic accounting rule for splitting value isn't harmful on the surface:

$$\text{Value} = \text{price plus accured interest}$$

What causes the harm is the formula for accrued interest. In a calculation left over from a time before calculators, accrued interest is calculated as a proportion of the next coupon on a bond. While there are many variations on the calculation of this proportion, the simplest one divides the actual number of days between the settlement date and the last bond coupon payment date by the total number of days between coupon payments.

Calculation of Accrued Interest

ABC Bank sells a 10-year, 10% coupon bond for an amount of money equal to 102% of par value, or $1,020 per bond. The next semi-annual coupon of $50 will be paid in 122 days, and it has been 60 days since the last coupon payment.

$$\text{Value} = \$1,020.00$$

$$\text{Accrued Interest} = 60 \ (\$50)/[60 + 122] = \$16.48$$

$$\begin{aligned} \text{Price} &= \text{Value} - \text{Accrued Interest} \\ &= \$1,020.00 - 16.48 \\ &= \$1,003.52 \text{ or } 100.352\% \text{ of par value} \end{aligned}$$

There is one fundamental flaw in these simple rules. In economic terms, the amount of accrued interest is an arbitrary calculation that has no economic meaning.[2] Why? The amount of accrued interest bears no relationship to the current level of interest rates. The accrued interest on the bond is calculated to be the same in an environment when interest rates are 3% as one where interest rates are 30%. The amount of accrued interest depends solely on the coupon on the bond, which reflects interest rate levels at the time of issue, not interest rates today. Since price is calculated as value minus an economically meaningless number, then price is an economically meaningless number as well. Unfortunately, the number referred to most often on a day-to-day basis in the financial industry is 'price', so those of us who focus on good numbers have to work backwards to remain focused on what's important—the value of the transaction, $1,020.[3] Market jargon labels true present value as 'dirty price', meaning price plus accrued interest. 'Clean price' means true present value minus accrued interest, i.e. the price quoted in the market. In our minds, the market has applied the words 'dirty' and 'clean' to the wrong definitions of price.

---

[2] One exception to this comment is the differential tax impact of accrued interest and price. It has long been acknowledged that no group has less influence on government policy than economists, so it is no surprise that the accountants devised the tax code.

[3] There are exceptions to this concept of accrued interest. Australia and Korea are two markets where there is no artificial division of 'value' into 'accrued interest' and 'price'.

From now on, when we say 'value', we mean true present value, i.e. 'dirty price', price plus accrued interest. In order to avoid confusion, we will always specify which concept of price we mean.

Present Value

A dollar received in the future is almost always[4] worth less than a dollar received today. This is more than just a reflection of inflation, it's a recognition that the market requires someone using the resources of others to pay 'rent' until those resources are returned. The implications of this fact are very important.

The basic present value calculation

If the value of one dollar received at time t_i is written $P(t_i)$, then the present value of an investment that generates n varying cash flows $C(t_i)$ at n times t_i in the future (for i equal to 1 through n), can be written as follows:

$$\text{Present value} = \sum_{i=1}^{n} P(t_i)C(t_i)$$

Example

Cash flow 1:	$100.00
Date received:	1 year from now
Cash flow 2:	$200.00
Date received:	10 years from now

Value of $1 *dollar received in the future*

Received in 1 year:	$0.90
Received in 10 years:	$0.50
Value	$= 100(0.9) + 200(0.5) = 190.00$

This simple formula is completely general. It is the heart of most banking calculations and much of finance. Note that the present value formula has the following features:

- it is independent of the number of cash flows;
- it is independent of the method of interest compounding;
- it assumes that cash flows are known with certainty.

---

[4] There have been a number of transactions in Japan at negative nominal interest rates in the late 1990s and in the early part of this decade.

The $P(t_i)$ values, the value of one dollar received at time t_i, are called discount factors. They provide the basis for all yield curve calculations—bond valuation, forward rates, yield to maturity, forward bond prices, and so on. How they are determined and how they link with other concepts is the essence of the remaining chapters of the book, and in particular we focus on them in Chapters 8 and 18. For the time being, we assume that these discount factors are known. That allows us to write down immediately a number of other formulas for valuation of securities where the contractual cash flows are known with certainty.

Calculating the Value of a Fixed Coupon Bond with Principal Paid at Maturity

If the actual dollar amount of the coupon payment on a fixed coupon bond is C and principal is repaid at time t_n, the value (price plus accrued interest) of the bond is:

$$\text{Value of Fixed Coupon Bond} = C \sum_{i=1}^{n} P(t_i) + P(t_n) \, \text{Principal}$$

Note that this formula applies regardless of how often coupon payments are made and regardless of whether the first coupon period is a full period in length.

Example

Principal amount:	$1,000.00
Interest paid:	semi-annually
Coupon rate:	10%
Coupon dollar amount:	$50.00
Periods to maturity:	4 semi-annual periods
Days to next coupon:	40 days

Value of $1 *dollar received in the future*	
Received in 40 days:	$0.99
Received in 6 months plus 40 days:	$0.94
Received in 1 year plus 40 days:	$0.89
Received in 1.5 years plus 40 days:	$0.83

Value	$= 50.00 \, (0.99 + 0.94 + 0.89 + 0.83) + 0.83(1,000)$
	$= 1,012.50$

Example

Principal amount:	$2,000.00
Interest paid:	annually
Coupon rate:	10%
Coupon amount:	$200.00
Periods to maturity:	3 annual periods
Days to next coupon:	350 days

Value of $1 *dollar received
    in the future*

Received in 350 days:	$0.95
Received in 1 year plus 350 days:	$0.86
Received in 2 years plus 350 days:	$0.76

Value	$= 200.00 \, (0.95 + 0.86 + 0.76)$
	$+ 0.76(2,000) = 2,034.00$

Calculating the Coupon of a Fixed Coupon Bond with Principal Paid at Maturity when Value is Known

If the value (price plus accrued interest) of a fixed coupon bond is known and the discount factors are known, the dollar coupon payment which leads a bond to have such a value is calculated by rearranging the previous formulas:

$$\text{Dollar Coupon Amount of Fixed Coupon Bond} = \frac{\text{Value} - P(t_n) \, \text{Principal}}{\sum_{i=1}^{n} P(t_i)}$$

Example

Principal amount:	$1,000.00
Interest paid:	semi-annually
Value:	$1,150.00
Periods to maturity:	4 semi-annual periods
Days to Next coupon:	40 days

Value of $1 *dollar received
    in the future*

Received in 40 days:	$0.99
Received in 6 months plus 40 days:	$0.94
Received in 1 year plus 40 days:	$0.89
Received in 1.5 years plus 40 days:	$0.83

Coupon Amount	$= (1,150 - 0.83*1,000)/(0.99 +$
	$0.94 + 0.89 + 0.83) = 87.67$
Coupon Rate	$= [2 \text{ payments} * \text{Amount}]/$
	$1,000.00 = 17.53\%$

Example

Principal amount:	$2,000.00
Interest paid:	annually
Periods to maturity:	3 annual periods
Days to next coupon:	350 days
Value:	$1,850.00

Value of $1 *dollar received in the future*

Received in 350 days:	$0.94
Received in 1 year plus 350 days:	$0.86
Received in 2 years plus 350 days:	$0.76

Coupon amount	$= (1,850 - 0.76*2,000)/(0.94$ $+ 0.86 + 0.76) = 128.91$
Coupon rate	$= [1 \text{ payment} * \text{Amount}]/2,000 = 6.45\%$

The Value of an Amortizing Loan

The value of an amortizing loan is the same calculation as that for a fixed coupon bond except that the variable C represents the constant level payment received in each period. There is no explicit principal amount at the end since all principal is retired in period-by-period payments included in the amount C. When the periodic payment dollar amount is known, the value of the loan is:

$$\text{Value of Amortizing Bond} = C \left[\sum_{i=1}^{n} P(t_i) \right]$$

Note again that this formula holds even for a short first period and for any frequency of payments, be they daily, weekly, monthly, quarterly, semi-annually, annually, or on odd calendar dates.

Example

Payment frequency:	semi-annually
Payment amount:	$500.00
Periods to maturity:	4 semi-annual periods
Days to next coupon:	40 days

Value of $1 *dollar received in the future*

Received in 40 days:	$0.99
Received in 6 months plus 40 days:	$0.94
Received in 1 year plus 40 days:	$0.89
Received in 1.5 years plus 40 days:	$0.83

Value	$= 500.00 (0.99 + 0.94 + 0.89$ $+ 0.83) = 1,825.00$

Calculating the Payment Amount of an Amortizing Bond when Value is Known

Like the fixed-coupon bond case, the payment amount on an amortizing loan can be calculated using the known amount for value (principal plus accrued interest) and rearranging the equation above for amortizing loans.

$$C = \text{Payment Amount on Amortizing Bond} = \frac{\text{Value}}{\sum_{i=1}^{n} P(t_i)}$$

Example

Payment frequency:	annually
Periods to maturity:	3 annual periods
Days to next coupon:	350 days
Value:	$1,850.00

Value of $1 *dollar received in the future*

Received in 350 days:	$0.95
Received in 1 year plus 350 days:	$0.86
Received in 2 years plus 350 days:	$0.76
Payment amount:	= (1,850)/(0.95 + 0.86 + 0.76)
	= 719.84

Risk management implications

In Chapters 4 and 6, we discussed the fact that the interest rate risk of a financial institution is the sum of the present value of its assets less the present value of its liabilities. We also noted that the width of the interest rate risk safety zone is at least consistent with the capital of the organization being invested in any maturity from one day to infinitely long, provided all other assets are match funded. In the example in Chapters 4 and 6, the asset of the simple financial institution was a three-year floating-rate loan that resets its interest rate semi-annually. We turn now to the valuation of this type of asset.

Calculating the Value of a Floating-Rate Bond or Loan with Principal Paid at Maturity

The calculation of the value of a floating-rate bond is more complicated than the valuation of a fixed-rate bond because future coupon payments are unknown. In order to value floating-rate bonds, we divide the formula for determining the coupon on the bond into two pieces—an index plus a fixed dollar spread over the index. We assume that the index is set at a level such that the value of a bond with one period (equal in length to $1/m$ years) to maturity and an interest rate equal to the index would be par value. This is equivalent to assuming that the yield curve (and its movements), which determines future values of the index, is the same as the yield curve we should use for valuing the floating-rate security. For example, we assume that the right yield curve for valuing all securities with rates reset based on the LIBOR rate should be valued at the LIBOR yield curve. We will relax this assumption below and in later chapters when we have more powerful tools to analyze more realistic assumptions about the value of a bond whose rate floats at the index plus zero spread. Using our simple assumptions for the time being, the present value of a floating-rate bond priced at the index level plus a fixed dollar amount (the 'spread') per period is equal to par value (the value of all future payments at an interest rate equal to the floating index plus the return of principal) plus the present value of the stream of payments equal to the spread received each period. The value of the stream of payments equal to the spread can be valued using the equation above for the value of an amortizing bond. Therefore the value of a floating-rate bond is:

$$\text{Value of Floating-Rate Bond} = P(t_1) \left[\left(1 + \frac{\text{index}}{m} \right) \text{Principal} \right]$$

$$+ \text{Spread} \left[\sum_{i=1}^{n} P(t_i) \right]$$

Note that the first term will be equal to the principal value, given our definition of the index, if the time to the first payment t_1 is equal to the normal length of the period between coupons. The first term will generally not be equal to the principal value if the length of the first period is shorter than its normal length, such as 17 days when the interval between interest rate resets is six months. Note also that the index may not be the same as the interest rate (which we will call the 'formula rate' from here on) used as the formula for setting the coupon on the bond. See the examples for valuation of bonds where the index rate and the formula rate are different.

Example

In this example, the coupon formula is based on LIBOR, which is a yield curve consistent with the credit risk of major international banks. In this example, our counterparty has a higher level of credit risk than a major international bank because the 'index value' which would cause a floating-rate note to have a present value equal to par value is LIBOR plus 1%, so the difference between the coupon rate on the floating-rate note and 'par pricing' is 2%–1%.

Coupon formula:	6-month LIBOR
	(adjusted[5]) + 2.00%
Index value:	6-month LIBOR + 1%
Principal amount:	2,000.00
Spread in dollar terms over and above	$(0.02-0.01) * 2,000/2$
par pricing:	$= 10.00$
Maturity:	2 years
Time to next coupon:	Exactly 6 months

Value of $1 received in the future

Received in 6 months:	0.96
Received in 1 year:	0.92
Received in 1.5 years:	0.87
Received in 2.0 years:	0.82

$$\text{Value} = 0.96 \left[\left(1 + \frac{\text{LIBOR} + 0.01}{2} \right) \text{Principal} \right]$$

$$+10.00\,[0.96 + 0.92 + 0.87 + 0.83] = 2,035.8$$

Example

This example is a variation of the same thing but with an important difference. The coupon formula is again based on LIBOR, but the best index value that would help us determine the pricing of a floating-rate security whose present value equals par value is the risk-free Treasury bill rate. In this example, the pricing which creates a floating-rate security with present value equal to par value is Treasury bills + 1%. The example helps us move from the Treasury yield curve to the LIBOR yield curve and back by giving us a formula that links the two. In the credit section of this book, we will take a more elegant approach than we use in this example:

Coupon formula:	6-month LIBOR + 2%
Index value:	Treasury bill + 1%
Rate relationship:	LIBOR = Treasury bill + 1.50%
Principal amount:	2,000.00

---

[5] Whenever 'LIBOR' (the London Interbank Offered Rate) is mentioned in the text that follows, we assume that the rate has been converted from the market convention of actual days/360 days per year to actual days/365 days per year by multiplying nominal LIBOR by 365/360.

Spread in dollar terms above the index value:	$(0.015 + 0.02 - 0.01) * 2{,}000/2 = 25.00$
First coupon rate:	7.00 at LIBOR $= 5.00$
Maturity:	2 years and 91 days
Time to next coupon:	91 days

Value of $1 *received in the future*

Received in 91 days:	0.98
Received in 6 months and 91 days:	0.95
Received in 1 year and 91 days:	0.91
Received in 1.5 years and 91 days:	0.86

$$\text{Value} = 0.98 \left[\left(1 + \frac{0.07}{2} \right) \text{Principal} \right] + 25.00 \left[0.95 + 0.91 + 0.86 \right]$$

$$= 2{,}096.60$$

Risk management implications

We now have enough tools to analyze the interest rate risk embedded in the simple financial institution we analyzed in Chapters 4 and 6. That financial institution had made a three-year, floating-rate loan with interest rates reset every six months at the financial institution's six-month certificate of deposit cost plus 2%.

What is the credit risk of the borrower on the loan? We don't know, which is the usual dilemma of an analyst required to analyze interest rate risk independently of credit risk. That is why an integrated treatment, the central theme of this book, is essential. Let's assume that the 'index value', which makes the loan have a present value of par, is the CD rate plus 1%.

Armed with this and the right set of present value factors, we can:

1. mark the assets and liabilities to market;
2. calculate the implied value of the equity of the financial institution;
3. change the discount factors to 'stress test' the calculations in 1 and 2 with respect to interest rate risk.

We will illustrate how to do this in more detail in subsequent chapters. We now turn to another set of basic tools that will help us do this for a broad range of assets and liabilities.

Compound Interest Conventions and Formulas

No one who has been in the financial world for long expects interest rates to remain constant. Still, when financial analysts perform traditional yield to maturity calculations, the constancy of interest rates is the standard assumption simply because of the difficulty of making any other choice. Particularly when discussing compound interest, constant interest rates is a very common assumption. This section discusses those conventions as preparation for the yield to maturity discussion later in this chapter. Using the techniques in Chapter 8, we can relax these simple but inaccurate assumptions.

The future value of an invested amount earning a simple interest rate of y compounded m times per year for n periods.

Almost all discussions of compound interest and future value depend on four factors:

- The constancy of interest rates;
- The nominal annual rate of interest;
- The number of times per year interest is paid;
- The number of periods for which interest is compounded.

$$\text{Future Value of Invested Amount} = (\text{Invested Amount})\left(1 + \frac{y}{m}\right)^n$$

Example

Invested amount:	100.00
Simple interest rate:	12%
Interest paid:	monthly
Investment period:	2 years

$$\text{Future Value} = 100.00 * \left(1 + \frac{0.12}{12}\right)^{24} = 126.97$$

The future value of an invested amount earning a simple interest rate of y compounded continuously for n years.

What happens if the compounding period becomes smaller and smaller, so that interest is compounded every instant, not every second or every day or every month? If we assume a simple interest rate of y invested for n years, the corresponding formula to the equation above is:

$$\text{Future Amount} = \text{Invested Amount}\,(e^{yn})$$

Many financial institutions actually use a continuously compounded interest rate formula for consumer deposits. As we will see in later chapters in this book, the continuous compounding assumption is a convenient mathematical shorthand for compound interest because derivatives of the constant $e = 2.7128\ldots$ to a power are much simpler (once one gets used to them) than the derivatives of a discrete compounding formula. The continuous time assumption also allows the use of the powerful mathematical tools called stochastic processes, which we introduce in Chapter 10.

Example

Invested amount:	100.00
Simple interest rate:	12%
Interest paid:	continuously
Investment period:	2 years and 180 days

$$\text{Future Value} = 100.00 \, e^{0.12 * (2 + (180/365))} = 134.88$$

Equivalent annual percentage rate

In order to easily compare potential investments where compounding assumptions are different, it is common to express the yield on the investment in terms of an 'annual percentage rate'. The annual percentage is the amount an investment would yield if:

- interest rates were constant and;
- interest is paid only once per year.

The annual percentage rate formula is a variation of the equations above where the investment period is regarded to be one year. It tells us how much interest would be earned during the one-year period. If interest is paid m times per year for an investment period of n periods, the annual percentage rate formula is:

$$\text{Annual Percentage Rate} = 100 \left[\left(1 + \frac{y}{n} \right)^m - 1 \right]$$

Note that the maturity n does not appear in the formula because it is mandated to be one year. For retail financial services such as lending and deposit-gathering, this U.S. government-mandated formula makes 'apples to apples' comparisons easier. For derivatives and risk management purposes, however, it can lead to problems. There is no substitute for the precise specification of the compounding frequency.

Example

Invested amount:	100.00
Simple interest rate:	12%
Interest paid:	monthly
Investment period:	2 years

$$\text{Annual Percentage Rate} = 100 \left[\left(1 + \frac{0.12}{12} \right)^{12} - 1 \right] = 12.68\%$$

The present value of a future amount if funds are invested at a simple interest rate of y compounded m times per year for n periods

A parallel question to the compound interest investment question is this: if we seek to have 100 dollars n periods in the future and funds have been invested at a constant rate y compounded m periods per year, how much needs to be invested initially? The answer is a rearrangement of our original formula for compounding of interest:

$$\text{Invested Amount} = \frac{\text{Future Value of Invested Amount}}{(1 + (y/m))^n}$$

Example

Future amount: 600.00
Simple interest rate: 10%
Interest paid: monthly
Investment period: 2 years

$$\text{Invested Amount} = \frac{600.00}{(1 + (0.10/12))^{24}} = 491.65$$

The present value of a future amount if funds are invested at a simple interest rate of y compounded continuously for n years

When interest is assumed to be paid continuously, the investment amount can be calculated by rearranging the equation for continuous compounding of interest:

$$\text{Invested Amount} = \frac{\text{Future Amount}}{e^{yn}} = \text{Future Amount} \, (e^{-yn})$$

Example

Future amount: 600.00
Simple interest rate: 12%
Interest paid: continuously
Investment period: 2 years and 180 days

$$\text{Invested Amount} = 600.00 \left[e^{-0.12 * \left(2 + \frac{180}{365} \right)} \right] = 444.86$$

Calculating the yield on a different compounding basis

It is often necessary to convert from one compounding basis to another. The formula for doing this is a variation of equations six and seven.

When converting from an interest rate of y paid m times per year for n periods to an interest rate of y^* paid p times per year for q periods (where n/m years $= q/p$ years), the formula is:

$$\text{Converted Yield } y^* = p \left[\left[\left(\frac{1+y}{m} \right)^n \right]^{1/q} - 1 \right]$$

Example

Original compounding basis
Yield: 10.00
Interest paid: monthly
Maturity: 24 months

Desired compounding basis
Interest paid: semi-annually
Maturity: 4 semi-annual periods

Note the maturity in each case is two years.

$$\text{Converted Yield } y^* = 2 \left[\left[\left(1 + \frac{0.1}{12} \right)^{24} \right]^{1/4} - 1 \right] = 10.21\%$$

When converting from an interest rate of y paid m times per year for n periods to an interest rate of y^* paid continuously for n/m years:

$$\text{Converted Yield } y^* = \frac{1}{(n/m)} \log \left[\left(1 + \frac{y}{m} \right)^n \right]$$

Example

Original compounding basis
Yield: 10.00
Interest paid: monthly
Maturity: 24 months

Desired compounding basis
Interest paid: continuously
Maturity: 2 years

Note the maturity in each case is two years.

$$\text{Converted Yield } y^* = \frac{1}{(24/12)}\log\left[\left(1+\frac{0.1}{12}\right)^{24}\right] = 9.96\%$$

When converting from an interest rate of y paid continuously for p years to an interest rate of y^* paid m times per year for n periods (where $p = n/m$):

$$\text{Converted Yield } y^* = m\left[\left[e^{yp}\right]^{\frac{1}{n}}-1\right]$$

Example
Original compounding basis
Yield: 9.00
Interest paid: continuously
Maturity: 2 years

Desired compounding basis
Interest paid: quarterly
Maturity: 8 quarters

Note the maturity in each case is two years.

$$\text{Converted Yield } y^* = 4\left[\left[e^{0.09*2}\right]^{\frac{1}{8}}-1\right] = 9.102\%$$

Compounding Formulas and Present Value Factors *P(t)*

In these sections, we have focused on the calculation of present value factors on the assumption that interest rates are constant, but compound at various frequencies. We could use this approach to calculate the present value factors that we used in all of the examples in the first part of this chapter, but as President Nixon famously said, 'That would be wrong.' Why? Because the yield curve is almost never absolutely flat. We deal with this issue in Chapter 8. With these compounding formulas behind us, the yield to maturity calculations can be discussed using a combination of the formulas in the second and third section of this chapter. The yield to maturity formula no longer plays an important role in modern interest rate risk management, but it is an important piece of market jargon and is a concept that is essential to communicating the 'present value' of a wide array of financial instruments.

Yields and Yield to Maturity Calculations

The concept of yield to maturity is one of the most useful and one of the most deceptive calculations in finance. Take the example of a five-year bond with a current value equal to its par value and with coupons paid semi-annually. The market is forecasting 10 different forward interest rates (which we discuss in the next section) that have an impact on the valuation of this bond. There are an infinite number of forward rate combinations that are consistent with the bond having a current value equal to its par value. What is the probability that the market is implicitly forecasting all 10 semi-annual forward rates to be exactly equal? Except by extraordinary coincidence, the probability is a number only the slightest bit greater than zero. Nonetheless, this is the assumption implied when we ask what the yield to maturity on ABC company's bond is. It's an assumption that is no worse than any other—but no better either, in the absence of any other information.

What if ABC company has two bonds outstanding—one of 10 years in maturity and another of five years of maturity? When an analyst calculates the yield to maturity on both bonds, the result is the implicit assumption that rates are constant at one level when analyzing the first bond and constant at a different level when analyzing the second bond. The implications of this are discussed in detail in Chapter 8. In Chapter 9, we will discuss a number of ways to derive more useful information from a collection of outstanding value information on bonds of a comparable type. As an example, if ABC company has bonds outstanding at all 10 semi-annual maturities, it is both possible and very easy to calculate the implied forward rates, zero-coupon bond prices (discount factors $P[t]$), and pricing on all possible combinations of forward bond issues by ABC company. The calculation of yield to maturity is more complex than these calculations, and it provides less information. Nonetheless, it's still the most often-quoted bond statistic other than 'clean price' (present value less accrued interest).

The formula for yield to maturity

For a settlement date (for either a secondary market bond purchase or a new bond issue) that falls exactly one 'period' from the next coupon date, the formula for yield to maturity can be written as follows for a bond which matures in n periods and pays a fixed coupon amount C m times per year:

$$\text{Value} = C\left[\sum_{i=1}^{n} P(t_i)\right] + P(t_n)[\text{Principal}]$$

$$\text{with } P(t_i) = \frac{1}{(1 + (y/m))^i}$$

Yield to maturity is the value of y that makes this equation true. This relationship is the present value equation for a fixed coupon bond, with the addition that the discount factors are all calculated by dividing one dollar by the future value of one dollar invested at a constant rate y for i periods with interest compounded m times per year. In terms of the present value concept, y is the internal rate of return on this bond.

Example

Bond principal value:	1,000.00
Interest paid:	semi-annually
Semi-annual coupon amount:	50.00
Bond value:	1,000.00

We can verify that yield to maturity is 10% by showing that the present value of the bond is equal to value, 1,000:

$$\text{Value} = 50 \sum_{i=1}^{4} [P(t_i)] + P(t_4)1000$$

$$\text{with } P(t_i) = \frac{1}{(1 + (0.10/2))^i}$$

$$\text{so Value} = 1,000.00$$

Yield to maturity for long or short first coupon payment periods

For most outstanding bonds or securities, there is almost always a short (or occasionally a long) interest payment period remaining until the first coupon payment is received. The length of the short first period is equal to the number of days from settlement to the next coupon, divided by the total number of days from the last coupon (or hypothetical last coupon, if the bond is a new issue with a short coupon date) to the next coupon. The method for counting days is specified precisely by the interest accrual method appropriate for that bond. We call this ratio of 'remaining days' to 'days between coupons' the fraction x.[6] Then the yield to maturity can be written as:

$$\text{Value} = C \left[\sum_{i=1}^{n} P(t_i) \right] + P(t_n)[\text{Principal}]$$

$$\text{with } P(t_i) = \frac{1}{(1 + (y/m))^{i-1+x}}$$

---

[6] We re-emphasize that the calculation of remaining days to days between coupons will vary depending on which of the common interest accrual methods are used to count the days.

where, as above, y is the value that makes this equation true.

Example

Bond maturity:	2 years and 91 days
Bond principal value:	1,000.00
Interest paid:	semi-annually
Semi-annual coupon amount:	50.00
Days to next coupon:	91
Days between coupons:	182

What is the present value if the yield to maturity y = 10%?

Present value =   1,024.695

Calculating yield to maturity using the Newton-Raphson method

If everyone who uses the term 'yield to maturity' had to be able to calculate yield without a computer, a high-tech dealing system, or (in the old days) a specialized bond calculator, the term never would have become popular to begin with. Looking at the equations in the previous section shows that the yield to maturity calculation is really an nth degree polynomial equation in the yield to maturity y. There is a relatively easy way out for those readers who, like the authors, successfully avoided exposure to solving polynomials other than quadratic functions. The Newton-Raphson method is an iterative approach to solving a non-linear equation like this one that is very effective for most yield to maturity calculations. This kind of non-linear equation-solver is used constantly in the remainder of this book so it's worthwhile to show the process of solving a non-linear equation in iterative fashion. In brief, the steps in solving for yield to maturity are as follows:

1. Rearrange the appropriate yield to maturity equation so that the right-hand side, which indicates the difference between the estimated value for a given yield and the actual value (the 'difference') is zero. Select the appropriate equation from the following:
   For normal length of time to the first coupon payment:

$$\text{Value Difference} = C \left[\sum_{i=1}^{n} P(t_i) \right] + P(t_n)[\text{Principal}] - \text{Value} = 0$$

$$\text{with } P(t_i) = \frac{1}{(1 + (y/m))^i}$$

For a long or short period to the first coupon payment:

$$\text{Value Difference} = C \left[\sum_{i=1}^{n} P(t_i) \right] + P(t_n)[\text{Principal}] - \text{Value} = 0$$

$$\text{with } P(t_i) = \frac{1}{(1 + (y/m))^{i-1+x}}$$

1. Guess a starting value for y. The coupon percentage (not the dollar amount of the coupon) is often a good starting point.
2. Calculate the derivative of the value difference equation above with respect to y, assuming the guessed value of y is correct. The derivatives of the two relevant equations are as follows:

For normal length of time to the first coupon payment:

$$\text{Derivative of Value Difference} = C \left[\sum_{i=1}^{n} Q(t_i) \right] + Q(t_n)[\text{Principal}]$$

$$\text{with } Q(t_i) = \frac{-i}{m \, (1 + (y/m))^{i+1}}$$

For a long or short period to the first coupon payment:

$$\text{Derivative of Value Difference} = C \left[\sum_{i=1}^{n} Q(t_i) \right] + Q(t_n)[\text{Principal}]$$

$$\text{with } Q(t_i) = \frac{-(i - 1 + x)}{m \, (1 + (y/m))^{i+x}}$$

3. Calculate the new estimated value of y from the following equation:

$$\text{New } y = \text{Old } y - \frac{\text{Difference Evaluated at Old } y}{\text{Derivative of Difference Evaluated at Old } y}$$

4. If the difference between the new estimated value of y and the previous guess for y, the 'old y', is less than the maximum allowable error (usually one basis point or 0.1 basis point for most applications), then stop. You have finished. If the difference is still wider than the maximum allowable error, go back to step 2 and repeat the process until the desired degree of accuracy is achieved.

While it is theoretically possible that this method may not converge, the method has always been effective in the authors' experience for normally

Figure 7.1: Newton-Raphson Method to Derive Yield to Maturity

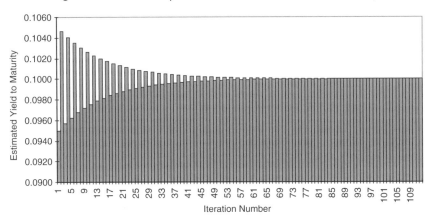

structured bonds. If the method does not converge for a given starting value of y, try a different starting value of y. The Newton-Raphson method provides a very quick and stable solution for almost every conceivable yield to maturity problem. Most common spreadsheet packages contain a solution method for non-linear problems[7] (like the yield to maturity formula), which allow the user to find yield to maturity without going through the steps above. In many cases, the yield to maturity on a bond is itself a function embedded in the spreadsheet software. Note that the yield to maturity on an amortizing instrument where all principal payments are incorporated in the level payment is calculated using exactly the same formula with the ending 'principal' set to zero.

Example

Using the fact that the present value in a previous example was 1,024.695, we use the Newton-Raphson method to derive yield to maturity. Using an initial guess of 9.5%, produces an iteration to an estimated value of y of 10%. The iteration to this solution is shown in Figure 7.1.

Calculating Forward Interest Rates and Bond Prices

What is the six-month interest rate that the market expects[8] to prevail two years in the future? Straightforward questions like this are the key to funding strategy or investment strategy at many financial institutions. Once discount factors (or, equivalently, zero-coupon bond prices) are known, making these calculations is simple.

---

[7] One example is the 'solver' function in the tools menu for Microsoft Excel.

[8] In later chapters, we will discuss 'risk neutral' interest rates and their relationship to the true expected value of future interest rates.

Implied forward interest rates on zero-coupon bonds

The forward interest rate t_i years in the future on a security that pays interest and principal at time t_{i+1} is:

$$\text{Forward Interest Rate} = \frac{100}{t_{i+1} - t_i} \left[\frac{P(t_i)}{P(t_{i+1})} - 1 \right]$$

This forward rate is the simple interest rate consistent with $1/(t_{i+1} - t_i)$ interest payments per year. For example, if t_i is two years and t_{i+1} is 2.5 years, then the forward interest rate is expressed on the basis of semi-annual interest payments.

Example

Value of $1 *dollar received in the future*
Received in 350 days: $0.88
Received in 1 year plus 350 days: $0.80

$$\text{Forward Rate} = \frac{100}{1} \left[\frac{0.88}{0.80} - 1 \right] = 10.00$$

This is the forward rate the market expects to prevail 350 days in the future on a one-year bond. The forward rate is expressed on the basis of annual compounding of interest.

Example

Value of $1 *dollar received in the future*
Received in 2 years: $0.80
Received in 2.5 years: $0.75

$$\text{Forward Rate} = \frac{100}{2.5 - 2} \left[\frac{0.80}{0.75} - 1 \right] = 13.33\%$$

The forward rate in this case assumes semi-annual interest payments consistent with the fact that the underlying instrument has a maturity of 0.5 years.

Implied forward zero-coupon bond prices

A parallel question to the question of the level of forward interest rates is: what is the forward price of a six-month zero-coupon bond two years in the future? The answer is a simple ratio. The price at time t_i of a zero-coupon bond with maturity at time t_{i+1} is:

$$\text{Implied Forward Zero Coupon Bond Price} = \frac{P(t_{i+1})}{P(t_i)}$$

We derive this simple formula using stochastic processes and no arbitrage arguments in later chapters.

Example
Value of $1 *dollar received in the future*

Received in 3 years:	$0.72
Received in 3.5 years:	$0.64
Implied zero-coupon bond price	= 0.64/0.72
	= 0.888889

Present value of forward fixed coupon bond

What is the present value of a bond to be issued on known terms some time in the future? The answer is a straightforward application of the basic present value formula. If the actual dollar amount of the coupon payment on a fixed coupon bond is C and principal is repaid at time t_n, the value (price plus accrued interest) of the bond is:

$$\text{Present Value of Forward Fixed Coupon Bond}$$

$$= C \left[\sum_{i=1}^{n} P(t_i) \right] + P(t_n)[\text{Principal}]$$

Example

Principal amount:	$1,000.00
Interest paid:	semi-annually
Coupon rate:	10%
Coupon amount:	$50.00
Periods to maturity:	4 semi-annual periods
Years to next coupon:	3 years

Value of $1 *dollar received in the future*

Received in 3 years:	$0.80
Received in 3.5 years:	$0.75
Received in 4 years 40 days:	$0.71
Received in 4.5 years:	$0.67

Present value $= 50.00\,(0.80 + 0.75 + 0.71 + 0.67)$
                                                       $+ 0.67(1{,}000)$
                                                       $= 816.5$

Implied forward price on a fixed coupon bond

There is another logical question to ask about a bond to be issued in the future on known terms. What would be the forward price, as of today, of the 'when issued bond', if we know its offering date? The answer is again a straight-forward application of the basic present value equation. If the actual dollar amount of the coupon payment on a fixed coupon bond is C and principal is repaid at time t_n, the forward value (price plus accrued interest) of the bond at the issuance date t_0 is:

Forward Value of Fixed Coupon Bond

$$= \frac{C\left[\sum_{i=1}^{n} P(t_i)\right] + P(t_n)[\text{Principal}]}{P(t_0)}$$

Example

Principal amount:	$1,000.00
Interest paid:	semi-annually
Coupon rate:	10%
Coupon amount:	$50.00
Periods to maturity:	4 semi-annual periods
Years to first coupon:	3 years

Value of $1 *dollar received in the future*

Received in 2.5 years:	$0.85
Received in 3 years:	$0.80
Received in 3.5 years:	$0.75
Received in 4 years 40 days:	$0.71
Received in 4.5 years:	$0.67

Present value $= [50.00\,(0.80 + 0.75 + 0.71 + 0.67)$
                                                       $+ 0.67(1{,}000)]$
                                                       $= 816.5$

Forward value $= 816.5/0.85$
                                                       $= 960.6$

Implied forward coupon on a fixed coupon bond

Finally, a treasurer may often be asked the implied forward issue costs (i.e. forward coupon rates) for a bond to be issued at par (or any other value). This question can be answered using a minor modification of another basic present value equation. For a bond to be issued at time t_0 with n interest payments and principal repaid at time t_n, the dollar amount of the coupon is given by the formula:

Dollar Coupon Amount of Fixed Coupon Bond

$$= \frac{P(t_0)(\text{Value at Issue}) - P(t_n)[\text{Principal}]}{\sum_{i=1}^{n} P(t_i)}$$

Example

Principal amount:	$1,000.00
Interest paid:	semi-annually
Value at issue:	$995.00
Periods to maturity:	4 semi-annual periods
Years to issuance:	2 years

Value of $1 dollar received in the future

Received in 2 years:	$0.86
Received in 2.5 years:	$0.81
Received in 3 years:	$0.75
Received in 3.5 years:	$0.70
Received in 4 years:	$0.65
Coupon amount	$= (0.86*995–0.65*1,000)$
	$/(0.81 + 0.75 + 0.70 + 0.65)$
	$= 70.687$
Coupon rate	$= [100*(2 \text{ payments})*\text{Amount}]$
	$/1,000.00$
	$= 14.14\%$

Other forward calculations

The same types of calculations can be performed for a very wide variety of other instruments and statistics. For instance, the forward yield to maturity can be calculated on a fixed coupon bond. Forward amortizing bond prices and payment amounts can be calculated as well. The present values and forward prices for literally any form of cash flow can be analyzed using the formulas presented above.

Conclusion

This chapter has summarized the building blocks of all financial market calculations—the concepts of present value, compound interest, yield to maturity, and forward bond yields and prices. All of these concepts are expressed using algebra. There are no mysteries here, yet the power of these simple concepts is great. Risk managers who make full use of present value and its implications have an advantage over the competition. Those who don't are disadvantaged in a very competitive world. As simple as these concepts are compared to the fixed income derivatives calculations we tackle in later chapters, they are still widely misunderstood and their powerful implications are ignored by the managers of many financial institutions.

At this point, there are probably more than a few readers thinking "yes, these concepts aren't difficult as long as someone gives you the discount factors—but where am I supposed to get them?" We give the answers to that question in Chapter 8 and (on a credit-adjusted basis) Chapter 18. There are so many potential ways to calculate the 'correct' discount factors that we purposely have chosen to speak about them generally in this chapter so that no one technique would obscure the importance of the present value calculations.

Exercises

Assume for purposes of the following exercises that today is January 15 2005 and that the prevailing market prices in the government bond market for the following zero-coupon bonds are as follows:

April 15 2005	0.974
October 15 2005	0.949
April 15 2006	0.921
October 15 2006	0.892
April 15 2007	0.862
October 15 2007	0.831
April 15 2008	0.798
October 14 2008	0.763
April 15 2009	0.725

Also, assume that all government bonds pay interest semi-annually, including both fixed and floating-rate instruments. Accrued interest is calculated according to the ratio of the actual days from the last interest payment to the total days between interest payments. Assume the par value of all government bonds is $1,000.

7.1 What is the present value of the 6% government bond maturing October 15 2007?

7.2 What is the amount of accrued interest on this bond? What would be the quoted 'price' in the U.S. market and other markets using similar accrued interest conventions?

7.3 Assuming there is no arbitrage in the market, what is the coupon that would prevail in the forward market if the government plans to issue a four-year bond at par on April 15 2005?

7.4 What would be the forward price on this bond if the government has announced in advance that the annual coupon rate will be 9%?

7.5   What are the semi-annual forward rates prevailing in the government bond market for six-month periods beginning April 15 2005?

7.6   If the government decided to issue today an amortizing bond with present value of $1,000 and equal payments on each April 15 and October 15 until maturity April 15 2009, what would the semi-annual payment have to be?

7.7   What is the yield to maturity on this amortizing bond?

7.8   What is the yield to maturity on the 6% bond in exercise 7.1?

7.9   What are the annual forward rates prevailing in the government bond market from April 15 2005, 2006, 2007, and 2008?

7.10 What are the continuously compounding yields to maturity for each of the discount government bonds whose prices are given above?

7.11 What is the quarterly compounded rate of interest on the government discount bond maturing on October 15 2008?

7.12 What is the present value of a government bond that pays the prevailing six-month government bond rate plus 0.50% semi-annually on each April 15 and October 15, maturing April 15 2009. Assume the coupon payment to be received April 15 2005 is an annual rate of 6%.

7.13 How much will the present value of the 6% bond in exercise 7.1 change if its yield to maturity goes up by 0.50%?

7.14 How much will the present value of the 6% bond in exercise 7.1 change if the continuously compounded yields to maturity on each of the zero-coupon bonds given above increase by 0.50%?

7.15 Assume that you hold $1,000 principal amount of the 6% bond maturing October 15 2007. Assume also that you can only hedge this position by taking a 'short' position in 7% government bonds maturing April 15 2006. If the continuous yields to maturity on all the discount bonds given above will increase by 0.50%, how much of the April 15 2006 bonds should be shorted to offset the risk of this scenario?

7.16 The ABC life insurance company's liabilities include policies on Ms Jones and Mr Smith. Ms Jones' insurance policy results in payments of $500 to ABC every April 15 and October 15 until her death. Mr. Smith's policy pays $750 to ABC on each April 15 and October 15. Ms Jones and Mr Smith's probabilities of dying have been determined from actuarial tables and adjustments to reflect (a) Ms Jones' high-risk lifestyle as a professor of finance at a well-known university and (b) Mr Smith's bungee-jumping hobby. The probabilities of death are:

Date	Ms Jones	Mr Smith
April 15 2007	10%	20%
October 15 2007	20%	30%
April 15 2008	30%	40%
October 15 2008	20%	10%
April 15 2009	20%	0%

Both Ms Jones' and Mr Smith's policies pay $10,000 upon their death.

(a) What is the net present value, discounted at the government securities yield curve, of ABC's cash flows on each policy? Assume that ABC is 'risk neutral' with regard to the probabilities of death, so no risk premium has to be reflected in the net present value calculation.

(b) Assume that the only bonds available for purchase in the government bond market are the following bonds, whose present values are consistent with the zero-coupon bond prices quoted above. How much, in terms of both principal amount and present value, of each bond does ABC have to buy to perfectly match the expected cash flows on these policies?

Coupons Prevailing in the Government Bond Market

Maturity Date	Coupon
April 15 2007	10%
October 15 2007	9%
April 15 2008	8%
October 15 2008	7.5%
April 15 2009	7%

ABC Company has decided not to follow the perfectly matched cash flow strategy in exercise 7.16(b). Instead, the company owes $10,000 principal amount of the 7.5% bonds due October 15 2003 and $15,000 of the 7% bonds due April 15 2009.

(c) What is the mark-to-market value of ABC company (market value of assets minus market value of liabilities), assuming that the government yield curve is the appropriate yield curve for discounting all of the company's assets and liabilities?

(d) By what percentage does the market value change if the continuous yield to maturity on each of the zero-coupon bond prices quoted above increases by 1%, and decreases by 1%?

CHAPTER 8

Yield Curve Smoothing[1]

Yield curve smoothing has long been the Rodney Dangerfield of risk management analytics. In spite of the importance of yield curve smoothing technology, the discipline has not received the respect that it deserves. In this chapter, we summarize some of the key principles of yield curve smoothing and illustrate two practical tests for determining which of two competing yield curve smoothing techniques is superior. As we saw in Chapter 7, the zero-coupon bond prices with t years to maturity $P[t]$ are essential to practical risk measurement and management. In Chapter 7, we assumed that the $P[t]$ values were given to us. In this chapter, we show exactly how to derive them from a wide variety of fixed income data and prices observable in the market.

The accuracy with which we derive yield curve data has become increasingly important in recent years because of the intense research focus among both practitioners and academics on credit risk modeling. In particular, the reduced-form modeling approach of Duffie and Singleton [1999] and Jarrow [2001] has the power to extract default probabilities and the 'liquidity premium' (the excess of 'credit spread' above and beyond expected loss) from bond prices and credit default swap prices. We discuss this in detail in Chapter 18 after our review of credit risk models, but it is important to mention here as one of the most critical reasons for ensuring that yield curve smoothing is performed well.

The Three 'Best' Approaches to Yield Curve Smoothing

Van Deventer and Imai [1996] explain that the 'best' approach to yield curve smoothing is not subject to debate once the criterion for 'best' is defined mathematically and once the objective of the user is specified.

Implicitly, among both practitioners and academics, the 'best' approach to yield curve smoothing is the approach that produces the 'most reasonable'

---

[1] This chapter is based on a www.riskcenter.com article by Donald R. van Deventer, 'Evaluating Yield Curve Smoothing Techniques with Implications for Credit Spreads,' January 2004, and Chapter 2 of van Deventer and Imai [1996].

outputs. When academics and market practitioners look at competing yield curve smoothing techniques, their evaluations of alternative yield curve smoothing techniques usually argue that the 'smoothest' yield curve output is the best. Furthermore, the 'smoothest' criterion can be applied alternatively to yields, prices, forward rates or credit spreads. We concentrate on the first three yield curve smoothing objectives (yields, prices, and forward rates) in this chapter and will address the issue of the smoothest credit spreads in Chapter 18.

The Definition of Smoothness

If the best yield curve smoothing technique is the one that produces the 'smoothest' output, we need a mathematical definition of smoothness. Hildebrand [1987] points out that the most common (but not the only) definition of smoothness is the function that minimizes Z, the integral of the function's squared second derivative over the relevant interval:

$$Z = \int_{t_1}^{t_2} [g''(s)]^2 ds$$

This smoothness function is used in disciplines ranging from engineering to computer graphics and has a long history that has been frequently overlooked in finance. A straight line, for example, is perfectly smooth because its second derivative is zero everywhere.

Once the criterion for 'best' is defined as the function g which minimizes the smoothness statistic Z, then the functional form for $g(s)$ can be unambiguously derived mathematically, with no debate about which function is best. Penter [1989] shows that a cubic spline produces the smoothest output for two of the three main objectives (zero yields and zero prices), and van Deventer and Imai [1996] use the same mathematics to prove which function produces the smoothest forward rate curve. That proof is given in Appendix 2 of this chapter. We know from this mathematical technique that:

1. A cubic spline of zero-coupon bond yields produces the smoothest zero yield curve;
2. A cubic spline of zero-coupon bond prices produces the smoothest zero-coupon bond price curve;
3. A quartic spline of forward rates produces the smoothest forward rate curve.

We will discuss all of these techniques in this chapter, but before we do, we need to ask an important question.

What is a 'Spline'?

A spline is a series of line segments drawn using a specific functional form between observable data points in such a way that the line segments join (or 'spline') together in a smooth way. A cubic spline is a set of N cubic polynomials that fit the observable data. A quartic spline is a series of N fourth-degree polynomials that fit the observable data. The calculus of variations is used to prove which functional form, of the infinite number of functional forms available, is smoothest given the objectives specified in 1, 2, and 3 above. This mathematical derivation is proof enough for the most mathematically-inclined practitioners. Appendix 1 illustrates this kind of proof for the maximum smoothness forward rate technique.

Why do we need this continuously drawn yield curve? If we own a portfolio of bonds that were originally 10-year bonds that we have been accumulating over the last decade, we could conceivably have cash flows on 10 years × 365 days = 3,650 potential payment dates. If we are going to apply the same accuracy standards to risk management at the enterprise level that have long been applied on the trading floor, we need a yield curve smoothing technology that has the potential to produce zero-coupon bond prices for 3,650 different payment dates over this 10-year horizon. That is where the spline technology comes in.

How can we prove that one smoothing technique is superior to another to someone who is more intuitive, someone who isn't convinced by a magic wand called the calculus of variations? There are two ways to do that, and we employ both in this chapter:

- **Calculate the smoothness statistic** for two competing models and show which one is smoother subject to the same constraints. If one of the techniques is either 1, 2, or 3 above, we know who the winner will be.
- **Do the 'Shimko' test for reasonableness**, which produces results very similar to the rankings we would get in the first test. We outline these tests in the next two sections.

Calculating the Smoothness Statistic for Two Competing Smoothing Methods

We can illustrate in spreadsheet software the relative smoothness of two competing smoothing methods. For purposes of this example, we assume the objective is to produce the 'smoothest possible zero-coupon bond yield curve'. This is case (1) above, and we can prove mathematically that a cubic spline of zero-coupon bond yields will be the smoothest, but we want to demonstrate this empirically and quantitatively, beyond just looking at competing graphs.

We start in Step 1 by using the smoothness function Z, which measures the smoothness of a function $g(t)$ over an interval from t_1 to t_2. Z is defined as:

$$Z = \int_{t_1}^{t_2} [g''(s)]^2 ds$$

Next, in Step 2 we define the constraints and the maturity period for the comparison between two competing functions g. For illustrative purposes, we assume that we want to make the comparison for the following observable data and constraints:[2]

- The time interval is from two years to five years in maturity;
- The value of the zero yield curve is 0.05 (5%) at two years;
- The value of the zero yield curve is 0.06 (6%) at five years;
- The first derivative of the zero yield curve is 0.001 at two years;
- The first derivative of the zero yield curve is 0 at five years.

The last four assumptions define four equations that must be satisfied. The latter two come from requirements that each line segment fit together smoothly with adjacent line segments and they are derived by joint estimation. We ignore that here, but we will discuss it in more detail later in this chapter.

The next step, Step 3, is to define the two competing functional forms or smoothing techniques that we want to compare. To compare them, we must describe them in mathematical form.

We assume that one of the yield curve smoothing techniques, Method A, is cubic spline of continuously compounded zero-coupon bond yields, which takes the form:

$$y(t) = a + bt + ct^2 + dt^3$$

in each time interval. For this example, we are only analyzing the time interval from two years to five years.

What if the competing smoothing technique, Method B, is a cubic spline fit to the natural log of the zero-coupon bond price $P(t)$? Using continuous compounding formulas, this function fits a cubic polynomial to the log of the zero-coupon bond price, which we can rewrite as follows:

$$\ln[P(t)] = \ln[\exp(-y(t)t)] = a + bt + ct^2 + dt^3$$

---

[2] We choose these assumptions for illustrative purposes only. If we were smoothing the swap curve with six line segments spanning zero to 10 years, we would calculate the total smoothness for the full 10 years, for example.

since the zero-coupon bond price and the zero-coupon bond yield are related by the continuous compounding formula. This means that the Method B smoothing method is the same as fitting the following function to zero yields:

$$y(t) = \frac{-a}{t} - b - ct - dt^2$$

The values we get for a, b, c, and d will be different for Methods A and B. The next step, Step 4, in the comparison is to define the constraints we want to impose mathematically.

Our assumptions require that:

$$y(2) = 0.05;$$
$$y(5) = 0.06;$$
$$y'(2) = 0.001;$$
$$y'(5) = 0;$$

for both smoothing methods, where $y(t)$ is the continuously compounded zero-coupon bond yield at time t and $y'(t)$ is the first derivative of the zero yield at time t.

We specify these equations and solve for a, b, c, and d in Step 5. Because the functional forms are different, a, b, c, and d have different values for the two methods. Since we have four equations in four unknowns in both cases, we can solve for a, b, c, and d directly in each case:

Values of a, b, c, and d	Cubic Spline of LN (Zero-Coupon Bond Price)	Cubic Spline of Zero Yields
a	−0.062963	0.063704
b	0.024444	−0.017222
c	−0.026222	0.006444
d	0.002370	−0.000630

The final step, Step 6, in the comparison is to calculate the smoothness statistic Z.

By taking the second derivative of both yield curve smoothing functions, using the values of a, b, c, and d, we can substitute into the formula for Z in Step 1 and calculate the smoothness statistic Z. We can see quantitatively that Method A, the cubic spline of zero yields, produces a smoother yield curve than Method B, because the smoothness statistic Z is lower for Method A over the two- to five-year intervals that we defined in our test:

		Cubic Spline of LN (Zero-Coupon Bond Price)	Cubic Spline of Zero Yields
Results of Calculations Value of t			
when evaluated at t_1	2	0.01901310	0.00017554
when evaluated at t_2	5	0.04743027	0.00020798
Smoothness Coefficient			
from t_1 to t_2		0.02841717	0.00003244

A perfectly smooth line has a smoothness coefficient of zero.

We can confirm this mathematical conclusion by plotting the derived yield curves. The smoothest line is the one which 'wiggles' the least and which on average is closest to a straight line between the observable 5 and 6% zero yields (the constraints on the first derivatives prevent our results from being a straight line).

Figure 8.1 illustrates that the cubic spline of zero yields, the solid line, is smoother.

Given the criterion we have chosen (produce the maximum smoothness zero yield), the cubic spline of zero yields will always win for any set of common constraints that apply equally to the two competing functional forms. If this is not the case, there is an error in the calculation.

Figure 8.1 Comparison of Zero Yield Curves for Two Different Smoothing Methods

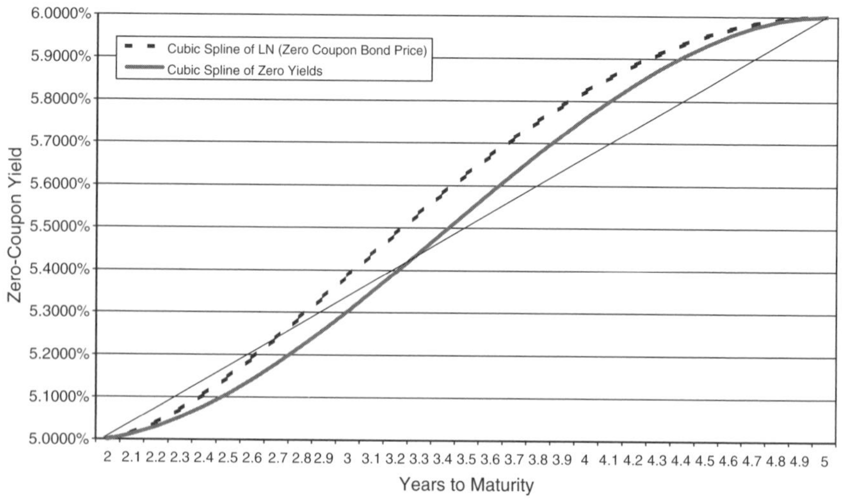

If we choose a different criterion for best yield curve (say the smoothest forward rate curve or the smoothest zero-coupon bond price curve), then the best functional form will not be a cubic spline of zero yields. It would be a quartic spline of forward rates in the former case and a cubic spline of zero-coupon bond prices in the latter case.

The Shimko Test

Van Deventer and Imai [1996] also report the results of another intuitive test suggested by David Shimko, and we report their results in Appendix 1 of this chapter. This test is not as mathematically rigorous as the smoothness calculation given above, but it has powerful appeal to practitioners to show the reasonableness of competing smoothing techniques.

The test that Shimko suggested works as follows:

1. Collect observable market data on bond prices or yields at N different maturities on M different observation dates for one bond issuer.
2. Determine which one of these N maturities is the most important to estimate accurately. Call this maturity point J.
3. Eliminate all M observations of data at maturity point J from the sample.
4. Smooth the remaining $N-1$ data points for each of the M dates.
5. Use the results of the smoothing to estimate the values that would have prevailed at maturity point J on each of the M observation dates.
6. Compare the theoretical values at maturity point J on the M observation dates with the actual observable market values.
7. The 'best' smoothing technique is the one with the smallest sum of the squared errors calculated in the previous step.

Van Deventer and Imai [1996] report that the maximum smoothness forward rate approach was the winner in this test on large samples of U.S. Dollar and Japanese yen interest rate swap data. In those tests, the seven-year swap rate was eliminated and alternative yield curve smoothing technologies were used to estimate what the seven-year swap rate would have been if it was observable. The maximum smoothness forward rate approach had the least estimation error in both yen and dollar samples.

Smoothing on Coupon-Bearing Data

The comparisons we have done above assumed that we had zero-coupon yields, zero-coupon bond prices, or forward rates. In fact, these quantities are not observable, but that does not affect the use of the comparisons above or any of the smoothing methods discussed above. The techniques are applied using exactly the same non-linear equation solving methods that apply to the calculation of simple yield to maturity.

If we want to use cubic spline yield smoothing on N observable bond prices of ABC company on a particular day and divide the yield curve into 10 one-year intervals from maturities zero to 10 years, we will have 10 cubic polynomials, one for each one year interval. We find the best fitting collection of 10 polynomials by following this process:

1. Guess the initial set of zero-coupon bond yields $y(0)$, $y(1)$, ..., $y(10)$.
2. Solve for a, b, c, and d using the techniques in van Deventer and Imai [1996] for each of the 10 line segments.
3. Calculate the theoretical value (price plus accrued interest) of each of the N bonds.
4. Calculate the sum of the squared valuation errors by comparing the theoretical bond values with the observable bond values (price plus accrued interest).
5. If this sum of squared errors is within a tolerance e, stop and output desired yield curve smoothing output (forward rates, theoretical bond values, zero-coupon yields, etc.) based on the final 10 sets of a, b, c, and d coefficients.
6. If the squared error is not within the tolerance e, guess a new set of y values using standard techniques and go back to Step 2.

This process has been used by more than a decade in enterprise-wide risk management software and is very fast on modern computers.

In some special cases (for example, a government bond market where all payment dates are August 15 and February 15), we can estimate the 'best y values' by linear regression because we know the present value of the bond is a linear combination of zero-coupon bond prices as we saw in Chapter 7. Take the case of a bond with four payments, a coupon dollar amount of C, and a principal amount of 1,000. Its present value is a linear combination of the four zero-coupon bond prices:

$$\text{Bond Value} = CP(1) + CP(2) + CP(3) + (C + 1,000)P(4)$$

Therefore, in the special case where we have more bonds (say M) than payment dates (say N), $M > N$, linear regression will give us the best fitting P values and these can be converted to y values. In this case, we only go through one iteration of the process above (because we know from linear regression that our initial y's can't be improved), but we still need to derive the splines that connect the known y values. We have to do this because we may be valuing transactions that have cash flows on dates other than the N payment dates for which we know the y values. This process of using linear regression to determine the y values is not yield curve smoothing, it is the calculation of inputs to yield curve smoothing.

Once the coefficients for two competing techniques have been obtained for coupon-bearing data, the comparison of smoothness statistics and the Shimko test are identical to the tests outlined above on zero-coupon yield data.

Using Yield Curve Smoothing Techniques[3]

In Chapter 7, the basics of present value, forward rates, and interest rate compounding were discussed on the assumption that the present value of $1 to be paid at various times in the future was known with certainty. The examples and exercises provided these 'discount factors', or zero-coupon bond prices. In the remainder of this chapter, we show how to derive the zero-coupon bond prices at any maturity using four basic techniques:

- Linear smoothing of zero-coupon bond yields;
- Cubic spline smoothing of zero-coupon bond yields;
- Cubic spline smoothing of zero-coupon bond prices;
- Maximum smoothness forward rates, a quartic spline of forward rates.

We will illustrate how to use the smooth curves we derive for each of these methods to calculate zero-coupon bond prices and zero-coupon bond yields, the yield curve data we required to solve all of the problems in Chapter 7. We leave the calculation of continuous forward rates to the interested reader, since discrete forward rate calculations were given in Chapter 7.

For purposes of these examples, we assume that we have derived the coefficients needed for each of the smoothing techniques using the methods discussed in the remainder of this chapter and its appendices. We assume that we derived the coefficients in this manner:

1. We had observable bond prices at various maturities from zero to 10 years.
2. We decided to divide the zero to 10-year interval into three segments, zero to two years, two years to five years, and five years to 10 years.
3. We will focus on examples that use the yield curve parameters for the two to five-year line segment. If we need zero-coupon bond prices or zero-coupon bond yields for maturities of less than two years, we use the coefficients for that line segment. If we need zero-coupon bond prices or bond yields for maturities over five years, we use the coefficients for that line segment.

We start with linear yield curve smoothing.

---

[3] We are grateful for the enormously helpful comments and insights of Oldrich Vasicek, Robert Jarrow, Volf Frishling, and Kenneth Adams on this chapter.

Example: Using linear yield curve smoothing of zero-coupon yields

After fitting three linear segments to the three time intervals and deriving the best fitting parameters, we know that zero-coupon bond yields in the interval from two to five years can be derived from the following equation:

$$y(t) = a + bt$$

To get the value of the continuous zero-coupon yield curve for the four-year maturity, $t = 4$ and

$$y(4) = a + b4$$

From the formula in Chapter 7 for continuous compounding, we know the zero-coupon bond prices in the interval from two to five years have the formula as shown in equation 8.9:

$$P[t] = e^{-y(t)t} = e^{-t(a+bt)}$$

To get the value of the zero-coupon bond price at $t = 4$ years, we substitute 4 for t:

$$P[4] = e^{-y(4)4} = e^{-4(a+b4)}$$

Using these formulas, we can solve all of the problems in Chapter 7 using linear yield curve smoothing of zero-coupon yields. We now turn to cubic spline smoothing of zero-coupon bond yields.

Example: Using cubic spline smoothing of zero-coupon yields

After fitting three line segments, which are cubic polynomials to the three time intervals, and deriving the best fitting parameters, we know that zero-coupon bond yields in the interval from two to five years can be derived from the following equation:

$$y(t) = a + bt + ct^2 + dt^3$$

To get the value of the continuous zero-coupon yield curve for the four-year maturity, $t = 4$ and

$$y(4) = a + b4 + c4^2 + d4^3$$

From the formula in Chapter 7 for continuous compounding, we know the zero-coupon bond prices in the interval from two to five years have the formula:

$$P[t] = e^{-y(t)t} = e^{-t(a+bt+ct^2+dt^3)} = e^{-(at+bt^2+ct^3+dt^4)}$$

To get the value of the zero-coupon bond price at $t = 4$ years, we substitute 4 for t:

$$P[4] = e^{-y(4)4} = e^{-4(a+b4+c4^2+d4^3)} = e^{-(a4+b4^2+c4^3+d4^4)}$$

Using these formulas, we can again solve all of the problems in Chapter 7 using cubic spline smoothing of zero-coupon yields. Next we investigate the use of cubic splines of zero-coupon bond prices.

Example: Using cubic spline smoothing of zero-coupon bond prices
The two smoothing methods we have illustrated so far are based on the smoothing of zero-coupon bond yields (or coupon-bearing bond prices which we do by guessing best fitting zero yields, smoothing, and iterating until we get the fit we want as discussed above). Now we turn to a common alternative, the fitting of a cubic spline to zero-coupon bond prices. Again, we focus on the line segment from two to five years. We know that the zero-coupon bond price is:

$$P(t) = a + bt + ct^2 + dt^3$$

To calculate the value of a zero-coupon bond price when we know a, b, c, and d and the maturity $t = 4$ years,

$$P(4) = a + b4 + c4^2 + d4^3$$

Using the continuous compounding formula from Chapter 7 again, we know that the zero-coupon bond yield can be written as:

$$y(t) = \frac{-1}{t} \ln[P(t)] = \frac{-1}{t} \ln[a + bt + ct^2 + dt^3]$$

When we need the zero-coupon bond yield for $t = 4$ years,

$$y(4) = \frac{-1}{4} \ln[P(4)] = \frac{-1}{4} \ln[a + b4 + c4^2 + d4^3]$$

Next, we turn to the maximum smoothness forward rate technique.

Example: Using maximum smoothness forward-rate smoothing

The maximum smoothness forward rate technique was introduced by Adams and van Deventer [1994] and corrected by van Deventer and Imai [1996]. It was designed specifically to correct a common problem with linear yield curve smoothing and the cubic spline technique. For many observations, those techniques lead to implausibly volatile forward rate curves. This technique is slightly more complex than the spline techniques but the results are consistently superior. It is now widely used by the world's most sophisticated financial institutions. Practical application of the technique takes advantage of the mathematical relationship between continuous forward rates, continuous zero-coupon yields, and continuous zero-coupon bond prices, which are outlined in Appendix 1 to this chapter. Firstly, we fit a quartic polynomial to forward rates in each of the three time intervals we have been using in this example. Between two years and five years, for example, the forward rate curve will be given by:

$$f(t) = a + bt + ct^2 + dt^3 + et^4$$

We assume that the techniques of Appendix 1 have been followed and we know the values of a, b, c, d, and e plus we know the values of zero-coupon bond yields at the 'knot points', the maturities at zero, two, five, and 10 years. We know them because (as discussed above) we have gone through the iterative process of guessing the y values at these knot points, solving for the forward rate curve, and then improving our guesses of the y values until we have the best possible fit of the observable (coupon-bearing bond) data. Since we know the y values at the knot points, we also know the values of the zero-coupon bond prices at the knot points, $P[0]$, $P[2]$, $P[5]$, and $P[10]$. This gives us the general formula for zero-coupon bond prices between knot points at maturity t_i and maturity $t_i - 1$:

$$P[t] = P[t_{i-1}] e^{-[a(t-t_{i-1})+(b/2)(t-t_{i-1})^2+(c/3)(t-t_{i-1})^3+(d/4)(t-t_{i-1})^4+(e/5)(t-t_{i-1})^5]}$$

$$\text{since } P[t] = P[t_{i-1}]e^{-\int_{i-1}^{t} f(s)\,ds}$$

In our example, we are focusing on the interval from two to five years, so t_{i-1} is 2. If we make this substitution for t_{i-1}, we can calculate the zero-coupon bond price at four years as in the equation above.

$$P[4] = P[2]e^{-[a(4-2)+(b/2)(4-2)^2+(c/3)(4-2)^3+(d/4)(4-2)^4+(e/5)(4-2)^5]}$$

In addition, if we substitute the continuous compounding formula from Chapter 7, we can derive the general formula for zero-coupon yields using the maximum smoothness forward rate method:

$$y[t] = -\frac{1}{t}\left[\ln P[t_{i-1}] - \left(a(t - t_{i-1}) + \frac{b}{2}(t - t_{i-1})^2 + \frac{c}{3}(t - t_{i-1})^3\right.\right.$$
$$\left.\left. + \frac{d}{4}(t - t_{i-1})^4 + \frac{e}{5}(t - t_{i-1})^5\right)\right]$$

When we want to derive the zero-coupon bond yield for the four-year maturity, we know:

$$y[4] = -\frac{1}{4}\left[\ln P[2] - \left(a(4 - 2) + \frac{b}{2}(4 - 2)^2 + \frac{c}{3}(4 - 2)^3\right.\right.$$
$$\left.\left. + \frac{d}{4}(4 - 2)^4 + \frac{e}{5}(4 - 2)^5\right)\right]$$

Using these formulas, we can again answer all of the interest rate valuation and risk questions posed in Chapter 7.

Now we turn back to the practical question—which one of these techniques should we use?

The Shimko Test for Yield Curve Smoothing

As we reported earlier in this chapter, there are two techniques for judging which yield curve smoothing technique is 'best'. The first technique is to calculate the smoothness statistic for the yield curve smoothing objective (zero-coupon bond prices, zero-coupon bond yields, or forward rates) and to choose the technique with the best smoothness. From the mathematical derivation of the techniques, we know in advance which technique will win. We prove mathematically in Appendix 2 that the maximum smoothness forward rate curve produces the smoothest forward rate curve of any mathematical function, for example.

The second technique is very practical and was suggested by David Shimko—eliminate one of the input data points, use all competing yield curve smoothing techniques, and then (using the examples in this chapter) calculate a theoretical value for the missing data point. If this is repeated over a very large data set, the best technique is judged to be the one which minimizes the squared pricing errors for the input data point, defined as the sum of the actual input data value minus the theoretical data input value[2] over all of the observations.

Adams and van Deventer [1994] showed that the maximum smoothness forward rate technique was consistently the best by the Shimko test on interest rate swap data for the U.S. and Japan. Their results are reproduced in Appendix 1.

Conclusion

Almost all market participants who are familiar with each of the smoothing techniques in this chapter and who have processed a lot of data choose the maximum smoothness forward rate technique as the best smoothing technique for practical risk management.

For those who are interested in the reasons why so many have reached this conclusion, the worked derivation of the cubic splines and the maximum smoothness forward rate technique in Appendix 1 should be helpful. For those who are mathematically inclined, Appendix 2 provides the proof that the maximum smoothness forward rate technique is the smoothest possible forward rate curve that one can derive.

For everyone else, we now turn back to practical risk management now that we have laid the foundations with the basic tools and techniques.

Exercises

The exercises in this chapter are all based on the assumption that the following rates are observable in the market. To answer these exercises, readers will need the techniques given in Appendix 1 to fit two line segments to this observable market data:

Instantaneous interest rate:	4.00%
3-year continuous yield	5.00%
10-year continuous yield	6.50%

8.1 What are the coefficients of a yield curve that is linear in time to maturity for continuously compounded yields, that are consistent with this observable market data?

8.2 Using this linear yield curve, what is the quarterly payment on an amortizing bond with 12 quarters to maturity and a present value of 100?

8.3 What are the semi-annual forward rates out to 10 years associated with this yield curve?

8.4 What are the coefficients of a cubic yield spline calculated such that the continuous yield curve is flat ($y' = 0$) at the 10-year maturity?

8.5 Using this cubic yield spline, what would the coupon be on a new bond issue with semi-annual coupons, all principal due in 10 years, and a present value equal to 99?

8.6 What are the coefficients of a cubic yield spline calculated such that the continuous yield curve is instantaneously straight ($y'' = 0$) at the 10-year maturity?

8.7 Using this yield curve, how would your answer to question 8.5 differ?

8.8 What are the coefficients of a cubic price spline calculated such that the continuous yield at the 10-year point (not the zero-coupon price curve) is flat ($y' = 0$) at the 10-year maturity?

8.9 What are the semi-annual 'par coupons' for bonds associated with this yield curve such that they all have present values of 100?

8.10 What are the coefficients of the maximum smoothness forward rate curve consistent with the observable data?

8.11 Using spreadsheet software, graph the forward rates associated with all five yield curves at quarterly intervals. Which forward rate curve would you select as the most realistic?

8.12 Using the maximum smoothness curve, what would be the par coupon (such that on the issue date the present value would be 100) for a semi-annual bond with a maturity of five years that will be issued in 18 months?

8.13 Using the maximum smoothness yield curve, what is the semi-annual payment on a level payment lease that will settle in one year and have a present value of $125,000 at that time?

8.14 Using the maximum smoothness yield curve, what semi-annual premium produces a life insurance policy with a net present value of zero, if the amount paid out upon death of the insured is $100,000 and there is a 50% probability of death in year nine and a 50% probability in year 10?

8.15 Ms Jones, the finance professor who lives dangerously, has borrowed $100,000 from an extremely unpleasant relative. She is due to repay it via a lump sum payment of $120,000 in two years, but she is tired of being 'nagged' about it by the relative. Assume that she doesn't care if she never sees this relative again. What is the best offer she should make the relative, using the maximum smoothness yield curve, for immediate repayment? What is Ms Jones' gain if the relative will settle for $75,000 cash today?

8.16 Assume that there are three securities observable in the market— an instantaneous interest rate of 4%, a one-year zero-coupon bond with an instantaneous yield of 4.5%, and a two-year bond with semi-annual interest payments that has a present value of 100 and a coupon of 4.75%. Find the cubic yield spline which is flat at two years ($y' = 0$) and which is consistent with the observable data. (Hint: Use the 'solver' tool in common spreadsheet software to find the two-year continuous yield, which when combined with the other two data points and a cubic yield spline, makes the bond's four payments have a present value of 100.)

Appendix 1
Worked Examples of Cubic Spline and Maximum Smoothness Forward-Rate Smoothing

We begin this appendix by reviewing the cubic spline approach to yield curve smoothing in sections 1 and 2. In section 3, we introduce the maximum smoothness forward rate approach and discuss the alternative implementations of this technique. We then go on to show how the maximum smoothness forward rate technique is applied to coupon bearing bond data in section 4. Our conclusions are then summarized in section five. Appendix 2 contains a restated proof of the maximum smoothness forward-rate approach.

Cubic spline yield smoothing
Cubic splines have historically been the method preferred for yield curve smoothing. In spite of the popularity of the cubic spline approach, market participants have often relied on linear yield curve smoothing as a technique that is especially easy to implement, but its limitations are well-known:

- Linear yield curves are continuous but not smooth; at each knot point there is a 'kink' in the yield curve.
- Forward rate curves associated with linear yield curves are linear and discontinuous at the knot points. This means that linear yield curve smoothing sometimes cannot be used with the Heath, Jarrow and Morton [1992] term structure model (which we cover in later chapters), since it usually assumes the existence of a continuous forward rate curve.
- Estimates for the parameters associated with popular term structure models like the extended Vasicek [1977] or Cox, Ingersoll and Ross [1985] models are unreliable because the structure of the yield curve is unrealistic. The shape of the yield curve, because of its linearity, is fundamentally incompatible with an academically sound term structure model, so resulting parameter estimates are often implausible.

The cubic spline approach, first applied to yield curve smoothing by McCulloch [1975], was designed to address the first of these concerns.

In the following sections, we show how to use the smoothing methods above in an example where we are given data at time zero, one, and two years on either (a) the simple interest yield on zero-coupon bonds, (b) the continuous yield on zero-coupon bonds, or (c) the zero-coupon bond price. We assume that simple interest yields are the following:

Instantaneous interest rate:	6.00%
1-year interest rate:	5.25%
2-year interest rate (annually compounded):	4.00%

Table 8.1 Examples of Various Smoothing Calculations

Base Case Assumptions

Period	Simple Interest	Continuous Yield	Discount Bond Price
0	6	0.060000	1.000000
1	5.25	0.051168	0.950119
2	4	0.039221	0.924556

Table 8.1 summarizes the equivalent continuously compounded yields and zero-coupon bond prices that are consistent with this data and that are used in subsequent sections. In section 4, we use the same data to calculate the maximum smoothness forward rate curve on the alternative assumption that the input data above represents the coupons on semiannual payment bonds trading at par. Figure 8.3 gives the results of the calculations for linear yield curve smoothing when we model the yield y as the linear function.

$$y(t) = a_i + b_i t \quad \text{for } i = 1, 2 \text{ with } t_{i-1} \leq t \leq t_i$$

In the linear smoothing case, there are four constraints that must be met. The yield curve is broken into segment 1 and segment 2. Segment 1 spans maturities from time zero to year one. Segment 2 spans the maturities from time one to time two. The four constraints require that the two segments equal the actual data. The results produce a yield curve such that $y = 0.06 - 0.00883t$ during the first segment and $y = 0.063116 - 0.01195t$ during the second segment. These results are produced by solving the four equations in four

Figure 8.2 Linear Smoothing

General Form:				$y = a + bt$			
			Coefficients in Equation				Constant
Constraint	Time	a1	b1	a2	b2		
Time 0: Must equal actual	0	1	0	0	0		0.06
Time 1: Must equal actual	1	1	1	0	0		0.051168
Time 1: Must equal actual	1	0	0	1	1		0.051168
Time 2: Must equal actual	2	0	0	1	2		0.039221
		Inverse Matrix					Answers
		1	0	0	0		0.06
		−1	1	0	0		−0.00883
		0	0	2	−1		0.063116
		0	0	−1	1		−0.01195

	a1	b1	a2	b2	
Calculated Coefficients	0.06	−0.00883	0.063116	−0.01195	
	Constraint	Calculated			
Check on constraints	Value	Value	Difference		
Time 0: Must equal actual	0.06	0.06	0		
Time 1: Must equal actual	0.051168	0.051168	0		
Time 1: Must equal actual	0.051168	0.051168	0		
Time 2: Must equal actual	0.039221	0.039221	0		

unknowns using matrix inversion. This can be done in simple spreadsheet software.

The mathematical rationale for the cubic polynomial

The choice of the cubic polynomial for smoothing is not arbitrary. It can be proven mathematically (see Schwartz [1989]), that there is no smoother function, of any functional form, that fits the observable data points and is continuous and twice differential at the knot points than a cubic spline. Smoothness is defined mathematically as the value Z given by the formula:

$$Z = \int_0^T [f''(s)]^2 ds$$

where the function f is used to smooth the observable data. If Z is 0, then the line is perfectly smooth. Function 1 is more smooth than function 2 if Z is less for function 1 than it is for function 2. If the objective of the analyst is the smoothest possible yield curve, then the cubic spline of yields produces the smoothest yield curve. If the objective of the analyst is the smoothest possible discount bond price function, then a cubic spline of zero-coupon bond prices produces the smoothest curve. Any other functional form, given these objectives, is inferior to cubic splines by the smoothness criterion. For more on smoothness, see Adams and van Deventer [1994].

Using cubic spline smoothing to smooth yields: A review

Assume that we are given zero-coupon bond yields $y_0, y_1, y_2, \ldots, y_n$, consistent with maturities $t_0, t_1, t_2, \ldots, t_n$. We assume without loss of generality that t_0 is 0. We fit the function:

$$y_i(t) = a_i + b_i t + c_i t^2 + d_i t^3$$

to the interval between t_i and t_{i-1}. Therefore we have $4n$ unknowns to solve, since we need to know a, b, c, and d for all n intervals between the $n+1$ data points. In order to solve for all of these a, b, c, and d values, we make use of the fact that these equations must fit the observable data points, that the first derivatives must be equal at the $n-1$ knot points $t_1, t_2, t_3, \ldots, t_{n-1}$, and that the second derivatives must also be equal at the knot points. We have the following equations which constrain the values of a, b, c, and d:

n equations requiring that the cubic polynomials fit the n data points t_1, $t_2, \ldots, t_n$

$$y(t_i) = a_i + b_i t_i + c_i t_i^2 + d_i t_i^3$$

for i from 1 to n.

n equations requiring that the cubic polynomials fit the n data points t_0, t_1, t_2,..., t_{n-1}

$$y(t_{i-1}) = a_i + b_i t_{i-1} + c_i t_{i-1}^2 + d_i t_{i-1}^3$$

for i from 1 to n.

$n-1$ equations requiring that the first derivatives of the cubic polynomials on each side of the knot points be equal:

$$b_i + 2c_i t_i + 3d_i t_i^2 - b_{i+1} - 2c_{i+1} t_i - 3d_{i+1} t_i^2 = 0$$

for i from 1 to $n-1$.

$n-1$ equations requiring that the second derivatives of the cubic polynomials on each side of the knot points be equal:

$$2c_i + 6d_i t_i - 2c_{i+1} - 6d_{i+1} t_i = 0$$

for i from 1 to $n-1$.

This gives us $4n - 2$ equations to solve for $4n$ unknowns. We need two more equations to complete the system. The first equation is usually chosen such that the yield curve is instantaneously straight ($y''(0) = 0$) at the left hand side of the yield curve:

$$2c_1 + 6d_1 t_0 = 0$$

The right hand side, or long end, of the yield curve offers the opportunity to impose another constraint. There are two common choices—either the yield curve can be set to be flat ($y'= 0$), or the yield curve can be set to be instantaneously straight ($y'' = 0$) at the longest maturity. We select one of the following equations to complete the system:

Either;

$$b_n + 2c_n t_n + 3d_n t_n^2 = 0$$

or;

$$2c_n + 6d_n t_n = 0$$

This gives us $4n$ equations and $4n$ unknowns, and all of the equations are linear in the unknowns. We can solve this set of linear equations simply using matrix inversion, which can be done in spreadsheet software or more complex software implementations.

Problems with cubic splines of yields

To summarize the problems with the cubic splines of yields, we recall that at each knot point we have set yields and the first two derivatives with respect to yields equal for each polynomial meeting at a given knot point:

$$y_i(t_i) = y_{i+1}(t_i)$$
$$y'_i(t_i) = y'_{i+1}(t_i)$$
$$y''_i(t_i) = y''_{i+1}(t_i)$$

In continuous time, the continuous forward rate $f(t)$ can be written as:

$$f(t) = y(t) + ty'(t)$$

We can write the derivatives of f in terms of the derivatives of y as follows:

$$f'(t) = 2y' + ty''$$
$$f''(t) = 3y'' + ty'''$$

At the knot points, this means that:

$$f_i(t_i) = f_{i+1}(t_i)$$
$$f'_i(t_i) = f'_{i+1}(t_i)$$
$$f''_i(t_i) \neq f''_{i+1}(t_i)$$

The second derivative of the forward rate curve will NOT be equal at the knot points since we have not constrained y''', the third derivative of the yield curve, to be equal at the knot points. This leads to the principal problems associated with the use of cubic yield (or price) splines:

- The forward rate curve is not twice differentiable at the knot points, so it is not 'smooth'. The first derivative of the forward rate curve will have a kink in it at each knot point.
- In addition, the forward rate curves associated with a cubic spline-based yield curve tend to be very volatile, particularly on the right hand side of the yield curve, to such a degree that their use can lead to implausible forward rate curves.

For these reasons, the maximum smoothness forward rate approach offers a number of advantages.

Examples of the use of the cubic yield spline

In order to make use of the results of any yield curve smoothing method, we have to be familiar with the continuous time links between zero-coupon bond prices, continuously compounded yields on zero-coupon bond prices (that is, continuous yields), and continuous forward rates.

In Chapter 7, we showed that a zero-coupon bond price can be calculated from its maturity and its continuously compounded yield to maturity from the equation:

$$P[\tau] = e^{-\tau y(\tau)}$$

The definition of a continuous forward rate is minus the percentage change in zero-coupon bond prices for an infinitely small change in years to maturity, as given by the following formula:

$$f[\tau] = -\frac{\partial P[\tau]/\partial \tau}{P[\tau]}$$

Since P can be written as a function of time to maturity, so can the forward rate:

$$f[\tau] = -\frac{\partial P[\tau]/\partial \tau}{P[\tau]}$$
$$= -\frac{\partial(e^{-\tau y[\tau]})/\partial \tau}{P[\tau]}$$
$$= y[\tau] + \tau y'[\tau]$$

Finally, it can be shown that P can be written as a function of forward rates alone:

$$P[\tau] = e^{-\int_0^\tau f[s]\,ds}$$

We can use these relationships to derive useful information from a cubic spline of yields. If a cubic spline of yields has been calculated, then the continuous yield at any point in time is given by a cubic polynomial:

$$y[\tau] = a + b\tau + c\tau^2 + d\tau^3$$

That means zero-coupon bond prices can be calculated using the formulas above:

$$P[\tau] = e^{-a\tau - b\tau^2 - c\tau^3 - d\tau^4}$$

Finally, continuous forward rates can be written as:

$$P_i(t) = a_i + b_i t + c_i t^2 + d_i t^3$$

We can apply these formulas to a concrete example.

Example 8.1

Assume that a cubic yield spline has been fitted to real data and that the cubic polynomial for the continuous yield y is such that $y[t] = 0.05 + 0.001t + 0.0002t^2 + 0.00001t^3$. Solving for the continuous yields at annual maturities gives the following:

Maturity	Continuous Yield
5	6.1250%
6	6.5360%
7	7.0230%
8	7.5920%
9	8.2490%
10	9.0000%

Example 8.2

Using the same cubic polynomial for the continuous yield y in Example 8.1, we can derive zero-coupon bond prices as follows:

Maturity	Zero-Coupon Bond Price
5	0.73620
6	0.67560
7	0.61164
8	0.54479
9	0.47597
10	0.40657

Note that, from the zero-coupon bond prices that are derived from the cubic yield spline, all of the calculations given in Chapter 7 can be done successfully.

Example 8.3

Again using the same cubic polynomial for the continuous yield y in Example 8.1, the continuous forward rates at each annual maturity are derived by substituting the appropriate time to maturity in the formula for continuous forward rates given above:

Maturity	Continuous Forward Rates
5	8.0000%
6	9.2240%
7	10.7120%
8	12.4880%
9	14.5760%
10	17.0000%

Example 8.4

As in the earlier section of the chapter, assume that we are given the following interest rates as input:

Instantaneous interest rate:	6.00%
1-year interest rate:	5.25%
2-year interest rate (annually compounded):	4.00%

Fit a cubic yield spline to this data.

Table 8.2 provides the coefficients a, b, c, and d, using cubic yield smoothing with the yield curve held flat at the right hand side of the curve.

Table 8.2 Cubic Yield Spline Smoothing Right Hand Side Constraint: $y' = 0$

	Time	Coefficients of equations								Equation Value
		a1	b1	c1	d1	a2	b2	c2	d2	
Time 0: Must equal actual	0	1	0	0	0	0	0	0	0	0.06
Time 1: Must equal actual	1	1	1	1	1	0	0	0	0	0.051168
Time 1: Must equal actual	1	0	0	0	0	1	1	1	1	0.051168
Time 2: Must equal actual	2	0	0	0	0	1	2	4	8	0.039221
Equal First Derivatives at T1	1	0	1	2	3	0	-1	-2	-3	0
Equal Second Derivatives at T1	1	0	0	2	6	0	0	-2	-6	0
Left Hand Side Constraint: $y' = 0$	0	0	0	2	0	0	0	0	0	0
Right Hand Side Constraint: $y' = 0$	2	0	0	0	0	0	1	4	12	0

	Inverse of Matrix									Answer
1	1	0	0	0	0	0	0	0		0.06
2	-1.28571	1.285714	0.428571	-0.42857	-0.28571	-0.07143	-0.28571	0.142857		-0.00623
3	0	0	0	0	0	0	0.5	0		-0.0026
4	0.285714	-0.28571	-0.42857	0.428571	0.285714	0.071429	-0.21429	-0.14286		-0.0026
5	1.714286	-1.71429	-0.57143	1.571429	1.714286	-0.57143	-0.28571	-0.85714		0.047534
6	-3.42857	3.428571	5.142857	-5.14286	-3.42857	1.142857	0.571429	2.714286		0.031165
7	2.142857	-2.14286	-4.71429	4.714286	2.142857	-0.71429	-0.35714	-2.57143		-0.0374
8	-0.42857	0.428571	1.142857	-1.14286	-0.42857	0.142857	0.071429	0.714286		0.009869

Coefficient	a1	b1	c1	d1	a2	b2	c2	d2
Calculated Value	0.060000	-0.006235	0.000000	-0.002597	0.047534	0.031165	-0.037399	0.009869

Constraint	Constraint Value	Calculated Value	Difference
Time 0: Must equal actual	0.06	0.060000	0.00
Time 1: Must equal actual	0.051168	0.051168	0.00
Time 1: Must equal actual	0.051168	0.051168	0.00
Time 2: Must equal actual	0.039221	0.039221	0.00
Equal First Derivatives at T1	0	0.000000	0.00
Equal Second Derivatives at T1	0	0.000000	0.00
Left Hand Side Constraint: $y' = 0$	0	0.000000	0.00
Right Hand Side Constraint: $y' = 0$	0	0.000000	0.00

The result of solving the eight equations in eight unknowns in Table 8.2 are the two cubic polynomials with the coefficients $a1$, $b1$, $c1$, and $d1$ for segment one from time zero to time one and with coefficients $a2$, $b2$, $c2$, and $d2$ for segment two from year one to year two.

Table 8.3 shows that, if we try to force the second derivative of the forward rate function f'' to be equal at each knot point, cubic yield smoothing reduces to a simple cubic function where a, b, c, and d are equal for each line segment.

Table 8.4 shows the parameters for the case when the right hand side of the yield curve is held instantaneously straight, $y'' = 0$.

Table 8.3 Cubic Yield Spline Smoothing Right Hand Side Constraint: $y' = 0$ and f'' equal

	Time	Coefficients of equations								Equation Value
		a1	b1	c1	d1	a2	b2	c2	d2	
Time 0: Must equal actual	0	1	0	0	0	0	0	0	0	0.06
Time 1: Must equal actual	1	1	1	1	1	0	0	0	0	0.051168
Time 1: Must equal actual	1	0	0	0	0	1	1	1	1	0.051168
Time 2: Must equal actual	2	0	0	0	0	1	2	4	8	0.039221
Equal First Derivatives at T1	1	0	1	2	3	0	-1	-2	-3	0
Equal Second Derivatives at T1	1	0	0	2	6	0	0	-2	-6	0
Equal f'' at T1	1	0	0	6	24	0	0	-6	-24	0
Right Hand Side Constraint: $y' = 0$	2	0	0	0	0	0	1	4	12	0

	Inverse of Matrix								Answer
1	1	0	0	0	0	0	0	0	0.06
2	-2	2	2	-2	-1	-0.5	0.166667	1	0.006232
3	1.25	-1.25	-2.75	2.75	1.25	0.75	-0.29167	-1.5	-0.02182
4	-0.25	0.25	0.75	-0.75	-0.25	-0.25	0.125	0.5	0.006753
5	1	-1	1	0	1	-1	0.166667	0	0.06
6	-2	2	2	-2	-2	2	-0.33333	1	0.006232
7	1.25	-1.25	-2.75	2.75	1.25	-1.25	0.208333	-1.5	-0.02182
8	-0.25	0.25	0.75	-0.75	-0.25	0.25	-0.04167	0.5	0.006753

	a1	b1	c1	d1	a2	b2	c2	d2
Coefficient	a1	b1	c1	d1	a2	b2	c2	d2
Calculated Value	0.060000	0.006232	-0.021816	0.006753	0.060000	0.006232	-0.021816	0.006753

Constraint	Constraint Value	Calculated Value	Difference
Time 0: Must equal actual	0.06	0.060000	0.00
Time 1: Must equal actual	0.051168	0.051168	0.00
Time 1: Must equal actual	0.051168	0.051168	0.00
Time 2: Must equal actual	0.039221	0.039221	0.00
Equal First Derivatives at T1	0	0.000000	0.00
Equal Second Derivatives at T1	0	0.000000	0.00
Left Hand Side Constraint: $y'' = 0$	0	0.000000	0.00
Right Hand Side Constraint: $y' = 0$	0	0.000000	0.00

Cubic spline price smoothing

The same basic approach to the smoothing of yield curves applies to the smoothing of zero-coupon bond prices, from which smooth yield curves can be derived. The basic steps are parallel to the yield smoothing case.

Using cubic spline smoothing to smooth zero-coupon bond prices

Assume that we are given zero-coupon bond prices $P[t_0], P[t_1], P[t_2], ..., P[t_n]$ consistent with maturities $t_0, t_1, t_2, ..., t_n$. We assume without loss of generality that t_0 is 0. We fit the function:

$$P_i(t) = a_i + b_i t_i + c_i t_i^2 + d_i t_i^3$$

to the interval between t_i and t_{i-1}. Therefore we have $4n$ unknowns to solve for, since we need to know a, b, c, and d for all n intervals between the $n + 1$ data points, as in the yield curve smoothing case. In order to solve for all of these a, b, c, and d values, we make use of the fact that these equations must fit the observable data points, that the first derivatives must be equal at the $n - 1$ knot points $t_1, t_2, t_3, ..., t_{n-1}$, and that the second derivatives also must be equal at the knot points. We have the following equations which constrain the values of a, b, c, and d:

Table 8.4 Cubic Yield Spline Smoothing Right Hand Side Constraint: $y'' = 0$

	Time	a1	b1	c1	d1	a2	b2	c2	d2	Equation Value
					Coefficients of equations					
Time 0: Must equal actual	0	1	0	0	0	0	0	0	0	0.06
Time 1: Must equal actual	1	1	1	1	1	0	0	0	0	0.051168
Time 1: Must equal actual	1	0	0	0	0	1	1	1	1	0.051168
Time 2: Must equal actual	2	0	0	0	0	1	2	4	8	0.039221
Equal First Derivatives at T1	1	0	1	2	3	0	-1	-2	-3	0
Equal Second Derivatives at T1	1	0	0	2	6	0	0	-2	-6	0
Left Hand Side Constraint: $y''=0$	0	0	0	2	0	0	0	0	0	0
Right Hand Side Constraint: $y''=0$	2	0	0	0	0	0	0	2	12	0

					Inverse of Matrix					Answer
	1	1	0	0	0	0	0	0	0	0.06
	2	-1.25	1.25	0.25	-0.25	-0.25	-0.08333	-0.29167	0.041667	-0.00805
	3	0	0	0	0	0	0	0.5	0	0
	4	0.25	-0.25	-0.25	0.25	0.25	0.083333	-0.20833	-0.04167	-0.00078
	5	1.5	-1.5	0.5	0.5	1.5	-0.5	-0.25	-0.25	0.058442
	6	-2.75	2.75	1.75	-1.75	-2.75	0.916667	0.458333	0.791667	-0.00338
	7	1.5	-1.5	-1.5	1.5	1.5	-0.5	-0.25	-0.75	-0.00467
	8	-0.25	0.25	0.25	-0.25	-0.25	0.083333	0.041667	0.208333	0.000779

Coefficient	a1	b1	c1	d1	a2	b2	c2	d2
Calculated Value	0.060000	-0.008053	0.000000	-0.000779	0.058442	-0.003379	-0.004674	0.000779

Constraint	Constraint Value	Calculated Value	Difference
Time 0: Must equal actual	0.06	0.060000	0.00
Time 1: Must equal actual	0.051168	0.051168	0.00
Time 1: Must equal actual	0.051168	0.051168	0.00
Time 2: Must equal actual	0.039221	0.039221	0.00
Equal First Derivatives at T1	0	0.000000	0.00
Equal Second Derivatives at T1	0	0.000000	0.00
Left Hand Side Constraint: $y'' = 0$	0	0.000000	0.00
Right Hand Side Constraint: $y'' = 0$	0	0.000000	0.00

n equations requiring that the cubic polynomials fit the n data points $t_1, t_2,\ldots, t_n$:

$$P(t_i) = a_i + b_i t_i + c_i t_i^2 + d_i t_i^3$$

for i from 1 to n.

n equations requiring that the cubic polynomials fit the n data points $t_0, t_1, t_2,\ldots, t_{n-1}$:

$$P(t_{i-1}) = a_i + b_i t_{i-1} + c_i t_{i-1}^2 + d_i t_{i-1}^3$$

for i from 1 to n.

$n-1$ equations requiring that the first derivatives of the cubic polynomials on each side of the knot points be equal:

$$b_i + 2c_i t_i + 3d_i t_i^2 - b_{i+1} - 2c_{i+1} t_i - 3d_{i+1} t_i^2 = 0$$

for i from 1 to $n-1$.

$n-1$ equations requiring that the second derivatives of the cubic polynomials on each side of the knot points be equal:

$$2c_i + 6d_i t_i - 2c_{i+1} - 6d_{i+1} t_i = 0$$

for i from 1 to $n-1$.

This gives us $4n-2$ equations to solve for $4n$ unknowns as in the yield smoothing case. We again need two more equations to complete the system. Unlike the yield case, however, constraining the right hand side of the zero-coupon price curve has to be examined with great care to make sure that the assumptions have economic meaning. For example, in the yield case, we constrained the first derivative of the smoothed curve such that $y' = 0$ at the far right hand side of the yield curve. The parallel constraint, requiring $P' = 0$ at the right hand side of the curve, has some powerful and harmful implications. The continuous forward rate consistent with the smoothed price curve can be written as:

$$f(t) = \frac{-\partial P(t)/\partial t}{P(t)}$$

Therefore, an assumption that P' is zero is equivalent to assuming that the forward rate is zero at that point on the curve. We have to reject this assumption as a candidate for one of our two remaining constraints.

As in the yield smoothing case, the first equation is usually chosen such that the yield at time 0 equals an observable short rate $y(0)$. In order to do so, we note that:

$$f(t) = \frac{-P'(t)}{P(t)} = -\frac{b + 2ct + 3dt^2}{P(t)}$$

At time zero, $P = 1$ and $f(0) = y(0)$, so this constraint becomes:

$$-b_1 = y(0)$$

There are two common choices for the constraint affecting the right hand side of the yield curve—either the yield curve can be set to be flat ($y' = 0$) or the price curve can be set to be instantaneously straight ($P'' = 0$) at the longest maturity. The first of these two possible constraints can be derived from the fact that:

$$y(t) = \frac{-1}{t} \ln [P(t)]$$

and:

$$y'(t) = \frac{1}{t^2} \ln [P] - \frac{1}{tP} (b + 2ct + 3dt^2)$$

If y' is set to zero at the right hand side of the yield curve, then this constraint can be written as:

$$\ln[P(t_n)] = -\frac{t_n}{P(t_n)}\left(b + 2ct_n + 3dt_n^2\right)$$

after multiplying both sides by t to the second power. P is a constant at the right hand side of the yield curve so this equation remains a linear equation in the parameters a, b, c, and d.

The other candidate for selection is the following equation, which constrains the second derivative $P'' = 0$ at the right hand side of the curve:

$$2c_n + 6d_n t_n = 0$$

As in the yield smoothing case, we can solve this system of $4n$ equations in $4n$ unknowns using matrix inversion and spreadsheet software.

Problems with cubic splines of prices

The problems with cubic splines of the zero-coupon price curve are the same as those resulting from the cubic spline of yield curves:

- the forward rate curve is not twice differentiable; the second derivative of the forward rate is discontinuous at the knot points, since we did not constrain the third derivative of the price functions to be continuous and the second derivative of the forward rate function depends on the third derivative of the price function:

$$f(t) = \frac{-P'(t)}{P(t)}$$

$$f'(t) = \frac{-P''(t)}{P(t)} + \frac{P'(t)^2}{P(t)^2}$$

$$f''(t) = \frac{-P'''(t)}{P(t)} + \frac{3P'(t)P''(t)}{P(t)^2} - \frac{2P'(t)^3}{P(t)^3}$$

- forward rate curves can be implausibly volatile, particularly on the right hand side of the yield curve

Examples of the use of the cubic price spline

We can use the continuous time linkages between zero-coupon bond prices, continuous yields, and continuous forward rates just as we did to derive practical calculations from the cubic price splines previously. Assume that for the cubic polynomial that spans yields five to 10, the zero-coupon bond price is given by the polynomial $P(t) = 1.00 - 0.03t - 0.00001t^2 - 0.00001t^3$. We also need to make use of the fact that:

$$f[\tau] = -\frac{\partial P[\tau]/\partial \tau}{P[\tau]}$$

so f can be calculated from the cubic price spline using the following relationship:

$$f[\tau] = \frac{-b - 2c\tau - 3d\tau^2}{a + b\tau + c\tau^2 + d\tau^3}$$

The continuous yield can be derived from the fact that:

$$y[\tau] = -\frac{1}{\tau}\ln[P(\tau)]$$

Example

What are the zero-coupon prices for five-, six-, seven-, eight-, nine- and 10-year maturities? We get the answer by substituting the proper value for t in the equation above.

Maturity	Zero-Coupon Bond Price
5	0.84850
6	0.81748
7	0.78608
8	0.75424
9	0.72190
10	0.68900

Example

What are the continuous zero-coupon bond yields for these same maturities? We make use of the equation above linking continuous yields and zero-coupon bond prices to derive the following:

Maturity	Continuous Yield
5	3.2857%
6	3.3588%
7	3.4385%
8	3.5256%
9	3.6208%
10	3.7251%

Example

What are the continuous forward rates at the five-, six-, seven-, eight-, nine-, and 10-year points on the yield curve? The answer is given by the relationship given above between forward rates and zero-coupon bond prices.

Maturity	Continuous Forward Rates
5	3.6358%
6	3.8166%
7	4.0212%
8	4.2533%
9	4.5172%
10	4.8186%

Example

Assume that we are given the following interest rates as input:

Instantaneous interest rate:	6.00%
1-year interest rate:	5.25%
2-year interest rate (annually compounded):	4.00%

Fit a cubic price spline to this data.

Table 8.5 gives a, b, c, and d for the cubic price smoothing case where the price curve is held instantaneously straight ($P'' = 0$) at the right hand side of the yield curve.

Table 8.5 Cubic Price Spline Smoothing Right Hand Side Constraint: $p'' = 0$

	Time	a1	b1	c1	Coefficients of equations d1	a2	b2	c2	d2	Equation Value
Time 0: Must equal actual	0	1	0	0	0	0	0	0	0	1
Time 1: Must equal actual	1	1	1	1	1	0	0	0	0	0.950119
Time 1: Must equal actual	1	0	0	0	0	1	1	1	1	0.950119
Time 2: Must equal actual	2	0	0	0	0	1	2	4	8	0.924556
Equal First Derivatives at T1	1	0	1	2	3	0	-1	-2	-3	0
Equal Second Derivatives at T1	1	0	0	2	6	0	0	-2	-6	0
Left Hand Side Constraint: $f = y(0)$	0	0	-1	0	0	0	0	0	0	0.06
Right Hand Side Constraint: $p'' = 0$	2	0	0	0	0	0	0	2	12	0
					Inverse of Matrix					Answer
	1	1	0	0	0	0	0	0	0	1
	2	0	0	5.55E-17	-5.6E-17	-5.6E-17	-2.8E-17	-1	0	-0.06
	3	-2.14286	2.142857	0.428571	-0.42857	-0.42857	-0.14286	1.714286	0.071429	0.006924
	4	1.142857	-1.14286	-0.42857	0.428571	0.428571	0.142857	-0.71429	-0.07143	0.003195
	5	2.571429	-2.57143	0.285714	0.714286	1.714286	-0.42857	-0.85714	-0.28571	1.008697
	6	-4.71429	4.714286	2.142857	-2.14286	-3.14286	0.785714	1.571429	0.857143	-0.08609
	7	2.571429	-2.57143	-1.71429	1.714286	1.714286	-0.42857	-0.85714	-0.78571	0.033016
	8	-0.42857	0.428571	0.285714	-0.28571	-0.28571	0.071429	0.142857	0.214286	-0.0055
Coefficient		a1	b1	c1	d1	a2	b2	c2	d2	
Calculated Value		1.000000	-0.060000	0.006924	0.003195	1.008697	-0.086092	0.033016	-0.005503	

Constraint	Constraint Value	Calculated Value	Difference
Time 0: Must equal actual	1	1.000000	0.00
Time 1: Must equal actual	0.950119	0.950119	0.00
Time 1: Must equal actual	0.950119	0.950119	0.00
Time 2: Must equal actual	0.924556	0.924556	0.00
Equal First Derivatives at T1	0	0.000000	0.00
Equal Second Derivatives at T1	0	0.000000	0.00
Left Hand Side Constraint: $y = y(0)$	0.06	0.060000	0.00
Right Hand Side Constraint: $p'' = 0$	0	0.000000	0.00

Table 8.6 shows the results for the cubic price spline is calculated such that yields on the far right hand side of the curve are held flat ($y' = 0$).

Table 8.6 Cubic Price Spline Smoothing Right Hand Side Constraint: $y' = 0$

	Time	a1	b1	c1	d1	a2	b2	c2	d2	Equation Value
					Coefficients of equations					
Time 0: Must equal actual	0	1	0	0	0	0	0	0	0	1
Time 1: Must equal actual	1	1	1	1	1	0	0	0	0	0.950119
Time 1: Must equal actual	1	0	0	0	0	1	1	1	1	0.950119
Time 2: Must equal actual	2	0	0	0	0	1	2	4	8	0.924556
Equal First Derivatives at T1	1	0	1	2	3	0	-1	-2	-3	0
Equal Second Derivatives at T1	1	0	0	2	6	0	0	-2	-6	0
Left Hand Side Constraint: $f = y(0)$	0	0	-1	0	0	0	0	0	0	0.06
Right Hand Side Constraint: $y' = 0$	2	0	0	0	0	0	-2.1632	-8.6528	-25.9584	0.078441
					Inverse of Matrix					Answer
	1	1	0	0	0	0	0	0	0	1
	2	4.44E-16	-4.4E-16	0	0	0	0	-1	0	-0.06
	3	-2.25	2.25	0.75	-0.75	-0.5	-0.125	1.75	-0.11557	0.002874
	4	1.25	-1.25	-0.75	0.75	0.5	0.125	-0.75	0.11557	0.007245
	5	3	-3	-1	2	2	-0.5	-1	0.462278	1.024899
	6	-6	6	6	-6	-4	1	2	-1.38683	-0.1347
	7	3.75	-3.75	-5.25	5.25	2.5	-0.625	-1.25	1.271265	0.077571
	8	-0.75	0.75	1.25	-1.25	-0.5	0.125	0.25	-0.34671	-0.01765

	a1	b1	c1	d1	a2	b2	c2	d2
Coefficient Calculated Value	1.000000	-0.060000	0.002874	0.007245	1.024899	-0.134697	0.077571	-0.017654

Constraint	Constraint Value	Calculated Value	Difference
Time 0: Must equal actual	1	1.000000	0.00
Time 1: Must equal actual	0.950119	0.950119	0.00
Time 1: Must equal actual	0.950119	0.950119	0.00
Time 2: Must equal actual	0.924556	0.924556	0.00
Equal First Derivatives at T1	0	0.000000	0.00
Equal Second Derivatives at T1	0	0.000000	0.00
Left Hand Side Constraint: $y = y(0)$	0.06	0.060000	0.00
Right Hand Side Constraint: $y' = 0$	0.078441	0.078441	0.00

Maximum smoothness forward rates

Adams and van Deventer [1994] attempt to remedy these problems of cubic spline smoothing with a new approach that addresses both problems directly:

- They seek to derive a forward rate curve that is continuous and twice differentiable, and;
- They derive the curve in such a way that the forward rate curve is the smoothest curve of any of the family of curves that are continuous, twice differentiable, and consistent with the observable data.

Again, we assume that there are n observable data points $t_1, t_2, t_3, \ldots, t_n$ and n observable zero-coupon bond prices $P[t_1], \ldots, P[t_n]$.

Deriving maximum smoothness forward rates

Adams and van Deventer [1994] show that the smoothest possible forward rate curve consists of a quartic forward rate function that is fitted between

---

[4] This theorem, contributed by Oldrich Vasicek, is a restated version of the theorem in Adams and van Deventer [1994] from van Deventer and Imai [1996].

each knot point. The conclusions regarding the maximum smoothness forward rate curve can be summarized in the following theorem:[4]

Theorem: The term structure $f(t)$, $0 \leq t \leq T$, of forward rates that satisfies the maximum smoothness criterion:

$$\min \int_0^T [f''(s)]^2 ds$$

while fitting the observed prices P_1, $P_2, \ldots, P_m$ of zero-coupon bonds with maturities $t_1, t_2, \ldots, t_m$ is a fourth order spline given by:

$$f(t) = e_i t^4 + d_i t^3 + c_i t^2 + b_i t + a_i \quad \text{for } t_{i-1} < t \leq t_i, i = 1, 2, \ldots, m+1$$

where $0 = t_0 < t_1 < t_2 < \cdots < t_m < t_{m+1} = T$.

The coefficients a_i, b_i, c_i, d_i, and e_i where $i = 1, 2, \ldots, m+1$ satisfy the equations:

$$e_i t_i^4 + d_i t_i^3 + c_i t_i^2 + b_i t_i + a_i = e_{i+1} t_i^4 + d_{i+1} t_i^3 + c_{i+1} t_i^2$$
$$+ b_{i+1} t_i + a_{i+1} \quad \text{for } i = 1, 2, \ldots, m$$

$$4 e_i t_i^3 + 3 d_i t_i^2 + 2 c_i t_i + b_i = 4 e_{i+1} t_i^3 + 3 d_{i+1} t_i^2 + 2 c_{i+1} t_i$$
$$+ b_{i+1} \quad \text{for } i = 1, 2, \ldots, m$$

$$12 e_i t_i^2 + 6 d_i t_i + 2 c_i = 12 e_{i+1} t_i^2 + 6 d_{i+1} t_i + 2 c_{i+1} \quad \text{for } i = 1, 2, \ldots, m$$

$$24 e_i t_i + 6 d_i = 24 e_{i+1} t_i + 6 d_{i+1} \quad \text{for } i = 1, 2, \ldots, m$$

$$\frac{1}{5} e_i (t_i^5 - t_{i-1}^5) + \frac{1}{4} d_i (t_i^4 - t_{i-1}^4) + \frac{1}{3} c_i (t_i^3 - t_{i-1}^3) + \frac{1}{2} b_i (t_i^2 - t_{i-1}^2)$$
$$+ a_i (t_i - t_{i-1}) = -\log \left(\frac{P_i}{P_{i-1}} \right) \quad \text{for } i = 1, 2, \ldots, m$$

The proof of this theorem is given in Appendix 2.

Using the maximum smoothness forward rate function in practice

The use of the maximum smoothness forward rate function in practice is more complex than the use of the cubic spline approach because there is a larger number of parameters to be determined. In the case where we have n observable data points, we have $5n$ unknowns since we need to find a, b, c, d, and e for each of the n segments of the forward rate curve. We have the following constraints that are essential to insure the reasonableness of the resulting forward rate, yield, and price curves:

$n-1$ equations requiring that the forward rates be equal at each knot point:

$$a_i + b_i t_i + c_i t_i^2 + d_i t_i^3 + e_i t_i^4 - a_{i+1} - b_{i+1} t_i - c_{i+1} t_i^2 - d_{i+1} t_i^3 - e_{i+1} t_i^4 = 0$$

at knot points for i from 1 to $n-1$. We also have:

$n-1$ equations requiring that the first derivative of the forward rates be equal at each knot point:

$$b_i + 2c_i t_i + 3d_i t_i^2 + 4e_i t_i^3 - b_{i+1} - 2c_{i+1} t_i - 3d_{i+1} t_i^2 - 4d_{i+1} t_i^3 = 0$$

at knot points for i from 1 to $n-1$. Unlike the cubic yield smoothing case and the cubic price smoothing approach, we specifically require that the second derivatives of the forward rate curve be equal at each knot point to insure that the curve is everywhere twice differentiable:

$n-1$ equations requiring that the second derivative of the forward rate curve be equal at each knot point:

$$2c_i + 6d_i t_i + 12e_i t_i^2 - 2c_{i+1} - 6d_{i+1} t_i - 12e_{i+1} t_i^2 = 0$$

$n-1$ equations requiring that the third derivative of the forward rate curve be equal at each knot point:

$$6d_i + 24e_i t_i - 6d_{i+1} - 24e_{i+1} t_i = 0$$

The next set of constraints come from the fact that:

$$P[t] = e^{-\int_0^t f(s)\,ds}$$

Since we are using a forward rate function broken into quartic segments and we have observable data, we can write:

$$P[t_i] = P[t_{i-1}]e^{-\int_{t_{i-1}}^{t_i} f(s)\,ds}$$

Rearranging this equation and expressing it as a linear function of the parameters a, b, c, d, and e gives the next set of constraints:

n constraints that the forward rate curves be consistent with observable data:

$$a_i(t_i - t_{i-1}) + \frac{b_i}{2}(t_i^2 - t_{i-1}^2) + \frac{c_i}{3}(t_i^3 - t_{i-1}^3) + \frac{d_i}{4}(t_i^4 - t_{i-1}^4) + \frac{e_i}{5}(t_i^5 - t_{i-1}^5)$$
$$= -\ln\left[\frac{P(t_i)}{P(t_{i-1})}\right]$$

for the n observable data points from $i = 1$ to n, noting that P for $t = t_0$ is 1.

So far, these constraints give us $4(n-1) + n$ or $5n - 4$ equations.

We require two other constraints of economic significance:

- That the forward rate curve be consistent with an observable short rate $y(0)$, or:

$$a_1 = y(0) = f(0)$$

- That the slope[5] of the forward rate curve at the right hand side of the yield curve be zero, i.e. $f' = 0$:

$$b_n + 2c_n t_n + 3d_n t_n^2 + 4e_n t_n^3 = 0$$

We can complete the system of $5n$ equations in $5n$ unknowns by imposing the additional constraints that the forward rate curve be instantaneously straight at both the left hand and right hand side of the curve, i.e. that:

$$f''(t_0) = 2c_1 + 6d_1 t_0 + 12e_1 t_0^2 = 0$$
$$f''(t_n) = 2c_n + 6d_n t_n + 12e_n t_n^2 = 0$$

We can then solve for each of the n sets of a, b, c, d, and e using matrix inversion.

---

[5] An imposition on the forward rate curve such as the constraint that follows does have an impact on the level of smoothness. The resulting forward curve will be less smooth than one for which such a constraint has not been imposed. Tibor Janosi has suggested that, instead of setting these constraints to zero, one should set the constraints equal to a value x and x is selected to be the value which produces the lowest smoothness statistic over the entire curve. Values of x are obtained by iterative solutions such as those of the Newton-Raphson technique discussed in Chapter 7.

Example of the use of the maximum forward-rate smoothing approach

Adams and van Deventer [1994] report on the relative performance of maximum smoothness forward rate smoothing as a predictor of true market yields. Adams and van Deventer performed this test of the accuracy of the maximum smoothness approach in comparison with five other smoothing methods. They collected observable market data, left out one observable data point, and then estimated the missing data point using each smoothing method. This calculation was repeated over a large number of daily observations and the mean absolute error associated with each smoothing method was calculated. Over 660 days of data in the U.S. dollar swap market, Adams and van Deventer found the mean absolute pricing errors in estimating the true seven-year U.S. dollar swap rate as follows:

Maximum smoothness forward rate smoothing:	0.0573%
Cubic price spline, $y'(10$ years$) = 0$:	0.0640%
Linear yield curve smoothing:	0.0691%
Cubic price spline, $p''(10$ years$) = 0$:	0.0790%
Cubic yield spline, $y'(10$ years$) = 0$:	0.0851%
Cubic yield spline, $y''(10$ years$) = 0$:	0.0898%

In results for the yen market over 848 daily observations, the maximum smoothness forward rate approach again was the most successful:

Maximum smoothness forward rate smoothing:	0.0111%
Linear yield curve smoothing:	0.0166%
Cubic yield spline, $y''(10$ years$) = 0$:	0.0192%
Cubic yield spline, $y'(10$ years$) = 0$:	0.0198%
Cubic price spline, $p''(10$ years$) = 0$:	0.0208%
Cubic price spline, $y'(10$ years$) = 0$:	0.0418%

In general, the technique considerably outperforms spline and linear smoothing techniques in all of the varieties outlined above. For this reason, it remains the most appropriate technique for most practical applications.

For purposes of the next three examples, we will assume that the maximum smoothness forward rate curve has been fitted to observable data and that the forward rate curve has the form $f(t) = 0.04 + 0.0001t + 0.0001t^2 + 0.000005t^3 + 0.000001t^4$. We also assume that the zero-coupon bond price in year five is 0.79. When using the maximum smoothness forward rate approach, we need to express the zero-coupon bond price as a function of the forward rate quartic polynomial:

$$f(t) = a + bt + ct^2 + dt^3 + et^4$$

Since we fit a different forward rate quartic polynomial over each time interval between 'knot points', we have a different zero-coupon price function between each set of knot points. For the interval between t_i and t_{i-1}, the zero-coupon bond price function is:

$$P[t] = P[t_{i-1}]\, e^{-[a(t-t_{i-1})+(b/2)(t-t_{i-1})^2+(c/3)(t-t_{i-1})^3+(d/4)(t-t_{i-1})^4+(e/5)(t-t_{i-1})^5]}$$

$$\text{since } P[t] = P[t_{i-1}]\, e^{-\int_{t_{i-1}}^{t} f(s)\,ds}$$

The continuous yield y is written as a function of forward rates in the following manner:

$$y[t] = -\frac{1}{t}\left[\ln P[t_{i-1}] - \left(a(t - t_{i-1}) + \frac{b}{2}(t - t_{i-1})^2 + \frac{c}{3}(t - t_{i-1})^3\right.\right.$$
$$\left.\left. +\frac{d}{4}(t - t_{i-1})^4 + \frac{e}{5}(t - t_{i-1})^5\right)\right]$$

Given these facts, we can derive the results in the three examples below and do any of the calculations in Chapter 7.

Example: Continuous yields

The continuous yield at the five-, six-, seven-, eight-, nine-, and 10-year points is calculated using the expression above, inserting the proper values for a, b, c, d, and e for the five- to 10-year interval on the yield curve.

Maturity	Continuous Yield
5	4.7144%
6	4.5988%
7	4.5291%
8	4.4996%
9	4.5114%
10	4.5697%

Example: Zero-coupon bond prices

Zero-coupon bond prices can be calculated from the integral of the forward rate curve and the zero-coupon bond price prevailing at the beginning of the relevant time interval.[6]

---

[6] The zero-coupon bond price prevailing at the beginning of the time interval is in turn calculated from the prior segments of the continuous forward rate curve.

Maturity	Zero-Coupon Bond Price
5	0.79000
6	0.75887
7	0.72831
8	0.69770
9	0.66629
10	0.63320

Example: Continuous forward rates

The continuous forward rates themselves are obtained directly from the quartic polynomial.

Maturity	Continuous Forward Rates
5	4.4250%
6	4.6576%
7	4.9716%
8	5.3856%
9	5.9206%
10	6.6000%

Note that all the calculations of Chapter 7 can be derived from a maximum smoothness forward rate function in a manner similar to the equations given above.

Table 8.7 Maximum Smoothness Forward-Rate Smoothing Right Hand Side Constraint: $f' = 0$

	Time			Coefficients of equations								Equation
		a1	b1	c1	d1	e1	a2	b2	c2	d2	e2	Value
Time 0: Must equal actual $y(0)$	0	1	0	0	0	0	0	0	0	0	0	0.06
Time 1: Must equal actual $\ln[P(t1)/P(t0)]$	1	−1	−0.5	−0.33333	−0.25	−0.2	0	0	0	0	0	−0.05117
Time 2: Must equal actual $\ln[P(t2)/P(t1)]$	2	0	0	0	0	0	−1	−1.5	−2.33333	−3.75	−6.2	−0.02727
Equal First Derivatives at T1	1	0	1	2	3	4	0	−1	−2	−3	−4	0
Equal Second Derivatives at T1	1	0	0	2	6	12	0	0	−2	−6	−12	0
Equal Third Derivatives at T1	1	0	0	0	6	24	0	0	0	−6	−24	0
Right Hand Side Constraint: $f' = 0$	2	0	0	0	0	0	0	1	4	12	32	0
Right Hand Side Constraint: $f'' = 0$	2	0	0	0	0	0	0	0	2	12	48	0
Left Hand Side Constraint: $f'' = 0$	0	0	1	0	0	0	0	0	0	0	0	0
equal f at t1	1	1	1	1	1	1	−1	−1	−1	−1	−1	0

					Inverse of Matrix							Answer
1	1	0	0	0	0	0	0	0	0	0		0.060000
2	1.78E-15	3.55E-15	0	−2.6E-16	0	0	0	1.11E-16	1	0		0.000000
3	−9.76744	−11.8605	2.093023	−0.48837	0.05814	0.040698	0.55814	−0.15116	−3.34884	−2.09302		−0.036250
4	12.32558	16.39535	−4.06977	0.866279	−0.1686	−0.09302	−1.1686	0.321705	3.261628	4.069767		0.011608
5	−4.12791	−5.72674	1.598837	−0.2689	0.113857	0.04845	0.530523	−0.15019	−0.99564	−1.59884		0.001748
6	6.813953	8.488372	−2.67442	1.290698	−0.71318	0.142442	−1.04651	0.387597	1.27907	1.674419		0.047442
7	−23.2558	−33.9535	10.69767	−2.16279	1.852713	−0.4031	4.186047	−1.55039	−4.11628	−10.6977		0.050234
8	25.11628	39.06977	−13.9535	1.255814	−1.72093	0.395349	−5.72093	2.174419	4.325581	13.95349		−0.111601
9	−10.9302	−17.5581	6.627907	−0.29651	0.684109	−0.16279	3.017442	−1.22868	−1.85465	−6.62791		0.061842
10	1.686047	2.761628	−1.07558	0.021802	−0.09932	0.024225	−0.51599	0.237403	0.28343	1.075581		−0.010810

Coefficient	a1	b1	c1	d1	e1	a2	b2	c2	d2	e2	
Calculated Value	0.060000	0.000000	−0.036250	0.011608	0.001748	0.047442	0.050234	−0.111601	0.061842	−0.010810	

Constraint	Constraint Value	Calculated Value	Difference
Time 0: Must equal actual $y(0)$	0.06	0.060000	0.00
Time 1: Must equal actual $\ln[P(t1)/P(t0)]$	−0.05117	−0.051168	0.00
Time 2: Must equal actual $\ln[P(t2)/P(t1)]$	−0.02727	−0.027273	0.00
Equal First Derivatives at T1	0	0.000000	0.00
Equal Second Derivatives at T1	0	0.000000	0.00
Equal Third Derivatives at T1	0	0.000000	0.00
Right Hand Side Constraint: $f' = 0$	0	0.000000	0.00
Right Hand Side Constraint: $f'' = 0$	0	0.000000	0.00
Left Hand Side Constraint: $f'' = 0$	0	0.000000	0.00
equal f at t1	0	0.000000	0.00

Example

The advantages of the maximum smoothness approach are apparent even using the simple example given above. Table 8.8 shows how a, b, c, d, and e are calculated for the maximum smoothness forward rate method.

Figure 8.3 graphs the continuous yields for each of the smoothing methods, and Figure 8.4 graphs the forward rates.

Figure 8.3 Continuous Yield Curves for Various Smoothing Methods

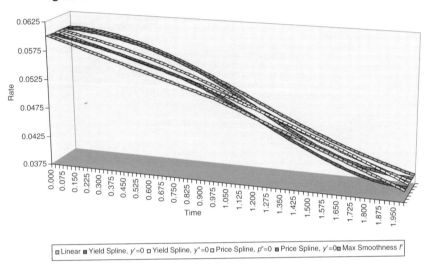

Figure 8.4 highlights the differences between the various methods most clearly, showing the discontinuity of the linear forward rate curve at year one and the tendency of the cubic splines to bend sharply up or down at the right hand side of the yield curve.

Smoothing coupon-bearing bond data or other data

It is logical, but incorrect, to conclude that the techniques discussed above apply only to the smoothing of zero-coupon bond yields or prices, since they are at the heart of the constraints imposed by each smoothing method. In reality, however, the same techniques can be used to create a smooth yield curve from almost any market data. In general, the process used in smoothing is as follows:

1. From observable market data (such as bond prices), select key maturity points.
2. Guess zero-coupon bond prices for these key maturity points.
3. Smooth the yield curve by the desired method.
4. Calculate the implied values of the observable market data (i.e. a bond price).

Figure 8.4 Continous Forward Rates for Various Yield Curve Smoothing Methods

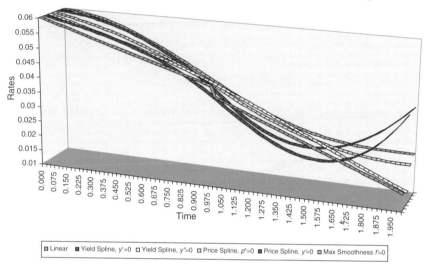

5. If the implied price is within the desired tolerance of the actual price, then the yield curve smoothing process is completed.
6. If the implied price is not within the desired tolerance, then improve the guess of zero-coupon bond prices and return to Step 3. Repeat until within tolerance.

The heart of this iterative method is the Step 6 'improvement' in the guess of zero-coupon bond prices. Normally, the successive substitution method is very effective in providing an efficient convergence to actual market prices.[7]

The successive substitution method requires that the unknown parameters which need to be identified by iteration be expressed in a form as follows:

$$x_n = h(x_1, x_2, ..., x_n)$$

In this formula, x_n is the variable to be obtained by iteration. The initial guess for x_n is input to the function h and a new value of x_n is produced. If this new x_n differs by less than the desired tolerance from the old x_n, the process is complete. If not, the process is repeated.

---

[7] In practice, the successive substitution method provides difficulties in only one case—the use of the cubic yield spline on data with observations with a long time gap (say from 10 to 30 years), a long maturity (like 30 years), and high interest rates. As part of the iteration, negative 30-year zero-coupon bond prices may result as part of an interim step in the calculation. With yields calculated as the log of prices, the iteration comes to a premature halt. This problem can be avoided in a number of ways.

We can change our assumptions about the example above to show how the maximum smoothness forward rate approach can be used on coupon-bearing bond data. Assume that the input data on yields (6% short rate, 5.25% one-year rate, and 4% two-year rate) represent coupon rates on new issue bonds issued at par with semi-annual payments. The parameters of the forward rate function are not the directly targeted variables of the iteration process. It is more efficient to iterate on key zero-coupon bond prices and smooth the results, iterating until we have a maximum smoothness forward rate curve for which bonds with the assumed coupons have a present value of par. Therefore, the direct inputs to the iteration process are the one-year and two-year zero-coupon bond prices $P(1)$ and $P(2)$. There are many choices for possible specifications for the two equations necessary to use the successive substitution method. One such set of equations uses the present value of each bond:

$$V_i = \sum_{j=1}^{n_i} \frac{P(t_j)C_i}{2} + P(t_{n_i})100$$

which is simply the present value of the semi-annual coupon payments $C_i/2$ and the ending principal, which we arbitrarily set at 100. Equations that produce efficient solutions from the successive substitution method take the following form in this example:

$$P(1) = (100 - V_1)/100 + P(1)$$
$$P(2) = (100 - V_2)/100 + P(2)$$

Both equations are derived by adding the appropriate present value factor to both sides of the equation which specifies that the present value of each bond should be 100. This completes Step 1 above.

In Step 2, we need a guess for the initial values of $P(1)$ and $P(2)$. A guess of high quality is that $P(1)$ and $P(2)$ have the values that they would have if the 5.25% and 4% coupons were zero-coupon bond yields. From our prior examples, this leads to initial guesses for $P(1)$ of 0.950119 and $P(2)$ of 0.924556.

Using this data as inputs, we smooth the yield curve, getting the a, b, c, d, and e parameters of Table 8.7. We then calculate zero-coupon bond prices for 0.5 years and 1.5 years and use them to calculate the V_i values—100.0567 for the one-year bond and 100.0198 for the two-year bond. We input the $P(1)$ and $P(2)$ values and the V_i values into the right hand side of the equations above to obtain new values for $P(1)$ and $P(2)$ of 0.950686 and 0.924358. We repeat this process for five iterations until the prices of the zero-coupon bonds change by less than 0.0000001, leaving us with a smooth forward rate curve and present values for the one and two-year bonds of 100.0000.

The same iterative approach can be used for all of the other yield curve smoothing techniques as well.

Conclusion

The maximum smoothness forward rate approach is a powerful technique for smoothing yield curves when the smoothness and continuity of the forward rate curve that results are important to the user. For most practical applications, these considerations are essential to obtaining a high-quality estimate of term structure model parameters for any of the popular term structure models. We have demonstrated the practical implementation of the maximum smoothness forward rate technique in comparison with four variations on the cubic spline approach and the linear smoothing technique that have been popular for years. The linear approach is often unusable since the forward rate curves are discontinuous, a violation of one of the often-used assumptions of the Heath, Jarrow and Morton [1992] term structure model. The cubic spline approaches produce discontinuous second derivatives of the forward rate curve. While not a technical violation of the Heath, Jarrow and Morton model, most market participants would prefer the smoothness of a forward rate curve that is continuous and twice differentiable. As shown in Adams and van Deventer [1994] using 848 daily observations from the yen swap market and 660 daily observations from the U.S. dollar swap market, the maximum smoothness forward rate approach is also more accurate in modeling true market yields.

Appendix 2

Proof of the Theorem[8]

Schwartz [1989] demonstrates that cubic splines produce the maximum smoothness discount functions or yield curves if the spline is applied to discount bond prices or yields respectively. In this appendix, we derive by a similar argument, the functional form that produces the forward rate curve with maximum smoothness. Let $f(t)$ be the current forward rate function, so that:

$$P(t) = \exp\left(-\int_0^t f(s)\,ds\right) \qquad \text{(A1)}$$

is the price of a discount bond maturing at time t. The maximum smoothness term structure is a function f with a continuous derivative that satisfies the optimization problem:

$$\min \int_0^T f''^2(s)\,ds \qquad \text{(A2)}$$

---

[8] This proof was kindly provided by Oldrich Vasicek. We also appreciate the comments of Volf Frishling, who pointed out an error in the proof in Adams and van Deventer [1994]. Robert Jarrow also made important contributions to this proof.

subject to the constraints:

$$\int_0^{t_i} f(s)\, ds = -\log P_i, \quad \text{for } i = 1, 2, ..., m. \tag{A3}$$

Here the $P_i = P(t_i)$, for $i = 1, 2, ..., m$ are given prices of discount bonds with maturities $0 < t_1 < t_2 < \cdots < t_m < T$.

Integrating twice by parts, we get the following identity:

$$\int_0^t f(s)\, ds = \frac{1}{2} \int_0^t (t - s)^2 f''(s)\, ds + t f(0) + \frac{1}{2} t^2 f'(0) \tag{A4}$$

Put

$$g(t) = f''(t), \quad 0 \le t \le T \tag{A5}$$

and define the step function:

$$u(t) = 1 \quad \text{for } t \ge 0$$
$$= 0 \quad \text{for } t < 0.$$

The optimization problem can then be written as:

$$\min \int_0^T g^2(s)\, ds \tag{A6}$$

subject to

$$\frac{1}{2} \int_0^T (t_i - s)^2 u(t_i - s) g(s)\, ds = -\log P_i - t_i f(0) - \frac{1}{2} t_i^2 f'(0) \tag{A7}$$

for $i = 1, 2, ..., m$. Let $\lambda_i = 66$ for $i = 1, 2, ..., m$ be the Lagrange multipliers corresponding to the constraints (A7). The objective then becomes:

$$\min Z[g] = \int_0^T g^2(s)\, ds + \sum_{i=1}^m \lambda_i \left(\frac{1}{2} \int_0^T (t_i - s)^2 u(t_i - s) g(s)\, ds \right.$$
$$\left. + \log P_i + t_i f(0) + \frac{1}{2} t_i^2 f'(0) \right) \tag{A8}$$

According to the calculus of variations, if the function g is a solution to (A8), then:

$$\frac{d}{d\varepsilon} Z[g + \varepsilon h]_{\varepsilon=0} = 0 \qquad \text{(A9)}$$

for any function $h(t)$ identically equal to $w''(t)$ where $w(t)$ is any twice differentiable function defined on $[0, T]$ with $w'(0) = w(0) = 0$.[9] We get:

$$\frac{d}{d\varepsilon} Z[g + \varepsilon h]_{\varepsilon=0} = 2 \int\limits_0^T \left[g(s) + \frac{1}{4} \sum_{i=1}^m \lambda_i (t_i - s)^2 u(t_i - s) \right] h(s)\, ds$$

In order that this integral is zero for any function h, we must have:

$$g(t) + \frac{1}{4} \sum_{i=1}^m \lambda_i (t_i - t)^2 u(t_i - t) = 0 \qquad \text{(A10)}$$

for all t between 0 and T. This means that:

$$g(t) = 12 e_i t^2 + 6 d_i t + 2 c_i \quad \text{for } t_{i-1} < t \leq t_i, \ i = 1, 2, ..., m + 1, \qquad \text{(A11)}$$

where

$$e_i = -\frac{1}{48} \sum_{j=i}^m \lambda_j$$

$$d_i = \frac{1}{12} \sum_{j=i}^m \lambda_j t_j \qquad \text{(A12)}$$

$$c_i = -\frac{1}{8} \sum_{j=i}^m \lambda_j t_j^2$$

and we define $t_0 = 0$, $t_{m+1} = T$. Moreover (A10) implies that g and g' (and therefore f'' and f''') are continuous. From (A4) we get:

$$f(t) = e_i t^4 + d_i t^3 + c_i t^2 + b_i t + a_i, \ t_{i-1} < t \leq t_i, \ i = 1, 2, ..., m + 1. \quad \text{(A13)}$$

---

[9] We are grateful to Robert Jarrow for his assistance on this point.

Continuity of f, f', f'' and f''' then implies that:

$$e_i t_i^4 + d_i t^3 + c_i t_i^2 + b_i t_i + a_i = e_{i+1} t_i^4 + d_{i+1} t_i^3 + c_{i+1} t_i^2 + b_{i+1} t_i$$
$$+ a_{i+1}, \quad i = 1, 2, \ldots, m \tag{A14}$$

$$4e_i t_i^3 + 3d_i t_i^2 + 2c_i t_i + b_i = 4e_{i+1} t_i^3 + 3d_{i+1} t_i^2$$
$$+ 2c_{i+1} t_i + b_{i+1}, \quad i = 1, 2, \ldots, m.$$

$$12e_i t_i^2 + 6d_i t_i + 2c_i = 12e_{i+1} t_i^2 + 6d_{i+1} t_i + 2c_{i+1}$$
$$24e_i t_i + 6d_i = 24e_{i+1} t_i + 6d_{i+1} \tag{A15}$$

The constraints (A3) become:

$$\frac{1}{5} e_i (t_i^5 - t_{i-1}^5) + \frac{1}{4} d_i (t_i^4 - t_{i-1}^4) + \frac{1}{3} c_i (t_i^3 - t_{i-1}^3) + \frac{1}{2} b_i (t_i^2 - t_{i-1}^2)$$
$$+ a_i (t_i - t_{i-1}) = - \log \left[\frac{P_i}{P_{i-1}} \right], \tag{A16}$$
$$i = 1, 2, \ldots, m$$

where we define $P_0 = 1$. This proves the theorem.

Interest Rate Analytics

CHAPTER 9

Duration and Convexity

The use of duration has gone through a curious evolution. As we discussed in Chapter 1, the use of duration as a tool for total balance sheet risk management met with more than five decades of resistance, in spite of the fact that duration and its variants have been standard techniques on trading floors for most of that time. From a twenty-first century perspective, it has become something more than just standard practice for interest rate hedging and risk analysis on the trading floor—the duration concepts are effectively the concepts upon which all advances in interest rate analytics are based.

On the other hand, from a total balance sheet management perspective, there are still many management teams at very large financial institutions who believe that net income simulation is a solid basis for risk management and that interest rate risk analytics used on the trading floor either don't apply or are too hard to understand.

In this chapter, we discuss the duration concepts in view of these two constituencies—one group which views duration as 'too simple' and which has moved on to more advanced techniques, and another group which views duration as 'too hard' to apply. As we discussed in Chapter 1, a lot of this difference in view is due to gaps between the generations and differences in educational experience. As one of the authors is the 'older generation', he advocates the latter explanation!

Even back in 1978, Jonathan Ingersoll, Jeffrey Skelton, and Roman Weil published an appreciation of Frederick R. Macaulay's 1938 work on duration entitled "Duration Forty Years Later." In that work, the authors pointed out a number of key aspects of duration and potential pitfalls of duration that we want to emphasize in this chapter. In this chapter, we introduce the concepts of duration and convexity as they have traditionally been used for 'bond math'. We then relate them to Macaulay's 1938 work. 'Standard practice' in financial markets has gradually drifted away from Macaulay's original concept of duration. In the three decades since Ingersoll, Skelton, and Weil published their article, the 'standard practice' has divided into two streams— the traditional adherents of 'bond math', and the term structure model school of thought, which we begin to outline in the next chapter. The purpose of this chapter is to re-emphasize the points made about duration by Ingersoll, Skelton and Weil and to highlight the errors that can result from deviating from Macaulay's original formulation of duration. Most of the vocabulary of financial markets still stems from the use of the traditional fixed income mathematics used in this chapter, but the underlying meanings have evolved as financial instruments and financial mathematics have become more complex. We turn to those concepts in Chapter 10, but for now, we focus on the history of the duration concept.

Macaulay's Duration: The Original Formula

As in Chapters 7 and 8, we use the basic valuation formulas for calculating the present value of a bond.

We define the price of a zero-coupon bond with maturity of t years as $P(t)$. We let its continuously compounded yield be $y(t)$, and we label the cash flow in period t as $X(t)$. As we discussed in Chapter 7, the present value of these cash flows is:

$$\text{Present Value} = \sum_{i=1}^{n} P(t_i)X(t_i)$$

$$= \sum_{i=1}^{n} e^{-y(t_i)t_i} X(t_i)$$

The last line substitutes the relationship between $y(t)$ and $P(t)$ when yields $y(t)$ are continuously compounded. Macaulay investigated the change in present value as each yield $y(t)$ makes a parallel shift of amount x, so the new yield at any maturity $y(t)^* = y(t) + x$. The change in present value that results is:

$$\frac{\partial \text{Present Value}}{\partial x} = \sum_{i=1}^{n} -t_i e^{-y(t_i)t_i} X(t_i)$$

$$= \sum_{i=1}^{n} -t_i P(t_i)X(t_i)$$

In the next few chapters, we address the empirical issue of how frequency yield curve movements in major markets take place in this parallel fashion. For the time being, let's assume that a parallel shift assumption is good enough that we need to at least measure our exposure to this kind of risk.

Macaulay defined duration as the percentage change (expressed as a positive number, which requires changing the sign in the equation above) in present value that results from this parallel shift in rates:

$$\text{Duration} = -\frac{\partial \text{Present Value}/\partial x}{\text{Present Value}}$$

$$= \frac{\sum\limits_{i=1}^{n} t_i P(t_i) X(t_i)}{\sum\limits_{i=1}^{n} P(t_i) X(t_i)}$$

From this formula, we can see the reason that duration is often called the 'present value-weighted average time to maturity' of a given security. The time to maturity of each cash flow t_i is weighted by the share of the present value of the cash flow at that time in total present value.

In the case of a bond with n coupon payments of C dollars (note that C is not the annual percentage interest payment unless payments are made only once per year) and a principal amount of 100, this duration formula can be rewritten as:

$$\text{Duration} = -\frac{\partial \text{Present Value}/\partial x}{\text{Present Value}}$$

$$= \frac{C\left[\sum\limits_{i=1}^{n} t_i P(t_i)\right] + t_n P(t_n) 100}{C\left[\sum\limits_{i=1}^{n} P(t_i)\right] + P(t_n) 100}$$

This form of duration, the form its inventor intended, has come to be known as Fisher-Weil duration. All discounting in the present value calculations is done at a different continuous yield to maturity $y(t_i)$ for each maturity. We know from Chapter 8 that we can get these continuous yields to maturity from the various yield curve smoothing techniques discussed in that chapter.

Using Duration for Hedging

How is the duration concept used for hedging? Let's examine the case where a huge financial institution has its entire balance sheet in one unit of a security with present value B_1. Let's also assume that the financial institution is uncomfortable with its risk level. One thing the financial institution could do is to try to buy the Jarrow-Merton put option that we discussed in Chapter 1. This put option would provide the financial institution with price insurance against the decline in value of this security. Let's assume instead, however, that the financial institution wants to hedge in a more traditional way. Let's assume that the financial institution wants to form a zero-risk portfolio that includes the hedging security (which has present value B_2). What amount of this second security should the financial institution use to hedge? Let the 'zero-risk' amount of the hedging security be w. Then the total value of this portfolio W is:

$$W = B_1 + w B_2$$

We want the change in the value of this hedged portfolio to be zero for infinitely small parallel shifts in the term structure of interest rates. We can call the amount of this shift x. For the hedge to be successful, we must have:

$$\frac{\partial W}{\partial x} = \frac{\partial B_1}{\partial x} + w\frac{\partial B_2}{\partial x} = 0$$

From this equation, we can calculate the right amount of B_2 to hold for a perfect hedge as:

$$w = -\frac{\partial B_1/\partial x}{\partial B_2/\partial x}$$

Notice that this formula doesn't directly include duration. We can incorporate the duration calculation by modifying the original equation for a perfect hedge as follows:

$$\frac{\partial W}{\partial x} = B_1\frac{\partial B_1/\partial x}{B_1} + wB_2\frac{\partial B_2/\partial x}{B_2}$$

$$= -B_1\text{Duration}[B_1] - wB_2\text{Duration}[B_2] = 0$$

Therefore the hedge amount w can be rewritten:

$$w = \frac{-B_1\text{Duration}[B_1]}{B_2\text{Duration}[B_2]}$$

Using either formula for w, we can establish the 'correct' hedge for the financial institution's portfolio. While we have discussed hedging as if the financial institution only owned one security, this traditional analysis applies equally well to a financial institution that owns millions of transactions whose risk is captured by the artificial 'security' we have described above. This hedging technique has the following characteristics:

- It is correct only for infinitely small parallel shifts in interest rates;
- It has to be 'rebalanced' like a Black-Scholes options delta hedge whenever:
  1. rates change;
  2. time passes.

The hedge will not be correct if there are large parallel jumps in interest rates, nor will it be correct for non-parallel shifts in interest rates. In other words, the basic theory of duration doesn't result in a 'buy and hold' hedge. This insight is perhaps the model's greatest contribution to the world of finance. At the same time, it leaves many management teams looking for the insurance policy against risk that they buy once and don't have to deal with again for many years.

Duration: The Traditional Market Convention

Over time, the conventional wisdom has evolved from Macaulay's original formulation of the duration concept. With the explosion in interest rate derivatives over the last two decades, the original formulation and its more modern relatives dominate among younger and more analytical interest rate risk experts. However, the 'evolved' Macaulay duration is experiencing a decline in popularity because it relies on traditional 'bond math' rather than the Fisher-Weil continuous compounding and the related concepts of Chapters 7 and 8. The reason for the change to 'bond math' from Macaulay's original formulation is a simple one—until relatively recently, it has been difficult for market participants to easily take the $P(t)$ values from the current yield curve using the techniques that were outlined in Chapter 8. Now that yield curve smoothing has become easier, this problem has declined in importance, but the market's simpler formulation persists in many areas of major financial institutions. The best way to explain the 'bond math' market convention for duration is to review the formula for yield to maturity.

The formula for yield to maturity

For a settlement date (for either a secondary market bond purchase or a new bond issue) that falls exactly one 'period' from the next coupon date, the formula for yield to maturity can be written as follows for a bond which matures in n periods and pays a fixed dollar coupon amount C m times per year as shown in Chapter 7:

$$\text{Price} + \text{Accrued Interest} = \text{Present Value} = C\left[\sum_{i=1}^{n} P(t_i)\right] + P(t_n) * \text{Principal}$$

$$\text{where } P(t_i) = \frac{1}{\left(1 + \frac{y}{m}\right)^i}$$

Yield to maturity is the value of y that makes this equation true. This relationship is the present value equation for a fixed coupon bond, with the addition that the discount factors are all calculated by dividing one dollar by the future value of one dollar invested at y for i periods with interest compounded m times per year). In other words, y is the internal rate of return on this bond. Note also that the present value of the bond, using these discount factors, and the price of the bond are equal since there is no accrued interest.

Yield to maturity for long or short first coupon payment periods

For most outstanding bonds or securities, as we saw in Chapter 7, the number of periods remaining usually contains a short (or occasionally a long) first period. The length of the short first period is equal to the number of days from settlement to the next coupon, divided by the total number of days from the last coupon (or hypothetical last coupon, if the bond is a new issue with a short coupon date) to the next coupon. The exact method of counting days for the purpose of this calculation depends on the interest accrual method associated with the bond (examples are actual/actual, the National Association of Securities Dealers 30/360 method in the U.S., or the Euro market implementation of the 30/360 accrual method). We call the fraction of remaining days (as appropriately calculated) to days between coupons (as appropriately calculated) x. Then the yield to maturity can be written:

$$\text{Present Value} = C \sum_{i=1}^{n} [P(t_i)] + P(t_n) * \text{Principal}$$

$$\text{where } P(t_i) = \frac{1}{(1 + (y/m))^{i-1+x}}$$

As in the case of even first coupon periods, y is the yield to maturity that makes this relationship true, the internal rate of return on the bond. Note that when x is 1, this reduces to the formula above for even-length first periods. For a review of the use of the Newton-Raphson method for calculating y, see Chapter 7.

Applying the yield to maturity formula to duration

The conventional definition of duration is calculated by applying the implications of the yield to maturity formula to the original Macaulay duration formula, which is given below:

$$\text{True Duration} = -\frac{\partial \text{Present Value}/\partial x}{\text{Present Value}}$$

$$= \frac{\sum_{i=1}^{n} t_i P(t_i) X(t_i)}{\sum_{i=1}^{n} P(t_i) X(t_i)}$$

We can rewrite this formula for a conventional bond by substituting directly into this formula on the assumptions that market interest rates are equal for all maturities at the yield to maturity y and that interest rates are compounded at discrete, instead of continuous, intervals. This results in the following changes:

- the discount factors $P(t_i)$, taken from the smoothed yield curve by Macaulay, are replaced by a simpler formulation which uses the same interest rate (the yield to maturity) at each maturity:

$$P(t_i) = \frac{1}{(1 + (y/m))^{i-1+x}}$$

- the time t_i is directly calculated as:

$$t_i = \frac{i - 1 + x}{m}$$

Using this formulation, the 'conventional' definition of duration for a bond with dollar coupon C and principal of 100 is:

$$\text{Conventional Duration} = \frac{C\left[\sum_{i=1}^{n} t_i P(t_i)\right] + t_n P(t_n)100}{\text{Present Value}}$$

$$= \left(C\left[\sum_{i=1}^{n} \frac{i-1+x}{m}\left(\frac{1}{(1+(y/m))^{i-1+x}}\right)\right] + \frac{n-1+x}{m}\left(\frac{1}{(1+(y/m))^{n-1+x}}\right)100\right)\Bigg/\text{Present Value}$$

This is just a discrete time transformation of Macaulay's formula. As shown below, however, it doesn't measure the percentage change in present value for a small change in the discrete yield to maturity, as shown in the next section.

Modified Duration

In the case of Macaulay duration, the formula was based on the calculation of:

$$\text{Duration} = -\frac{\partial \text{Present Value}/\partial x}{\text{Present Value}}$$

$$= \frac{\sum_{i=1}^{n} t_i P(t_i) X(t_i)}{\sum_{i=1}^{n} P(t_i) X(t_i)}$$

The second line of the equation immediately above results from the fact that the yield to maturity of a zero-coupon bond with maturity t_i, written as $y(t_i)$, is continuously compounded. The conventional measure of duration, given in the previous section, is not consistent with Macaulay's derivation of duration when interest payments are discrete instead of continuous. What happens to the percentage change in present value when the discrete yield to maturity (instead of the continuous yield to maturity analyzed by Macaulay) shifts from y to $y+z$ for infinitely small changes in z? Using the yield to maturity formula as a starting point and differentiating with respect to z, we get the following formula, which is called modified duration:

$$
\text{Modified Duration} = \left(C \left[\sum_{i=1}^{n} \frac{(i-1+x)}{m} \left(\frac{1}{(1+(y/m))^{i+x}} \right) \right] \right.
$$

$$
\left. + \frac{n-1+x}{m} \left(\frac{1}{1+(y/m)^{n+x}} \right) 100 \right) \Big/ \text{Present Value}
$$

$$
= \frac{\text{Conventional Duration}}{1+(y/m)}
$$

This modified duration measures the same thing that Macaulay's original formula was intended to measure—the percentage change in present value for an infinitely small change in yields. The Macaulay formulation and the conventional duration are different for the following reasons:

- The Macaulay measure (most often called Fisher-Weil duration) is based on continuous compounding and correctly measures the percentage change in present value for small parallel changes in these continuous yields. The conventional duration measure, a literal translation to discrete compounding of the Macaulay formula, does *not* measure the percentage change in price for small changes in discrete yield to maturity. The percentage change in present value is measured by conventional modified duration. When using continuous compounding, 'duration' and 'modified duration' are the same.
- The Macaulay measure uses a different yield for each payment date instead of using the yield to maturity as the appropriate discount rate for each payment date.

The impact of these differences in assumptions on hedging are outlined below.

The Perfect Hedge: The Difference between the Original Macaulay and Conventional Durations

Both the original Macaulay (Fisher-Weil) and conventional formulation of duration are intended to measure the percentage change in value for a parallel shift in yields. The percentage change is measured as the percentage change in present value—it is important to note that it is *not* the percentage change in *price* (present value − accrued interest) that is measured. The difference between a hedge calculated based on the percentage change in present *value* (the *correct* way) versus a hedge based on the percentage change in *price* (the *incorrect* way) can be significant if the bond to be hedged and the instrument used as the hedging instrument have different amounts of accrued interest. The impact of this 'accrued interest' effect varies with the level of interest rates and the amount of accrued interest on the underlying instrument and the instrument used as a hedge. If payment dates on the two bonds are different and the relative amounts of accrued interest are different, the hedge ratio error can exceed 5%.

The second source of error when using modified duration to calculate hedge ratios is the error induced by using the yield to maturity as the discount rate at every payment date instead of using a different discount rate for every maturity. The hedging error (relative to Fisher-Weil duration) from this source can easily vary from –2% to +2% as a linear yield curve takes on different shapes. The hedge ratio error is obviously most significant when the yield curve has a significant slope.

Convexity and its Uses

The word 'convexity' is heard every day on trading floors around the world, and yet it's a controversial subject. It is usually ignored by leading financial academics, and it's an important topic to two diverse groups of financial market participants—adherents to the historical yield—to maturity bond mathematics that predates the derivatives world and the use of term structure models that is the central topic of this book, and modern 'rocket scientists' who are compelled to translate the latest in derivatives mathematics to hedges that work. This section is an attempt to bridge the gap between these constituencies.

Convexity: A general definition

The duration concept, reduced to its most basic nature, involves the ratio of the first derivative of a valuation formula f to the underlying security's value:

$$\text{Duration} = \frac{-f'(y)}{f(y)}$$

The variable y could be any stochastic variable that determines present value according to the function f. It may be yield to maturity, it may be the short rate in a term structure model, etc. It is closely related to the delta hedge concept, which has become a standard hedging tool for options-related securities. The underlying idea is exactly the same as that discussed at the beginning of this chapter: for infinitely small changes in the random variable, the first derivative (whether called 'duration' or 'delta') results in a perfect hedge if the model incorporated in the function f is 'true'. So far in our discussion, the constituencies mentioned above are all in agreement.

As we showed in the section above, the duration and modified duration concepts are *not* 'true' whenever the yield curve is not flat. The academic community and the derivatives hedgers agree on this point and neither group would be satisfied with a hedge ratio based on the discrete yield to maturity formulas presented in this chapter, despite their long established place in the history of fixed income markets. All three constituencies agree, however, that when the random variable in a valuation formula 'jumps' by more than an infinitely small amount, a hedging challenge results.

Leading academics solve this problem by either assuming it away or by breaking a complex security into more liquid 'primitive' securities and assembling a perfect hedge that exactly replicates the value of the complex security. In the case of a non-callable bond, the perfect hedge is the portfolio of zero-coupon bonds that exactly offsets the cash flows of the underlying bond portfolio. Traditional practitioners of bond math and derivatives experts often are forced to deal with the fact that no perfect hedge exists or the required rebalancing of a hedge can only be done at discrete, rather than continuous, intervals.

The fundamental essence of the convexity concept involves the second derivative of a security's value with respect to a random input variable y. It is usually expressed as a ratio to the value of the security, as calculated using the formula f:

$$\text{Convexity} = \frac{f''(y)}{f(y)}$$

It is very closely linked with the gamma calculation (the second derivative of an option's value with respect to the price of the underlying security).

When a security's value makes a discrete jump because of a discrete jump in the input variable y, the new value can be calculated to any desired degree of precision using a Taylor expansion, which gives the value of the security at the new input variable level, say $y + z$, relative to the old value at input variable level y:

$$f(y+z) = f(y) + f'(y)z + f''(y)\frac{z^2}{2!} + \cdots + f^{[n]}(y)\frac{z^n}{n!} + \cdots$$

Rearranging these terms and dividing by the security's original value $f(y)$, gives us the percentage change in value that results from the shift z:

$$\frac{f(y+z) - f(y)}{f(y)} = \frac{f'(y)}{f(y)} z + \frac{f''(y)}{f(y)} \frac{z^2}{2!} + \cdots + \frac{f^{[n]}(y)}{f(y)} \frac{z^2}{n!} + \cdots$$

$$= (\text{Duration}) z + (\text{Convexity}) \frac{z^2}{2!} + \text{Error}$$

The percentage change can be expressed in terms of duration and convexity and an error term. Note that 'modified duration' should replace 'duration' in this expression if the random factor is the discrete yield to maturity. We will see in Chapter 10 that this Taylor expansion is very closely related to Ito's Lemma, the heart of the stochastic mathematics we introduce in Chapter 10. These techniques, combined with the yield curve smoothing technology of Chapter 8, form the basis for an integrated analysis of interest rate risk and credit risk, which is increasingly popular today.

Convexity for the present value formula

For the case of the present value of a security with cash flows of X_i per period, payments m times per year, and a short first coupon of x periods, the convexity formula can be derived by differentiating the present value formula twice with respect to the yield to maturity y and then dividing by present value:

$$\text{Convexity} = \left[\sum_{i=1}^{n} X(t_i) \left(\frac{-(i-1+x)}{m} \right) \left(\frac{-(i-1+x)-1}{m} \right) \right.$$
$$\left. * \left(\frac{1}{1+(y/m)} \right)^{-(i-1+x)-2} \right] \Big/ \text{Present Value}$$

When present value is calculated using the continuous time approach

$$\text{Present Value} = \sum_{i=1}^{n} e^{-t_i y(t_i)} X(t_i)$$

then the continuous compounding or Fisher-Weil version of convexity is:

$$\text{Convexity} = \frac{\left[\sum_{i=1}^{n} t_i^2 P(t_i) X(t_i) \right]}{\text{Present Value}}$$

Hedging Implications of the Convexity Concept

To the extent that rebalancing a hedge is costly or to the extent that the underlying random variable jumps rather than moves in a continuous way, the continuous rebalancing of a duration (or delta) hedge will be either expensive or impossible. In either case, the 'best hedge' is the hedge that comes closest to a 'buy and hold' hedge, a hedge that can be put in place and left there with no need to rebalance until the portfolio being hedged has matured or been sold. A hedge which matches both the duration (or modified duration in the case of a hedger using a present value based-valuation formula) and the convexity of the underlying portfolio will come closer to this objective than most simple duration hedges. Consider the case of a financial institution with a portfolio that has a value P and two component securities (say mortgages and auto loans) with values S_1 and S_2. Denoting first and second derivatives of value with respect to the random factor and duration by D and convexity by C, the best hedge ratios w_1 and w_2 for a hedge using both securities S_1 and S_2 can be obtained by solving the same kind of equations we used above in the duration case. We need to solve either:

$$P' = w_1 S'_1 + w_2 S'_2$$
$$P'' = w_1 S''_1 + w_2 S''_2$$

or:

$$PD_P = w_1 S_1 D_1 + w_2 S_2 D_2$$
$$PC_P = w_1 S_1 C_1 + w_2 S_2 C_2$$

for the hedge ratios w_1 and w_2.

Consider the following examples of duration and convexity on both a Fisher-Weil basis and on a discrete basis. Assume that the yield curve smoothing process has generated zero-coupon bond yields on a continuously compounded basis of:

Maturity	Continuous Yield
0.5	5.00%
1.0	5.75%
1.5	6.25%
2.0	6.50%

We want to analyze the duration and convexity of a bond with two years to maturity, semi-annual payments, and a coupon of 12%. The present value of the bond can be calculated as 110.05777 using the techniques discussed in Chapter 7. The Fisher-Weil duration is 1.84395.

Table 9.1 Fisher-Weil Duration

Coupon:	12.00%
Principal	100
Payments Per Year	2

Years to Maturity	Zero Yield	Discount Factor	Cash Flow	Present Value	Time Weighted Present Value
0.5	5.00%	0.97531	6.00	5.85186	2.92593
1	5.75%	0.94412	6.00	5.66473	5.66473
1.5	6.25%	0.91051	6.00	5.46306	8.19459
2	6.50%	0.87810	106.00	93.07812	186.15623
Total				110.05777	202.94149
Fisher-Weil Duration					**1.84395**

The Fisher-Weil convexity can be calculated in a similar way to be 3.5593. The same calculation can be done on a discrete basis. Step 1 is to use the Newton-Raphson method to solve for the yield to maturity on the bond that gives its present value of 110.05777. This yield is 6.5526%. We then use this constant yield of 6.5526% to calculate new discount factors, multiply them by the cash flow and years to maturity for each payment, and we divide the sum

Table 9.2 Fisher-Weil Convexity

Coupon:	12.00%
Principal	100
Payments Per Year	2

Years to Maturity	Zero Yield	Discount Factor	Cash Flow	Present Value	Time Sqaured Weighted Present Value
0.5	5.00%	0.97531	6.00	5.8519	1.4630
1	5.75%	0.94412	6.00	5.6647	5.6647
1.5	6.25%	0.91051	6.00	5.4631	12.2919
2	6.50%	0.87810	106.00	93.0781	372.3125
Total				110.0578	391.7320
Fisher-Weil Convexity					**3.5593**

Table 9.3 Duration and Modified Duration

Yield to Maturity	6.5526%
Coupon:	12.00%
Principal	100
Payments Per Year	2

Years to Maturity	Yield to Maturity	Discout Factor	Cash Flow	Present Vallue	Time Weighted Present Value
0.5	6.5526%	0.96828	6.00	5.8097	2.9048
1	6.5526%	0.93756	6.00	5.6254	5.6254
1.5	6.5526%	0.90782	6.00	5.4469	8.1703
2	6.5526%	0.87902	106.00	93.1759	186.3517
Total				110.0578	203.0522
Duration					**1.8450**
Modified duration					**1.7864**

of these calculations by present value to get a traditional duration of 1.8450. This is quite close to Fisher-Weil duration, but as noted above, the traditional duration number does not measure the percentage change in price for small changes in yield to maturity, which is our objective. This is measured by modified duration, which can be calculated as 1.7864, a dramatically different number from Fisher-Weil duration.

Table 9.4 Convexity

Yield to Maturity	6.5526%
Coupon:	7.00%
Principal	100
Payments Per Year	2

Years to Maturity	Yield to Maturity	$(i-1+x)/m$	$(i+x)/m$	Cash Flow	Convexity Discount Factor	Time Weighted Total
0.5	6.5526%	0.5	1.0	6.00	0.9078	2.7234
1	6.5526%	1.0	1.5	6.00	0.8790	7.9112
1.5	6.5526%	1.5	2.0	6.00	0.8511	15.3204
2	6.5526%	2.0	2.5	106.00	0.8241	436.7895
Total						462.7444
Convexity						**4.2046**

Convexity can be calculated in a similar way. We arrive at a figure of 4.2046, again significantly different from the Fisher-Weil version of convexity.

Hedging a Bank Balance Sheet, Hedging an Insurance Company's Equity, or Hedging a Pension Fund's Assets and Liabilities: Conclusion

The concepts we have illustrated in this chapter generally assume a very simple position of a trader or a financial institution—there is generally only one security in the portfolio and only one hedging instrument. In practical application, traders have 10, 50, 100, or 100,000 positions and financial institutions have 50,000, 1 million, or 20 million positions. The process of measuring the change in the value of the position (some of which are assets and some of which are liabilities), is identical whether there is one position or millions. We illustrate the calculation of these interest rate deltas or durations in the next few chapters. The calculation of the perfect hedge is also the same from a total balance sheet perspective with one modest variation. As we saw in Chapters 1–6, the interest rate risk of the proceeds of the financial institution's equity is irrelevant to shareholders as long as all of the other assets are funded in such a way that there is a constant hedged cash flow from them. If this assumption is correct, then the financial institution cannot go bankrupt from interest rate risk and the financial institution is in the safety zone. Using this concept, the hedging techniques of this chapter would be applied to all assets and liabilities except those which are funded with the capital of the financial institution.

Over the last 56 years, the market's conventional definition of duration has drifted from Macaulay's original concept to a measure that appears similar but which can be very misleading if used inappropriately. Fortunately, the trends in interest rate risk management are now swinging forcefully back to the original Macaulay concept. As Ingersoll, Skelton, and Weil point out, the Macaulay formulation offers considerable value as a guide to the correct hedge if one takes a 'back to basics' approach: the measure should focus on the percentage change in present value, not price, and the discount rate at each maturity should reflect its actual continuous yield to maturity as obtained using the techniques in Chapter 8. Assuming the yield to maturity is the same for each cash flow or coupon payment on a bond can result in serious hedging errors. The duration (or modified duration) approach to hedging is a strong foundation on which to build a hedging program, if properly modified to recognize the expense of rebalancing the hedge or the likelihood of discrete jumps in the underlying random variable that prevent an economical, continuous rebalancing of the hedge. The convexity approach provides a useful guide to maximizing hedging efficiency, but the term convexity has outlasted the simple convexity formula commonly used for bonds. The formula itself has been supplanted by the concepts we will introduce in subsequent chapters.

How do we calculate these concepts for a bond option? How do we calculate them for a first to default swap? How do we calculate them for a mortgage that prepays? How do we calculate them for a savings deposit without an explicit maturity? That is a task to which we will turn after a little more foundation in interest rate risk analytics.

Exercises

Use the following zero-coupon bond prices to derive continuous yields to maturity that will allow you to answer the following questions. Assume that the zero-coupon bond prices have been obtained from one of the yield curve smoothing techniques in Chapter 8 and that you believe the technique to be the appropriate one in today's market. Assume today is January 15 2005.

April 15 2005	0.974
October 15 2005	0.949
April 15 2006	0.921
October 15 2006	0.892
April 15 2007	0.862
October 15 2007	0.831
April 15 2008	0.798
October 14 2008	0.763
April 15 2009	0.725

9.1   Using the Fisher-Weil duration formula, what is the duration of the 6% semi-annual payment bond that matures April 15 2008?

9.2   You own $2,000 principal amount of the bond in Exercise 9.1. The only hedging instrument you can use to hedge your position, because of liquidity considerations, is the zero-coupon bond maturing October 15 2006. Assuming infinitely small parallel shifts in zero-coupon bond yields, how much (in terms of principal amount) of the October 15 2006 zero-coupon bond should you sell short to perfectly hedge your position in the 6% bonds due April 25 2008?

9.3   Assume that the accrued interest calculation method appropriate for the 6% bonds in Exercise 9.1 shows that the short first period to the April 15 2005 coupon is exactly half a period in length. What is the yield to maturity on this bond? Using the yield to maturity formula, what is the traditional duration on this bond? What is the modified duration?

9.4   Calculate the modified duration of the October 15 2006 zero-coupon bond after calculating its yield to maturity on a semi-annual basis (use the techniques in Chapter 7 to make this adjustment).

9.5   Using the modified duration concept, how much of the October 15 2006 zero-coupon bonds should you sell short to hedge the $2,000 of 6% bonds due 2008, based on your answers in Exercises 9.3 and 9.4? How much does this answer deviate from the answer to Exercise 9.2?

9.6 Which hedge ratio will generally get you the best hedge, the ratio in Exercise 9.2 or the ratio in Exercise 9.5?

9.7 Using the continuously compounded Fisher-Weil approach, what is the continuous convexity of the 6% bonds maturing 2008?

9.8 Using the discrete yield to maturity approach to convexity, what is the convexity of the 6% bonds maturing in 2008?

9.9 Assume you can use both the October 15 2006 zero-coupon bond and the October 15 2008 zero-coupon bond to hedge your $2,000 position in the 6% bonds due 2008. Using the Fisher-Weil duration and convexity calculations, what should your position be in the two zero-coupon bonds for the hedge which perfectly matches both the Fisher-Weil duration and convexity of the 6% bonds due 2008?

9.10 Continuing the assumptions of Exercise 9.9, but using the discrete yield to maturity formula-based modified duration and convexity formulas, what should your position be in the two zero-coupon bonds for the hedge which perfectly matches both the modified duration and the discrete convexity of the 6% bonds due 2008?

9.11 What are the Fisher-Weil convexity and duration of the two life insurance policies described in Exercise 7.16? Using the Fisher-Weil duration and convexity formulas, how much of the zero-coupon bonds due October 15 2006 and October 15 2008 should you own to match the Fisher-Weil duration and convexity of the life policies?

CHAPTER 10

Duration as a Term Structure Model[1]

In Chapter 9, we were introduced to Frederick Macaulay's duration concept. At the heart of the duration concept is the implicit assumption that rates at all maturities move at the same time in the same direction by the same absolute amount. For example, we may assume that the amount of change for the yield to maturity of all bonds observable in the market at all maturities is one basis point. This assumption about how rates move can be labeled a 'term structure model'. At the same time, it is known on trading floors all over the world as 'PVBP', the present value of a basis point, a common measure of risk.

The purpose of this chapter is to introduce the concept of term structure models and the procedure for evaluating the reasonableness of a given term structure model. We then apply this procedure to the duration term structure model in the last section of the chapter. In Chapters 11–13, we go on to fully implement the term structure model concept so that we can calculate the credit-adjusted value of the Jarrow-Merton put option, the best measure of integrated credit and interest rate risk, as outlined in Chapter 1. We attempt to define precisely how much risk we have and what the hedge is that is necessary to move us to where we want to be on the risk/return spectrum.

What is a Term Structure Model and Why Do We Need One?

When analyzing fixed income portfolios, the value of a balance sheet, or a fixed income option it is not enough to know where interest rates currently are. It is not possible to know where rates will be in the future with any certainty. Instead, we can analyze a portfolio or a specific security by making an assumption about the random process by which rates will move in the future. Once we have made an assumption about the random (or 'stochastic') process

---

[1] An earlier version of this chapter appeared as Chapter 4 of van Deventer and Imai [1996].

by which rates move, we can then derive the probability distribution of interest rates at any point in the future. Without this kind of assumption, we cannot analyze interest rate risk effectively.

The same comments apply equally well to portfolios of common stocks and equity derivatives, because of the well-known links between equity prices and interest rates that we analyze in Chapters 14 and 15.

Most importantly, risk-free interest rates have repeatedly been shown to be statistically significant determinants of defaults in the North American market.[2] We discuss this linkage in detail in Chapters 16–18.

For all of these reasons, we need a more robust way to model interest rate movements than the bond math of the modified duration concept. We need to utilize the same tools for interest rate analytics that Black and Scholes [1973] used in the options market. We turn to that task now.

The Vocabulary of Term Structure Models

The mathematics for analyzing something whose value changes continuously, but in a random process, is heavily used in physics, and these tools from physics have been responsible for most of the derivatives valuation formulas used in finance in the last three decades. We need to spend a little time on these mathematical techniques because of the power they bring to a clear understanding of risk and what to do about it.

In this stochastic process mathematics used in physics, the change in a random variable x over the next instant is written dx. The most common assumption (but not the only assumption) about the random jumps in the size of a variable x is that they are normally distributed. The 'noise' or shock to the random variable is assumed to come from a random number generator called a Wiener process. It is a random variable, say z, whose value changes from instant to instant, but which has a normal distribution with mean zero and standard deviation of one. For example, if we assume that the continuously compounded zero-coupon bond yield $y(t)$ for a given maturity t jumps continuously with mean zero and standard deviation of one, we would write:

$$dy = dz$$

In stochastic process mathematics, all interest rates are written as decimals, such as 0.03 instead of 3, so the assumption that rates jump each instant by one (which means 100%) is too extreme. We can scale the jumps of interest rates by multiplying the noise generating Wiener process by a scale factor. In the

---

[2] See Kamakura Risk Information Services-Credit Risk Technical Guide, version 2.2, November 2003.

case of interest rates, this scale factor is the 'volatility' of the stochastic process driving interest rate movements. This volatility is related to, but different from, the volatility of stock prices assumed by Black and Scholes to be log-normally distributed. In the Black-Scholes model, the return on stock prices is assumed to be normally distributed, not stock prices themselves. In our simple interest rate model, the change in interest rates is assumed to be driven by this normally distributed 'shock term' z with changes dz. We label this interest rate volatility σ. In that case, the stochastic process for the movement in yields is:

$$dy = \sigma\,dz$$

The volatility term allows us to scale the size of the shocks to interest rates up and down. We can set this interest rate volatility scale factor to any level we want, although normally it would be set to levels that most realistically reflect the movements of interest rates. We can calculate this implied interest rate volatility from the prices of observable securities such as interest rate caps, interest rate floors, or callable bonds. We will show the relationship between interest rate volatility and the volatility of the Black-Scholes model in Chapter 15 on the random interest rates version of the Merton model.

The yield that we have modeled above is a random walk, a stochastic process where the random variable drifts randomly with no trend up or down. As time passes, ultimately the yield will rise to infinity or fall to negative infinity. This isn't a very realistic assumption about interest rates, which usually move in cycles of three to seven years, depending on the country and the central bank's approach to monetary policy. How can we introduce interest rate cycles to our model? We need to introduce some form of drift in interest rates over time. One form of drift is to assume that interest rates change by some formula as time passes:

$$dy = \alpha(t)\,dt + \sigma\,dz$$

The formula above assumes that on average, the change in interest rates over a given instant will be the change given by the function $\alpha(t)$, with random shocks in the amount of $\sigma\,dz$. This formula is closely linked to the term structure models proposed by Ho and Lee [1986] and Heath, Jarrow, and Morton [1992]. Both of these models make it easy to fit actual observable yield curve data exactly with a simple assumption about how interest rates move. The function $\alpha(t)$ can be chosen to fit a yield curve smoothed using the techniques of Chapter 8 exactly. We go into more detail on both of these term structure models in Chapter 11.

The assumption about yield movements above isn't satisfactory in the sense that it is still a random walk of interest rates, although there is the drift term $\alpha(t)$ built into the random walk. The best way to build the interest rate cycle into the random movement of interest rates is to assume that the interest rate drifts back to some long-term level, except for the random shocks from the dz term. One process that does this is:

$$dy = \alpha(\gamma - y)\,dt + \sigma\,dz$$

This is the Ornstein-Uhlenbeck process, which is at the heart of the Vasicek [1977] model, which we introduce in Chapter 11. The term α is called the 'speed of mean reversion'. It is assumed to be a positive number. The larger it is, the faster y drifts back toward its long-term mean γ, and the shorter and more violent interest rate cycles will be. Since α is positive, when y is above γ, it will be pulled down except for the impact of the shocks which emanate from the dz term. When y is less than γ, it will be pulled up.

In almost every term structure model, the speed of mean reversion and the volatility of interest rates play a key role in determining the value of securities which are either interest options or which have interest rate options embedded in them. More importantly, this simple term structure model is so powerful and analytically attractive that it is at the heart of both the random interest rate version of the Merton model (Chapter 15) and the more modern reduced form credit models of Duffie and Singleton [1999] and Jarrow [1999, 2001] which we discuss in Chapter 16.

For that reason, it's important to understand a little more about how these interest rate models are derived.

Ito's Lemma

Once a term structure model has been chosen, we need to be able to draw conclusions about how securities, whose values depend on interest rates, should move around. For instance, if a given interest rate y is assumed to be the random factor that determines the price of a zero-coupon bond P, it is logical to ask how the zero-coupon bond price moves as time passes and y varies. The formula used to do this is called Ito's lemma.[3] Ito's lemma puts the movement in the bond price P in stochastic process terms like this:

$$dP = P_y dy + \frac{1}{2}P_{yy}(dy)^2 + P_t$$

where the subscripts denote partial derivatives. This formula looks very much like the Taylor series expansion that we used in our discussion on convexity

---

[3] For more on Ito's lemma, see Shimko [1992] for implementations in applied finance.

in Chapter 9. The change in the price of a zero-coupon bond equals its first derivative multiplied by the change in y plus one-half of its second derivative multiplied by the volatility of y plus the 'drift' in prices over time. The terms dy and $(dy)^2$ depend on the stochastic process chosen for y. If the stochastic process is the Ornstein-Uhlenbeck process given above, we can substitute the values for dy and $(dy)^2$. If we do this, then the movements in P can be rewritten:

$$dP = P_y\left[\alpha(\gamma - y)\,dt + \sigma\,dz\right] + \frac{1}{2}P_{yy}\sigma^2\,dt + P_t\,dt$$

$$= \left[P_y\alpha(\gamma - y) + \frac{1}{2}P_{yy}\sigma^2 + P_t\right]dt + P_y\sigma\,dz$$

$$= g(y, t)\,dt + h(y, t)\,dz$$

For any stochastic process, the dy term is the stochastic process itself. The term $(dy)^2$ is the instantaneous variance of y. In the case of the Ornstein-Uhlenbeck process, it is the square of the coefficient of dz, σ^2. The term $g(y, t)$, which depends on the level of rates y and time t, is the drift in the bond price. The term $h(y, t)$ is the bond price volatility in the term structure model sense, not the Black-Scholes sense.[4] We have neatly divided the expression for movements in the bond's price into two pieces. The first term depends on the level of interest rates and time, and the second term depends on the dz term, which introduces random shocks to the interest rate market. If dz or h were always zero, then interest rates would not be random. They would drift over time, but there would be no surprises. Not surprisingly, we will devote a lot of time to discussing the hedging that eliminates these interest rate shocks.

Ito's lemma for more than one random variable

What if the zero-coupon bond price depended on two random variables, x and y? Then we would be dealing with a 'two-factor' term structure model, to which we turn in Chapter 12. The formula for the movement in the bond's price for such a two-factor term structure model is given by Ito's lemma as follows:

$$dP = P_x\,dx + P_y\,dy + \frac{1}{2}P_{xx}(dx)^2 + \frac{1}{2}P_{yy}(dy)^2 + P_{xy}(dxdy) + P_t$$

The instantaneous correlation between the two Wiener processes Z_x and Z_y which provide the random shocks to x and y, is reflected in the formula for

---

[4] See the next chapter for the relationship between volatility in the Black-Scholes sense and the term structure model sense.

the random movement of P by the instantaneous correlation coefficient rho; $(dxdy)$ is defined as $\rho\sigma_x\sigma_y$. The sigmas are the instantaneous variances of the two variables driving this term structure model, parallel to the variance of our original 'single factor' term structure model above. David Shimko [1992] has an excellent discussion of how to apply this kind of arithmetic to many problems in finance. Our need is restricted to term structure models, so we now turn to the construction of a single factor term structure model based on the duration concept.

Using Ito's lemma to build a term structure model

In their pioneering work, Heath, Jarrow and Morton [1992] clearly outline the steps that must be followed in developing a term structure model. There are potentially hundreds of alternative term structure models but their derivation has a common core. The steps involved in building a term structure model almost always follow this process:

(1) Make an assumption about the random (stochastic) process that interest rates follow that is consistent with market behavior in general.
(2) Use Ito's lemma to specify how zero-coupon bond prices move.
(3) Impose the constraint that there not be riskless arbitrage in the bond market via the following steps:
    (a) Use a bond of one maturity (in the case of a one factor model) to hedge the risk of a bond which has another maturity.[5]
    (b) After eliminating the risk of this 'portfolio', impose the constraint that this hedged portfolio earns the instantaneous (short-term) risk-free rate of interest.
(4) Solve the resulting partial differential equation for zero-coupon bond prices.
(5) Examine whether this implies reasonable or unreasonable conditions in the market.
(6) If the economic implications are reasonable, proceed to value other securities with the model. If they are unreasonable, reject the assumption about how rates move as a reasonable basis for a term structure model.

We will illustrate this process by analyzing the economic implications of the assumption of parallel yield curve shifts underlying the traditional duration analysis. We are converting the 1938 duration concept into a twenty-first century term structure model.

---

[5] If there are two random factors driving movements in interest rates, two bonds would be necessary to eliminate the risk of these random factors. N bonds would be necessary for an N factor model.

Duration as a Term Structure Model

In this section, we use the continuous compounding formulas discussed in Chapter 7 to analyze the yield to maturity y_i on a zero-coupon bond with maturity t_i and its value P:

$$P(t_i) = e^{-y_i t_i}$$

We want to examine what happens when all yields at time zero y_0 shift by a parallel amount x, with x being the same for all maturities. After the shift of x, the price of a zero-coupon bond with maturity $\tau = T - t$ (t is the current time in years and T is the maturity date of the bond in years, for a net maturity of $T - t$) will be:

$$P(\tau) = e^{-(y_0 + x)\tau}$$

where $y = y_0 + x$. We assume that x is initially zero and that we are given today's yield curve and know the values of y for all maturities.

We now make our assumption about the term structure model for interest rates. We assume that the movements in x follow a random walk, that is, we assume that changes in x have no drift term and that the change in x is normally distributed as follows:

$$dx = \sigma \, dz$$

The scale factor σ controls the volatility of the parallel shifts x. We now proceed to Step 2 of the previous section by using Ito's lemma to specify how the zero-coupon bond price for a bond with time to maturity $T - t$ moves. We use the formulas for the first and second derivatives of the bond price P and our knowledge of what dx and $(dx)^2$ are. Ito's lemma says:

$$
\begin{aligned}
dP &= P_x \, dx + \frac{1}{2} P_{xx} \, (dx)^2 + P_t \\
&= -\tau P \sigma \, dz + \frac{1}{2} \tau^2 P \sigma^2 \, dt + y P \, dt \\
&= \left[\frac{1}{2} \tau^2 P \sigma^2 + y P \right] dt - \tau P \sigma \, dz \\
&= g(y, t) P \, dt + h(y, t) P \, dz
\end{aligned}
$$

because

$$
\begin{aligned}
y &= y_0 + x \\
\tau &= T - t \\
P &= \exp^{-y\tau}
\end{aligned}
$$

$$P_x = -\tau P$$

$$P_{xx} = \tau^2 P$$

$$P_t = y P$$

$$g(y, t) = \frac{1}{2}\tau^2\sigma^2 + y$$

$$h(y, t) = -\tau\sigma$$

We now go to Step 3 as outlined in the previous section. We want to form a portfolio of one unit of bond one with maturity τ_1 and w units of the bond two with maturity τ_2. This is exactly the same kind of hedge construction that we did in Chapter 9. The value of this portfolio is:

$$W = P_1 + w P_2$$

We then apply Ito's lemma to changes in the value of the portfolio as the parallel shift amount x moves:

$$dW = dP_1 + w\, dP_2$$

$$= g_1 P_1\, dt + h_1 P_1\, dz + w\,[g_2 P_2\, dt + h_2 P_2\, dz]$$

$$= [g_1 P_1 + w g_2 P_2]\, dt + [h_1 P_1 + w h_2 P_2]\, dz$$

As in Step 3(b) above, we want to eliminate the interest rate risk in this portfolio. Since all interest rate risk comes from the random shock term dz, eliminating the interest rate risk means choosing w such that the coefficient of dz is zero. This means that the proper hedge ratio w for zero interest rate risk is:

$$w = \frac{-h_1 P_1}{h_2 P_2} = \frac{\tau_1 P_1}{\tau_2 P_2}$$

Substituting this into the equation above means:

$$dW = \left[g_1 P_1 + \frac{\tau_1 P_1}{\tau_2 P_2} g_2 P_2 \right] dt$$

Now we impose the 'no arbitrage' condition. Since the interest rate risk has been eliminated from this portfolio, the instantaneous return on the portfolio

dW should equal the riskless[6] short-term rate (the rate y with maturity 0, $y(0)$) times the value of the portfolio W:

$$dW = r(P_1 + wP_2)\, dt$$
$$= [g_1 P_1 + wg_2 P_2]\, dt$$

Rewritten, this means that:

$$\frac{rP_1 - \big((1/2)\tau_1^2\sigma^2 + y_1\big)\,P_1}{\tau_1 P_1} = \frac{rP_2 - \big((1/2)\tau_2^2\sigma^2 + y_2\big)\,P_2}{\tau_2 P_2} = k$$

This ratio has to be equal for any two maturities or there will be riskless arbitrage opportunities in this bond market. We define this ratio k as the 'market price of risk'. Choosing bond one and dropping the subscript one means that the yield y must satisfy the following relationship:

$$rP - \frac{1}{2}\tau^2\sigma^2 P - yP = k\tau P$$

Rearranging means that the yield y for any maturity must adhere to the following relationship:

$$y(\tau) = r - k\tau - \frac{1}{2}\tau^2\sigma^2$$

This equation comes from Step 4 in the section above. For a no arbitrage equilibrium in the bond market under a parallel shift in the yield curve, the yield y must be a quadratic function of time to maturity τ. If the function is not quadratic, there would be riskless arbitrage in the market. This is a surprising and little understood implication of the assumption of parallel yield curve shifts in the market. Clearly, the implication that yields are quadratic is good news and bad news. The good news is that the yield curve math is simple and can fit a lot of observable yield curves over some portion of their range. The bad news is the basic shape of the quadratic function!

---

[6] We have implicitly assumed in this chapter that we are modeling the risk-free term structure. We will relax this assumption in later chapters.

Conclusions About the Use of Duration's
Parallel Shift Assumptions

Unfortunately, the assumption that yields move in parallel fashion results in a number of conclusions that don't make sense if we impose the no-riskless-arbitrage conditions: First, interest rates can have only one 'hump' in the yield curve. This hump will occur at maturity:

$$\tau = -\frac{k}{\sigma^2}$$

Much more importantly, beyond a certain maturity, yields will turn *negative* since sigma is positive. Yields will be zero for two values of T defined by setting y equal to zero and solving for the maturities consistent with the yield of zero:

$$T = -\frac{k}{\sigma^2} \pm \sqrt{\frac{2r}{\sigma^2} + \frac{k^2}{\sigma^4}}$$

For normal values of k, these values of T define a range over which y will be positive. Outside of that range, yields to maturity will be negative. Forward rates are also quadratic and have the form:

$$f(\tau) = r - 2k\tau - \frac{3}{2}\tau^2\sigma^2$$

because forward rates are related to yields by the formula:

$$f(\tau) = y(\tau) + \tau y'(\tau)$$

as shown in Chapter 8. Zero-coupon bond prices are given by:

$$P(\tau) = e^{-y(\tau)\tau} = e^{-r\tau + k\tau^2 + (1/2)\sigma^2\tau^3}$$

These features of a parallel shift-based term structure model pose very serious problems. If the parallel yield curve shift assumption is used, as it is when we use the traditional duration approach to hedging, the resulting bond market is either:

(a) inconsistent with the real world because of negative yields, if we impose the no arbitrage conditions, or;
(b) enabling riskless arbitrage if we let yields have a shape that is not quadratic in the term to maturity.

In either case, the model is unacceptable for use by market participants because its flaws are so serious. The most important point of this chapter, however, is to show how we can move in a systematic way from an assumption about how interest rates move to explicit formulas for forward rates, zero-coupon bond prices, zero-coupon bond yields, and many other complex securities. We have laid the groundwork for extending the models to be consistent with observable yield curves. Most importantly, we have laid the groundwork for valuing the Jarrow-Merton put option that quantifies interest rate risk and credit risk in a fully integrated way.

In the next chapter, we turn to our next task. We use the same sort of analysis to identify some more attractive alternative models of the term structure that will provide a solid and realistic foundation for integrated interest rate risk and credit risk analysis.

Example

Before moving on, however, we want to show how the duration term structure model that we have derived in this chapter, can be fitted to observable yields. The *Wall Street Journal* reported closing prices for U.S. Treasury strips (zero-coupon bonds) at the following levels on March 25 1996:

Table 10.1 Closing Prices for U.S. Treasury Strips as at March 25 1996

Maturity	Price	Years to Maturity	Yield
5/15/96	99.28	0.14	5.163%
11/15/96	96.70	0.64	5.207%
11/15/97	91.30	1.64	5.539%
11/15/98	86.03	2.64	5.691%
11/15/99	80.89	3.64	5.820%
11/15/00	76.02	4.65	5.902%
11/15/01	71.22	5.65	6.011%
11/15/02	66.78	6.65	6.075%
11/15/03	62.36	7.65	6.176%
11/15/04	58.16	8.65	6.267%
11/15/05	54.20	9.65	6.347%
11/15/06	50.42	10.65	6.430%
11/15/07	46.92	11.65	6.496%
11/15/08	43.64	12.65	6.554%
11/15/09	40.05	13.65	6.703%
11/15/10	37.61	14.65	6.674%
11/15/11	34.89	15.65	6.727%
11/15/12	32.42	16.65	6.763%
11/15/13	30.11	17.65	6.799%

Continued

Table 10.1 (cont'd) Closing Prices for U.S. Treasury Strips as at March 25 1996

Maturity	Price	Years to Maturity	Yield
11/15/14	27.97	18.65	6.830%
11/15/15	26.00	19.65	6.854%
11/15/16	24.17	20.66	6.874%
11/15/17	22.53	21.66	6.881%
11/15/18	21.02	22.66	6.885%
11/15/19	19.66	23.66	6.876%
11/15/20	18.34	24.66	6.877%
11/15/21	17.22	25.66	6.856%
11/15/22	16.22	26.66	6.823%
11/15/23	15.38	27.66	6.769%
11/15/24	14.56	28.66	6.722%

The yield shown above is the continuously compounded yield to maturity. What values of r, k, and sigma in our simple term structure model provide the best fit to this actual data?

Using spreadsheet software to find the best fitting parameters (minimizing the sum of the squared error versus the actual continuous yields) gives the following results:

$$k = -0.00149839$$
$$\text{sigma} = 0.00825377$$
$$r = 5.234\%$$

The fit to the observed zero-coupon yield curve using these parameters is actually quite good, as shown in this graph:

Figure 10.1 Actual U.S. Treasury Strip Yields Versus Best Fitting Duration Model March 25, 1996

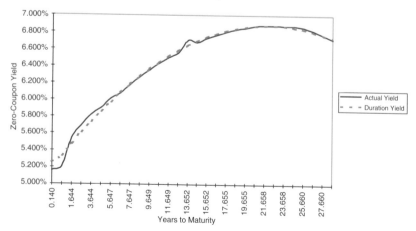

The fitted yield curve is quite a good match for the actual yield curve, with errors beyond six years in maturity of generally less than two basis points. Nonetheless, there are many problems using this approach in practice, as illustrated in the following examples.

Example: At what maturity will there be a peak in the yield curve?

Using the values for k, r, and sigma above, the formula at the beginning of this section indicates a peak at 21.99 years. Beyond that point, the yield curve steadily declines and will reach negative infinitely when the maturity gets long enough.

Example: At what maturities will yields turn negative?

Using the formulas above, yields turn negative in two places since the yield curve is a quadratic function of time to maturity. Yields reach zero for maturities of –22.95 years (which isn't relevant) and 66.94 years (which is relevant). Outside of these points, yields will be negative.

These examples indicate the dangers of the assumptions behind the duration approach—either the yield curve is locally 'no-arbitrage' with the undesirable quadratic form, or arbitrage will be possible. Even in the local 'no arbitrage' yield curve environment, arbitrage will be possible once it is admitted that consumers will hold cash rather than invest at negative interest rates. We turn to more attractive solutions in the next chapter, because the term structure model approach is very powerful and essential to risk management. We just need to fine-tune it to make it more realistic.

EXERCISES

Assume for the next four exercises that zero-coupon bond yields prevailing in the market are such that r is 6.00%, the three-year continuous yield is 8.00%, and the 20-year yield is 8.25%.

10.1 What values of k and sigma are consistent with this yield curve?

10.2 What is the highest point on the yield curve and at what maturity does it occur? What is the lowest point on the yield curve, and at what maturity does it occur?

10.3 At what maturities will the yield curve reach zero?

10.4 Would you buy a 99-year bond in this market? Why or why not? Assume for the next four exercises that the yield curve has the following features: r is 7%, the five-year yield is 6.25%, and the 20-year yield is 8.00%.

10.5 What values of k and sigma are consistent with this yield curve?

10.6   What is the highest point on the yield curve and at what maturity does it occur? What is the lowest point on the yield curve, and at what maturity does it occur?

10.7   At what maturities will the yield curve reach zero?

10.8   Would you buy a 99-year bond in this market? Why or why not?

CHAPTER 11

The Vasicek and Extended
Vasicek Models[1]

I n this chapter, we introduce four term structure models that are based on increasingly realistic assumptions about the random movement of interest rates. As we saw in Chapter 10, the historically popular assumption that the yield curve shifts in a parallel fashion can be consistent with a 'no arbitrage' economy, but only if the yield curve is quadratic and only if yields become negative beyond a given point on the yield curve. For this reason, we need a richer set of assumptions about yield curve movements that allow us to derive a theoretical yield curve whose shape is as close as possible, if not identical, to observable market yields and whose other properties are realistic. Again, why do we care about term structure models? We are looking for an integrated framework that allows us to analyze interest rate risk and credit risk using a common analytical base that produces pricing, valuation and hedging of these risks jointly. Most importantly, we want to be able to value the Jarrow-Merton put option discussed in Chapter 1 that best measures the total integrated risk that the company faces.

This chapter will be too mathematical for many practitioners and too simple for many hard-core 'rocket scientists'. We ask both groups for their patience, as our objective in this chapter is to show clearly the links between good theory and best practice in risk management. We shall cite other references for additional reading as and when appropriate.

We start with the simplest possible model. We will use the same assumptions for each of the four models we review in this chapter. We will assume bond prices in all four models depend solely on a single random factor, the short-term rate of interest. We will relax that assumption in Chapter 12, but it is safe to say that this single factor model for the risk-free term structure provides the current foundation for the credit risk models of Duffie and

---

[1] An earlier version of this chapter appeared in Chapter 5 of van Deventer and Imai [1996].

Singleton [1999] , Jarrow and Turnbull [1995], and Jarrow [1999, 2001] that define the current state of the art.

As we go through each of these four single factor term structure models, we go through the same steps as Chapter 10 to derive the form that zero-coupon bond prices and yields must have for the risk-free bond market to be a no arbitrage market:

- We specify the stochastic process for the movements in interest rates.
- We use Ito's lemma to derive the stochastic movements in zero-coupon bond prices.
- We impose no arbitrage restrictions to generate the partial differential equation that determines zero-coupon bond prices.
- We solve this equation for bond prices, subject to the boundary condition that the price of a zero-coupon bond with zero years to maturity must be one.

The four models we discuss all assume that changes in the short-term rate of interest are normally distributed. This assumption is a little more questionable in Japan's low rate environment than it is in other countries, but it pays huge dividends in processing speed (because of fast closed form solutions) and software quality as we discuss in Chapter 43. All of these issues are of major importance to an institution that has a large number of assets and liabilities or one that needs a large number of random scenarios to accurately measure and hedge risk. The four term structure models we review in this chapter are all special cases of the Heath, Jarrow and Morton [1992] framework, which we discuss in Chapter 12. The four models we select for this chapter are as follows:

1. Parallel rate shock model, where changes in the short-term risk-free rate r are random with no drift over time. This is the same as the continuous time duration model reviewed in Chapter 10. It was originally introduced by Robert Merton. Because the model has zero drift in rates over time, it does not generally exactly match the observable yield curve.

2. The extended parallel rate shock model, which matches the observable yield curve exactly. Changes in the short-term risk-free rate of interest r are a random walk with non-zero drift, allowing a perfect fit to an observable yield curve. We label this model the 'extended' Merton model or Ho and Lee model.

3. A non-parallel rate shift model, in which changes in the risk-free short-term rate of interest r allow for interest rate cycles. Analytically, we would say that changes in r follow the 'Ornstein-Uhlenbeck' process with a drift term, and r is reverting to a constant long-term value plus normally distributed shocks (the Vasicek model). It is this 'mean reversion' that causes cycles in interest rates.

4. A non-parallel rate shift model, which fits the observable yield curve exactly. In this model, changes in *r* follow the Ornstein-Uhlenbeck process again. The drift in *r* is such that we match the observable yield curve. This model is called the 'extended' Vasicek or Hull and White model.

Each of these models has strengths and weaknesses. We discuss each in term. Most importantly, we need to emphasize how these models will be used.

- **Risk-free yield curve**. We use these models to fit risk-free yield curves. We build the credit models of Chapters 14–18 on top of them to get the yield curves for risky issuers.
- **Valuation**. We use these models because of their rich array of high-speed, high accuracy closed form (algebraic) solutions that allow for best practice information technology implementation.
- **Simulation**. As we discuss in Chapter 12 and many other chapters, especially Chapters 39 to 44, we can simulate interest rate scenarios with many more complex assumptions about yield curve movements. Given a simulated interest rate environment in period 39 and scenario 147, however, we will get the fastest mark-to-market value for fixed income securities using the closed form solutions of a single factor model that is consistent with the environment in period 39 that was simulated in scenario 147.

Can we use these single factor models for a risky issuer's yield curve, like the interest rate swap curve?

Yes, but we have to beware of the limitations of this approach. Valuing a swaption using a term structure model based on the swap curve embeds the implicit assumption that the counterparty will not default, because (as we will see below) this possibility is ignored until we reach Chapters 14–18. In reality, the possibility that the counterparty might default before they can exercise the swaption decreases the cost of the swaption to you. We shall deal with these issues in the rest of this book, but we ignore them in this introduction to term structure modeling.

The Merton Term Structure Model: Parallel Yield Curve Shifts

One simple assumption about the short-term risk-free interest rate *r* is that it follows a simple random walk[2] with a zero drift over time. In Chapter 10, we

---

[2] To be precise, a Gaussian random walk.

applied this assumption to zero-coupon bond yields of all maturities and required that this random shift in rates be the same for all maturities. Robert Merton [1970] applied the random walk assumption to the short-term rate of interest r and derived what this means for the rest of the yield curve. Using the 'stochastic process' vocabulary from Chapter 10, we can write the change in r as:

$$dr = \sigma \, dZ$$

The change in the short-term rate of interest r equals a constant sigma times a random shock term, where Z represents a standard Wiener process with mean zero and standard deviation of one. The constant sigma is the instantaneous volatility of interest rates, which we can scale up and down to maximize the goodness of fit versus the observable yield curve. We will be careful to distinguish between interest rate volatility and the volatility of zero-coupon bond prices throughout the remainder of this book. From Chapter 10, we know that Ito's lemma can be used to write the stochastic process for the random changes in the price of a zero-coupon bond price as of time t with maturity T:

$$dP = P_r dr + \frac{1}{2} P_{rr} (dr)^2 + P_t \, dt$$

The change in the bond's price equals its first derivative with respect to r multiplied by the change in r, plus a term multiplied by the second derivative of the bond's price and a drift term, the derivative of the bond's price with respect to the current time t. In this random walk model, the variance of the interest r is $(dr)^2 = s^2$, so the expression above can be expanded to read:

$$dP = P_r \sigma \, dz + \frac{1}{2} P_{rr} \sigma^2 \, dt + P_t \, dt$$

Our goal is to find the formula for P as a function of the short rate r. Once we do this, we can vary the time to maturity T and derive the shape of the entire yield curve and how the yield curve moves in response to changes in r.

The next step in doing this is to impose the condition that no arbitrage is possible in the bond market. Since we have only one random factor in the economy, we know that we can eliminate this risk factor by hedging with only one instrument. If we had n independent risk factors, we would need n instruments to eliminate the n risks. Let's assume that an investor holds one unit of a zero-coupon bond, bond 1, with maturity T_1. The investor forms a portfolio of amount W, which consists of the one unit of bond 1 and w units of bond 2, which has a maturity T_2. The bond with maturity T_2 is the hedging instrument. The value of the portfolio is:

$$W = P_1 + w P_2$$

What is the proper hedge ratio w, and what are the implications of a perfect hedge for bond pricing? We know from Ito's lemma that the change in the value of this hedged portfolio is:

$$dW = dP_1 + wdP_2$$

$$= P_{1_r}\sigma \, dz + \left(\frac{1}{2}P_{1_{rr}}\sigma^2 + P_{1_t}\right) dt + w\left[P_{2_r}\sigma \, dz + \left(\frac{1}{2}P_{2_{rr}}\sigma^2 + P_{2_t}\right) dt\right]$$

Gathering the coefficients of the random shock term dZ together gives:

$$dW = \left(\frac{1}{2}P_{1_{rr}}\sigma^2 + P_{1_t}\right) dt + w\left(\frac{1}{2}P_{2_{rr}}\sigma^2 + P_{2_t}\right) dt + \left[P_{1_r} + w P_{2_r}\right]\sigma \, dZ$$

We repeat the process we followed in Chapter 10 to arrive at the zero risk hedge. If we choose w, the hedge amount of bond 2, such that the coefficient of the random shock term dZ is zero, then we have a perfect hedge and a riskless portfolio. The value of w for which this is true is:

$$w = \frac{-P_{1_r}}{P_{2_r}}$$

Note that this is identical to the hedge ratio we found for the duration-based parallel shift model in Chapter 10. If we use this hedge ratio, then the instantaneous return on the portfolio should exactly equal the short-term rate of interest multiplied by the value of the portfolio:

$$dW = rW \, dt = (r P_1 + r w P_2) \, dt$$

If this is not true, then riskless arbitrage will be possible. Imposing this condition and rearranging the equation above gives us the following relationship:

$$dW = (r P_1 + r w P_2) \, dt = \left(\frac{1}{2}P_{1_{rr}}\sigma^2 + P_{1_t}\right) dt + w\left(\frac{1}{2}P_{2_{rr}}\sigma^2 + P_{2_t}\right) dt$$

We then substitute the expression for w above into this equation, eliminate the dt coefficient from both sides, rearrange, and divide by interest rate volatility sigma to get the following relationship:

$$-\lambda = \frac{(1/2)P_{1_{rr}}\sigma^2 + P_{1_t} - rP_1}{\sigma P_{1_r}} = \frac{(1/2)P_{2_{rr}}\sigma^2 + P_{2_t} - rP_2}{\sigma P_{2_r}}$$

For any two maturities T_1 and T_2, the no arbitrage condition requires that this ratio be equal. We call the negative of this ratio λ,[3] the market price of risk. For normal risk aversion, the market price of risk should be positive because in a risk-averse market, riskier (longer maturity) bonds should have a higher expected return than the short rate r and because the rate sensitivity of all bonds P_r is negative. Since the choice of T_1 and T_2 is arbitrary, the market price of risk ratio must be constant for all maturities. *It is the fixed income equivalent of the Sharpe ratio*, which measures 'excess return' per unit of risk with the following statistic:

$$\text{Sharpe Ratio} = \frac{\text{Expected Return} - \text{Risk Free Return}}{\text{Standard Deviation of Return}}$$

We will return to the Sharpe ratio and the strong parallels between equilibrium in the fixed income and the equity markets frequently in this book. In our case, the numerator is made up of the drift in the bond's price:

$$\text{Drift} = \text{Expected Return} = \frac{1}{2}P_{rr}\sigma^2 + P_t$$

which also equals the expected return since the shock term or stochastic component of the bond's price change on average has zero expected value.

We now solve the equation above for any given bond with maturity T and remaining time to maturity $T-t = \tau$ as of time t, under the assumption that lambda (the market price of risk) is constant over time. Rearranging the equation above gives the following partial differential equation:

$$\lambda\sigma P_r + \frac{1}{2}P_{rr}\sigma^2 + P_t - rP = 0$$

which must be solved subject to the boundary condition that the price of the zero-coupon bond upon maturity T must equal its principal amount 1:

$$P(r, T, T) = 1$$

---

[3] We insert the minus sign in front of λ to be consistent with other authors' notation and subsequent chapters.

We use a common method of solving partial differential equations, the educated guess. We guess that P has the solution:

$$P(r, t, T) = P(r, \tau) = e^{rF(\tau)+G(\tau)}$$

where $T - t = \tau$ and we need to solve for the forms of the functions F and G. We know that:

$$P_r = F(\tau)P$$
$$P_{rr} = F(\tau)^2$$
$$P_t = -P_\tau = (-rF' - G')P$$

Substituting these values into the partial differential equation and dividing by the bond price P gives the following:

$$\lambda \sigma F + \frac{1}{2}\sigma^2 F^2 - rF' - G' - r = 0$$

We know from Merton [1970] and the similar equation in Chapter 10 that the solution to this equation is:

$$F(\tau) = -\tau$$
$$G(\tau) = -\frac{\lambda \sigma \tau^2}{2} + \frac{1}{6}\sigma^2 \tau^3$$

and therefore the formula for the price of a zero-coupon bond is given by:

$$P(r, t, T) = P(r, \tau) = e^{-r\tau - (\lambda \sigma \tau^2/2) + (1/6)\sigma^2 \tau^3}$$

This is nearly the same bond pricing equation that we obtained in Chapter 10 under the assumption of parallel shifts in bond prices. It has the same virtues and the same liabilities of the duration approach:

- It is a simple analytical formula;
- Zero-coupon bond prices are a quadratic function of time to maturity;
- Yields turn negative (and zero-coupon bond prices rise above one) beyond a certain point;
- If interest rate volatility σ is zero, zero-coupon bond yields are constant for all maturities and equal to r.

From the Chapter 7 formula for continuous compounding:

$$P(r, \tau) = e^{-y(\tau)\tau}$$

the zero-coupon bond yield formula can be calculated as:

$$y = r + \frac{1}{2}\lambda\sigma\tau - \frac{1}{6}\sigma^2\tau^2$$

The last term in this formula ultimately becomes so large as time to maturity increases that yields become negative. Setting $y' = 0$ and solving for the maximum level of y (the 'hump' in the yield curve) shows that this occurs at a time to maturity of:

$$\tau^* = \frac{3\lambda}{2\sigma}$$

and that the yield to maturity at that point is:

$$y(\tau^*) = r + \frac{3}{8}\lambda^2$$

Note that the peak in the yield curve is independent of interest rate volatility, although the location of this hump is affected by interest rate volatility. As volatility increases, the hump moves to shorter and shorter maturity points on the yield curve. We can also determine the point at which the zero-coupon bond yield equals zero using the quadratic formula. This occurs when the yield curve reaches a time to maturity of:

$$\tau^* = \frac{3\lambda}{2\sigma} + \frac{3}{\sigma}\sqrt{\frac{\lambda^2}{4} + \frac{2r}{3}}$$

The market price of risk is normally expected to be positive, so this formula shows rates will turn negative at a positive term to maturity τ^*.

The price volatility of zero-coupon bonds is given by:

$$\sigma P_r = -\tau\sigma P$$

Another useful tool that we can derive from this term structure model is the percentage change in the price of zero-coupon bonds for small changes in the short rate r. Under the Merton term structure model this sensitivity to r is:

$$r - \text{duration} = -\frac{P_r}{P} = -\frac{-\tau P}{P} = \tau$$

therefore the rate sensitivity of a zero-coupon bond in this model is its time to maturity in years. We label this percentage change 'r-duration' to contrast it with Macaulay's measure of price sensitivity discussed in earlier chapters, where price is differentiated with respect to its continuous yield to maturity. We can calculate the 'r-duration' of coupon-bearing bonds using the same logic. The hedge ratio w given above for hedging of a bond with maturity T_1 with a bond maturing at T_2 is:

$$w = \frac{-P_{1_r}}{P_{2_r}} = -\frac{\tau_1 P_1}{\tau_2 P_2}$$

The Merton term structure model gives us very important insights into the process of deriving a term structure model. Its simple formulas make it a useful expository tool, but the negative yields that result from the formula are a major concern. It leads to a logical question—can we 'extend' the Merton model to fit the actual yield curve perfectly? If so, this, superficially at least, would allow us to avoid the negative yield problems associated with the model. We turn to this task next.

The Extended Merton Model

Ho and Lee [1986] extended the Merton model to fit a given initial yield curve perfectly in a discrete time framework. In this section, we derive the equivalent model using continuous time and the no arbitrage approach of Chapter 10 and the previous section. This basic 'extension' technique is common to all term structure models generally used in major financial institutions. In the extended Merton case, we assume that the short rate of interest is again the single stochastic factor driving movements in the yield curve. Instead of assuming that the short rate r is a random walk, however, we assume that it has a time dependent drift term $a(t)$:

$$dr = a(t)\, dt + \sigma\, dZ$$

As before, Z represents a standard Wiener process that provides random shocks to r; Z has mean zero and standard deviation of one. The instantaneous standard deviation of interest rates is again the constant sigma, which we can scale up and down to fit observable market yields. Appendix 1 shows how to derive zero-coupon bond prices in this model using exactly the same procedures as the previous section. The only difference is that we allow the change in the short-term rate of interest to follow the drift term $a(t)$. When we apply the no arbitrage conditions and derive zero-coupon bond prices, we get the following formula:

$$P(r, t, T) = e^{-r\tau - (\lambda\sigma\tau^2/2) + (1/6)\sigma^2\tau^3 - \int_t^T a(s)(T-s)ds}$$

Note that this is identical to the formula for the zero-coupon bond price in the Merton term structure model with the exception of the last term. The value of the zero-coupon bond is one when $t = T$ as the boundary condition demands.

Like the Merton term structure model, the price volatility of zero-coupon bonds is given by[4]:

$$\sigma P_r = -\tau\sigma P$$

and the percentage change in price of zero-coupon bonds for small changes in the short rate r is:

$$r\text{-duration} = -\frac{P_r}{P} = -\frac{-\tau P}{P} = \tau$$

The behavior of the yield to maturity on a zero-coupon bond in the extended Merton-Ho and Lee model is always consistent with the observable yield curve since the expression for yield to maturity:

$$y(\tau) = r + \frac{\lambda\sigma\tau}{2} - \frac{1}{6}\sigma^2\tau^2 + \frac{1}{\tau}\int_t^T a(s)(T-s)\,ds$$

contains the 'extension term':

$$\text{extension}(\tau) = \frac{1}{\tau}\int_t^T a(s)(T-s)\,ds$$

The function $a(s)$ is chosen such that the theoretical zero-coupon yield to maturity y and the actual zero-coupon yield are exactly the same. The function $a(s)$ is the 'plug' that makes the model fit and corrects for 'model error', which would otherwise cause the model to give implausible results. Since any functional form for yields can be adapted to fit a yield curve precisely,[5] it is

---

[4] We could change the sign of this expression to make it positive since the sign of the Wiener process dZ is arbitrary.

critical in examining any model for plausibility to minimize the impact of this extension term. Why? Because the extension term itself contains no economic content.

In the case of the Ho and Lee model, the underlying model would otherwise cause interest rates to sink to negative infinity, just as in the Merton model. The extension term's magnitude, therefore, must offset the negative interest zero-coupon bond yields that would otherwise be predicted by the model. As maturities get infinitely long, the magnitude of the extension term will become infinite in size. This is a significant cause for concern, even in the extended form of the model. One of the most important attributes of term structure model selection is to find one which best captures the underlying economics of the yield curve so that this extension is minimized for the entire maturity spectrum.

The Vasicek Model

Both the Merton model and its extended counterpart the Ho and Lee model, are based on an assumption about random interest rate movements that imply that, for any positive interest rate volatility, zero-coupon bond yields will be negative at every single instant in time for long maturities beyond a critical maturity τ. The extended version of the Merton model, the Ho and Lee model, offsets the negative yields with an extension factor that must grow larger and larger as maturities lengthen. Vasicek [1977] proposed a model that avoids the certainty of negative yields and eliminates the need for a potentially infinitely large extension factor. Even more importantly, the Vasicek model produces realistic interest rate cycles. Vasicek accomplishes this by assuming that the short rate r has a constant interest rate volatility sigma like the models above, with an important distinction— the short rate exhibits mean reversion around the long-term average level of interest rates, which he calls μ:

$$dr = \alpha(\mu - r)\,dt + \sigma\,dZ$$

The change in the short-term rate of interest r is a function of a 'drift' term and a shock term where:

r is the instantaneous short rate of interest;
α is the speed of mean reversion;
μ is the long-term expected value for r, and;
σ is the instantaneous standard deviation of r.

---

[5] For example, consider this term structure model, where zero-coupon bond yields are a linear function of years to maturity: $y(\tau) = 0.05 + 0.01\tau$. It is clearly a ridiculous model, but it can be made to fit the yield curve exactly in a manner similar to the Ho and Lee model.

Z is the standard Wiener process with mean zero and standard deviation of one, exactly like we have used in the first two examples. The difference from previous models comes in the drift term, which gives this stochastic process its name—the Ornstein-Uhlenbeck process. The drift term in the stochastic process proposed by Vasicek pulls the short rate r back toward μ, so μ can be thought of as the long-term level of the short rate. When the short rate r is above μ, the first term tends to pull r downward since a is assumed to be positive. When the short rate r is below μ, r tends to drift upward. The second term of the stochastic process, of course, applies random shocks to the short rate, which may temporarily offset the tendencies toward mean reversion of the underlying stochastic process. The impact of mean reversion is to create realistic interest rate cycles, with the level of alpha determining the length and 'violence' of rises and falls in interest rates. What are the implications of this model for the pricing of bonds? We derive the zero-coupon bond pricing formula in Appendix 2. The zero-coupon bond pricing formula is an exponential function with two terms, one of which is a function of the short-term rate of interest r:

$$P(r, t, T) = e^{-F(t,T)r - G(t,T)}$$

$$= \exp\left[-rF(\tau) - \left(\mu + \frac{\lambda\sigma}{\alpha} - \frac{\sigma^2}{2\alpha^2}\right)[\tau - F(\tau)] - \frac{\sigma^2 F^2(\tau)}{4\alpha}\right]$$

where the function F is defined in Appendix 2 as:

$$F(t, T) = F(\tau) = \frac{1}{\alpha}\left(1 - e^{-\alpha\tau}\right)$$

The continuously compounded zero-coupon bond yield in the Vasicek model is easy to derive from the compound interest expression given in Chapter 7. We use the definition of function G in Appendix 2:

$$y(\tau) = -\frac{1}{\tau}\ln[P(\tau)] = -\frac{1}{\tau}[-rF(\tau) - G(\tau)]$$

$$= \frac{F(\tau)}{\tau}r + \frac{G(\tau)}{\tau}$$

As time to maturity gets infinitely long, we can calculate the infinitely long zero-coupon bond yield maturity as:

$$y(\infty) = \mu + \frac{\lambda\sigma}{\alpha} - \frac{\sigma^2}{2\alpha^2}$$

This yield to maturity is positive for almost all realistic sets of parameter values, correcting one of the major objections to the Merton term structure model, without the necessity to extend the yield curve with a time dependent drift in the short rate of interest r.

What does duration mean in the context of the Vasicek model? Macaulay defined duration, as we saw in Chapters 9 and 10, as the percentage change in bond prices with respect to (the parallel shift in) yield to maturity in a continuous time context. The parallel shift in the Macaulay model was the single stochastic factor driving the yield curve. In the Vasicek model, the short rate r is the stochastic factor. We define 'r-duration' as above—the percentage change in the price of a bond with respect to changes in the short rate r:

$$r\text{-duration} = \frac{-P_r}{P} = \frac{F(\tau)P}{P} = F(\tau) = \frac{1}{\alpha}\left[1 - e^{-\alpha\tau}\right]$$

This function F is a powerful tool that we can use for hedging in the Vasicek model and its extended version, which we cover in the next section. The hedge ratio necessary to hedge one unit of a zero-coupon bond with a remaining maturity of τ_1 using a bond with remaining maturity of τ_2 is:

$$w = -\frac{P_{1_r}}{P_{2_r}} = -\frac{F(\tau_1)P[\tau_1]}{F(\tau_2)P[\tau_2]}$$

a hedge ratio substantially different from that using the Merton or Ho and Lee models:

$$w = -\frac{\tau_1 P[\tau_1]}{\tau_2 P[\tau_2]}$$

In practical use, it is this difference in hedge ratios that allows us to distinguish between different models. The ability to extend a model, as in the previous section, renders all extendible models equally good in the sense of fitting observable data. In reality, however, the explanatory power of various term structure models can be substantially different. Ultimately, the relative performance of each model's hedge ratios and its ability to explain price movements of traded securities with the fewest parameters are what differentiates the best models from the others. We discuss the testing of interest rate models extensively in Chapter 21.

The stochastic process proposed by Vasicek allows us to calculate the expected value and variance of the short rate at any time in the future s from the perspective of current time t. Denoting the short rate at time t by $r(t)$, the expected value of the short rate at future time s is:

$$E_t[r(s)] = \mu + [r(t) - \mu]e^{-\alpha(s-t)}$$

The standard deviation of the potential values of r around this mean value is:

$$\text{Standard Deviation}_t\,[r(s)] = \sqrt{\frac{\sigma^2}{2\alpha}\left[1 - \exp^{-2\alpha(s-t)}\right]}$$

Because $r(s)$ is normally distributed, there is a positive probability that $r(s)$ can be negative. As pointed out by Black [1995], this is inconsistent with a no arbitrage economy in the special sense that consumers hold an option to hold cash instead of investing at negative interest rates. The magnitude of this theoretical problem with the Vasicek model[6] depends on the level of interest rates and the parameters chosen. In general, it should be a minor consideration for most applications. Very low interest rates in Japan in the last decade, with short rates often under 0.02%, did lead to high probabilities of negative rates using both the Vasicek and extended Vasicek models when sigma was set to match observable prices of caps and floors. Although the price of a floor with a strike price of zero was positive during this period[7], indicating that the market perceived a real probability of negative rates, the best fitting values of sigma for all caps and floors prices indicated a probability of negative rates that was unrealistically large. For most economies, the Vasicek and extended Vasicek models are very robust with wide-ranging benefits from practical use. We discuss alternative models in Chapter 12.

The Extended Vasicek-Hull and White Model

Hull and White [1990] bridged the gap between the observable yield curve and the theoretical yield curve implied by the Vasicek model by extending, or stretching, the theoretical yield curve to fit the actual market data. A theoretical yield curve which is identical to observable market data is essential in practical application, since a model which does not fit actual data will propagate errors resulting from this lack of fit into hedge ratio calculations and valuation estimates for more complex securities. This defeats the entire purpose of the risk management exercise, and it is a contributor to the losses at National Australia Bank, which we discussed in Chapter 1. No sophisticated user would be willing to place large bets on the valuation of a bond option or other derivative security by a model that cannot fit observable bond prices.

---

[6] The same objection applies to the Merton and Ho and Lee models and a wide range of other models that assume a constant volatility of interest rates, regardless of the level of short-term interest rates.

[7] Lehman Brothers was quoting a floor price on six-month yen LIBOR with a three-year maturity and a strike price of zero at one basis point bid, three basis points offered during the fall, 1995.

Hull and White apply the identical logic as the previous section, but they allow the market price of risk term λ to drift over time, instead of assuming it is constant, as in the Vasicek model. If we assume this term drifts over time, what are the implications for the pricing formula for zero-coupon bonds?

Hull and White use the time-dependent drift term in interest rates, theta, where theta in turn depends on a time-dependent market price of risk:

$$\theta(t) = \alpha\mu + \lambda(t)\sigma$$

Hull and White derive the zero-coupon bond price in the Extended Vasicek model using this assumption as shown in Appendix 3:

$$P(r, t, T) = e^{-F(t,T)r - G(t,T)}$$

$$= \exp\left[-rF(\tau) - \int_t^T F(s, T)\theta(s)\,ds \right.$$

$$\left. + \left(\frac{\sigma^2}{2\alpha^2}\right)[\tau - F(\tau)] - \frac{\sigma^2 F^2(\tau)}{4\alpha} \right]$$

The zero-coupon bond price is again an exponential function with two terms, one which is multiplied by the random short-term rate of interest r, and the other which contains the functions F and G. Function F is defined the same way as in the previous section. Function G contains the extension term and is defined in Appendix 3. As in the Vasicek model, the price sensitivity of a zero-coupon bond is given by the formula:

$$r\text{-duration} = \frac{-P_r}{P} = \frac{F(\tau)P}{P} = F(\tau) = \frac{1}{\alpha}\left[1 - e^{-\alpha\tau}\right]$$

This is the same formula as in the regular Vasicek model.

Now that we have completed the process of deriving these models, let's get back to the practical work of risk management—measuring our risk and deciding how to hedge if we are uncomfortable with the risk level that we derive.

An Example of the Hedging Implications of Term Structure Models Compared to the Duration Approach

So far, our discussion in this chapter has been purely theoretical, but the practical implications for hedging a position in the bond or swap market are very powerful. In order to compare the traditional duration approach with the term structure model approach, let's use a practical example. We assume that the current yield curve prevails in the money and bond markets.

As in typical U.S. or Euro currency money markets, we assume that the interest rates for six-month and one-year maturities are stated on an actual/360 day basis. In order to keep the example simple, we assume that there are exactly 182.5 days to maturity on the six-month instrument. Accordingly, the interest that would be paid on a money market instrument with a six-month maturity and the stated 6% coupon would be:

$$\text{Interest} = \frac{\$100 * 0.06 * 182.5}{360}$$

Therefore, the zero-coupon bond price with a six-month maturity can be calculated using the formula:

$$\text{Zero-Coupon Bond Price} = \frac{1}{1 + (\text{Actual Days} * \text{Coupon})/360}$$

The one-year instrument is also assumed to have interest paid only at maturity, like the London interbank offered market, and to have interest quoted on the same 'actual/360' day basis. The zero-coupon bond price is calculated in the same way. All of the other instruments are assumed to be standard semi-annual payment bonds quoted on the U.S. '30/360' day basis.[8] The zero-coupon bond prices associated with each maturity can be calculated recursively using the known zero-coupon bond prices for shorter maturities and the following formula for the price $P[t_n]$ of a zero-coupon bond with maturity t_n:

$$P[t_n] = \frac{1 - (C/2)\left[\sum_{i=1}^{n-1} P[t_i]\right]}{(C/2) + 1}$$

This formula assumes that a 6% coupon, for example, is stated as 0.06 and that it is paid semi-annually on a principal amount of $1. By using this formula, we arrive at the zero-coupon bond prices given above. If the date is not

---

[8] Note that this does *not* mean that interest is calculated on the basis of a 360-day year. A 10% bond would pay two equal coupons of $5 each if the principal was $100, unlike an actual/360 day instrument. The '30/360' is really short-hand, that signifies that accrued interest (which is irrelevant to this example) is divided among 12 months of equal length.

Table 11.1 Observable Market Yield Curve

Years to Maturity	Par Yield	Yield Basis	Zero-Coupon Bond Price
0.5	6.000%	Actual/360	0.970481197
1.0	6.500%	Actual/360	0.938171868
1.5	6.750%	30/360	0.905037929
2.0	7.000%	30/360	0.871034604
2.5	7.500%	30/360	0.830672569
3.0	8.000%	30/360	0.787869301

complete enough to use this recursive formula, we can use one of the yield curve smoothing techniques discussed in Chapter 8.

We now want to answer a very practical question:

How much of the one-year instrument should we sell short (or issue as a liability) in order to hedge the interest rate risk on a $100 position in the three-year bond?

Table 11.1 assumes that all of the instruments currently trade at present values equal to their $100 par values. We will compare three 'duration' formulas:

- Traditional modified duration;
- The Ho and Lee model 'r-duration';
- The Extended Vasicek 'r-duration'.

In Chapter 9, we used the modified duration formula for a semi-annual payment bond with an even payment period to the first coupon payment and n payments remaining.

For both the Ho and Lee and Extended Vasicek models, interest rate risk is measured by 'r-duration', the change in value with respect to changes in the short rate of interest r. For a semi-annual bond with n payments to maturity, the r-duration for the Ho and Lee model is:

$$\text{Ho-Lee } r\text{-duration} = \frac{-\partial NPV/\partial r}{NPV}$$

$$= \frac{(C/2)\sum_{i=1}^{n} t_i P[t_i] + t_n P[t_n]}{NPV}$$

The r-duration for the Extended Vasicek model is:

$$\text{Extended Vasicek } r\text{-duration} = \frac{-\partial NPV / \partial r}{NPV}$$

$$= \frac{(C/2) \sum_{i=1}^{n} F[t_i] P[t_i] + F[t_n] P[t_n]}{NPV}$$

$$F[t_i] = (1/\alpha) \left[1 - e^{-\alpha t_i} \right]$$

The hedge ratio for each duration measure is consistent with the hedge ratios, labeled w above, which we have calculated throughout this chapter. For all three duration measures, the hedge ratio would be calculated as:

$$\text{Hedge Ratio} = \frac{-D_1 V_1}{D_2 V_2}$$

where D_i is the duration instrument for instrument i and V_i is the net present value[9] of one unit of security i. In the current example, V_i is the par value of 100 for each instrument.

Table 11.2 compares the various duration measures in the assumed yield curve environment—the modified duration, Ho and Lee, and Extended Vasicek approach. The Extended Vasicek approach can be calibrated at various speeds of mean reversion (alpha). Using a very low level (0.0001) and a fairly representative level for alpha (0.10), calculate the following duration measures for each instrument:

Table 11.2 Modified Duration, Ho and Lee and the Extended Vasicek Model

Years to Maturity	Modified Duration	Ho-Lee r-duration	Extended Vasicek r-duration for Various Alpha Values	
			0.0001	0.10
0.5	0.4852	0.4998	0.4998	0.4875
1.0	0.9382	0.9844	0.9844	0.9372
1.5	1.4042	1.4514	1.4513	1.3493
2.0	1.8365	1.9004	1.9002	1.7261
2.5	2.2416	2.3242	2.3239	2.0641
3.0	2.6211	2.7221	2.7217	2.3654

[9] Note that here we mean true present value (price + accrued interest), not simple 'price'.

The Ho and Lee duration measures can be calculated as the limit of the Extended Vasicek model's duration measure as alpha approaches zero. We might also ask what alpha values in the Extended Vasicek model are required to match the duration as measured by the modified duration approach. A little iteration produces the matching alphas:

The modified duration approach implies a degree of 'mean reversion', as measured by alpha, which is not consistent across maturities. How different are the hedging implications of these three models?

Using the duration measures given in Table 11.3 and adding the Extended Vasicek measures for alpha of 0.2 and 0.3, gives the following hedge ratios as shown in Table 11.4:

Table 11.3 Alpha Needed To Match Modified Duration

Maturity	Alpha
0.5	0.1188
1.0	0.0977
1.5	0.0440
2.0	0.0340
2.5	0.0291
3.0	0.0256

Table 11.4 Summary of Hedge Ratios

Hedging Three-Year Bond with One-Year Bond

Duration Measure	Amount of 1-year Bond to Hedge \$100 3-year Bond
Modified Duration	279.38
Ho and Lee	276.52
Extended Vasicek	
alpha = 0.0001	276.49
alpha = 0.1000	252.40
alpha = 0.2000	231.89
alpha = 0.3000	214.42

The modified duration approach results in a hedging amount of the one-year bond that is higher than any other model—279.38. We would sell short, or issue 279.38 of the one-year bond to hedge a three-year bond position of 100 under the modified duration measure. The Ho and Lee model indicates a hedge of 276.52, and the Extended Vasicek model indicates hedging amounts ranging from the Ho and Lee value (as alpha approaches zero), and 214.42 when alpha is 0.3. All three models fit the observable yield curve perfectly. Only the Extended Vasicek model, however, can be parameterized to fit actual market conditions by adjusting alpha. Neither the modified duration approach nor the Ho and Lee approach contain an extra degree of freedom that allows this kind of adjustment. This is one of the primary reasons why the Extended Vasicek approach is increasingly popular among practitioners.

Note also that the level of interest rate volatility σ does not impact hedge ratios as long as both the instrument being hedged and the hedging tool come from the same market and are subject to interest rate shocks with the same σ. We will come back to this point in later chapters.

Conclusion

In this chapter we have reviewed four popular term structure models, their derivation, and their use in the hedging of coupon-bearing bonds. A practical example shows that only the Extended Vasicek model is adjustable to reflect the actual sensitivity of the long end of the yield curve to movements in shorter-term interest rates. This allows a precise adjustment of hedges to fit market conditions unique to the sub-market or the country being considered. It also requires care in the choice of this parameter, alpha, for an erroneous choice has significant implications. We return to the parameter estimation problem in Chapter 13 and the implications for term structure model testing in Chapter 21. Suffice to say that in almost every market, a carefully implemented hedging problem using the Extended Vasicek model or richer term structure models, such as the Heath, Jarrow and Morton model, will produce better hedges than models which don't offer the same ability to adjust to local market conditions.

Exercises

For purposes of the exercises, we assume that zero-coupon bond prices have the same values as in Chapter 7. We also assume that today is January 15 2005 and that the prevailing market prices in the government bond market for the following zero-coupon bonds are as follows:

April 15 2005	0.974
October 15 2005	0.949

April 15 2006	0.921
October 15 2006	0.892
April 15 2007	0.862
October 15 2007	0.831
April 15 2008	0.798
October 14 2008	0.763
April 15 2009	0.725

11.1 Assume that we know that alpha is 0.05 and sigma is 0.01 for the Extended Vasicek model which best fits observable derivatives securities prices. What is the r-duration for each of the zero-coupon bonds above?

11.2 What is the volatility of the price of each of the zero-coupon bonds above?

11.3 Using the definition of convexity in Chapter 9, what is the 'r-convexity' of each of the zero-coupon bonds above?

11.4 Given the r-durations of the bonds in Exercise 11.1, how much of the April 15 2009 zero-coupon bonds should be shorted to hedge a position of $3,000 principal amount of the April 15 2008 zero-coupon bonds?

11.5 What is the r-duration of a semi-annual payment bond with a coupon of 6% and a maturity of April 25 2008?

11.6 How much of the April 15 2009 zero-coupon bond should be shorted to hedge a position of $100,000 principal amount of the bond in Exercise 11.5?

11.7 The ABC Bond Index is the key index by which fixed income investment managers' performance is measured, both in terms of risk and return. The index consists of two bonds, an 8% coupon bond due April 15 2008 with principal outstanding of $1,000 and a 5% coupon bond due April 15 2009 with principal outstanding of $2,000. Both bonds pay semi-annually. What is the r-duration of the ABC Bond Index?

11.8 Amalgamated Insurance Company invests the proceeds from life insurance premium payments to match the ABC Bond Index. AIC can borrow or lend an infinite amount of money at the overnight rate of interest. It is currently holding assets in cash of $1 billion dollars. The investment committee of AIC has authorized the chief investment officer to buy the 7% semi-annual bonds maturing April 15 2007 in whatever amount necessary, in combination with overnight lending or borrowing, so the interest rate risk (defined as r-duration) of AIC's portfolio matches the ABC Bond Index. What should the chief investment officer do?

11.9 What values of r, alpha, sigma, mu and the market price of risk
        lambda produce Vasicek model bond prices which best match the
        zero-coupon bond prices in the market? (Hint: use common spread-
        sheet software to minimize the sum of squared errors of estimated
        versus actual zero-coupon bond prices).

11.10 Convert the zero prices given above and the zero prices from the
        best fitting Vasicek model zero prices at the same maturities to con-
        tinuously compounded yields. How much 'extension' (difference in
        yields) is necessary on this particular day?

Appendix 1

Deriving Zero-Coupon Bond Prices in the Extended Merton Model

Ito's lemma gives us the same formula for changes in the value of a zero-
coupon bond P, except for substitution of the slightly more complex
expression for dr:

$$dP = P_r \, dr + \frac{1}{2} P_{rr} (dr)^2 + P_t \, dt$$

$$= P_r [a(t) \, dt + \sigma \, dz] + \frac{1}{2} P_{rr} \sigma^2 \, dt + P_t \, dt$$

We form a no arbitrage portfolio with value W, as in the first section in this
chapter, so that the coefficient of the dZ term is zero. We get the same hedge
ratio as given in the original Merton model:

$$w = \frac{-P_{1_r}}{P_{2_r}}$$

By applying the no arbitrage condition that $dW = rW$, we are led to a no
arbitrage condition closely related to that of the original Merton model:

$$-\lambda = \frac{P_{1_r} a(t) + \frac{1}{2} P_{1_{rr}} \sigma^2 + P_{1_t} - r P_1}{\sigma P_{1_r}} = \frac{P_{2_r} a(t) + \frac{1}{2} P_{2_{rr}} \sigma^2 + P_{2_t} - r P_2}{\sigma P_{2_r}}$$

In the Ho and Lee model, the market price of risk must be equal for any
two zero-coupon bonds with arbitrary maturities T_1 and T_2. In the Ho and Lee
case, the market price of risk again is the fixed income counterpart of the
Sharpe ratio, with expected return on each bond equal to:

$$\text{Drift} = \text{Expected Return} = P_r a(t) + \frac{1}{2} P_{rr} \sigma^2 + P_t$$

Now the value of the zero-coupon bond price P for any given maturity is fixed by the shape of the yield curve which Ho and Lee seek to match perfectly. Our mission in solving the partial differential equation in the Ho and Lee model is to find the relationship between the drift term $a(t)$ and the bond price P. The partial differential equation, which must be solved, comes from rearranging the no arbitrage condition above, and our continued assumption that lambda is constant:

$$P_r[a(t) + \lambda\sigma] + \frac{1}{2}P_{rr}\sigma^2 + P_t - rP = 0$$

which must hold, subject to the fact that the value of a zero-coupon bond must equal one at maturity.

$$P(r, T, T) = 1$$

We use an educated guess to postulate a solution and then see what must be true for our guess to be correct (if it is possible to make it correct). We guess that the solution P is closely related to the Merton model:

$$P(r, t, T) = e^{-r\tau + G(t,T)}$$

We need to find the function G which satisfies the partial differential equation. We take the partial derivatives of P and substitute them into the partial differential equation:

$$P_r = -\tau P$$
$$P_{rr} = \tau^2 P$$
$$P_t = (r + G')P$$

When we substitute these partial derivatives into the partial differential equation and simplify, we get the following relationship:

$$-[a(t) + \lambda\sigma]\tau + \frac{1}{2}\sigma^2\tau^2 + G' = 0$$

We solve this differential equation in G by translating the derivative of G with respect to the current time t (not τ) into this expression:

$$G(t, T) = -\frac{\lambda\sigma\tau^2}{2} + \frac{1}{6}\sigma^2\tau^3 - \int_t^T a(s)(T - s)\, ds$$

Therefore, the value of a zero-coupon bond in the extended Merton-Ho and Lee model is given by the equation:

$$P(r, t, T) = e^{-r\tau - (\lambda\sigma\tau^2/2) + (1/6)\sigma^2\tau^3 - \int_t^T a(s)(T-s)\,ds}$$

Appendix 2

Deriving Zero-Coupon Bond Prices in the Vasicek Model

We use the notation of Chen [1992] to answer this question using the same process as in the Merton and Ho and Lee models. By Ito's lemma, movements in the price of a zero-coupon bond is:

$$dP = P_r\,dr + \frac{1}{2}P_{rr}(dr)^2 + P_t\,dt$$

$$= P_r[\alpha(\mu - r)\,dt + \sigma\,dz] + \frac{1}{2}P_{rr}\sigma^2\,dt + P_t\,dt$$

Using exactly the same no arbitrage argument that we used previously, we can eliminate the dZ term by choosing the hedge ratio necessary to eliminate interest rate risk (which is what dZ represents). The partial differential equation consistent with a no arbitrage bond market in the Vasicek model is:

$$P_r[\alpha(\mu - r) + \lambda\sigma] + \frac{1}{2}P_{rr}\sigma^2 + P_t - rP = 0$$

and, as above, it must be solved subject to the boundary condition that a zero-coupon bond's price at maturity equals its principal amount, one:

$$P(r, T, T) = 1$$

The market price of risk λ is assumed to be constant. As a working assumption, we guess that the zero-coupon bond price has the solution:

$$P(r, t, T) = P(r, \tau) = e^{-rF(\tau) - G(\tau)}$$

where F and G are unknown functions of $\tau = T - t$. If our working assumption is correct, we will be able to obtain solutions for F and G. We know that:

$$P_r = -FP$$

$$P_{rr} = F^2 P$$

$$P_t = (-r F_t - G_t) P$$

By replacing the derivatives of the zero-coupon bond price P in the partial differential equation above and rearranging, we know that the following relationship must hold:

$$r[\alpha F - F_t - 1] + \left[\frac{1}{2} F^2 \sigma^2 - F(\alpha \mu + \lambda \sigma) - G_t \right] = 0$$

This relationship must hold for all values of r, so the coefficient of r must be zero:

$$\alpha F - F_t - 1 = 0$$

We can solve this partial differential equation by rearranging it until we have:

$$\frac{\alpha F_t}{1 - \alpha F} = -\alpha$$

We then take the integral of both sides such that:

$$\int\limits_t^T \frac{\alpha F_t(s, T)}{1 - \alpha F(s, T)} \, ds = - \int\limits_t^T \alpha \, ds$$

Evaluating the integrals on both sides of the equation leaves the relationship:

$$\ln \left[1 - \alpha F(t, T) \right] = -\alpha (T - t)$$

Calculating the exponential of both sides defines F:

$$F(t, T) = F(\tau) = \frac{1}{\alpha} \left(1 - e^{-\alpha \tau} \right)$$

To determine the value of the function G, we must solve the partial differential equation:

$$\frac{1}{2} F^2 \sigma^2 - F(\alpha \mu + \lambda \sigma) - G_t = 0$$

or

$$G_t = \frac{1}{2} F^2 \sigma^2 - F(\alpha\mu + \lambda\sigma)$$

We can calculate that:

$$\int_t^T F(s, T)\, ds = \frac{1}{\alpha}[\tau - F(\tau)]$$

and that

$$\int_t^T F^2(s, T)\, ds = \frac{1}{\alpha^2}[\tau - F(\tau)] - \frac{F^2(\tau)}{2\alpha}$$

We can take the integral of both sides of the equation above to solve for G:

$$\int_t^T G_s(s, T)\, ds = \int_t^T \left[\frac{1}{2} F(s, T)^2 \sigma^2 - F(s, T)(\alpha\mu + \lambda\sigma)\right] ds$$

$$= \frac{1}{2}\sigma^2 \left[\frac{1}{\alpha^2}(\tau - F(\tau)) - \frac{F^2(\tau)}{2\alpha}\right] - \frac{\alpha\mu + \lambda\sigma}{\alpha}[\tau - F(\tau)]$$

$$= \left[\frac{\sigma^2}{2\alpha^2} - \mu - \frac{\lambda\sigma}{\alpha}\right][\tau - F(\tau)] - \frac{\sigma^2}{4\alpha} F^2(\tau)$$

Since

$$\int_t^T G_s(s, T)\, ds = G(T, T) - G(t, T)$$

and since $G(T, T)$ must be zero for the boundary condition that $P(T, T) = 1$,

$$G(t, T) = G(\tau) = \left[\mu + \frac{\lambda\sigma}{\alpha} - \frac{\sigma^2}{2\alpha^2}\right][\tau - F(\tau)] + \frac{\sigma^2}{4\alpha} F^2(\tau)$$

This means that the value of a zero-coupon bond in the Vasicek model is:

$$P(r, t, T) = e^{-F(t, T)r - G(t, T)}$$

$$= \exp\left[-rF(\tau) - \left(\mu + \frac{\lambda \sigma}{\alpha} - \frac{\sigma^2}{2\alpha^2} \right)[\tau - F(\tau)] - \frac{\sigma^2 F^2(\tau)}{4\alpha} \right]$$

Appendix 3

Valuing Zero-Coupon Bonds in the Extended Vasicek Model

The partial differential equation changes only very slightly from the one we used in the third section of this chapter:

$$P_r[\alpha(\mu - r) + \lambda(t)\sigma] + \frac{1}{2}P_{rr}\sigma^2 + P_t - rP = 0$$

subject to the usual requirement that the bond's price equals one at maturity:

$$P(r, T, T) = 1$$

We can rewrite the partial differential equation as:

$$P_r[(\alpha\mu + \lambda(t)\sigma) - \alpha r] + \frac{1}{2}P_{rr}\sigma^2 + P_t - rP = 0$$

and using the definition:

$$\theta(t) = \alpha\mu + \lambda(t)\sigma$$

we can simplify the partial differential equation to the point that it looks almost identical to that of the Ho and Lee model earlier in the chapter:

$$P_r[\theta(t) - \alpha r] + \frac{1}{2}P_{rr}\sigma^2 + P_t - rP = 0$$

As in the third section in this chapter, we assume that the solution to the pricing of zero-coupon bonds takes the form:

$$P(r, t, T) = P(r, \tau) = e^{-rF(\tau) - G(\tau)}$$

where F and G are unknown functions of $\tau = T - t$. Using the partial derivatives of P under the assumption that we have guessed the functional form correctly, we know that the following relationship must hold:

$$r[\alpha F - F_t - 1] + \left[\frac{1}{2}F^2\sigma^2 - F\theta(t) - G_t\right] = 0$$

From Appendix 2, we can prove:

$$F(t, T) = F(\tau) = \frac{1}{\alpha}\left(1 - e^{-\alpha\tau}\right)$$

We now must solve for G given the following equation:

$$G_t = \frac{1}{2}F^2\sigma^2 - F\theta(t)$$

We do this by taking the integral of both sides and making use of the integral of F^2 which was given in Appendix 2 to arrive at the solution for G:

$$G(t, T) = G(\tau) = \int_t^T F(s, T)\theta(s)\,ds - \frac{\sigma^2}{2\alpha^2}[\tau - F(\tau)] + \frac{\sigma^2}{4\alpha}F^2(\tau)$$

Therefore, under the extended Vasicek model, the value of a zero-coupon bond is given by the formula:

$$P(r, t, T) = e^{-F(t,T)r - G(t,T)} = \exp\left[-rF(\tau) - \int_t^T F(s, T)\theta(s)\,ds\right.$$

$$\left. + \left(\frac{\sigma^2}{2\alpha^2}\right)[\tau - F(\tau)] - \frac{\sigma^2 F^2(\tau)}{4\alpha}\right]$$

CHAPTER 12

Alternative Term Structure Models[1]

In Chapter 11, we presented a number of one-factor models of the term structure of interest rates. These models all assume that the term structure we are studying is the risk-free term structure, where the probability of default by the issuer is zero. In this chapter, we consider alternative models that offer a richer array of potential movements in the term structure of interest rates, while preserving the implicit assumption that default will not occur. In Chapters 16–18, we broaden our analysis to include multi-factor models of the yield curve that explicitly incorporate the probability of default. For example, the Shimko, Tejima, and van Deventer extension of the Merton model, which we discuss in Chapter 16, is a two-factor term structure model in the guise of a discussion of the valuation of risky debt. The two risky variables were the short rate of interest r, which drives the risk-free yield curve's movements, and the value of the underlying assets being financed.

There is a very wide variety of alternative term structure models to the basic Vasicek model (and its close relative, the extended Vasicek or Hull and White model) that we have used to illustrate the basic term structure approach to risk management. Each of the alternative models has distinct advantages and disadvantages, which we survey briefly here. The Vasicek family of models has tractability as its greatest strength. The Gaussian nature of interest movements means that a wide range of analytical solutions to the valuation of fixed income securities and derivatives is available, as we will see in later chapters. In Chapter 17, we will study the reduced form credit models of Duffie and Singleton [1999] and Jarrow [1999–2001], both of which are constructed on the Hull and White/Extended Vasicek framework. The ability to use these advanced credit models built upon a simple but powerful random interest rates framework is key to achieving the ability to value the Jarrow-Merton put option as an index of risk that we first introduced in Chapter 1.

---

[1] An earlier version of this chapter appeared as Chapter 18 in van Deventer and Imai [1996].

The strength of the Extended Vasicek model is also its weakness: the model allows for negative interest rates, and historical interest rates in almost all major markets show evidence of a dependence on more than one-factor. These weaknesses of the model vary in importance, depending on the state of the economy. As this book is written, the yen LIBOR rate has been near zero for many years and it doesn't appear likely to rise soon. The standard levels of interest volatility that we have been using throughout this book have ranged from 0.005 to 0.02, and anything in that range would imply a very high probability of negative rates in the Japanese market. While observable interest rate floor prices in yen have traded at a small positive price for a floor at zero, Black's [1995] argument that market participants will use their 'option' to hold cash in order to avoid negative interest rates is a very persuasive one. In today's yen market, a model which does not allow for negative interest rates has significant attractions.

Similarly, the explanatory power of a one-factor model varies with the economy. We show in the next chapter that the one-factor extended Vasicek model has a very good ability to explain 54 simultaneous U.S. dollar swaption prices at a wide variety of strike prices and maturities. Similarly, except for the low level of yen rates, yen yield curve movements have been very well-behaved over a long period of time and a single factor model has great power to model historical movements. Canadian and Australian experience, however, has featured very complex yield curve movements where two or more factors would add realism to a term structure model.

The last decade has seen a burst of innovation in yield curve modeling and the number of approaches is now almost uncountable, ranging from the 'LIBOR market model' popular with interest rate derivatives traders to alternative models popular in the market for mortgage-backed securities. In this chapter, we trace the major types of term structure models that can provide a framework for integrated interest rate risk and credit risk, the major objective of this book.

The second section of this chapter reviews alternative one-factor interest rate models, most of which allow avoidance of negative interest rates. The third section provides an introduction to two-factor models. The fourth section introduces the three-factor model of Chen [1994]. The fifth section briefly reviews the Heath, Jarrow, and Morton approach, and the sixth section summarizes the considerations in term structure model selection.

Alternative One-Factor Interest Rate Models

The Cox, Ingersoll, and Ross (CIR) [1985] model, which the authors derive in a general equilibrium framework, has been as popular in the academic community to the same degree as the Vasicek model has been among financial market participants. It is therefore appropriate that we begin our discussion of one-factor model alternatives to the Vasicek model with a review of the CIR approach.

The CIR model

The Cox, Ingersoll and Ross model has been particularly influential because the original version of the paper was in circulation in the academic community at least since 1977, even though the paper wasn't formally published until 1985. CIR assume that the short-term interest rate is the single stochastic factor driving interest rate movements, and that the variance of the short rate of interest is proportional to the level of interest rates. This has the highly desirable property of preventing negative short rates of interest, and it means that interest rate volatility is higher in periods of high interest rates than it is in periods of low interest rates. The realism of this assumption depends on which financial market is being studied, but casual empiricism would lead one to believe that it's a more desirable property when modeling the U.S. (1978–1985), Brazil, or Mexico than it would perhaps be for Japanese financial markets today.

The authors assume that stochastic movements in the short rate take the form:

$$dr = k(\mu - r)\,dt + \sigma\sqrt{r}\,dz$$

The change in interest rates will have a mean reverting drift term, which causes interest rate cycles, just like the extended Vasicek and Vasicek models. The interest rate shock term has the same volatility as the Vasicek model but it is multiplied by the square root of the short-term rate of interest. CIR show that the value of a zero coupon bond with maturity $\tau = T - t$ takes the form:

$$P(r, \tau) = A(\tau)\,e^{-B(\tau)r}$$

$$A(\tau) = \left[\frac{2\gamma e^{(\gamma+\lambda+k)(\tau/2)}}{g(\tau)}\right]^{(2k\mu)/\sigma^2}$$

$$B(\tau) = \frac{-2(1 - e^{-\gamma\tau})}{g(\tau)}$$

where

$$g(\tau) = 2\gamma + (k + \lambda + \gamma)(e^{\gamma\tau} - 1)$$

$$\gamma = \sqrt{(k + \lambda)^2 + 2\sigma^2}$$

The authors also derive an analytical solution for the price of a European call option on a zero-coupon bond.

In practical application, the CIR model has met with mixed results in spite of the strong theoretical attractiveness of the no-negative-interest-rates feature of the model. Hull and White [1990] note that the extended version of the model, which would exactly fit an observable yield curve, may not fit some yield curve shapes where instantaneous forward rates turn negative. For the reasons noted by Black [1995], this problem normally can be corrected by using the maximum smoothness forward rate technique of Chapter 8, instead of linear smoothing or cubic spline smoothing which can frequently result in negative forward rates.

Flesaker [1993] notes a more serious constraint on practical use: the difficulty of estimating parameters for the CIR model because of the existence of many local optimums. We discuss this topic at some length in the next chapter. Finally, Pearson and Sun [1994] test a two-factor version of the CIR model for nominal interest rates and conclude 'the extended CIR model ... fails to provide a good description of the Treasury market.' The empirical work on term structure models in general is still in its early stages, even after 20 years of research, and we feel that the CIR model deserves to remain a strong candidate for practical use pending testing of the extended version of the model in a widely variety of economic environments.

The Dothan model

Dothan [1978] provides a model of short rate movements where the short-term riskless rate of interest r follows a geometric Wiener process. The short rate has a lognormal distribution and will therefore always be positive:

$$dr = \sigma r \, dz$$

The resulting analytical solution for zero-coupon bond prices is quite complex. The Dothan model, while sharing one of the attractive properties of the CIR model, lacks the 'mean reversion' term which causes interest rate cycles, one of the key features necessary in a realistic term structure model:

$$k(\mu - r)$$

This term's omission makes the Dothan model much less realistic than the CIR or Vasicek models.

The Longstaff model

Longstaff [1989] proposes a model in which the variance of the short rate is proportional to the level of the short rate, like the CIR model, and the mean version of the short rate is a function of its square root:

$$dr = k(\mu - \sqrt{r}) \, dt + \sigma \sqrt{r} \, dz$$

The resulting pricing equation for zero-coupon bonds is very unique in comparison to other term structure models in that the implied yield to maturity on zero-coupon bonds is a non-linear function of the short rate of interest:

A, B, and C are complex functions of the term structure model parameters and are described in Longstaff.

$$P(r, \tau) = A(\tau)e^{B(\tau)r + C(\tau)\sqrt{r}}$$

In empirical tests, Longstaff concludes that the non-linearity of yields does bring additional explanatory power to the model but that '...the actual pricing of even intermediate term discount bonds may be more complex than can be accommodated within the context of a single-state-variable model.'[2]

The Black, Derman, and Toy model

Black, Derman, and Toy [1990] suggest another model which avoids the problem of negative interest rates and allows for time dependent parameters. The stochastic process specifies the percentage change in the short-term rate of interest as a mean reverting function of the natural logarithm of interest rates:

$$d[(\ln(r)] = [\theta(t) - \phi(t)\ln(r)] \, dt + \sigma(t) \, dz$$

The model has many virtues from the perspective of financial market participants. It combines the ability to fit the observable yield curve (like the Ho and Lee and extended Vasicek models) with the non-negative restriction on interest rates and the ability to model the volatility curve observable in the market. The model's liability is the lack of tractable analytical solutions, which are very useful in (a) confirming the accuracy of numerical techniques and (b) valuing large portfolios where speed is essential. We will devote a considerable amount of time to this in Chapter 43, where information technology considerations come to the fore.

The Black and Karasinski model

Black and Karasinski [1991] further refine the Black, Derman, and Toy approach with the explicit incorporation of time-dependent mean reversion:

$$d[(\ln(r)] = \phi(t) [\ln[\mu(t)] - \ln(r)] \, dt + \sigma(t) \, dz$$

This modification allows the model to fit observable cap prices, one of the richest sources of observable market data incorporating interest rate volatility

---

[2] Longstaff [1989], p. 222.

information. The authors describe in detail how to model bond prices and interest derivatives using a lattice approach. The model, like its predecessor the Black, Derman, and Toy model, is quite popular among financial market participants.

Two-Factor Interest Rate Models

As we discuss below, one of the challenges in specifying a two-factor model is selecting which two factors are the most appropriate. In Chapters 16 and 17, we discuss credit models where the two factors of the risky debt term structure model are the riskless short rate of interest and either (a) the value of the asset being financed (in the Shimko, Tejima, and van Deventer extension of the Merton credit model) or (b) a macro factor driving default, as in the Jarrow credit model. In this section, we review a number of two-factor models that are based on various assumptions about the two risky factors which best model a risk-free yield curve.

The Brennan and Schwartz model

Brennan and Schwartz [1979] introduced a two-factor model where both a long-term rate and a short-term rate follow a joint Gauss-Markov process. The long-term rate is defined as the yield on a consol (perpetual) bond. Brennan and Schwartz assume that the log of the short rate has the following stochastic process:

$$d[\ln(r)] = \alpha[\ln(l) - \ln(p) - \ln(r)] dt + \sigma_1 dz_1$$

The short rate r moves in response to the level of the consol rate l and a parameter p relating the "target value" of $\ln[r]$ relative to the level of $\ln(l)$. Brennan and Schwartz show that the stochastic process for the consol rate can be written:

$$dl = l[l - r + \sigma_2^2 + \lambda_2\sigma_2] dt + l\sigma_2 dz_2$$

Lambda in this expression is the market price of long-term interest rate risk. Longstaff and Schwartz proceed to test the model on Canadian government bond data, with good results.

The two-factor CIR model

Chen and Scott [1992] derive a two-factor model in which the nominal rate of interest I is the sum of two independent variables y_1 and y_2, both of which follow the stochastic process specified by CIR:

$$dy_i = k_i(\theta_i - y_i) dt + \sigma_i \sqrt{y_i} dz_i$$

Chen and Scott show that the price of a discount bond in this model is:

$$P(y_1, y_2, t, T) = A_1 A_2 e^{-B_1 y_1 - B_2 y_2}$$

where A and B have the same definition as in the CIR model, with the addition of the appropriate subscripts. The authors go on to value a wide range of interest rate derivatives using this model. The end result is a powerful model with highly desirable properties and a wealth of analytical solutions.

The two-factor Vasicek model

Hull and White [1993] show that there is a similar extension for the Vasicek model when the nominal interest rate *I* is the sum of two factors r_1 and r_2. The value of a zero-coupon bond with maturity *tau* is simply the product of two factors P_1 and P_2 which have exactly the same functional form as the single factor Vasicek model, except that one is driven by r_1 and the other by r_2:

$$V(r_1, r_2, \tau) = P_1(r_1, \tau) P_2(r_2, \tau)$$

Both stochastic factors are assumed to follow stochastic processes identical to the normal Vasicek model:

$$dr_i = \alpha_i (\mu_i - r_i) \, dt + \sigma_i \, dz_i$$

This model, which hasn't yet received the attention from financial market participants that it deserves, seems to offer a great deal of potential because it preserves the simplicity of the original extended Vasicek/Hull-White model while extending its power.

The Longstaff and Schwartz stochastic volatility model

Longstaff and Schwartz [1992] propose a model in which two stochastic factors, which are assumed to be uncorrelated, drive interest rate movements. The factors *x* and *y* are assumed to follow the stochastic processes:

$$dx = (\gamma - \delta x) \, dt + \sqrt{x} \, dz_1$$

$$dy = (\eta - \upsilon y) \, dt + \sqrt{y} \, dz_2$$

The authors demonstrate that both the short-term interest rate *r* and the variance of changes in the short rate *V* are linear functions of *x* and *y*:

$$r = \alpha x + \beta y$$

$$V = \alpha^2 x + \beta^2 y$$

Longstaff and Schwartz derive the value of a discount bond in this economy to be:

$$V(x, y, \tau) = E_1(\tau)\, e^{E_2(\tau)x + E_3(\tau)y}$$

where:

$$E_1(\tau) = A^{2\gamma}(\tau) B^{2\eta}(\tau)\, e^{k\tau}$$

$$E_2(\tau) = (\delta - \Phi)[1 - A(\tau)]$$

$$E_3(\tau) = (\nu - \Psi)[1 - B(\tau)]$$

$$A(\tau) = \frac{2\Phi}{(\delta + \Phi)[e^{\Phi\tau} - 1] + 2\Phi}$$

$$B(\tau) = \frac{2\Psi}{(\nu + \Psi)[e^{\Psi\tau} - 1] + 2\Psi}$$

$$\Phi = \sqrt{2\alpha + \delta^2}$$

$$\Psi = \sqrt{2\beta + \nu^2}$$

$$k = \gamma(\delta + \Phi) + \eta(\nu + \Psi)$$

Longstaff and Schwartz describe procedures for valuing interest rate-related derivatives under this framework in great detail.

Chen's Three-Factor Term Structure Model

As factors are added to a term structure model, it becomes more realistic and more complex. Chen [1994] introduces a three-factor term structure model where the short-term rate of interest is random and mean-reverting around a level which is also random. Moreover, Chen also assumes that the volatility of the short rate is random:

$$dr = k(\theta - r)\, dt + \sqrt{\sigma}\sqrt{r}\, dz_1$$

$$d\theta = \nu(\bar{\theta} - \theta)\, dt + \zeta\sqrt{\theta}\, dz_2$$

$$d\sigma = \mu(\bar{\sigma} - \sigma)\, dt + \eta\sqrt{\sigma}\, dz_3$$

The short rate r is mean reverting around the long run level σ. The volatility of the short rate is written by Chen as σ. The long-term level of interest rates theta is itself random and mean-reverting around a long-term level. The volatility of the short rate is also mean-reverting with a form much like the CIR specification. Chen goes on to derive, with considerable effort, closed-form solutions for this richly-specified model.

Chen's model demonstrates that there is a rich array of choices for financial market participants who require the additional explanatory power of a two- or three-factor model and who are willing to incur the costs, which we discuss below, of such models. Perhaps the richest approach to multi-factor risk management, however, is that of Heath, Jarrow, and Morton, to which we now turn.

The Heath, Jarrow, and Morton Approach

Heath, Jarrow, and Morton, (HJM) [1992] take a dramatically different approach to the selection of the stochastic 'state variables' and at the same time they provide a general framework for the derivation of all term structure models. Almost all of the models discussed both in this chapter and in previous chapters focus on the short rate of interest as a state variable. In the case of the two- and three-factor models in the previous sections, the selection of what the variables actually should be is part of the art of skillful practical application.

The HJM approach to term structure modeling is dramatically different. The current term structure in its entirety, much as Ho and Lee assumed in our discussions in Chapter 11, is the 'state variable'. We know from Chapters 7 and 8 that the term structure can be described analytically by the entire range of zero-coupon bond yields, zero-coupon bond prices, or continuous forward rates, such as the maximum smoothness forward rate curve that we derive in Chapter 8. HJM focus their analysis on forward rates because of the ease of exposition that results. The single factor version of the HJM model says that the change in forward rates as of current time t with maturity at time u can be described by a volatility function, a drift function, and one Wiener process supplying shocks to the term structure:

$$f(t + dt, u) - f(t, u) = \sigma(x, y, z) \, dz + \text{drift}(x, y, z) \, dt$$

The variables x, y, and z represent arbitrary arguments in the volatility and drift functions.

Constant single factor volatility

If the volatility function is a constant, then HJM show that the model reduces to the continuous time limit of the Ho and Lee (extended Merton) model that we discuss in Chapter 11.

Exponentially declining volatility

If the volatility function is chosen such that:

$$\sigma(u - t) = \sigma_0 \, e^{-\alpha(u-t)}$$

then the single-factor version of HJM reduces to the single-factor extended Vasicek/Hull and White model. The two parameters in the equation above have the same volatility and speed of mean reversion implications as in the extended Vasicek discussion in Chapter 11.

CIR version of HJM

The Cox, Ingersoll, and Ross model is shown to be a special case of the HJM approach if the volatility function is a deterministic function g times the square root of spot rate (the forward rate as of time t with maturity t):

$$\sigma(x, y, z) = g(u - t)\sqrt{f(t, t)}$$

Other volatility structures

The richness of the HJM approach stems from the fact that a wide variety of other volatility structures can be chosen to more precisely match either historical or observable volatility of the term structure. This provides a tremendous flexibility in modeling derivatives like caps, floors, and swaptions where the pricing of the derivative is directly tied to interest rate volatility.

Two-Factor HJM modeling

When there is more than one stochastic factor driving evolution of the term structure, the first equation in this section is written instead as:

$$f(t + dt, u) - f(t, u) = \sigma_1(x, y, z)\, dz_1 + \sigma_2(x, y, z)\, dz_2 + \text{Drift}(x, y, z)\, dt$$

As in the single-factor case, the kind of specifications which can be made are almost limitless.

Most of the time (although there are exceptions), the evolution of the term structure in the HJM model is path-dependent, i.e. it depends on the exact history of term structure evolution because, in general, an up-move in rates followed by a down-move in rates does not lead to the same yield curve as the down-up evolution. This means that the use of the bushy tree or monte carlo approaches, which we discuss in later chapters, must be used. As HJM point out, though, there are a number of path-independent variations of HJM as well.

The HJM approach is rapidly becoming the standard method for term structure modeling on Wall Street because of the generality of its application, the realism offered by matching yield curve and volatility structures, and the relatively good speed of numerical solutions based on this approach. For a very thorough and readable discussion of the implementation of this approach, see Jarrow [1996].

Term Structure Model Selection

The selection of a term structure model is more than a model choice. Choosing the number of factors and a specific model almost inevitably implies a given degree of accuracy in parameter estimation and restricts the user to a specific numerical technique for security valuation. For example,

- Selecting a two-factor HJM model usually restricts the user to a bushy tree solution of American option valuation and will produce parameters with less individual statistical significance than the parameters in a single-factor model.
- Selecting the Black-Karasinski model means that no analytical solutions are available and that both parameter estimation and hedging will depend on a binomial or trinomial tree.
- Selecting the single-factor extended Vasicek model maximizes speed and the availability of analytical solutions, at some cost in realism of term structure movements.

The choice of a model, then, can't be unbundled from the resulting requirements for parameter estimation and the requisite numerical solutions.

For this reason, it is not necessarily true that more stochastic factors will improve the quality of the valuation and hedging of a particular security. Back-testing and out-of-sample testing are necessary to compare the joint hypothesis of Model A/Parameter Estimation Approach A/Numerical Technique A with Model B/Parameter Estimation Approach B/Numerical Technique B.

In general, we can make the following observations regarding the practical use of alternative term structure models:

- Models with mean reversion work better in practice than models without mean reversion.
- Numerical techniques produce deltas and gammas of much lower quality than analytical techniques. The rDelta[3] that result from numerical techniques have a 'stair-step' nature that can't be avoided except by dramatically increasing the number of time steps used.
- Models with few analytical solutions require more processing time. While they may have theoretical attractions, some of the net 'theory benefits' will be offset by the inaccuracy induced by a user who must summarize transaction data to reduce runtime. Net-net, the lower quality theory, applied to each record individually, can produce a better answer in many circumstances than higher quality theory applied to aggregated data. Consider two five-year caps, one at a 9% strike and the other at an 11%

---

[3] The first derivative of the security's value with respect to the short rate of interest, as discussed in Chapter 11.

strike. An analyst who adds them together and uses an average strike of 10% to get his high-powered term structure model's calculation time down will get a much lower quality answer than one who doesn't.[4]

- Reducing the number of time steps when evaluating an American option to improve calculation time results in dramatic errors. A 30-year callable mortgage with 360 possible call dates has a much different value than a 30-year mortgage with 20 call dates. A three-factor model using a bushy tree approach with 20 time steps will produce a less accurate answer than a one-factor model assuming 100 time steps.

- Historical parameter estimation produces lower quality parameter estimates if there are a lot of parameters because of multi-colinearity. For example, the Brennan and Schwartz two-factor model, which is based on a long rate and a short rate, is very inaccurate in the yen market in practical use not because of problems with the theory, but because multi-colinearity in the regression analysis can render the parameter estimates statistically insignificant.

- Models which contain true economic meaning outperform models which are purely based on historical data with no underlying meaning, all other things being equal. For example, a model which explains term structure movements on the basis of movements in the real rate of interest, inflation, and the value of the underlying risky asset being financed, will almost always outperform a model based on changes in the level, slope and bend in the yield curve.

Which two factors?

In focusing on two-factor models with true economic meaning, we ask the question which two factors are the most important. The answer would normally include the following factors:

- The short real rate of interest;
- The long real rate of interest;
- The instantaneous rate of inflation;
- The long-term expected level of inflation;
- The instantaneous credit spread;
- The long-term expected credit spread;
- The value of the asset being financed;
- The parallel shift in the yield curve;
- The spread between the short rate and the long rate;
- The instantaneous default intensity (probability of default over a short time interval).

---

[4] This happens every day in every major bank around the world.

The best choice of factors will depend on the problem at hand, and the proof of which choice is 'best' will have to be based on more than logic alone.

As market participants ourselves, the authors believe that a competition between two alternative joint choices of models/parameters/numerical techniques can only be resolved by extensive historical and out-of-sample testing of hedging accuracy, since almost all models can fit observable data well. We analyze this in Chapter 21.

Exercises

For purposes of Exercises 12.1–12.4, assume the Cox, Ingersoll and Ross term structure model parameters are as follows:

$$\mu = 0.12$$

$$k = 0.08$$

$$\sigma = 0.015$$

$$\lambda = 0.01$$

12.1 What is the price of zero-coupon bonds with maturities of one, two, and three years in the CIR model?

12.2 How different are these prices from the prices that would prevail in the Vasicek model if all of the parameters had the same values?

12.3 What is the rDelta in the CIR model?

12.4 Assume you own two-year zero-coupon bonds with a face value of $100. You are concerned about 'model risk', so you want to hedge your exposure with a hedge that involves equal market values of the one-year zero-coupon bond and the three-year zero-coupon bond (assume that there is no liquidity in the two-year maturity). Using the CIR model, what should the proper hedge amount be in the one-year and three-year bonds to eliminate the interest rate risk of your position?

For purposes of Exercises 12.5–12.10, assume that the two-factor Vasicek model applies. We assume that risk factor one is the riskless rate of interest and that risk factor two is the credit spread on bonds issued by the major New Jersey investment banking firm Golden, Spats & Co. We assume parameter values for risk factor one are:

$$\mu = 0.09$$

$$k = 0.1$$

$$\sigma = 0.015$$

$$\lambda = 0.01$$

We assume the parameters for risk factor two, the credit spread,[5] are

$$\mu = 0.02$$

$$k = 0.05$$

$$\sigma = 0.002$$

$$\lambda = 0.001$$

12.5 What would zero-coupon bond prices be for Golden, Spats at one year and one and a half years?

12.6 What would be the price of a one-year forward contract on an 18-month GS&Co. zero-coupon bond?

12.7 What are the rDeltas in this specification of a two-factor Vasicek model for (a) the riskless rate of interest and (b) the credit spread?

12.8 Assume that GS&Co. has issued you, Metropolis Life Insurance Company, $100 principal amount of the one-year forward on the 18 month GS&Co. zero-coupon bond at an exercise price of $90. You can hedge this position only with a one-year bond and a two-year bond, the only maturities where there is liquidity in GS&Co. zero-coupon bonds. How much of each bond should you use to hedge?

12.9 What concerns would you have in using this specification of a risky debt model?

---

[5] These parameter estimates are hypothetical and are not based on actual data.

CHAPTER 13

Estimating the Parameters of Term Structure Models[1]

In Chapter 11, we discussed the single-factor term structure models that are the foundation for the modern credit models of Jarrow and Turnbull [1995], Duffie and Singleton [1999], and Jarrow [1999, 2001]. As we noted in Chapter 12, these single factor term structure models and the multi-factor credit models associated with them are essential for the algebraic ('closed form') valuation of the complex instruments that we discuss in the remainder of this book. As we noted in Chapter 12, we need to maximize the use of algebraic solutions over numerical solutions because of their advantages in speed, accuracy and quality of implementation in large systems. This is a point we return to in Chapter 43 on information technology considerations.

That being said, we also use term structure models for simulating future environments. After future environments have been created, we have the real option to do valuation in two ways—to use the same term structure model that created the environment for valuation, or to use a simpler term structure model that has algebraic valuation capabilities that are faster, given the simulated yield curve. The world's most sophisticated financial institutions do both. For either purpose, we need to have the ability to estimate the parameters of the term structure models that we are going to employ. We turn to that task in a practical way in this chapter.

Introduction to Term Structure Model Parameter Estimation

Many discussions of the use of term structure models in risk management overlook the real difficulties of estimating the parameters for use in such models. Market participants have become used to the idea of estimating parameters from observable market data as a result of the popularity of the

---

[1] An earlier version of this chapter appeared as Chapter 19 in van Deventer and Imai [1996].

Black-Scholes option pricing model and the accepted market practice of estimating volatility for use in the model from market option prices. 'Implied volatility' is the value of volatility in the Black-Scholes model, which makes the theoretical price equal to the observable market price. The same basic concepts are just as necessary, but harder to do, in a term structure model context for reasons we explain in this chapter. In the first part of this chapter, we base our comments on a data set that includes 2,320 days of Canadian Government Bond data provided by a major Canadian financial institution. The data spanned the time period January 2 1987 to March 6 1996. Thereafter, we turn to U.S. swaption data provided by one of the leading New York derivatives dealers.

Figure 13.1 Historical Movements in Canadian Government Bond Rates, 1987–1996

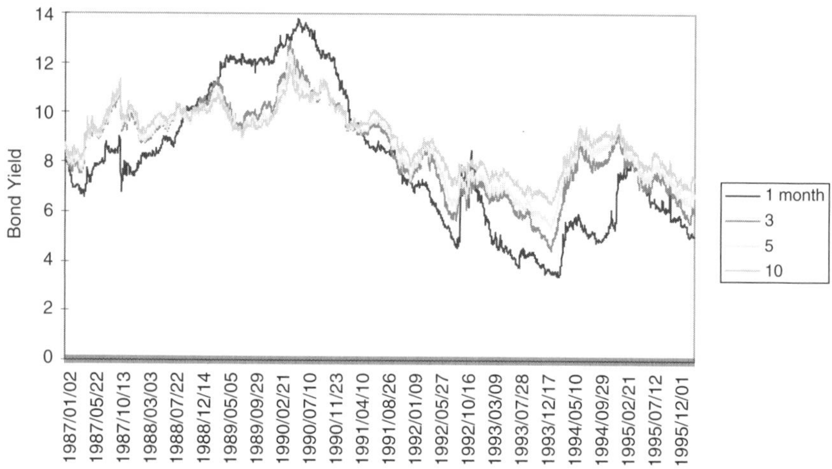

Estimation procedures for term structure models have not progressed as rapidly as the theory of the term structure itself, and leading edge practice is undergoing rapid change. In the view of the authors, there is a hierarchy of approaches of varying quality for determining the appropriate parameters. In this chapter, we follow a number of approaches:

1. *Traditional academic approach*, following theory precisely to estimate the stochastic process for the short-term riskless rate of interest, in this case the one-month Canadian government bill yield. This approach is generally not satisfactory in any market and we found it to be unsatisfactory on Canadian data as well.

2. *Volatility curve approach*, matching parameters to the historical relative volatilities of bond yields at different maturities. This approach worked moderately well.

3. *Advanced historical volatility approach*, in which we used a two step process to (a) fit relative yield changes on all 2,320 days based on the

theoretical relationship between the short rate and longer term yields by regression analysis, and then (b) fit term structure model parameters to the regression coefficients.

4. *Single day yield curve fitting*, which is the yield curve equivalent of implied volatility using the Black-Scholes model.

5. *Option-based derivative price fitting*, which the authors feel is the most satisfactory method in markets that have a rich array of option-related derivatives prices.

We discuss each of these methods in turn.

Traditional Academic Approach

In this section, we focus on the process we would use for a single-factor term structure model for expository purposes, but a very similar approach would be used for a multi-factor term structure model. Almost all single factor term structure models assume that the sole random factor driving interest rates is the short-term rate of interest.[2] Each term structure model assumes a particular formula for these random movements. In the Vasicek model, this formula is:

$$dr = \alpha(\mu - r)\,dt + \sigma\,dz$$

where alpha is the speed of 'mean reversion', μ is the constant long-term expected value of the short-term rate, and sigma is interest rate volatility, as explained in Chapter 11. In the extended Vasicek or Hull and White model, the μ term is not constant—it varies over time, but it is not random. The market price of risk, the fixed income equivalent of the Sharpe ratio, is the fourth parameter in the Vasicek model. The traditional academic approach estimates these parameters by running the regression equation:

$$\Delta r = A + Br + \varepsilon$$

using the shortest observable interest rate as a proxy for r (which is an instantaneous interest rate according to the theory). In the Vasicek model, the theoretical parameters can be related to the regression parameters since:

$$\alpha = -B$$

and

$$\mu = -\frac{A}{B}$$

---

[2] The duration term structure model of Chapter 10 is an exception.

For an example of an elegant analysis of a number of theoretical models' parameters, see Chan, Karolyi, Longstaff and Sanders [1992]. The latter study, while carefully done, suffers from the typical outcome of such studies—in no case does the assumed stochastic process explain more than 3% of the variation in the short-term rate of interest. We find the same problem when running the above regression on 2,320 days of data using the one-month Canadian bill rate as the short rate proxy. The regression equation has literally zero explanatory power (an R^2 of 0.0007) and neither A nor B are statistically significant. Therefore we conclude that this approach is not useful in the Canadian market. The following scatter diagram informally confirms the lack of correlation between the level of interest rates and the change in the level of the short rate. The Vasicek model would have led us to expect a negative correlation, since alpha is a positive number.

Figure 13.2 Change in One-Month Canadian Treasury Bill Rate versus Level of One-Month Rate, 1987–1996

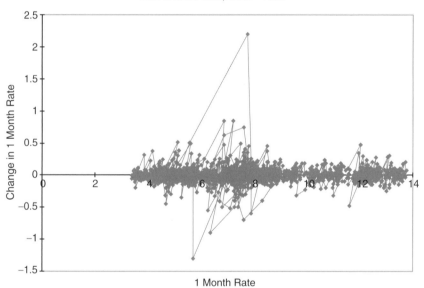

In almost all major markets, this approach leads to similar results. The short rate is often the control mechanism for monetary policy and thus reflects a much more complex set of variables than one equation can capture. This is one of the motivations for the multi-factor term structure models discussed in Chapter 12 and the multi-factor simulation approaches we also discussed in that chapter.

In Chapter 21, we apply the techniques of model testing common in credit risk analysis to U.S. interest rates, so this is a topic we will revisit.

Volatility Curve Approach

Many market participants use parameter estimates that are consistent with the historical relative degree of volatility of longer-term 'yields' in relationship to the short rate. Under the Vasicek and Extended Vasicek models, the volatility of zero-coupon bond yields is:

$$\text{Var}\,[y(\tau)] = f(\tau)^2\sigma^2$$

where:

$$f(\tau) = \frac{1 - e^{-\alpha\tau}}{\alpha\tau}$$

since zero-coupon yields in both versions of the model can be written as linear functions of the short rate r:

$$y(\tau) = f(\tau)r + g(\tau)$$

Therefore, market participants calculate observable variances for bond yields[3] and then choose values of sigma and alpha which best fit historical volatility. The most precise method for doing this is to use the advanced yield curve smoothing techniques of Chapter 8 to calculate zero-coupon continuous yields at all of the key maturities for all of the observation dates. The method chosen for yield curve smoothing does have an impact on the term structure model parameters estimated, so yield curve smoothing has an importance above and beyond the yield curve itself. Here, we take a short cut and illustrate the process by par bond coupon rates as proxies for zero-coupon bond yields. We take the following approach:

1. Collect yield volatilities for various maturities. For Canada, these maturities are one month, two months, three months, six months, and then one, two, three, four, five, seven, 10 and 25 years.
2. Estimate initial values for the speed of mean reversion and interest rate volatility. Typical guesses would be 0.10 for alpha and 0.01 (which is 1%) for interest rate volatility.
3. Use enterprise risk management software or a spreadsheet to calculate by iteration the best fitting values for alpha and sigma given the yield volatilities and initial guesses of parameter values.

The results of this analysis for Canada are summarized in Table 13.1:

---

[3] Market participants often take the short cut of approximating zero-coupon yields by the par bond coupon levels at each maturity, the same approach we take here in the interest of brevity. This simplification leads to some error and we recommend the precise calculation of zero yields via yield curve smoothing.

Table 13.1 Variance in Canadian Government Interest Rates (January 2 1987 to March 6 1996: Interest Rates and Variance are in Percent)

| | Canadian Treasury Bills | | | | | Canadian Government Bond Years to Maturity | | | | | | |
	1 month	2 months	3 months	6 months	1 year	2	3	4	5	7	10	25
Actual Variance	7.677	8.346	7.433	6.842	6.529	3.880	3.044	2.623	2.237	1.909	1.471	0.996
Estimated Variance	7.943	7.745	7.552	7.008	6.051	4.564	3.496	2.717	2.143	1.389	0.794	0.140
Error	−0.266	0.602	−0.119	−0.166	0.478	−0.684	−0.452	−0.095	0.094	0.520	0.677	0.856
Squared Error	0.071	0.362	0.014	0.028	0.228	0.468	0.204	0.009	0.009	0.270	0.458	0.732

Best Fitting Parameter Values:

Alpha $\quad$ 0.305172

Sigma $\quad$ 2.854318%

Maturity Tau	0.083333	0.166667	0.25	0.5	1	2	3	4	5	7	10	25

The best fitting alpha value was 0.305. This is a fairly large speed of mean reversion and reflects the relatively large variation in short-term Canadian rates, relative to long-term rates, over the sample period. Interest rate volatility was also high at 0.0285. At the current low levels of Canadian interest rates, this volatility level would clearly be too high. Comparable figures for the U.S. swap market, based on a fit to 54 swaptions prices, which we discuss in a later section, were a speed of mean reversion of 0.05379 and an interest rate volatility of 0.01369. With the prevalence of low interest rates around the world in recent years, the values of both the speed of mean reversion and interest rate volatility continue to fall.

Advanced Volatility Curve Approach

In the previous section, we derived parameters for a single-factor term structure model. A more flexible approach takes the linear relationship between the short rate and zero-coupon bond yields that would be consistent with a one-factor model, but we actually test whether the single factor model is in fact 'true'. We use the relationship between zero yields at any maturity and the short rate:

$$y(\tau) = f(\tau)r + g(\tau)$$

for any given maturity τ. We then fit a linear regression equation of the form:

$$dy(\tau) = A(\tau) + B(\tau)\,dr$$

to yields at a given maturity τ. We then run this regression equation for zero yields of various maturities. Of course A and B will be different for each maturity as theory predicts. We know that:

$$B(\tau) = f(\tau)$$

so, after getting estimates of B for n different maturities over a historical data period, we can then find the values of alpha which produce the best fit to the observed values of B. For the Canadian market, we performed a regression of par bond coupon yields (as proxies for zero-coupon bond yields) on the one-month Canadian Government bill rate. The results of these regressions showed a higher implied mean reversion speed at shorter maturities:

The best fitting alpha at three years was a very high 1.00921. At 25 years, the alpha at 0.296 is much more consistent with the historical variances reported in the previous section. Table 13.2 provides a strong clue that a multi-factor model would add value (assuming there are no other problems, such as parameter estimation and the valuation of American options, that are strong disadvantages of multi-factor models) in the Canadian market. This is true of most markets where recent interest rate fluctuations have been large and where current rate levels are near historical lows.

Table 13.2 Implied Speed of Mean Reversion by Historical Sensitivity to Movements in the Canadian Treasury Bill Rate, 1987–1996
Yield $= m *$ short rate $+ b$

	3-Year Bond Yield	10-Year Bond Yield	25-Year Bond Yield
Coefficient of Short Rate	0.31430	0.17709	0.13505
Standard Error	0.01960	0.01573	0.01349
t-score	16.03177	11.26116	10.01270
R^2	0.09985	0.05189	0.04422
Best Fitting Alpha	1.00921	0.56275	0.29600

Implied Parameters from an Observable Yield Curve

Most market participants feel more comfortable basing analysis on parameter values implied from observable securities prices than on historical data *when observable prices are sufficient for this task*. For example, if the only observable data is the yield curve itself, we can still attempt to fit the actual data to the theory by maximizing the goodness of fit from the theoretical model. In many markets around the world, the yield curve itself *is* the only observable interest rate 'derivative'. In the Vasicek model, as explained in previous chapters, the price of a zero-coupon bond is given by the relationship:

$$P(\tau) = e^{-F(\tau)r - G(\tau)}$$

where:

$$F(\tau) = \frac{1}{\alpha}\left[1 - e^{-\alpha\tau}\right]$$

$$D = \mu + \frac{\sigma\lambda}{\alpha} - \frac{\sigma^2}{2\alpha^2}$$

$$G(\tau) = D[\tau - F(\tau)] + \frac{\sigma^2}{4\alpha}F(\tau)^2$$

and μ is the long-term expected value of the short rate, λ is the market price of risk, and α and σ are the speed of mean reversion and the level of interest rate volatility. In the extended Vasicek (Hull and White) model, only alpha and sigma are explicitly identified. Zero-coupon bond prices have the form:

$$P(\tau) = e^{-F(\tau)r - G(\tau) - H(\tau)}$$

where *H* is a 'plug' which forces the theoretical model to fit the observable data correctly.

We want the model we estimate to have the maximum goodness of fit, which means that we want to minimize the 'extension' in the extended Vasicek model. This is consistent with our stress on the underlying economic logic of the factors we could select in the multi-factor term structure model discussion in Chapter 12. This prejudice means we want to minimize the value of the function *H* over the yield curve range we are fitting. We do this by creating the best fitting Vasicek yield curve and allowing calculation of the function *H* at a later stage. We have four unknowns in the Vasicek model. To maximize goodness of fit, we can pull a large number of zero-coupon bond prices from the observable yield curve using the yield curve smoothing techniques of Chapter 8 and try to find the parameters which fit the observable yield curve as well as possible.

In first class derivatives software, the authors feel strongly that it is essential to have access to a sophisticated, non-linear regression package to estimate the parameters. For purposes of this section, we have used simple spreadsheet software to better illustrate the process of estimation. Because the simple spreadsheet software lacks the power of the approach used by the best non-linear regression routines, we have arbitrarily set the market price of risk to zero and the long-term expected value of the short rate $r(\mu)$ to equal the 10-year bond yield. We then find the best fitting alpha and sigma. The quality of the result depends on whether the shape of the yield curve on that day happens to be very similar to that which the Vasicek model would imply. This is a common conclusion, as pointed out by the former head of derivatives research at Merrill Lynch (see Flesaker [1993]), and one of the reasons why market participants often feel compelled to supplement current yield curve data with historical parameter data.

To illustrate the yield curve fitting approach, we took yield curve data for the beginning, middle, and end of the data set and we picked the days for which the 10-year Canadian government bond yield reached its highest and lowest points. We used maturities at one month, six months, two, three, four, five, seven, and 10 years so that we could use the same input data for all five of the dates chosen. The results of this analysis, using simple spreadsheet software to obtain parameters, were as follows:

Table 13.3 Best Fitting Parameters for Selected Yield Curves

Canadian Government Bond Market
Extended Vasicek Model
Using Common Spread Sheet Non-Linear Equation Solver

	Extended Vasicek Parameters at Various Points in Rate Cycle Using Common Spread Sheet Non-Linear Equation Solver				
Environment	**Date Beginning**	**Highest Rates**	**Data Mid-Point**	**Lowest Rates**	**Date Ending**
Date	January 2 1987	April 19 1990	August 1 1991	January 28 1994	March 6 1996
Mean Reversion	0.01462	0.25540	0.62661	0.70964	0.58000
Volatility	0.00000	0.05266	0.00000	0.00000	0.00100
Market Price of Risk	0.00000	0.00000	0.00000	0.00000	0.00000
Long-Term R	0.08730	0.11950	0.09885	0.06335	0.07600
Estimate Quality	**Low**	**Medium**	**Low**	**Low**	**Low**

Note: Spreadsheet solver capabilities are limited. Market Price of Risk and Long-term Expected Short Rate were arbitrarily set to Displayed Values with Optimization on Speed of Mean Reversion and Volatility

The results were consistent with other approaches in generally showing a high degree of mean reversion. The lack of power in spreadsheet non-linear equation-solving is reflected in the low or zero values for interest rate volatility and illustrates the need for *other data* (caps, floors, swaptions, bond options prices, etc.) and more powerful techniques for obtaining these parameters. We found common spreadsheet packages could not obtain a reasonable solution for March 6 1996 with two unknowns due to the straightness of the yield curve. In the Cox, Ingersoll, and Ross model, which we discussed in Chapter 12, it is the authors' experience that the problem of local optimums is much more serious than it is with the Vasicek model. Even using a powerful non-linear regression technique, we found that it was not possible to converge to a solution for Cox, Ingersoll, and Ross parameters on 40% of 848 observations in the yen swap market on which we tested the Cox, Ingersoll, and Ross model. In the Vasicek model, it is important to take care in modeling the situation in which alpha approaches zero. This is a frequent cause of failed parameter estimates, particularly when using common spreadsheet software.

The Best Approach: Fitting Parameters to Volatility-Sensitive Instruments

Given these results, we think it is essential to use parameters estimated from observable caps, floors, and swaptions data (or other option-related securities prices[4]) to the extent it is available. These are the market instruments most sensitive to interest rate volatility. Using these instruments is also consistent with the equity market practice of implying stock price volatility from observable prices on options on common stock.

To illustrate the power of this approach in the interest rate derivatives market, we turn now to U.S. dollar data on European swaption prices observable in August 1995.[5] At the time the data was obtained, there were 54 observable swaption prices. A swaption, as discussed earlier, gives the holder the right to initiate a swap of predetermined maturity and fixed-rate level on an exercise date in the future. We estimated extended Vasicek model parameters by

---

[4] In the U.S. market, there are a fairly large number of callable U.S. Treasury securities whose prices provide some guide to interest rate volatility. When rates are infinitely high, the value of the call option is zero, therefore the power to extract parameter estimates is greatest when bond prices trade roughly in the range between 95 and par value. Also in the U.S. market, there are more than 400 callable U.S. agency securities, which may actually provide the richest source of information on term structure model parameters for a nearly risk-free yield curve.

[5] The data used in this section was provided by one of the largest U.S. dollar swap dealers in the world.

choosing the speed of mean reversion (alpha) and interest rate volatility (sigma) which minimized the sum of the squared errors in pricing these 54 swaptions.[6] The 'price' of the swaption was obtained by converting the Black-Scholes volatility quotation for the swaption price to the percentage of notional principal that the equivalent dollar swaption price represented. The exercise periods on the swaptions were six months, one, two, three, four, and five years. The underlying swap maturities were six months, one, two, three, four, five, six, seven, and 10 years. Figure 13.3 shows the relative pricing performance of swaptions with a six-month exercise period for all nine observable maturities.

Figure 13.3 Market European Swaption Prices versus Extended Vasicek Estimated Prices, U.S. Dollars, August 1995, Swaption Exercise Period: 6 Months

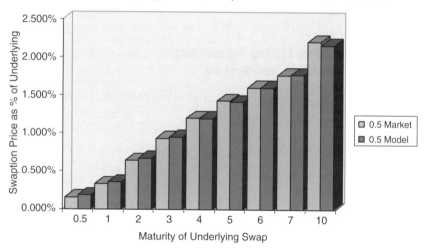

The largest absolute mispricing error of the six-month swaptions was five basis points. The market price of a 10-year swaption was 2.21% of notional principal, compared to a model price of 2.16%. For swaptions with a one-year exercise period, the fit was also excellent, as shown in the Figure 13.4.

The largest mispricing was at seven years, where the model indicated 2.39% as the price versus an actual of 2.23% of notional principal. For swaptions of two years in exercise price, the performance was better still.

------

[6] Note that another criterion could have been to select the parameters which minimized the sum of the squared percentage error in pricing the swaptions.

Figure 13.4 Market European Swaption Prices versus Extended Vasicek Estimated Prices, U.S. Dollars, August 1995, Swaption Exercise Period: 1 Year

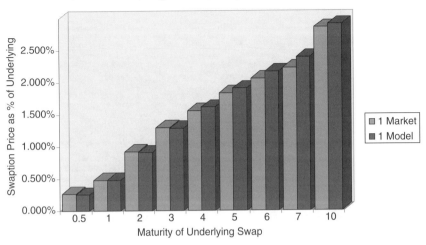

Figure 13.5 Market European Swaption Prices versus Extended Vasicek Estimated Prices, U.S. Dollars, August 1995, Swaption Exercise Period: 2 Years

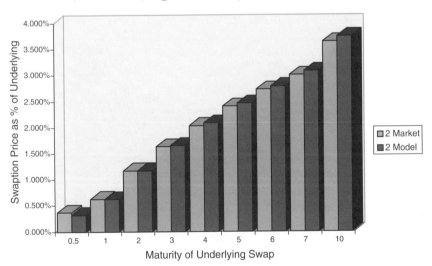

The largest mispricing for a two-year exercise period was 10 basis points of notional principal (a model price of 3.74% versus true market price of 3.64%). The three-year results indicated a maximum error of only six basis points at seven years (model price of 3.42%, compared to 3.36% in reality).

Figure 13.6 Market European Swaption Prices versus Extended Vasicek Estimated Prices, U.S. Dollars, August 1995, Swaption Exercise Period: 3 Years

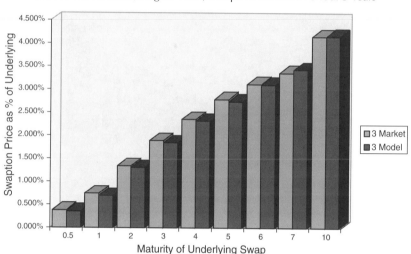

For four-year swaptions, the maximum error was 16 basis points at four years (3.03% market price compared to a 2.87% model price).

Figure 13.7 Market European Swaption Prices versus Extended Vasicek Estimated Prices, U.S. Dollars, August 1995, Swaption Exercise Period: 4 Years

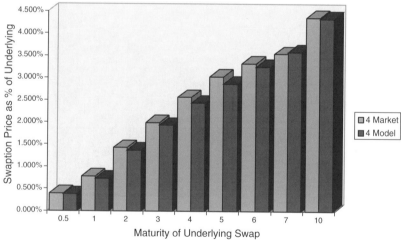

The five year results were also good, with a worst-case error of 15 basis points at seven years due to a model price of 3.63% compared to a true market value of 3.48%.

Overall, the extended Vasicek model's performance was very good. The average model error was literally zero basis points with a mean absolute error

Figure 13.8 Market European Swaption Prices versus Extended Vasicek Estimated Prices, U.S. Dollars, August 1995, Swaption Exercise Period: 5 Years

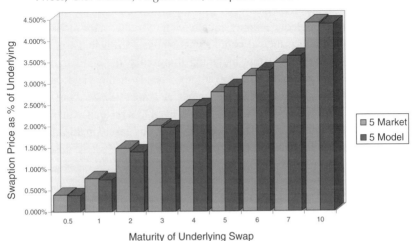

of five basis points of notional principal, even though only two parameters (in addition to the current yield curve) were used to price 54 securities. Compare this to the Black model for commodity futures, which is often used for swaptions and caps and floors pricing. The Black model required 54 different implied volatility values to match actual market prices, even though the model in theory assumes that one volatility parameter should correctly price all 54 swaptions. Volatilities in the Black model ranged from 0.13 to 0.226, a very wide range that should indicate the need for caution to swaption market participants regarding the use of the Black model, results of the 'LIBOR market' term structure model notwithstanding.

In summary, the extended version of the Vasicek model, when applied to swaption prices, proved two things:

- Swaptions provide a rich data set with good convergence properties that allow market participants to use even common spreadsheet software to obtain high quality term structure parameter estimates.
- The accuracy of the extended Vasicek model, using only two parameters held constant over 54 swaptions, is far superior to that of the Black commodity futures model in predicting actual market prices.

Moreover, if we allow interest rate volatility to vary by swaption quote, we get results that match the market perfectly while varying by less than implied volatilities using the Black commodity model. In estimating term structure parameters, the lesson is clear. A rich data set of current prices of securities with significant optionality are necessary to provide an easy-to-locate global optimum for almost any popular term structure model.

Parameter Estimation for Multi-Factor Models

While we have focused on parameter estimation for single factor models in this chapter, the same procedures apply equally well to multi-factor models. Market participants often add principal components analysis to their list of parameter estimation options (with factors including things like the short rate, the long rate/short rate spread, and a measure of the 'bend' in the yield curve). This approach is practical and popular but comes at a cost—since there is no economic rationale for factors like 'bend', there is even less assurance than usual that the future will be like the past. This means simulations based on this kind of popular but ad hoc model have to be taken with more than the usual 'dose of salt'.

Exercises

13.1 Assume that the historical zero-coupon bond yield variance (in percentage form) have been the following:

1 year:	4.25%
2 years:	3.54%
3 years:	3.23%
5 years:	2.75%
7 years:	2.13%
10 years:	1.95%

What are the best fitting values of sigma and alpha in the Vasicek model?

13.2 Assume that regressions of the zero-coupon bond yield on the short-term rate of interest have produced the following values:

1 year:	0.74
3 years:	0.52
5 years:	0.36
7 years:	0.24
10 years:	0.16

What are the best fitting values of sigma and alpha in the Vasicek model?

13.3 What are the best fitting Vasicek parameters for the following zero-coupon bond prices? Assume that the model will be extended to a perfect fit after the unextended Vasicek model is made to fit as well as possible.

1 year:	0.92
2 years:	0.83
3 years:	0.74
5 years:	0.58
7 years:	0.47
10 years:	0.35

13.4 What form does the Vasicek model take as alpha approaches zero? What impact does this fact have on parameter estimation?

Credit Risk Models

CHAPTER 14

An Introduction to Credit Risk: Using Market Signals in Loan Pricing and Performance Measurement

In the first thirteen chapters of this book, the fundamental emphasis has been to lay the foundation for an integrated treatment of credit risk and interest rate risk. We now introduce the analysis of credit risk, building on the foundation we have established with our prior focus on the term structure of interest rates. For an excellent overview of the challenges of managing credit risk, the authors highly recommend Caouette, Altman, and Narayanan (1998).

Market Prices for Credit Risk

Our primary focus in this chapter is to introduce the use of market prices in credit risk analysis. In subsequent chapters we discuss the state of the art models that are used with this market data to construct an integrated approach to market risk and credit risk. Our primary focus in this and later chapters is on 'best practice', but before we do that, it is important to add a word of warning about past practice and highlight some of its dangers.

For a large insurance company or pension fund, the use of market signals in credit risk analysis is accepted without question because so much of the fixed income portfolio consists of bonds issued by large highly-rated issuers. This is definitely not the case in the banking industry, especially with the demise of the purely wholesale-oriented commercial banks such as First Chicago, Continental Illinois, J.P. Morgan, and the Industrial Bank of Japan. Today, outside of the investment portfolio, the dominant majority of transactions on the balance sheet of the bank are extensions of credit to small businesses and retail clients who don't have ratings and don't issue debt in their own name that is readily traded in the market place. For these institutions, using market prices of credit risk in the management of the bank was a larger 'leap of faith'.

Using market prices for credit risk analysis has enormous benefits to all financial institutions and we will spend a lot of time in subsequent chapters on

259

the execution of these ideas. Some of the major benefits can be summarized as follows:

- *Increased accuracy in pricing:* Financial institutions create value-added for their owners by skillful asset selection and asset pricing. Market prices of credit risk can be used to sharply improve the accuracy of pricing on credit extended to all counterparties from retail clients to sovereigns.
- *Increased clarity in corporate strategy:* A skillful use of market prices allows senior management to see more clearly where value has been created in asset selection. More importantly, it allows senior management to see where future opportunities lie. Most importantly, senior management can also clearly see which areas to avoid.
- *Increased sophistication in risk management:* Market prices for credit risk provide invaluable insights about the correlation of risks among borrowers and about the macro-economic factors driving the correlation in default. This allows a sophisticated financial institution to hedge its portfolio of risks with respect to changes in these macro factors. This reduces the sharp cyclicality of the credit cycle.
- *Increased precision in measuring the safety and soundness of financial institutions:* Market prices of credit risk have helped regulators and shareholders alike more quickly and more accurately measure the safety and soundness of financial institutions.

We discuss each of these benefits in turn after a brief review of the kinds of market data that is critical in this regard.

Critical Sources of Market Data on Credit Risk

Up until quite recently, financial institutions weighted credit risk analysis very heavily toward the use of historical data:

- historical rates of default;
- historical movements in credit ratings;
- historical transition matrices of movements from one ratings category to another.

We discuss these historical data techniques with a critical eye in the next chapter. It is impossible to avoid these techniques in a large financial institution, but it is important to supplement them heavily with market data from sources like these:

Bond prices
There are many vendors who sell very large databases of daily bond prices spanning most of the developed countries and literally more than 100,000 different

bond issues. An institution which does not use this data extensively in setting corporate strategy, asset pricing, and risk management policies is destined to under-perform and is more likely to end up as a troubled institution. The use of these bond prices should be very pervasive around the institution, not just restricted to one or two specialists in an analytical group.

Credit default swap prices

The boom in innovation in credit default swaps in the last decade has provided financial institutions with another view of the credit risk of the top 300 to 500 credits in the world on a daily basis. The use of credit default swap pricing has many benefits:

Transparency: The pricing of the credit default swap itself makes the market's assessment of the reference name's credit risk clearly apparent in the simplest of ways—it's the insurance premium for credit risk. There's no need to use the advanced techniques for measuring credit spread that we discuss in Chapter 18.

'On the run' maturities: Credit default swaps are most frequently quoted at five-year maturities, but also at one- and three-year maturities for the most popular reference names. These maturities are the maturities at which many new transactions are done in lending markets, so it provides a concentrated view of credit risk at key maturities. Bond prices, by contrast, are scattered at many maturities and data at key 'new issue' maturities is sparse by definition, since all outstanding issues now have shorter maturities.

Cyclicality: The history of credit default swaps shows the cyclicality of credit risk at a constant maturity very clearly. We return to the drivers of this cyclicality in depth in Chapter 17 when discussing reduced form credit models.

Recovery rates: Credit default swaps are commonly traded in two forms—the digital default swap, which essentially pays $1 upon default, and the more common credit default swap structure which pays only the 'loss given default' as carefully defined in ISDA contract language. Comparing the pricing of these two structures allows financial institutions to get the market's view on the expected magnitude of 'loss given default', supplementing the notoriously sparse loss given default data maintained by most financial institutions and the rating agencies.

First to default swaps

The recent boom in 'first to default swaps' provides the market's view on the implicit correlation between the (standard) five reference credits underlying the first to default swap quoted. The reference names might be IBM, GM, British Airways, the Republic of Korea, and Toyota. If all of the reference names are likely to default at exactly the same time and if they all have similar probabilities of default, the pricing on the first to default swap will be very close to the pricing on a credit default swap for any one of the reference names. If, by contrast, there is very little correlation between the reference names from a credit risk perspective, first to default swap pricing will approach five times the cost of the credit default swap on any one of the reference names since it is five times more likely to have to pay on the swap.

The market's view on this degree of correlation is valuable and we discuss it at length in later chapters, particularly in the context of counterparty credit risk. There is one important *caveat emptor* with respect to first to default swaps—those who truly believe that the pairwise correlation between any two counterparties is equal for all pairs will be eaten alive in the market place!

Collateralized debt obligations

Pricing in the collateralized debt obligation market can potentially provide the same kind of implied correlation estimates among larger portfolios of 100 or so reference names, which typically make up the collateral pool on a CDO. Price transparency in this market has been very poor, in part because of the typical arbitrage cycle on Wall Street where 'smart people take money from dumb people' early in the life of a new and complex instrument.[1] An increase in price transparency offers similar benefits as the first to default swap market in understanding the market's implied correlation in defaults among the reference collateral.

Interest rate swap prices

Large international financial institutions are typically the counterparties on the dominant proportion of interest rate swaps in major currencies. Historical movements in interest rate swap spreads, then, potentially reflect (directly and indirectly) credit spreads of these large financial institutions. A major international pension fund, for instance, has shown the median default probabilities for large international financial banks[2] are highly statistically significant in explaining movements in interest rate swap spreads even in the era of highly-rated 'special purpose vehicles' designed to insulate the swap market from credit risk.

Equity prices

As we will see in Chapter 16 on the Merton model of risky debt and in Chapter 17 on reduced form models, equity prices contain extremely valuable information on credit quality on a much larger universe of companies than it

---

[1] Quote from a young trader at Barings Securities after his first year on the trading floor, circa 1998.

[2] Specifically, the Kamakura Risk Information Services 'Jarrow Chava' default probabilities, KDP-jc, provided by Kamakura Corporation.

is possible to find in the bond markets or the markets for over the counter-credit derivatives. Different modeling technologies make use of this information in different ways, but the explanatory power of equity markets is undeniable at this point among sophisticated market participants.

We now return to the practical use of this market credit information.

Increased Accuracy in Pricing

Some of the uses of market credit information are very basic and yet substantially improve financial institutions' performance. For example, one major lender in the Asia-Pacific region was lending to a borrower in Japan at yen LIBOR plus 1.50% when the bonds of the borrower were trading at 9% over the Japanese government bond rate. The maturities of the bond and the loan were similar, and the loan was unsecured just like the bond. The head of international lending sheepishly admitted that they had mispriced the loan and that the bank would have been much better off just buying the bonds. As simple as this comparison is, it is shocking how few financial institutions make this comparison in their lending activities—even though it's standard in their bond trading activities.

In Chapter 41, we will revisit the topic of performance measurement in detail but a preview of that chapter is useful here. In a presentation to a risk management group, two executives of J.P. Morgan explained how the credit default swap market had changed the bank's thinking on measuring the shareholder value added on lending transactions.[3] A loan, they explained, was the economic equivalent of buying a Treasury bond with the same maturity and entering into a credit default swap to provide credit protection on the borrower. Therefore the bank measured the shareholder value added on a loan as the excess of the loan's interest rate over the sum of the Treasury yield and the pricing on the credit default swap. Very simple. Very accurate. No capital allocation. No bureaucracy needed. More on this in Chapter 41.

Increased Clarity in Corporate Strategy

From a corporate strategy point of view, one of the most critical decisions faced by senior management is the proper asset allocation for the institution. Where is shareholder value added the greatest? As we saw in the previous section, credit default swap pricing is providing new insights on a small subset of major corporate and sovereign names. More than that, however, we can use

---

[3] Presentation to the North American Asset and Liability Management Association, September 2001, Toronto.

market prices of debt, equity and credit derivatives to compare asset classes and to answer questions such as the following:

- How much of the 'credit spread' (see Chapter 18) is the loss component and how much is the liquidity component (i.e. everything other than the risk-adjusted potential loss)?
- How correlated are credit risk-adjusted returns in various sectors?
- What are the drivers of credit risk in each of these sectors?

Van Deventer and Imai [2003] analyze these issues in detail and we will devote considerable time to them in later chapters as well.

Increased Sophistication in Risk Management

Financial institutions have always needed to know how to simulate true credit adjusted portfolio performance for every counterparty, from retail borrowers to major sovereign and corporate credit. They have always needed to know the default probability for each borrower and the macro factors which drive that default probability and which cause correlation in events of default. If we don't use the market prices of credit risk discussed above, we have to make some simple assumptions to approximate true credit risk. Representative examples are the Moody's Investors Service 'diversity score' concept and the simple correlation and default probability assumptions in Standard & Poor's CDO Evaluator.[4]

If we use the credit information discussed above, however, we can make some substantial improvements in risk assessment from the transaction level (say a single first to default swap) to the portfolio level, the full balance sheet of a large financial institution.

We do this in detail in Chapters 39–44.

Increased Precision in Measuring the Safety and Soundness of Financial Institutions

Van Deventer and Imai [2003] discuss the New Capital Accords from the Basel Committee on Banking Supervision in detail. The proposed capital accords are well-intentioned, but highly convoluted. More importantly, they result in financial ratios that have not yet been proven as predictors of financial institutions failure.

---

[4] See the web sites for each of the rating agencies for more detail on these concepts.

The market signals on credit risk discussed above offer valuable market signals on the risk of major international financial institutions because their:

- bond credit spreads are visible in the market place;
- risk as embedded in traditional and digital credit default swaps is visible in the market place;
- default probabilities can be derived from stock prices and other data as we describe in Chapters 16 and 17.

All of these measures will outperform the Basel capital calculations as predictors of financial institutions failure. In part, this is the result of the fact that the Basel process constrains the risk assessment to one financial ratio. The Jarrow-Chava approach (see Chapter 17) allows *any* financial ratio to be added as an explanatory variable—an unconstrained approach. If the Basel ratio has predictive power, the Jarrow-Chava approach can use it along with all the other key explanatory variables such as stock prices and macro factors. The Jarrow-Chava approach cannot be outperformed by any single financial ratio, because that ratio can be used as an input to Jarrow-Chava.

For that reason, efficient use of all available market-based credit information is the key to success in assessing the safety and soundness of financial institutions world-wide.

We discuss this in detail in the next four chapters.

CHAPTER 15

Traditional Approaches to Credit Risk: Ratings and Transition Matrices

Almost every financial institution uses credit ratings actively in both individual asset selection and in portfolio management. Ratings have a history measured in decades and they will be used actively many decades from now. That being said, rating agencies and experts in internal ratings now face substantial pressure, both commercial and conceptual, from providers of quantitative default probabilities both inside and outside of the organization. In this chapter, we summarize some of the strengths and weaknesses of a traditional ratings approach for comparison with the quantitative approaches that increasingly dominate risk management and credit derivatives pricing.

Ratings: What They Do and Don't Do

For many years Moody's Investors Service and Standard & Poor's Corporation were essentially the only providers of credit risk assessment on large corporations and sovereign issuers of debt. This has changed dramatically, recently, with a plethora of new credit rating agencies being set up around the world to challenge the older rating agencies.

Why is Competition Emerging in the Rating Agency Business?

This is an interesting question that sheds a lot of light on the credit modeling process and their answers provide essential background to Chapters 16–18.

Competing rating agencies and vendors of default probabilities have emerged for a number of reasons, just some of which are noted here:

- The '**granularity**' of ratings offered by the major rating agencies is low. The number of ratings grades (AAA, AA, A, BBB, BB, B, CCC, CC, and D for Standard & Poor's, for example) is small, so companies with ratings are divided into only nine groups. Market participants need a much higher degree of precision that the rating alone allows, even giving credit for the pluses and minuses attached to each rating.

- The **annual default rates by rating are very volatile** over time, so there is considerable uncertainty about what the default probability is that is associated with each rating. Ratings are an ordinal measure of credit risk, rather than a quantitative default probability.
- **Ratings change very infrequently**, so market participants are getting a view of an issuer's credit that changes only every six to 12 months at most.
- Ratings take the long 'through the cycle view' so **they show relatively little of the cyclicality** that many analysts believe is the key to credit risk management.
- The **ratings universe is a very small percentage** of the total number of counterparties that a typical financial institution would lend to (retail clients, small business clients and corporate clients totaling in the millions at some large banks), so an institution relying on ratings as its primary credit risk management tool is forced, by definition, to take a piecemeal approach to enterprise credit risk management. Each class of counterparties ends up having a different type of rating, some internal and some external.
- Rating agencies are normally paid by the structurer of a complex CDO or the issuer of the securities, so there is substantial **commercial pressure** on the agencies for a 'good' rating.
- Rating agencies have a substantial 'non-rating' consulting business arm, so they are increasingly being scrutinized as having **potential conflicts of interest**, such as the major accounting firms before they offloaded their consulting arms in the last decade.

This doesn't mean that ratings don't have considerable value in the credit risk process, but it does mean that their usefulness is bounded by a number of constraints.

Figure 15.1 Historical One Year Default Rates by Standard & Poor's Rating, 1981–2002

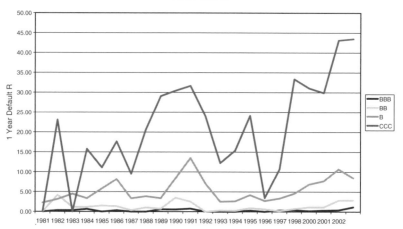

Figure 15.1 shows the average annual default rates by initial rating in each calendar year from 1981 to 2002 from Standard & Poor's Corporation. It shows the high volatility of default rates, even for issuers with the same rating, over the 1981–2002 period. All rating agencies have a similar challenge, because default risk changes over the credit cycle and ratings generally don't. This is one of the major reasons that quantitative credit models are attractive to their users—they have the ability to capture the cyclicality of risk as the business cycle comes about.

When we look at the figures for historical default rates (see Table 15.1), the challenge of setting credit ratings becomes apparent. Note that for companies rated BBB through to CCC, the average default rate is less than two standard deviations from zero, i.e. by normal statistical measures we could reach the

Table 15.1 Historical One Year Default Rates by S&P Rating

	Standard & Poor's Rating on January 1			
Year	**BBB**	**BB**	**B**	**CCC**
1981	0.00	0.00	2.22	0.00
1982	0.34	4.19	3.11	23.08
1983	0.33	1.17	4.49	0.00
1984	0.67	1.16	3.33	15.79
1985	0.00	1.52	5.80	11.11
1986	0.33	1.34	8.19	17.65
1987	0.00	0.38	3.35	9.52
1988	0.00	1.05	3.86	20.69
1989	0.58	0.72	3.37	29.09
1990	0.56	3.53	8.45	30.43
1991	0.77	2.53	13.49	31.67
1992	0.00	0.00	7.08	24.00
1993	0.00	0.34	2.53	12.24
1994	0.00	0.26	2.62	15.38
1995	0.31	0.92	4.19	24.14
1996	0.00	0.63	2.71	3.45
1997	0.35	0.18	3.34	10.71
1998	0.40	0.75	4.56	33.33
1999	0.18	1.13	6.87	31.08
2000	0.34	1.13	7.71	29.89
2001	0.39	2.83	10.72	43.10
2002	1.16	2.88	8.47	43.48
Average	0.31	1.30	5.48	20.90
Standard Deviation	0.31	1.17	3.02	12.52

incorrect conclusion that the ratings did not have statistical significance as predictors of default. This conclusion is not correct as we show in Chapter 18 on credit model testing. Almost all quantitative and qualitative measures of credit risk are similar in this regard, and more subtle testing procedures are needed to tell them apart from a performance perspective.

The great competitive strength of the older rating agencies is the existence of this history which they can use as proof of their long-standing skill, through many cycles, in ranking companies by riskiness.

As van Deventer and Imai [2003] point out, the rating agencies are made up of some very intelligent people and their ratings have stood the test of time. They can be supplemented with some valuable tools in these dimensions:

- Converting ratings to default probabilities;
- Adding internal ratings and default probabilities to expand coverage of counterparties;
- Adding macro factors which drive risk, in order to meet the challenge of Chapter 1;
- Adding databases done on a monthly basis rather than the annual basis typical of rating agency performance;
- Analyzing the random changes in ratings from one level to another.

We briefly discuss each of these issues as they relate directly to credit modeling in Chapters 16 and 17 and we perform the testing in Chapter 18.

Converting Ratings to Default Probabilities

As Table 15.1 shows, it is hard to be satisfied with the risk assessment we would get from any ratings process if we use the average default probability over a long period of time associated with each rating. By that measure, almost no ratings tool has an average default probability more than two standard deviations from zero. The default incidence varies tremendously over time and this variation is predictable.

In Chapter 17, we introduce the reduced form credit models and the use of logistic regression to link historical default rates to a set of explanatory variables. Ratings can be used with logistic regression (even if the rating is the only input) to maximize the quality of the default probability given the rating and the other variables (such as proxies for economic conditions, stock price indices, etc.).

There is no reason to simply use average default experience associated with the rating, and there are many good reasons not to do so. This comment applies to all ratings technologies including:

- Retail 'credit scores';
- Small business ratings;

- Internal ratings of all classes of borrowers;
- Rating agency ratings.

Expanding Coverage with Internal Ratings and Default Probabilities

While the major rating agencies are covering a wider and wider percentage of the corporate universe, the fraction of financial institution counterparties with third party ratings is very low for most commercial banks (and reasonably low for other types of financial institutions).

The best solution for the coverage problem is to supplement third party ratings with internal ratings and default probabilities that we discuss in Chapters 16 and 17.

Why is there a need for internal ratings if there are high-quality default probabilities? The authors would argue that there isn't a need for internal ratings if the estimation of default probabilities has been performed effectively. Nonetheless, we recognize that ratings are a part of banking culture and will be around, however unnecessary, as the appendix of credit risk measures, an organ of limited usefulness that is easier to leave in place than to remove unless they have gone truly bad.

Many institutions use a 10- or 20-point internal ratings scale with the same nomenclature for all classes of counterparties, retail, small business, large corporate, and sovereign. As one banker explained "A small business rated a five should have the same risk as a retail client rated a five."

As Table 15.1 shows for S&P ratings, this desire for consistency is logical and understandable. It is doable by definition for well-crafted default probabilities (since a 5% probability of default has the same meaning whether it refers to a company or a person), but is very hard to do for any type of ratings technology. If losses by ratings grade are cyclical, then actual loss experience for companies rated '5' will only be the same as loss experience for home mortgage borrowers rated '5' by coincidence, even if they are the same on average. The responses to the credit cycle will be different for different types of borrowers, and the presence of collateral further complicates the attempt to generate consistency.

There is an even bigger reason to use default probabilities rather than internal ratings—quantitative default probabilities can be generated from history, but internal ratings can't, if the people or ratings procedures haven't been in place during that history. We discuss this in more detail in Chapters 16 and 17.

Adding Macro Factors to Capture Cyclicality

One of the best ways to supplement ratings in order to understand, through the cycle, variability in default experience, is with the type of macro-economic variables that affect both the structural types of credit models and the reduced form models that we discuss in Chapters 16 and 17. Without this addition to the logistic regression that links ratings to default experience, the exercise would be a frustrating one and the ability to predict loss experience won't be much better than using the average default experience for the ratings class, which we showed above.

Monthly versus Annual Data

For all classes of borrowers, no financial institution has ever had credit or default data that was in excess of its needs. For this reason alone, it is very important for default studies and default databases to be done on a monthly basis, rather than an annual basis. A monthly database can always be converted to annual, but the converse is not true.

Moreover, the importance of various explanatory variables changes with the forecasting horizon. An annual database is a crude merging of borrowers who default in one, two, three, four, five, six, seven,... and 12 months. Keeping a more transparent view of the actual time to default is essential to the performance measure we do in Chapter 18.

Transition Matrices: Analyzing the Random Changes in Ratings from One Level to Another

One of the techniques most often used to supplement the ratings process is the transition matrix. Table 15.2 below shows the annual ratings transition matrix for Standard & Poor's ratings on average over the 1981–2002.[1]

Table 15.2 Average One-Year Transition Rates, 1981–2002

Standard &Poor's Rating	AAA	AA	A	BBB	BB	B	CCC	D	Rating Withdrawn	Rounding Error	Total
AAA	89.37	6.04	0.44	0.14	0.05	0.00	0.00	0.00	3.97	−0.01	100.00
AA	0.57	87.76	7.30	0.59	0.06	0.11	0.02	0.01	3.58	0.00	100.00
A	0.05	2.01	87.62	5.37	0.45	0.18	0.04	0.05	4.22	0.01	100.00
BBB	0.03	0.21	4.15	84.44	4.39	0.89	0.26	0.37	5.26	0.00	100.00
BB	0.03	0.08	0.40	5.50	76.44	7.14	1.11	1.38	7.92	0.00	100.00
B	0.00	0.07	0.26	0.36	4.74	74.12	4.37	6.20	9.87	0.01	100.00
CCC	0.09	0.00	0.28	0.56	1.39	8.80	49.72	27.87	11.30	−0.01	100.00

---

[1] Ratings Performance 2002: Default, Transition, Recovery and Spreads, Standard & Poor's Corporation, February 2003.

The transition matrix works like this. The rating (internal or external) is captured at the beginning of a period (normally annually but the authors recommend monthly). The probability of moving to a different rating or default is captured in each column for a company starting with the rating describing that row. For example, a company starting the year with a BBB rating from Standard & Poor's has an 84.44% probability of ending the year with the same rating. The same company has a 4.15% probability of being rated A at the end of the year, and a 0.37% probability of defaulting (a rating of D). Except for rounding error, the sum of the transition probabilities in each row should sum to one (100%).

Depending on the periodicity of the data, the transition matrix can be 'compounded' to obtain transition probabilities for different timeframes.

These transition matrices can be used in two ways, which parallel the use of credit models in Chapters 16 and 17:

- **For simulation**, the path-dependent movement from one rating to another, occasionally ending in default, can be simulated for every counterparty. This is an essential feature in enterprise risk management software.[2]
- **For valuation, pricing and hedging**, Jarrow, Lando, and Turnbull [1997] present an elegant model for valuation, pricing, and hedging of defaultable instruments using a model of discrete steps toward bankruptcy (via transition matrices of ratings). This model uses a random interest rate framework (like those we discussed in Chapters 11 and 12) and allows the analyst to value credit risky bonds and loans, with and without embedded options, and options on those loans and bonds. Few financial institutions have fully appreciated the power that the Jarrow, Lando, and Turnbull approach brings to internal ratings, in part because the reduced form models of Chapter 17 have proven to be even more powerful.

The Jarrow-Merton Put Option

To conclude, let us recall the big picture objectives of Chapters 1 and 2. We want to both measure interest rate and credit risk on an integrated basis and also be able to do something about it if we are uncomfortable with the level of risk we have. We want to compute the value of the Jarrow-Merton put option (say in one year at the par value of the liabilities of the financial institution) on

---

[2] For example, Kamakura Corporation's Kamakura Risk Manager enterprise risk management system allows users to simulate transition from one rating to another, interacting in a logical way with prepayment options, loan loss provisions, and cash flow arrival timing. One major lender processes two million transactions each day through this simulation software.

the value of company assets, which is the best coherent estimate of the risk the institution has taken on.

In simple terms, we want to know 'what is the hedge' if our risk is too large.

With the exception of the Jarrow, Lando, and Turnbull approach, the use of credit ratings leaves us short of the goal line. The link between ratings and pricing, valuation and hedging is very tenuous in most financial institutions.

That is not the case with state of the art term structure models, which reflect a full valuation, hedging, and pricing framework. We analyse this in Chapter 16.

Structural Credit Models: An Introduction to the Merton Approach

I n Geneva in December 2002, Robert Merton was speaking to a large conference audience of 400 risk managers when a question arose from the back of the room. "Professor Merton," the questioner started, "what else do you recommend to financial institutions using commercial versions of your credit model?" After a long pause, Professor Merton said, "Well, the first thing you have to remember is that the model is 28 years old." This is both the strength and the weakness of the Merton model. As it ages it is better understood and more widely used. At the same time, more extensive credit model testing like that in van Deventer and Imai [2003] has been mandated by the Basel Committee on Banking Supervision. As test results of the type we discuss in Chapter 18 accumulate, the weaknesses of the model are becoming more starkly apparent. In this chapter, we address the strengths and weaknesses of the Merton model from an intuitive and theoretical perspective. In Chapter 17, we move to the more modern reduced form models like those behind the new Loss Distribution Model launched by the Federal Deposit Insurance Corporation of the U.S. on December 10 2003. In Chapter 18, we look at the two modeling technologies in a unified way for testing as required under the proposed New Capital Accords from the Basel Committee on Banking Supervision.

Structural Models: A Personal History

The application of quantitative techniques to credit risk analysis at first resulted in the same sort of resistance that quantitative measurement of interest rate risk did, as explained in Chapters 1 and 2. The early converts to the Merton approach were passionate about its promise, and one of the authors was certainly in that category. Don van Deventer was so impressed with the model that he became the first person to market a commercial version of the model in Japan in the very early 1990s. In 1993, he and Dennis Uyemura extolled its virtues in their book *Financial Risk Management in Banking* [1993]. By the time that book was published, potential clients of the Merton default probability service had begun to make logical and sensible suggestions about how to improve the model. Taking these criticisms seriously, Shimko, Tejima and van Deventer [1993] extended the Merton model to include random interest rates and asset values correlated with interest rates, as we discuss below. Van Deventer and Imai [1996] discuss both the original Merton model and the random interest rate version of it. By 1995, the initial reduced form model of Jarrow and Turnbull [1995] was published and we began working with Professor Jarrow. Van Deventer and Imai [2003] recount how Professor Jarrow came upon the reduced form approach. Professor Jarrow argued that the choice of capital structure by management was a dynamic process that was an endogenous function of the company's financial condition and economic conditions. He questioned whether he could solve such a complex problem in a usable way if he extended the structural approach. The reduced form model that he (along with Duffie and Singleton [1999] and many others) has developed has set a new standard for credit model performance that we discuss in Chapters 17 and 18. Recent research reconciles the two approaches, arguing that market participants have less information than management (which acts as if the Merton model was true), leading market participants to act as if the reduced form approach is true.

After the launch of the Kamakura Risk Information Services (KRIS) default probability product in November 2002, the authors have worked extensively with major financial institutions to better understand the practical use and performance of the KRIS Merton models, the KRIS reduced form model, and a hybrid model which has the Merton default probability as an input. Our discussions in Chapters 16–18 reflect the insights that we have gained on a U.S. database which spans 1989 to the present, with more than 1.2 million monthly observations, a research database from 1963 to 1998 with another 1.4 million monthly observations, and a very large international database.

The Intuition of the Merton Model

The intuition of the Merton model is dramatically appealing, particularly to Don van Deventer, a former treasurer at a major bank holding company who used the model's insights to formulate financial strategy. Merton [1974] was a pioneer in options research at MIT at the time that Black and Scholes [1973] had just published their now well-known options model. One of the reasons for the enduring popularity of the credit model is the even greater popularity of the Black-Scholes model. The Black-Scholes model is simple enough that it can be modeled in popular spreadsheet software. Because of this simplicity, Hull [1993] and Jarrow and Turnbull [1996] note with chagrin that traders in interest rate caps and floors frequently use the related Black commodity options model, even though it implicitly assumes interest rates are constant. In the same way, extensive use of the Merton model will persist for decades even though it is now clear that other modeling techniques for credit risk are more effective. As background for a review of those models in Chapters 17 and 18, we now turn to the Merton model and its many variations.

Merton's great insight was to recognize that the equity in a company can be considered an option on the assets of the firm. More formally, he assumes that the assumptions that Black and Scholes apply in their stock options model can be applied to the assets of corporations. Merton [1974] assumes that the assets of corporations are completely liquid and traded in frictionless markets. He also assumes that interest rates are constant, and that the firm has only one zero-coupon debt issue outstanding. He assumes, like Black and Scholes, a one-period world where management choices are made at time zero and the consequences of those decisions would become apparent at the end of the single period.

Given these assumptions, what happens at the end of the single period at time T? If the value of company assets $V(T)$ is greater than the amount of debt that has to be paid off K, then the excess value $V(T) - K$ goes to equity holders in exactly the same way as if the company was liquidated in the liquid markets Merton assumes. If the value of company assets is less than K, then equity holders get nothing. More importantly, from a *Basel II* perspective, debt holders have a loss given default of $K - V(T)$. Loss given default is built into the Merton model, an insight many market participants have overlooked.

The payoffs on the common stock of the firm are identical to that of an option at current time t with these characteristics:

- The option has maturity $T - t$, the same maturity as the debt. The original maturity of the option was $T - 0$.
- The option has a strike price equal to the amount of debt K.
- The option's value is determined by the current value of company assets $V(t)$ and their volatility σ.

We label this call option, the value of the company's equity, $C(V(t), t, T, K)$. Then Merton invokes an argument of Nobel prize winners Modigliani and Miller [1958]. Merton assumes that the value of company assets equals the value of its equity plus the value of its debt. That means we can express the value of the company's debt as:

$$D(V(t), t, T, K) = V(t) - C(V(t), t, T, K)$$

That, in essence, is the heart of the Merton model intuition. Alternative versions of the Merton model are relatively minor variations around this theme. Many versions in fact are just alternative methods of estimating the Merton parameters.

In the next few sections, we summarize some of the variations on the Merton model. After that, we turn to practical use of the Merton model.

The Basic Merton Model

In order to be precise about the Merton model and related default probabilities, we need to be more precise about the assumptions used by Black, Scholes and Merton[1].

r: Interest rates are constant at a continuously compounded rate r.

σ: The value of company assets has a constant instantaneous variance of the return on company assets, $\sigma(V(t), t)^2 = \sigma$.

K: K is the amount of zero-coupon debt payable at maturity, time T.

Black, Scholes and Merton assume that the value of company assets follows a lognormal distribution and that there are no dividends on these assets and no other cash flows from them during the period. Formally, we can write the evolution of the value of company assets over time as:

$$\frac{dV(t)}{V(t)} = \alpha \, dt + \sigma \, dW(t)$$

$W(t)$ is normally distributed with mean zero and variance t—it is the 'random number generator' which produces shocks to the value of company assets. The magnitude of these shocks is scaled by the volatility of company assets, σ. The term α is the drift in the value of company assets. We discuss its value later in this chapter, but we don't need to spend time on that now. From this formula, we know that $V(t)$, the value of company assets, is lognormally distributed. Taking advantage of these facts, the value of company assets at a future point in time can be written as:

$$V(t) = V(0) \, e^{[(\alpha - (1/2)\sigma^2)t + \sigma W(t)]}$$

We can use this equation to get the value of company assets and its distribution at maturity T. $W(t)$, as mentioned previously, is normally distributed with mean zero and variance t (standard deviation of $\sqrt{t}$). This allows us to get the well-known 'distance to default' in the Merton model. We can do this

---

[1] For readers who would like a more detailed explanation of options concepts, the authors recommend Ingersoll [1987], Hull [1993] and Jarrow and Turnbull [1996].

by first rewriting the formula for the value of company assets to get the instantaneous return on company assets. The return on company assets is normally distributed because W is normally distributed:

$$y(t) = \frac{1}{t}\left[(\alpha - \frac{1}{2}\sigma^2)t + \sigma W(t)\right]$$

The distance from default is the number of standard deviations that this return is (when $t = T$, the date of maturity) from the instantaneous return just needed to 'break even' versus the value of debt that must be paid, K. We can write this breakeven return as $y(K, T)$ or:

$$y(K, T) = \frac{1}{T}\ln\left[\frac{K}{V(0)}\right]$$

The standard deviation of the return on company assets $y(t)$ when $t = T$ is $\sigma/\sqrt{T}$ so we can write the distance to default $z(T)$ as:

$$z(T) = \frac{y(T) - y(K, T)}{\sigma/\sqrt{T}}$$

Later in this chapter, we discuss how this distance to default or the Merton default probabilities themselves can be mapped to actual historical default rates. In order to use the Merton default probabilities, we need to evaluate α. We turn to that in the next section.

Making use of the derivation so far, Merton shows that the value of company equity $C(V(0), 0, T, K)$ is equal to the value of a Black-Scholes call option:

$$C[V(0), 0, T, K] = V(0)N(d_1) - KP(0, T)N(d_2)$$

$N()$ is the cumulative normal distribution function that can be found in any popular spreadsheet package. The variable $d_1 = \ln[V(0)/KP(0, T)]$, and $d_2 = d_1 - \sigma\sqrt{(T - 0)}$. The expression $P(0, T)$ is the zero-coupon bond price as of time zero of \$1 paid at time T, discounting at the constant risk-free interest rate r. We discussed the continuously compounded value for P in Chapter 7. Using the Modigliani and Miller argument that the value of company assets must equal the sum of the value of this call option, the value of the debt D gives us:

$$V(0) = C[V(0), 0, T, K] + D[V(0), 0, T, K]$$

Rearranging this gives the Merton formula for risky debt. The second expression takes advantage of the symmetrical nature of the normal distribution.

$$D[V(0), 0, T, K] = V(0) - V(0)N(d_1) + KP(0, T)N(d_2)$$
$$= V(0)N(-d_1) + KP(0, T)N(d_2)$$

As we have stated throughout this book, our objective is to formulate an integrated approach to interest rate risk and credit risk that provides pricing, hedging, and valuation. Ultimately, we want to be able to value the Jarrow-Merton put option on the assets of our company or business unit that provides the best measure of 'risk'.

Therefore it is very important to note that all of the Black-Scholes hedging concepts can be applied to the Merton model of risky debt.

The **delta** of risky debt shows the change in the value of risky debt that results from a change in the value of company assets:

$$\text{Delta} = \frac{\partial D}{\partial V} = 1 - N(d_1) > 0$$

The value of risky debt rises when the value of company assets V rises. The gamma of risky debt is the second derivative of the Merton risky debt formula with respect to the value of company assets:

$$\text{Gamma} = \frac{\partial_2 D}{\partial V^2} = \frac{-f(d_1)}{V\sigma\sqrt{T}} < 0$$

Similarly, we can derive derivatives for changes in time, volatility, and the level of interest rates, in a way parallel to that of the Black-Scholes model.

$$\text{Theta} = \frac{\partial D}{\partial t} = \frac{Vf(d_1)\sigma}{2\sqrt{T}} + rKP(0, T) \quad N(d_2) > 0$$

$$\text{Vega} = \frac{\partial D}{\partial \sigma} = -V\sqrt{T} \quad f(d_1) < 0$$

$$\text{Rho} = \frac{\partial D}{\partial r} = -TKP(0, t) \quad N(d_2) \leq 0$$

Note that we can hedge our position in risky debt by taking the appropriate positions in the assets of the company, just like a trader of stock options can hedge their position in options with a replicating position in the underlying common stock. Similarly, in the Merton model, both the value of the debt and the value of the common stock are functions of the value of company assets. This means that a position in the debt of the company can be hedged with the appropriate 'short' position in the common stock of the company. Note however that when the value of common stock approaches zero, this hedge will break down in practice, for sound theoretical reasons. The value of debt can keep declining as the value of company assets declines, but the stock price can't go below zero.

Finally, note that we can do pricing, hedging and valuation in the Merton model without any discussion whatsoever of default probabilities and loss given default. They are totally unnecessary, since the valuation formulas take into account all possible values of company assets, the probability of default at each asset level, and the loss given default at each asset level. This is obvious from a theoretical point of view, but it is often forgotten by practitioners who follow this process:

1. Estimate the Merton model of risky debt;
2. Derive the Merton default probability;
3. Apply this default probability to calculate the value of a debt instrument.

If our objective is valuation and hedging, steps 2 and 3 are unnecessary given the sound theoretical structure that Merton has laid out.

Before turning to the subject of default probabilities, we emphasize this point by discussing valuation of a bond with many payments.

Valuing Multi-Payment Bonds with the Merton Model of Risky Debt

How do we apply the single-period Merton model to value a bond with many payments, for example, a 10-year bond with semi annual payments? To do the valuation, we need 20 zero-coupon bond prices to apply the present value techniques of Chapter 7. Remember, if we have a smoothed yield curve using the techniques in Chapter 8, we don't need the Merton model for valuation because we can extract the 20 zero-coupon bond prices we need directly from the yield curve with no need to resort to the Merton theory. When we say 'use the Merton model' for valuation, what we are really saying is this—how do we fit the parameters of the model to coupon-paying bonds with observable prices? We will return to this issue below when we discuss parameter fitting. Let's say we have a three-year bond with an observable price, a five-year bond with an observable price and a 10-year bond with an observable price. How can we fit the Merton model to this data? If all the bonds have the same payment dates (say June 15 and December 15), then we can guess the value of debt to be paid off K, the value of company assets $V(0)$, and the volatility of company assets σ. We are immediately confronted with a conflict with model assumptions because we see from the smoothed risk-free yield curve that the value of the continuously compounded zero yield r will not be constant, there will be 20 different values, one for each payment date.

At this point, users of the Merton model get to the 'quick and dirty' nature of application that is consistent with using the constant interest rate Black model to value interest rate caps! Given the 20 values of the risk-free rate, in our example we have three pricing equations for the bonds and three variables to solve for—K, $V(0)$, and σ. At the same time, theory says we should also be fitting the model to the stock price, but we don't know which of the 20 maturities that we are using is most relevant to the stock price.

Let's squint our eyes, hold our nose, and get this done. As a practical matter, the authors would fit the model to the shortest maturity observable debt issue, the longest observable debt issue, and stock price. For any pricing error that arises, we can extend the model just like we extended the Vasicek term structure model to get the Hull and White model. We can use the techniques of Chapter 13 to find the best fitting Merton parameters just like we did for term structure model parameters.

How should we do this? What should we 'extend' to fit the observable term structure for, say, IBM using the Merton model? Users can extend K, the value of debt to be paid off, to be different at each maturity. Another option is to extend the volatility of company assets with σ. A final option is to allow for drift in the value of company assets. All of these are acceptable alternatives. Van Deventer and Imai [2003] show, using data from First Interstate Bancorp new issue spreads, that the pricing error can be large when using the Merton model without some form of extension.

Valuing European Options on Coupon Bonds Using the Merton Model

In Chapter 24, we talk about the valuation of options on bonds in a single-factor term structure model. In order to obtain a solution, it is necessary to note that the value of a zero-coupon bond and the value of a coupon-bearing bond is a monotonic function of the single factor in the term structure model. We can calculate the 'break even' level of the single factor in the term structure model that triggers exercise of the option, and valuation is straightforward.

In the same way, the value of company assets in the Merton model is the single risk factor in the Merton risky debt 'term structure model'. By varying the value of company assets, we can calculate what level of company assets would trigger the exercise of a bond option and proceed to valuation from that fact.

As U.S. former president Richard Nixon once said, 'But that would be wrong'. Precisely, But no more wrong than the traders who are using the constant interest rate Black model to value interest rate caps, one of the great contradictions between theory and practice. We make these compromises in the spirit of the 80/20 rule that Uyemura and van Deventer [1993] discuss extensively.

We can do the same to use the Merton model as a bond option model. Note however, that all of the variation in the bond's price is attributed to changes in the value of company assets, not changes in the risk-free term structure, since r is assumed to be constant.

Most quantitative analysts with a longer-term career horizon would be uncomfortable using the Merton model for valuing any kind of bond option, which is one of the reasons why the reduced form model framework is so much more attractive in both theory and practice.

We now turn to the probability of default in the Merton model.

Estimating the Probability of Default in the Merton Model

As shown previously, we don't need the Merton model default probabilities for valuation, pricing and hedging in the Merton framework. The model implicitly considers all possible default probabilities and the associated loss given default for each possible ending value of company assets $V(T)$. As an index of risk, however, the default probabilities are potentially important (we measure *how* important in Chapter 18).

One of the curious features of the Black-Scholes options model in the Merton context, is that the drift term in the return on company assets α doesn't affect the valuation formulas just like the drift in the return on a common stock doesn't affect its option pricing. We do need to know α when it comes to the probability of default on an empirical or statistical basis (as opposed to the risk neutral default probabilities that are implicitly embedded in the valuation formulas).

Jarrow and van Deventer [1998] derive the empirical default probabilities using Merton's inter-temporal capital asset pricing model. That model recognizes that the value of company assets of all companies are not independent. They will be priced in a market that recognizes the benefits of diversification, that knows, for example, that lending to a suntan lotion company and an umbrella-maker diversifies away weather risk. These benefits of correlation in the returns on company assets affect the expected return on the assets. Jarrow and van Deventer note that when interest rates are constant, the expected return on the assets of company i in Merton's [1973] equilibrium asset pricing model must be:

$$\alpha_i = r + \frac{\sigma_i \rho_{iM}}{\sigma_M}(\alpha_M - r)$$

where r is the continuously compounded risk-free rate, the subscript M refers to the 'market' portfolio or equivalently, the portfolio consisting of all assets of all companies in the economy, and ρ_{iM} denotes the correlation between the return on firm i's asset value and the return on the market portfolio of all companies' assets.

Given this formula for α, the probability of default in the Merton model becomes:

$$\text{Probability (Default)} = \text{Probability} \, (V_i(T) < K)$$
$$= N \left(\frac{\ln(K / V_i(0)) - \mu_i T}{\sigma_i \sqrt{T}} \right)$$

The variable μ is defined as:

$$\mu_i = -\frac{1}{2}\sigma_i^2 + (1 - b_i)r + b_i a_M$$

where $b_i = (\sigma_i \rho_{iM})/\sigma_M$ is the ith firm's beta, which measures the degree to which the return on the assets of the ith company is correlated with the return on the assets of all companies.

When interest rates are not constant, α takes on a more complex form, as we discuss in a later section, and the Merton default probability formula changes.

Implying the Value of Company Assets and their Return Volatility σ

The market value of company assets in the Merton model is not observable, nor is its volatility. If the asset volatility is known, we can solve implicitly for the value of company assets $V(0)$ by solving the equation relating the total value of the company's equity (stock price S multiplied by number of shares outstanding M) to the Black-Scholes call option formula:

$$MS = C[V(0), 0, T, K] = V(0)N(d_1) - KP(0, T)N(d_2)$$

The volatility of the return on company assets is not observable, but we can observe the stock price history of the firm and calculate the volatility of the return on the stock σ_c in typical Black-Scholes fashion. In Appendix 1, we use Ito's lemma in the same way we did earlier in the book, when we introduced term structure models of interest rate movements. This allows us to link the observable volatility of equity returns σ_c to the volatility of the returns on company assets σ:

$$\frac{\sigma_c C}{C_V V} = \sigma$$

Together with the call option formula above, we have two equations in two unknowns $V(0)$ and σ. We solve for both of them and create a time series of each. From these time series on the value of company assets for all companies, we can calculate the betas necessary to insert in the default probability formula above. The expected return on the assets of all companies is usually estimated as a multiple of the risk-free rate in such a way that model performance (as we discuss in Chapter 18) is optimized.

An alternative derivation of the volatility of company asset returns

There is an alternative method for deriving the implied volatility of the return on company assets. Since the equity of the company is a call option on the value of company assets, a call option on the common stock of the company is an option on an option. Geske [1979] derived a closed-form valuation for compound options (CC). We can replace the equation linking equity return volatility with asset return volatility with Geske's compound options formula. If there are M shares of common stock outstanding at price S and if the value of a call option on one share is X, then the total value of a call option on all common shares as a function of the value of company assets V takes this form:

$$MX = CC\,[V(0), T, K] = \{V(0)N_2(h + \sigma\sqrt{T}, k + \sigma\sqrt{T_1}, \rho)$$
$$- K_1 P(0, T_1)N_2(h, k, \rho)\} - KP(0, T)N(h)$$

$$h = \frac{\ln[V(0)/V^* P(0, T)] - (\sigma^2 T)/2}{\sigma\sqrt{T}}$$

$$k = \frac{\ln[V(0)/K_1 P(0, T_1)] - (\sigma^2 T_1)/2}{\sigma\sqrt{T_1}}$$

$$\rho = \sqrt{T/T_1}$$

Here, T is the expiration date of the option on the common stock of the company at a strike price of K. The equity of the company (which itself has a 'maturity' equal to that of risky debt) is an option on the assets of the firm with a maturity date of T_1 and an exercise price (the amount of debt to be paid off) of K_1. V^* is the value of company assets at time T which triggers exercise of the option on the common stock. $N_2(x, y, z)$ is the bivariate normal distribution. $P(0, T)$ is the time zero value of a risk-free zero-coupon bond which pays \$1 at time T.

This again gives us two equations in two unknowns, so we can imply values for $V(0)$ and σ as we did with the alternative equation for the volatility of returns on company assets. The two methods are less than fully satisfactory. A relatively small percentage of listed companies have traded options with observable prices, and these options have quite short maturities. Assuming away the 'volatility smile' problem (see Rubinstein [1995]), using this method would produce very short-term estimates for the volatility of company assets. Moreover, we would find ourselves generally using this method for the biggest companies, who on average, are the highest quality credits in the market place. The other method of estimating the value of company asset returns is typically done using a fairly long-term volatility of returns on the common stock—σ_c. This is the standard for equity beta calculations, and it often helps to avoid the worst case scenario where the stock price has been near zero for such a long time that the historical volatility is zero (implying a low default probability even if the value of company assets is low)—producing an inaccurate default probability estimate even though the company concerned is obviously high-risk.

Mapping the Theoretical Merton Default Probabilities to Actual Defaults

Falkenstein and Boral [2000] note that the theoretical values of Merton default probabilities produced in this manner typically result in large bunches of companies with very low default probabilities and large bunches of companies with very high default probabilities. In both cases, the Merton default probabilities are generally much higher than the actual levels of default experienced as shown in Figure 16.1 below:

Figure 16.1 The Actual Default Rate on Theoretical Merton Default Probabilities is Much Less Than The Model Predicts; this is Corrected by Mapping to Actual Defaults

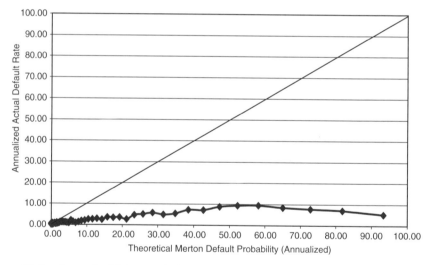

If the theoretical Merton default probabilities were perfectly aligned with actual default rates, the XY chart linking actual and theoretical default rates would fall exactly on the line rising from the lower left hand corner to the upper right hand corner. In Figure 16.1, we have divided a universe of 1.2 million Merton default probabilities into 100 equal-sized samples of 12,000 observations, each after arranging the sample in order from lowest default probability to highest default probability. We then plotted the actual default rate experienced against the mid-point of our one-percentile samples. The zero[th] percentile has the lowest 12,000 observations, the first percentile has the next highest 12,000 observations, and so on until we reach the

99th percentile, which contains the 12,000 highest default probabilities. As Figure 16.1 shows, there was an actual default rate of less than 10% even on the 99th percentile group, which had a midpoint theoretical Merton default probability of 95%. This tendency of the Merton model to create too many false positives can be controlled by a careful mapping of the theoretical default probabilities to actual default rates. As we can see from Figure 16.1, if this is done correctly, the mapped Merton default probabilities should never exceed 10% because no one-percentile sample has a default rate higher than 10%.

We discuss the results of this mapping exercise in Chapter 18. How is the mapping actually done? We can map either the distance of default to actual default probabilities or we can map the theoretical Merton default probability to actual default rates.

In either case, the mapping is normally a monotonic mapping that changes the level of default probabilities but not the ordinal ranking of companies by riskiness. As we note in Chapter 18, this mapping therefore does not change the ROC accuracy ratio, the standard statistical measure of model performance for 0/1 events like bankruptcy. There are many monotonic functions that we can use for this purpose, including the logistic regression technique which we discuss in Chapter 17.

The Merton Model When Interest Rates are Random

As mentioned in the introduction to this chapter, one of the earliest concerns expressed about the accuracy of the Merton model was its reliance on the assumption that interest rates are constant, exactly as in the Black-Scholes model. Shimko, Tejima and van Deventer [1993] solved this problem by applying Merton's option model with random interest rates to the risky debt problem. The random interest rates version of Black-Scholes can be used with any of the single factor term structure models, which we reviewed in Chapter 11, which is one of the reasons for their importance in this book.

When interest rates are random, the value of the company's equity is a random interest rates option on the value of company assets with a valuation formula given in van Deventer and Imai [2003].

Using this random interest rates-based valuation formula, we then solve for the value of risky debt exactly as we did above using the Modigliani and Miller relationship. In fitting the parameters of the model, we estimate the term structure parameters exactly as in Chapter 13. We then use the same procedures as above to estimate the implied value of company assets, $V(0)$, the implied volatility of the returns on company assets, and the implied correlation between the returns on company assets and interest rates.

Van Deventer and Imai [2003] extensively address this version of the Merton model of risky debt and show how it can be used to allocate firm capital when interest rate risk and credit risk are both present.

One difference in using this model is that the expected return on the value of company assets depends on correlations from both the market for company assets and the risk-free bond market.

The Merton Model with Early Default

Another variation on the Merton problem is focused on another objection to the basic structure of the Merton model—default never occurs as a surprise. It either occurs at the end of the period or it doesn't, but it never occurs prior to the end of the period. Analysts have adopted the 'down and out' option in order to trigger early default in the Merton model. In this form of the model, equity is a 'down and out' call option on the assets of the firm. Equity becomes worthless if the value of company assets falls to a certain barrier level, often the amount of risky debt that must be repaid at the end of the period K. Adopting this formulation, the total value of company equity again equals an option on the assets of the firm, but this option is a down and out option.

The value of the barrier in this formula conceptually should be the minimum value of company assets that will provide the cash flow to meet debt obligations and the costs of producing the minimum level of the company's products that would insure survival. This is a difficult figure to estimate, and it's one reason why some analysts have gone further to model this mysterious barrier as a random value. It also serves as justification for Professor Jarrow's intuition that capital structure choices are dynamic functions of the value of company assets and other random factors like interest rates.

Loss Given Default in the Merton Model

As mentioned earlier in this chapter, analysts are divided between those who seek to use the Merton model for valuation, pricing and hedging, and those who use it to estimate default probabilities and then in turn try to use the default probabilities and loss given default for pricing, valuation and hedging outside the Merton model structure. The former group is truer to the model, because the Merton model incorporates all potential probabilities of default and loss given default in its valuation formulas. For this reason, there is no need to specify default probabilities and loss given default for valuation of the model—they are endogenous, just like the Black-Scholes model considers all potential rates of return on common stock in the valuation of an option on the common stock.

Loss given default is the expectation (with respect to the value of company assets (V)) for the amount of loss $K - V(T)$ which will be incurred given that the event of default has occurred. The derivation of loss given default in the model is left as an exercise for the reader.

Copulas and Correlation Between the Events of Default of Two Companies

The Merton model is fitted to market data in a univariate manner, i.e. one company at a time. As a result, there is no structure in the risky debt model itself that describes how the events of default of two companies would be correlated. Because this correlation is not derived from the model's structure, many analysts *assume* a correlation structure[2]. This contrasts sharply with the implementation of the reduced form models in Chapter 17, where the correlation between the events of default of all companies is jointly derived when the model is fitted.

Now let's go back to the Merton case. Let's assume that we need to estimate the correlation that causes two companies to have defaults and default probabilities that are not independent. If we are true to the model we could make the argument that the returns on the value of company assets for both companies has correlation ρ:

$$\frac{dV_a}{V_a} = \mu_a \, dt + \sigma_a \, dZ_a$$

$$\frac{dV_b}{V_b} = \mu_b \, dt + \sigma_b \, dZ_b$$

$$(dZ_a \, dZ_b) = \rho \, dt$$

The correlation of the returns on the assets of both companies can be estimated using the formulas above from the historical implied series on the value of company assets. This is the proper specification for correlation in the 'copula' method of triggering correlated events of default.

There are a number of other ways of doing the same thing. If the analyst has an observable probability that both companies will default between time t and T, then the value of the correlation coefficient ρ can be implied from the Merton model default probability formulas and the joint multivariate normal distribution of the returns on company assets for the two companies (or five companies in the common first to default swap structure). There is no reason to assume that the pairwise correlation between all pairs of companies is the same—in fact, this is a serious error in analyzing first to default swap pricing.

There are other methods of triggering correlated default that are much simpler and more direct than imposing a correlation on the Merton structure. The fastest and most efficient from a computer science point of view is the correlated binomial distribution. We can directly compute the joint distribution of

---

[2] Private conversation with Robert Jarrow, February 4 2004.

default events without the need to resort to the multivariate monte carlo simulation necessary with the ad hoc correlation in the Merton structure.

There are two more elegant alternatives that the authors prefer. First choice is the reduced form models to which we now turn. A second choice, which stays true to the Merton theory, is to specify the macroeconomic factors driving the returns on company assets and to allow them to drive the correlations in the events of default.

Challenges in Using the Merton Model: A Preview

In Chapter 19, we present a detailed suite of test results using huge databases for reduced form, Merton and hybrid models. The results, which are well-known to many sophisticated users of credit models, will disappoint many fans of the intuition embedded in the Merton model, the authors included!

Nonetheless, in the Basel II era, we cannot afford to avoid this reality. We have to examine the causes of the differential in model performance and constantly use this analysis to refine credit modeling techniques.

Van Deventer and Imai [2003] extensively summarize the strengths and concerns with each of the models they review, including the Merton and Shimko, Tejima, van Deventer random interest rates version of the Merton model. In their view, the key factors that contribute to the model performance issues in the Merton model can be summarized as follows:

- The model implicitly assumes a highly volatile capital structure by positing that the dollar amount of debt stays constant while the value of company assets varies randomly.
- The model (in traditional form) assumes interest rates are constant, but they are not.
- The model assumes that company assets are traded in a perfectly liquid market so the Black-Scholes replication arguments can apply. In reality, most corporate assets are illiquid, which makes the application of the Black-Scholes model inappropriate in both theory and practice.
- The model does not allow for early default—default only occurs at the end of the period.
- The model's functional form is very rigid and does not allow the flexibility to incorporate other powerful explanatory variables in default probability prediction.

Finally, from a portfolio management point of view, we prefer a model where the correlation in defaults can be derived, not assumed. As we have emphasized throughout this book, we are seeking pricing, valuation and hedging at both the transaction level and the portfolio level. The Merton model leaves us wondering 'how do I hedge?' We show in Chapter 19 that many naïve models of default have a greater accuracy in the ordinal ranking of companies by riskiness than the Merton model. This result, which is well known to the largest and most sophisticated users of default models, motivates the more modern reduced form approach, to which we now turn.

Appendix 1

In the Merton model of risky debt, the volatility of returns on company assets (not the volatility of the value of assets), σ, is a critical parameter but it is not observable.

We can observe the historical volatility of returns on the company's common stock (note, this is *not* the same as the volatility of the stock price or standard deviation of the stock price). By linking this observable historical volatility of common stock returns by formula to the historical volatility of company asset returns, we can derive the value of the volatility of company asset returns σ.

Assumptions

The value of company assets V follows the same stochastic process as specified in Black-Scholes:

$$\frac{dV}{V} = \alpha \, dt + \sigma \, dZ$$

We will use Ito's lemma to expand the formula for the value of equity, the Black-Scholes call option $C[V(0), 0, T, K]$, and then link its volatility to the volatility of company assets σ.

Using Ito's Lemma to Expand Changes in the Value of Company Equity

Merton's assumptions lead to the conclusion that the value of company assets is a call option on the assets of the firm $C[V(0), 0, T, K]$. Using Ito's lemma as we did in the chapter on term structure models, we can write the stochastic formula for changes in stock price as a function of V:

$$dC = C_V \, dV + \frac{1}{2} C_{VV} (dV)^2 \, dt + C_t \, dt$$

Substituting for dV gives:

$$dC = C_V (V\alpha \, dt + V\sigma \, dZ) + \frac{1}{2} C_{VV} (dV)^2 \, dt + C_t \, dt$$

We can then rearrange, separating the drift from the stochastic terms:

$$dC = \left[C_V V r \, dt + \frac{1}{2} C_{VV} (dV)^2 \, dt + C_t \, dt \right] + C_V V \sigma \, dZ$$

The equation above is for the change in stock price C. The volatility of stock price (*not* return on the stock price) is $C_V V \sigma$. We can get the expression for the volatility of the return on the stock price by dividing both sides by stock price C:

$$\frac{dC}{C} = \frac{\left[C_V V r \, dt + (1/2) C_{VV} (dV)^2 \, dt + C_t \, dt \right]}{C} + \frac{C_V V \sigma}{C} \, dZ$$

Therefore, the market convention calculation for the volatility of the return on common stock σ_C (which is observable given the observable stock price history) is:

$$\sigma_C = \frac{C_V V \sigma}{C}$$

We solve this equation for σ to express the volatility of the return on the assets of the firm as a function of the volatility of the return of the firm's common stock:

$$\frac{\sigma_C C}{C_V V} = \sigma$$

This formula can be used for σ in the Merton model of risky debt.

CHAPTER **17**

Reduced Form Credit Models

The challenges associated with the Merton model discussed in Chapter 16 were not the only motivators of researchers looking for a more comprehensive, all-encompassing framework for risk management. Many sophisticated bankers were looking for a synthesis between models of default for major corporations and the credit scoring technology that has been used for decades to rate the riskiness of retail and small business borrowers. The Merton model's restrictive assumptions and inflexible functional form mean that it cannot provide this comprehensive framework, although it could serve as an input to a more comprehensive approach.[1] Indeed, the only firm offering a small business implementation of the Merton model discontinued the product in recent years. The framework long sought by bankers, the reduced form modeling framework, has blossomed dramatically in the years since the Jarrow-Turnbull paper was published in 1995. On December 10 2003, the Federal Deposit Insurance Corporation announced that it was adopting the reduced form modeling framework for its new Loss Distribution Model (see the website of the FDIC for details of the model), after many years of studying the Merton model as an alternative.

In this chapter, we introduce the basic concepts of the reduced form modeling technology and the reasons that it has gained such quick popularity.[2]

The Jarrow-Turnbull Model, 1995

Many researchers trace the first reduced form model to Jarrow and Turnbull [1995], and we start our review of the reduced form model with that paper.

---

[1] For an example of such a hybrid model, see the test results in Chapter 19.

[2] Interested readers who would like more technical details on reduced form models should see van Deventer and Imai [2003], Duffie and Singleton [2003], Lando [2004], and Schonbucher [2003]. See also the many technical papers in the research section of the Kamakura Corporation website, www.kamakuraco.com.

Jarrow and Turnbull's objective was to outline a modeling approach that would allow valuation, pricing and hedging of derivatives where the:

- asset underlying the derivative security might default or;
- writer of the derivative security might default.

This kind of compound credit risk is essential to properly valuing the Jarrow-Merton put option on the assets of a financial institution, which we discussed as the best single integrated measure of the total risk of all types that a financial institution has. This compound approach to default is also at the very core of the New Capital Accords [2003] proposed by the Basel Committee on Banking Supervision because of the prevalence of compound default risks in typical bank loan guaranties and in derivatives markets. In addition, analyzing compound credit risk is a substantial departure from the popular Black-Scholes approach that is all-pervasive in the market place. The Black-Scholes model assumes that the company:

- whose common stock underlies an option on the common stock will not default and;
- the counterparty who has written the call option and has an obligation to pay if the option is 'in the money' will not default.

Ignoring this kind of compound default risk can lead to very large problems, like the potential loss of $500 million that J.P. Morgan had at risk in the Asia crisis in 1997–1998.[3] The Merton model discussed in the last chapter is not flexible enough to provide the kind of framework that Jarrow and Turnbull were seeking[4].

The Jarrow-Turnbull framework

Jarrow and Turnbull assume a frictionless economy where two classes of zero-coupon bonds trade.[5] The first class of bonds are risk-free zero-coupon bonds $P(t, T)$, where t is the current time and T is the maturity date. They also introduce the idea of a 'money market fund' $B(t)$ which represents the compounded proceeds of $1 invested in the shortest term risk-free asset starting at time zero. The second class of bonds trading are the risky zero-coupon

---

[3] See van Deventer and Imai [2003] for a discussion of this incident, which illustrates the need for a higher standard for 'best practices' in risk management.

[4] See Jarrow and Turnbull for a discussion of the complexities of using a Geske [1979]-style compound options approach to analyze compound credit risks.

[5] This assumption is necessary for the rigorous academic framework of the model but not for the model's practical implementation.

bonds of XYZ company, which potentially may default. These zero-coupon bonds have a bond price $v(t, T)$. For expositional purposes, Jarrow and Turnbull assume that interest rates and the probability of default are statistically independent.[6] They assume that the time of bankruptcy T^* for firm XYZ is exponentially distributed with parameter 1. They assume that there is a Poisson bankruptcy process driven by the parameter μ, which they assume to be a positive constant less than 1.[7] Jarrow and Turnbull assume that the risk-free interest rates are random and consistent with the extended Merton term structure model (the continuous time version of the Ho and Lee model) that we studied in Chapter 11. They also assume that in the event of bankruptcy, $1 of XYZ zero-coupon debt pays a recovery rate $\delta < 1$ on the scheduled maturity date of the zero (not at the time of default). When bankruptcy occurs, the value of XYZ zero-coupon debt falls to $\delta P(T^*, T)$ because the payment at maturity falls from $1 to δ, but the payment of δ is now certain and risk-free. The value of δ can be different for debt of different seniorities. For expositional purposes, Jarrow and Turnbull assume that the recovery rate is constant. We relax that assumption in the next section.

Jarrow and Turnbull show that the value of a defaultable zero-coupon bond in this model is:

$$v(t, T) = \left[e^{-\lambda\mu(T-t)} + (1 - e^{-\lambda\mu(T-t)})\delta \right] P(t, T)$$

We can interpret this formula in a practical way by noting a few points. The product $(\lambda\mu)$ is the continuous probability of default at any instant in time. The quantity:

$$1 - e^{-\lambda\mu(T-t)}$$

is the (risk neutral) probability that XYZ company defaults between time t and maturity of the zero-coupon bond T. The quantity:

$$e^{-\lambda\mu(T-t)}$$

is the (risk neutral) probability that company XYZ does *not* default between time t and maturity of the zero-coupon bond at time T. With this in mind, we

---

[6] Jarrow and Turnbull discuss how to relax this assumption, which we do in the next section.

[7] This again means that default risk and interest rates (for the time being) are not correlated. The parameter μ technically represents the Poisson bankruptcy process under the martingale process, the risk neutral bankruptcy process.

can see that Jarrow and Turnbull have reached a very neat and, with hindsight, simple conclusion that the value of a zero-coupon bond in the Jarrow-Turnbull model is the probability-weighted present value of what the bond holder receives if we know there is no default (in which case we have the equivalent of a risk-free bond, $P(t, T)$), and what we receive if we know for certain that default will occur, the recovery rate multiplied by the risk-free zero-coupon bond price $\delta P(\tau, T)$.

This clever result depends on the assumption that default and interest rates are not correlated. Like the Shimko, Tejima and van Deventer [1993] version of the Merton model, we relax this assumption in the next section.

Jarrow and Turnbull then go on to derive closed form solutions for a number of important securities prices:

- European call option on XYZ Company's defaultable zero-coupon bond;
- Defaultable European call option on XYZ's defaultable zero-coupon bond (where the writer of the call option might default, assuming its default probability is independent of both interest rates and the bankruptcy of XYZ);
- European call option on XYZ Company's defaultable common stock.

The Jarrow-Turnbull modeling framework is a very important extension of the risk management analytics we have discussed so far, because it provides an integrated and flexible framework for analyzing interest rate risk and credit risk, the central objective of this book.

We have one task left, and that is to discuss the extension of the approach above to interest rate-dependent and macroeconomic factor-dependent default.

The Jarrow Model

The Jarrow [1999–2001] model is an important extension of the Jarrow-Turnbull [1995] model, which was perhaps the first reduced form model to experience wide-spread commercial acceptance. Many other researchers, most notably Duffie and Singleton [1999], have done very important work on reduced form models but in the remainder of this chapter we will concentrate on Jarrow's work because of the continuity with the Jarrow-Turnbull model we discussed in the previous section.

In the early days of the credit derivatives markets, dealers turned to the Merton model for pricing purposes. Dealers soon realized that the credit default swap market prices were consistently different from those indicated by the Merton model for many of the reasons we have discussed in Chapter 16. Dealers were under considerable pressure from both management, risk managers, and external auditors to adopt a modeling technology with better pricing accuracy. Dealers' instinct for self-preservation was an added incentive.

The Jarrow-Turnbull model was the first model which allowed the matching of market prices and provided a rational economic basis for the evolution of market prices of everything from corporate debt to credit derivatives.

The original Jarrow-Turnbull model [1995] assumes that default is random but that default probabilities are non-random time-dependent functions. The Jarrow [1999–2001] model extends the Jarrow-Turnbull model in a large number of significant respects. First, default probabilities are assumed to be random, with explicit dependence of default probabilities on random interest rates and an arbitrary number of lognormally distributed risk factors. These lognormally distributed risk factors are extremely important in modeling correlated default, a critical factor in the U.S. as van Deventer and Imai [2003] show. Van Deventer and Imai also demonstrate the strong links between macroeconomic factors and credit risk, a phenomenon we explore further in Chapter 19.

Jarrow goes beyond the Jarrow-Turnbull framework by explicitly incorporating a liquidity factor that affects the prices of bonds, but not equity. This liquidity factor can be random and is different for each bond issuer. In addition, the liquidity parameter can be a function of the same macro risk drivers that determine the default intensity, a phenomenon that many researchers note in Chapter 18. Although we use the term 'liquidity factor', we intend the term to describe everything affecting bond prices above and beyond potential losses due to default. This can include things like bid-offered price spreads, the impact on market prices of the sale of large holdings of a specific bond issue (i.e. the Long Term Capital Management incident), general risk aversion in the fixed income market, and so on.

The Jarrow model also allows for the calculation of the implied recovery given default δ_i. This parameter, which can be random and driven by other risk factors, is defined by Jarrow as the fractional recovery of δ where v is the value of risky debt a fraction of an instant before bankruptcy at time τ and the subscript i denotes the seniority level of the debt.

$$\text{Recovery} = \delta_i(\tau)v(\tau-, T : i)$$

This is a different recovery structure than Jarrow-Turnbull, where the recovery rate was specified as a fraction of the principal value to be received at maturity T.

Duffie and Singleton [1999] were the first to use this specification for the recovery rate. They recognized that the traditional bankers' thinking on the recovery rate, expressed as percentage of 'principal', made the mathematical derivation of bond and credit derivatives prices more difficult. They also recognized that thinking of recovery as a percentage of principal was too limiting—what is the principal on an 'in the money' interest rate cap? On a foreign exchange option? On an undrawn loan commitment? Expressing recovery as a percentage of value one instant before bankruptcy is both more powerful and more general. We can easily convert it back to the traditional 'recovery rate as a percentage of principal' to maximize user-friendliness of the concept.

The hazard rate, or 'default intensity', in the Jarrow model is given by a linear combination of three terms:

$$\lambda(t) = \lambda_0 + \lambda_1 r(t) + \lambda_2 Z(t)$$

This is a much simpler expression than the default probability we discussed in the derivation of the Merton credit model in Chapter 16, and it is much richer than the structure of Jarrow-Turnbull. The first term, λ_0, can be made time-dependent, extending the credit model exactly like we extended term structure models in Chapter 11. The term $Z(t)$ is the 'shock' term with mean zero and standard deviation of one which creates random movements in the macro factor(s) (like oil prices, in the case of ExxonMobil), which drives default for that particular company.[8] Movements in this macro factor are generally written in this form:

$$dM(t) = M(t)[r(t)\,dt + \sigma_m\,dZ(t)]$$

The change in the macro factor, say oil prices, is proportional to its value and drifts upward at the random risk-free interest rate $r(t)$, subject to random shocks from changes in $Z(t)$, multiplied by the volatility of the macro factor, σ_m. While the default intensity in the Jarrow model, as we have written it, describes interest rates and one macro factor as drivers of default, it is easy to extend the model to an arbitrary number of macro factors. This is because the sum of a linear combination of normally distributed variables such as $Z(t)$ is still normally distributed. In this book, we will use the one factor notation for expositional purposes. Please note that the incorporation of these macroeconomic drivers of default means that the default probabilities (and default intensities) are correlated due to their dependence on common factors. This is a very important step forward from Jarrow-Turnbull where the default probabilities of the two companies in that example were uncorrelated with each other and with interest rates.

In the Jarrow model, interest rates are random, but the term structure model chosen is a more realistic model than the extended Merton model. The term structure model assumed for the riskless rate of interest is a special case of the

---

[8] In more mathematical terms, $Z(t)$ is standard Brownian motion under a risk neutral probability distribution Q with initial value zero that drives the movements of the market index $M(t)$.

Heath, Jarrow and Morton [1992] framework commonly known as the Hull-White or Extended Vasicek model. In our Chapter 16 discussion of the Shimko, Tejima and van Deventer model, we used the original Vasicek [1977] term structure model. This is the easiest model to manipulate, and it has the virtue of being so straightforward that a good spreadsheet analyst can implement the model. For practical use, though, it is critical that the risk-free interest rate assumptions be completely consistent with the current observable yield curve (and any other interest rate derivatives on that yield curve). The Extended Vasicek model contains an extension from the original Vasicek model, which allows the theoretical yield curve to exactly match the actual yield curve. In this model, as we discussed in Chapter 11, the short-term rate of interest, $r(t)$, drifts over time in a way consistent with interest rate cycles, subject to random shocks from the Brownian motion $W(t)$, which like $Z(t)$, has mean zero and standard deviation of 1.[9]

$$dr(t) = a[\bar{r}(t) - r(t)]\, dt + \sigma_r\, dW(t)$$

Zero-Coupon Bond Prices in the Jarrow Model

Jarrow shows that the price of a zero-coupon bond can be derived that explicitly incorporates the interactions between the default intensity, interest rates, and the macro factor. The results are simple enough to be modeled in spreadsheet software, especially the case where the coefficients of short-term interest rates and the macro factors are zero. We discuss practical implementation of this version of the Jarrow model below.

The Jarrow Model and the Issue of Liquidity in the Bond Market

One of the many virtues of reduced form models is the ability to fit parameters to the model from a wide variety of securities prices. The type of data of most interest to lenders is bond prices or credit derivatives prices. Since a large company like IBM has only one type of common stock outstanding, while it could have 10, 20 or 30 bond issues outstanding, it is logical to expect that there is less liquidity in the bond market than in the market for common stock. Jarrow makes an explicit adjustment for this in his model by introducing a very general formulation for the impact of liquidity on bond market prices. This is a very powerful feature of the model that reduces the question

---

[9] The expression for random movements in the short rate is again written under a risk neutral probability distribution.

of bond market liquidity to a scientific question (how best to fit a parameter which captures the liquidity impact), rather than a philosophical question of whether or not bond prices can be used to calculate the parameters of a credit model. Note that there can be either a liquidity discount or liquidity premium on the bonds of a given issuer, and there is no implicit assumption by Jarrow that the liquidity discount is constant—it can be random and is flexible in its specifications, consistent with the research we discuss in Chapter 18.

Jarrow's original [1999–2001] model shows how the Jarrow credit model can be fitted to bond prices and equity prices simultaneously or it can be fitted to bond prices alone. Jarrow and Yildirum [2002] show how the model can be fitted to credit derivatives prices and Chava and Jarrow [2002a, 2002b] fit the model to historical data on defaults.

The Jarrow-Merton Put Option as a Risk Index and a Practical Hedge

As we have noted throughout this book, our objective is an integrated treatment of credit risk and interest rate risk. We want a coherent measure of integrated risk, like the Jarrow-Merton put option we first mentioned in Chapter 1. In addition to measuring risk accurately, we want to be able to do something about it. Indeed, one of the key objectives of the credit risk process is practical action—the effective hedging of credit risk. In the Merton model, the single risk driver of default is the value of company assets. For portfolio hedging, we need to know the value of company assets for all companies and how they are correlated, what macro risk drivers affect them, and what the mathematical link is between these macro factors and the value of company assets. None of these links between macro factors and the value of company assets is specified in the Merton credit model, although there are various ways we can use other work of Robert Merton to build this framework. Market practitioners tend to assume the structure of the correlation, rather than deriving it as in the Jarrow framework.

The Jarrow model is much better suited to hedging credit risk on a portfolio level than the Merton model, because the link between the (N) macro factor(s) reflected in M and the default intensity is explicitly incorporated in the model. Take the example of Exxon, whose probability of default is driven by interest rates and oil prices, among other things. If $M(t)$ is the macro factor oil prices, it can be shown that the size of the hedge that needs to be bought or sold to hedge one dollar of risky zero-coupon debt with market value v under the Jarrow model is given by:

$$\partial v_l(t, T : i)/\partial M(t)$$
$$= -[\partial \gamma_i(t, T)/\partial M(t) + \lambda_2(1 - \delta_i)(T - t)/\sigma_m M(t)]v_l(t, T : i)$$

The variable v is the value of risky zero-coupon debt and gamma is the liquidity discount function representing the illiquidities often observed in the debt market. There are similar formulas in the Jarrow model for hedging coupon-bearing bonds, defaultable caps, floors, credit derivatives and so on.

Van Deventer and Imai [2003] show that the steps in hedging the macro factor risk for any portfolio are identical to the steps that a trader of options has been taking for 30 years (hedging their net position with a long or short position in the common stock underlying the options):

- Calculate the change in the value (including the impact of interest rates on default) of all retail credits with respect to interest rates.
- Calculate the change in the value (including the impact of interest rates on default) of all small business credits with respect to interest rates.
- Calculate the change in the value (including the impact of interest rates on default) of all major corporate credits with respect to interest rates.
- Calculate the change in the value (including the impact of interest rates on default) of all bonds, derivatives, and other instruments.
- Add these 'delta' amounts together.
- The result is the global portfolio 'delta', on a default-adjusted basis, of interest rates for the entire portfolio.
- Choose the position in interest rate derivatives with the opposite delta.
- This eliminates interest rate risk from the portfolio on a default-adjusted basis.

We can replicate this process for any macro factor that impacts default, such as exchange rates, stock price indices, oil prices, the value of class A office buildings in the central business district of key cities, etc.

Most importantly:

- We can measure the default-adjusted transaction level and portfolio risk exposure with respect to each macro factor.
- We can set exposure limits on the default-adjusted transaction level and portfolio risk exposure with respect to each macro factor.
- We know how much of a hedge would eliminate some or all of this risk.

It can be shown that all other risk, other than that driven by macro factors, can be diversified away. This hedging and diversification capability is a powerful step forward from where most financial institutions found themselves at the close of the twentieth century.

Fitting the Jarrow Model to Bond Prices, Credit Derivatives Prices, and Historical Default Databases

One of the many advantages of the reduced form modeling approach is its rich array of closed form solutions. These include closed form solutions for zero-coupon bond prices, coupon-bearing bond prices, credit default swap prices, first to default swap prices and many others. This means that there are many alternatives for fitting the Jarrow model parameters. We discuss a few of them in the following section.

Fitting the Jarrow model to debt prices

Later in this chapter, we analyze an example of how to fit the Jarrow model to observable prices of risky debt. Third party bond price vendors offer databases with daily or weekly prices on more than 100,000 different risky debt issues. Prices can be obtained for almost every issuer with a rating from the major rating agencies. Once these prices have been obtained, there are two major approaches for fitting the Jarrow parameters:

Fitting to current price data only

The first method would be to fit the Jarrow parameters to currently observable prices only. The steps in the fitting are as follows:

1. Assume a structure of the liquidity function in the Jarrow model. For example, a liquidity function that is effectively linear in years to maturity could be adopted. Say the assumed structure contains two parameters a and b.
2. Collect the N observable bond prices.
3. Using a non-linear equation solver, find the combination of a, b, λ_0, λ_1, and λ_2 which minimizes the sum of squared errors on the observable bonds.
4. Eliminate any remaining pricing errors by making λ_0 a time-dependent variable. The original value of λ_0 is useful to obtain because it is the value which minimizes the amount of extension, exactly as we fitted the Hull and White term structure model in Chapter 11 by finding the Vasicek parameters which are best fitting as a first step.

We illustrate this process in an example below.

Fitting to current price data and historical price data

If we are willing to accept the hypothesis that the impact of interest rates and macroeconomic factors on the default probability of a particular company is fairly stable over time, one can improve the quality of parameter estimates by adding historical data to the estimation procedure. Let's assume that the analyst has five years of daily price data for, say, IBM bonds. The following procedure takes advantage of this data.

1. Assume a structure of the liquidity function in the Jarrow model. For example, a liquidity function that is effectively linear in years to maturity could be adopted. Say the assumed structure contains two parameters a and b.
2. Collect the $N(i)$ observable bond prices on each observation date i, for the whole sample $i = 1, M$ observations.
3. Using a non-linear equation solver over the entire sample, find the combination of a, b, λ_0, λ_1, and λ_2 which minimizes the sum of squared errors on the observable bonds.
4. λ_1 and λ_2 are the coefficients of interest rates and the macro factors on default. We hold these parameters constant over the whole sample and then go back over the sample and refit the parameters a, b, and λ_0 for each day in the sample, allowing them to change daily.
5. Eliminate any remaining bond pricing errors on a given day by making λ_0 a time (to maturity) dependent variable. The original value of λ_0 for that day, as above, is useful to obtain because it is the value which minimizes the amount of extension, exactly as we fitted the Hull and White term structure model in Chapter 11 by finding the Vasicek parameters which are best fitting as a first step.

Fitting the Jarrow model to credit derivatives prices

The procedure for fitting the Jarrow model to credit derivatives prices is exactly the same as fitting the Jarrow model to bond prices, except of course that the closed form solution that is being used is the credit derivatives formula in the Jarrow model, not the bond price formula. Because most counterparties with traded credit derivatives will have only one to three maturities at which prices are visible, using a longer history of credit derivatives prices as described in the second method above will be even more helpful than it is in the bond market.

Fitting the Jarrow model to a historical database of defaults

The Kamakura Corporation launched its Kamakura Risk Information Services (KRIS) default probability products in November 2002. Among the default probabilities offered by Kamakura was the first ever reduced form default probability model, along with the Kamakura Merton default probability and a hybrid model using a reduced form model structure with the Merton model as one of many explanatory variables. We discuss the accuracy and performance of these models in the next chapter.

Fitting the reduced form model to historical bankruptcy data was explored extensively by Chava and Jarrow [2002a, 2002b] and van Deventer and

Imai [2003]. This fitting process involves advanced hazard rate modeling, an extension of the credit scoring technology that has been used for retail and small business default probability estimation for many decades. The distinction between credit scoring and hazard rate modeling is very important. Typically, credit scoring analysis uses the most recent information available on a set of non-defaulting counterparties and the last set of information available on the defaulting counterparties. Hazard rate modeling makes use of all information about all counterparties at every available time period, in order to explain, for example, why Enron defaulted in December 2001 instead of at some earlier time.

The Kamakura Corporation's KRIS default probability service includes more than 1.2 million monthly observations on over 8,000 companies for North America alone. In the North American sample, more than 1,600 companies have failed. A company failure is denoted as a 'one' in the bankruptcy variable, and the lack of failure is denoted as a 'zero'. Since the entire history of a company is included, Enron will have many observations that are 'zeros' and only one observation which is a 'one', the December 2001 observation.

All of the companies are modeled together and a set of explanatory variables are gathered which best predict default. In addition to interest rates and macro factors that are part of the theory of the Jarrow model, other factors that are known to be important are added as appropriate. These include financial ratios, other macroeconomic variables, multiple inputs from the stock price and its history for each company, company size, industry variables and so on. As we will see in Chapter 19, the result is a very powerful model highly capable of discriminating among companies by both long-term and short-term risk. Logistic regression is the tool that is used to estimate the parameters or coefficients multiplying each input variable, as explained in detail by van Deventer and Imai.

Chava and Jarrow [2002a, 2002b] discuss how these hazard-rate modeling-based default probabilities can be converted to the Jarrow theory we discuss above and related to the parameters λ_0, λ_1, and λ_2.

Fitting the Jarrow Model to Retail, Small Business, and Governmental Counterparties

While the Jarrow-Turnbull and Jarrow models have been discussed in the context of a corporate counterparty, there is no reason to restrict the models' application to corporations alone. They can be applied with equal effectiveness to retail client default modeling, small business default modeling, and to the modeling of defaults by sovereign entities. The only difference is the inputs to the logistic regression model like that which we discussed in the preceding paragraphs. Other than that, all of the analysis is identical.

For example, consider sovereigns that issue debt, but for whom there are no observable prices (say, Kazakhstan); historical estimation using logistic regression is the normal fall-back estimation procedure. To do such estimation of the Jarrow model for sovereigns would require construction of a historical database of sovereigns and their financial attributes and a variable showing default/no default in various points in time.

In many countries there is a large amount of bond issuance by cities, towns, municipal special purpose entities, and other government entities besides the national government itself. The prices of the bonds issued by these entities are sometimes heavily affected by special tax features, such as the exemption of municipal bonds from federal income tax in the U.S. Jarrow default probabilities can be fitted to this group as well, both from bond prices (if they are high quality) and by logistic regression from a historical default database.

Example: Fitting the basic Jarrow Bond model parameters to the credit spread curve

In the basic Jarrow model where the default intensity $\lambda_0(t)$ (the probability of default over the next instant at time t) is constant, Jarrow shows that the zero-coupon credit spread at time t with maturity at time T is the sum of two components, a liquidity component and an expect loss component. The liquidity component is broadly defined to include everything that is not expected loss.

Credit Spread (CS) (t, T) = Liquidity Component + Expected Loss Component

The Jarrow model is very general with respect to the functional form of the liquidity component. For practical implementation, however, it is extremely powerful and simple to assume that the liquidity component of the credit spread is a linear function of the years to maturity $T - t$.

$$\text{Liquidity Component} = a_0 + a_1 \times (T - t),$$

where a_0 and a_1 are constants, T is date of payment and t is the current date. Thus $(T - t)$ is years to payment date.

The expected loss component is not a function of years to maturity because the default intensity λ_0 is assumed (for purposes of the example in this section only) to be constant. The recovery rate δ in the Jarrow model is also assumed to have a very general form. To make the mathematics of the derivation and usage of the model as simple as possible, as mentioned above, δ is *not* defined as the recovery as a percentage of a bond's principal, the traditional bond market convention. Instead, the recovery rate is expressed as a percentage of the 'security's value' an instant before bankruptcy. This is a more general assumption because the 'security' may not be a bond—it could be a foreign exchange put option that is defaultable, or it could be an interest rate swap or an option on a common stock where it is not clear what the traditional fixed income definition of 'principal' should be. We can easily convert back and forth, however, between the definition of δ and the more traditional definition of recovery rate as a percentage of bond principal. With that bit of background, we can define the expected loss component of the zero-coupon credit spread:

$$\text{Expected Loss Component} = \lambda_0 (1 - \delta),$$

where λ_0 is the Jarrow default intensity and δ is the recovery rate.

As we saw above, the zero-coupon credit spread observed between risky and risk-free bonds is composed of the liquidity components and the expected loss component

$$\text{Credit Spread } (t, T) = \text{Liquidity Component} + \text{Expected Loss Component}$$

And given our assumptions,

$$\text{Credit Spread } (t, T) = [a_0 + a_1 (T{-}t)] + \lambda_0 (1 - \delta)$$

Note that there is a different credit spread for each maturity, and therefore a different credit spread for each cash flow associated with a particular bond or other security. If we rearrange the credit spread into a constant term and a term that is linear in years to maturity we get:

$$\text{Credit Spread } (t, T) = X + B (T - t)$$

where the constant X has both a liquidity and expected loss component:

$$X = a_0 + \lambda_0 (1 - \delta)$$

and where the coefficient of years to maturity B is simply:

$$B = a_1$$

Therefore if we can empirically estimate X and B, we can extract the Jarrow parameters from X and B in a number of ways.

There are four common methods for extracting the remaining Jarrow parameters from the equation

$$X = a_0 + \lambda_0 (1 - \delta)$$

1. **Set a_0 equal to zero and solve for δ_{implied}.** This works if the left side of the possible range in which a_0 must lie (for the recovery rate to be between zero and one) is negative and the right side is positive. It doesn't work if the constraints on a_0 require it to be a positive number.

This is a common choice because it conveniently reduces the number of variables we need to use.

2. **Set δ to be a figure identified from a rating agency or other historical experience and solve for a_0.** This is also a common choice, but it is not helpful if determining the implied recovery rate is our main objective.

3. **Override λ_0 until it falls in a range in which we can again use Alternative 1.** If the estimates of λ_0 are volatile, a moving average of λ_0 can be used to accomplish this objective. This is also a defensible option.

4. **Solve for the ratio k between the minimum allowable a_0 value and maximum allowable a_0 value (for the recovery rate to be between zero and one), which minimizes the standard deviation of a_0. The recovery rate can be shown to be constant and equal to this k. See below.**

We discuss fitting of the yield curve to risky bonds in more detail in Chapter 18.

Research supporting this assumption as a good first approximation is included in Appendix 1 of this chapter, using the First Interstate Bancorp credit spread data in van Deventer and Imai [2003]. The average R^2 on linear regressions fitted as a function of maturity to 427 weeks of new issue credit spreads for First Interstate Bancorp from 1984 to 1993 was 95%. The lowest R^2 of any observation was 85%.

ACME Company bond example for two coupon-bearing bonds

This section provides a worked example of the determination of implied Jarrow parameters from traded bond prices.

We assume that the following traded bond information is available on September 5 2003:

Today's	9/5/2003
Bond A	
Coupon	5%
Maturity	7/31/2016
Principal	100.00
Dirty Price (Price + Accrued Interest)	$91.00
Seniority	Senior
Bond B	
Coupon	6%
Maturity	8/27/2021
Principal	100.00
Dirty Price (Price + Accrued Interest)	$93.50
Seniority	Senior

How should an investor benchmark the Jarrow models to decide whether or not to buy bond C, for which he's received an offer from an investment banking firm?

General calculation steps

Step 1: Calculate the risk-free zero yields for the present value factors for the payment dates from raw risk-free bond prices or yields. We recommend the maximum smoothness forward rate technique as discussed in Chapter 8 for this calculation. Let's assume that we have done that and obtained the following zero-coupon risk-free yields for the payment dates associated with Bond A.

Today's Date   9/5/2003

Bond A Payment Dates	Bond A Years to Maturity	US Treasury Zero-Coupon Yields
1/31/2004	0.41	4.0446%
7/31/2004	0.90	4.0995%
1/31/2005	1.41	4.1549%
7/31/2005	1.90	4.2095%
1/31/2006	2.41	4.2649%
7/31/2006	2.90	4.3195%
1/31/2007	3.41	4.3749%
7/31/2007	3.90	4.4295%
1/31/2008	4.41	4.4849%
7/31/2008	4.91	4.5398%
1/31/2009	5.41	4.5952%
7/31/2009	5.91	4.6498%
1/31/2010	6.41	4.7052%
7/31/2010	6.91	4.7598%
1/31/2011	7.41	4.8152%
7/31/2011	7.91	4.8698%
1/31/2012	8.41	4.9252%
7/31/2012	8.91	4.9801%
1/31/2013	9.41	5.0355%
7/31/2013	9.91	5.0901%
1/31/2014	10.41	5.1455%
7/31/2014	10.91	5.2001%
1/31/2015	11.41	5.2555%
7/31/2015	11.91	5.3101%
1/31/2016	12.41	5.3655%
7/31/2016	12.91	5.4204%

Today's Date   9/5/2003

Bond B Payment Dates	Bond B Years to Maturity	US Treasury Zero-Coupon Yields
2/27/2004	0.48	4.0527%
8/27/2004	0.98	4.1076%
2/27/2005	1.48	4.1630%
8/27/2005	1.98	4.2176%
2/27/2006	2.48	4.2730%
8/27/2006	2.98	4.3276%
2/27/2007	3.48	4.3830%
8/27/2007	3.98	4.4376%
2/27/2008	4.48	4.4930%
8/27/2008	4.98	4.5479%
2/27/2009	5.48	4.6033%
8/27/2009	5.98	4.6579%
2/27/2010	6.48	4.7133%
8/27/2010	6.98	4.7679%
2/27/2011	7.48	4.8233%
8/27/2011	7.98	4.8779%
2/27/2012	8.48	4.9333%
8/27/2012	8.98	4.9882%
2/27/2013	9.49	5.0436%
8/27/2013	9.98	5.0982%
2/27/2014	10.49	5.1536%
8/27/2014	10.98	5.2082%
2/27/2015	11.49	5.2636%
8/27/2015	11.98	5.3182%
2/27/2016	12.49	5.3736%
8/27/2016	12.99	5.4285%
2/27/2017	13.49	5.4839%
8/27/2017	13.99	5.5385%
2/27/2018	14.49	5.5939%
8/27/2018	14.99	5.6485%
2/27/2019	15.49	5.7039%
8/27/2019	15.99	5.7585%
2/27/2020	16.49	5.8139%
8/27/2020	16.99	5.8688%
2/27/2021	17.49	5.9242%
8/27/2021	17.99	5.9788%

Step 2: In the simplest form of the Jarrow model, the model implies that the credit spread is linear in the form Credit Spread $= X + B$(years to maturity). In Step 2, we assume this form and guess the Jarrow parameters of X and B. We assume that $X = 0.004$ and $B = 0.001$. That gives us the following implied credit spreads:

Bond A Payment Dates	Bond A Years to Maturity	US Treasury Zero-Coupon Yields	Bond A Credit Spread
1/31/2004	0.41	4.0446%	0.4405%
7/31/2004	0.90	4.0995%	0.4904%
1/31/2005	1.41	4.1549%	0.5408%
7/31/2005	1.90	4.2095%	0.5904%
1/31/2006	2.41	4.2649%	0.6408%
7/31/2006	2.90	4.3195%	0.6904%
1/31/2007	3.41	4.3749%	0.7408%
7/31/2007	3.90	4.4295%	0.7904%
1/31/2008	4.41	4.4849%	0.8408%
7/31/2008	4.91	4.5398%	0.8907%
1/31/2009	5.41	4.5952%	0.9411%
7/31/2009	5.91	4.6498%	0.9907%
1/31/2010	6.41	4.7052%	1.0411%
7/31/2010	6.91	4.7598%	1.0907%
1/31/2011	7.41	4.8152%	1.1411%
7/31/2011	7.91	4.8698%	1.1907%
1/31/2012	8.41	4.9252%	1.2411%
7/31/2012	8.91	4.9801%	1.2910%
1/31/2013	9.41	5.0355%	1.3414%
7/31/2013	9.91	5.0901%	1.3910%
1/31/2014	10.41	5.1455%	1.4414%
7/31/2014	10.91	5.2001%	1.4910%
1/31/2015	11.41	5.2555%	1.5414%
7/31/2015	11.91	5.3101%	1.5910%
1/31/2016	12.41	5.3655%	1.6414%
7/31/2016	12.91	5.4204%	1.6912%

Bond B Payment Dates	Bond B Years to Maturity	US Treasury Zero-Coupon Yields	Bond B Credit Spread
2/27/2004	0.48	4.0527%	0.4479%
8/27/2004	0.98	4.1076%	0.4978%
2/27/2005	1.48	4.1630%	0.5482%
8/27/2005	1.98	4.2176%	0.5978%
2/27/2006	2.48	4.2730%	0.6482%
8/27/2006	2.98	4.3276%	0.6978%
2/27/2007	3.48	4.3830%	0.7482%
8/27/2007	3.98	4.4376%	0.7978%
2/27/2008	4.48	4.4930%	0.8482%
8/27/2008	4.98	4.5479%	0.8981%
2/27/2009	5.48	4.6033%	0.9485%
8/27/2009	5.98	4.6579%	0.9981%
2/27/2010	6.48	4.7133%	1.0485%
8/27/2010	6.98	4.7679%	1.0981%
2/27/2011	7.48	4.8233%	1.1485%
8/27/2011	7.98	4.8779%	1.1981%
2/27/2012	8.48	4.9333%	1.2485%
8/27/2012	8.98	4.9882%	1.2984%
2/27/2013	9.49	5.0436%	1.3488%
8/27/2013	9.98	5.0982%	1.3984%
2/27/2014	10.49	5.1536%	1.4488%
8/27/2014	10.98	5.2082%	1.4984%
2/27/2015	11.49	5.2636%	1.5488%
8/27/2015	11.98	5.3182%	1.5984%
2/27/2016	12.49	5.3736%	1.6488%
8/27/2016	12.99	5.4285%	1.6986%
2/27/2017	13.49	5.4839%	1.7490%
8/27/2017	13.99	5.5385%	1.7986%
2/27/2018	14.49	5.5939%	1.8490%
8/27/2018	14.99	5.6485%	1.8986%
2/27/2019	15.49	5.7039%	1.9490%
8/27/2019	15.99	5.7585%	1.9986%
2/27/2020	16.49	5.8139%	2.0490%
8/27/2020	16.99	5.8688%	2.0989%
2/27/2021	17.49	5.9242%	2.1493%
8/27/2021	17.99	5.9788%	2.1989%

Step 3: Next, we calculate the risky zero yields by adding the credit spread to the risk-free yield for that payment date. Note that that there exists a different spread for every payment date, and that the credit spread is not just assumed to be constant for all maturities out to the maturity date. If only one bond price is available, a short-term proxy (for example commercial paper) needs to be incorporated, but in this example we have two bond prices.

Bond A Payment Dates	Bond A Years to Maturity	US Treasury Zero-Coupon Yields	Bond A Credit Spread	Bond A Zero Yield
1/31/2004	0.41	4.0446%	0.4405%	4.4852%
7/31/2004	0.90	4.0995%	0.4904%	4.5899%
1/31/2005	1.41	4.1549%	0.5408%	4.6957%
7/31/2005	1.90	4.2095%	0.5904%	4.7999%
1/31/2006	2.41	4.2649%	0.6408%	4.9057%
7/31/2006	2.90	4.3195%	0.6904%	5.0099%
1/31/2007	3.41	4.3749%	0.7408%	5.1157%
7/31/2007	3.90	4.4295%	0.7904%	5.2199%
1/31/2008	4.41	4.4849%	0.8408%	5.3257%
7/31/2008	4.91	4.5398%	0.8907%	5.4304%
1/31/2009	5.41	4.5952%	0.9411%	5.5363%
7/31/2009	5.91	4.6498%	0.9907%	5.6404%
1/31/2010	6.41	4.7052%	1.0411%	5.7463%
7/31/2010	6.91	4.7598%	1.0907%	5.8504%
1/31/2011	7.41	4.8152%	1.1411%	5.9563%
7/31/2011	7.91	4.8698%	1.1907%	6.0604%
1/31/2012	8.41	4.9252%	1.2411%	6.1663%
7/31/2012	8.91	4.9801%	1.2910%	6.2710%
1/31/2013	9.41	5.0355%	1.3414%	6.3769%
7/31/2013	9.91	5.0901%	1.3910%	6.4810%
1/31/2014	10.41	5.1455%	1.4414%	6.5869%
7/31/2014	10.91	5.2001%	1.4910%	6.6910%
1/31/2015	11.41	5.2555%	1.5414%	6.1969%
7/31/2015	11.91	5.3101%	1.5910%	6.9010%
1/31/2016	12.41	5.3655%	1.6414%	7.0069%
7/31/2016	12.91	5.4204%	1.6912%	7.1116%

Bond B Payment Dates	Bond B Years to Maturity	US Treasury Zero-Coupon Yields	Bond B Credit Spread	Bond B Zero Yield
2/27/2004	0.48	4.0527%	0.4479%	4.5007%
8/27/2004	0.98	4.1076%	0.4978%	4.6054%
2/27/2005	1.48	4.1630%	0.5482%	4.7113%
8/27/2005	1.98	4.2176%	0.5978%	4.8154%
2/27/2006	2.48	4.2730%	0.6482%	4.9213%
8/27/2006	2.98	4.3276%	0.6978%	5.0254%
2/27/2007	3.48	4.3830%	0.7482%	5.1313%
8/27/2007	3.98	4.4376%	0.7978%	5.2354%
2/27/2008	4.48	4.4930%	0.8482%	5.3413%
8/27/2008	4.98	4.5479%	0.8981%	5.4460%
2/27/2009	5.48	4.6033%	0.9485%	5.5518%
8/27/2009	5.98	4.6579%	0.9981%	5.6560%
2/27/2010	6.48	4.7133%	1.0485%	5.7618%
8/27/2010	6.98	4.7679%	1.0981%	5.8660%
2/27/2011	7.48	4.8233%	1.1485%	5.9718%
8/27/2011	7.98	4.8779%	1.1981%	6.0760%
2/27/2012	8.48	4.9333%	1.2485%	6.1818%
8/27/2012	8.98	4.9882%	1.2984%	6.2865%
2/27/2013	9.49	5.0436%	1.3488%	6.3924%
8/27/2013	9.98	5.0982%	1.3984%	6.4965%
2/27/2014	10.49	5.1536%	1.4488%	6.6024%
8/27/2014	10.98	5.2082%	1.4984%	6.7065%
2/27/2015	11.49	5.2636%	1.5488%	6.8124%
8/27/2015	11.98	5.3182%	1.5984%	6.9165%
2/27/2016	12.49	5.3736%	1.6488%	7.0224%
8/27/2016	12.99	5.4285%	1.6986%	7.1271%
2/27/2017	13.49	5.4839%	1.7490%	7.2330%
8/27/2017	13.99	5.5385%	1.7986%	7.3371%
2/27/2018	14.49	5.5939%	1.8490%	7.4430%
8/27/2018	14.99	5.6485%	1.8986%	7.5471%
2/27/2019	15.49	5.7039%	1.9490%	7.6530%
8/27/2019	15.99	5.7585%	1.9986%	7.7571%
2/27/2020	16.49	5.8139%	2.0490%	7.8630%
8/27/2020	16.99	5.8688%	2.0989%	7.9677%
2/27/2021	17.49	5.9242%	2.1493%	8.0736%
8/27/2021	17.99	5.9788%	2.1989%	8.1777%

Step 4: We calculate the present value discount factors for the risky yield curve for each payment date using continuous compounding of interest (because our risk-free yields and Jarrow credit spreads are all on a continuously compounded basis):

Bond A Payment Dates	Bond A Years to Maturity	US Treasury Zero-Coupon Yields	Bond A Credit Spread	Bond A Zero Yield	Bond A Present Value Factors
1/31/2004	0.41	4.0446%	0.4405%	4.4852%	0.9820
7/31/2004	0.90	4.0995%	0.4904%	4.5899%	0.9594
1/31/2005	1.41	4.1549%	0.5408%	4.6957%	0.9360
7/31/2005	1.90	4.2095%	0.5904%	4.7999%	0.9127
1/31/2006	2.41	4.2649%	0.6408%	4.9057%	0.8886
7/31/2006	2.90	4.3195%	0.6904%	5.0099%	0.8646
1/31/2007	3.41	4.3749%	0.7408%	5.1157%	0.8400
7/31/2007	3.90	4.4295%	0.7904%	5.2199%	0.8156
1/31/2008	4.41	4.4849%	0.8408%	5.3257%	0.7908
7/31/2008	4.91	4.5398%	0.8907%	5.4304%	0.7661
1/31/2009	5.41	4.5952%	0.9411%	5.5363%	0.7411
7/31/2009	5.91	4.6498%	0.9907%	5.6404%	0.7166
1/31/2010	6.41	4.7052%	1.0411%	5.7463%	0.6918
7/31/2010	6.91	4.7598%	1.0907%	5.8504%	0.6676
1/31/2011	7.41	4.8152%	1.1411%	5.9563%	0.6431
7/31/2011	7.91	4.8698%	1.1907%	6.0604%	0.6193
1/31/2012	8.41	4.9252%	1.2411%	6.1663%	0.5953
7/31/2012	8.91	4.9801%	1.2910%	6.2710%	0.5719
1/31/2013	9.41	5.0355%	1.3414%	6.3769%	0.5486
7/31/2013	9.91	5.0901%	1.3910%	6.4810%	0.5261
1/31/2014	10.41	5.1455%	1.4414%	6.5869%	0.5036
7/31/2014	10.91	5.2001%	1.4910%	6.6910%	0.4819
1/31/2015	11.41	5.2555%	1.5414%	6.1969%	0.4603
7/31/2015	11.91	5.3101%	1.5910%	6.9010%	0.4396
1/31/2016	12.41	5.3655%	1.6414%	7.0069%	0.4190
7/31/2016	12.91	5.4204%	1.6912%	7.1116%	0.3992

Bond B Payment Dates	Bond B Years to Maturity	US Treasury Zero-Coupon Yields	Bond B Credit Spread	Bond B Zero Yield	Bond B Present Value Factors
2/27/2004	0.48	4.0527%	0.4479%	4.5007%	0.9787
8/27/2004	0.98	4.1076%	0.4978%	4.6054%	0.9560
2/27/2005	1.48	4.1630%	0.5482%	4.7113%	0.9326
8/27/2005	1.98	4.2176%	0.5978%	4.8154%	0.9091
2/27/2006	2.48	4.2730%	0.6482%	4.9213%	0.8850
8/27/2006	2.98	4.3276%	0.6978%	5.0254%	0.8610
2/27/2007	3.48	4.3830%	0.7482%	5.1313%	0.8364
8/27/2007	3.98	4.4376%	0.7978%	5.2354%	0.8120
2/27/2008	4.48	4.4930%	0.8482%	5.3413%	0.7871
8/27/2008	4.98	4.5479%	0.8981%	5.4460%	0.7624
2/27/2009	5.48	4.6033%	0.9485%	5.5518%	0.7375
8/27/2009	5.98	4.6579%	0.9981%	5.6560%	0.7130
2/27/2010	6.48	4.7133%	1.0485%	5.7618%	0.6882
8/27/2010	6.98	4.7679%	1.0981%	5.8660%	0.6640
2/27/2011	7.48	4.8233%	1.1485%	5.9718%	0.6396
8/27/2011	7.98	4.8779%	1.1981%	6.0760%	0.6158
2/27/2012	8.48	4.9333%	1.2485%	6.1818%	0.5918
8/27/2012	8.98	4.9882%	1.2984%	6.2865%	0.5685
2/27/2013	9.49	5.0436%	1.3488%	6.3924%	0.5453
8/27/2013	9.98	5.0982%	1.3984%	6.4965%	0.5228
2/27/2014	10.49	5.1536%	1.4488%	6.6024%	0.5004
8/27/2014	10.98	5.2082%	1.4984%	6.7065%	0.4787
2/27/2015	11.49	5.2636%	1.5488%	6.8124%	0.4572
8/27/2015	11.98	5.3182%	1.5984%	6.9165%	0.4366
2/27/2016	12.49	5.3736%	1.6488%	7.0224%	0.4161
8/27/2016	12.99	5.4285%	1.6986%	7.1271%	0.3963
2/27/2017	13.49	5.4839%	1.7490%	7.2330%	0.3769
8/27/2017	13.99	5.5385%	1.7986%	7.3371%	0.3584
2/27/2018	14.49	5.5939%	1.8490%	7.4430%	0.3401
8/27/2018	14.99	5.6485%	1.8986%	7.5471%	0.3227
2/27/2019	15.49	5.7039%	1.9490%	7.6530%	0.3056
8/27/2019	15.99	5.7585%	1.9986%	7.7571%	0.2894
2/27/2020	16.49	5.8139%	2.0490%	7.8630%	0.2734
8/27/2020	16.99	5.8688%	2.0989%	7.9677%	0.2583
2/27/2021	17.49	5.9242%	2.1493%	8.0736%	0.2436
8/27/2021	17.99	5.9788%	2.1989%	8.1777%	0.2297

Step 5: The next step is to identify the cash flows on each bond at each payment date:

	Bond Cash Flows	
	At Maturity	**Other Dates**
Bond A	102.50	2.50
Bond B	103.00	3.00

Step 6: We then apply the present value factors to get the theoretical present value of both bonds given the values that we have assumed for X and B. We compare the theoretical present value with the observable dirty price (price plus accrued interest) and calculate the sum of squared pricing errors:

	Market Value	**Theory Value**	**Squared Error**
Bond A	91.00	85.37	31.68
Bond B	93.50	85.73	60.43
Total			92.12

Step 7: Next we use the solver function in simple spreadsheet software to solve for the values of X and B, which minimizes the sum of squared pricing errors. We are able to match observable market prices exactly with these new values of X and B. Note that all of the credit spreads have changed at every maturity:

Credit Spread = X + B Years to Maturity

Let X = ⟨ 0.002726 ⟩ ◄── These are the values that we will use in
Let B = ⟨ 0.000504 ⟩   future steps. We're close to the end!

Bond Cash Flows	
At Maturity	**Other Dates**
102.50	2.50
103.00	3.00

	Market Value	Theory Value	Squared Error
Bond A	91.00	91.00	0.00
Bond B	93.50	93.50	0.00
Total			0.00

Bond A Years to Maturity	US Treasury Zero-Coupon Yields	Bond A Credit Spread	Bond A Zero Yield	Bond A Present Value Factors
0.41	4.0446%	0.2930%	4.3376%	0.9826
0.90	4.0995%	0.3182%	4.4176%	0.9608
1.41	4.1549%	0.3436%	4.4985%	0.9386
1.90	4.2095%	0.3685%	4.5780%	0.9165
2.41	4.2649%	0.3939%	4.6589%	0.8939
2.90	4.3195%	0.4189%	4.7384%	0.8714
3.41	4.3749%	0.4443%	4.8192%	0.8485
3.90	4.4295%	0.4693%	4.8988%	0.8259
4.41	4.4849%	0.4947%	4.9796%	0.8029
4.91	4.5398%	0.5199%	5.0596%	0.7802
5.41	4.5952%	0.5453%	5.1405%	0.7572
5.91	4.6498%	0.5702%	5.2200%	0.7347
6.41	4.7052%	0.5956%	5.3009%	0.7119
6.91	4.7598%	0.6206%	5.3804%	0.6896
7.41	4.8152%	0.6460%	5.4612%	0.6672
7.91	4.8698%	0.6710%	5.5408%	0.6453
8.41	4.9252%	0.6964%	5.6216%	0.6232
8.91	4.9801%	0.7216%	5.7016%	0.6017
9.41	5.0355%	0.7470%	5.7825%	0.5802
9.91	5.0901%	0.7719%	5.8620%	0.5594
10.41	5.1455%	0.7973%	5.9429%	0.5386
10.91	5.2001%	0.8223%	6.0224%	0.5184
11.41	5.2555%	0.8477%	6.1032%	0.4983
11.91	5.3101%	0.8727%	6.1828%	0.4789
12.41	5.3655%	0.8981%	6.2636%	0.4595
12.91	5.4204%	0.9233%	6.3436%	0.4408

Bond B Payment Dates	Bond B Years to Maturity	US Treasury Zero-Coupon Yields	Bond B Credit Spread	Bond B Zero Yield	Bond B Present Value Factors
2/27/2004	0.48	4.0527%	0.2968%	4.3495%	0.9794
8/27/2004	0.98	4.1076%	0.3219%	4.4295%	0.9576
2/27/2005	1.48	4.1630%	0.3473%	4.5103%	0.9353
8/27/2005	1.98	4.2176%	0.3723%	4.5899%	0.9132
2/27/2006	2.48	4.2730%	0.3977%	4.6707%	0.8905
8/27/2006	2.98	4.3276%	0.4227%	4.7503%	0.8681
2/27/2007	3.48	4.3830%	0.4481%	4.8311%	0.8452
8/27/2007	3.98	4.4376%	0.4731%	4.9106%	0.8225
2/27/2008	4.48	4.4930%	0.4985%	4.9915%	0.7995
8/27/2008	4.98	4.5479%	0.5236%	5.0715%	0.7768
2/27/2009	5.48	4.6033%	0.5490%	5.1523%	0.7538
8/27/2009	5.98	4.6579%	0.5740%	5.2319%	0.7313
2/27/2010	6.48	4.7133%	0.5994%	5.3127%	0.7086
8/27/2010	6.98	4.7679%	0.6244%	5.3923%	0.6863
2/27/2011	7.48	4.8233%	0.6498%	5.4731%	0.6639
8/27/2011	7.98	4.8779%	0.6748%	5.5526%	0.6420
2/27/2012	8.48	4.9333%	0.7002%	5.6335%	0.6200
8/27/2012	8.98	4.9882%	0.7253%	5.7135%	0.5985
2/27/2013	9.49	5.0436%	0.7507%	5.7943%	0.5771
8/27/2013	9.98	5.0982%	0.7757%	5.8739%	0.5563
2/27/2014	10.49	5.1536%	0.8011%	5.9547%	0.5355
8/27/2014	10.98	5.2082%	0.8261%	6.0343%	0.5154
2/27/2015	11.49	5.2636%	0.8515%	6.1151%	0.4954
8/27/2015	11.98	5.3182%	0.8764%	6.1946%	0.4760
2/27/2016	12.49	5.3736%	0.9019%	6.2755%	0.4567
8/27/2016	12.99	5.4285%	0.9270%	6.3555%	0.4381
2/27/2017	13.49	5.4839%	0.9524%	6.4363%	0.4197
8/27/2017	13.99	5.5385%	0.9774%	6.5159%	0.4020
2/27/2018	14.49	5.5939%	1.0028%	6.5967%	0.3845
8/27/2018	14.99	5.6485%	1.0278%	6.6763%	0.3677
2/27/2019	15.49	5.7039%	1.0532%	6.7571%	0.3511
8/27/2019	15.99	5.7585%	1.0781%	6.8366%	0.3352
2/27/2020	16.49	5.8139%	1.1035%	6.9175%	0.3196
8/27/2020	16.99	5.8688%	1.1287%	6.9975%	0.3046
2/27/2021	17.49	5.9242%	1.1541%	7.0783%	0.2899
8/27/2021	17.99	5.9788%	1.1791%	7.1579%	0.2759

Step 8: The next step is to retrieve the Jarrow parameters from the values we have found for X and B. We know that the credit spread:

$$CS = a_0 + a_1 \times (T - t) + \lambda_0 (1 - \delta)$$

where:

$a_1 = B$ from step 4 above;
$a_0 + \lambda_0 (1 - \delta) = X$ from step 4 above;

so we have determined a_1. We now turn to the other parameters, which are determined by the value of X.

> Now we need to split the credit spread into the liquidity and expected loss piece
> Credit Spread $= X + B$ Years to Maturity
>
> Let $X =$ 0.002726
> Let $B =$ 0.000504

Zero-Coupon Credit Spread

In the Basic-Jarrow Model $= [a_0 + a_1(T - t)] + \lambda_0 (1 - \text{Recovery Rate})$

This piece is the 'liquidity' piece.
λ_0 is instantaneous default intensity in the Jarrow model.
Rearranging this equation and using the X and B from above, we know that

$$0.002726 + 0.000504 (T - t) = [a_0 + a_1(T - t)] + \text{Lambda}_0 (1 - \text{Recovery Rate})$$

So we can derive the Jarrow parameters from these relationships:

$$0.002726 = a_0 + \lambda_0 (1 - \text{Recovery Rate})$$
$$0.000504 = a_1$$

So the only remaining task is to determine how much of intercept in this linear relationship is related to liquidity (the a_0) and how much is related to.

We do that in the next step.

Step 9: There are three basis choices for determining the value of the other Jarrow parameters. One alternative, the maximum smoothness recovery rate, is a subject of future research.

There are a number of choices that we can make in this regard.

1. **Assume that the liquidity parameter a_0 is 0**

   $0.2726\% = a_0 + \lambda_0(1 - \text{Recovery Rate})$ is the relationship from the previous

   page, so if $a_0 = 0$

   $0.2726\% = \lambda_0(1 - \text{Recovery Rate})$ we have and if the recovery

   $0.9087\% = \lambda_0$ rate is 70% then:

   Note: This approach is common in the credit derivatives market but we believe
   that it results in a very conservative estimate of the default intensity
   (much higher than it really is).

2. **Use the maximum smoothness recovery rate method with KDP-jc derived from historical defaults. We cover that elsewhere.**

3. **Use the liquidity factor a_0 from a comparable traded instrument (say bonds issued by another, more frequent issuer)**

   In fitting the model to observable bond prices of that issuer you may conclude
   that $a_0 = 0.12\%$. Then:

   $0.2726\% = 0.12\% + \text{Lambda}_0 (1 - \text{Recovery Rate})$ and we can solve for

   Lambda$_0$ again:

   $0.5087\% = \text{Lambda}_0$

What have we accomplished by this process?
1. We have benchmarked the Jarrow credit models using primary market pricing information on only two bonds;
2. We have the default intensity and default probability for the issuer;
3. We have the liquidity parameters on the bonds;
4. We have the treasury yield curve.
5. We can now use the power of the Jarrow models to:
   a. Mark-to-market the untraded Bond C to do rich/cheap analysis;
   b. Simulate the periodic and cumulative loss rates on the bonds;
   c. Simulate scheduled cash flows and defaults on each bond in every period;
   d. Do a credit-adjusted value-at-risk on an entire portfolio of bonds by many issuers;
   e. Simulate loss experience on any seniority 'tranche' if the bonds are embedded in a CDO;
   f. Value each tranche for rich/cheap analysis;
   g. Simulate the cash flows on a fully default-adjusted basis on each tranche;
   h. Do proforma performance analysis versus a benchmark analysis (say versus the Lehman Government Index); and much more.

The Term Structure of Default Probabilities

In the Jarrow model, like in the real world, the probability of default for any given issuer varies over time as the macro factors driving the default probabilities change. Many examples are given by Donald R. van Deventer and Kenji Imai in their book *Credit Risk Models and the Basel Accords* (John Wiley & Sons, 2003). For this reason the annualized default probability for any company varies with the time horizon covered and the outlook for the macro factors during that time horizon. Even independent of changes in macro factors, the default risk of the company changes. Most of the correlated defaults observed in the market, however, are caused by the joint impact of macro factors on the default probabilities of all companies, as noted by Linda Allen and Anthony Saunders in Bank for International Settlements *Working Paper* 126. These macro factors impact both the term structure of default probabilities for each company and the correlation in their default probabilities and in their events of default.

In a rapidly improving economy (say, the U.S. economy in mid-2003) the short-term outlook for a company driven by cyclical factors would be very positive. The term structure of default probabilities would be sloping downward. In a rapidly deteriorating economy, the term structure of defaults would be sloping upward. Figure 17.1 shows the evolution of forward annualized monthly default probabilities, conditional on the company surviving for the number of months specified. The company is AT&T Wireless and the default probabilities (KDP) are provided by Kamakura Corporation as of February 26 2004.

Figure 17.1 Forward Annualized Monthly Default Probabilities for AT&T Wireless, February 26 2004

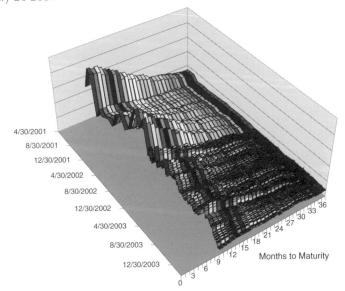

These forward default probabilities were benchmarked by adjusting the weightings of the explanatory variables to fit a forecasting horizon from the current month to 36 months forward. We can see dramatic and reasonable evolutions in default probabilities as AT&T emerged from the NASDAQ-related credit trauma of 2001–2002. During this time, the company's credit rating didn't change, but its credit quality dramatically did.

Correlations in Default Probabilities

In the same way, the Jarrow models fitted to historical default databases illustrate the parallels between default probabilities and interest rates:

- Default probabilities have a term structure just like interest rates;
- Changes in interest rates and macro-economic factors make the term structure of default probabilities rise and fall over time;
- Like interest rates, short-term default probabilities rise and fall by much more than long-term default probabilities, which may be the effective average of default probabilities over many credit cycles;
- The difference between a strong credit and a weak credit is not their short-term default probability when times are good. In good times, both will have a low probability of default. The difference can be seen most clearly when times are bad.

Macro factors cause correlated movements in the short-term default probabilities for both strong and weak credits. As we will see in Chapter 19, the Merton model of risky debt surprisingly misses much of this correlation.

A few examples will illustrate this phenomenon. Figure 17.2[10] shows the Jarrow short-term default probabilities for Bank of America (BAC) and Bank

Figure 17.2 Short-Term Default Probabilities for Bank of America and Bank One

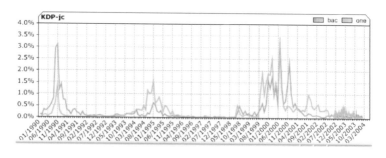

---

[10] This data and the following examples are provided by Kamakura Corporation's KRIS default probability service, version 3.0.

One (ONE) as they move through three recessions in 1990–1991, 1994–5, and 2001–2002.

The simple five-year monthly correlation of their Jarrow default probabilities is 74%.

The second example is British Airways (BAB) versus American Airlines (AMR) during the spring of 2003 when AMR was near bankruptcy. Figure 17.3 shows a high degree of sympathetic movement in these two firms, even across international boundaries, dating back to the 1990–1991 recession.

Figure 17.3 Short-Term Default Probabilities for British Airways and American Airlines

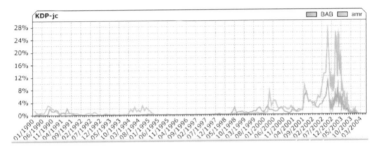

The correlation in their default probabilities over the most recent five years was 82%.

The next example compares BBB-rated Sears (S) versus AA-rated Walmart. The graph clearly illustrates what all practical lenders know—the difference between a strong credit and a weaker one is not their default probabilities when times are good. Almost no one defaults in a strong economy. The difference comes in the bad times, when the short-term default probability of the weaker credit, in this case Sears, substantially increases, even though there is also movement upwards in Walmart's default probabilities as well.

Figure 17.4 Short-Term Default Probabilities for Sears and Walmart

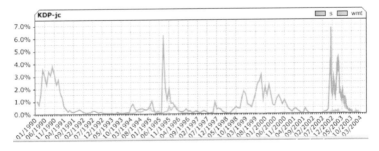

On average, Sears has higher and more volatile default probabilities than Walmart. A long-term default probability for Sears will be higher than Walmarts'; a short-term default probability for the two firms will be nearly identical in good times and very different in bad times.

Finally we compare Ford (F) and Merrill Lynch (MER). A commonly used model for rating collateralized debt obligations[11] assumes that the correlation in defaults for two firms in different industries is zero. We can see from Figure 17.6 that this assumption is simply not accurate for Ford and Merrill Lynch:

Figure 17.5 Short-Term Default Probabilities for Ford and Merrill Lynch

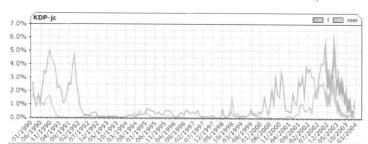

Both firm's default probabilities vary dramatically over time, and they both increase substantially in times of economic weakness. The five-year monthly correlation of their default probabilities is 68%. Clearly, default risk is correlated across national borders and across industry boundaries, and the Jarrow model captures it powerfully.

Conclusion

In this chapter, we have introduced the Jarrow-Turnbull and Jarrow models of risky debt. They offer powerful closed form solutions for practical issues that are central to the integrated treatment of interest rate risk and credit risk. We have shown how to fit the Jarrow model to debt prices, credit derivatives prices, and historical default data-bases. We have shown how an identical approach, with different explanatory variables, can be applied to:

- retail counterparties;
- small business counterparties;
- municipalities;
- sovereigns.

---

[11] Standard & Poor's CDO Evaluator is one of many packages that make this assumption.

Finally, we have shown through practical examples that the Jarrow reduced form models clearly illustrate both the term structure of default probabilities for any type of counterparty and the correlation of default probabilities for any two counterparties.

This kind of correlated risk is what drives the 'fat tails' in losses that endanger financial institutions. An understanding of this issue is essential to both the integrated measure of risk via the Jarrow-Merton put option and to the hedging of portfolio level credit risk with macro hedges using stock price index futures and interest rate derivatives.

In the next chapter, we spend more time on fitting the model to interest rate data, and then in Chapter 19 we compare performance of the Merton and Jarrow models.

Appendix 1

Converting default intensities to discrete default probabilities

The reduced form models are attractive because they allow for default or bankruptcy to occur at any instant over a long time frame. Reduced form default probabilities can be converted from:

- continuous to monthly, quarterly or annually;
- from monthly to continuous or annually;
- from annually to monthly or continuous.

This section shows how to make these changes in periodicity on the simplifying assumption that the default probability is constant over time. When the default probability is changing over time, and even when it is changing randomly over time, these time conversions can still be made although the formulas are slightly more complicated.

Converting monthly default probabilities to annual default probabilities

In estimating reduced form and hybrid credit models from a historical data-base of defaults, the analyst fits a logistic regression to a historical default data-base that tracks bankruptcies and the explanatory variables on a monthly, quarterly or annual basis. The default probabilities obtained will have the periodicity of the data (i.e. monthly, quarterly or annually). We illustrate conversion to a different maturity by assuming the estimation is done on monthly data. The probability that is produced by the logistic regression, P, is the probability that a particular company will go bankrupt in that month. By definition, P is a monthly probability of default. To convert P to an annual basis, assuming P is constant, we know that:

$$\text{Probability of no bankruptcy in a year} = (1-P)^{12}$$

Therefore the probability of going bankrupt in the next year is:

$$\text{Annual probability of bankruptcy} = 1-(1-P)^{12}$$

The latter equation is used to convert monthly logistic regression probabilities to annual default probabilities.

Converting annual default probabilities to monthly default probabilities

In a similar way, we can convert the annual probability of default, say A, to a monthly default probability by solving the equation:

$$A = 1-(1-P)^{12}$$

for the monthly default probability given that we know the value of A.

$$\text{Monthly probability of default } P = 1-(1-A)^{1/12}$$

Converting continuous instantaneous probabilities to an annual default probability or monthly default probability

In Jarrow [1999], Professor Jarrow writes briefly about the formula for converting the instantaneous default intensity $\lambda(t)$ (the probability of default during the instant time t) to a default probability that could be monthly, quarterly or annual:

"For subsequent usage the term structure of yearly default probabilities (under the risk neutral measure) can be computed via:

$$Q_t(\tau \leq T) = 1 - Q_t(\tau > T)$$

where;

$$Q_t(\tau > T) = E_t\left(e^{-\int_t^T \lambda(u)\,du}\right)$$

and $Q_t(\cdot)$ is the time t conditional probability."

In this section, we interpret Professor Jarrow's formula. $Q_t(\tau \le T)$ is the probability at time t that bankruptcy (which occurs at time τ) happens before time T. Likewise, $Q_t(\tau > T)$ is the probability that bankruptcy occurs after time T. Professor Jarrow's formula simply says that the probability that bankruptcy occurs between now (time t) and time T is one minus the probability that bankruptcy occurs after time T. He then gives a formula for the probability that bankruptcy occurs after time T:

$$Q_t(\tau > T) = E_t \left(e^{-\int_t^T \lambda(u)\,du} \right)$$

E_t is the expected value of the quantity in parentheses as of time t. Because we are using the simplest version of the Jarrow model in this appendix, $\lambda(t)$ is constant so we can simplify the expression for $Q_t(\tau > T)$:

$$Q_t(\tau > T) = e^{-\lambda(T-t)}$$

Converting continuous default probability to an annual default probability

The annual default probability A when λ is constant and $T-t = 1$ (one year) is:

$$A = 1 - Q_t(\tau > T) = 1 - e^{-\lambda}$$

Converting continuous default probability to a monthly default probability

The monthly default probability M when λ is constant and $T - t = 1/12$ (one twelfth of a year) is:

$$M = 1 - Q_t(\tau > T) = 1 - e^{-\lambda(1/12)}$$

Converting an annual KDP to a continuous default intensity

When the annual default probability A is known and we want to solve for λ, we solve the equation above for λ as a function of A:

$$\lambda = -\ln(1 - A)$$

Converting a monthly default probability to a continuous default intensity

In a similar way, we can convert a monthly default probability to a continuous default intensity by reversing the formula for M. This is a calculation we would do if we had a monthly default probability from a logistic regression and we wanted to calculate λ from the monthly default probability:

$$\lambda = -12 \ln (1 - M)$$

These formulas are normally embedded in best practice enterprise-wide risk management software so that the user doesn't need to make these calculations themselves.

CHAPTER 18

Credit Spread Fitting and Modeling[1]

Chapters 16 and 17 provided an extended introduction to structural and reduced form credit modeling techniques. As emphasized throughout this book, we need to employ the credit models of our choice as skillfully as possible in order to provide our financial institution with the ability to price credit risky instruments, to calculate their theoretical value in comparison to market prices, and to hedge our exposure to credit risk. The most important step in generating this output is to fit the credit models as accurately as possible to current market data.

If we do this correctly, we can answer these questions:

- Which of the 15 bonds outstanding for Ford Motor Company is the best value at current market prices?
- Which of the 15 bonds should I buy?
- Which should I sell short or sell outright from my portfolio?
- Is there another company in the auto sector whose bonds provide better risk-adjusted value?

Answering these questions is the purpose of this chapter.

Introduction to Credit Spread Smoothing

The accuracy of yield curve smoothing techniques has taken on increased importance in recent years because of the intense research focus among both practitioners and academics on credit risk modeling. In particular, the reduced form modeling approach of Duffie and Singleton [1999] and Jarrow [1999, 2001] has the power to extract default probabilities and the 'liquidity premium' (i.e. the excess of credit spread above expected loss) from bond prices and credit default swap prices.

---

[1] Portions of this chapter were published on the web site www.riskcenter.com in January 2004.

In practical application, there are two ways to do this estimation. The first method, which is also the most precise, is to use the closed form solution for zero-coupon credit spreads in the respective credit model and to solve for the credit model parameters that minimize the sum of squared pricing error for the observable bonds or credit default swaps. This form of credit spread fitting includes both the component that contains the potential losses from default and a liquidity premium like that in the Jarrow model we discussed in Chapter 17. It also allows for the model to be extended to exactly fit observable bond market data in the same manner as the Hull and White/Extended Vasicek term structure model discussed in Chapters 10–12. This approach is used in the enterprise risk software system Kamakura Risk Manager[2] offered by Kamakura Corporation, for example.

The second method, which is used commonly in academic studies of credit risk, is to calculate credit spreads on a 'credit model independent basis' in order to later study which credit models are the most accurate. We discuss both methods in this chapter. We turn to credit model independent credit spreads first.

The Credit Spread: A Credit Model-Independent Risk Measure

In Chapters 1–4, we discussed the difference between 'common practice' and 'best practice' in risk management in general. Before showing how yield curve smoothing can improve fixed income calculations and credit spread calculations in particular, it is important to compare best practice to long-established market conventions for credit spread quotations. We start by summarizing the common market convention ('common practice') for quoting credit spreads.

The market convention for credit spreads

Credit spreads are quoted to bond-buying financial institutions by investment banks every day. What is a credit spread? From a common practice perspective, the credit spreads being discussed daily in the market involve the same kind of simple assumptions as the yield to maturity and duration concepts that we reviewed in Chapters 9 and 10.

The following steps are usually taken in the market convention approach to quoting the credit spread on the bonds of ABC Company at a given instant in time relative to a risk-free curve such as the U.S. Treasury curve:

1. Calculate the simple yield to maturity[3] on the bond of ABC Company given its value (price plus accrued interest) and its exact maturity date.

---

[2] For more information on Kamakura Risk Manager, see www.kamakuraco.com.

[3] See Chapter 1 in *Financial Risk Analytics: A Term Structure Model Approach for Banking, Insurance and Investment Management* by Donald R. van Deventer and Kenji Imai for details on this calculation.

2. Calculate the simple yield to maturity on the 'on the run' U.S. Treasury bond with the closest maturity date. This maturity date will almost never be identical to the maturity date of the bond of ABC company.
3. Calculate the credit spread by subtracting the risk-free yield to maturity from the yield to maturity on the ABC Company bond.

This market convention is simple, but inaccurate for many reasons:

- The yield to maturity calculation assumes that zero-coupon yields to each payment date of the given bond are equal for every payment date— **it implicitly assumes the risk-free yield curve is flat**, but if credit spreads are being calculated for credit risky bonds with two different maturity dates, a different 'flat' risk-free curve will be used to calculate the credit spreads for those two bonds because the risk-free yield to maturity will be different for those two bonds.
- The yield to maturity calculation usually implicitly assumes **periods of equal length** between payment dates (which is almost never true in the U.S. for semi-annual bond payment dates).
- The **maturity dates on the bonds don't match** exactly except by accident.
- The **payment dates on the bonds don't match** exactly except by accident.
- The **zero-coupon credit spread is assumed to be flat**.
- Differences in coupon levels on the bonds, which can dramatically impact the yield to maturity and therefore credit spread, are ignored.
- Often, timing differences in bond price information are ignored. Many academic studies, for example, calculate credit spreads based on bond prices reported monthly. Since the exact timing of the pricing information is not known, it is difficult to know which date during the month should be used to determine the level of the risk-free yield curve.
- Call options embedded in the bond of ABC Company are often ignored, because they can't be calculated independently of the credit model used. For example, the value of a call option on a bond that is '10 years, non-call five' depends on the probability that the issuer will default in the first five years before the call option can be exercised.

The market convention for fitting credit spreads is very simple, but these problems with the methodology are very serious problems. This kind of inaccuracy is no longer tolerated by traders in fixed income derivatives like caps, floors, swaps, swaptions, and so on based on the LIBOR curve. Better analytics for credit spread modeling are now moving into the market for corporate, sovereign, and municipal bonds as well and for very good reason—if you don't use the better technology, you'll be 'picked off' by traders who do.

We turn next to a credit model independent method for fitting the credit spread.

A Better Convention for Credit Model-Independent Credit Spreads

The credit spread calculation that is the market convention has only one virtue—it is simple. Like the yield to maturity calculation (which assumes the risk-free zero-coupon bond curve is flat), it assumes a flat credit spread at every payment date on the bond. Moreover, if the credit spread is calculated for two bonds of the same issuer with the same payment dates but with different maturity dates, the zero-coupon credit spread assumed for the same payment date will be different for the two bonds. For example, if ABC Company's bonds maturing June 15 2028 are trading at 250 basis points over Treasury bonds and the bonds maturing June 15 2011 are trading at 125 basis points over Treasury bonds, we have this problem: the zero-coupon bond credit spreads on June 15 2005 are assumed to be 250 basis points for the 2028 bond and 125 basis points for the 2011 bond. This inconsistency occurs because the credit spread is not derived from joint estimation that analyzes both bonds at the same time. This is a serious error that can be easily avoided as we discuss later in this chapter.

We start by proposing a better methodology for analyzing the credit spread of one bond of a risky issuer that avoids most of the problems of the market convention. This methodology continues to assume, however, that the credit spread for each bond of a risky issuer is the same at all payment dates.

We can derive a more precise calculation of credit spread on a 'credit model independent basis' if we use the yield curve smoothing technology introduced in Chapter 8. This method was first proposed by Jarrow, van Deventer and Wang [2003] and has been in commercial use since 1993.[4] Assume there are M payments on the ABC Company bond and that all observable non-call U.S. Treasury bonds are used to create a smooth, continuous Treasury yield curve using the techniques we described in Chapter 8. Then the continuous credit spread x on the ABC bond can be constructed like this:

1. For each of the M payment dates on the ABC Company bond, calculate the continuously compounded zero-coupon bond price and zero-coupon yield from the U.S. Treasury smoothed yield curve. These yields will be to actual payment dates, not scheduled payment dates, because the day count convention associated with the bond will move scheduled payments forward or backward (depending on the convention) if they fall on weekends or holidays.

2. Guess a continuously compounded credit spread of x that is assumed to be the same for each payment date.

---

[4] As mentioned above, this method has been a standard calculation of the Kamakura Risk Manager enterprise-wide risk management system since 1993.

3. Calculate the present value of the ABC bond using the M continuously compounded zero-coupon bond yields $y(i) + x$, where $y(i)$ is the zero-coupon bond yield to that payment date on the risk-free curve. Note that $y(i)$ will be different for each payment date but that x is assumed to be constant for all payment dates.

4. Compare the present value calculated in Step 3 with the value of the ABC bond (price plus accrued interest) observed in the market.

5. If the theoretical value and observed value are within a tolerance e, then stop and report x as the credit spread. If the difference is outside the tolerance, improve the guess of x using standard methods and go back to Step 3.[5]

6. Spreads calculated in this manner should be confined to non-callable bonds or used with great care in the case of callable bonds.

This method is commonly used by many of the world's largest financial institutions.

Yield curve smoothing technology is at the heart of this credit spread calculation because the M payment dates on ABC Company's bonds require zero-coupon U.S. Treasury yields on dates that are unlikely to be payment dates or maturity dates observable in the U.S. Treasury market. Yield curve smoothing is even more important (a) in countries where the number of risk-free bonds observable is far fewer (like Japan) or (b) when smoothing is being done directly on the risky bond issuer's yield curve itself. ABC Company may have only five bonds with observable prices, for example, compared to more than 200 in the U.S. Treasury market. In the rest of this chapter, we talk about two alternative methods for smoothing the ABC Company yield curve.

We can illustrate this improved credit model independent credit spread with data from the Ford Motor Company's bond obtained from the National Association of Securities Dealers (NASDAQ) bond price reporting system. On September 18 2003, the credit spread calculated from market price[6] of the Ford Motor Company BBB-rated 6.625% bonds due October 1 2028 was 2.40%. To do this calculation, we used the risk-free zero-coupon bond yields for every October 1 and April 1 payment dates on the Ford bond. For the purposes of this example, we used maximum smoothness forward rate curve smoothing which we discussed in Chapter 8.

---

[5] Chapter 1 of van Deventer and Imai's *Financial Risk Analytics* illustrates one method commonly used for this purpose.

[6] To be precise, the credit spread is calculated from the true present value (market price plus accrued interest) of the Ford bond.

The credit spreads calculated in this manner for the Ford Motor Company bonds are shown in Figure 18.1 below:

Figure 18.1 Credit Spread on Ford Motor Company 6.625% Bonds due 2028

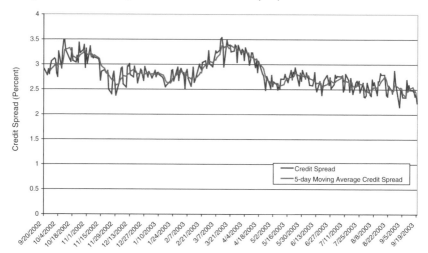

We have plotted both the raw credit spread and a five-day moving average. The variation in the credit spread is small and reflects the normal price volatility (due to the mix of bid and offered prices and hour to hour changes in market conditions) typical of the NASDAQ-reported bond prices.

The calculation presented in this section resolves a number of problems with the market convention calculation for credit spreads while still preserving its simplicity—the calculation is done on one bond at a time and assumes the zero-coupon credit spread is flat and constant for each payment date:

- We are using different zero-coupon bond yields for the risk-free yield curve on each of the October 1 and April 1 payment dates for the Ford Motor Company 6.625% bonds due 2028. The market convention instead uses the yield to maturity on the nearest 'on the run' Treasury bond and assumes that this discount rate is the same at each October 1 and April 1 payment date.
- We are using the actual number of days between October 1 and April 1, not assuming the difference between those dates is exactly 0.5 years.
- We are using the Treasury yields for the exact payment dates, so we avoid the mismatch in maturity dates in the market convention between the October 1 2028 maturity of the Ford bonds and the maturity date of the 'on the run' Treasury bond.
- Therefore we avoid completely the market convention's problem that payment dates on the risky and risk-free bonds don't match.

- We have eliminated the distorting impact of the coupon level on the risk-free 'on the run' Treasury bond since we are using all observable Treasury bond prices to create the maximum smoothness forward rate curve and zero-coupon bond yield curve for Treasuries.

We turn now to a still better approach—joint estimation of a credit spread curve using all observable Ford Motor Company bond prices simultaneously to derive the curve.

Joint Estimation of a Smooth Credit Curve

In Chapter 8 we explained that the 'best' approach to yield curve smoothing is not subject to debate once the criterion for 'best' is defined mathematically and once the objective of the user is specified. The same is true for credit spreads.

Implicitly, among both practitioners and academics, the 'best' approach to yield curve smoothing is the approach that produces the 'most reasonable' outputs. In Chapter 8, we saw that comparisons of alternative yield curve smoothing techniques were made on the basis that the 'smoothest' yield curve output is the best. Further more, the 'smoothest' criterion can be applied alternatively to zero-coupon bond yields, zero-coupon bond prices, continuous forward rates or credit spreads.

In Chapter 8, we used the smoothness definition of Hildebrand [1987]. He pointed out that the most common (but not the only) definition of smoothness is the function that minimizes Z, the integral of the function's squared second derivative over the relevant interval:

$$Z = \int_{t_1}^{t_2} [g''(s)]^2 \, ds$$

Using this definition and the analogies to yield curve smoothing in Chapter 8, we can show mathematically that there are two principal choices for smoothing the continuous credit spread curve:

1. A cubic spline of zero-coupon credit spreads produces the smoothest zero yield credit spread curve;
2. A quartic spline of forward credit spreads produces the smoothest forward credit spread curve.

In practical use, both of these methods produce very good results because they smooth the yield curve of the risky issuer relative to the continuous Treasury yield curve that we can derive using any of the smoothing techniques in Chapter 8. This is vastly superior to smoothing the risky issuer's yield curve looking only at the risky issuer's bond prices and ignoring the shape of the Treasury curve.

Figure 18.2 Assumed Risk-Free Zero-Coupon Yield Curve

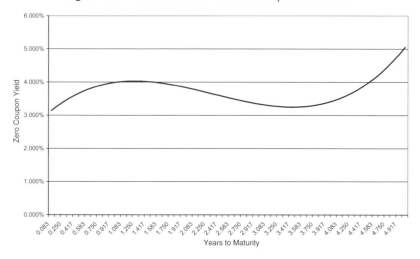

Figure 18.2 shows why this is necessary. Consider smoothing the yield curve of a risky corporate bond issuer when the risk-free curve has this hypothetical zero-coupon yield curve.

This yield curve could have been derived by using any of the six yield curve smoothing methods discussed in Chapter 8, fitted to observable risk-free bond prices, risk-free 'on the run' bond yields, and so on. We take this curve as a given as we have dealt with the process for determining this curve in Chapter 8.

Now consider an issuer of credit risky securities who has the following securities observable in the market place:

- One-month commercial paper with one twelfth of one year to maturity and a price plus accrued interest (present value) of 0.996257022. This is equivalent to a continuously compounded zero-coupon yield to maturity of 4.50% using the formulas of Chapter 7.
- A bond issue with exactly four years remaining until maturity and a coupon of 10.00% payable semi-annually. Price plus accrued interest (present value) is 109% of the $100 par value.

We examine three of the many possible alternatives for deriving the yield curve for this risky issuer to illustrate the main points of this chapter:

1. Linear smoothing of the zero-coupon yield curve as in Chapter 8;
2. Linear smoothing of the credit spread;
3. Maximum smoothness credit spread forward smoothing.

We implement them one by one and compare their results.

Linear Yield Curve Smoothing of the Zero-Coupon Yield Curve

We use the techniques of Chapter 8 to smooth the zero-coupon continuous yield curve on the assumption that the zero-coupon bond yield is:

$$y(t) = a + bt$$

where t is the yield to maturity and $y(t)$ is the continuously compounded zero-coupon bond yield. We know that:

$$y(1/12) = 0.045 = a + b\,(1/12)$$

since the zero yield at one month to maturity is observable.[7] We assume that we need the zero-coupon yield curve from time zero to five years to maturity to price obligations up to five years in maturity for this risky issuer. We don't know the value for the five-year zero yield to maturity. We guess that $y(5) = k$, an arbitrary initial guess. That gives us two more equations:

$$y(5) = a + b5 = k$$
Present value of four-year bond $= 109$

We have three unknowns a, b, and k. We also have three equations. We can use the non-linear equation solver in common spreadsheet software to arrive at the solution:

$$0.044380198 = a$$
$$0.007437621 = b$$
$$8.157\% = 0.08157 = k.$$

After completing the other two smoothing methods, we will compare their implications.

Linear Smoothing of the Credit Spread

Another of the many ways to solve for the yield curve of the risky issuer is to assume that the continuously compounded credit spread with t years to maturity has the form:

$$c(t) = a + bt$$

---

[7] Best practice implementation uses exact day count instead of assuming each month is 1/12 of a year. We use the simpler method for illustrative purposes only.

This is a convenient specification because we know the continuous yield curve for the risk free curve at every maturity since we have used the techniques of Chapter 8 on the risk-free curve. From that continuous yield curve, we can directly take the risk-free zero yields $r(t)$ for any maturity t.

For maturities of one month and five years we know:

$$r(1/12) = 3.140\% = 0.0314$$
$$r(5) = 5.050\% = 0.0505$$

Again, we guess that the five-year zero-coupon bond yield for the risky bond issuer is our initial guess k. We again have three equations in three unknowns:

$$k = 0.0505 + c(5) = 0.0505 + a + b5$$
$$4.50\% = 0.0314 + c(1/12) = 0.0314 + a + b(1/12)$$
$$\text{Present value of four-year bond} = 109$$

The solutions to this system of three equations in three unknowns can be found (using spreadsheet software again) to be:

$$0.013055882 = A$$
$$0.006568994 = B$$
$$9.64\% = 0.0964 = k$$

Again, we will review the implications after deriving risky bond yields by one more method.

Maximum Smoothness Credit Spread Forward Smoothing

In this section, we calculate the credit spread and risky issuer's yield curve on the assumption that the 'forward credit spread' has a shape that is consistent with the maximum smoothness forward credit spread that one can obtain given the constraints that we impose. The maximum smoothness forward credit spread $c_f(t)$ is simply the forward rate for the risky curve at maturity t $y_f(t)$ minus the forward rate for the risk-free curve at time t $r_f(t)$:

$$c_f(t) = y_f(t) - r_f(t)$$

We know from Chapter 8 that the maximum smoothness forward credit spread can be proven mathematically to be a quartic function of the form:

$$c_f(t) = a + bt + ct^2 + dt^3 + et^4$$

We do not include the proof in this chapter but it is exactly analogous to the proof of the maximum smoothness forward rate technique for the risk-free yield curve given in Chapter 8.

For the purposes of our example here we can choose any number of line segments for the forward credit spread. Since we have two observable securities prices at one month and four years and because we need to have the zero-coupon yield curve out to five years, it is conventional to use three line segments, all of which have the quartic form, for the forward credit spread curve:

- The first line segment, from zero to 1/12 years in maturity;
- The second line segment, from 1/12 to four years in maturity;
- The third line segment, from four years to five years in maturity.

For this example, we will use only one line segment that spans the entire range from zero years to five years to maturity to simplify the exposition. Following the Chapter 8 exposition for maximum smoothness forward rates, we know that the:

- zero-coupon yield at 1/12 years to maturity must be 4.50%;
- The present value of the four-year bond must be 109.

For the first two methods we used in this section, these were enough equations to solve for the two unknowns a and b after guessing a value for the five-year credit spread k and adding a third equation that insures that the equation produces a credit spread of k. Following Chapter 8, we add the equation for k and then require that the forward credit spread has a second derivative equal to zero at time zero, a first derivative equal to zero at year five, and a second derivative equal to zero at year five:

$$k = \text{five-year zero-coupon credit spread};$$
$$c_f''(0) = 0;$$
$$c_f'(5) = 0;$$
$$c_f''(5) = 0.$$

This gives us a total of six equations in six unknowns (a, b, c, d, e, and k). We can solve this in Excel using the convenient formulas in Chapters 7 and 8 for the risky issuer's zero-coupon bond prices, zero-coupon bond yields, and zero-coupon forward rates. We note that the risky issuer's credit spread is $c(t) = y(t) - r(t)$, the risky issuer's forward rate is $y_f(t)$, the risky issuer's forward credit spread is $c_f(t) = y_f(t) - r_f(t)$, and the risky issuer's zero-coupon bond price is $P[t]$:

$$P[t] = e^{-\int_0^\tau y_f(s)\,ds}$$

Since P can be written as a function of time to maturity, so can the forward rate:

$$y_f[t] = -\frac{\partial P[t]/\partial t}{P[t]}$$

$$= -\frac{\partial(e^{-ty[t]})/\partial t}{P[t]}$$

$$= y[t] + t\,y'[t]$$

We use these equations and the solver function in spreadsheet software to arrive at the values for the six unknowns:

$$0.012908 = a$$
$$0.016683 = b$$
$$0.000000 = c$$
$$-0.000667 = d$$
$$0.000067 = e$$
$$0.0421 = 4.21\% = c(5) = y(5) - r(5) = k$$

Comparing Alternative Techniques for Smoothing the Yield Curve of a Risky Issuer

We can now compare the results from these three representative methods. Figure 18.3 shows that the linear yield smoothing method is likely to produce strange forward rates based on the graph of continuous zero-coupon bond yields for the three methods.

Figure 18.3 Zero-Coupon Yields on Risk-Free Yield Curve and Three Smoothed Risky Yield Curves

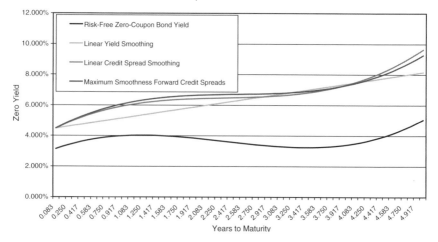

When we graph zero-coupon credit spreads for the three methods, we can see that the linear yield curve smoothing method produces implausible credit spreads with two humps and a downward slope toward the five-year point. This unrealistic conclusion would lead a careful user to reject this method in almost all circumstances.

Figure 18.4 Zero-Coupon Credit Spreads for Three Smoothing Approaches

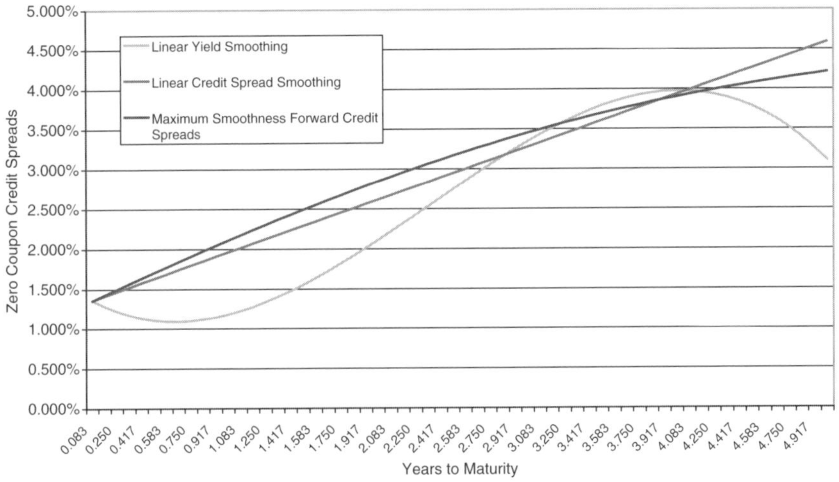

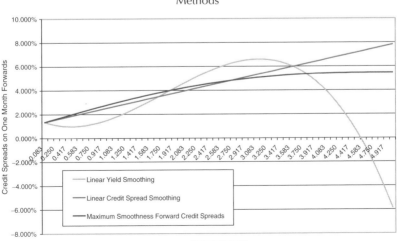

Next, we plot one-month credit spread forwards (alternatively continuously compounded credit spread forwards), for all three methods. Our conclusions from Figure 18.4 are confirmed in that the one-month forward credit spread for linear yield curve smoothing implausibly turns negative:

Figure 18.5 Credit Spreads on One Month Forward Rates for Three Smoothing Methods

The difference between linear credit spread smoothing and maximum smoothness forward credit spreads in this example is small. The maximum smoothness method shows realistic flattening of the forward credit spread curve. More importantly, in all circumstances, this method minimizes the probability that the forward credit spread turns negative at some point in the relevant yield curve range. For this reason, most careful users would choose this method of credit spread smoothing for fitting observable fixed income securities prices to a smooth curve.

Fitting the Loss Portion of the Credit Spread

We have now completed an example of the most important task in modeling the impact of credit risk on yields—the gross level of the credit spread at all maturities. This methodology is far superior to both the market convention and the single bond credit spread estimation that we discussed at the beginning of this chapter, because all observable bonds of a risky issuer are considered simultaneously in this smoothing method, and the credit spread curve applies to all of the risky issuer's bonds (we exclude callable bonds from this exercise, as well as bonds of dissimilar seniority).

The next task in credit spread smoothing is to divide the credit spread into two portions, the portion related to the default probability and the recovery rate, and the part related to all other factors. We call this second part the liquidity component of the credit spread, since it includes things like the premium required to compensate for illiquidity on sale, bid/offered spreads, general risk aversion not elsewhere included, and so on.

In Chapter 17, we showed how the credit risk-related component of the credit spread has a particular functional form in the Jarrow reduced form models. The form of the liquidity function in the Jarrow model can take on any functional form, much like the extension of the Vasicek yield curve model from its theoretical value to the actual observable market yields as discussed in Chapter 11. This 'extension' is at the heart of the Extended Vasicek/Hull and White term structure model and we use exactly the same approach to 'extend' the credit component of the Jarrow model to fit the credit spread exactly. This 'extension' is the liquidity component.

In general, we have two basic methodologies for doing this:

1. Derive the continuous credit spread $c(t)$ as above and then calculate the liquidity component by subtracting the best fitting credit risk components, which we label $m(t)$. The liquidity component is then $l(t)$ which we write:

$$l(t) = c(t) - m(t)$$

2. Specify the form and parameters for the liquidity component based on values for other comparable credits for which such parameters are known.

Common choices are to assume that the liquidity component is linear in years to maturity so, $l(t) = u + wt$ or to assume that $l(t)$ is an exponential function, allowing the yield curve to be upward-sloping, downward-sloping, or humped. In this case:

$$l(t) = \exp(u + wt + zt^2)$$

The first method is the normal choice when we have two or more observable fixed-rate instruments outstanding for the issuer. The 'best fitting credit risk components' are those parameters for the Jarrow model described in Chapter 17 which minimize the fitting error versus the smoothed yield curve. By using the 'best fitting credit risk components' or parameters of the Jarrow model, we minimize the amount of the 'plug' or extension that is used to span the gap between the theoretical credit model and the observable yield curve.

The second method is used when there is only one bond or less for the risky issuer and we are forced to use the parameters from another issuer as a proxy for the issuer we are analyzing.

Estimating the Recovery Rate from Observable Market Data

One of the great advantages of the reduced form credit risk models is that parameters can be derived from observable bond market prices. This is problematic for the single period Merton model of risky debt. It too can be extended in various ways to become a pseudo-multiperiod model—one assumption that accomplishes this is that a different amount of zero-coupon debt matures on each payment date of an observable group of bonds, so we can assure a perfect fit to these bond prices. Unlike the reduced form models, however, the Merton model is a single period model by its very nature and this kind of simple extension is cumbersome and involves a considerable amount of model risk.

In the case of the Jarrow model, a price history on a number of risky bonds can be combined with a history of Jarrow-Chava default probabilities like those discussed in Chapter 17. When we combine data in this way, we have enough degrees of freedom to imply recovery rates over time from observable bond prices. A convenient assumption for doing this is to assume a form for the liquidity component that is tractable and solve for the implied recovery rate that results in the 'maximum smoothness' movements in the parameters of the liquidity component.

We leave this fascinating topic for further exposition at another time. Suffice it to say that this methodology for implied recovery rates provides much more stable estimates than databases of actual recoveries, because they converge by definition to the actual recovery rate experienced by a troubled company.

Recent Academic Work on the Credit Spread

There has been a recent flurry of interesting academic papers on modeling the entire credit spread. In most cases, the authors use the market convention for credit spread so their conclusions are tentative, but the results are still illuminating. In general, the papers show that the liquidity component of the credit spread may well be driven by the same macro-economic factors that contribute to the default probability of a risky issuer (and perhaps the recovery rate).

We briefly discuss four papers in this section.

John Y. Campbell and Glen B. Taksler, "Equity Volatility and Corporate Bond Yields", May 2002

Campbell and Taksler use credit spreads calculated on monthly Treasury rates, which is potential source of error, but their conclusions are nonetheless interesting. Credit spread is calculated as the simple difference in yield to maturity, in accordance to the market convention discussed in the beginning of this chapter. They compile a database of 43,000 credit spread observations, but only 22,000 are usable after adding explanatory variables. They use ordinary least squares, not logistic regression, to fit credit spread with a number of explanatory variables. They conclude that the 180-day standard deviation of excess return on the common stock is a key variable driving the total credit spread. This conclusion is consistent with both common specifications for reduced form models of the credit spread and common implementations of the Merton model, with the caveat that the Merton model does not explicitly provide for a liquidity component of credit spreads.

Pierre Collin-Dufresne, Robert S. Goldstein, J. Spencer Martin, "The Determinants of Credit Spread Changes," June 26 2000.

This study can explain about 25% of the movements in corporate bond spreads. Contrary to the expectation of many, including the authors of this book, the authors of the study were unable to find any common set of factors that explain correlated movements in credit spreads across issuers. The study applies a structural model of credit risk, unlike the largely reduced form approach of Campbell and Taksler. The study uses the Warga database, whose quality is of concern because the bond price data is monthly, making synchronization of bond spreads with explanatory variables difficult. The study uses linear smoothing of bond yields. The study uses contemporaneous returns on the S&P500 as an explanatory variable, contrary to much empirical work in the private sector which shows that a longer-term return has considerably more explanatory power in predicting both default and credit spreads. The authors use linear least squares and test other variables like interest rates, leverage, stock returns and stock index returns as potential risk factors driving total credit spreads.

Jing-zhi Huang and Weipeng Kong, "Explaining Credit Spread Changes: Some New Evidence from Option-Adjusted Spreads of Bond Indexes", June 2003.

The authors conclude that 'our analysis confirms that credit spread changes for high-yield bonds are more closely related to equity market factors and also provides evidence in favor of incorporating macroeconomic factors into credit risk models.' Unfortunately the study uses bond index data, not raw bond data, which contributes an unknown amount of error into the study. The study uses weekly and monthly observations. Option-adjusted spreads are used, but these cannot be determined without the formal assumption of a credit model since the value of the prepayment option is a function of the probability of default. The authors did not incorporate this fact in the OAS calculation, but its conclusions are still of interest. The authors use ordinary least squares and maturity buckets of 1–10 years, 10–15 years, and 15+ years instead of the exact maturity dates on the bonds underlying the bond indexes. This study is consistent with the incorporation of macro factors in reduced form models.

Edwin J. Elton, Martin J. Gruber, Deepak Agrawal, and Christopher Mann, "Explaining the Rate Spread on Corporate Bonds," Journal of Finance, February 2001.

This study also uses the monthly Warga database. The authors go a step further than the other authors in correctly focusing on zero-coupon yields, not coupon-bearing yield spreads. The method used by the authors is not as precise as that described in this chapter, however. The authors also correctly identify the state tax effect on the corporate bond spread.[8] The authors are unique among the studies in this section in using a transition matrix to estimate the expected loss component of the credit spread, rather than using the Jarrow-Chava approach of Chapter 17. Since this study assumes implicitly that macro factors do not influence expected loss, it attributes all of the movement in credit spread related to macro factors to the liquidity component of spreads. This study is based on quite a small grouped data set but its conclusions are interesting and the methodology is very careful in the estimation of zero-coupon yields for the risky issuers. The conclusion that macro factors drive credit spreads is consistent with the reduced form models studied in Chapter 17.

---

[8] The risk-free bond curve in the U.S. is exempt from taxation at the state level, while the risky bond yield curve is subject to state taxes. It is therefore correct to say that some part of the 'liquidity' component of the credit spread is due to this tax differential.

Conclusion

Academic work on macroeconomic factors driving credit spreads is compatible with the reduced form models of Chapter 17, although the methodology for deriving credit spreads is considerably less precise than the methods outlined in this chapter.

In this chapter, we have shown how the credit spread on one risky bond can be derived from the bond's present value and the risk-free yield curve by taking advantage of the yield curve smoothing technology of Chapter 8. We have also shown that the techniques of Chapter 8 can also be applied to the credit spread itself, rather than to zero-coupon bond yields or bond prices. We conclude that using a technique that maximizes the smoothness of forward credit spreads is the only method that minimizes the possibility that forward credit spreads will be negative or implausibly variable. By using this approach to yield curve smoothing, we can derive the liquidity component of credit spreads and imply the recovery rate consistent with bond prices when Jarrow-Chava default probabilities are available.

Chapter 19 discusses credit model testing procedures.

Interest Rate and Credit Model Testing

Tests of Credit Models Using Historical Data[1]

The proposed New Capital Accord (henceforth, Basel II) by the Basel Committee on Banking Supervision places heavy emphasis on the role of credit risk in measuring the safety and soundness of financial institutions. For that reason, it is critical from both a shareholder value point of view and a regulatory point of view that financial institutions have a clear understanding of the accuracy and performance of the credit models employed for that purpose.

Without knowledge of the accuracy of the models,

- How can regulators know whether the financial institution's capital is too high or too low?
- How can shareholders know whether the reserve for loan losses is adequate or not?
- How can the CEO certify that the financial statements of the company are accurate?
- How can the institution have confidence that a hedge of its portfolio credit risk will work?
- How can the institution have confidence in its own survival?

These are critical questions, to say the least, and they are the major motivators of the emphasis on credit model testing in this chapter. The Basel Accords' contribution to credit risk modeling has been two-fold. Firstly, the Accords stress the need to apply credit risk models to the entire balance sheet, not just to credit-related derivatives like credit default swaps. Secondly, the Accords stress the need for quantitative proof that the models perform well. Performance measurement is critical both across credit risk categories and

---

[1] This chapter is based on van Deventer and Wang [2003] and Jarrow and van Deventer [2004].

over time, i.e. through the peaks and troughs of credit cycles. See Allen and Saunders [2003] in *Working Paper* 126 of the Bank for International Settlements for more on the importance of cyclicality in credit risk modeling.

The result of these key developments has been a surge of interest in reduced form models and increased implementation of these models around the world in financial institutions of all types, with applications to retail clients, private companies, listed companies and sovereigns. A prominent example is the December 10 2003 announcement by the Federal Deposit Insurance Corporation that it has adopted a reduced form model-related Loss Distribution Model that we mentioned in Chapter 17.[2] The FDIC announcement is just another confirmation of a wholesale movement away from the older structural models of credit risk like the original Merton [1974] risky debt model and more recent extensions like Shimko, Tejima and van Deventer [1993], which we discussed in Chapter 16.

Given the plethora of credit risk models now available, how and why did the FDIC conclude that the reduced form model offered the most promise? More generally, how should a bank seeking to use credit risk models in credit risk management assess its relative performance and, then, implement them in practice? The answer to this difficult question is the subject of this chapter. In this chapter, we devote an extensive discussion to the testing of credit models on historical default data. In Chapter 20, we turn to tests of credit models on market data.

An Introduction to Credit Model Testing

The Merton model discussed in Chapter 16 has many virtues, but the reduced form modeling technology of Chapter 17 is a much more modern and powerful approach. Still, as noted in Chapter 16, use of the Merton model will continue indefinitely just as the Black model (with its assumptions of constant interest rates) persists in the market for interest rate caps or floors. The purpose of this chapter is to insure that users of both the Merton and reduced form modeling approaches clearly understand the performance of the models they employ for the reasons cited in the previous section.

One of the dilemmas facing the Basel Committee on Banking Supervision is the paucity of data on credit model performance. The primary reasons why there is so little evidence on the performance of credit models fall into two categories. The first is the considerable expense and expertise needed, both in

---

[2] Please see Jarrow, Bennett, Fu, Muxoll, and Zhang, 'A General Martingale Approach to Measuring and Valuing the Risk to the FDIC Insurance Funds', *Working Paper*, November 23 2003. Available on www.kamakuraco.com or on the website of the Federal Deposit Insurance Corporation.

terms of finance and computer science, to assemble the data and computer coding to provide a consistent methodology for testing credit models in a way that the proposed Basel II requires. Van Deventer and Imai [2003] note that the Basel II requires that banks to prove to their regulatory supervisors that the credit models they use perform 'consistently and meaningfully.'[3] Typically, the only institutions which have the capability to assemble these kinds of databases are extremely large financial institutions and commercial vendors of default probabilities. Prior to the commercialization of default probabilities by Moody's KMV, studies of default were based on a very small number of defaulting observations. Falkenstein and Boral [2000] cite academic papers by Altman [1968] (33 defaults), Altman [1977] (53 defaults), and Blum [1974] (115 defaults) to illustrate the relatively small sample sizes used to draw inferences about bankruptcy probabilities prior to 1999. By way of contrast, Kamakura Corporation's commercial default database includes more than 1,600 failed company observations and its research database, which spans a longer period, contains more than 2,000 failed companies for North America alone.

For major financial institutions that have incurred the expense of a large default database, the results of model testing are highly valuable and represent a significant competitive advantage over other financial institutions which do not have the results of credit model performance tests. For example, there is a large community of arbitrage investors actively trading against users of the Merton default probabilities when the arbitrage investors perceive the signals sent by the Merton model to be incorrect.

Among the vendor community, the majority of vendors offer a single default probability model. This presents a dilemma for potential consumers of commercial default probabilities. A vendor of a single type of credit model has two reasons not to publish quantitative tests of performance. The first reason is that the tests may prove that the model is inferior and ultimately may adversely affect the vendor's commercial prospects. Perhaps for this reason, most vendors require clients to sign license agreements that forbid the clients from publicizing any results of the vendor's model performance. The second reason is more subtle. Even if quantitative performance tests are good, the fact that the vendor offers only one model means that the vendor's tests will be perceived by many as biased in favor of the model that the vendor offers.

Four former employees of Moody's Investors Service have set the standard for quantitative model test disclosure in a series of papers—Andrew Boral, Eric Falkenstein, Sean Keenan, and Jorge Sobehart. The authors respect the important contributions of Boral, Falkenstein, Keenan, and Sobehart to the integrity of the default probability generation and testing process.

---

[3] Section 302, p. 55, "The New Basel Capital Accord", Basel Committee on Banking Supervision, May 31, 2001.

The need for such tests is reflected in the frequently heard comments of default probability users who display a naïveté with respect to credit models which will ultimately result in their failure to meet the credit model testing requirements of Basel II. We present some samples in the next section, which illustrate the need for better understanding of credit model testing.

Misunderstandings About Credit Model Testing

A commonly heard comment on credit model performance goes like this:

> *'I like Model A because it showed a better early warning of the default of Companies X, Y and Z.'*

Many users of default probabilities make two critical mistakes in assessing default probability model performance. They choose a very small sample (in this case three companies) to assess model performance and use naïve criteria for good performance. Assessing model performance on only three companies or 50 or even 100 in a universe of 8,000–10,000 in the total universe of U.S. corporations needlessly exposes the potential user to: (a) an incorrect conclusion just because of the noise in the small sample; and (b) to the risk of data mining by the default probability vendor, who (like a magician doing card tricks) can steer the banker to the three or 50 or 100 examples which show the model in the best light. A test of the whole sample eliminates these risks. Analysts should demand this of both internal models and models purchased from third parties.

The second problem this banker's quote has is the performance criteria. The implications of this comment are two fold:

- I can ignore all false predictions of default and give them zero weight in my decision.
- If Model A has higher default probabilities than Model B on a troubled credit, then model A must be better than model B.

Both of these implications should be grounds for a failing grade by banking supervisors. The first comment, ignoring all false positives, is sometimes justified by saying 'I sold Company A's bonds when its default probabilities hit 20% and saved my bank from a loss of $1.7 million, and I don't care if other companies which don't default have 20% default probabilities because I would never buy a bond with a 20% default probability anyway.' Why, then, did the bank have the bond of Company A in its portfolio? And what about the bonds that were sold when default probabilities rose, only to have the bank miss out on gains in the bond's price that occurred after the sale. Without knowledge of the gains avoided, as well as the losses avoided, the banker has shown a striking 'selection bias' in favor of the model they are currently using. This selection bias will result in any model being judged good by a true believer. We give some examples below.

The second implication exposes the banker and the vendor to a temptation that can be detected by the tests we discuss below: The vendor can make any model show 'better early warning' signs than any other model simply by raising the default probabilities. If the vendor of model B wants to win this banker's business, all they have to do is multiply all of their default probabilities by six or add an arbitrary scale factor to make their default probabilities higher than model A. The banker making this quote would not be able to detect this moral hazard because they do not use the testing regime mentioned below. The authors can't resist pointing out that using the summer temperature in Fahrenheit as a credit model will outpredict any credit model by this criteria if the company defaults in July or August in the Northern Hemisphere.

Eric Falkenstein and Andrew Boral[4] [2000] of Moody's Investors Service address the issue of model calibration directly:

'Some vendors have been known to generate very high default rates, and we would suggest the following test to assess those predictions. Firstly, take a set of historical data and group it into 50 equally populated buckets (using percentile breakpoints of 2%, 4%, ... 100%). Then consider the mean default prediction on the x-axis with the actual, subsequent bad rate on the y-axis. More often than not, models will have a relation that is somewhat less than 45% (i.e., slope <1), especially at these very high-risk groupings. This implies that the model purports more power than it actually has, and more importantly, it is mis-calibrated and should be adjusted.'

We present the results of the Falkenstein and Boral test later in this chapter. We also present a second type of test to detect this kind of bias in credit modeling below. If a model has a bias to levels higher than actual default rates, it is inappropriate for Basel II to use because it will be inaccurate for pricing, hedging, valuation, and portfolio loss simulation.

Another quotation illustrates a similar point of view that is inconsistent with Basel II compliance in credit modeling:

'That credit model vendor is very popular because they have correctly predicted 10,000 *of the last* 10,500 *small business defaults.'*

Again, this comment ignores false predictions of default and assigns zero costs to false predictions of default. If any banker truly had that orientation, the Basel II credit supervision process will seek them out with a vengeance because the authors hereby propose a credit model at zero cost that outperforms the commercial model referred to above:

100% Accurate Prediction of Small Business Defaults: The Default Probability for All Small Businesses is 100%.

---

[4] Page 46.

This naïve model correctly predicts 10,500 of the last 10,500 defaults. It is free in the sense that assigning a 100% default probability to everyone requires no expense or third party vendor since any one can say the default probability for everyone is 100%. As the banker quoted above, it is consistent with a zero weight on the prediction of false positives. Most financial institutions admit that false positives are important. As one major financial institution commented, one model 'correctly predicted 1,000 of the last three defaults'.

Once this is admitted, there is a reasonable basis for testing credit models.

The Two Components of Credit Model Performance

The performance of models designed to predict a yes or no–zero or one–event, like bankruptcy, has been the focus of mathematical statistics for more than fifty years. For an excellent summary of statistical procedures for evaluating model performance in this regard, see Hosmer and Lemeshow [2000]. These performance tests, however, have only been applied to default probability modeling in recent years. Van Deventer and Imai [2003] provide an overview of these standard statistical tests for default probability modeling. Related papers are van Deventer and Outram [2002] and van Deventer and Wang [2003]. Jarrow, van Deventer and Wang [2003] and van Deventer and Imai [2003] apply an alternative hedging approach to measuring credit model performance. We discuss each of these alternative testing procedures in turn. In this chapter, we focus on testing models on historical bankruptcy data. In Chapter 20, we test models based on market data.

Basel II requires that financial institutions have the capability to test credit model performance and internal ratings to ensure that they consistently and meaningfully measure credit risk. There are two principal measures of credit risk model performance. The first is a measure of the correctness of the ordinal ranking of the companies by riskiness. For this measure, we use the so-called receiver operating characteristics (ROC) Accuracy Ratio, whose calculation is reviewed briefly in the next section. The second is a measure of the consistency of the predicted default probability with the actual default probability, which Falkenstein and Boral [2000] call 'calibration'. This test is necessary to ensure the accuracy of the model for pricing, hedging, valuation and portfolio simulation. Just as importantly, it is necessary to detect a tendency for a model to bias default probabilities to the high side as Falkenstein and Boral note, which overstates the predictive power of a model by the naïve criteria of the first quote in the introduction.

We discuss each of these tests in turn in the next two sections.

Measuring Ordinal Ranking of Companies by Credit Risk

The standard statistic for measuring the ordinal ranking of companies by credit riskiness is the ROC accuracy ratio. The ROC accuracy ratio is closely related to, but different than, the cumulative accuracy profiles used by Jorge Sobehart and colleagues [2000], formerly at Moody's Investors Service and now at Citigroup, in numerous publications in recent years.

The receiver operating characteristics (ROC) curve was originally developed in order to measure the signal to noise ratio in radio receivers. The ROC curve has become increasingly popular as a measure of model performance in fields ranging from medicine to finance. It is typically used to measure the performance of a model that is used to predict which of two states will occur (sick or not sick, defaulted or not defaulted, etc.). van Deventer and Imai [2003] go into extensive detail on the meaning and derivation of the ROC accuracy ratio, which is a quantitative measure of model performance.

In short, the ROC accuracy ratio is derived in the following way:

- Calculate the theoretical default probability for the entire universe of companies in a historical database that includes both defaulted and non-defaulted companies.
- Form all possible pairs of companies such that the pair includes one defaulted 'company' and one non-defaulted 'company'. To be precise, one pair would be the December 2001 defaulted observation for Enron and the October 1987 observation for General Motors, which did not default in that month. Another pair would include defaulted Enron, December 2001, and non-defaulted Enron, November 2001, and so on.
- If the default probability technology correctly rates the defaulted company as more risky, we award one point to the pair.
- If the default probability technology results in a tie, we give half a point.
- If the default probability technology is incorrect, we give zero points.
- We then add up all the points for all of the pairs, and divide by the number of pairs[5].

The results are intuitive and extremely clear on model rankings:

- A perfect model scores 1.00 or 100% accuracy, ranking every single one of the defaulting companies as more risky than every non-defaulting company.

---

[5] This calculation can involve a very large number of pairs. The current commercial database at Kamakura Corporation involves the comparison of 1.4 billion pairs of observations, but on a modern personal computer, as of this writing, processing time for the exact calculation is slightly over one hour. Processing time using a very close approximation is less than one minute.

- A worthless model scores 0.50 or 50%, because this is a score that could be achieved by flipping a coin.
- A score in the 90% range is extremely good.
- A score in the 80% range is very good, and so on.

Van Deventer and Imai provide worked examples to illustrate the application of the ROC accuracy ratio technique. The ROC accuracy ratio can be equivalently summarized in one sentence:

It is the average percentile ranking of the defaulting companies in the universe of non-defaulting observations.

We turn now to the Kamakura Corporation database, which we shall use to apply the ROC accuracy ratio technology. Results will be summarized for the North American database, which includes all listed companies for which the explanatory variables were available.

The Predictive ROC Accuracy Ratio: Techniques and Results

The Kamakura Risk Information Services database is a monthly database. Other researchers have used annual data, including the work of Sobehart and colleagues noted above. Annual data has been used in the past because of the researchers' interest in long-term bankruptcy prediction. One of the purposes of this chapter is to show how monthly data can be used for exactly the same purpose, and to show how accuracy changes as the prediction period grows longer.

The basic Jarrow-Chava [2002a, 2002b] model uses logistic regression technology to combine equity market and accounting data for default probability prediction consistent with the reduced form modeling approach of Chapter 17. Jarrow and Chava provide a framework that shows that these default probability estimates are consistent with the best practice reduced form credit models of Jarrow [1999–2001] and Duffie and Singleton [1999].

We turn now to the ROC accuracy ratios for the Jarrow-Chava reduced form modeling approach.

The predictive capability of the Jarrow-Chava reduced form model default probabilities

Basel II is reasonably tentative in its consideration of default probability models because of a lack of information regarding the predictive capabilities of the models. This section shows that the technology for measuring predictive capability is transparent and straightforward. We show that the reduced form modelling approach has a high degree of accuracy even when predicting from a distant horizon.

The standard calculation for the ROC accuracy ratio is always based on the default measure in the period of default (which could be a month if using monthly data, or a year if using yearly data). In order to address Basel and financial institutions management questions about the 'early warning' capability of default probability models, it is useful to know the accuracy of credit models at various time horizons, not just in the period of default.

We know that, in their past, companies which defaulted were at some point the same as other companies and their default probabilities were probably no different from those of otherwise similar companies. In order words, if we took their default probability in that benign era and used that to calculate the ROC accuracy ratio, we would expect to see an accuracy ratio of 0.50 or 50%, because at that point in their history the companies are just 'average' and so are their default probabilities.

Therefore, our objective is to see how far in advance of default the ROC accuracy ratio for the defaulting companies rises from the 50% level on its way to achieving the standard ROC accuracy ratio in the month of default.

Measuring the predictive ROC accuracy ratio

We calculate the time series of predictive ROC accuracy ratios in the following way:

- We again form all possible pairs of one defaulted company and one non-defaulted company. Instead of defining the 'default date' and associated default probability for Enron as December, 2001, however, we step back one month prior to default and use the November time period for Enron as the default date and the November 2001 default probability as the 'one-month predictive' default probability.
- We calculate the ROC accuracy ratio on this basis.
- We lengthen the prediction period by one more month again.
- We recalculate which default probability we will use in the ROC comparison for each of the defaulted companies (in the second iteration, we will use the October 2001 default probability for Enron, not November).
- We repeat the process until we have studied the predictive period of interest and have calculated the predictive ROC accuracy ratio for each date.

Results for the Jarrow-Chava database, 1963–1998

We illustrate the results first for the basic Jarrow-Chava model [2002a, 2002b] based on 1.3 million monthly observations from 1963–1998. That model uses two accounting ratios, equity volatility and returns, and company size to predict default. In subsequent sections, we report results for the substantially enhanced version of the Jarrow-Chava model offered as part of Kamakura Risk Information Services.

Figure 19.1 shows that the ROC accuracy ratio is well above the 50% level for the basic Jarrow-Chava default probability series even five years prior to default over the 1.4 billion pairs of default probability comparisons. The ROC accuracy ratio rises steadily as default comes closer and closer, ending at the 92.74% accuracy reported by van Deventer and Imai [2003].

The rise in the predictive ROC accuracy ratio is easier to see in tabular form. Twelve months prior to default, the accuracy ratio is 78.54%. Two years prior

Figure 19.1 ROC Accuracy Ratios from 60 Months Prior to Default to Month of Default KDP-jc Jarrow-Chava Reduced Form 1 Year Default Probability for All Listed U.S. Companies, 1963–1998

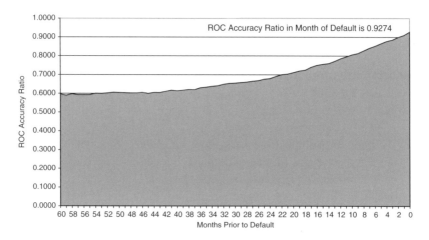

to default, the predictive accuracy ratio is 67.97%, which means the default probabilities for the companies that would ultimately default were already higher than 67.97% of all non-defaulting companies in all time periods. Three years prior to default the accuracy ratio was still at 63%, and five years before default it was 59.65%. Was this 59.65% estimate of the ROC accuracy ratio statistically different from the 50% accuracy ratio that we would expect if the defaulting companies were so far from default that they were 'just average'? The answer is yes—because of the 1.3–1.4 billion comparisons we are making to determine the accuracy ratio, the standard deviation on our estimate of the accuracy ratio is very small and, at the five-year time horizon, we are more than 7,000 standard deviations from the 50% mark.

Put another way, defaulting companies have default probabilities higher than 60% of all companies 54 months before default. They have default probabilities higher than 70% of all companies 22 months prior to default. They have default probabilities higher than 80% of all companies 10 months before

Table 19.1 Predictive ROC Accuracy Ratio of KDP-jc, 1963–1998, Listed U.S. Companies

Months Prior to Bankruptcy	ROC Accuracy Ratio	Number of Observations	Number of Defaults	Number of Comparisons	Standard Deviation of Estimated ROC Accuracy Ratio	Number of Standard Deviations from .5 ROC Accuracy Ratio
60	0.5965	1,346,701	979	1,317,461,838	0.0000135	7,140
59	0.5902	1,347,633	979	1,318,374,266	0.0000135	6,659
58	0.5973	1,348,564	979	1,319,285,715	0.0000135	7,206
57	0.5932	1,349,496	979	1,320,198,143	0.0000135	6,894
56	0.5928	1,350,430	979	1,321,112,529	0.0000135	6,865
55	0.5933	1,351,365	979	1,322,027,894	0.0000135	6,906
54	0.6009	1,352,301	979	1,322,944,238	0.0000135	7,494
53	0.5999	1,353,239	979	1,323,862,540	0.0000135	7,419
52	0.6023	1,354,175	979	1,324,778,884	0.0000134	7,608
51	0.6059	1,355,109	979	1,325,693,270	0.0000134	7,891
50	0.6047	1,356,046	979	1,326,610,593	0.0000134	7,800
49	0.6037	1,356,983	979	1,327,527,916	0.0000134	7,725
48	0.6024	1,357,921	979	1,328,446,218	0.0000134	7,626
47	0.6024	1,358,860	979	1,329,365,499	0.0000134	7,629
46	0.6053	1,359,799	979	1,330,284,780	0.0000134	7,857
45	0.5993	1,360,739	979	1,331,205,040	0.0000134	7,393
44	0.6044	1,361,682	979	1,332,128,237	0.0000134	7,793
43	0.6039	1,362,625	979	1,333,051,434	0.0000134	7,756
42	0.6108	1,363,569	979	1,333,975,610	0.0000133	8,300
41	0.6174	1,364,513	979	1,334,899,786	0.0000133	8,825
40	0.6141	1,365,457	979	1,335,823,962	0.0000133	8,566
39	0.6169	1,366,402	979	1,336,749,117	0.0000133	8,792
38	0.6211	1,367,348	979	1,337,675,251	0.0000133	9,130
37	0.6202	1,368,295	979	1,338,602,364	0.0000133	9,061
36	0.6300	1,369,243	979	1,339,530,456	0.0000132	9,855
35	0.6335	1,370,193	979	1,340,460,506	0.0000132	10,144
34	0.6384	1,371,143	979	1,341,390,556	0.0000131	10,550
33	0.6413	1,372,096	979	1,342,323,543	0.0000131	10,794
32	0.6489	1,373,049	979	1,343,256,530	0.0000130	11,433
31	0.6536	1,374,003	979	1,344,190,496	0.0000130	11,835
30	0.6549	1,374,957	979	1,345,124,462	0.0000130	11,950
29	0.6582	1,375,912	979	1,346,059,407	0.0000129	12,237
28	0.6604	1,376,870	979	1,346,997,289	0.0000129	12,431
27	0.6650	1,377,828	979	1,347,935,171	0.0000129	12,835
26	0.6688	1,378,786	979	1,348,873,053	0.0000128	13,172
25	0.6763	1,379,746	979	1,349,812,893	0.0000127	13,844
24	0.6797	1,380,705	979	1,350,751,754	0.0000127	14,155
23	0.6906	1,381,664	979	1,351,690,615	0.0000126	15,160
22	0.7002	1,382,624	979	1,352,630,455	0.0000125	16,070
21	0.7038	1,383,585	979	1,353,571,274	0.0000124	16,422
20	0.7109	1,384,546	979	1,354,512,093	0.0000123	17,121
19	0.7201	1,385,509	979	1,355,454,870	0.0000122	18,049
18	0.7247	1,386,474	979	1,356,399,605	0.0000121	18,527
17	0.7400	1,387,438	979	1,357,343,361	0.0000119	20,158
16	0.7502	1,388,404	979	1,358,289,075	0.0000117	21,301
15	0.7557	1,389,371	979	1,359,235,768	0.0000117	21,940
14	0.7594	1,390,337	979	1,360,181,482	0.0000116	22,381

Table 19.1 Predictive ROC Accuracy Ratio of KDP-jc, 1963-1998, Listed
U.S. Companies (*Cont'd*)

Months Prior to Bankruptcy	ROC Accuracy Ratio	Number of Observations	Number of Defaults	Number of Comparisons	Standard Deviation of Estimated ROC Accuracy Ratio	Number of Standard Deviations from .5 ROC Accuracy Ratio
13	0.7709	1,391,307	979	1,361,131,112	0.0000114	23,782
12	0.7854	1,392,278	979	1,362,081,721	0.0000111	25,656
11	0.7951	1,393,251	979	1,363,034,288	0.0000109	26,992
10	0.8063	1,394,226	979	1,363,988,813	0.0000107	28,625
9	0.8133	1,395,201	979	1,364,943,338	0.0000105	29,704
8	0.8270	1,396,176	979	1,365,897,863	0.0000102	31,951
7	0.8412	1,397,152	979	1,366,853,367	0.0000099	34,514
6	0.8520	1,398,129	979	1,367,809,850	0.0000096	36,661
5	0.8653	1,399,106	979	1,368,766,333	0.0000092	39,587
4	0.8776	1,400,083	979	1,369,722,816	0.0000089	42,639
3	0.8851	1,401,061	979	1,370,680,278	0.0000086	44,708
2	0.8992	1,402,039	979	1,371,637,740	0.0000081	49,108
1	0.9098	1,403,017	979	1,372,595,202	0.0000077	52,999
0	0.9274	1,403,898	979	1,373,457,701	0.0000070	61,044

default. By the month of default, again, they have default probabilities higher than 92.74% of all non-defaulting companies over all time periods.

This is an impressive showing for the Jarrow-Chava reduced form default probabilities over one of the largest commercially available default databases in the U.S., with 1.4 million monthly observations. Of course these monthly observations can be converted to annual observations for comparative annual analysis as well.

These concrete results can be used directly by financial institutions to meet the requirements for the Internal Ratings Based Approach in the New Capital Accords proposed by the Basel Committee on Banking Supervision. The results are based on statistical approaches that are standard in mathematical statistics and standard in fields from electronics to medicine to finance. Moreover, the statistical significance of the results can also be determined and replicated by financial institutions themselves who purchase the default database or use their own proprietary databases.

Mapping the Merton Model to Actual Defaults and the Impact on ROC Accuracy Ratio

In comparing different versions of the Merton credit model, one of the key issues is the 'mapping of theoretical default probabilities to actual default experience'. Different users of the Merton model do this in varying ways, but almost all users of the Merton model have one characteristic in common:

> *The theoretical Merton default probabilities are mapped to actual default experience in a way that changes the absolute level of the default probabilities but not the ordinal ranking of the companies in the universe.*

This has a very important implication for the ROC accuracy ratios of the Merton model:

> *The methodology used for mapping theoretical default probabilities to actual default experience will not change the ROC accuracy ratio for the Merton model if it preserves the ordinal ranking of companies by riskiness.*

Stating it more simply, the ROC accuracy ratio only measures ordinal accuracy, not calibration or consistency between expected and actual defaults. This point is obvious but often overlooked by naïve users who believe that the mapping methodology improves accuracy. As far as the ROC accuracy ratio goes, this belief is without foundation. The only benefit to a better mapping technology is shown below in measuring the consistency between actual and expected defaults. This is a different issue than measuring the accuracy of the ordinal ranking of companies.

Reduced Form Model Versus Merton Model Performance

To date, other than in papers by the four alumni of Moody's Investors Service mentioned above, there have been very few studies of credit model performance on a common platform of historical defaults and at various forecasting horizons. In this section, we turn to that task. We compare the accuracy of the ordinal ranking of credit risk for three credit models distributed by the Kamakura Corporation:

Reduced form credit model

- **KDP-jc**, Kamakura Default Probabilities from an advanced form of the Jarrow-Chava [2002] approach. The model uses six basic inputs, which are transformed to twelve explanatory variables, including financial ratios, equity market data, macro factors and two other variables.

Structural credit models

- **KDP-ms**, Kamakura Default Probabilities using the 'best' Merton approach with proprietary mapping to actual default experience by Kamakura.

Hybrid credit models

*   **KDP-jm**, Kamakura Default Probabilities combining the Jarrow and Merton approaches in a hybrid model within the logistic regression framework. The KDP-ms Merton default probability is added as an additional explanatory variable to the Jarrow-Chava variables in KDP-jc to form KDP-jm.

Figure 19.2 shows the ROC accuracy ratios for version 2.2 of all three of the models based on data from 1989 to July 2003. It shows clearly that the accuracy of the credit risk ranking of both the KDP-jc Jarrow-Chava reduced form model and the hybrid KDP-jm model are superior to the KDP-ms Merton model for all forecasting horizons of 15 months and less prior to default. By the month of default, the performance differential is in excess of 15%, a very large difference over the one million-observation sample size of default probabilities for the 1989–2003 period. In the 15–30 month forecasting horizon, the KDP-jm Jarrow-Merton hybrid model and the KDP-ms Merton model are close in accuracy, with the KDP-jc Jarrow-Chava model slightly less accurate.

Figure 19.2 Kamakura Default Probabilities Predictive ROC Accuracy Ratios in the Months Prior to Bankruptcy January, 1989–July 2003

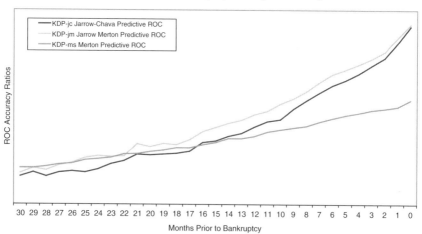

With this kind of precision in ranking of models by accuracy for any user-defined forecasting horizon, there should be no question about the superiority of Model A versus Model B when it comes to the Basel II requirements for credit model testing. The performance advantage of the reduced form models is even more striking when the relative weighting of the input variables is optimized for the forecasting horizon. We will report on those results in a future publication.

Consistency of Estimated and Actual Defaults

Falkenstein and Boral [2000] correctly emphasize the need to do more than measure the correctness of the ordinal ranking of companies by riskiness. One needs to determine whether a model is correctly 'calibrated', in the words of Falkenstein and Boral, that is whether the model has default probabilities that are biased high or low. As noted in the example in the introduction, a naïve user of credit models can be convinced a model has superior performance just because it gives higher default probabilities for some subset of a sample. A test of consistency between actual and expected defaults is needed to see whether this difference in default probability levels is consistent with actual default experience or just an *ad hoc* adjustment or noise.

A simple example is enough to show why this comparison of actual and expected defaults has to be done period-by-period, not just over the sample as a whole.

Consider the following example:

- Assume we know the actual average probability of default for all listed companies in the U.S. from 1963–1998 and that all companies in the U.S. have this probability of default.
- Assume that this default probability is constant over the 1963–1998 (an assumption common to many CDO modeling approaches).
- Assume that there is no correlation between the default probabilities of any two companies (another common assumption in CDO modeling).

How consistent would the actual number of defaults and the expected number of defaults have been, given these assumptions?

We take the following steps:

1. Based on the number of companies that are listed in the U.S. at the start of each year, we calculate the confidence intervals on the high and low numbers of default that should occur in that year, if our assumption that there is zero correlation is true.
2. We then compare the actual number of defaults to our confidence interval.
3. When we do this analysis, we know the following:
   a. Over the entire period 1963–1998, our expected number of defaults will exactly match the U.S. total (which is a much better perform-ance than we would get in forecasting CDO defaults);
   b. We can calculate the 99.5% number of defaults;
   c. We can calculate the 0.5% number of defaults;
   d. If our credit modeling assumptions are good, we will have a high degree of consistency between actual and expected defaults, falling out of the confidence interval only 1% of the time.

Figure 19.3 Actual Number of U.S. Bankruptcies vs. Predicted Bankruptcies Assuming No Correlation Between Companies and Over Time

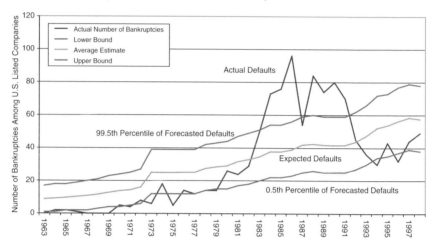

Figure 19.3 shows the results of the forecasting exercise described above.

As Figure 19.3 shows, even though we correctly forecast the 1,120 bankruptcies that occurred in the U.S. over the 1963–1998, we were dramatically wrong on timing and our assumption that there is no correlation among listed companies in the U.S. seems to be seriously wrong. Over almost all of the 40-year period, we are at or below the 0.5% percentile level or over the 99.5% percentile level when it comes to actual number of bankruptcies—we are out of the 99% range of probability much of the time. We can measure how often in Figure 19.4 below.

Table 19.2 shows that in 18 of the 36 years studied, exactly half the time, actual defaults were outside 99% confidence interval in our simulation, even

Table 19.2 Stimulated Number of Defaults Using Average U.S. Default Probability and Assuming No Correlation Among U.S. Companies

	Number of Listed Companies in U.S.			Actual Number of Bankruptcies	Lower Bound of 0.5th Percentile	Expected Number of Defaults at 50th Percentile	Upper Bound at 99.5th Percentile	Outside of 99% Probability Range?
Year	Not Bankrupt	Bankrupt	Total					
1963	1252	0	1252	0	1	8.8	17	yes
1964	1297	2	1299	2	1	9.1	18	
1965	1373	2	1375	2	2	9.7	18	
1966	1449	1	1450	1	2	10.2	19	yes
1967	1545	0	1545	0	2	10.8	20	yes
1968	1645	0	1645	0	3	11.5	21	yes
1969	1821	0	1821	0	4	12.8	23	yes

Table 19.2　Stimulated Number of Defaults Using Average U.S. Default Probability and Assuming No Correlation Among U.S. Companies (*Cont'd*)

	Number of Listed Companies in U.S.			Actual Number of Bankruptcies	Lower Bound of 0.5th Percentile	Expected Number of Defaults at 50th Percentile	Upper Bound at 99.5th Percentile	Outside of 99% Probability Range?
Year	Not Bankrupt	Bankrupt	Total					
1970	1949	5	1954	5	4	13.7	24	
1971	2042	4	2046	4	5	14.4	25	yes
1972	2277	8	2285	8	6	16.0	27	
1973	3560	6	3566	6	12	25.0	39	yes
1974	3532	18	3550	18	12	24.9	39	
1975	3543	5	3548	5	12	24.9	39	yes
1976	3563	14	3577	14	12	25.1	39	
1977	3567	12	3579	12	12	25.1	39	
1978	3905	14	3919	14	14	27.5	42	
1979	4036	14	4050	14	15	28.4	43	yes
1980	4133	26	4159	26	15	29.2	44	
1981	4493	24	4517	24	17	31.7	47	
1982	4669	29	4698	29	18	33.0	49	
1983	4885	50	4935	50	20	34.6	51	
1984	5302	73	5375	73	22	37.7	54	yes
1985	5299	76	5375	76	22	37.7	54	yes
1986	5448	96	5544	96	23	38.9	56	yes
1987	5913	54	5967	54	25	41.9	59	
1988	5959	84	6043	84	26	42.4	60	yes
1989	5890	74	5964	74	25	41.9	59	yes
1990	5850	80	5930	80	25	41.6	59	yes
1991	5870	70	5940	70	25	41.7	59	yes
1992	6195	45	6240	45	27	43.8	62	
1993	6717	36	6753	36	30	47.4	66	
1994	7401	30	7431	30	34	52.2	72	yes
1995	7616	43	7659	43	35	53.8	73	
1996	8001	32	8033	32	37	56.4	77	yes
1997	8281	44	8325	44	39	58.4	79	
1998	8154	49	8203	49	38	57.6	78	
Grand Total*		1120	159551	1120	622	1120	1650	18

though on average we predicted exactly the right number of defaults over the 36 years. This shows that model calibration over time, not just over a 'one period' sample, is very important. We now turn to similar tests for the most recent release of default probabilities from Kamakura Corporation's Kamakura Risk Information Systems Database.

Recent Results from North America

In this and subsequent sections, we report test results for the KRIS version 3.0 default probabilities on a sample of 1.1 million observations from

North America from 1989 to the present. Similar tests performed solely on that subset of the universe that has debt ratings from the major rating agencies score much higher than what is reported below.

The standard ROC accuracy ratios introduced above are reported for three credit models:

- KDP-jc, the Jarrow-Chava reduced form Kamakura Default Probability based on historical estimation of default probabilities using macroeconomic factors, financial ratios, and various inputs from the equity market.
- KDP-ms, the Kamakura implementation of the Merton structural model of risky debt.
- KDP-jm, the Jarrow-Merton hybrid model which uses KDP-jc and KDP-ms jointly to predict default.

The ROC accuracy ratios for the three models are as follows[6]:

93.62%, KDP-jc Jarrow-Chava reduced form model;
91.83%, KDP-jm Jarrow-Merton hybrid model;
83.42%, KDP-ms Merton structural model.

These results show that the reduced form KDP-jc model significantly outperforms the Merton model in an ordinal ranking of companies by credit riskiness. The ROC accuracy ratio for KDP-ms is similar to the Merton implementation of Jorge Sobehart, Sean Keenan, and Roger Stein [2000] and Eric Falkenstein and Andrew Boral [2000], when they were at Moody's Investors Service. The results show that 6.48% of the non-defaulting observations for the KDP-jc model (100−93.62) are higher than the average default probability for defaulting observations. The same figure for the Merton model is 16.68 (100 − 83.42). This means that the Merton model has almost three times the number of false positives than the Jarrow-Chava reduced form model.

Even more importantly, this is true for any mapping of the Merton default probabilities from their theoretical values to actual defaults, which preserves the ordinal ranking of the companies by riskiness.[7] This is because the ROC accuracy ratio does not change if the ordering of the observations is not changed.

---

[6] Complete results are described in the Kamakura Risk Information Services Technical Guide, version 3.0, February 2004. This confidential document is distributed to KRIS clients and to financial services regulatory agencies upon request.

[7] Mapping in such a way that the ranking of companies is not changed is very common in the industry.

We now turn to another important model test, the comparison of performance versus naïve 'single variable' credit models.

Performance of Credit Models versus Naïve Models of Risk

Knowing the absolute level of accuracy is extremely useful, but it is just as important to know the relative accuracy of a credit model versus naïve models of credit risk. A typical 'naïve' model would be one that uses only one financial ratio or equity market statistic to predict default.

It is well-known among industry experts that many financial ratios outperform the Merton model in the ordinal ranking of riskiness. This result, however, seems unknown to many academics and financial services regulators, so we present representative results here[8].

ROC accuracy ratios for Merton model versus selected naïve models

89.20%, Relative ranking of the current stock price versus the stock price for the last N years;

88.10%, Percentile ranking among all company stock prices on that day;

87.33%, One-year excess return on the stock versus equity index;

87.37%, One-month equity volatility;

85.33%, Company size;

83.42%, KDP-ms, Merton structural model.

This observation that the Merton model underperforms common financial ratios has economic and political implications for the practical use of credit models:

> *Can management of a financial institution or bank regulators approve a model whose performance is inferior to a financial ratio that management and bank regulators would not approve as a legitimate modeling approach on a stand-alone basis?*

Of course, the answer is no. This finding is another factor supporting the use of reduced form models, which by construction, outperform any naïve model depending on a single financial ratio.[9]

---

[8] Based on 1.1 million monthly observations consisting of all listed companies in North America for which data was available from 1989–2003, Kamakura Risk Information Services data-base, version 3.0.

[9] Recall that the hazard rate estimation procedure determines the 'best' set of explanatory variables from a given set. In the estimation procedure previously discussed, a single financial ratio was a possible outcome, and it was rejected in favor of the multi-variable models presented.

Consistency of Actual and Expected Defaults

Van Deventer and Wang [2003] also present a test to measure the performance of models over the credit cycle, an important issue as noted by Allen and Saunders [2003] in BIS *Working Paper* 126. Figure 19.4 shows the actual number of company failures in North America from 1990 to 2003 versus the number of defaults that would be expected under each of the three credit models listed above.

Figure 19.4 Comparison of Monthly Actual Bankrupticies versus Expected Bankruptcies, KRIS 3.0.

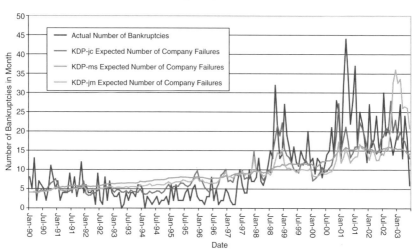

van Deventer and Wang propose a quantitative measure of the consistency between actual and expected defaults–the adjusted R^2 of the regression equation:

$$\text{Actual Defaults} = a + b \text{ (Expected defaults)}$$

Using annual time periods, the Jarrow-Chava model scores the best by this measure with an adjusted R^2 of 87%. The Merton model ranks second at 79%, and the hybrid model third with 70%. This also establishes that the Jarrow-Chava approach is better at modeling default level changes over the credit cycle.

The Falkenstein and Boral Test

Eric Falkenstein and Andrew Boral [2000], formerly of Moody's Investors Service, suggested another consistency test between actual and expected defaults. They suggest the following test:

- Order the universe of all default probability observations from lowest to highest.
- Create N 'buckets' of these observations with an equal number in each bucket.
- Measure the default probability boundaries that define the low end and high end of each bucket.
- Measure the actual rate of default in each bucket.
- The actual default rate should lie between the lower and upper boundary of the bucket for most of the N buckets.

Falkenstein and Boral propose this test because the implied 'early warning' of a credit model can be artificially increased by multiplying the default probabilities by some arbitrary ratio like five. If the model was properly calibrated before this adjustment, the result of multiplication by five will result in an expected level of defaults that is five times higher than actual defaults, which would be unacceptable both to management and to financial institutions regulators under the New Capital Accords. Recent anecdotal evidence is consistent with reports that different vendors' default probabilities can differ by a factor of five or six.

If there is an accidental or intentional bias in default probabilities, the adjusted R^2 test in the prior section will detect date-related or credit-cycle related biases. If the bias is related to the absolute level of the of the default probabilities, the Falkenstein and Boral test applies.

Figure 19.5 applies the Falkenstein and Boral test using 100 time buckets for version 3.0 of Kamakura Corporation's KDP-jc Jarrow Chava reduced form model:

Figure 19.5 Comparison of Upper and Lower Bound of KDP-jc in Each Percentile with Actual Annualized Default Rate, 1,158,256 Observations, January 1989–June 2003

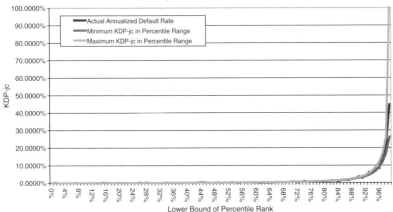

The light gray line defines the upper default probability in each of the 100 buckets. Each bucket has 11,583 observations. The medium gray line defines the lower default probability bound of each bucket. The darkest gray line is the actual frequency of defaults. Figure 19.6 shows a very high degree of consistency in the KDP-jc modeling of actual versus expected defaults.

Figure 19.6 displays the same results on a logarithmic scale.

Figure 19.6 Comparison of Upper and Lower Bound of KDP-jc in Each Percentile with Actual Annualized Default Rate, KRIS 3.0, 1,158,256 Observations, January 1989–June 2003

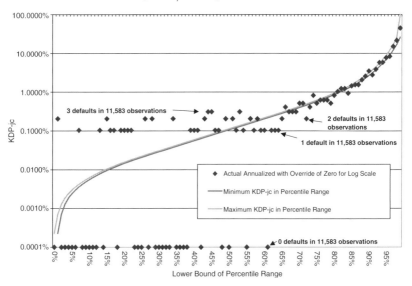

The Falkenstein and Boral test does not work well for the lower default probability buckets due to small sample size issues having to do with the discreteness of a default event. As indicated in Figure 19.7, it is impossible for the actual default frequency to fall between the upper and lower bounds of the bucket because 0 defaults out of 11,583 is below the lower bound and one default out of 11,583 is above the upper bound. Only one of the buckets has an actual number of defaults (two defaults out of 11,583) outside of the 99% confidence interval in the lower default probability ranges. Consequently, this test is most useful for the intermediate buckets.

Figure 19.7 shows the same results for the Kamakura implementation of the Merton model.

Again, the consistency of actual and expected defaults is very high.

Another test suggested by Eric Falkenstein[10] is to plot the distribution of actual defaults by the percentile of the default probabilities. The 1st percentile

---

[10] Private conversation with one of the authors, fall 2003.

Figure 19.7 Comparison of Upper and Lower Bound of KDP-ms in Each Percentile with Actual Annualized Default Rate, KRIS 3.0, 1,158,256 Observations, January 1989–June 2003

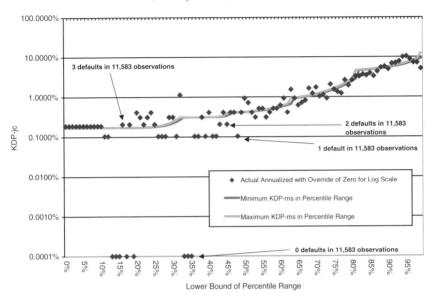

Figure 19.8 Percent of Total Bankruptcies by Percentile for KDP-jc and Theoretical Merton, January 1989 to June 2003

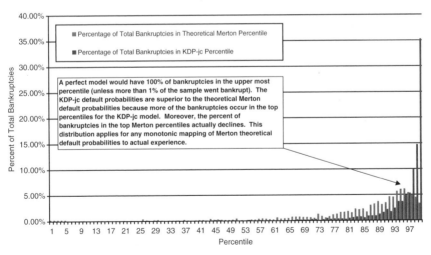

(the lowest 11,583 of the 1,158,268 default probabilities in the sample) should have the lowest number of defaults and the 100th percentile should have the highest.

Figure 19.8 shows these test results for the Merton model and KDP-jc. KDP-jc shows a better performance because the actual default experience is more heavily concentrated in the highest default probability percentile buckets. In contrast, the default rate actually declines in the highest percentile buckets for the Merton model. The difference can be measured quantitatively using a Chi-squared test as suggested in van Deventer and Imai [2003].

Implications of Model Testing for Basel Compliance and Practical Use of Credit Models

As Robert Merton pointed out in a quotation used in Chapter 16, the Merton model is now more than 29 years old. It remains popular in industry and regulatory circles, but for the first time there is a well-established scientific basis for measuring the performance of credit models on the same historical default data in two key dimensions:

- Ordinal ranking of firms by credit riskiness;
- Consistency of actual and expected defaults.

Before such tests became available, many well-intentioned bankers were unable to correctly assess credit model performance because of a lack of data and, as noted by Falkenstein and Boral, there was a tendency for some models to produce higher default probabilities than actual default experience could justify.

This bias is harmful in two respects. Unless the tests outlined in this chapter are performed, it can result in an inaccurate ranking of model performance. More importantly, if this bias is not detected, all calculations using such a model would produce inaccurate pricing, valuation, hedging and portfolio loss simulation. This compounding of effects is contrary to the principles laid out in Basel II, even though the Basel Committee clearly had the legacy of the older Merton model in mind when drafting its proposals.

A scientific approach to testing multiple models reveals that reduced form and hybrid models offer superior performance by both the criteria listed above. Furthermore, many financial ratios are more accurate in ranking companies by riskiness than the Merton model for every monotonic mapping of theoretical default probabilities to actual default experience. Practical bankers and skilled regulators need accurate model test results to generate value added for their shareholders.

We add to those tests using market data in the next chapter.

CHAPTER 20

Tests of Credit Models Using Market Data

In Chapters 16 and 17, we reviewed the structural and reduced form models of credit risk. Our interest in the models and how well they work is more than academic. We are looking for a comprehensive framework for enterprise risk management that creates true risk-adjusted shareholder value. We want to be able to accurately value the Jarrow-Merton put option on the value of the firm's assets that is the best comprehensive measure of integrated credit risk and interest rate risk. If risk is outside of the 'safety zone' discussed in earlier chapters, we want to know the answer to a critical question: what is the hedge? If we cannot answer this question, our credit risk modeling efforts are just an amusement with no practical use.

For this reason, it is critical to study the relative accuracy of the two major contending schools of thought in credit risk modeling, above and beyond the literal requirements of the Basel Committee on Banking Supervision that van Deventer and Imai [2003] discuss in detail. The nature of the Jarrow-Merton put option as a measure of risk is very similar to the structure of the Merton model of risky debt, so we approach market data tests of credit models with some optimism. Nonetheless, we know that the tests on historical data that we reviewed in Chapter 19, showed that the Merton model of risky debt was out-performed as a measure of credit risk by models as simple as the one-year excess return on the company's stock.

In this chapter, we trace recent developments in using market data to test credit models and outline directions for future research.

Testing Credit Models: The Analogy with Interest Rates

In Chapters 11 and 12, we examined competing theories of movements in the risk-free term structure of interest rates. In Chapter 13, we reviewed various methods of estimating the parameters of those models and in the next chapter we go one step further to explicitly test interest rate model performance. In this chapter, our task is similar, except that the term structure model we are testing is a term structure with credit risk.

Market data test 1: Accuracy in fitting observable yield curves and credit spreads

Continuing the term structure model analogy, one of the easiest and most effective market data tests of a credit model is to see how well the model fits observable yield curve data. All credit models take the existing risk-free yield curve as given, so we can presume we have a smooth and perfectly fitting continuous risk-free yield curve using one of the techniques of Chapter 8. Given this risk-free curve, there is an obvious test of competing credit models: which model best fits observable credit spreads?

As we discuss in Chapter 18, the market convention for credit spreads is a crude approximation to the exact day count precision in credit spread estimation that we propose as an alternative in Chapter 18. It would be better if we could measure model performance on a set of data that represents market quotations on the basis of credit spreads that we know are 'clean'. There are many sources of this kind of data, ranging from interest rate swap quotations (where the credit issues are complex), to credit default swaps, which we discuss below. Van Deventer and Imai [2003][1] present another source, the credit spreads quoted by investment bankers weekly to First Interstate Bancorp, which at the time was the seventh largest bank holding company in the U.S. This data series is reproduced in an appendix by van Deventer and Imai.

They then propose a level playing field for testing the ability of the reduced form and Merton models to fit these credit spreads by restricting both models to their two parameter versions, with these two parameters re-estimated for each data point. The parameters were estimated in a 'true to the model' fashion. For the Merton model, for instance, it is assumed that the equity of the firm is an option on the assets of the company. Van Deventer and Imai assume this assertion is true, and solve for the implied value of company assets and their volatility such that the sum of squared error in pricing the value of company equity and the two-year credit spread was minimized. The two-year credit spread was chosen because it was the shortest maturity of the observable credit spreads and therefore closest to the average maturity of the assets held by a bank holding company like First Interstate.

For the Jarrow model, van Deventer and Imai select the simplest version of the model in which the liquidity function discussed in Chapter 17 is a linear function of years to maturity and in which the default intensity $\lambda(t)$ is assumed constant. These assumptions imply (see Jarrow [1999]) that the zero-coupon credit spread is a linear function of years to maturity.

---

[1] Chapter 7

Van Deventer and Imai show that the Jarrow model substantially outperforms the Merton model in its ability to model credit spreads for First Interstate. The Merton model tended to substantially under price credit spreads for longer maturities, a fact noted by many market participants. The Merton model also implies that short-term credit spreads will be zero for a company that is not extremely close to bankruptcy, while the Jarrow liquidity parameter means the model has enough degrees of freedom to avoid this implication.

Figure 20.1 shows the adjusted R^2 on a simple linear regression, repeated for each observation, that seeks to explain credit spread as a linear function of years to maturity.

Figure 20.1 R^2 on Regression Fitting Linear Credit Spread to First Interstate Bancorp New Issue Credit Spreads at 2, 3, 5, 7 and 10 years, 1984–1993

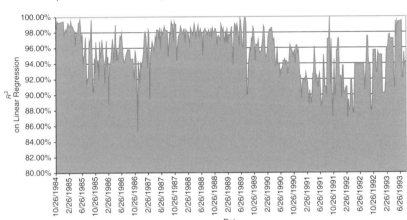

On average, over the entire First Interstate sample, the assumption of linearity of credit spreads explained 95% of the variation in credit spreads within a given observation. The worst fitting observation is shown in Figure 20.2 below, a day when there was a distinct 'bend' in the First Interstate credit spread curve.

In the tests we have described so far, we are essentially testing the credit model equivalent of the Vasicek term structure model, i.e. we are using the pure theory and not extending the model to perfectly fit observable data like we do using the extended Vasicek/Hull and White term structure model. We now turn to a test that allows us to examine model performance even for models that fit the observable term structure of credit spreads perfectly.

Figure 20.2 Credit Spread on First Interstate New Issues at 2, 3, 5, 7 and 10 years on November 21 1986 with R^2 of 85.39 on Linear Regression as Function of Maturity

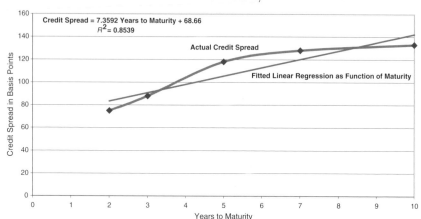

Market data test 2: Tests of hedging performance

From a trader's perspective, a model that can't fit observable data well is a cause for caution, but not a fatal flaw. The well-known 'volatility smile' in the Black-Scholes options model doesn't prevent its use, but it affects the way the parameters are estimated. After this tweaking of the model, it provides useful insights on hedging of positions in options. How do the Jarrow and Merton models compare in this regard?

Jarrow and van Deventer [1998] present such a test, again using data from First Interstate Bancorp. They implement basic versions of the Jarrow and Merton models and assume that they are literally true. They then calculate how to hedge a one-week position in First Interstate two-year bonds, staying true to the theory of each model. In the Merton model, this leads to a hedge using U.S. Treasuries to hedge the interest rate risk and a short position in First Interstate common stock to hedge the credit risk. In the Jarrow model, it was assumed that the macro factors driving the default intensities $\lambda(t)$ were interest rates and the S&P500 index, so U.S. Treasuries and the S&P500 futures contracts were used to hedge.

Jarrow and van Deventer report that the hedging error using the Jarrow model was on average only 50% as large as that of using the Merton model over the entire First Interstate sample.

More importantly, they report the surprising conclusion that the Merton model fails a naïve model test like those we examined in Chapter 19—a simple duration model produced better hedging results than the Merton model.

This surprised Jarrow and van Deventer and many other observers, so Jarrow and van Deventer turned to the next test to understand the reasons for this poor performance.

Market data test 3: Consistency of model implications with model performance

Jarrow and van Deventer investigated the poor hedging performance of the Merton model in detail to understand why the hedging performance of the model was so poor. They ran a linear regression between hedging error and the amount of Merton hedges (in Treasuries and common stock of First Interstate). The results of this standard diagnostic test were again a shock—the results showed that instead of selling First Interstate common stock short to hedge, performance would have been better if a long position had been taken out in common stock instead. While the authors don't recommend this as a hedging strategy to anyone, it illustrates what Jarrow and van Deventer found—the movements of stock prices and credit spreads are much more complex than the Merton model postulates. As we can confirm from the first derivatives of the value of risky debt given in Chapter 16, the Merton model says that when the value of company assets rises, stock prices should rise and credit spreads should fall. The opposite should happen when the value of company assets falls, and neither should change if the value of company assets is unchanged.

If the Merton model is literally true, this relationship between stock prices and credit spreads should hold true 100% of the time. Van Deventer and Imai report the results of Jarrow and van Deventer's examination of the First Interstate credit spread and stock price data—only 40–43% of the movements in credit spreads (at two years, three years, five years, seven years and 10 years) were consistent with the Merton model. This is less than could be achieved with a credit model that consists of using a coin flip to predict directions in credit spreads. This result explains why going short the common stock of First Interstate produced such poor results.

Van Deventer and Imai report the results of similar tests involving more than 20,000 observations on credit spreads of bonds issued by companies like Enron, Bank One, Exxon, Lucent Technologies, Merrill Lynch and others. The results consistently show that only about 50% of movements in stock prices and credit spreads are consistent with the Merton model of risky debt. These results have been confirmed by many others and are presented more formally in a recent paper by Jarrow, van Deventer and Wang [2003].[2]

What causes this surprising result? To which sectors of the credit spectrum do the findings apply? First Interstate had credit ratings that ranged from AA to BBB over the period studied, so it was firmly in the investment grade range of credits. Many have speculated that the Merton model would show a higher

---

[2] The treasury department of a top ten U.S. bank holding company reported, much to its surprise, that their own 'new issue' credit spreads showed the same low level of consistency with the Merton model as that reported for First Interstate.

degree of consistency on lower quality credits. Research is being done intensively at the time of writing and we look forward to the concrete results of that research.

For the time being, we speculate that the reasons for this phenomenon are as follows:

- Many factors other than the potential loss from default affect credit spreads, as the academic studies outlined in Chapter 18 have found. This is consistent with the Jarrow specification of a general 'liquidity' function that can itself be a random function of macro factors.
- The Merton assumption of a constant, unchanging amount of debt outstanding, regardless of the value of company assets, may be too strong. Debt covenants and management's desire for self-preservation may lead a company to overcompensate, liquidating assets to pay down debt when times are bad.
- The Merton model of company assets trading in frictionless efficient markets may miss the changing liquidity of company assets, and this liquidity of company assets may well be affected by macro factors.

What are the implications of the First Interstate findings for valuation of the Jarrow-Merton put option as the best indicator of company risk? In spite of the strong conceptual links with the Merton framework, the Merton model itself is clearly too simple to value the Jarrow-Merton put option with enough accuracy to be useful.

What are the implications of the First Interstate findings for bond traders? They imply that even a trader with perfect foresight of changes in stock price one week ahead would have lost money more than 50% of the time if they used the Merton model to decide whether to go long or short the bonds of the same company. Note that this conclusion applies to the valuation of risky debt using the Merton model—it would undoubtedly be even stronger if one were using Merton default probabilities because they involve much more uncertainty in their estimation, as we saw in Chapter 16.

What are the implications of the First Interstate findings for the Jarrow model? There are no such implications, because the Jarrow model per se does not specify the directional link between company stock prices and company debt prices. This specification is left to the analyst who uses the Jarrow model and derives the best fitting relationship from the data.

Market data test 4: Comparing performance with credit spreads and credit default swap prices

There is a fourth set of market data tests that we can perform which is the subject of a very important segment of current research—comparing credit model performance with credit spreads and credit default swap quotations as predictors of default. This is a 'naïve model' test much like those posed in Chapter 19 using historical default data.

The results of these tests on a large sample are eagerly anticipated by market participants. If a credit model outperforms credit spreads and credit default swap prices in predicting default, the model will be used for arbitrage.

What if the models underperform credit spreads and credit default swap prices? They will still be used extensively, but perhaps more judiciously, because 99% of bank credit is extended to obligors without bond ratings and without the ability to issue bonds. Just as importantly, knowledge of credit spreads doesn't automatically tell us what the total risk of the entire portfolio is. We need a better-understood analytical link to value the risk of the institution as a whole and to understand how to hedge interest rate risk and credit risk from a portfolio perspective.

We look at this issue after turning to market data tests of interest rate models in the next chapter.

CHAPTER 21

Tests of Interest Rate Models Using a Credit Risk Approach

Throughout this book we have emphasized the links between credit risk and interest rate risk in order to determine the appropriate valuation and hedging of the risk that a financial institution or corporation has taken on. The level of risk is measured by the value of the put option proposed by Robert Jarrow and Robert Merton in Chapter 1. For example, what is the cost of a put option on the current assets of the corporation at a strike price equal to 100% of the par value of its liabilities and a maturity of one year? Just as importantly, having calculated this risk measure, we want to know what macro factor hedges of this risk level can be put in place to guard against adverse movements in the institution's risk.

In order to do this, we need to be able to calculate the risk-adjusted value of each asset and we must be able to calculate the value of a put option on a portfolio of assets. We turn to that task beginning in the next chapter. Before doing so, however, we need to complete our discussion of model testing that we began in Chapters 19 and 20. Model testing is required both by the New Capital Accords of the Basel Committee of Banking Supervision and by best practice in risk-adjusted shareholder value creation. A failure to understand model performance is dangerous, not only to shareholders, but also to management. In the National Australia Bank foreign exchange incident outlined in Chapter 1, as of this writing, the chairman of the board, the chief executive officer, the board member in charge of risk management, the head of risk management, and five members of the foreign exchange department have been dismissed.[1] In short, a clear understanding of risk is essential to understanding the quality of our calculation of the Jarrow-Merton put option.

In Chapters 19 and 20, we showed how historical default data and market prices can be used to test the validity and relative accuracy of credit models. In Chapter 18, we showed how market data can be used to fit models of the credit spread observable in the market. In this chapter, we apply similar

---

[1] *Australian Financial Review*, March 25–26 2004.

'credit risk-type' tests to supplement our work on term structure models in Chapters 11–13. The term structure models we discussed in Chapters 11 and 12 each have a number of implications that stem from their theory, just as the Merton model has implications for the relative movements in stock prices and credit spreads that we discussed in Chapter 20.

In the case of the risk-free term structure models, just as in the credit model case, we need to know how accurate our assumptions are. We turn to this task now.

Testing Term Structure Analytics Using a Credit Risk Approach

The credit model testing procedures outlined in Chapters 19 and 20 can be applied to address a number of questions about the risk-free term structure:

- Is a one-factor model of the risk-free term structure accurate? How accurate? Do we need a two or three-factor model?
- Is the implicit assumption of one-factor models that all zero-coupon bond yields have 100% correlation correct?
- Are interest rate movements parallel or do they show a non-zero speed of mean reversion, implying non-parallel movements?
- Is interest rate volatility independent of the level of interest rates?
- Does the choice of yield curve smoothing techniques have an impact on measured interest rate volatility?
- Which interest rate smoothing method works 'the best' over a long period of history?
- When are the implications of yield curve smoothing techniques worth reexamining?

We address each of these questions in turn using data on the U.S. Treasury market provided by Kamakura Corporation's Kamakura Risk Information Services.

One-Factor versus Multi-Factor Models of the Risk-Free Term Structure

In Chapters 11 and 12, we discussed the fact that modern credit risk models, which assume random interest rates, almost always have been constructed on one-factor models of the risk-free term structure of interest rates, particularly the Vasicek and extended Vasicek term structure model used by Shimko, Tejima and van Deventer [1993], Duffie and Singleton [1999], and Jarrow [1999–2001]. The Jarrow-Turnbull [1995] model uses the Ho and Lee/extended Merton approach. How good are these assumptions about the term structure model?

If the extended Vasicek and Ho and Lee models are absolutely true, interest rate movements at all maturities should have 100% correlation with each other. Table 21.1 shows that interest rates in the U.S. Treasury market have correlations with each other that range from 85% to almost 100%, depending on the maturities being discussed.

Table 21.1 Correlation of Daily U.S. Treasury Rates, January 1 1982 to February 15 2002

	U.S. Treasury Maturity										
Maturity	1 Month	3 Months	6 Months	1 Year	2 Years	3 Years	5 Years	7 Years	10 Years	20 Years	30 Years
1 Month	1.0000	1.0000	0.9958	0.9861	0.9671	0.9523	0.9220	0.9047	0.8848	0.9184	0.8505
3 Months		1.0000	0.9959	0.9862	0.9672	0.9523	0.9219	0.9046	0.8847	0.9181	0.8504
6 Months			1.0000	0.9961	0.9824	0.9698	0.9421	0.9257	0.9064	0.9329	0.8727
1 Year				1.0000	0.9935	0.9845	0.9613	0.9466	0.9293	0.9512	0.8978
2 Years					1.0000	0.9977	0.9849	0.9749	0.9617	0.9718	0.9358
3 Years						1.0000	0.9940	0.9870	0.9770	0.9816	0.9555
5 Years							1.0000	0.9983	0.9939	0.9923	0.9804
7 Years								1.0000	0.9981	0.9961	0.9888
10 Years									1.0000	0.9983	0.9955
20 Years										1.0000	0.9992
30 Years											1.0000

Source: Kamakura Risk Information Services

If we have a time horizon of 20 years or less, the correlations of interest rates are almost all in excess of 90%. Whether this is sufficiently 'true' to be used as a core assumption depends on the analyst, but it is a level of accuracy very similar to that of the best credit model ROC accuracy ratios discussed in Chapter 19.

Another test of the appropriateness of a one-factor model parallels the test of the relationship between credit spreads and stock prices in Chapter 20. For example, what percentage of the time does the 20-year Treasury bond yield move in the same direction as three-month Treasury bill yields? All one-factor models of the term structure imply this percentage should be 100%. We measure this percentage and its standard deviation given its binomial distribution (i.e. one = consistent with a one-factor model, zero = not consistent). We then apply the same procedures as the Merton tests to measure whether we should reject the assumption of a single-factor model.

Parallel Versus Non-Parallel Yield Curve Shifts

The next test that we can apply is a test to measure whether movements in interest rates are parallel shifts (as implied by the Ho and Lee/extended

Merton model), or non-parallel shifts (as implied by the Vasicek and extended Vasicek/Hull and White approach. We can test this econometrically as suggested in Chapter 13 by fitting the speed of mean reversion α and measuring whether it is statistically different from zero.

Another test is more simple. We can take the standard deviation of observed interest rates over an extended period of time. If the parallel yield curve shift assumption is true, we would expect these standard deviations to be the same for all maturities. The chart below shows that the standard deviation of the absolute level of U.S. Treasury rates has been roughly the same across the maturity spectrum, with rates in the middle of the yield curve showing somewhat higher standard deviations than short-term and long-term rates.

Table 21.2 Standard Deviation of U.S. Treasury Yields, 1962 to 2003

					U.S. Treasury Maturity						
Maturity	1 Month	3 Months	6 Months	1 Year	2 Years	3 Years	5 Years	7 Years	10 Years	20 Years	30 Years
Standard Deviation of Daily Interest Rates	2.5139	2.5138	2.6325	2.8589	3.0587	2.6829	2.5904	2.4390	2.4999	2.6074	2.3207

Source: Kamakura Risk Information Services

The same calculation based on daily changes in interest rates again is roughly consistent with the assumption of parallel interest rate movements implied by the Ho and Lee/extended Merton model:

Table 21.3 Standard Deviation of Daily Changes in U.S. Treasury Yields, 1962 to 2003

					U.S. Treasury Maturity						
Maturity	1 Month	3 Months	6 Months	1 Year	2 Years	3 Years	5 Years	7 Years	10 Years	20 Years	30 Years
Standard Deviation of Daily Interest Rates	0.0872	0.0868	0.0830	0.0936	0.0980	0.0827	0.0779	0.0812	0.0699	0.0658	0.0745

Source: Kamakura Risk Information Services

We can test this quantitatively by applying a chi-squared test of equal standard deviations, much as van Deventer and Imai [2003] did in testing the default rates of internal credit models.

Interest Rate Volatility and Interest Rate Levels

The Ho and Lee and Vasicek family of models are popular for analysis because of the ease of calculations that stem from the implicit assumption that the volatility of interest rates is independent of interest rate levels. The Cox, Ingersoll and Ross model (see Chapter 12) and others do not make this assumption—interest rate volatility is explicitly assumed to rise when interest rates rise.

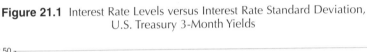

Figure 21.1 Interest Rate Levels versus Interest Rate Standard Deviation, U.S. Treasury 3-Month Yields

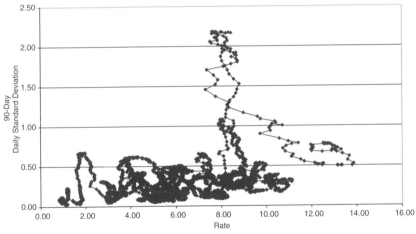

Figure 21.1 plots the three-month Treasury bill rate in the U.S. versus the 90-day standard deviation of changes in the three-month bill rate.

Visual inspection would lead one to conclude that for most of the sample, the correlation between interest rate levels and volatility has been weak, but there was one period where the correlation was significant. We measure this quantitatively below.

Figure 21.2 is the same graph for 10-year U.S. Treasury yields and shows a much different picture.

Figure 21.2 Interest Rate Levels versus Interest Rate Standard Deviation, U.S. Treasury 10-Month Yields.

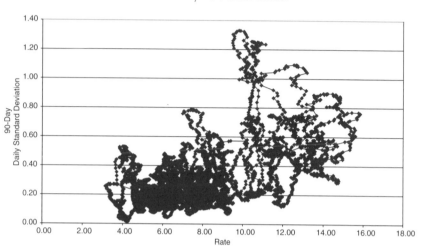

The correlation between rate levels and volatility is much more striking in the case of 10-year yields. We summarize this correlation for the period 1962–2003 in the U.S.:

Table 21.4 Correlation of Daily U.S. Treasury Rates and 90-day Standard Deviation, January 1 1982 to February 15 2002

	U.S. Treasury Maturity										
Maturity	1 Month	3 Months	6 Months	1 Year	2 Years	3 Years	5 Years	7 Years	10 Years	20 Years	30 Years
Correlation	0.2676	0.2699	0.3388	0.4884	0.4513	0.4381	0.4440	0.4541	0.4596	0.5449	0.5108

Source: Kamakura Risk Information Services

The data shows that the correlation between interest rates and their volatility increases as the maturity lengthens.

At the very least, this indicates that modeling based on the Ho and Lee extended Vasicek models should include stress tests of interest rate volatility.

Implications of Yield Curve Smoothing for Interest Rate Modeling

In this section, we point out that the method chosen for yield curve smoothing does have strong implications for various measures of interest rate model performance. In Chapter 8, we discussed six yield curve smoothing techniques ranging from a simple assumption that zero-coupon bond yields are linear functions of yield to maturity, to the maximum smoothness yield curve smoothing technique and four implementations of cubic spline smoothing.

One important measure of model performance, as we saw above, is to measure whether interest rate movements are parallel at different maturities. Figure 21.3 shows the standard deviation of movements in the one-month U.S. Treasury rates and one-month U.S. Treasury forwards out to 30 years in maturity for all six smoothing techniques.

Figure 21.3 Standard Deviation of Daily U.S. Treasury One-Month Forward Rates by Maturity of Forward Rate, 1982–2001.

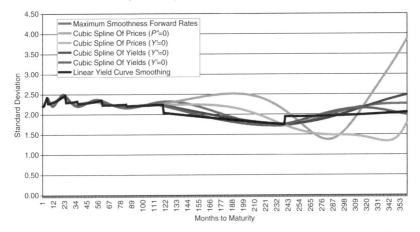

While the movements of one-month forward rates are roughly parallel on average, the standard deviation observed depends upon the yield curve smoothing technique employed.

The same can be said about the daily changes in one-month forward rates. The measured standard deviation in forward rates depends upon the yield curve smoothing technique employed:

Figure 21.4 Standard Deviation of Daily Changes in U.S. Treasury Monthly Forward Rates, 1982–2001

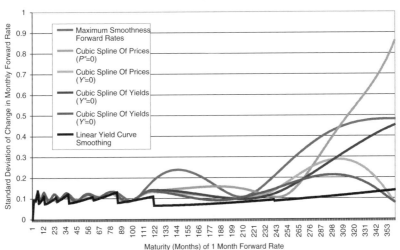

Standard deviations for almost all techniques are higher for forward rate maturities between observable points on the yield curve (such as the 15 year point, midway between 10 and 20-year yields). In spite of the crudeness of forward rates implied by linear yield curve smoothing on one day (forward rates are sloping step functions with large jumps at observable data points), the linear yield curve technique is a strongly competing 'naïve model' when the criterion for 'best model' is the minimum standard deviation of changes in U.S. Treasury monthly forward rates over the entire data set.

Another measure of model performance is to measure the correlation of monthly forward rates, not just the correlation of U.S. Treasury yields themselves. Figure 21.5 plots the correlation between one-month U.S. Treasury yields with monthly U.S. Treasury rate forwards out to 30 years. It shows that correlation declines steadily with the maturity of the forward rate, but the absolute level of correlation depends upon the yield curve smoothing technique used, turning negative in one case.

Figure 21.5 Correlation Between One-Month U.S. Treasury Rate and Forward U.S. Treasury Rates, 1982–2001

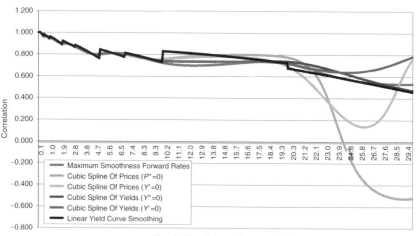

Another important observation to make is how critically potentially 'bad data' can impact forward rates on any given day. Figure 21.5 shows U.S. Treasury yields on three days in December 1982. The yields themselves don't seem to move much at all, but they end up having strong implications on forward rates implied from the three yield curves:

Figure 21.6 U.S. Treasury Yield Curve, December 17, 20 and 21 1982.

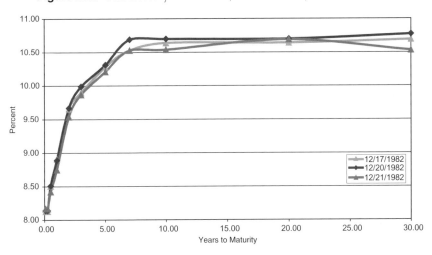

In tabular form, we can see that the changes in yields are small in absolute terms but their joint movements imply large movements in forward rates.

Table 21.5 U.S. Treasury Yields, December 17–21 1982

	Years to Maturity										
Maturity	1 Month	3 Months	6 Months	1 Year	2 Year	3 Years	5 Years	7 Years	10 Years	20 Years	30 Years
12/17/1982	8.13	8.13	8.51	8.91	9.66	9.90	10.28	10.53	10.64	10.64	10.69
12/20/1982	8.14	8.14	8.51	8.89	9.67	9.99	10.31	10.69	10.70	10.70	10.77
12/21/1982	8.17	8.17	8.42	8.75	9.54	9.87	10.21	10.53	10.54	10.69	10.53

In particular, the 16 basis point jump in the seven-year Treasury yields from December 17 to December 20 dramatically impacts implied forward rates. The same is true for the one basis point fall on December 21 in the 20-year yield when the seven and 10-year yields fell 16 basis points and the 30-year rate fell 24 basis points:

Even the maximum smoothness forward rate technique, designed to produce the most plausible and smooth forward rates, is unable to cope with this kind of strange movement in Treasury yields. The December 17–21 1982 period was the period producing the greatest movement in 30-year monthly

Table 21.6 Changes in U.S. Treasury Yields, December 17–21 1982

Maturity	Years to Maturity										
	1 Month	3 Months	6 Months	1 Year	2 Years	3 Years	5 Years	7 Years	10 Years	20 Years	30 Years
12/17/1982	8.13	8.13	8.51	8.91	9.66	9.90	10.28	10.53	10.64	10.64	10.69
12/20/1982	8.14	8.14	8.51	8.89	9.67	9.99	10.31	10.69	10.70	10.70	10.77
Change in Yields	0.01	0.01	0.00	−0.02	0.01	0.09	0.03	0.16	0.06	0.06	0.08
12/20/1982	8.14	8.14	8.51	8.89	9.67	9.99	10.31	10.69	10.70	10.70	10.77
12/21/1982	8.17	8.17	8.42	8.75	9.54	9.87	10.21	10.53	10.54	10.69	10.53
Change in Yields	0.03	0.03	−0.09	−0.14	−0.13	−0.12	−0.10	−0.16	−0.16	−0.01	−0.24
12/17/1982	8.13	8.13	8.51	8.91	9.66	9.90	10.28	10.53	10.64	10.64	10.69
12/21/1982	8.17	8.17	8.42	8.75	9.54	9.87	10.21	10.53	10.54	10.69	10.53
Change in Yields	0.04	0.04	−0.09	−0.16	−0.12	−0.03	−0.07	0.00	−0.10	0.05	−0.16

forward rates using the maximum smoothness forward rate technique and the graph of the forward rates derived are shown in Figure 21.7:

Figure 21.7 Monthly U.S. Treasury Forward Rates, Maximum Smoothness Forward Rate Technique December 17, 20 and 21 1982

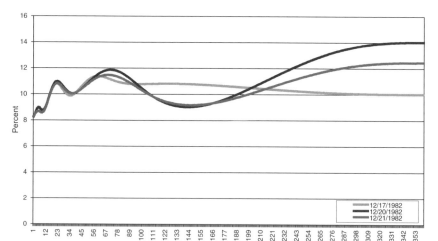

The forward rates derived are smooth, as we would expect from this technique, and they show a plausible flatness at the 30-year point as the model imposes. What is concerning is the 400 basis point movement in implied forward rates from December 17 to December 20, a result triggered by the rate movements discussed above. Forward rates decline somewhat on December 21.

The point here is that bad data can result in even the highest quality yield curve smoothing technology producing movements in forward rates that at times seem implausible. This will impact tests of term structure model performance for all smoothing methods, so the user of yield curve smoothing data should beware of this unavoidable model risk.

Implications for Integrated Analysis of Credit Risk and Model Risk

The techniques we used in Chapters 19 and 20 to test credit risk models provide added insight to term structure models as well. This is important because models of the risk-free term structure are the very foundation of the credit risk models we will use in the following chapters to measure integrated credit risk and interest rate risk using the Jarrow-Merton put option.

The data above shows that the one-factor model assumption is fairly consistent with U.S. data for maturities out to 20 years, if the accuracy standard is at the 90% plus accuracy that we demand from the best credit models. The assumption of parallel yield curve shifts, as simple as it is, seems surprisingly consistent with U.S. data over a long period. Interest rate volatility does appear correlated with interest rate levels, especially at the longer maturities, making models like the Cox, Ingersoll and Ross models worthy of additional study. Finally, valuation using yield curve smoothing and tests of term structure model performance using yield curve smoothing depend critically on which yield curve smoothing technique is used. Stress testing the yield curve smoothing technique to detect model risk in this regard is important to perform regularly.

We now turn to the calculation of integrated credit risk and interest rate risk.

Risk Management Applications, Instrument by Instrument

CHAPTER 22

Valuing Credit Risky Bonds

O ur ultimate objective in this section of the book is to calculate the value of the Jarrow-Merton put option on the assets of the firm, which Jarrow and Merton propose as the best measure of total risk. Total risk combines interest rate risk, credit risk, foreign exchange risk, and so on. In order to value this option, we need to be able to value all of the instruments on the financial institution's balance sheet. We derive the value of the option on all assets from the value of the portfolio of the underlying instruments on which the option is exercised.

In addition to valuation, we need to know how to simulate the value that the financial instrument may take at multiple points in the future and in multiple scenarios.

We go through this process in a systematic pattern. We start first with straight bonds, bonds with credit risk and bonds with no credit risk. In the next chapter, we extend this analysis to credit derivatives and collateralized debt instruments. In Chapter 24, we get to the 'option' portion of the exercise by studying options on bonds. We follow with valuation techniques for a string of related financial instruments thereafter, bringing it all together in Chapters 39 to 44.

We turn now to the valuation of bonds with and without credit risk. We then turn to simulation of future values.

The Present Value Formula

In Chapter 7, we reviewed the basic case where the value of a financial instrument was the sum of the present value of each cash flow. The expression $P(t)$ is the present value of a dollar received at time t from the perspective of time zero. The expression $C(t)$ is the cash flow to be paid at time t.

$$\text{Present value} = \sum_{i=1}^{n} P(t_i)C(t_i)$$

Do we need to say any more than this about bond valuation? Surprisingly, the answer is yes.

Valuing bonds with no credit risk

Fortunately, in the case of bonds with a default probability of zero, valuation is as simple as the formula above. In a no arbitrage economy with frictionless trading, the present value formula above applies. As we noted in Chapter 7, 'present value' does not mean 'price', it means 'price plus accrued interest'.

Where do we get the values of the discount factors $P(t)$? We get them from the yield curve smoothing techniques discussed in Chapter 8. We derive the P values by using one of the six key techniques discussed in Chapter 8:

- Linear smoothing of zero-coupon bond yields;
- Cubic splines (four alternatives);
- Maximum smoothness forward rates.

Given these P values and the terms of the bond, its valuation is very simple. What about simulating future values? That is not as easy.

Simulating the future values of bonds with no credit risk

The Jarrow-Merton put option that is our ultimate valuation objective can be thought of as a European option, valued on only one date, or it can be thought of as an American option with many possible exercise dates. The European option analogy is a way of thinking about risk that is consistent with traditional value at risk concepts—risk matters on only one date, we can ignore intervening cash flows, and analyze the single date we choose as important. Common choices are 10-day horizons, one-month horizons, and one-year horizons. The longer the horizon, the more tenuous this way of thinking becomes.

Most analysts, including the authors, believe that a multi-period approach to the Jarrow-Merton put option and risk in general is essential. How do we calculate the variation in the value of a bond with no credit risk over time?

We use the term structure model approaches of Chapters 11 and 12 and the parameter fitting techniques of Chapter 13. In Chapter 21, we present some evidence on how well the term structure models work in practice. The steps in simulating the risk-free term structure can be summarized as follows:

1. Capture today's continuous zero-coupon yield curve using a yield curve smoothing technique.
2. Choose a term structure model and calculate its parameters.
3. Choose a time step to step forward in time, delta t, to arrive at time step one.
4. Calculate the random value for scenario one for the N risk factors at time step one.
5. Re-smooth the yield curve at time step one. If you are being true to the term structure model, this is already done. If you are using a more ad hoc

simulation, you apply the yield curve smoothing techniques of Chapter 8 to smooth the yield curve between the values of the yields whose simulated values you know, (for instance, you may be simulating a four-factor yield curve where the short rate, the one-year rate, the five-year rate and the 20-year rate are the risk factors).

6. Repeat steps 3–5 until you have completed the simulation to M time steps, completing scenario j (and of course for the first scenario $j = 1$).
7. Repeat steps 3–6 for a total of N scenarios.

At each point in time, in each scenario, we can calculate the value of the risk-free bond using the formula above. The number of cash flows and the time before they arrive will of course change as time passes.

We return to this process in detail when discussing callable bonds and interest rate lattices in Chapter 30.

This seems simple enough—what about the credit risky case?

Valuing bonds with credit risk

Is the process of valuing bonds with credit risk any different from valuing bonds without credit risk? As we saw in Chapter 18, we need to do more work to fit credit risky bonds to observable market data and we need to be able to separate out the credit loss-related portion of the credit spread from the liquidity portion as we discussed then.

What if we do that? Having done that and having calculated the value of a risky zero-coupon bond with maturity t $P(t)$, can we use the formula for value given above?

$$\text{Present value} = \sum_{i=1}^{n} P(t_i)C(t_i)$$

Robert Jarrow [2004] provides the answer in a recent paper. The necessary and sufficient conditions for using the present value formula can be summarized as follows:

- The present value formula can be used correctly if the recovery rate δ is constant and the same for all bonds with the same seniority, the assumption used by Jarrow and Turnbull [1995].
- The present value formula can be used if the recovery rate is random and depends only on time and seniority.
- If the default process is a Cox process (like the reduced form models in Chapter 17), then a sufficient condition to use the present value formula is for recovery to be a fraction of the bond's price an instant before default.

In reduced form models, then, the present value formula can be used in a straightforward way. In the Merton model and its variations, things are not so easy.

Problems with Valuing Coupon Bonds in the Merton Model

Van Deventer and Imai [2003] show, in an extensive analysis, that the Merton model of Chapter 16 is quite difficult to use in a coupon-bearing credit risky bond context. They show that the model has very large pricing errors even if it is carefully fitted to be true to the model. They fit the model so that the value of the common stock of a firm (in their example First Interstate Bancorp) is equal to an option on the assets of the firm, and they further impose the condition that the two-year credit spread is consistent with observable market prices. At long maturities, the Merton model is shown to very heavily under price the credit spread for reasonable parameter values.

This can be overcome by 'extending the model' to fit an observable credit risky yield curve, but what about the recovery rate issues raised by Professor Jarrow? As we showed in Chapter 16, the recovery rate in the Merton model is random. It depends on the value of company assets at the time of bankruptcy. If the amount of money due at maturity on the underlying bonds is B, the recovery rate is 100% if the value of company assets at maturity is exactly equal to B. If the value of company assets at maturity is zero, then the recovery rate is zero. This has implications for Jarrow's three conditions for the use of the present value formula:

- The first condition cannot be used because the Merton recovery rate is not constant.
- The second condition is problematic for the Merton model for two reasons. First of all, there is only one zero-coupon bond in the model, so it doesn't deal at all with the issue of bonds of different seniorities and with bonds with different maturity dates. The first issue is an easy extension, and the second is not. Secondly, there is 'recovery' at only one date, the date the bond matures, and there is no recovery rate at any other times because there is no probability of bankruptcy on those dates (unless one is using the 'knock out' option version of the Merton model, as discussed in Chapter 16).
- The third condition does not apply, since the structure of the Merton model is not a Cox process.

Suffice it to say that the use of the present value formula to value credit risky coupon bonds in a Merton framework is not for the faint at heart.

It involves some heroic extensions of the model and a passion for the Merton structure that dominates the passion to be true to the Merton model itself. This is a contradiction that many practitioners accept, but one which should cause us to lose sleep at night.

Simulating the Future Values of Bonds with Credit Risk

Simulating the value of risky bonds involves a straightforward number of steps using the reduced form models. We discuss the Merton model simulation in the next section.

For the reduced form model, the steps are as follows:

1. Simulate the risk-free term structure as given above.
2. Choose a formula and the risk-drivers for the liquidity component of credit spread as discussed in Chapter 18.
3. Choose a formula and the risk-drivers for the default intensity process in the Jarrow model as discussed in Chapter 17.
4. Simulate the random values of the drivers of liquidity risk and the default intensity for M time periods over N scenarios, consistent with the risk-free term structure.
5. Calculate the default intensity and the liquidity component at each of the M time steps and N scenarios. Note that these will be changing randomly over time because interest rates and other factors are 'driving' each of them. This is essential to capturing cyclicality in bond prices and defaults.
6. Apply the Jarrow model as we have done in Chapters 17 and 18 to get the zero-coupon bond prices for each maturity relevant to the bond.
7. Calculate the bond's value at each of the M time steps and N scenarios, conditional on the company not defaulting in that period or in a prior date.

This is slightly but not much more complicated than the risk-free bond simulation. It relies on the identical interest rate scenarios and simulation process. Note that if the simulation is done for many companies with common risk factors driving default, we will see correlated default behavior that we have discussed throughout this book.

For the Merton model, however, things are not as straightforward.

Simulating the Future Values of Bonds with Credit Risk in the Merton Model

When we wish to simulate future risky bond prices using the Merton model, we have the same kind of problem we had with valuation. The fundamental assumptions of the model are inconsistent with best practice in risk management—we need a random interest rate multi-period framework, and the Merton model is a constant interest rate single-period framework. Let's wave a magic wand and make all of these problems disappear for the moment. How would we bend the Merton model to use for multi-period simulation?

1. We assume that interest rates are random and use the Shimko, Tejima and van Deventer framework instead of the original Merton constant interest rate framework.
2. We estimate the initial value of company assets V and its volatility for each company from equity prices and their history as discussed in Chapter 16.
3. We specify the random factors driving the value of company assets V and the functional form that links them to V. These are not in the original Merton paper.
4. We simulate these random factors over M time steps and N scenarios.
5. We simulate the random change in the value of company assets V forward to time step 1 given the value of random factors driving V. If there is a coupon payment on bond k on this date, we deduct that payment amount from the simulated value of V to get its adjusted value the instant after the payment. If there is no payment on this date, use the original simulated value of V. Given V, we calculate the zero-coupon bond prices in the Merton model for all maturities needed on that date (i.e. all dates on which there is future cash flow) even though the Merton model assumes there is only one bond and one payment date.
6. Using the adjusted value of V, we repeat steps 2 and 3 and simulate forward for the M time steps, deducting coupon payments wherever they occur. If at any point, V is less than the required payment, the company defaults and the recovery rate is specific to that time step and scenario.
7. Repeat steps 5-6 for N scenarios.
8. We calculate the coupon bond value in each scenario, conditional on the company not having defaulted.

The good news is that we can specify a mechanical process that resembles the Merton model in concept, but we are very inconsistent with the theory. The falls in asset values due to bond payments, for example, is not consistent with the original theory. The specification of the links between the risk factors driving the value of company assets is implicit in other work of Robert Merton that we hint at in Chapter 16, but we haven't made it explicit. Suffice it to say that common risk factors can cause correlated movements in asset values of two companies and correlated events of default.

The authors don't recommend this process as it can lead to many unintended consequences (like the serious mispricing found by van Deventer and Imai [2003]).

Valuing the Jarrow-Merton Put Option

If we have a portfolio of straight bonds on the asset side of our financial institution, we are almost ready to value the Jarrow-Merton put option on the assets of the firm. We will defer that until we reach Chapter 24, but the goal is near at hand. We move first to the discussion of credit default swaps and collateralized debt obligations because they help set a more general portfolio context for the problem.

CHAPTER 23

Credit Derivatives and Collateralized Debt Obligations

The boom in credit derivatives structures and volumes in the last decade has had the same impact on credit risk modeling technology that interest rate derivatives had on modeling in that discipline. Much of the credit modeling that we discussed in Chapters 17 and 18 had its roots in the need of market participants to hedge credit derivatives exposure and to mark-to-market their exposure once the transaction that has been done is no longer 'on the run', and therefore no longer consistent with the maturities for which pricing is observable.

In this chapter, we continue our discussion of an integrated treatment of interest rate risk and credit risk, following the pattern of straight bonds discussed in Chapter 22. Along the way, we point out potential pitfalls for the end user of credit derivatives and collateralized debt obligations that stem from market conventions that are overly simplistic and seriously understate the risk inherent in the credit derivatives structure.

The focus of this chapter is on pricing, valuation, hedging and simulation with the same ultimate goal of this book: being able to measure and hedge risk in a fully integrated way, as captured by the Jarrow-Merton put option that we discussed beginning in Chapter 1. We will not focus on the details of transaction terms and structures, which are covered in depth by a number of others including Tavakoli [2001], Ranson [2003] and Rutledge and Raynes [2003]. Our focus is on analyzing credit derivatives in the context of a highly accurate enterprise-wide risk management framework with a complete integration of credit risk and interest rate risk.

Credit Default Swaps: Valuation and Simulation

Credit default swaps have grown very popular because of the difficulty in hedging single-name credit risk by shorting the common stock of the issuer or the publicly traded bonds of the issuer. Shorting the common stock of a company is less than satisfactory for a very important reason. Shorting the common stock of a bond issuer only covers the risk of the debt holder until the common stock price falls very low and finally reaches a point where the gain on common stock sold short can no longer cover losses on a bond position even if 100% of the common stock outstanding is shorted. This point is easy to confirm if one uses the Merton structure in Chapter 16 and the first derivatives of common stock and the value of company debt with respect to changes in the value of company assets. Debt holders can still lose value as the value of company assets falls, long after the common stock price has hit zero. The second concern with hedging a debt position with a short position in common stock has been pointed out by many authors beginning with Jarrow and van Deventer [1998] and continuing through van Deventer and Imai [2003] and Jarrow, van Deventer and Wang [2003]. We summarized the results of those tests in Chapters 19 and 20. The links between the value of the common stock of a company and the pricing of its debt are much more complicated than the single factor Merton model of risky debt postulates. Van Deventer and Imai show how traders with a perfect forecast of equity prices one to seven business days ahead would have lost money more than half the time using the Merton model of risky debt to determine whether to go long or short the bond. In the same way, they show that for high-grade bond issuers like First Interstate Bancorp, using the Merton model of risky debt to hedge debt exposure produces hedges with twice the hedging error as a reduced form model.[1]

Another alternative to hedging the debt of a risky issuer is to sell short another debt issue of the same issuer in the right proportions. Clearly, if this were easy to do, one would either sell the debt issue being hedged outright or sell it short. Short sales of risky debt are rarely an option because of the illiquidity of the bond market (which is explicitly incorporated in the Jarrow model of risky debt discussed in Chapter 17). For that reason, the development of the credit default swap market has been met with enthusiasm by market participants over the last decade.

Two credit default swap structures are common in the market place. In the first structure, which we call the traditional structure, the credit protection provider pays the purchaser of credit protection the 'recovery amount' associated with the notional principal of the credit default swap after a specified time frame from the carefully defined event of default. In the second structure, the provider of credit protection essentially pays $1 upon the occurrence

---

[1] Readers interested in examining this phenomenon for themselves can find the entire First Interstate Bancorp new issue credit spread history in van Deventer and Imai [2003].

of an event of default. By comparing the pricing on the two structures for the same issuer and the same maturity, we can imply the recovery rate and loss given default implicit in market prices.

The conceptual benefits of these derivatives structures to financial institutions are powerful, but the market is maturing as a number of concerns are beginning to slow the rapid growth in the credit default swap market:

Liquidity: As of this writing, bid/offered prices for credit protection are typically limited to 1,000 to 1,500 counterparty names in the U.S. dollar and Euro markets on any given day. Actually trades occur on one third to one half of these names on any given day. In the months leading up to the bankruptcy of Enron in December 2001, for example, one leading electronic exchange for credit protection recorded trades in Enron credit derivates on less than one third of the business days in November 2001.

Counterparty concentration concerns: The number of credit protection providers is limited to some of the world's largest financial institutions, because a small firm with limited creditworthiness presents few benefits to the buyer of credit protection regardless of the reference name for which credit protection is being purchased. As a result, the overwhelming majority of credit derivatives transactions have 10–20 of the world's largest financial institutions as the providers of credit protection. Purchasers of credit protection have two major concerns with this development. Firstly, they have a large concentration of transactions with a small number of counterparties, leading them to cap their exposure to the leading market-markers in credit default swaps. Secondly, there is a high correlation among the default probabilities of the leading credit default swap market-makers and leading industrial corporations on which credit protection is being provided.

Consider the correlation between the reduced form model default probabilities[2] for General Motors and the following major banks and securities firms:

Citigroup	45.2%
Goldman Sachs	44.5%
Lehman Brothers	42.7%
Merrill Lynch	41.5%
UBS	33.1%.

We can see from the 14-year history of default probabilities for General Motors and Merrill Lynch that there is a sharp rise in the default probabilities

---

[2] Default probabilities shown below are from Kamakura Risk Information Services, version 3.0, from Kamakura Corporation (www.kamakuraco.com). The correlations reported are correlations of monthly data over a five-year period.

for both GM and Merrill when the U.S. economy is in recession, as was the case in 1990–1991, 1994–1995, and 2001–2002:

Figure 23.1 Historical Default Probabilities for General Motors and Merrill Lynch

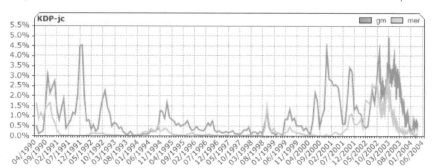

Cost: The third factor constraining the growth of the credit swap market is the cost of doing a transaction and, perhaps, unwinding it once the transaction is complete. As is always the case with derivatives, the bid-offered spread for these over the counter transactions is much greater than the equivalent transaction would be if it were traded on an exchange. Market participants are taking active steps to increase the efficiency of trading in these instruments, as pricing of the bid-offered spread has become an issue for large volume players in this market.

We turn now to the valuation and simulation of traditional credit default swaps and digital default swaps.

Valuation of traditional and digital Credit Default Swaps

Valuation and simulation of credit default swaps highlight the differences between the Merton credit model of Chapter 16 and the reduced form models introduced in Chapter 17. Typical transactions involve a five-year life with 10 'insurance payments' made semi-annually by the buyer of credit protection. How do we handle this multi-payment convention? It's no problem in the reduced form model structure, which is multi-period by definition. For the Merton single period structure, it's more of a problem. We can deal with this issue in an ad-hoc way in the Merton model framework:

Valuing Credit Default Swaps in the Merton framework

Consider a Merton model for the risky debt of General Motors where our Merton model has a five-year life. How would we value a five-year credit default swap if the price of credit protection is purchased at time zero?

Credit default swap: The credit default swap is a put option on the risky debt of General Motors. The put option can be valued using the Geske compound option formula that we discussed in Chapter 16 in the context of estimating the implied volatility of the value of company assets in the Merton model. This formulation implies that payment on the credit derivative is made only at the five-year point, not at the time of bankruptcy (or a contractually agreed number of business days later). Specifying the Merton model in its barrier options form is one way to allow for early payout on a credit default swap, but the put option on risky debt becomes more complex to value. Assuming away this complexity, what is the level of semi-annual insurance payments that has the same present value as the time zero value of the put option on GM's debt? We use the knowledge of Chapter 22 to find the level of constant insurance payments with the same present value as the put option, extracted using the credit spread smoothing techniques of Chapter 18. In the reduced form model structure, as pointed out in Chapter 22, these zero coupon prices for GM properly reflect the possibility of bankruptcy.

Please note that the Merton structure does not allow for the fact that a liquidity premium in credit spreads above and beyond the loss component is also reflected in credit default swap prices.

This formulation assumes that the provider of credit protection is default-free. We modify that assumption in the context of first to default swaps below.

Digital default swaps in the Merton structure: A digital default swap in the Merton structure is a digital put option on the assets of the firm with a strike price equal to the value of maturing debt B at the end of the five-year period. We can use the digital put and call options formulas in Jarrow and Turnbull [1996] for this purpose. We again have to make an ad hoc adjustment for the 10 semi-annual credit protection payments as discussed in the previous section.

Again, we are implicitly assuming that the provider of the credit protection is default-free, an assumption we relax below.

Valuing Credit Default Swaps in the reduced form modeling structure

Jarrow [1999] provides a valuation framework for credit default swaps that explicitly allows for the fact that there may be illiquidity in the bond markets, which is in return reflected in risky bond prices. Jarrow and Yildirum [2001] value credit derivatives in a simpler framework where bonds are assumed to trade in completely frictionless markets. They assume that interest rates are random, consistent with Chapter 17, and that the recovery rate is constant.[3] The probability of default of the reference name is driven by a constant default intensity component and by an interest rate-driven component. The resulting valuation formula depends on the reduced form model parameters

λ_0 and λ_1 as in Chapter 17. The coefficient of the macro factors driving default λ_2 is assumed by Jarrow and Yildirum to be zero. A more general framework is given by Jarrow [1999].

Digital Default Swaps in the reduced form model structure

Jarrow [1999] similarly shows that the value of a digital default swap when the default intensity λ_0 is constant can be written:

$$I_t(T)1_{\{\tau > t\}} = \lambda_0 \int_t^T v(t, s : e)\, ds = \lambda_0 \int_t^T p(t, s)e^{-\lambda_0(s-t)}\, ds$$

In this expression, the expression $v(t, s, i)$ refers to the time t zero coupon bond of the risky issuer with maturity s and seniority i. The expression $p(t, s)$ is a risk-free zero coupon bond as of time with maturity s. The integrals in this expression recognize that default can occur any time between time t and the maturity of the credit protection at time T.

Jarrow shows how this expression changes as interest rates and macro factors are allowed to drive the default intensities.

We now take the first step toward the valuation of collateralized debt obligations by discussing first to default swaps.

First to Default Swaps

In recent years, another credit derivative structure has become common, particularly among hedge funds, as a way to arbitrage the pricing of credit default swaps on individual reference names. These structures are called first to default or basket swaps. In the typical structure, the life of the credit protection is five years and there are five reference names in the 'basket'. The credit protection provider pays upon the first (and only the first) event of default for any of the five names.

The key to pricing of this structure is the amount of correlation among the events of default of the five reference names. If all have the same constant default intensity and if they have no correlation in the event of default, the first to default swap basket should cost five times as much as a credit default swap on any one of the names since it is five times more likely to default. On the other hand, if the five reference names have identical default intensities, and 100% correlation in the events of default, the pricing on the basket will

---

[3] Jarrow [1999] allows the recovery rate to be random and to depend on the same macro factors as those that drive the default probabilities of the issuer.

be exactly the same as the pricing on the credit default swap on any one of these names because they always default together.

The correlation in the events of default can be modeled, as always, in either the Merton or reduced form model framework.

Correlations: Which correlations?

In modeling the first to default swap structure, market participants frequently confuse the meaning of the term correlation. Correlation can mean three things, and in two of the three cases the term has a model-specific meaning:

Correlation in the value of company assets in the Merton framework, which is definitely not the same as the other two meanings of the term correlation. Note that the correlation in the value of company assets between firms A and B can be 100%, but the correlation in the events of default will not be, except if the two firms A and B have identical default probabilities.

Correlation in default intensities due to dependence on common macro factors like interest rates and the S&P 500 in a U.S. context. The correlation between the default intensities of companies A and B in the reduced form modeling context depends on the magnitude of the parameters λ_0, λ_1, and λ_2 for each of the two companies A and B.

Correlation in the events of default, not the default probabilities themselves. This is the correlation between the two vectors for Companies A and B, which have zero in a period when the company did not default and one when the company does default. For two solvent companies, obviously, these vectors have nothing but zeros, so the correlation in the events of default cannot be implied by the historical data on events of default for Companies A and B.

We will try to make these distinctions clear in what follows:

Modeling First to Default Swaps in the Merton Framework

Valuing first to default swaps in the Merton framework requires some ad hoc adjustments to the model. Among the ad hoc adjustments we need to make are the following:

1. We assume default probabilities for all five names in the basket are non-random (many assume they are constant) over the five-year period of the swap.
2. We assume that correlation in the events of default can be correctly modeled by modeling the appropriate correlation in the returns on company assets in the Merton framework. These correlations are

the unobservable correlations in the unobservable time series of the value of company assets for the five firms (or sovereigns) in the basket.

3. We ignore intervening cash flows during the five-year period.
4. We ignore the single-period nature of the Merton model since we have 10 intervening payments to the protection provider unless default occurs before the payment date.
5. We use only one yield curve to discount cash flows, even if the five firms in the basket have dramatically different risk levels and yield curves.

Market participants imply the common pairwise correlation (i.e. assuming the pairwise correlation in the value of company assets is the same number for all pairs of companies in the basket) that makes the monte carlo-simulated value of the first to default swap trade at current market prices. This implied common correlation is generally used as market slang just like 'implied vol' is used in equity and fixed income options. Only the naïve should assume that the use of this Merton/copula framework is regarded as best practice by arbitrageurs. Hedge funds are mercilessly arbitraging this first to default swap market, taking money from those who are too simplistic in their approach.

Modeling First to Default Swaps in the reduced form model framework

Jarrow [1999] shows that the present value of a contract which pays \$1 if both firms 1 and 2 default prior to time T has the following formula, where the subscripts for 1 and 2 denote the firm:

$$V_t \mathbf{1}_{\{\tau_1 > t, \tau_2 > t\}} = p(t, T) - E_t \left(e^{-\int_t^T [r(u) + \lambda_1(u)] du} \right) - E_t \left(e^{-\int_t^T [r(u) + \lambda_2(u)] du} \right)$$
$$+ E_t \left(e^{-\int_t^T [r(u) + \lambda_1(u) + \lambda_2(u)] du} \right)$$

The expression E_t denotes the risk neutral expected value of the expressions in brackets as of time t. Jarrow goes on to show how closed form solutions can be obtained to value basket swaps in the reduced form model context.

We can arrive at the same conclusion by aggressively simulating the macro factors driving the default intensities in the reduced form models, simulating default/no default in a multi-period way, and taking the right risk-adjusted present value of the cash flows that result. We outline this procedure below in the context of collateralized debt obligations.

Counterparty Credit Risk as a First to Default Swap

The Jarrow formula in the previous section shows us how to model counterparty credit risk. Assume that Company A is buying digital default swap protection on Company C with Company B as the insurance provider.

We know that this transaction pays:

- zero if Company A defaults before Company B or Company C (since Company A defaults on the credit insurance premiums);
- zero if Company B defaults before Company C;
- $1 if Company C defaults (a) before Companies A and B but (b) before the credit protection contract expires.

We can use this knowledge to simulate the counterparty credit risk using either the Merton or Jarrow reduced form model framework discussed above.

Collateralized Debt Obligations

Collateralized debt obligations are generalized versions of first to default swaps, second default swaps, third to default swaps and so on. In a typical CDO structure, there may be 100 underlying reference names with a (roughly) equal amount of (actual or notional) principal associated with each of the reference names. If the underlying collateral is in the form of bonds issued by the 100 reference names, the proceeds of the issuance of senior, subordinated and equity tranches of the CDO are used to buy these bonds. If the underlying collateral is in the form of credit default swaps (a so-called 'synthetic' CDO), then the proceeds of the issurance of the tranches are used to buy a bond of a single issuer, and are paid to the CDO tranche holders over time depending on how many of the reference names default. The fact that all of the cash in the synthetic structure is invested in one reference name is a *huge factor* in differentiating between the so-called 'cash flow' CDOs (the bond structure) and the synthetic CDO structure. This concentration of risk must not be ignored in CDO analysis.

The value and cash flow generated by the underlying reference names in the CDO is identical in its nature to what we discussed in Chapters 22 and the first part of this chapter. The only difference is that the cash flow is parceled out according to the priorities of the tranches. If there is only one tranche (i.e. the equity tranche), CDO analysis is no different from credit risk portfolio analysis. If there are two tranches, the first cash flows go to the senior tranche as specified in the CDO indenture, ('the waterfall') and the remaining cash flows (if any) go to the equity tranche, and so on.

The simulation of which cash flows go to whom is at the heart of CDO analysis, as is the simulation of correlated defaults. The investment banking community and the rating agencies have aggressively advocated a method of analysis that dramatically understates the worst case losses from a CDO portfolio, and users of this analysis should recognize that (if they take the analysis seriously) they will grossly overpay for CDO tranches.

The typical industry standard calculation[4] contains many implicit errors:

- Default probabilities are assumed to be non-random over the life of the CDO (usually 5–10 years).
- Macro factors therefore do not cause a rise and fall in default probabilities over the credit cycle.
- Modest correlation in the events of default has to be induced by using a Merton /copula structure. This structure commonly assumes that there is no correlation between the returns on the value of company assets between company A and company B if they are in different industries. It also assumes that the correlation in the value of company assets is 30% within the same industry.
- All intervening cash flows are ignored.
- Random interest rates are ignored.

The result of all of these simplifying assumptions is a dramatic understatement of risk much like the analysis we did of correlated defaults in the U.S. market in earlier chapters.

We turn to proper valuation, simulation and hedging of credit derivative structures in the next section.

Valuing and simulating cash flows and defaults for Credit Default Swaps, First to Default Swaps and CDOs

The correct procedure for valuing credit default swaps (traditional or digital), first to default swaps and CDOs is to follow a slight variation on the process we outlined in a corporate bond context in Chapter 22.

Simulating the future values of Credit Default Swaps, First to Default Swaps and CDO reference collateral and tranches

Simulating the value of various credit derivatives structures using the reduced form approach takes the following procedure. We discuss the Merton model simulation in the next section.

For the reduced form model, the steps are as follows:

1. Simulate the risk-free term structure of interest rates as given in Chapter 22.

---

[4] The correlation figures given here are for the 'CDO Evaluator' provided to structurers by one of the major rating agencies, but most of the rating agencies take a closely related approach.

2. Choose a formula and the risk-drivers for the liquidity component of credit spread as discussed in Chapter 18.

3. Choose a formula and the risk-drivers for the default intensity process in the Jarrow model as discussed in Chapter 17. The macro factors driving correlated risk can be estimated using historical default data and historical macro factors using logistic regression or from observable market prices of bonds.

4. Simulate the random values of the drivers of liquidity risk and the default intensity for M time periods over N scenarios, consistent with the risk-free term structure.

5. Calculate the default intensity and the liquidity component at each of the M time steps and N scenarios. Note again, as in Chapter 22, that these will be changing randomly over time because interest rates and other factors are driving each of them. This is essential to capturing cyclicality in bond prices and defaults that create correlated defaults and which have a major impact on the equity tranches and junior tranches of CDOs.

6. Simulate the default/no default of each reference name at each of the M time steps and N scenarios.

7. Calculate the payments made on the derivative structure, given the number and amount of defaults to that date in each scenario.

8. Apply the Jarrow model as we have done in Chapters 17 and 18 to get the zero-coupon bond prices for the risk-free curve and for each reference name in the CDO collateral pool or underlying the first to default swap or credit derivative.

9. Calculate the derivative's value at each of the M time steps and N scenarios, conditional on the number of defaults among the reference names that have occurred to that point in the simulation.

This is slightly but not that much more complicated than the risk-free bond simulation discussed in Chapter 22. It relies on the identical interest rate scenarios and simulation process. Note that if the simulation is done for many companies with common risk factors driving default, we will see correlated default behavior that we have discussed through out this book.

As discussed in Chapter 22, for the Merton model, things are not as straightforward.

Simulating the Future Values of Bonds with Credit Risk in the Merton Model

When we wish to simulate future values and pay-offs on credit derivatives using the Merton model, we have the same kind of problem we had with valuation. The fundamental assumptions of the model are inconsistent with best practice in risk management—we need a random interest rate multi-period framework and the Merton model is a constant interest rate single-period framework. As in Chapter 22, we make the following adjustments to the model:

1. We assume that interest rates are random and use the Shimko, Tejima and van Deventer framework instead of the original Merton constant interest rate framework.

2. We estimate the initial value of company assets V and its volatility for each company from equity prices and their history as discussed in Chapter 16.

3. We specify the random factors driving the value of company assets V and the functional form that links them to V. These are not in the original Merton paper.

4. We simulate these random factors over M time steps and N scenarios.

5. We simulate the random change in the value of company assets V forward to time step 1 given the value of random factors driving V. If there is a coupon payment on bond k on this date, we deduct that payment amount from the simulated value of V to get its adjusted value the instant after the payment. If there is no payment on this date, we use the original simulated value of V. Given V, we calculate the zero coupon bond prices in the Merton model for all maturities needed on that date (i.e. all dates on which there is future cash flow), even though the Merton model assumes there is only one bond and one payment date.

6. Using the adjusted value of V, we repeat steps 2 and 3 and simulate forward for the M time steps, deducting coupon payments wherever they occur. If at any point V is less than the required payment, the company defaults and the recovery rate is specific to that time step and scenario.

7. Repeat steps 5–6 for N scenarios.

8. We calculate the coupon bond value in each scenario, conditional on the company not having defaulted.

9. We calculate the payoffs to each tranche (if more than one) on the credit derivative.

10. We calculate the risk-adjusted expected value of the cash flows on the credit derivative on this basis.

As in Chapter 22, the authors don't recommend this process, as it can lead to many unintended consequences (like the serious mispricing found by van Deventer and Imai [2003]). At least, however, it is more accurate than the ad hoc copula approach promulgated by the rating agencies that ignores the macro factors driving default all together.

Valuing the Jarrow-Merton Put Option

We have analyzed the reference names in a first to default swap or in a collateralized debt obligation just as if they were loans in a bank lending portfolio or private placements on the books of a pension fund or insurance company. The next step is to integrate them with the liabilities of the institution so that we can evaluate the Jarrow-Merton put option as an integrated measure of company risk. We turn to that task in Chapter 24.

European Options on Bonds[1]

In this section of the book, we lay the foundation for valuation and simulation of most financial instruments that are owned by major financial institutions. Our purpose in doing so is to provide a basis for the integration of interest rate risk and credit risk so that we can calculate the value of the put option that Robert Jarrow and Robert Merton propose as the best measure of integrated risk.

In this chapter, we introduce a general approach for the valuation of fixed income derivatives and then focus specifically on the valuation of a European option on bonds. In the first part of the chapter, we lay this framework on the assumption that both the underlying bond and our counterparty on the bond option are default-free. We relax this assumption at the end of the chapter, laying the framework for the Jarrow-Merton option valuation that we highlight in Chapters 39–44.

In this chapter and the rest of this book, we focus on the Vasicek model rather than the Extended Vasicek model. Shimko, Tejima and van Deventer [1993] used the Vasicek model when they generalized the Merton model of risky debt to allow for random interest rates, as we discussed in Chapter 16. Jarrow [1999–2001] and Duffie and Singleton [1999] used the extended Vasicek model in the reduced form credit models we discussed in Chapter 17.

We use the Vasicek model in the rest of this book for a simple reason. The Vasicek model allows for easier exposition and it provides a solid foundation for the financial market participant or serious student of finance who wants to 'extend' the results of derivatives securities valuation in the Vasicek model to find the Extended Vasicek result. For most derivative securities, this extension is a modest one. Closed form solutions are available for both models, which

---

[1] An earlier version of this chapter appeared as Chapter 6 of van Deventer and Imai [1996].

is why they are so popular as the risk-free term structure model underlying the credit models of Chapters 16–17.

This chapter introduces the concept of risk neutral interest rates and the relationship between this powerful concept and the risk-free term structure models we discussed in Chapter 11. We then use the insights of the risk neutral approach to value European options on bonds and then discuss doing this on a credit risk-adjusted basis at the end of the chapter.

An Introduction to Risk Neutral Interest Rates and the No-Arbitrage Assumption

Over the last 50 years, monetary economists have devoted a considerable amount of time to the discussion of 'liquidity premiums' embedded in the risk-free term structure of interest rates.[2] Ingersoll [1987] gives a very lucid summary of the theories that seek to explain the liquidity premium. Usually, the discussions of the liquidity premium focus on the long-standing debate about whether forward rates represent only the market's expectations of future interest rates or whether forward rates also include a premium for risk. One of the most popular theories of the term structure is the 'local expectations hypothesis', which holds that bond market participants are indifferent to risk and that the expected return on bonds of all maturities must therefore equal the short-term risk-free rate of interest. The linkage between this theory of the term structure of interest rates and the Vasicek model helps illustrate the 'risk neutral' approach.[3]

In Chapter 11, we introduced the Vasicek model in which short-term interest rates move randomly according to the stochastic process:

$$dr = \alpha(\mu - r)\,dt + \sigma\,dz$$

Using the hedging argument from Chapter 11, risk-free arbitrage requires that zero-coupon bonds for all maturities are related to the market price of risk lambda by the following equation:

$$\frac{P_r\alpha(\mu - r) + (1/2)\sigma^2 P_{rr} + P_t - rP}{\sigma P_r} = -\lambda$$

---

[2] Note that in this chapter the phrase 'liquidity premium' refers to a premium in the risk-free term structure associated with interest rate risk. In Chapter 18 and other chapters in this book, 'liquidity premium' refers to the difference between total credit spread and the loss component of credit spread for a 'credit risky' issuer.

[3] See Ingersoll [1987] for an in-depth discussion of the links between the local expectations hypothesis and term structure models.

This bond market version of the Sharpe ratio says that the ratio of expected return on the bond less the risk-free return on the bond, rP, divided by its standard deviation must be the same for bonds of all maturities. If lambda is positive[4], investors receive an extra return or 'liquidity premium' for holding bonds with higher price volatility. If lambda is zero, investors are 'risk neutral' and the expected return on all bonds is the risk-free rate. When lambda is zero, we can rearrange the equation above such that:

$$\frac{P_r\alpha(\mu - r) + (1/2)\sigma^2 P_{rr} + P_t}{P} = r$$

The numerator of this expression is the expected change in the bond's price that we get by calculating dP using Ito's lemma as in Chapters 4 and 5 and then taking its expected value.[5] The expression says:

$$\frac{dP}{P} = r$$

The percentage return on bonds of all maturity equals the risk-free rate. If investors are 'risk neutral', then the Vasicek model with lambda equals zero applies.

What if investors are *not* risk neutral? Is the concept of risk neutrality useful in valuing fixed income and foreign exchange derivatives? The answer is definitely yes. For any degree of risk aversion, as measured by the market price of risk lambda, we can derive a related stochastic process for interest rates that is consistent with a 'pseudo' economy where investors are risk neutral and the same bond prices would prevail.[6] We assume that observable interest rates move according to the Vasicek model stochastic process above. For what stochastic process would (a) the same bond prices prevail and (b) investors be risk neutral? We guess that the stochastic process has the form:

$$d\tilde{r} = a(\tilde{r}, t)\, dt + \sigma\, dz$$

---

[4] Note that P_r is negative and that the minus sign in front of lambda corrects for the fact that the denominator on the left hand side of the equation, the volatility of the bond's price, is negative.

[5] The expected value of any function h times the stochastic term $dz\, E[h\, dz]$ is zero, so the random term in the Ito's lemma expansion disappears on taking the expectation. See Shimko [1992] for an artistic exposition of this point.

[6] See Jarrow [1996] for an extensive discussion of the construction of the 'pseudo' probabilities behind the risk neutral stochastic process for interest rates.

where the tilde denotes the risk neutral process. If the process is truly risk neutral, the expected return on all bonds will equal the short rate r, which by standard assumption is equal to the current risk neutral interest rate:

$$\frac{P_{\tilde{r}}a(\tilde{r}, t) + (1/2)\sigma^2 P_{\tilde{r}\tilde{r}} + P_t}{P} = r = \tilde{r}$$

We rearrange this equation and divide by sigma times the first derivative of the bond's price P_r to get:

$$\frac{P_{\tilde{r}}\, a(\tilde{r}, t) + (1/2)\,\sigma^2\, P_{\tilde{r}\tilde{r}} + P_t - \tilde{r}P}{\sigma P_{\tilde{r}}} = 0$$

This is the equilibrium bond pricing equation under the risk neutral interest rate process. For what value of the function $a(\tilde{r}, t)$ is this valuation equation identical to the valuation equation using the observable stochastic process given above? It is identical if:

$$a(\tilde{r}, t) = \alpha(\mu - r) + \lambda\sigma$$

so the equivalent risk neutral stochastic process for interest rates is simply a shift in the drift term of the short-term interest rate:

$$d\tilde{r} = [\alpha(\mu - \tilde{r}) + \lambda\sigma]\, dt + \sigma\, dz$$

The risk neutral process is always assumed to be such that the risk neutral short rate at the current time t and the observable short rate at that time are equal. There is a close link between the existence of this risk neutral-equivalent stochastic process and the assumption of a no-arbitrage economy.

Jamshidian [1990] summarizes these links by noting that for any one-factor model of interest rates, there are eight equivalent conditions that assure a no-arbitrage economy:

1. The market price of risk is the same for bonds of all maturities.
2. The expected drift in the observable short rate r can be expressed as the product of the difference between the volatility of a bond with maturity T and the market price of risk times the volatility of the observable short rate.
3. The short rate r at an arbitrary point t in the future can be expressed as a particular stochastic integral of the volatilities of bond prices plus the forward rate for time t prevailing at time zero.

4. The forward rate at time T as of an arbitrary point t in the future can be expressed as a particular stochastic integral of the volatilities of bond prices plus the forward rate for time T prevailing at time zero.

5. Bond prices prevailing at any point in time equal the risk neutral discounted expected value of future risk neutral short-term interest rates.

6. The relative prices of a zero-coupon bond with maturity T and a 'money market fund' consisting of the compounded reinvestment of $1 at time zero at the short-term risk neutral rate of interest, are martingales[7] with respect to the risk neutral process for interest rates.

7. The forward rates as of time T from the perspective of time t are martingales with respect to a 'T-maturity forward risk-adjusted expectation'.

8. Forward bond prices are martingales with respect to the forward risk-adjusted expectation.

See Heath, Jarrow and Morton [1992] and Jamshidian [1990] for a precise mathematical specification of these points.

Relationship Between the Expected Short Rate, Expected Risk Neutral Short Rate, and Forward Rates

The local expectations hypothesis holds that the expected return on bonds of all maturities is the short rate of interest. In addition, most debates on the nature of the liquidity premium in the term structure of interest rates revolve around the relationship between forward rates and expected future short rates. In the Vasicek model, it is important to make it clear that neither the expected observable short rate of interest nor the expected risk neutral short rate at some arbitrary future date will, in general, equal the forward rate prevailing for that maturity.

Vasicek [1977][8] showed that the observable short rate r expected to prevail at time s in the future from the perspective of time t is:

$$E_t[r(s)] = \mu + [r(t) - \mu] e^{-\alpha(s-t)}$$

---

[7] Informally, a variable is a martingale if its expected value for a given stochastic process (in this case, the risk neutral process) at some point in the future equals its current value. See Arnold [1974] or Karatzas and Shreve [1991] for a formal mathematical definition. See Jarrow [1996] for more on the 'money market fund' analogy.

[8] See equation 25 in Vasicek.

Jamshidian[9] shows that the expected value of the risk neutral short rate expected to prevail at time s in the future from the perspective of current time t[10] is:

$$E_t[\tilde{r}(s)] = \mu + \frac{\lambda\sigma}{\alpha} + \left[r(t) - \left(\mu + \frac{\lambda\sigma}{\alpha}\right)\right]e^{-\alpha(s-t)}$$

$$= E_t[r(s)] + F(s-t)\lambda\sigma$$

where

$$F(s-t) = \frac{1}{\alpha}\left[1 - e^{-\alpha(s-t)}\right]$$

The forward rate f prevailing at time t for maturity at time s is:

$$f_t(s) = \mu + \frac{\lambda\sigma}{\alpha} + \left[r(t) - \left(\mu + \frac{\lambda\sigma}{\alpha}\right)\right]e^{-\alpha(s-t)} - \frac{\sigma^2}{2}F(s-t)^2$$

$$= E_t[\tilde{r}(s)] - \frac{\sigma^2}{2}F(s-t)^2$$

$$= E_t[r(s)] + F(s-t)\lambda\sigma - \frac{\sigma^2}{2}F(s-t)^2$$

These formulas clearly show that forward rates will not equal either the expected value of the observable short rate or the expected value of the risk neutral short rate unless interest rate volatility sigma is zero. This is true even under the local expectations hypothesis ($\lambda = 0$). This distinction between forward rates and the two variations on expected future short rates will be important to keep in mind in the next section.

A General Valuation Formula for Valuation of Interest Rate-Related Securities in the Vasicek Model

In this section, we present the general Jamshidian solution for the valuation of interest rate-related securities under the Vasicek model. It is simplest to do this in terms of the risk neutral interest rate process. Using the results from the first section of this chapter, we define the 'risk neutral drift' in the risk neutral short-term interest rate to be consistent with Jamshidian as:

$$\tilde{\mu} = \mu + \frac{\sigma\lambda}{\alpha}$$

---

[9] See page 208 of Jamshidian [1989].

[10] Remember that the current short rate r and the current risk neutral short rate are equal by assumption, so no notational distinction is necessary.

so we can write the risk neutral stochastic process for the short rate as:

$$d\tilde{r} = [\alpha(\mu - \tilde{r}) + \lambda\sigma]\,dt + \sigma\,dz$$
$$= \alpha(\tilde{\mu} - \tilde{r})\,dt + \sigma\,dz$$

Following Jarrow [1996] and Jamshidian [1989], we can also define the value of a money market fund with an original principal amount at beginning time t of $1, which is continually reinvested at the risk neutral interest rate until time s as:

$$B(t, s) = e^{Y(t, s)}$$

where

$$Y(t, s) = \int_t^s \tilde{r}(u)\,du$$

What is the value of a security which pays a continuous cash flow at a function $h[r(t), t]$ which depends on time t and the level of the observable (not risk neutral[11]) short rate r and a terminal cash flow $g[r(T), T]$ when it matures at time T?

We know from Chapter 11 that a zero-coupon bond must satisfy a partial differential equation that restricts its excess expected return over the observable short-term interest rate r, all divided by the price volatility of the security, to equal the market price of risk lambda. In the Vasicek model, the market price of risk lambda is assumed to be a constant.[12] Shimko [1992] shows that the same concept applies for a security which has cash flow prior to maturity according to some function $h[r(t), t]$. The value of a security paying continuous cash flow h and cash flow g at maturity must satisfy the partial differential equation[13] for its value V such that:

$$\alpha(\tilde{\mu} - r)V_r + \frac{1}{2}\sigma^2 V_{rr} + V_t - rV + h(r, t) = 0$$

---

[11] Derivative contracts, for instance, pay based only on observable interest rates, not risk neutral rates.

[12] This assumption is relaxed in the Extended Vasicek (Hull and White) version of the model. The derivation which follows is almost identical for the extended version of the Vasicek model.

[13] Note again that the observable short rate r and the risk neutral rate are the same at current time t.

subject to the boundary condition that at maturity T:

$$V(r, T) = g(r)$$

There are two different expressions for the general solution to this valuation problem. The first solution is useful for numerical solution techniques like binomial and trinomial lattice techniques:

$$V(r, t) = E_{r,t} \left[\frac{g[\tilde{r}(T)]}{B(t, T)} + \int_t^T \frac{h[\tilde{r}(s), s]}{B(t, s)} \, ds \right]$$

Jamshidian, citing Friedman [1975], shows that the value V of any security can be written simply as the (risk neutral) expected value of the terminal cash flow g at time T divided by the value of the money fund $B(t, T)$, plus the continuous sum of the continuous cash flow at time s h divided by the value of the money fund $B(t, s)$, *but cash flows g and h are determined as functions of the risk neutral interest rate instead of the observable interest rate r.* This is the heart of the lattice calculation techniques which are constructed based on the risk neutral interest rate process, use cash flows determined by risk neutral interest rates, and discount by the value of the money fund B. We discuss how to construct such lattices in Chapter 30.

The most convenient form of the solution formula for V to use in obtaining closed form solutions for security values is given as Jamshidian's equation 5:

$$V(r, t) = P(r, t, T)E[g(R_{r,t,s})] + \int_t^T P(r, t, s)E[h(R_{r,t,s}, s)] \, ds$$

The value V is the simple present value of the 'expected' cash flows from functions g and h except that expected cash flows are *not* evaluated based on the probability distribution for either the observable short rate r or the risk neutral short rate. Instead, cash flows are evaluated as if the 'short rate' R has:

$$\text{mean}_R(r, t, s) = f(r, t, s) = re^{-\alpha(s-t)} + \alpha F(s - t)\tilde{\mu} - \frac{\sigma^2}{2}F(s - t)^2$$

$$\text{variance}_R = \text{var}_{r,t}[r(s)] = v^2(t, s) = \frac{\sigma^2}{2\alpha}\left[1 - e^{-2\alpha(s-t)}\right]$$

$$F(s - t) = \frac{1}{\alpha}\left[1 - e^{-\alpha(s-t)}\right]$$

In other words, we evaluate the expected values of the cash flows *g* and *h* as if the short rate had a mean equal to the forward rate with maturity equal to the timing of the cash flow and the same variance as the observable short rate will have at that time (say time *s*) from the perspective of current time *t*. How can this be? We know from the second section of this chapter that the forward rate equals neither the expected observable short rate nor the expected risk neutral short rate. The reason for this surprising conclusion is given in Appendix 1. We illustrate the use of the formula above to evaluate European options on risk-free bonds in the next section.

The Value of European Options on a Zero-Coupon Bond

We can use the closed form solutions formula above to value a European call option on a zero-coupon bond. We assume that the call option is to be valued at current time *t*. It is an option to purchase a risk-free zero-coupon bond with maturity at time T_2 that is exercisable at a purchase price *K* at time T_1. The derivation is shown in Appendix 2.

The value of the call option as of time *t* given the observable short rate *r* is:

$$V(r, t, T_1, T_2, K) = P(r, t, T_2)N(h) - P(r, t, T_1)KN(h - \sigma_P)$$

where *N* is the standard cumulative normal distribution. We use the following definitions:

$$h = \frac{1}{\sigma_P} \ln \left[\frac{P(r, t, T_2)}{KP(r, t, T_1)} \right] + \frac{\sigma_P}{2}$$

$$\sigma_P = vF_1$$

The latter expression is the standard deviation of the price of the T_2 maturity zero-coupon bond's price.

Readers familiar with the Black-Scholes options model will notice a strong similarity to the pricing formula in that model. The similarities occur because the zero-coupon bond's price is lognormally distributed since its yield is linear in the short rate of interest and the yield is therefore normally distributed. There are very important differences in this formulation compared to the Black-Scholes model that are worth noting:

- The volatility of the bond's price declines over time and reaches zero at maturity, which is fully captured by the Jamshidian formulation. It is not captured by the Black-Scholes model if applied to bond options, since the bond price volatility is assumed to be constant in the

Black-Scholes model. As we noted earlier, many traders in caps, floors and swaptions erroneously accept the Black model's assumption of constant bond price volatility, which is a partial explanation for the volatility 'smile' observed when using the Black model for caps, floors and swaptions.

- The Jamshidian formulation looks through bond price fluctuations to the economic source of the fluctuations, random interest rates, and provides an internally consistent methodology for bond option valuation. Using the Black-Scholes model for bond options pricing relies on the dangerous inconsistency that bond options are being valued using a model that assumes interest rates are constant.

- The Jamshidian formula, in combination with the Vasicek or Extended Vasicek term structure model, provides a consistent approach that allows cross-hedging of a one-year option on a three-year zero-coupon bond with the appropriate hedging amount of two-year bonds. The Black-Scholes model does not provide an explanation of the relationship between price changes on bonds with different maturities.

- The Jamshidian formulation provides all of the same richness of hedging tools, including the term-structure model equivalent of the 'Greeks':

$$r\text{Delta} = \frac{\partial V}{\partial r}$$

$$r\text{Gamma} = \frac{\partial^2 V}{\partial r^2}$$

$$r\text{Vega} = \frac{\partial V}{\partial \sigma}$$

$$r\text{Theta} = \frac{\partial V}{\partial t}$$

The Jamshidian formulation is far more powerful in explaining observable caps and floors prices, as we will see in later chapters.

European puts on zero-coupon bond prices

The Jamshidian technique applies to European put options as well. Put-call parity requires that the sum of a long position in a European call and a short position in a European put at the same strike price K is the equivalent of a long position in a forward contract on the zero-coupon bond with maturity T_2 at an exercise price of K at time T_1. The present value of the forward bond contract, which we know from Chapter 7, can be shown to be:

$$\text{Call}(r, t, T_1, T_2, K) - \text{Put}(r, t, T_1, T_2, K) = P(r, t, T_2) - P(r, t, T_1)K$$

as it should be. This results simply from the fact that:

$$N(-h) = 1 - N(h)$$

because of the symmetry of the normal cumulative distribution function.

Options on Coupon-Bearing Bonds

Jamshidian notes that the price of any security with a positive amount of contractual cash flows a_i at n points of time in the future is a monotonically decreasing function of the short rate of interest r. Therefore, the zero-coupon bond formulas for European options can be applied directly to the problem of European options on coupon-bearing bonds. For each cash flow date, the strike price K_i is set to equal the zero-coupon bond price as of the exercise date T such that the present value of the remaining payments on the security as of time T exactly equal the true strike price on the entire security K. The interest rate r^* is the short term interest rate at which this is true:

$$\sum_{i=j}^{n} a_i P(r^*, T, T_i) = K$$

and;

$$K_i = P(r^*, T, T_i)$$

Jamshidian shows that the value of a European option on the entire security is the weighted sum of options on each cash flow:

$$\text{Option}(r, t, T, K) = \sum_{i=j}^{n} a_i \, \text{Option}(r, t, T, T_i, K_i)$$

An example of the use of this formula is given in the next section.

Options on coupon-bearing bonds: An example

Throughout the first half of the 1990s, step-up coupon bonds were popular among issuers and investors alike. In this section, we analyze a step-up coupon bond with a six-year maturity and semi-annual coupons at 6% for the first three years and 8% for the last three years. We assume that the bonds are callable at par on the interest payment date three years from now (after interest has been paid on that date). The rising coupon structure on this type of bonds was rarely relevant to issuers, who typically combined the bonds with an interest rate swap to convert the proceeds to a floating rate instrument tied to the London Interbank Offered Rate at a spread well below the normal financing costs available to the issuer. The issuers were beneficiaries of a large arbitrage due to the fact than many investors, attracted by the higher coupon in the latter half of the life of the bond, placed a lower value on the issuer's ability to call the bonds than most market participants. In this section, we use the Jamshidian bond pricing formula to price this hypothetical step-up coupon bond issue.

The bond is composed of two securities. The first part is the bond itself, which we analyze as if it were non-callable by taking the simple present value of cash flows.

Table 24.1 Step-Up Coupon Bond Scheduled Cash Flow

Maturity	Interest	Principal	Total
0.5	30		30
1.0	30		30
1.5	30		30
2.0	30		30
2.5	30		30
3.0	30		30
3.5	40		40
4.0	40		40
4.5	40		40
5.0	40		40
5.5	40		40
6.0	40	1,000	1,040

We do this present value calculation using the parameters for the Vasicek term structure model given in Table 24.2 below.

The bonds, if we ignore the value of the call option, have a present value of 996.59. This is the value many investors believed they were receiving when they were offered the bonds at a price plus accrued interest of, say, 98% of par, or 980. Unfortunately, we now have to calculate the value of the call option and subtract this value from the simple present value of the bonds to get the true value of this 'packaged' security.

Step one is to determine what value of the short rate r, assuming it is now three years forward, will cause the bonds to have a present value of exactly 1,000 (par value) on that date. Using the 'solver' function in a common spreadsheet software package, we see that the breakeven level of r is 7.8412%.

Table 24.2 Step-Up Coupon Bond Present Value of Scheduled Payments

Term Structure Model Parameters

Alpha	0.05000
Mu	0.08000
Sigma	0.01500
Lambda	0.01000
r	6.7500%

Maturity	F(T)	D	G(T)	Zero Price	Cash Flow	Present Value
0.5	0.49380	0.03800	0.00051	0.96672	30	29.00
1.0	0.97541	0.03800	0.00200	0.93441	30	28.03
1.5	1.44513	0.03800	0.00443	0.90305	30	27.09
2.0	1.90325	0.03800	0.00775	0.87265	30	26.18
2.5	2.35006	0.03800	0.01191	0.84321	30	25.30
3.0	2.78584	0.03800	0.01687	0.81472	30	24.44
3.5	3.21086	0.03800	0.02259	0.78716	40	31.49
4.0	3.62538	0.03800	0.02902	0.76053	40	30.42
4.5	4.02968	0.03800	0.03614	0.73481	40	29.39
5.0	4.42398	0.03800	0.04391	0.70997	40	28.40
5.5	4.80856	0.03800	0.05229	0.68601	40	27.44
6.0	5.18364	0.03800	0.06125	0.66289	1,040	689.41
Total Present Value of Cash Flow						**996.59**

Table 24.3 Calculation of Breakeven *r* at 3-Year Point

Break-even *r* in 3-years   7.8412%

Maturity	F(T)	D	G(T)	Zero Price	Cash Flow	Present Value
0.5	0.49380	0.03800	0.00051	0.96153	40	38.46
1.0	0.97541	0.03800	0.00200	0.92451	40	36.98
1.5	1.44513	0.03800	0.00443	0.88892	40	35.56
2.0	1.90325	0.03800	0.00775	0.85471	40	34.19
2.5	2.35006	0.03800	0.01191	0.82186	40	32.87
3.0	2.78584	0.03800	0.01687	0.79032	1,040	821.94
Total Present Value of Cash Flows						**1,000.00**

As shown in the previous section, we can now calculate a call option on this step-up coupon bond even though it has more than one cash flow by combining the values of call options on each cash flow using the zero prices in Table 24.3 as the adjusted strike prices. This calculation shows that the total value of the call option is 32.96.

Table 24.4 Calculation of European Call Option Value

Break-even r in 3-years				7.8412%							
T1 Maturity	T2 Maturity	$P(T1)$	$P(T2)$	Strike Price K	$F(T2-T1)$	$v(T1)$	Sigma P	h	Value of Call on on $1	Cash Flow	Total Call Value
3.0	3.5	0.81472	0.78716	0.96153	0.49380	0.02415	0.01192	0.41052	0.00593	40	0.24
3.0	4.0	0.81472	0.76053	0.92451	0.97541	0.02415	0.02355	0.42215	0.01136	40	0.45
3.0	4.5	0.81472	0.73481	0.88892	1.44513	0.02415	0.03490	0.43350	0.01632	40	0.65
3.0	5.0	0.81472	0.70997	0.85471	1.90325	0.02415	0.04596	0.44456	0.02083	40	0.83
3.0	5.5	0.81472	0.68601	0.82186	2.35006	0.02415	0.05675	0.45535	0.02493	40	1.00
3.0	6.0	0.81472	0.66289	0.79032	2.78584	0.02415	0.06727	0.46587	0.02864	1,040	29.79
Total Value of European Option to Call the Bond											**32.96**

The total value of the package offered to investors is 996.59 – 32.96, or 963.63. Investors who thought that they were getting a bargain at 980 actually paid more than 16 too much.

Differences of opinion about the right price of securities are what makes a market. As we have seen in this chapter, bond option pricing is more of a science and somewhat less of an art than it has been in the past, thanks to the pioneering work of Black, Scholes, Vasicek, and Jamshidian who combined both approaches to reach the conclusions of this chapter. With these tools, both issuers and investors will have a more accurate view of fair value. We now turn to the Jarrow-Merton put option and the credit risk adjustment of these formulas.

The Jarrow-Merton Put Option in the Absence of Credit Risk

We can use the coupon-bearing bond put option formula from the previous two sections to illustrate the valuation of the Jarrow-Merton put option as an integrated risk measure in the special case where the company's liabilities are all insured by a default-free government and where it invests solely in default-free bonds. Assume without loss of generality, that all of the asset cash flows and liability cash flows fall on n dates. Since all of these cash flows are default-free, we can aggregate them without a loss of generality. Let the sum of all of the asset cash flows on each date i for $i = 1, n$ be denoted by b_i. Let the sum of all of the asset cash flows on each date i for $i = 1, n$ be denoted by c_i. The net cash flows on the n dates is defined as $a_i = b_i - c_i$. This is exactly parallel to Jamshidian's coupon-bearing bond formula above. What strike price is relevant to this problem? One strike price that is relevant to the government insuring the liabilities of the company is a strike price of $K = 0$. This corresponds to an option to 'put' the equity of the company to the government insurer when the value of the equity is zero or below. This put option will be exercised when the company is effectively bankrupt and the government insurance payments will be necessary. The maturity of the put option is assumed to be equal to the time to the first net cash outflow $(a_i < 0)$ since bankruptcy is impossible if $a_i > 0$; the value of the put option with a maturity prior to the first cash outflow will be zero.

Clearly, the valuation of this put option becomes more complicated (a) if the assets held by the company are not free of credit risk and (b) if the company itself can default. We turn to these issues in the next section.

Valuing Options on a Defaultable Zero-Coupon Bond

If the issuer of a zero-coupon bond can default, bond options get much more interesting. In the case of the Merton model, a call option to buy the defaultable zero-coupon bond assumed by Merton was discussed in Chapter 16. The value of this option is a monotonically decreasing function of the value of company assets, which have a normally distributed return as discussed in Chapter 16, so the compound options approach of Geske can be used to solve this problem. Note that the multivariate normal distribution is used in both the Geske formula and by Jamshidian (see Appendix 1), since the problems are closely related.

In the reduced form model of Jarrow discussed in Chapter 17, the value of an option on a zero-coupon bond is given by Jarrow [1999]. The formula closely resembles the Jamshidian formula given above with appropriate adjustments for the loss given default on the defaultable zero-coupon bond. Jarrow goes on to show there is also a closed form solution for a call option on a coupon-bearing bond, resembling that of Jamshidian, when the default intensity is constant. When the default intensity is driven by interest rates and macro factors as described in Chapter 17, lattice techniques or monte carlo simulation are needed to value options on defaultable coupon-bearing bonds. The same is true where the writer of the option can default on his obligations as well.

We next turn to other financial instruments that must be valued before we can analyze the Jarrow-Merton measure of integrated risk in Chapters 39–44.

Exercises

24.1 Using the Vasicek parameter assumptions of the example above, what is the value at the beginning of the six-year period of a three-year call option to buy a six-year zero-coupon bond at a price of 88?

24.2 What is the price of a three-year put option at the same strike price of 88?

24.3 What is the present value of a three-year forward contract to buy a zero-coupon bond with current maturity of six years at a price of 98?

24.4 What combination of European calls and European puts on this six-year zero-coupon bond replicates the value of a three-year forward contract at a price of 88?

24.5 What is the value of this combination?

24.6 How does that value compare to the answer you gave to 24.3?

24.7 What is the value of a three-year put at par value on the step-up coupon bond described in the example above? Do this calculation without using Jamshidian's put option formula.

24.8 Calculate the 'Greeks' for the term structure model European call option formula: rDelta, rGamma, rTheta, and rVega. Should there be another Greek for the speed of mean reversion factor, alpha? Even if you think the answer is no, calculate rAlpha any way.

24.9 Recalculate the value of the call option in the example above for maturities of 0.5, 1, 1.5, 2, 2.5, 3.5, 4, 4.5, 5 and 5.5 years.

24.10 What relationship should an American call option on these bonds have to the European call options in the example above and problem 24.9?

24.11 Calculate the value of the step-up coupon bonds in the example above for r of 2, 4, 6, 8 and 10% on two bases: assuming the bonds are non-callable and assuming they are callable after three years as described. Describe the differences in interest rate sensitivity that you observe.

24.12 Assume you are the new chief investment officer at a life insurance company that owns more step-up coupon bonds than it should. Your predecessor has gone on to manage money for a well-known southern California municipality under considerable duress. You own $1,000 principal amount of the callable step-up bond in the example above and you want to hedge the risk that the bonds will be called with a four-year zero-coupon bond (the only maturity at which you have any liquidity). How much of that four-year zero should you buy or sell? Remember, hedge the call option only.

Appendix 1

Derivation of the Closed Form Valuation Formula

The formula in which cash flows are determined by risk neutral interest rates and discounted by the value of the money market fund B, comes directly from stochastic process mathematics. It is important to understand how this formula is related to the formula for numerical solutions, which has become so popular for numerical valuation of fixed income securities and interest rate derivatives. The closed form valuation formula is just as powerful, so we devote considerable effort here to rationalizing these two solutions (which appear at first glance to be at odds with each other), by elaborating on the derivation shown in the appendix to Jamshidian [1989].

Jamshidian shows that the expected value in the formula for numerical solutions can be rewritten in terms of the multivariate normal probability density function p, which depends on the initial short rate r, current time t, future time s, the risk neutral interest rate at time s r', and the yield on the money market fund $Y(t, s)$ since r' and Y are both random and jointly normally distributed:

$$V(r, t) = \int_{-\infty}^{\infty} \int_{-\infty}^{\infty} \frac{g(r')}{B(t, T)}\, p[r, t, T, r', Y(t, T)]\, dY\, dr'$$

$$+ \int_{t}^{T} \int_{-\infty}^{\infty} \int_{-\infty}^{\infty} \frac{h(r', s)}{B(t, s)}\, p[r, t, s, r', Y(t, s)]\, dY\, dr'\, ds$$

To link the numerical solution formula and the closed form solution formula, we need to evaluate further the integral:

$$G(r, r', t, s) = \int_{-\infty}^{\infty} \frac{1}{B(t, s)}\, p[r, t, s, r', Y]\, dY = \int_{-\infty}^{\infty} e^{-Y(t,s)}\, p(r, t, s, r', Y)\, dY$$

To do this, we make use of the following facts concerning the mean, variance, and covariance of risk neutral rates and the money market yield Y:

$$E_{r,t}[\tilde{r}(s)] = m_r = e^{-\alpha \tau} r + \alpha F(\tau)\tilde{\mu}$$

$$\text{var}_{r,t}[\tilde{r}(s)] = v_r^2 = \frac{\sigma^2}{2\alpha}\left[1 - e^{-2\alpha\tau}\right]$$

$$E_{r,t}[Y(t, s)] = m_y = \tau\tilde{\mu} + (r - \tilde{\mu})F(\tau)$$

$$\text{var}_{r,t}[Y(t, s)] = v_y^2 = \frac{\sigma^2}{2\alpha^3}\left[4e^{-\alpha\tau} - e^{-2\alpha\tau} + 2\alpha\tau - 3\right]$$

$$\text{cov}_{r,t}[\tilde{r}(s), Y(t, s)] = \rho v_r v_y = \frac{\sigma^2}{2}F(\tau)^2$$

$$\tau = s - t$$

Now the probability density function for any two variables x_1 and x_2 with a joint multivariate normal distribution, means m_1 and m_2, standard deviations σ_1 and σ_2, and correlation *rho* can be written:

$$f(x_1, x_2) = \frac{1}{2\pi\sigma_1\sigma_2\sqrt{(1-\rho^2)}} \exp\left[\frac{-1}{2(1-\rho^2)} \left[\left(\frac{x_1 - m_1}{\sigma_1} \right)^2 \right. \right.$$

$$\left. \left. -2\rho\left(\frac{x_1 - m_1}{\sigma_1} \right)\left(\frac{x_2 - m_2}{\sigma_2} \right) + \left(\frac{x_2 - m_2}{\sigma_2} \right)^2 \right] \right]$$

After a tedious calculation, it is possible to show that:

$$f(x_1, x_2) = n(x_1, m_1, \sigma_1)\, n\left(x_{21}, m_1 + \sigma_2\rho x_1, \sigma_2\sqrt{1-\rho^2} \right)$$

where n is the single variate normal density function for variable x with mean m and standard deviation s such that:

$$n(x, m, \sigma) = \frac{1}{\sigma\sqrt{2\pi}} e^{(-1/2)((x-m)/\sigma)^2}$$

It can also be shown that:

$$\int_{-\infty}^{a} e^{bs}\, n(s, m, \sigma)\, ds = e^{b(m + (b\sigma^2/2))} N(a, m + b\sigma^2, \sigma)$$

where $N(a, m, \sigma)$ is the cumulative normal distribution function for a variable a with mean m and standard deviation σ. Accordingly, we can rewrite the formula as follows:

$$G(r, r', t, s) = \int_{-\infty}^{\infty} e^{-Y} f(r', Y)\, dY$$

$$= \int_{-\infty}^{\infty} e^{-Y} n(r', m_r, v_r)\, n\left(Y, m_y + v_y\rho r', v_y\sqrt{1-\rho^2} \right) dY$$

$$= n(r', m_r, v_r) \int_{-\infty}^{\infty} e^{-Y} n\left(Y, m_y + v_y\rho r', v_y\sqrt{1-\rho^2} \right) dY$$

$$= n(r', m_r, v_r)\, e^{-(m_y + v_y\rho r' - ((1-\rho^2)v_y^2/2))}$$

$$= P(r, t, s)n[r', f(s - t), v_r]$$

which is Jamshidian's equation 13. $f(s-t)$ is the forward rate for maturity at time s from the perspective of time t. This bridges the gap between the numerical solutions and closed form solutions equation and shows why the forward rate becomes the mean of the distribution used to evaluate closed form solutions even though neither the mean of the observable short rate nor the mean of the risk neutral short rate equals the forward rate.

Appendix 2

Deriving the Value of a European Call Option on a Zero-Coupon Bond

In this appendix we show the derivation of a European call option on a default-free zero-coupon bond. Because it is a European option exercisable only at time T_1, there is no intermediate cash flow (function $h = 0$ in the numerical solutions and closed form solutions formulas) and cash flow g at maturity is:

$$g(R, T_1) = P(R, T_2) - K \quad \text{if } R < s^*,$$
$$= 0 \quad \text{if } R \geq s^*$$

The call option has a payoff only if the price of a zero-coupon bond with maturity at T_2 is greater than K as of time T_1. This comes about only if the short rate R as of time T_1 is less than a critical level s^* defined by solving this equation for s^*:

$$K = P(s^*, \tau) = e^{-F(\tau)s^* - G(\tau)}$$

where, using the notation of Chen [1992]:

$$\tau = T_2 - T_1$$

$$F(\tau) = \frac{1}{\alpha}\left(1 - e^{-\alpha\tau}\right)$$

$$D = \tilde{\mu} - \frac{\sigma^2}{2\alpha^2} = \mu + \frac{\sigma\lambda}{\alpha} - \frac{\sigma^2}{2\alpha^2}$$

$$G(\tau) = D[\tau - F(\tau)] + \frac{\sigma^2}{4\alpha}F(\tau)^2$$

so that:

$$s^* = -\frac{\ln(K) + G(\tau)}{F(\tau)}$$

The value of the call option as of time t given the observable short rate r is:

$$V(r, t, T_1, T_2, K) = P(r, t, T_1) \int_{-\infty}^{s^*} \left(e^{-sF(\tau) - G(\tau)} - K\right) n[s, f(T_1 - s), v] \, ds$$

where n is the normal density function, f is the forward rate as of time t prevailing for maturity at time T_1 and v is the standard deviation of the short rate (both observable and risk neutral) which will prevail as of T_1 from the perspective of time t:

$$f(r, t, T_1) = re^{-\alpha(T_1 - t)} + \alpha F_1 \tilde{\mu} - \frac{\sigma^2}{2} F_1^2$$

$$v(r, t, T_1) = \sqrt{\frac{\sigma^2}{2\alpha} \left(1 - e^{-2\alpha(T_1 - t)}\right)}$$

and we use the abbreviations:

$$F(T_i - t) = F_i$$
$$G(T_i - t) = G_i$$
$$F(T_2 - T_1) = F_\tau$$
$$G(T_2 - T_1) = G_\tau$$
$$f(T_1 - t) = f_1$$

We can quickly simplify this expression so that:

$$V(r, t, T_1, T_2, K) = P(r, t, T_1)\left[e^{-G(\tau)} \int_{-\infty}^{s^*} e^{-sF(\tau)} n[s, f_1, v] \, ds \right.$$

$$\left. -K \int_{-\infty}^{s^*} n(s, f_1, v) \, ds \right]$$

$$V(r, t, T_1, T_2, K) = P(r, t, T_1)\left[e^{-F_\tau f_1 - G_\tau + (F_\tau^2 v^2)/2} N\left(F_\tau v + \frac{s^* - f_1}{v}\right) \right.$$

$$\left. - KN\left(\frac{s^* - f_1}{v}\right)\right]$$

This expression can be simplified considerably using the fact that:

$$-G_\tau - f_1 F_\tau + \frac{F_\tau^2 v^2}{2} = -\ln[P(r, t, T_1)] + \ln[P(r, t, T_2)]$$

and that:

$$\frac{s^* - f_1}{v} = \frac{\ln\left((P(r, t, T_2)/KP(r, t, T_1)\right)}{vF_1} - \frac{1}{2}vF_1$$

to arrive at Jamshidian's formulation for the value of a European option on a zero-coupon bond:

$$V(r, t, T_1, T_2, K) = P(r, t, T_2)N(h) - P(r, t, T_1)KN(h - \sigma_P)$$

where N is the standard cumulative normal distribution and we use the following definitions:

$$h = \frac{1}{\sigma_P} \ln\left[\frac{P(r, t, T_2)}{KP(r, t, T_1)}\right] + \frac{\sigma_P}{2}$$

$$\sigma_P = vF_1$$

The latter expression is the standard deviation of the price of the T_2 maturity zero-coupon bond's price.

CHAPTER 25

Forward and Futures Contracts[1]

I n this chapter, we continue the process of valuing the most common instruments on the balance sheet of major financial institutions around the world. Valuation enables us to efficiently perform a multi-period simulation of cash flows and future values for these instruments, both of which are critical to the ultimate objective—measuring interest rate risk and credit risk in a consistent framework, via the Jarrow-Merton put option introduced in Chapter 1.

Our focus in this chapter is on forward contracts and futures contracts for interest–rate-related instruments. Careful attention to this issue is important both from a correct hedging analysis and from an accounting perspective. Major banks need to carefully analyze their derivatives hedging programs under International Accounting Standard 39 and the related U.S. Financial Accounting Standard 133. This chapter lays the groundwork for the correlation requirements of those standards, both in terms of valuation and cash flow.

Financial forward and futures contracts are critical everyday tools of risk management and investment management. Their popularity is probably best summarized by the three-month Eurodollar contract traded on the Chicago Mercantile Exchange. Open interest in these contracts has long exceeded trillions of dollars, even for the most long-dated contracts. This chapter illustrates the important distinctions between forward and futures contracts of different types, using the tools of Chapter 24 that we developed in the context of valuing options on zero-coupon and coupon-bearing bonds. We start first with various forward contracts and then cover futures contracts.

Forward Contracts on Zero-Coupon Bonds

The most basic forward contract is a forward contract on the price of a zero-coupon bond. In this section and the rest of the chapter, we need to make an

---

[1] An earlier version of this chapter appeared as Chapter 7 in van Deventer and Imai [1996].

important distinction between the *value* of an existing contract on the books of an investment manager, insurance firm, or bank and the *price* of the forward contract quoted in the market. Before making this distinction clear, a real world example of a forward contract on zero-coupon bonds is useful. In this case, the best example is provided by the 90-day Bank Bill futures contract traded on the Sydney Futures Exchange. For purposes of this section, we will ignore daily mark-to-market requirements and analyze this contract as a forward, not a futures, contract. We will do the true futures analysis later in the chapter.

Contract:	90-day Bank Bills, Sydney Futures Exchange
Quotation basis:	100-yield in percent, quoted to two decimal places
Assumed maturity of underlying bill:	90 days
Valuation formula:	Bank Bill Contract Price $= \dfrac{365\,(1,000,000)}{365 + (90 * \text{yield}/100)}$

The bank bill contract assumes the underlying instrument pays simple interest on an actual/365 day basis and has a maturity of 90 days. Essentially, the price of the contract is the price of a 90-day zero-coupon bond with principal amount of A\$ 1 million at maturity. The calculation is the same as those we used in Chapter 7. One of the key features of the Sydney Bank Bill contract, as opposed to the LIBOR contracts we discuss below, is that the value of an 0.01% change in yield depends on the level of interest rates rather than being a constant dollar amount like the Eurodollar contract:

Yield (%)	A\$ Value of 0.01% Yield Increase
9.00%	A\$ 23.60
10.00%	A\$ 23.49
11.00%	A\$ 23.37
12.00%	A\$ 23.26

Note that the quotation method (100 − yield) is irrelevant to valuation— only the underlying cash flow described by the valuation formula matters for valuation purposes.

For notational convenience, we do the valuation analysis assuming that the principal amount on the underlying instrument is A\$1 instead of A\$ 1 million.

We know from Chapter 7 that the forward price of this bond should be the ratio of zero-coupon bond prices:

$$\text{Forward Bond Price}\,(r, t, T_1, T_2) = \frac{P(r, t, T_2)}{P(r, t, T_1)}$$

where T_2 is the maturity date of the underlying instrument (in years), T_1 is the maturity date of the forward contract, and t is the current time. This result doesn't depend on any particular term structure model since it can be derived using arbitrage arguments alone:

How is this result relevant to the valuation of a zero-coupon bond forward using the Vasicek model[2] and the results of Chapter 24? Noting that:

$$T_2 = T_1 + \frac{90}{365}$$

in the case of the Sydney Futures Exchange contract, we analyze the value of a Sydney Bank Bill *Forward*. Like all of the valuation formulas in Chapters 10, 11, and 24, the value V of this existing contract must satisfy the general Vasicek model partial differential equation:

$$V_r \alpha(\tilde{\mu} - r) + \frac{1}{2}\sigma^2 V_{rr} + V_t - rV = 0$$

We assume that the existing forward contract has a zero-coupon bond exercise price K, which equates to a quoted exercise yield Y^* by inverting the valuation formula like this:

$$Y^* = \frac{36,500}{90}\left[\frac{1,000,000}{K} - 1\right]$$

Using the notation of Chapter 24, the exercise price is equivalent to an instantaneous short rate in the Vasicek model of s^* such that:

$$K = P(s^*, T_1, T_2) = e^{-F_\tau s^* - G_\tau}$$

where F and G are as defined in Chapter 24 and the subscript refers to the maturity $T_2 - T_1$:

$$\tau = T_2 - T_1$$

---

[2] Again, similar results would be obtained for other term structure models and we use the Vasicek model here because of the ease of exposition relative to other models.

We know from Jamshidian's general valuation formula that the value of the forward contract is equal to the present value of the expected value of the cash flow on the contract's maturity date, evaluated as if the mean of the short rate is equal to the instantaneous forward rate for T_1:

$$V(r, t, T_1, T_2, K) = P(r, t, T_1) \int_{-\infty}^{\infty} \left(e^{-sF_\tau - G_\tau} - K \right) n[s, f_1, v] \, ds$$

with f_1 denoting the instantaneous forward rate prevailing at time t with maturity time T_1 and with v representing the same standard deviation of the short rate as of time T_1 from the perspective of time t. This expression simplifies to:

$$V(r, t, T_1, T_2, K) = P(r, t, T_1) \left[\frac{P(r, t, T_2)}{P(r, t, T_1)} - K \right]$$

$$= P(r, t, T_2) - P(r, t, T_1) K$$

The price of an existing zero-coupon bond forward contract equals the current value of the underlying instrument (the price of a zero-coupon bond maturing at T_2) less the present value of the strike price, valued with maturity equal to the exercise date.

What about the observable market price of a forward contract on a zero-coupon bond? We call this observable market price Q. We know that no cash is required to purchase such a contract, therefore its value must be zero or arbitrage would be possible. We also know that at the instant a contract is purchased, the strike price K will equal the quoted market price Q. Therefore we can solve for Q to get the same result we found in Chapter 1:

$$V(r, t, T_1, T_2, K) = 0 = P(r, t, T_1) \left[\frac{P(r, t, T_2)}{P(r, t, T_1)} - Q \right]$$

So

$$Q(r, t, T_1, T_2) = \frac{P(r, t, T_2)}{P(r, t, T_1)} = \text{Forward Zero-Coupon Bond Price}$$

The observable market price (in zero-coupon bond terms) equals the forward bond price.

$$Y^* = \frac{36{,}500}{90} \left[\frac{1{,}000{,}000}{\text{Forward Zero-Coupon Bond Price}} - 1 \right]$$

In yield terms as quoted on the Sydney Futures Exchange, the quoted yield will be as in Chapter 24, all of the term structure model equivalent of the Greeks apply to both V and Q, with the key statistics being the first derivatives with respect to the random short rate r in the Vasicek model:

$$r\text{Delta}(V) = \frac{\partial V}{\partial r}$$

$$r\text{Delta}(Q) = \frac{\partial Q}{\partial r}$$

Later in this chapter, we deal with the implications of daily margin requirements and the possibility that there could be a default (a) either by the Exchange itself or (b) on the instrument underlying the forward contract in keeping with our interest in an integrated treatment of interest rate risk and credit risk. The analysis in this section implicitly assumes that both the Exchange and the underlying instrument are default-free.

Forward rate agreements

The design of the Sydney Futures Exchange Bank Bill Contract is one of a relatively small number of contracts where the underlying instrument is a zero-coupon bond. It is most common for the underlying instrument to be expressed in term of an interest rate. Perhaps the most common forward contract with this structure is the forward rate agreement (FRA), where the counterparties agree on a strike rate K at maturity T_1 based on an underlying rate for an instrument maturing at T_2. The cash flow at time T_2 from the FRA is proportional to the FRA rate at maturity and the strike rate K:

$$\text{Cash Flow} = B(\text{FRA Rate}[T_1] - K)$$

where the coefficient B reflects the notional principal amount, the maturity of the underlying instrument, and the interest quotation method used for the FRA contract (i.e. actual/360 days, actual/365 days, etc.). In this section, we analyze the case where this interest differential is paid at the maturity of the underlying instrument, T_2. Conventional FRAs normally pay in an economically equivalent way, paying the present value of this interest rate differential at the maturity of the FRA contract, T_1.

We value the contract as if cash flowed at time T_1 by taking the simple present value of T_2 cash flow from the perspective of time T_1 (the standard

FRA convention):

$$\text{Present Value}\,[T_1] = P(\tau)B[\text{FRA Rate} - K]$$

$$= P(\tau)B\left[\frac{1}{P(\tau)} - 1 - K\right]$$

$$= B[1 - P(\tau)(1 + K)]$$

Using Jamshidian's formula and the approach in Chapter 24, we know the value of an existing FRA contract which pays at time T_2 is the present value of expected T_1 cash flow (present value), evaluated on the assumption that the short rate r has a mean equal to the instantaneous forward rate at time T_1:

$$V(r, t, T_1, T_2, K) = P(r, t, T_1)\int_{-\infty}^{\infty} B\left[1 - e^{-sF_r - G_r}(1 + K)\right]n(s, f_1, v)\,ds$$

$$= B[P(r, t, T_1) - (1 + K)P(r, t, T_2)]$$

$$= BP(r, t, T_2)\,[\text{Forward Rate} - K]$$

The value of an existing FRA contract which pays at the T_2 maturity of the underlying instrument is the present value (based on a T_2 maturity) of the difference between the forward rate and the strike price.

What will be the observable FRA quotation Q for a contract which pays at the maturity of the underlying instrument? For a newly quoted instrument the value must be zero and the strike price K will be equal to Q. Solving for Q gives:

$$Q(r, t, T_1, T_2) = \frac{P(r, t, T_1)}{P(r, t, T_2)} - 1 = \text{Forward Rate}$$

What if the rate differential between the FRA rate and K is paid on an undiscounted basis at time T_1? We answer that question in the next section.

Eurodollar futures-type forward contracts

What if the market convention regarding FRA payment was that the forward rate agreement pays its cash flow:

$$\text{Cash Flow} = B(\text{FRA Rate}\,[T_1] - K)$$

at the T_1 maturity of the FRA contract instead its present value at time T_1 or payment in cash at the T_2 maturity of the underlying instrument? An FRA that pays in this manner is essentially equivalent to a Eurodollar Futures contract with no mark-to-market margin (i.e. a Eurodollar futures-type forward). Such a Eurodollar futures-type forward, if modeled after the Chicago Mercantile Exchange Eurodollar futures contract, would pay $25 for every one basis point differential between the settlement yield on the futures-type forward and the strike price. Unlike the Sydney Futures Exchange Bank Bill future discussed earlier in this chapter, the dollar value of a basis point change in quoted yield is the same for all levels of interest rates under this type of contract. The cash flow at time T_1 under this kind of contract is:

$$\text{Cash Flow} = B\left(\frac{1}{P(\tau)} - 1 - K\right)$$

so we can use Jamshidian's formula to calculate the value of a Eurodollar futures-type forward contract with strike K:

$$V(r, t, T_1, T_2, K) = P(r, t, T_1) \int_{-\infty}^{\infty} B\left(\frac{1}{P(\tau)} - [1 + K]\right) n(s, f_1, v_1)\, ds$$

Again, using a key formula from Chapter 24 and simplifying gives:

$$V(r, t, T_1, T_2, K) = BP(r, t, T_1)\left[\left(\frac{P(r, t, T_1)}{P(r, t, T_2)}\right)e^{F_\tau^2 v_1^2} - (1 + K)\right]$$

$$= BP(r, t, T_1)\left[(\text{Forward Rate} + 1)\, e^{F_\tau^2 v_1^2} - (1 + K)\right]$$

The value of a true forward rate agreement in place at a strike price of K is the present value of the difference between an adjustment factor times one plus the forward rate less the sum of one plus the strike rate. This adjustment factor reflects the volatility of the short rate at time T_1 from the perspective of time t:

$$v_1^2 = \frac{\sigma^2}{2\alpha}\left[1 - e^{-2\alpha(T_1 - t)}\right]$$

If the volatility of interest rates σ is zero, then v_1 becomes zero and the Eurodollar futures-type forward becomes a simple present value times the difference between the forward rate and the strike price. We will see later also that a zero value for σ causes futures prices to equal forward prices. As long as interest rate volatility σ is not zero, however, a volatility adjustment is necessary for correct valuation of outstanding Eurodollar futures-type forwards.

What will be the market price of a Eurodollar futures-type forward that pays at its maturity T_1? As in the first and second sections of this chapter, the value of a new contract must be zero and its market price Q will equal the strike price of that contract. The quoted price of such a contract will be:

$$Q(r, t, T_1, T_2) = \left(\frac{P(r, t, T_1)}{P(r, t, T_2)} \right) e^{F_\tau^2 v_1^2} - 1$$

$$= [\text{Forward Rate} + 1] \, e^{F_\tau^2 v_1^2} - 1$$

The forward rate observable in the market equals one plus the forward rate, times a volatility adjustment factor, less one. When interest rate volatility is zero, the Eurodollar futures-type forward contract rate will equal the simple forward rate.

Futures on Zero-Coupon Bonds: The Sydney Futures Exchange Bank Bill Contract

From this point on in the chapter, we deal with true futures contracts. A 'true' futures contract has daily mark-to-market requirements, with cash flow on an existing contract occurring continuously through its life. Ending cash flow is essentially zero, since the full amount of the change in observable futures prices over the life of the contract will have already been paid in cash through the continuous mark-to-market requirements. We will ignore initial margin payments and the return of these initial payments since they represent a simple zero-coupon bond type adjustment to the formulas which follow.

Like the previous three sections, there is an important distinction between the market value of an existing futures position V and the observable market price of a futures contract Q. The first three sections showed the distinct differences between V and Q for three different types of forward contracts. In this section and the remainder of the chapter, we note the following:

The market value V of an existing futures position will always be zero since (a) the market price of a new futures contract must be zero to avoid arbi-trage and (b) a previously taken futures position is continuously made equivalent to a new position by continuous margin payments. The observ-able market price Q of the future contract and the initial strike rate K on the futures transaction, put in place at time t_0, are related by the fact that cash payments of at least $M = K - Q$, the cumulative net loss (gain) on the futures contract, must have been made to (withdrawn from) the margin account since initiation of the transaction at time t_0. The balance of the margin account is unknown since parties with a positive margin balance may use the cash proceeds for any purpose.

This important comment notwithstanding, a trader is always thinking about their gains or losses in terms of the original rate at which the futures contract was purchased K and the current market price Q. It is critical to note that this differential will have already impacted the financial institution's balance sheet (i.e. the cash account) and the trader's focus on the differential K−Q reflects only a partial view of the impact of the futures contract on the institution. Most sophisticated institutions are taking both views of the impact of a futures contract, the trader's view and the true daily cash flow pattern via the margin accounts.

These comments require a careful vocabulary to bridge the gap between the jargon of market participants and financial reality. To a market participant, the 'value of a futures contract' is $Q-K$, even though the margin account balance would be $\text{Max}\,(0, K-Q)$ rather than always being $Q-K$. These same market participants are rarely aware of the margin account balance, which is normally managed by an operational group. To a financial economist, the value is zero. Fortunately, the interest rate risk of a futures position to both groups is the change in Q that results from a change in interest rates, as captured by movements in the single stochastic factor r (given our assumption for expositional purposes that the Vasicek term structure model applies). Taking care to remember this distinction between viewpoints, we ignore the market value of an existing futures position V and concentrate on determining the observable market price Q.

For the remainder of this chapter, we deviate temporarily from the solution technique we used in Chapter 24 and the first half of this chapter and return to our 'trial and error' solution techniques used in Chapters 10 and 11. The reason, as noted by Chen [1992] is that 'trading in futures markets requires no initial investment'[3] and, moreover, that value V is always zero due to margin requirements. Therefore, when we derive the partial differential equation for the observable market price of a futures contract Q, the usual term rQ that results from the no-arbitrage condition is missing:

$$Q_r\alpha(\tilde{\mu} - r) + \frac{1}{2}\sigma^2 Q_{rr} + Q_t = 0$$

This equation represents the fundamental partial differential equation for the determination of the observable futures price. For every futures contract, the boundary condition at maturity requires that futures price at expiration equals the market price of the underlying instrument.

Returning to the Sydney Futures Exchange Bank Bill futures contract, the boundary condition requires that the observable market price of a futures

---

[3] See page 99 of Chen [1992].

contract at expiration T_1 equals the market price of a zero-coupon bond (a bank bill) with the maturity of the instrument underlying the futures contract:

$$Q(r, t, T_1, T_2) = P(r, T_1, T_2) = P(\tau)$$

We guess that the solution to the price of a Sydney Futures Exchange Bank Bill futures contract (zero-coupon bond futures contract) takes the form:

$$Q(r, t, T_1, T_2) = \left[\frac{P(r, t, T_2)}{P(r, t, T_1)}\right] e^{-Z} = e^{-r(F_2 - F_1) - (G_2 - G_1) - Z}$$

on the assumption that the forward bond price must be important to the solution. Solving for Z gives us the formula for a futures contract on a zero-coupon bond:

$$Q(r, t, T_1, T_2) = \left[\frac{P(r, t, T_2)}{P(r, t, T_1)}\right] e^{-(\sigma^2/2) F_\tau F_1^2}$$

$$= (\text{Forward Zero Coupon Bond Price}) \, e^{-(\sigma^2/2) F_\tau F_1^2}$$

The zero-coupon bond futures contract will have an observable market price equal to the forward zero-coupon bond price times an adjustment factor which depends on the volatility of interest rates σ and the interest rate sensitivity F_1 of a zero-coupon bond with maturity of T_1. If interest rate volatility σ is zero, the futures price will equal the forward price of a zero-coupon bond. Note also that the exponent of the adjustment factor contains the term σF_1, which is the instantaneous price variance of a zero-coupon bond with maturity T_1. As the contract nears maturity, this variance reduces to zero.

The interest rate risk of a position in the Sydney Futures Exchange Bank Bill futures contract, or any other zero-coupon bond futures contract, can be calculated using the usual term structure model "Greeks" for sensitivity analysis:

$$r\text{Delta} = \frac{\partial Q}{\partial r}$$

$$r\text{Gamma} = \frac{\partial^2 Q}{\partial r^2}$$

$$r\text{Theta} = \frac{\partial Q}{\partial t}$$

$$r\text{Vega} = \frac{\partial Q}{\partial \sigma}$$

$$r\text{Alpha} = \frac{\partial Q}{\partial \alpha}$$

Futures on Coupon-Bearing Bonds: Example Using the SIMEX Japanese Government Bond Future

Futures contracts on coupon-bearing bonds are a modest extension of the zero-coupon bond price futures formula. Let us consider the contract specifications of the original Singapore International Monetary Exchange's Japanese government bond (JGB) contract:

Notional Principal	¥ 50,000,000
Maturity	10 years
Coupon Rate	6%

In actual operation, there will be a number of JGB issues that are 'deliverable' under the Simex contract. The seller of the futures contract has a 'delivery option' which allows the seller of the futures contract to deliver the 'cheapest to deliver' bond if the seller of the futures contract chooses to hold the contract to maturity. If there are N deliverable bonds, the exchange will calculate a delivery factor F_i which specifies the ratio of the principal amount on the ith deliverable bond to the notional principal of ¥ 50,000,000 that is necessary to satisfy delivery requirements.

One of the bonds at any given time is the 'cheapest to deliver'. After multiplying the yen coupon amounts and yen principal amount on this bond times the delivery factor, we will have the j maturities and cash flow amounts underlying the bond future. The market price of the bond future (as long as only one bond is deliverable) is the sum of zero-coupon bond futures prices (assuming one yen of principal on each zero-coupon bond future) times these cash flow amounts C_i:

$$Q_{\text{Bond}}(t, T_0) = \sum_{i=1}^{j} Q(r, t, T_i)C_i$$

T_0 is the maturity date of the bond futures contract. The sensitivity analysis of bond futures, assuming only one bond is deliverable, is the sum of the sensitivities for the zero-coupon bond futures portfolio which replicates the cash flows on the bond.

What about the value of the delivery option? Let us assume that there are two deliverable bonds. Using the insights of Jamshidian's approach to coupon-bearing bond options valuation, we know that there will be a level of the short rate r, which we label $s*$, such that the two bonds are equally attractive to deliver as of time T_0. Above $s*$, bond one is cheaper to deliver. Below $s*$, bond two is cheaper to deliver. We can solve the partial differential equation for futures valuation subject to the boundary conditions that the futures price converges to bond one's deliverable value above $s*$ and to bond two's deliverable value below s^*. We also impose the condition that the first and second derivatives of the futures price are smooth at a short rate level of s^*. The result is a special weighted average of the futures prices that would have prevailed if each bond was the only deliverable bond under the futures contract. There are other options embedded in common U.S. and Japanese bond tracks that can be analyzed in a related way.

Eurodollar and Euroyen Futures Contracts

Money market futures have evolved to a fairly standard structure around the world. The SIMEX futures contracts in U.S. dollars, yen, and (before the advent of the Euro) Deutsche marks are all on three-month instruments with a constant currency amount paid at maturity per basis point change in the price of the contract. The per basis point value of rate changes under each contract is as follows:

U.S. Dollars	US$ 25.00
Yen	2,500 yen
Marks	25 marks

In each case, the futures price must be equal to the underlying three-month interest rates, multiplied by the notional principal amount and the appropriate day count factor to convert the rate to an annual basis. At maturity, the futures price (actually, the futures rate times notional principal) Q must meet this boundary condition:

$$Q(r, t, T_1, T_2) = B \left[\frac{1}{P(r, T_1, T_2)} - 1 \right]$$

B represents the notional principal and annualization factor, T_1 is the maturity of the futures contract in years, and T_2 is the maturity of the underlying three-month instrument so T_2 is roughly 0.25 greater than T_1.

The futures contract must satisfy the same partial differential equation as in the previous section:

$$Q_r \alpha(\tilde{\mu} - r) + \frac{1}{2} \sigma^2 Q_{rr} + Q_t = 0$$

The solution to this equation, subject to the boundary condition on the futures price at its maturity date, is:

$$Q(r, t, T_1, T_2) = B \left[\left(\frac{P(r, t, T_1)}{P(r, t, T_2)} \right) e^{-(\sigma^2/2\alpha^2)[(F_2 - F_1)(1 + \alpha F_2) - (F_t + \alpha F_t^2)]} - 1 \right]$$

The market price of the futures contract (ignoring the annualization factor and notional principal embedded in *B*) is one over the forward bond price, multiplied by an adjustment factor, minus one.

This formula reduces to the forward rate if interest rate volatility σ is zero. It shows that there are significant differences in the interest sensitivity of money market futures contracts which pay a constant currency amount per basis point and futures contracts on zero-coupon bonds. Interest rate sensitivity parameters are calculated in the same way as in the prior sections.

Defaultable Forward and Futures Contracts

Jarrow and Turnbull [1995] show that, in special circumstances, the adjustment made in the price of a defaultable instrument is a simple ratio times the value of the same instrument if it were not defaultable. Many market participants simulate future values and cash flows of financial forwards and futures on the implicit assumption that default will not occur. The realization that default of the futures exchange itself is a possibility, however, should not come as a surprise to anyone who is familiar with the high correlation in the default probabilities between major financial institutions that we discussed in the context of first to default swaps and collateralized debt obligations. How should this risk be analyzed?

Experience in the Asia crisis shows very clearly that major macro factors like interest rates and foreign exchange rates are highly correlated with the default probabilities and credit spreads of institutions in the affected countries and any other institutions dealing heavily in instruments of that country. Van Deventer and Imai [2003] give numerous examples of the former phenomenon, and the extensive losses of the Credit Suisse Group in trading Russian bonds in the late 1990s is a concrete example of the latter.

Since the macro factors impact forward prices, futures prices and the default probabilities of the counterparties dealing in the forwards and futures, the neat separation of the credit-adjusted value of futures and forwards that Jarrow and Turnbull found will not apply.

A careful monte carlo simulation like that specified in Chapter 23 is essential to recognizing the slim, but real possibility, of the default of the futures exchanges in times of crisis. A counterparty on a forward contract is more likely to be another financial institution or corporation. Depending on the credit model and term structure model specified, a closed form solution for this counterparty risk can potentially be obtained even recognizing, for example, that interest rates drive both the payoff on the forward contract and the default probability of the counterparty. Rather than doing this mathematical derivation, a carefully structured monte carlo simulation can capture the same effects. We return to this theme in Chapters 39–44 in detail.

Exercises

For purposes of the exercises that follow, assume that the parameters of the Vasicek term structure model are as follows:

alpha, speed of mean reversion:	0.05
sigma, interest rate volatility:	0.015
lambda, market price of risk:	0.01
mu, long-term expected value of r:	0.09
r, current short rate of interest:	0.06

25.1 What would be the observable market price for a forward contract on a zero-coupon bond whose maturity today is three years if the maturity of the forward contract is one year?

25.2 What would be the value of an existing forward contract on the bond in exercise 25.1 if the exercise price on the forward contract is 0.83?

25.3 What would be the quoted yield on the 90-day bank bill forward contact with one year to expiration if the terms of the contract were identical to the Sydney Futures Exchange's 90 Bank Bill future, except for the fact that the contract is a forward, rather than a future?

25.4 What would be the quoted yield on the 90-day bank bill contract in Exercise 25.3 if the contract was a futures contract, not a forward contract?

25.5 What would be the observable market price on a forward contract with one year to maturity on a six-month instrument where the cash payment in one year would be $25 per basis point differential between the forward rate at expiration and the forward rate at initiation of the contract?

25.6 What would be the observable market price of the contract in 24.5 if it was a futures contract instead of a forward contract?

25.7 What would be the observable market price on a forward rate agreement with the terms in Exercise 25.6?

25.8 What would be the observable market price for a bond futures contract with one year to maturity on an underlying instrument which has five years to maturity, a principal amount of $100,000, and an annual coupon of 8%?

25.9 [Advanced] Calculate analytical expression for the *rDeltas* for:
   a. A forward contract on a zero-coupon bond;
   b. A forward rate agreement;
   c. A forward contract like a forward rate agreement, except that the cash amount paid at the expiration of the contract is $25 per

basis point of rate differential, not the present value of the rate differential at the expiration of the underlying instrument;

d. A futures contract on a zero-coupon bond;

e. A futures contract which pays like the forward contract in 25.9c;

f. A bond futures contract with N semi-annual coupons of C and principal B.

25.10 [Advanced] Use your answers to Exercise 25.9 to solve the following hedging problem. An insurance company has a two-year security with quarterly interest payments in its portfolio. The principal amount is $10 million and the coupon level is 6%. The company will hedge the first one year of interest rate risk by issuing a one-year security with quarterly interest payments. The second year of interest rate risk exposure can be hedged using the following instruments, all of which have maturity dates identical to the payment dates on the two-year loan:

a. forward contracts on a three-month zero-coupon bond;

b. forward rate agreements on a three-month instrument paying on an actual/365 day basis;

c. forward contract which pays $25 per basis point at the maturity of the forward contract according to the rate differential between the original forward rate and the rate on the underlying three-month instrument;

d. futures contracts on three-month zero-coupon bonds;

e. a futures contract which pays like the forward contract in 25.10.c.

Assume that there is no credit risk either on the two-year security or the futures contracts. Assume also that forward and futures contracts come in any denomination.

How much of the one year security should be issued, in combination with the futures contracts, for zero interest rate risk (the answer is *not* the obvious answer). How many of each of the futures contracts (using solely one type of contract at a time) would be employed to complete the hedge?

CHAPTER 26

European Options on Forward and Futures Contracts

This chapter continues our analysis of standard instruments found on the balance sheet of large financial institutions as we continue with our objective of establishing a unified measure of interest rate and credit risk. In order to value the Jarrow-Merton put option proposed in Chapter 1 as the best measure of total risk, we need a methodology for valuation and for simulation of cash flows and values at many future dates. As in Chapter 25, we need this capability for European options on forward and futures contracts for three reasons:

- To understand correct hedging amounts from a shareholder value-added perspective, as discussed in the early chapters of this book;
- To meet the requirements of International Accounting Standard 39 and Financial Accounting Standard 133;
- To meet the requirements of the New Capital Accord of the Basel Committee of Banking Supervision.

This chapter combines the valuation formulas for futures and forwards from Chapter 25 and the options approach from Chapter 24. Readers who believe that we can derive analytical solutions based on Chapters 24–25 may wish to skip this chapter as the derivation is similar to that of the last two chapters. As in Chapters 24 and 25, we use the Vasicek model to illustrate how to derive valuation formulas for this important class of instruments, and then we discuss analyzing defaultable options on forwards and futures.

Valuing Options on Forwards and Futures: Notations and Useful Formulas

Valuing options on forward and futures contracts can be done analytically in three ways. Firstly, as in the original Black-Scholes article on stock options, one can specify a partial differential equation and appropriate boundary conditions and solve for the correct option pricing formula. Secondly, we can take advantage of the first Jamshidian general solution for security pricing under the Vasicek model, which we then use to find numerical solutions. We explain how to do this in later chapters. Thirdly, we can use the second Jamshidian valuation formula from Chapter 24 to obtain analytical solutions. Market participants generally prefer analytical solutions over numerical solutions because both the speed and the accuracy of the analytical solution are superior, assuming the underlying term structure model would be used in both the analytical and the numerical approach.

In this chapter, we take frequent advantages of the following notation, adapted from Chen [1992]:

$$F_i = F(t, T_i) = \frac{1}{\alpha} \left[1 - e^{-\alpha(T_i - t)} \right]$$

$$F_{ij} = F(T_i, T_j) = \frac{1}{\alpha} \left[1 - e^{-\alpha(T_j - T_i)} \right]$$

$$F_{ij} = \frac{F_i - F_j}{\alpha F_i - 1}$$

$$D = \mu + \frac{\sigma \lambda}{\alpha} - \frac{\sigma^2}{2\alpha^2} = \tilde{\mu} - \frac{\sigma^2}{2\alpha^2}$$

$$G_i = G(t, T_i) = D[T_i - t - F_i] + \frac{\sigma^2 F_i^2}{4\alpha}$$

$$G_{ij} = D[T_j - T_i - F_{ij}] + \frac{\sigma^2 F_{ij}^2}{4\alpha}$$

$$v_i = v(t, T_i) = \sqrt{\frac{\sigma^2}{2\alpha} \left(1 - e^{-2\alpha(T_i - t)} \right)}$$

$$v_{ij} = v(T_i, T_j) = \sqrt{\frac{\sigma^2}{2\alpha} \left(1 - e^{-2\alpha(T_j - T_i)} \right)}$$

$$P_i = P(r, t, T_i) = e^{-r F_i - G_i}$$

$$P_{ij} = P(r, T_i, T_j) = e^{-r F_{ij} - G_{ij}}$$

Otherwise, we will be using the same notation as in Chapters 24 and 25. We denote the forward rate from the perspective of current time t and maturity T_i as f_i. We know from Chapter 24 that:

$$-G_{ij} - f_i F_{ij} + \frac{F_{ij}^2 v_i^2}{2} = \ln\left[\frac{P(r, t, T_j)}{P(r, t, T_i)}\right]$$

Using this expression and an equation from Chapter 24 provides a useful formula we use later in valuing options on FRAs:

$$\int_{-\infty}^{\infty} P_{0i}\, n(s, f_0, v_0)\, ds = \frac{P_i}{P_0}$$

We can also derive a useful expression for the expected value of the ratio of two coupon bonds with maturities T_i and T_j, evaluated as of time T_0 on the assumption that the short rate r has a normal density function n with mean f_0 and standard deviation v_0:

$$\int_{-\infty}^{\infty} \frac{P(s, T_0, T_j)}{P(s, T_0, T_i)}\, n(s, f_0, v_0)\, ds = \frac{P(r, t, T_j)}{P(r, t, T_i)}\, e^{v_0^2(F_{0i}^2 - F_{0i}F_{0j})}$$

These powerful formulas are central to the results of this chapter.

European Options on Forward Contracts on Zero-Coupon Bonds

Let us consider a European call option on a forward contract with maturity T_1 on a zero-coupon bond with maturity T_2. We also assume that the maturity of the option is T_0. What is the value of the option if the exercise price is K and the current time is time t? We know from the Jamshidian formula in Chapter 24 that the value of the option is:

$$V(r, t, T_0, T_1, T_2, K) = P_0 \int_{-\infty}^{s^*} \left[\frac{P_{02}}{P_{01}} - K\right] n(s, f_0, v_0)\, ds$$

The constant s^* is the value of the short rate r at time T_0 at which the forward bond price exactly equals the strike price K:

$$s^* = -\left[\frac{\ln(K) + G_{02} - G_{01}}{F_{02} - F_{01}}\right]$$

The forward bond price will only be greater than K when r at time T_0 is less than s^*. Using the formulas in the previous section and a key valuation formula from Chapter 24, gives the solution to the value of a European call option on a forward zero-coupon bond contract:

$$V(r, t, T_0, T_1, T_2, K) = P_0 \left(\frac{P_2}{P_1} \right) e^{v_0 \left(F_{01}^2 - F_{01} F_{02} \right)} N \left(\frac{s^* - f_0}{v_0} + v_0 [F_{02} - F_{01}] \right)$$
$$- P_0 K N \left(\frac{s^* - f_0}{v_0} \right)$$

As mentioned in Chapter 24, this term structure model-based option on forward bonds provides two critical improvements over the Black constant interest rate extension of the Black-Scholes model to futures contracts: it recognizes that the volatility of the forward bond's price is declining over time, and it provides a full explanation of term structure movements which allows for 'delta hedging', via the *rDelta* calculation, of the option position with bonds of any maturity (since the Vasicek model we are using is a single factor model).

European Options on Forward Rate Agreements

In this section, we analyze the European option to buy a forward rate agreement at the FRA strike rate of K. We assume that the option expires at time T_0, the FRA matures at time T_1, and the underlying zero-coupon bond matures at time T_2. The cash flow on the option at time T_0 is the time T_0 value of the FRA, less K:

$$\text{Cash Flow} = BP_{02} \left[\left(\frac{P_{01}}{P_{02}} - 1 \right) - K \right]$$

where B is a factor which represents both underlying notional principal and the annualization factor (i.e. actual days/360, actual days/365) which goes into the FRA cash flow calculation. Simplifying the cash flow expression and applying the Jamshidian valuation formula from Chapter 24 provides the value of the option on the FRA:

$$V(r, t, T_0, T_1, T_2, K) = P_0 \int_{s^*}^{\infty} [B P_{01} - (1 + K) B P_{02}] \, n(s, f_0, v_0) \, ds$$

Using the equations in the first section of this chapter and noting that there are non-zero cash flows only when r at time T_0 is above s^* gives the option value:

$$V(r, t, T_0, T_1, T_2, K) = B\left[P_1 N\left(\frac{f_0 - s^*}{v_0} - v_0 F_{01} \right) \right.$$

$$\left. -(1 + K) P_2 N\left(\frac{f_0 - s^*}{v_0} - v_0 F_{02} \right) \right]$$

Like all of the other term structure model-based formulas of this book, the complete array of sensitivity parameters, including *rDelta* and *rGamma*, are available to market participants.

European Options on a Eurodollar Futures-type Forward Contract

In this section, we analyze an option based on the observable market price of a Eurodollar futures-type option which pays a constant currency amount per basis point at the maturity of the forward contract. The underlying forward contract is the forward contract counterpart to the terms for standard three-month U.S. Dollar, yen and Euro futures contracts. We let the factor B represent both notional principal and an annualization factor. The time T_0 cash flow will be non-zero only if the short rate r at time T_0 is above a critical level s^*.

Let us consider an option whose cash flow is proportional to the difference between the forward contract rate and the strike price K on the exercise date K. The cash flow at time T_0, using the formula for Eurodollar futures-type forwards from Chapter 25, is:

$$\text{Cash Flow} = B\left[\left(\frac{P_{01}}{P_{02}} e^{F_{12}^2 v_{01}^2} - 1 \right) - K \right]$$

if the short rate at time T_0 is greater than a critical level s^*. This critical level is the short rate level at which the Eurodollar futures-type forward rate just equals the strike rate K. The rate s^* is implied by the equality of the forward rate and K:

$$\frac{P_{01}}{P_{02}} e^{F_{12}^2 v_{01}^2} - 1 = K$$

The level of s^* for which this is true is:

$$s^* = -\left[\frac{\ln(1+K) + G_{01} - G_{02} - F_{12}^2 v_{01}^2}{F_{01} - F_{02}}\right]$$

Using the Jamshidian formula and the relationships in the first section of this chapter leads to the solution:

$$V(r, t, T_0, T_1, T_2, K) = P_0 \int_{s^*}^{\infty} \left(\frac{P_{01}}{P_{02}} e^{F_{12}^2 v_{01}^2} - 1 - K\right) n(s, f_0, v_0)\, ds$$

This expression, like the other formulas in this chapter, can be rearranged to closely resemble the Black-Scholes options formula:

$$V(r, t, T_0, T_1, T_2, K) = P_0 \frac{P_1}{P_2} e^{F_{12}^2 v_{01}^2 + v_0^2(F_{02}^2 - F_{01}F_{02})} N\left(\frac{f_0 - s^*}{v_0} - v_0(F_{01} - F_{02})\right)$$
$$- P_0(1 + K)N\left(\frac{f_0 - s^*}{v_0}\right)$$

European Options on Futures on Zero-Coupon Bonds

Chen [1992] provides the solution for the valuation of options on zero-coupon bond futures like the Sydney Futures Exchange Bank Bill futures contract. The cash flow on such an option is:

$$\text{Cash Flow} = \frac{P_{02}}{P_{01}} e^{-(\sigma^2/2)F_{12}F_{01}^2} - K$$

where the left hand side of this expression is the value of the underlying futures contract as of time T_0. This cash flow occurs as long as the short rate r at time T_0 is less than a critical level s^*, at which the value of the futures contract at time T_0 exactly equals K. This occurs where:

$$-s^*(F_{02} - F_{01}) - (G_{02} - G_{01}) - \frac{\sigma^2}{2} F_{12} F_{01}^2 = \ln(K)$$

$$s^* = -\left[\frac{\ln(K) + G_{02} - G_{01} + (\sigma^2/2)F_{12}F_{01}^2}{F_{02} - F_{01}}\right]$$

or:

$$V(r, t, T_0, T_1, T_2, K) = P_0 \int\limits_{-\infty}^{s^*} \left(\frac{P_{02}}{P_{01}} e^{-(\sigma^2/2)F_{12}F_{01}^2} - K \right) n(s, f_0, v_0) \, ds$$

The value of the option fits the Jamshidian formulation.

Evaluating this integral using the same approach as previous sections leads to the option value:

$$V(r, t, T_0, T_1, T_2, K) = P_0 \frac{P_2}{P_1} e^{v_0^2(F_{01}^2 - F_{01}F_{02}) - (\sigma^2/2)F_{12}F_{01}^2}$$

$$N\left(\frac{s^* - f_0}{v_0} + v_0(F_{02} - F_{01}) \right) - P_0 K N\left(\frac{s^* - f_0}{v_0} \right)$$

This expression can be rearranged to show the relationship between the option and the futures price, as in Chen:

$$V(r, t, T_0, T_1, T_2, K) = P_0 \frac{P_2}{P_1} e^{(\sigma^2/2)F_0^2(F_{02} - F_{01}) - (\sigma^2/2)F_{12}F_1^2}$$

$$N\left(\frac{s^* - f_0}{v_0} + v_0(F_{02} - F_{01}) \right) - P_0 K N\left(\frac{s^* - f_0}{v_0} \right)$$

$$= P_0[\text{Futures Price}] \, e^{(\sigma^2/2)F_0^2(F_{02} - F_{01})}$$

$$N\left(\frac{s^* - f_0}{v_0} + v_0(F_{02} - F_{01}) \right) - P_0 K N\left(\frac{s^* - f_0}{v_0} \right)$$

All the usual term structure model sensitivity calculations, including rDelta and rGamma, can be done on these expressions, although one should take care to note that the forward rate prevailing at time t for maturity at time T_0, which we write as f_0, is a function of the short rate r.

European Options on Futures on Coupon-Bearing Bonds

As noted in Chapter 25, a future on a coupon-bearing bond can be analyzed as a collection of futures contracts on zero-coupon bonds. Similarly, a European option on a coupon-bearing bond futures contract can be analyzed using the Jamshidian approach to options on coupon-bearing bond options, discussed in Chapter 24. Actual bond futures contracts have embedded in them other options, such as the 'delivery option', discussed in Chapter 25.

Even with these complications, the approach of this chapter can be taken to provide a surprisingly tractable analytical answer for European option values without the need to resort unnecessarily to numerical solutions that introduce approximation error for reasons due to computer science, not due to financial theory. For more information on this approach, please contact the authors. American options require numerical techniques, which we discuss in later chapters.

Options on Eurodollar, Euroyen and Euromark Futures Contracts

From Chapter 25, we know that the observable market price at time T_0 of a money market futures contract maturing at time T_1 on an underlying instrument maturing at time T_2 and paying a constant currency amount per basis point of rate change will be:

$$Q(r, T_0, T_1, T_2) = B \left[\frac{P_{01}}{P_{02}} e^{-(\sigma^2/2\alpha^2)[(F_{02}-F_{01})(1+\alpha F_{02})-(F_{12}+\alpha F_{12}^2)]} - 1 \right]$$

if the notional principal is \$1. We analyze the case of a call option on a futures contract like the U.S. Dollar LIBOR futures contract traded in Chicago. Although almost all market participants concentrate on the futures rate, say 12%, the contract is actually quoted on the basis of an index, defined as:

$$\text{Index} = 100 - \text{Futures Rate}$$

A 'call option' to buy the index at 90 will pay the buyer of the call the index value at maturity (say 92, corresponding to a rate of 8%) less the strike price (90) times the notional principal amount consistent with the futures contract. Under this call option, the buyer receives payment when the futures rate falls (index rises) below (above) his exercise rate (exercise index level). Therefore the cash payoff on this call option is:

$$\text{Cash Flow} = K - Q(r, T_0, T_1, T_2)$$

for r below a critical level s^*, defined as the level of r at T_0 where the futures rate just equals the strike rate K. The critical level s^* is:

$$s^* = - \left[\left(\ln(1+K) + (G_{01} - G_{02}) \right. \right.$$
$$\left. \left. + \frac{\sigma^2}{2\alpha^2} \left[(F_{02} - F_{01})(1 + \alpha F_{02}) + (F_{12} + \alpha F_{12}^2) \right] \right) \middle/ (F_{01} - F_{02}) \right]$$

The value of this European call option is:

$$V(r, t, T_0, T_1, T_2, K)$$

$$= -BP_0 \frac{P_1}{P_2} e^{-(\sigma^2/2\alpha^2)[(F_{02}-F_{01})(1+\alpha F_{02})-(F_{12}+\alpha F_{12}^2)]+v_0^2(F_{02}^2-F_{01}F_{02})}$$

$$N\left(\frac{s^* - f_0}{v_0} - v_0(F_{01} - F_{02})\right)$$

$$+ P_0 B(1 + K)N\left(\frac{s^* - f_0}{v_0}\right)$$

Defaultable Options on Forward and Futures Contracts

As we noted in Chapter 25, Jarrow and Turnbull [1995] show that, in special circumstances, the adjustment made to the price of a defaultable instrument is a simple ratio times the value of the same instrument if it was not defaultable. Can we analyze the possibility of a default on the options in this chapter in the same way?

As we noted in Chapter 25, the answer is no. Since the macro factors impact options prices, forward prices, futures prices and the default probabilities of the counterparties dealing in the forwards and futures, the neat separation of the credit-adjusted value of futures and forwards that Jarrow and Turnbull found for simpler instruments will not generally apply. This doesn't mean that this approach can't be used as a first approximation, but it will significantly understate risk. As J.P. Morgan found out in 1998 in a well-known incident with S.K. Securities of Korea, the default probability of the counterparty can be dangerously correlated with the amount of money they owe you.[1] This is because the same macro factor drives both the legally required payoff on the security at hand and it drives the default probability of the counterparty. A true credit-adjusted valuation requires the kind of 'scenario specific' default probabilities that are embedded in the rich flexibility of the reduced form models discussed in detail in Chapter 17.

How do we simulate future values and cash flows on options on futures and forwards in a true default-adjusted fashion? Again, a careful monte carlo simulation like that specified in Chapter 23 is essential to recognizing the slim, but real, possibility of the default of the futures Exchanges in times of crisis.

---

[1] See van Deventer and Imai [2003] for a detailed discussion of this incident.

Similarly, the default of our counterparty on an over-the-counter option on futures and forwards could be analyzed analytically or numerically. As suggested in the previous chapter, rather than doing this mathematical derivation, a carefully structured monte carlo simulation can capture the same effects. This is the principal topic in Chapters 39–44.

Exercises

For purposes of the exercises that follow, assume that the parameters of the Vasicek term structure model are as follows:

alpha, speed of mean reversion:	0.05
sigma, interest rate volatility:	0.015
lambda, market price of risk:	0.01
mu, long-term expected value of r:	0.09
r, current short rate of interest:	0.06

26.1 What is the value of a one-year European option to buy a forward contract with two years remaining on a three-year zero-coupon bond, if the exercise price on the option is 0.90?

26.2 What is the value of a European put option on the same forward contract at the same exercise price and same maturity for the option?

26.3 What is the value of a one-year option to exercise a forward rate agreement with a two-year maturity on an underlying instrument which will have a three-month maturity at the maturity of the FRA, if the strike FRA rate on the option is 6%?

26.4 What is the value of the same option if the underlying two-year contract pays $25 per basis point for every basis point that the forward contract closes above the 6% strike rate at the maturity of the forward contract?

26.5 What is the value of a one-year option to buy a two-year futures contract on a zero-coupon bond which currently has three years to maturity at a strike price of 0.95?

26.6 What is the value of a one-year call option to buy the U.S. Dollar three-month LIBOR Eurodollar futures contract with a two-year maturity at an index rate of 91 (futures interest rate of 9%)?

CHAPTER 27

Caps and Floors[1]

Introduction to Caps and Floors

We are making step-by-step progress in valuing the financial instruments that might be found on the balance sheet of a major financial institution. To reiterate, our ultimate objective is the full valuation of the Jarrow-Merton put option on the balance sheet of the financial institution as the best measure of integrated credit risk and interest rate risk. The Jarrow-Merton put option is also an excellent basis for capital allocation, which is discussed in Chapters 39–44. In this chapter we turn to interest rate caps and floors using the tools from Chapter 26 extensively.

Interest rate caps and floors have become perhaps the most popular interest rate option-based instrument. They provide an invaluable tool for financial managers interested in controlling their exposure to extremely high or extremely low interest rates. They also provide an excellent basis for the estimation of term structure model parameters as we discussed in Chapter 13. Common uses of caps and floors include the following examples:

- Limiting the maximum rate paid on a floating-rate loan by purchasing a cap;
- Limiting the exposure to an effective floor[2] on non-maturity consumer deposit rates paid by the bank by purchasing a floor in the open market;
- Hedging the prepayment risk on a mortgage portfolio;
- Hedging the cancellation risk on a portfolio of life insurance policies;

---

[1] This chapter is an updated version of Chapter 9, van Deventer and Imai [1996].

[2] For many years, U.S. bankers felt that there was an interest rate floor on consumer savings deposits, a rate below which savings deposit rates could not go. Now that we have extensive experience with extremely low interest rates in Japan, it is apparent that this floor is effectively zero. What many initially thought was a floor was more likely the lagged response of consumer savings deposit rates to changing market rates. See Chapter 33 for more on this issue.

- Insuring that the performance of a fixed income portfolio can only improve as rates rise.

The purchaser of a cap effectively purchases an insurance policy against interest rate increases. Let us consider a hedger who has a floating-rate loan tied to three-month U.S. dollar LIBOR. By purchasing a 10% cap, the hedger insures that they will never pay more than 10% on the loan after subtracting payments from the seller of the cap. If rates rise to 12%, the hedger pays 12% on the loan, but receives 2% from the person who sold the cap, for a net expense of 10%.

Caps and floors are both traded outright and embedded in common banking and insurance industry assets and liabilities. A number of market conventions deserve mention here. Firstly, payment for the cap or floor typically takes place at time zero when the contract is traded outright. Embedded in a loan or deposit, the cap or floor price would be disguised as an interest rate differential relative to the identical loan or deposit with no cap or floor. Secondly, the cap or floor strike rate is stated on the same basis as the underlying interest rate. For example, the buyer of the LIBOR cap above is quoted a strike rate of 10% versus LIBOR. Both LIBOR and the cap strike rate interest amounts are calculated on an actual/360 day basis. In other markets, actual/365 days calculations are common. Both the LIBOR rate and the cap or floor rate will normally be set from the same reference point (the same 'screen' provided by a vendor of real time information, such as Reuters, Telerate, or Bloomberg) and use the same method for counting business days and the same holiday convention.

We abstract from these market conventions in this chapter to ease exposition. For purposes of this chapter, a strike rate quoted as 10% for a LIBOR cap on for a 91-day period would be converted to a decimal strike rate K using the following: formula:

$$K = 0.10 \frac{91}{360}$$

In applying the formulas below, the strike rate should be converted to this 'K format' to allow us to abstract from day count and accrual methods in what follows.

Another important market convention is the use of Black's [1976] futures model for the quotation of caps and floors prices that we have mentioned often in previous chapters. The Black-Scholes [1973] option model was perhaps the biggest innovation in financial theory in the twentieth century, but its well-justified popularity should not obscure the reasons cited in Chapter 24 for using a term structure model approach instead to model interest rate derivatives. Hull [1993] presents a very lucid explanation of the use of the Black [1976] approximation to cap and floor valuation and the reasons why a term structure model approach works better, the popular 'LIBOR market' term structure model not withstanding.

A commonly asked question is this: If most of the traders in the market are using the Black model, won't I be making a mistake by using something else? The short answer is an emphatic 'no'. We showed in Chapter 13 that the term structure model approach fits actual quoted prices better than the Black model, which has to considerably 'bend' to fit observable prices. We also show in Chapter 34 that the term structure model approach fits observable foreign exchange options data better than the conventional modification of the Black-Scholes model for the foreign exchange market. Finally, the true test of a model is the one which provides the best hedge. We can do this using the techniques applied to credit model hedging in van Deventer and Imai [2003]. As we've noted in Chapter 24, the Black-Scholes model assumes constant interest rates and we have to do a two-stage analysis that incorporates term structure model analytics after the fact to find a hedge. We think it's better to do this from the outset, and that's confirmed by the data in Chapter 13. The market convention of quoting caps and floors prices in terms of Black-Scholes volatilities means market participants have to convert that quotation into an up-front dollar price for analysis, valuation and hedging, but that is true even for traders who still rely solely on the Black model for their analytics.

At this point, we take advantage of our work in previous chapters to illustrate cap and floor pricing under a term structure model approach.

Caps as European Options on Forward Rate Agreements

In Chapter 26, we analyzed the European option to buy a forward rate agreement at the FRA strike rate of K. We assumed in Chapter 26 that the option expires at time T_0, the FRA matures at time T_1, and the underlying zero-coupon bond matures at time T_2. The cash flow on the option at time T_0 is the time T_0 value of the FRA, less K:

$$\text{Cash Flow} = BP_{02}\left[\left(\frac{P_{01}}{P_{02}} - 1\right) - K\right]$$

where B is a factor which represents both underlying notional principal and the annualization factor (i.e. actual days/360, actual days/365) which goes into the FRA cash flow calculation. Cash flow will be positive if r at time T_0 exceeds the critical level $s*$

$$s* = -\left[\frac{\ln(1 + K) + G_{01} - G_{02}}{F_{01} - F_{02}}\right]$$

The value of an option on the FRA was given in Chapter 26 as:

$$V\,(r, t, T_0, T_1, T_2, K)$$

$$= B\left[P_1 N\left(\frac{f_0 - s^*}{v_0} - v_0 F_{01}\right) - (1 + K)\,P_2 N\left(\frac{f_0 - s^*}{v_0} - v_0 F_{02}\right)\right]$$

Looking at the cash flows for an option on an FRA shows that a cap is really just a special case of an option on an FRA, where the exercise date of the option on the FRA (T_0 in Chapter 26) is the same as the expiration date of the FRA, T_1. We make this change to the valuation formula for an option on an FRA. All subscripts of zero become one, and we note that F_{11} and G_{11} are both zero. The value of a 'caplet' which matures at time T_1 and with a cap at the rate K (subject to the qualifications mentioned in the previous section) on an interest rate derived from an underlying instrument maturing at time T_2 is:

$$V\,(r, T_1, T_2, K) = B\left[P_1 N\left(\frac{f_1 - s^*}{v_1}\right) - (1 + K)\,P_2 N\left(\frac{f_1 - s^*}{v_1} - v_1 F_{12}\right)\right]$$

$$s^* = \frac{\ln(1 + K) - G_{12}}{F_{12}}$$

B is notional principal, and:

$$P_i = P(r, t, T_i)$$

This formula is also identical to the put option formula for zero-coupon bonds in Chapter 24. It represents a put on $1 + K$ units of a zero-coupon bond with maturity T_2 and a strike price of one at time T_1 on the sum of those $1 + K$ units.

Forming Other Cap-Related Securities

A wide variety of cap and floor derivatives can be constructed with this basic building block as a tool:

- Floor prices are calculated in an equivalent way using the formula for a call option on a zero-coupon bond in Chapter 24.
- Longer-term caps are constructed as the sum of a number of caplets.

- Longer-term floors are constructed as the sum of a number of floorlets.
- Collars represent a combination of caps and floors (typically purchasing a cap and selling a floor).
- Costless collars are created by finding the floor rate K_f, such that the value of the floor exactly equals the value of the cap with cap rate K_c (or vice versa).

Measuring the Credit Risk of Counterparties on Caps and Floors

All of our comments in Chapters 24–26 regarding the valuation of 'vulnerable' caps and floors apply here as well. Since the default probability of our counterparty on the cap or floor is very likely to be driven by interest rate levels, the credit risk-adjusted valuation of caps and floors will involve either a complex closed form solution in a reduced form model or (more likely) the equivalent monte carlo simulation with explicit interest rate drivers of our counterparties' default probabilities, like that in the Kamakura Risk Manager enterprise risk management software suite offered by Kamakura Corporation. Clearly, a 10-year cap on interest rates purchased from a soon-to-be bankrupt savings and loan association (driven into bankruptcy by high interest rates in the U.S.) is much less valuable than the same cap on U.S. interest rates provided by Swiss bank UBS AG or Dutch bank ABN-Amro since their exposure to U.S. interest rate risk is so much less than a savings and loan association in the late 1970s, just prior to the worst spike in interest rates in U.S. history.

Best practice requires that we take this into account in order to avoid the $1 trillion in losses that U.S. tax-payers suffered from failed financial institutions. The FDIC Loss Distribution Model announced on December 10 2003 (and discussed frequently in this book) does exactly this.

Exercises

For purposes of the exercises that follow, assume that the parameters of the Vasicek term structure model are as follows:

alpha, speed of mean reversion:	0.05
sigma, interest rate volatility:	0.015
lambda, market price of risk:	0.01
mu, long-term expected value of r:	0.09
r, current short rate of interest:	0.06

Assume that three-month periods are exactly 0.25 years long and that LIBOR is quoted on an actual/365 day basis (instead of market practice of actual/360).

27.1 What are the values of each of the eight caplets that make up the value of a two-year cap on three-month LIBOR at 10% (note: $K = 0.025$)?

27.2 What is the value of the two-year cap?

27.3 What are the values of each of the eight floorlets that make up the value of a floor on three-month LIBOR at 6% (note: $K = 0.015$)?

27.4 What is the value of the two-year floor?

27.5 What is the value of a two-year collar on three-month LIBOR with a cap at 10% and a floor at 6%?

27.6 What is the *rDelta* of each caplet?

27.7 What is the *rDelta* of the two-year cap?

27.8 What is the *rDelta* of each floorlet?

27.9 What is the *rDelta* of the two-year floor?

27.10 What is the *rDelta* of the two-year collar?

27.11 You are the derivative trader for caps and floors at Golden, Spats & Co., a major Newark dealer. You have been ordered to hedge your position in the two-year collar with zero-coupon bonds (you sold the collar to an industrial company Placem & Gamble). All quarterly maturities are available out to two years with good liquidity. What should be your position in each zero-coupon bond? Assume you believe one-factor term structure models are a good approximation to reality but that it's safer to 'match maturities' whenever possible to get the best fit, even if the term structure model turns out to be less than perfect.

Interest Rate Swaps and Swaptions

CHAPTER **28**

Introduction to Interest Rate Swaps

Interest rate swaps have become the most successful over-the-counter derivative security in the world, and for this reason it is particularly important that we include their credit-adjusted valuation in this book. This is true even when our counterparties offer transactions through an AAA-rated special purposes vehicle, because the default probabilities of the major U.S. financial institutions are highly correlated, as are credit spreads. The credit spreads on two bonds issued by Merrill Lynch and Goldman Sachs recently were shown to have a correlation of 95% when using the precise credit spread smoothing process discussed in Chapter 18.[1] This means that a guarantee by Bank A of an investment bank's special purpose vehicle has much less value than a guarantee by another entity with a much lower correlation in default probabilities and events of default, as we discussed in the context of first to default swaps in Chapter 23.

Valuation and simulation of interest rate swaps and swaptions is also critical to meet the accounting requirements for hedges under International Accounting Standard 39 and Financial Accounting Standard 133.

The most common plain vanilla interest rate swap between two counterparties calls for counterparty A to make fixed-rate payments at even intervals (normally semi-annual) to counterparty B and for counterparty B to make floating-rate payments, typically at three-month or six-month intervals, to counterparty A. Seen from the perspective of counterparty A, the swap has the same net cash flow as if counterparty A issued a fixed-rate bond and purchased a floating-rate bond (except in the case of default, where the principal amount is relevant in the bond case but not in the swap case). From the perspective of counterparty B, the swap cash flows are identical to the case where counterparty B purchases a fixed-rate bond with the proceeds of a floating-rate bond issue (again, except in the base of default).

---

[1] Source: Kamakura Corporation internal memorandum, April 2004.

471

Why are interest rate swaps so popular? The primary reasons include the vast liquidity of the swap markets in the major currencies, the low issuance costs compared to traditional bonds even under a medium-term note program or shelf registration, the ease of reversing a position with an offsetting transaction, and the lack of daily mark-to-market margin requirements for swap market participants of good quality. Operationally, a swap is much less work than a similar position in interest rate futures with the daily mark-to-market requirements.

Most market participants value swaps as if both the fixed and the floating side involved principal payments at maturity. Since the amounts net to zero, this is a good approximation when both parties have zero credit risk. As the credit risk of each party diverges from zero, this becomes a more dangerous assumption, so we won't use it in this chapter.

Valuing the Floating-Rate Payments on a Swap

In Chapter 7, we valued various floating-rate securities on the assumption that principal became due at maturity. In this section, we value the floating-rate payments only and ignore the ending principal payments. Consider the value at an interest rate reset date T_0 of interest paid at the current market levels on an underlying bond with maturity at T_1. The present value of this interest payment as of time T_0 is:

$$\text{Present Value} = P_{01}\left(\frac{1}{P_{01}} - 1\right) = 1 - P_{01}$$

Using the Jamshidian valuation formula in Chapter 24 and the related valuation equation, gives us the value of the interest rate payment as of the current time t:

$$V(r, t, T_0, T_1) = P_0 \int_{-\infty}^{\infty} (1 - P_{01})\, n(s, f_0, v_0)\, ds = P_0 - P_1$$

If in the future, we will receive N floating-rate payments at dates $T_1, \ldots, T_N$, priced on reset dates $T_0, T_1, \ldots, T_{N-1}$, the stream of floating-rate payments will be worth:

$$V(r, t, T_0, T_N) = \sum_{i=1}^{N} V(r, t, T_{i-1}, T_i) = \sum_{i=1}^{N} (P_{i-1} - P_i) = P_0 - P_N$$

The value of floating-rate payments at market levels equals the difference between values of a zero-coupon bond maturing at the first reset date and one maturing on the last payment date. If the current time t is the first reset date:

$$V(r, t, T_0, T_N) = 1 - P_N$$

If we had analyzed the problem as a floating-rate bond with principal paid at time T_N, the present value of principal would be P_N and the sum of the principal and interest portions would be par value, or one. If the first coupon has already been set (on a previous reset date) to a currency amount C_0 and there is a spread over the pricing index with a constant currency amount s, the value of the floating-rate payments consistent with Chapter 7 is:

$$V(r, t, T_0, T_N, s, C_0) = P_0 C_0 + P_0 - P_N + s \sum_{i=1}^{N} P_i$$

The Observable Fixed Rate in the Swap Market

A fixed-rate swap normally pays a fixed currency amount C at each payment date. The present value of this payment on M payment dates is taken directly from Chapter 7:

$$\text{Value}(r, t, T_1, T_M) = C \sum_{i=1}^{M} P_i$$

How could we calculate the market value on a swap if for some reason we could not observe it on dealing screens? Aside from the bid-offered spread, the market value of a new swap should be zero. Therefore the market level of the fixed-rate payment C will be the level C such that the present value of the fixed-rate payments exactly equals the present value of the floating-rate payments:

$$C \sum_{i=1}^{M} P_i = 1 - P_N$$

If T_N and T_M are the same dates, the equation above effectively requires that C be set at the level such that the present value of a bond with coupon C equals par value:

$$C \sum_{i=1}^{N} P_i + P_N = 1$$

An Introduction to Swaptions

A swaption is an agreement between two counterparties which allows counterparty A to enter into an interest rate swap with a pre-agreed fixed-rate payment C at the option of counterparty A. Swaptions come in two forms. The 'constant maturity' form of swaption prescribes that the interest rate swap has a set maturity, say five years, regardless of when the swaption was exercised. For example, if the exercise period on the swaption is two years, the underlying swap would end up being a five- year swap regardless of whether the swaption was entered into after three months, 12 months or two years. The 'fixed maturity date' swaption prescribes a maturity date for the swap at the signing date of the contract, and therefore the effective maturity of the swap will shorten if exercise is delayed. Consider a three-year swaption of the fixed maturity type on a swap with an original maturity of 10 years. If the swaption is exercised after two years, the swap that is entered into will have an eight-year life.

Both forms are common. If the swaption is a European swaption, the two methods are equivalent.

Valuation of European Swaptions

The valuation of European swaptions is a direct application of Jamshidian's formula for options on coupon-bearing bonds. As shown previously in this chapter, the market value of a new swap must be such that the fixed-rate on the swap would cause a coupon-bearing bond with the same payment frequency and maturity date[2] to trade at par. This means we can ignore the floating-rate side of the swap for purposes of valuation.[3] Therefore a swaption that allows the holder to receive the fixed-rate side of the swap is a call option to buy the equivalent underlying bond. A swaption which allows the holder to pay the fixed-rate side of the swap is a put option on the equivalent underlying bond. Having made this translation, the formula is identical to that of Chapter 24's options on coupon-bearing bonds.

Valuation of American Swaptions

Because of the intervening cash flows on swaps, there is the possibility of early exercise on an American swaption and therefore the European swaption valuation approach is only a rough approximation to the value of an American swaption. Correct valuation requires the numerical methods we analyze in Chapter 30.

---

[2] And for purposes of this chapter, credit risk.
[3] We could not ignore the floating side if the floating side involved a non-zero spread from the pricing index.

Defaultable Interest Rate Swaps and Swaptions

As discussed in the introduction of this chapter, even the existence of AAA-rated special purpose vehicles does not insulate a financial market participant from the risk of default by a counterparty on an interest rate swap or swaption. As van Deventer and Imai [2003] demonstrate with numerous examples from the Asia crisis that began on July 2 1997, interest rates drive default probabilities of most major corporations and financial institutions.[4]

Therefore we need to take the same approach as that discussed in Chapters 24–27, using monte carlo simulation of interest rate-driven default probabilities to measure the valuation and future distribution of values and cash flows on a credit-adjusted basis.

Exercises

For purposes of the exercises that follow, assume that the parameters of the Vasicek term structure model are as follows:

alpha, speed of mean reversion:	0.05
sigma, interest rate volatility:	0.015
lambda, market price of risk:	0.01
mu, long-term expected value of r:	0.09
r, current short rate of interest:	0.06

28.1 What is the present value of an existing $100 million swap with three years and three months to maturity, semi-annual LIBOR payments, a spread to LIBOR of zero, a fixed rate of 8%, and current floating-rate coupon of 6.5% (use actual/365 day interest for simplicity)? Assume you pay fixed rate and receive floating.

28.2 What is the *rDelta* of this swap position?

28.3 If you were going to hedge the interest rate risk of this swap with a position in two-year zero-coupon bonds, what should the size and direction (long or short) of the two-year zero-coupon bond position be?

28.4 How much would you pay for the right, two years from today, to enter into a five-year swap with semi-annual payments, a fixed rate of 7%, and a notional principal of $50 million. Assume the floating-rate side is LIBOR 'flat'.

28.5 What would the value of the same swaption be if the exercise period was one year, three years, four years, and five years? Which European

---

[4] Statistical evidence in this regard is available to clients of Kamakura Risk Information Services default probability service in the KRIS Technical Guide, Version 3.0, 2004.

swaption price would best approximate the value of an American swaption which allowed you to enter into the five-year 7% swap at any time in the next five years?

28.6 What is the *rDelta* of the swap in 28.4?

28.7 Assume that 10 seconds ago you bought the swaption giving you the right to pay fixed on the 7% five-year swap two years from now. Five seconds ago, your boss, anticipating adverse market movements, ordered all open trading positions hedged immediately. Your only outlet is a bond broker offering a two-way price in a four-year zero-coupon bond. What should you do? Assume immediate resignation is not an option since bonuses are paid next month.

CHAPTER 29

Exotic Swap and Option Structures[1]

Introduction to Exotic Swaps and Options

A difference of opinion makes a market, and that is the major rationale for the development of the market in exotic swaps and exotic options. A second and less happy rationale is the willingness of some market participants to buy and sell securities without much knowledge of their true value. In our quest for an integrated measure of interest rate risk and credit risk, we need to be able to handle these exotic structures as they will be found on the balance sheet of many institutions both on the buy side and the sell side. At the same time, two of the authors are ex-investment bankers. We recognize the endless quest of investment bankers to invent structures that they can value more accurately than their clients. The real purpose of this chapter is not only to value specific structures but to show that this approach is general enough to apply to new structures as they emerge.

In the first sections of this chapter we show how the techniques of Chapters 24–28 can be used to value securities that, at least at one point in their life, were considered 'exotic'. Exotic means both 'strange' and 'difficult to value', and it is the latter that often motivates the originators of exotic structures. The examples in this chapter are taken from actual deals found in the swap portfolio of some major U.S. Government-guaranteed agencies.

At the end of the chapter, we discuss how to incorporate the potential default of our counterparty so that we can incorporate these kinds of transactions in our valuation of the Jarrow-Merton put option as a comprehensive risk measure. We will return to this discussion in detail in Chapters 39–44.

Arrears Swaps

In most interest rate swaps, the floating-rate payment is based on LIBOR in the relevant currency. If the swap calls for six-month LIBOR, the LIBOR rate

---

[1] This chapter is a modified version of Chapter 11, van Deventer and Imai [1996].

is set on a reference date approximately six months before the cash interest payment will normally be made. In an arrears swap, the LIBOR rate and payment amount will be made 'in arrears', that is, shortly before the cash payment must be made. How do we value this kind of swap?

We start by analyzing the value of one arrears payment. We want the value at current time t of an arrears swap where the payment is determined and made at time T_0 based on a reference rate derived from a zero-coupon bond with a maturity at time T_1. The cash flow at time T_0 is:

$$\text{Cash Flow} = \frac{1}{P_{01}} - 1$$

if we assume a notional principal of \$1.

The value at current time t of a security that pays this amount at time T_0 comes from the general Jamshidian valuation formula:

$$V(r, t, T_0, T_1) = P_0 \int_{-\infty}^{\infty} \left(\frac{1}{P_{01}} - 1 \right) n(s, f_0, v_0)\, ds$$

which we can simplify using the valuation formulas in Chapter 24 to derive the value at time t as:

$$V(r, t, T_0, T_1) = \frac{P_0^2}{P_1} e^{F_{01}^2 v_0^2} - P_0$$

The value of N arrears payments made at $T_1, \ldots, T_N$ is:

$$V(r, t, T_1, T_N) = \sum_{i=1}^{N} V(r, t, T_i, T_{i+1}) = \sum_{i=1}^{N} \left[\frac{P_i^2}{P_{i+1}} e^{F_{i,i+1}^2 v_i^2} - P_i \right]$$

Equilibrium pricing calls for the net value of an arrears swap versus a traditional floating-rate swap plus a spread s (which may be positive or negative) to have a net value of zero.[2] Since the market value of the floating side of a traditional swap with dollar spread s to LIBOR is:

$$V(r, t, T_1, T_N) = 1 - P_N + s \sum_{i=1}^{N} P_i$$

---

[2] Again, we ignore the bid-offered spread.

The equilibrium spread s for which an arrears swap has an efficient market value of zero is:

$$s = \frac{P_N - 1 + \sum_{i=1}^{N} \left[\left(P_i^2 / P_{i+1} \right) e^{F_{i,i+1}^2 \, v_i^2} - P_i \right]}{\sum_{i=1}^{N} P_i}$$

In an efficient market, new swaps will be priced at this spread over LIBOR. Existing swaps would be priced based on the existing terms using the formulas above.

Digital Option

Another category is the 'digital' category of derivatives that pays either one or zero depending on the level of a random variable. Given our focus on fixed income derivatives, let us consider the value of a derivative security which pays \$1 at time T_0 if a short-term interest rate (such as LIBOR) is less than or equal to a critical level K. We assume that the underlying instrument has a maturity of time T_1. Cash flow is non-zero at time T_0 only if the short-term interest rate is below a critical level s^* such that:

$$s^* = \frac{\ln(1 + K) - G_{01}}{F_{01}}$$

According to Chapter 24 and the valuation formulas in it, the value of such a security is:

$$V(r, t, T_0, T_1, K) = P_0 \int_{-\infty}^{\infty} \ln(s, f_0, v_0) \, ds = P_0 N \left(\frac{s^* - f_0}{v_0} \right)$$

This same kind of approach can be applied to all kinds of digital structures.

Digital Range Notes

What if the security only pays \$1 if the short-term rate is between critical levels K_1 and K_2? These critical levels translate into short rates s_1 and s_2 such that:

$$s_i = \frac{\ln(1 + K_i) - G_{01}}{F_{01}}$$

The value of one payment of these 'digital range notes', viewed from the perspective of time t, is:

$$V(r, t, T_0, T_1, s_1, s_2) = P_0 \int_{s_2}^{s_1} \ln(s, f_0, v_0)\, ds$$

$$= P_0 \left[N\left(\frac{s_1 - f_0}{v_0}\right) - N\left(\frac{s_2 - f_0}{v_0}\right) \right]$$

Range Floater

Another popular derivative is the so-called 'range floater'. Consider a security which pays LIBOR when LIBOR is less than a critical level K, and zero otherwise. Cash flow is determined at time T_0 based on the level of an underlying zero-coupon bond with maturity T_1. The security pays LIBOR only if the short rate is below a critical level s_i, defined as follows:

$$s_i = \frac{\ln(1 + K_i) - G_{01}}{F_{01}}$$

The value of this single payment of a range floater as of current time t is:

$$V(r, t, T_0, T_1, s_1) = P_0 \int_{-\infty}^{\infty} P_{01} \left(\frac{1}{P_{01}} - 1\right) n(s, f_0, v_0)\, ds$$

$$= P_0 N\left(\frac{s_i - f_0}{v_0}\right) - P_1 N\left(\frac{s_i - f_0}{v_0} + v_0 F_{01}\right)$$

What about the case where the range floater pays only between critical LIBOR levels K_1 and K_2, which translate into critical levels of the short rate at time T_0 of s_1 and s_2 (defined as s_i above)? One payment of this range floater can be shown to be:

$$V(r, t, T_0, T_1, s_1, s_2) = P_0 \int_{s_2}^{s_1} P_{01} \left(\frac{1}{P_{01}} - 1\right) n(s, f_0, v_0)\, ds$$

$$= P_0 \left[N\left(\frac{s_1 - f_0}{v_0}\right) - N\left(\frac{s_2 - f_0}{v_0}\right) \right]$$

$$- P_1 \left[N\left(\frac{s_1 - f_0}{v_0} + v_0 F_{01}\right) - N\left(\frac{s_2 - f_0}{v_0} + v_0 F_{01}\right) \right]$$

If there are multiple payments in the range floater structure, the value of the whole structure is the sum of its parts.

Min-Max Floater

Another security that was extremely popular for a time was the 'min-max floater'. The security paid LIBOR as long as LIBOR was below a critical level X, which translated into a critical short rate level s^* at time T_0 of:

$$s^* = \frac{\ln(1 + X) - G_{01}}{F_{01}}$$

Above X, the security pays K - LIBOR. The general Jamshidian solution to this valuation problem is given by:

$$V(r, t, T_0, T_1, X, K) = P_0 \int_{-\infty}^{s^*} P_{01} \left(\frac{1}{P_{01}} - 1 \right) n(s, f_0, v_0) \, ds$$

$$+ P_0 \int_{s^*}^{\infty} P_{01} \left[K - \left(\frac{1}{P_{01}} - 1 \right) \right] n(s, f_0, v_0) \, ds$$

The solution again relies on the valuation equation from Chapter 24 and gives the value for one min-max floater payment as:

$$V(r, t, T_0, T_1, X, K) = P_0 \left[2N \left(\frac{s^* - f_0}{v_0} \right) - 1 \right]$$

$$+ P_1 (K + 1) - P_2 (2 + K) N \left(\frac{s^* - f_0}{v_0} + v_0 F_{01} \right)$$

Other Derivative Securities

Literally almost any fixed income derivative structure can be analyzed in this framework due to the generality of the solutions in Chapter 24 and the richness of the Vasicek term structure model. All of these analytical solutions have related sensitivity statistics, of which *rDelta* is the most important. As a result, explicit hedge ratios can be calculated directly. The largest area of derivatives that cannot be valued in this type of analytical, closed form solution is that of derivatives that include an American option. We turn to that problem in the next chapter. Before doing so, however, we look at the impact of credit risk on the valuation formulas above.

Credit Risk and Exotic Derivatives Structures

For all of the instruments we have analyzed in Chapters 22–29, we face a common dilemma. If we assume that the default probability of our counterparty is independent of the factors which drive payoffs on the instrument, then we make the same (potentially huge) mistake which J.P. Morgan made in the famous 1998 incident with SK Securities discussed in depth by van Deventer and Imai [2003]. This assumption is very seductive, because as Jarrow and Turnbull show, for many structures the impact of credit risk on the value of a structure just becomes a simple multiplier of the original valuation formula.

As is the case with the other structures discussed in the last few chapters, the authors believe that such an assumption is particularly dangerous in the case of derivative instrument credit risk (even in the presence of AAA-rated special purpose vehicles) for two reasons. Firstly, interest rates clearly have an impact, and potentially a substantial impact, on the default probabilities of financial institutions as we have learned time and time again in incidents ranging from the savings and loan crisis in the U.S. to the Asia crisis. This increased default risk comes not necessarily from interest rate mismatches but from the increase in the default probabilities of almost every counterparty on the balance sheet of the financial institution. Secondly, there is a tremendous concentration of market share in the derivatives business and the default of any one of those institutions has a double impact. It will adversely affect 10–20% of the derivatives transactions on the books of the institution (since market shares of the major derivatives players are typically in the 10–20% range) and it will cause an important market disruption as a huge wave of derivatives have to be analyzed and replaced with another counterparty, whose default probability is highly correlated with the institution that has defaulted.

For that reason, we think the valuation and simulation of interest rate exotic structures have to be analyzed using the same process outlined beginning in Chapters 22 and 23:

1. Default probabilities of derivatives counterparties are explicitly linked to interest rates;
2. Interest rate simulation will impact both the payoffs due on the structure and the default probabilities and zero-coupon bond prices of the risky counterparty;
3. The true credit-adjusted value and cash flow can then be accurately derived.

Any other strategy is the financial equivalent of 'sticking your head in the sand' and ignoring the problem instead of facing the reality of the problem. Fortunately for shareholders, depositors and deposit insurance funds of various

Nations, regulators from the Basel Committee on Banking Supervision to the FDIC in the U.S. are focusing on this issue with the intensity it deserves.

We do the same in Chapters 39–44.

Exercises

For purposes of the exercises that follow, assume that the parameters of the Vasicek term structure model are as follows:

alpha, speed of mean reversion:	0.05
sigma, interest rate volatility:	0.015
lambda, market price of risk:	0.01
mu, long-term expected value of r:	0.09
r, current short rate of interest:	0.06

29.1 What is the value of a security which pays the three-month LIBOR rate one year from now on a notional principal of $100 million if the three-month LIBOR rate is determined (a) on the payment date (an arrears swap payment) and (b) three months before the payment date (the normal method)?

29.2 What is the *rDelta* of each of the securities in Exercise 29.1?

29.3 What is the value of a security that pays $1 at the beginning of every quarter for four quarters beginning one year from now, if three-month LIBOR is (a) 8% or below, (b) between 10% and 8%? Assume LIBOR is measured on the first day of the quarter and payment is made that day.

29.4 What is the value of a security that pays LIBOR quarterly for the next four quarters only if LIBOR is between 6% and 7%?

29.5 What is the value of a security that pays (a) LIBOR quarterly if LIBOR is less than 8% and (b) 17% − LIBOR if LIBOR is greater than 8%. Assume the security has a one-year maturity and the first coupon has already been set at 8%.

29.6 What is the *rDelta* of the security in 29.5?

29.7 What amount of one-year zero-coupon bonds is necessary to hedge a position in the security in 29.5?

29.8 Is the security in 29.5 suitable for investment by a governmental entity? Why or why not?

CHAPTER 30

American Fixed Income Options[1]

Introduction to American Options

In Chapters 24–29, we emphasized the valuation of securities where the option embedded in the security was exercisable at only one date. These European options, as we have shown, generally have explicit analytical solutions in the Vasicek family of term structure models, so numerical techniques are neither necessary nor desirable when they can be avoided. Usually the interaction of the security's payoffs with the credit risk of the counterparty means that in most cases we will have to resort to numerical techniques.

As we will see below, numerical techniques have some disadvantages that are usually due to computer science considerations: they are normally more calculation-intensive, which reduces speed, and almost all steps taken to improve speed by reducing the complexity of the numerical calculation introduce an error that can often be significant. That is why, throughout this book, we strongly recommend the use of closed form solutions when they are available. Often, however, they are not available and one of those cases involves American style options on fixed income instruments where there are multiple exercise dates.

The Jarrow-Merton put option, the key integrated risk measure that we focus on in this book, can be thought of as an American option. The bank deposit insurance provided by the Federal Deposit Insurance Corporation is effectively an American put option on the value of deposits provided to depositors and paid for by the banks themselves (if priced correctly) and taxpayers (if priced incorrectly).

American options, in order to avoid arbitrage, must satisfy the same partial differential equation that we used in the Vasicek model in Chapter 11. In addition, there is a boundary condition similar to the boundary condition imposed in Chapters 11 and 24 that requires the value of the security at maturity

---

[1] This chapter is based on Chapter 12 of van Deventer and Imai [1996].

to equal its cash flow at maturity. In the case of American options, however, there is an additional boundary condition that requires that the holder of the option act rationally throughout the period during which the option can be exercised.[2] Consider the typical Japanese or American fixed-rate mortgage. We cover this topic in detail in Chapter 31 and 32, but we can briefly summarize the nature of these securities by saying that the holder of the mortgage (who may or may not be the original lender), receives a constant cash flow C. If the option to prepay is exercised, the holder of the cash flow receives a principal amount B, which depends on the time to maturity *tau*. Rational behavior requires the holder of this prepayment option (the borrower), to act to minimize the value of the security, so at any time to maturity *tau* the value of the security is:

$$\text{Value}[\tau] = \text{Minimum}[B(\tau), \text{Value if Prepayment Option Unexercised}]$$

If ever the value of the security if the option to prepay were greater than the value of prepaying, the holder prepays according to this boundary condition. We will see that the imposition of this seemingly simple constraint creates a problem so complex that, generally speaking, no analytical solutions for value are known.

As we discuss later in this chapter, the borrower also holds an option to default. Default becomes rational (subject to transactions costs like those which we discuss in the next chapter) when the value of the home becomes worth less than the principal due on the loan. A Federal Reserve study in the mid 1990s reported that the default rate on U.S. mortgages increased by five times when the value of the home was less than the principal on the loan. As we have noted elsewhere in this book, as many as 50% of home mortgages in Mexico defaulted in the mid 1990s for the same reason.[3]

We devote the remainder of this chapter to discussing the alternative valuation techniques for valuation of American fixed income options and their strengths and weaknesses. Most of the weaknesses revolve around the ability of the various techniques to mimic the boundary condition above. We concentrate through most of the chapter on Hull and White's [1990, 1993, 1994] popular trinomial lattice to illustrate the principles of the valuation of American options. At the end of the chapter, we return to the issue of a default by the mortgage borrower.

---

[2] We relax this assumption in the next chapter.

[3] The authors are grateful to Dr. Fausto Membrillo Hernandez of IPAB in Mexico City for this observation.

The reason for devoting the bulk of this and the two following chapters to American fixed income options is that almost all financial institutions have the majority of their balance sheets devoted to American fixed income options, explicitly or implicitly. A brief list of examples shows how critical this topic is. Typical American options on financial institution balance sheets include the following:

- The right to terminate a life insurance policy in return for receipt of its surrender value;
- The right to resign as the customer of an investment management firm;
- The right to prepay a mortgage loan;
- The right to withdraw as a bank from the consumer deposit gathering business;
- The right to withdraw almost any consumer bank deposit either at par or upon the payment of an early withdrawal penalty;
- The right of a corporate borrower to declare bankruptcy;
- The right of a financial institution to pay dividends;
- The right to exercise a foreign exchange option;
- The right to exercise a standard swaption contract.

The list of examples is almost endless. Needless to say, the topic at hand is a critical one.

An Overview of Numerical Techniques for Fixed Income Option Valuation

Financial market participants generally use one of six approaches to the valuation of fixed income options:

- Analytical solutions;
- Monte carlo simulation;
- 'Bushy trees';
- Finite difference methods;
- Binomial lattices;
- Trinomial lattices.

We all turn first to analytical solutions, like the present value formula and the Black-Scholes model, when we are aware that such analytical solutions exist. That is why the first 29 chapters of this book were primarily devoted to analytical solutions. In the case of American fixed income options, we generally have no alternative but to turn to a numerical technique. We discuss the five alternatives in turn and recommend that readers consult the excellent book by Robert Jarrow [1996] for additional material on this critical topic.

Monte Carlo simulation

Monte carlo simulation is justifiably popular in financial markets and in this book, but it must be used with great care. Adams and van Deventer [1993] have discussed the reasons for such caution in detail. In general, monte carlo simulation is slow and a rough approximation that is best restricted to problems that cannot be solved by any other method, (i.e. by analytical methods, lattice approaches, or by finite difference methods). Even though we will rely on monte carlo simulation in Chapters 39–44 for integrated interest rate risk and credit risk, we will do so selectively, combining monte carlo simulation with closed form solutions in a highly efficient way.

Monte carlo simulation is most appropriately used for problems that involve path dependence[4] or three or more random variables.[5] Monte carlo simulation has a number of liabilities, however. In the case of the valuation of mortgage-related securities, we discuss a number of specific problems with monte carlo simulation in Chapter 32. In general, however, monte carlo simulation's limitations can be summarized as follows:

- As Hull notes, 'one limitation of the monte carlo simulation approach is that it can be used only for European-style derivative securities'.[6] The boundary condition, which we specified above, cannot be correctly analyzed in monte carlo simulation since it is a forward-looking technique that projects from today into the future. To correctly value an American option, we measure value (as we see below) by working backwards from maturity to calculate value, assuming at each decision point that the option holder acts rationally. Monte carlo works by projecting one interest rate path at a time, so there is not enough information at any point on that path to correctly analyze whether or not an American option holder should prepay. For this reason, monte carlo simulation almost always requires the user to specify a decision rule regarding what the holder of the option should do in any given interest rate scenario, often in the form of a prepayment table or prepayment function in the case of a prepayment option. This is 'putting the cart before the horse', since the user has to guess how the option will be exercised before the user knows what the option is worth. Rather than going through this error-filled exercise, we think most users would get better results by just guessing the value of the option directly!

---

[4] Even in the case of path dependence, however, the use of monte carlo simulation is technically incorrect, as noted by Hull [1993].

[5] See Hull [1993], pages 329-334, for more on this point.

[6] See Hull [1993], page 334.

- The calculation speed of monte carlo techniques is slow for problems where there is a small number of random variables. It does have a speed advantage for problems with a large number of random variables, and it is this case which is typical for a complete analysis of integrated interest rate risk and credit risk.

- Monte carlo simulation by definition does not use all possible scenarios for valuation. There are an infinite number of interest rate scenarios, and monte carlo simulation, due to its speed problems, inevitably requires the user to use too few scenarios in the interests of time. In Chapters 39–44, we devote some time to this issue of the number of scenarios necessary to achieve statistical significance of a risk measure like value at risk.

- As a result of using less than all possible scenarios, monte carlo simulations have sampling error, which results from 'throwing the dice' too few times. Many users of monte carlo simulation are under the mistaken impression that the beautiful probability distribution that is displayed on their computer screen reflects the true uncertainty about the value of a security as measured by monte carlo. Nothing could be farther from the truth. If you call a major securities firm to get a bid on a mortgage security, you get a bid in the form of one number, not a probability distribution. The beautiful probability distribution reflects the inaccuracy or sampling error of the technique itself, and this kind of graph reflects a weakness of monte carlo, not a strength. This kind of sampling error can lead to very serious problems when calculating hedge amounts.

- To reduce sampling error to a meaningful level, a large number of simulations are normally required to get a stable answer and a sampling error small enough to allow decision-making to be based on the monte carlo results.[7]

- Sampling error becomes even more important when basing hedges on the results of monte carlo simulation. The authors feel that the primary purpose of the calculations in this book are to define action, rather than simply to describe the amount of risk an institution currently has. Knowing how much risk you have without knowing what to do about it is nearly useless from both a credit risk and an interest rate risk perspective. With monte carlo simulation, it is very easy to overestimate the

---

[7] In discussions with sophisticated institutions with many years experience with monte carlo simulation, Bank of America executives stated that 2,000 to 10,000 iterations were necessary for a stable answer, while Tokyo Mitsubishi Bank argued that 5,000 to 10,000 runs were essential. Recent evidence indicates that even these numbers may be way too low for particular risk management problems. A risk management expert at a very large New York bank expressed extreme concern that some line units in his bank were basing management actions on as few as 100 iterations per monte carlo calculation. We revisit these issues in Chapters 39–44.

accuracy of the results which often have a large sampling error. Consider a hedger who values their portfolio using 200 simulations via monte carlo. The result shows a value of 100 and a sampling error standard deviation of, say, two. This means that there is roughly a 65% probability that the true value lies between 98 and 102. In order to determine the proper amount of the hedge, the analyst shifts rates up by 10 basis points and repeats the analysis, getting a value of 99 and a sampling error standard deviation of two again. The analyst concludes that the delta of the portfolio is $100 - 99 = 1$ and wants to base the hedge on this result. This is fine, as far as it goes, but the delta has sampling error also. The sampling error on the delta is a function of the sampling error on the two simulation runs, and it is calculated as follows:

$$\sigma_{\text{hedge}\Delta} = \sqrt{\sigma_{\text{run1}}^2 + \sigma_{\text{run2}}^2}$$

- In the example given, the sampling error of the hedge delta of 1.00 works out to be 2.828. What does it mean for the precision of the hedge? It means that there is a 36.2% chance that the hedge amount is not only the wrong magnitude *but the wrong SIGN*! This is a career-ending type of error that has happened often enough on Wall Street that it's become a familiar story.[8]
- The delta from a monte carlo simulation can only be derived from doing the calculation twice (or preferably three times for securities with high convexity), further aggravating its speed disadvantages.
- Monte carlo simulations must be done on the basis of the 'risk neutral' distributions of all random variables, an adjustment which many users fail to make.

On the plus side, monte carlo simulation has a number of advantages which should not be overlooked:

- It is sometimes the only alternative where the cash flow is path dependent, as imprecise as it might be in that case.
- It has speed advantages for problems with a large number of variables. Generally, these mean three or more variables. This is typically the case

---

[8] A major New York bank reported a loss of more than $100 million after discovering the monte carlo simulation routine it was using to value its portfolio was producing a gamma (or second derivative) with the wrong sign; the loss was the magnitude of the mark-to-market error discovered after using a more sophisticated technique to value the same portfolio.

for the integrated interest rate risk and credit risk analysis that is the central focus of this book.

- It is relatively simple to implement.

What are our conclusions about monte carlo simulation? First of all, it is a tool that all users should have access to. Monte carlo simulation is widely available for less than $400 as an add-in to common spreadsheet software and, at this price, everyone should buy it. More sophisticated software packages which don't clearly display the sampling error of both value and hedges derived from monte carlo simulation calculations should be used with extreme caution. With this caveat, monte carlo simulation is essential to the complete integrated analysis of credit risk and interest rate risk. Finally, monte carlo needs to be supplemented with the other techniques in this chapter in order to be used with efficiency and accuracy. For example, in a multi-period monte carlo simulation that requires valuation at each point in time, closed form solutions should be used for this valuation when they are available, and the other techniques discussed below can be used when they are not available. In no case should it be necessary to use monte carlo simulation to value a European option. The authors believe this 'hybrid monte carlo' approach is firmly established as the best practice approach for integrated risk management, subject to the caveats above.

Finite difference methods

Finite difference methods are more complex but more general solution methods commonly used in engineering applications. Finite difference methods provide a direct general solution of the partial differential equation (that defines the price of a callable security), unlike lattice methods, which model the evolution of the random variables. These methods fall into two main groups, *explicit* and *implicit* finite difference methods. The explicit finite difference methods are equivalent to the lattice methods. Implicit methods are more robust in the types of problems that they can handle, but implicit methods are computationally more difficult. Both methods usually use a grid-based calculation method, rather than the lattice approach, to arrive at numerical solutions.

Finite difference methods can be used to solve a wide range of derivative product valuation problems, and they are not restricted to a small number of stochastic processes (i.e. normal or lognormal) that describe how the random variable moves. These methods can be used to value both American and European-style options. Like lattice methods, the valuation by finite difference methods is performed by stepping backwards through time. This is a one-stage process under the finite difference method; there is no need to model the evolution of the random variable before the valuation can be performed.

The authors believe that the finite difference method, in its grid rather than a lattice implementation, is a very useful tool for most institutions but its use to date in the financial services industry has been on single instrument valuation in a derivatives trading context, rather than a tool that has been successfully embedded in an enterprise-wide risk management system.

Binomial lattices

A binomial lattice (sometimes called a binomial tree) is a discrete time model for describing the movement of a random variable whose movements at each node on the tree can be reduced to an up or down movement with a known probability. The model is usually specified so that an upward movement followed by a downward movement gives the same value as a downward movement followed by an upward movement; this means there will be three possible values of the random variable at the end of the second time interval and $k + 1$ possible values at the end of time interval k.

Starting at a known value, x_0, of the variable at time zero, the two possible values of the variable at the end of the first time interval can be predicted by multiplying by two carefully calculated values u and d:

$$\text{higher value} = u * x_0$$
$$\text{lower value} = d * x_0$$

Since each node has two branches, the process can be repeated to predict the values at all the nodes in the tree. The values of u and d depend on the stochastic process for x; let us consider the binomial tree for stock price movements when the random stock price is lognormally distributed. If the coefficients of the equation describing how the stock price moves are constant, then there are simple formulas for the values of u and d which best approximate the true movement in the stock price. Jarrow [1996] uses the binomial tree concept for modeling interest rate movements, and Jarrow and Turnbull [1996] show how the same kind of tree (with appropriate modifications) can be used for modeling stock price movements.

Valuation with the binomial tree requires two passes through the lattice; on the first pass, which is forward from time zero, the values of the stock price or interest rate at each node are calculated and on the second pass, which is backwards, the values of the derivative security at each node are calculated. The proper fitting of the lattice is much like the process described below for the trinomial lattice. The evolution of the random variable in the first pass through the lattice is determined by the parameters of the stochastic process and the size of the discrete time step. Unlike the monte carlo method, subsequent forward passes will always produce the same values.

The binomial lattice can be used to value American-style options as well as European-style options.

Bushy trees

Lattice techniques are computationally efficient in that the lattices 'recombine', i.e. an interest rate increase followed by a decrease leads to the same interest rate as a decrease followed by an increase. For some stochastic processes, this recombination does not occur, particularly in the context of attractive assumptions about forward rate movements under the Heath, Jarrow and Morton [1992] model. In this case, that lattice takes on the structure of a 'busy tree' which has branches that split over and over but never recombine with other branches. The result is a reasonably efficient process for approximating the assumed stochastic process for interest rates and the ability to value complex securities that are path-dependent or which involve American options. As the number of time steps grows, the number of branches grows very rapidly, This has restricted the use of bushy trees to some extent in practice. The technique offers many of the advantages, however, but few of the disadvantages of monte carlo simulation when the number of random variables is small and the nature of the stochastic process assumed does not allow for recombining branches of the tree. See Jarrow [1996] for a very clear and thorough illustration of how the bushy tree technique should be employed.

Trinomial lattices

In a number of papers with important theoretical and practical implications, Hull and White [1990, 1993, 1994] developed the trinomial lattice valuation technique which has quickly established itself as the standard valuation technique, not only for the Vasicek model and its extended version (the Hull and White model), but also for a number of other single factor term structure models which are Markov in nature. This section borrows heavily from Hull and White [1994] in describing the workings of the trinomial lattice. A trinomial lattice (sometimes called a trinomial tree) is a discrete time model for describing the movement of a random variable whose movements at each node on the tree can be reduced to one of three possibilities—an up movement, a down movement or no change. The model is specified so that an upward movement followed by a downward movement and a downward movement followed by an upward movement give the same value as two movements where no change occurs. This means that there will be three possible values of the random variable at the end of the first time interval and $k + 2$ possible values at the end of time interval k. This recombining feature maximizes the efficiency of the calculation.

The additional outcome at each node provides an additional degree of freedom which enhances the power of the model. Trinomial lattices can be used to model almost any Markov stochastic process, including ones in which the parameters are functions of time and the random variable itself.

In modeling interest rate-related derivatives, it allows rates to be modeled so that the current term structure of interest rates and term structure of rate volatility are matched exactly by the modeling process. This offsets the more complicated calculations of the values at the ends of each branch. The trinomial lattice can be used to value American as well as European style options.

Four basic constraints are imposed on the three branches at each node of the tree:

1. The sum of the probabilities of each branch must be one. We call these probabilities p_u, p_m, and p_d (for the up, middle and down probabilities).

$$p_u + p_m + p_d = 1$$

2. The mean change in the short-term interest rate from the given node to the attached three nodes must be consistent with the theoretical expected change for the term structure model used.
3. The variance of change in the short rate from the current node to the next three nodes must be consistent with the theoretical value for the variance.
4. The probabilities must all be positive.

A fifth constraint may appear necessary to experienced users of lattice techniques or market participants with experience in considerably low interest rate environments like Japan from 1995 through this writing in 2004. The Vasicek model and its extended version allow a theoretical possibility of negative interest rates, even with a no-arbitrage derivation. Jamshidian [1989] calls this 'local no-arbitrage', since, as pointed out by Black [1995] interest rates should be considered as options. If rates are negative and market participants have the alternative of costlessly holding cash with zero interest, they will. If market participants have the option of holding cash, nominal interest rates can never turn negative or 'global arbitrage' would be possible. Black [1995] proposes a method of avoiding these problems, but we are unable, at this time, to devote the attention to this refinement that it deserves. We assume that the possibility of negative rates does not pose practical problems for the rest of the chapter. The four constraints above have a number of implications for the lattice. We follow the implementation procedure prescribed by Hull and White [1994]. In the previous chapters of this book, we have focused on the Vasicek model, in which the observable short-term rate of interest follows the stochastic process:

$$dr = \alpha[\mu - r] \, dt + \sigma \, dz$$

In Chapters 25–29, we used Jamshidian's closed form solutions equation where securities were valued as if the short rate of interest had a normal distribution with mean equal to the forward rate at a given maturity and the same variance as the Vasicek model's short rate. In implementing the trinomial lattice, we turn now to Jamshidian's numerical solutions equation, where securities are valued in a different way; cash flow dependent on the short-term rate of interest r is calculated as if r has the distribution of the risk neutral short-term interest rate. The discount factor is the accumulated value of the money market account (see Jarrow [1996] for more on this approach), which is defined as the accumulated value of an account with an initial balance of $1, which is continually reinvested in the money market account.

The stochastic process for the risk neutral short rate (which we call r in this section) in the Hull and White (extended Vasicek) model is:

$$dr = [\theta(t) - \alpha r]\, dt + \sigma\, dz$$

where theta has the definition:

$$\theta(t) = \frac{\tilde{\mu}(t)}{\alpha}$$

using the notation of Chapters 11 and 24.

Hull and White construct a trinomial lattice for the risk neutral short rate where the time steps have length Δt. If r_0 is the initial value of r at time zero on the lattice, the value of r at any subsequent node takes the form:

$$r = r_0 + k\,\Delta r$$

where k is an integer and can be either positive or negative. Step one in the Hull and White process for construction the lattice is to build an interim tree for r under the simplified assumptions that:

$$\theta(t) = 0$$
$$r_0 = 0$$

This effectively means that risk neutral r has the stochastic process:

$$dr = -\alpha\, dt + \sigma\, dz$$

This is a special case of the Vasicek model where:

$$\mu = 0$$

We know in the Vasicek model that the expected value of r at any time in the future is, when *mu* is zero:

$$E_t[r(s)] = r(t)e^{-\alpha(s-t)}$$

Over the time interval Δt, we know by subtracting the initial r from both sides that:

$$E[r(t + \Delta t) - r(t)] = r(t)[e^{-\alpha \Delta t} - 1] = r(t)M$$

where:

$$M = e^{-\alpha \Delta t} - 1$$

The variance of the change in the short rate over this interval Δt is the same as in the Vasicek model:

$$V = \frac{\sigma^2}{2\alpha}\left[1 - e^{-2\alpha \Delta t}\right]$$

We then determine the size of the time step Δt and set:

$$\Delta r = \sqrt{3V}$$

in order to minimize the errors of the numerical solution. Hull and White define node (i, j) on the tree as the node where $t = i\Delta t$ and $r = j\Delta r$. At most tree branches, there is an up shift in r of Δr, a middle branch with no change, and a downshift of Δr. In this case, the probabilities which meet the first three constraints are:

$$p_u = \frac{1}{6} + \frac{j^2 M^2 + jM}{2}$$

$$p_m = \frac{2}{3} - j^2 M^2$$

$$p_d = \frac{1}{6} + \frac{j^2 M^2 - jM}{2}$$

This will not always be the case, given constraint number four which requires the probabilities to all be positive. For positive alpha, for large values of j, the branching style has to change from the normal pattern:

$$\text{up branch} = +\Delta r$$

$$\text{middle branch} = 0$$

$$\text{down branch} = -\Delta r$$

to the downshift pattern:

$$\text{up branch} = 0$$

$$\text{middle branch} = -\Delta r$$

$$\text{down branch} = -2\Delta r$$

This change to the downshift pattern should occur at the smallest integer greater than $-0.184\,M$ (the non-integer value of j at which probabilities would otherwise become zero). Hull and White call this value $j_{\max}$. When the downshift pattern applies, the probabilities on the tree should be:

$$p_u = \frac{7}{6} + \frac{j^2 M^2 + 3jM}{2}$$

$$p_m = -\frac{1}{3} - j^2 M^2 - 2jM$$

$$p_d = \frac{1}{6} + \frac{j^2 M^2 + jM}{2}$$

Likewise, when j is small (a large negative number) it becomes necessary to switch to the *up shift pattern*:

$$\text{up branch} = +2\Delta r$$

$$\text{middle branch} = +\Delta r$$

$$\text{down branch} = 0$$

This should happen, Hull and White recommend, at a '$j_{\min}$' value equal to $-j_{\max}$.

We now illustrate the construction of these probabilities given a specific example. We construct a lattice with two time steps, one at two years and another at four years. We label the lattice starting point node A. The tree splits into three branches at the two-year maturity. The up node is labeled B, the middle node C, and the down node is D. At four years, the three branches from node B are E (up), F (middle), and G (down). From node C, the branches in the same order are F, G, and H. From node D, they are G, H, and I. At both two years and four years, zero-coupon bond prices are observable. The values are 0.88163 and 0.77018. We seek to construct a tree that matches these prices exactly. We will then use it to price bond options.

BASE CASE TREE: Outline of Nodes

Maturity	**0**	**2**	**4**
			E
		B	F
	A	C	G
		D	H
			I
Zero Price	1.00000	0.88163	0.77018

In order to later use Jamshidian's European bond option formula, these zero prices are actually 100% consistent with the Vasicek (not extended Vasicek) model. We used an alpha value of 0.08, interest volatility of 0.02, a market price of risk of 0.01, and a long-term expected value of the short rate of 0.10 (10%). We assumed a short rate of 0.06, and using the notation of Chapters 11 and 24, we calculated the zero prices cited above. We now proceed to lattice construction.

alpha =		0.08000
sigma =		0.02000
lambda =		0.01000
mu =		0.10000
Delta T =	size of time step =	2.00000
M =	expected value of [delta r/r] =	−0.14786
V =		0.00068
delta r =		0.04532
r		0.06000
D		0.07125

Maturity	**2**	**4**
F	1.84820	3.42314
G	0.01509	0.05575
Zero Bond Price	0.88163	0.77018

Delta r is 0.04532 on this lattice. Using these parameters, the up, middle and down probabilities associated with Node A are 0.16667, 0.66667, and 0.16667 respectively

Once the probabilities have been determined, the next step is to determine the value of $1 received in the event a given node is reached. We call these values $Q(i,j)$. The values of Q for all the nodes $m+1$ time steps from the start of the lattice are given by:

$$Q_{m+1,j} = \sum_k Q_{m,k}\, \text{prob}(k,j)e^{-(y_m+k\Delta r)\Delta t}$$

where k denotes all of these rate paths which connect with node $Q_{m+1,j}$. All other rate paths are excluded from the calculation. The variable y_m is a parallel shift up or down in the interest rates for all nodes m time steps from the start of the lattice. We assume that we have observable zero-coupon bond prices $P(0,m)$ consistent with the economy at time zero with maturities consistent with all time steps, including time step m. The variable y_m is calculated such that:

$$P(0, m+1) = \sum_{j=-n_m}^{n_m} Q_{m,j}e^{-(y_m+j\Delta r)\Delta t}$$

The coefficient of delta t in the exponent we refer to as 'adjusted r'. After rewriting this equation:

$$P(0, m+1) = e^{-y_m\Delta t}\left[\sum_{j=-n_m}^{n_m} Q_{m,j}e^{-j\Delta r\Delta t}\right]$$

we can solve for y_m:

$$y_m = -\frac{1}{\Delta t}\ln\left[\frac{P(0, m+1)}{\sum\limits_{j=-n_m}^{n_m} Q_{m,j}e^{-j\Delta r\Delta t}}\right]$$

With this as background, we can solve for all of the probabilities, Q values, and y values that exactly price a portfolio of zero-coupon bonds with maturities equal to the maturity at each time step. We know y_0 is given by the zero-coupon bond price $P(0,1)$ with maturity equal to the maturity of the first time step. We also know that the $Q(0,0)$ value is one. We fill out the lattice as follows:

1. Fill in the Q values for time step one.
2. Solve for y_1.
3. Using y_1, solve for the Q values for time step two.
4. Solve for y_2.
5. Continue until the end of the lattice.

We know the short rate for the first period, which is calculated from the two-year zero-coupon bond price using Chapter 1. The continuously compounded rate is 6.2989%. Given this rate for r, we can calculate the present value of a security which pays a $1 if we end up at node B. The Q value for node B is 0.14694. The values for nodes C and D are 0.58776 and 0.14694.

Using the formulas above for our sample lattice, we get the following results:

Table 30.1 Trinomial Lattice Worksheet

Node	A	B	C	D	E	F	G	H	I
j	0	1	0	−1	2	1	0	−1	−2
Initial r	0.00000	0.04532	0.00000	−0.04532	0.09064	0.04532	0.00000	0.04532	−0.09064
Up Probability	0.16667	0.10367	0.16667	0.25153	0.06253	0.10367	0.16667	0.25153	0.35825
Mid Probability	0.66667	0.64481	0.66667	0.64481	0.57922	0.64481	0.66667	0.64481	0.57922
Down Probability	0.16667	0.25153	0.16667	0.10367	0.35825	0.25153	0.16667	0.10367	0.06253
Pu + Pm + Pd	1.00000	1.00000	1.00000	1.00000	1.00000	1.00000	1.00000	1.00000	1.00000
Q		0.14694	0.58776	0.14694	0.01214	0.16095	0.40658	0.17596	0.01455
Shift		0.06826	0.06826	0.06826					
adjusted r (y)		0.11358	0.06826	0.02294					

Valuing Securities on the Lattice: European and American Calls

We now use this simple lattice to value a European call option on a zero-coupon bond with four years to maturity. We assume that the exercise period on the option is two years. We know from Chapter 24 that the value of this call option is:

$$V(r, 2, 4, K) = P(r, t, 4)N(h) - KP(r, t, 2)N(h - \sigma_P)$$

where:

$$\sigma_p = \frac{\sigma^2}{2\alpha}\left[1 - e^{-2\alpha 2}\right]\frac{1}{\alpha}\left[1 - e^{-\alpha 2}\right]$$

and:

$$h = \frac{\ln\left[(P(r, t, 4)/P(r, t, 2)K)\right]}{\sigma_P} + \frac{\sigma_P}{2}$$

We can calculate this option value for a wide variety of strike prices and compare to the values indicated by the lattice.

How is the lattice used to calculate this option value? In practice, we would use a lattice with many time steps to minimize errors. For illustration purposes, we will use the simple lattice we have constructed already in spite of the errors that will result. Exercise is a possibility at nodes B, C, and D. At node B, the cash flow from exercising the option will be the maximum of zero and the difference between the value of a four-year zero-coupon bond (which now has two years remaining) and the strike price K:

$$\text{Cash Flow} = \text{Maximum}(0, e^{-\text{adjusted } r\Delta t} - K)$$

We make the same cash flow calculation at nodes C and D. The value of the option is:

$$\text{Lattice Option Value} = Q_B \text{ Cash Flow}_B + Q_C \text{ Cash Flow}_C$$

$$+ Q_D \text{ Cash Flow}_D$$

In order to illustrate some basic principles of the use of lattices, we compiled this chart of theoretical (Jamshidian) call option values at various strike prices and the lattice valuations at the same strike prices:

Table 30.2 Comparison of Lattice and Jamshidian Closed Form Solutions for Call Option on Zero-Coupon Bond with Maturity of Four Years and Exercise Period on Call of Four Years

Jamshidian Calculations
Sigma P 0.002344

Strike Price	Yield to Strike	Jamshidian Model h	Value	Lattice Value	Difference
0.00	1381.55%	11732.45	0.77018	0.77018	0.00000
0.05	149.79%	1220.60	0.72609	0.72609	0.00000
0.10	115.13%	924.84	0.68201	0.68201	0.00000
0.15	94.86%	751.83	0.63793	0.63793	0.00000
0.20	80.47%	629.07	0.59385	0.59385	0.00000
0.25	69.31%	533.86	0.54977	0.54977	0.00000
0.30	60.20%	456.06	0.50568	0.50568	0.00000
0.35	52.49%	390.29	0.46160	0.46160	0.00000
0.40	45.81%	333.31	0.41752	0.41752	0.00000

Table 30.2 Comparison of Lattice and Jamshidian Closed Form Solutions for Call Option on Zero-Coupon Bond with Maturity of Four Years and Exercise Period on Call of Four Years (*Cont'd*)

Jamshidian Calculations
Sigma P 0.002344

Strike Price	Yield to Strike	Jamshidian Model		Lattice Value	Difference
		h	Value		
0.45	39.93%	283.05	0.37344	0.37344	0.00000
0.50	34.66%	238.09	0.32936	0.32936	0.00000
0.55	29.89%	197.43	0.28528	0.28528	0.00000
0.60	25.54%	160.30	0.24119	0.24119	0.00000
0.65	21.54%	126.14	0.19711	0.19711	0.00000
0.70	17.83%	94.52	0.15303	0.15303	0.00000
0.75	14.38%	65.08	0.10895	0.10895	0.00000
0.76	13.72%	59.43	0.10013	0.10013	0.00000
0.77	13.07%	53.85	0.09132	0.09132	0.00000
0.78	12.42%	48.35	0.08250	0.08250	0.00000
0.79	11.79%	42.91	0.07368	0.07368	0.00000
0.80	11.16%	37.54	0.06487	0.06534	−0.00047
0.81	10.54%	32.24	0.05605	0.05799	−0.00194
0.82	9.92%	27.01	0.04723	0.05065	−0.00341
0.83	9.32%	21.84	0.03842	0.04330	−0.00488
0.84	8.72%	16.73	0.02960	0.03595	−0.00635
0.85	8.13%	11.68	0.02079	0.02861	−0.00782
0.86	7.54%	6.68	0.01197	0.02126	−0.00929
0.87	6.96%	1.75	0.00318	0.01391	−0.01073
0.88	6.39%	−3.12	0.00000	0.01104	−0.01104
0.89	5.83%	−7.95	0.00000	0.00957	−0.00957
0.90	5.27%	−12.71	0.00000	0.00810	−0.00810
0.91	4.72%	−17.43	0.00000	0.00663	−0.00663
0.92	4.17%	−22.09	0.00000	0.00516	−0.00516
0.93	3.63%	−26.71	0.00000	0.00370	−0.00370
0.94	3.09%	−31.27	0.00000	0.00223	−0.00223
0.95	2.56%	−35.78	0.00000	0.00076	−0.00076
0.96	2.04%	−40.25	0.00000	0.00000	0.00000
0.97	1.52%	−44.67	0.00000	0.00000	0.00000
0.98	1.01%	−49.05	0.00000	0.00000	0.00000
0.99	0.50%	−53.38	0.00000	0.00000	0.00000
1.00	0.00%	−57.67	0.00000	0.00000	0.00000

For strike prices from zero up to 0.79, the lattice values are identical to the Jamshidian theoretical values. For strike prices between 0.80 and 0.95, the lattice values begin to deviate significantly from theoretical values, as you would expect given that we are essentially trying to replicate the theoretical value with a one-step lattice that has only three branches. The deviations can be displayed graphically to summarize the strike regions in which error is serious:

Figure 30.1 Errors in Using Simple Trinomial Lattice, as Percentage of Lattice Value, Plotted by Zero-Coupon Bond Option Strike Price

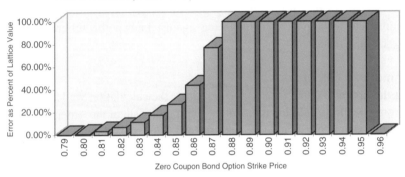

Errors basically grow large because this highly simplified version of the lattice continues to show some value to the call option from strike prices of 0.88 or over even when the theory would indicate that the option should be essentially worthless in this strike price range.

Figure 30.2 Actual Values versus Lattice Estimated Values of 2-Year Option to Buy 4-Year Zero-Coupon Bond, as Function of Exercise Price

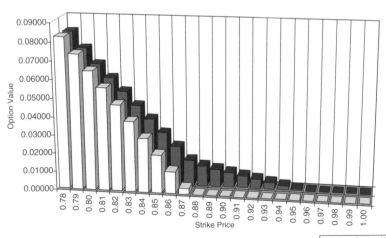

This exercise simply illustrates that error is inevitable when using numerical methods. In some cases, the technique will work perfectly over a wide range of values, as this simple example indicates. For particular strike prices, errors creep in. The user has to take care to adjust the characteristics of the lattice (chiefly the number of time steps), input parameters, etc. to minimize errors and not expect an overly precise answer from any numerical technique. Benchmarking against known theoretical answers is essential.

American call option

If the option was an American call option, the calculation we have just done would be the calculation done on the expiration date of the American call, say at time step m. Step one time step forward, back toward the start of the lattice to time step $m-1$. At time step $m-1$, cash flow will be:

$$\text{Cash Flow} = \text{Maximum}(\text{value if exercised at time step } m, e^{-\text{adjusted } r \Delta t} - K)$$

The value if left unexercised to time step m is simply the one-period present value, weighted by the probabilities, of the cash flow above:

$$\text{Value if exercised at time step } m = \sum_{j=\text{up, mid, down}} e^{-\text{adjusted } r_{m-1} \Delta t} \text{Probability}(m, j)$$
$$* \text{Maximum}(0, e^{-\text{adjusted } r_{m,j} \Delta t} - K)$$

In this manner, almost any fixed income security or derivative security can be valued on the lattice with a level of precision consistent with the analyst's choice of the size of the time steps.

In the next chapter, we modify our approach to allow for the irrational exercise of options, and we apply this combined discipline to mortgage-related securities in Chapter 32.

Lattice construction when default is possible

How does the possibility of default affect the call option on an ABC Company 10-year bond that is callable at any time after five years?

The credit model and the option are not separable because they impact each other in the following ways:

- The value of the call option is reduced by the possibility that ABC company defaults before it is able to exercise the call option;
- The value of the call option is reduced by the possibility that ABC's default probability is so high when exercising the call is

rational that it cannot raise the cash to retire the bonds by calling them;

- The potential losses from default are reduced by the possibility that the bonds have been called before default can occur.

This complex interaction is typical of multi-payment callable instruments that range from home mortgages to auto loans to bonds issued by corporations and governmental agencies. How is the lattice construction modified to handle this interaction, particularly in the key case (our constant focus) where interest rates and perhaps other macro-economic factors are drivers of default probability levels?

Jarrow and Turnbull [1995] describe this process in detail. At each node on the lattice, the default probability of the counterparty will take on a different value because the default probabilities vary by time and level of interest rates. Also at each node on the lattice, the company can either default or not default. If the company is in default, the payoff on the security is its defaulted value (in the Jarrow-Turnbull [1995] case, this is principal times recovery rate; in the Jarrow [1999, 2001] and Duffie-Singleton [1999] models, this is the recovery rate times the value of the security just an instant before default).

Jarrow [1999] goes on to show in detail how to construct lattice valuation techniques for the Jarrow model described in Chapter 17 where the default intensity is a linear combination of three terms:

$$\lambda(t) = \lambda_0(t) + \lambda_1 r(t) + \lambda_2 Z(t)$$

where $r(t)$ is the random rate of interest at time t and $Z(t)$ is the random excess return on the macro-factor driving default intensities for this risky counterparty. In the Jarrow model $r(t)$ and $Z(t)$ can have any arbitrary degree of correlation.

This lattice capability is one of the most powerful virtues of the reduced form modeling approach and one of its greatest strengths as a basis for integrated interest rate risk and credit risk analysis.

Does the same approach apply to the Shimko-Tejima-van Deventer [1993] random interest rates version of the Merton model? In a sense, yes. Risk-free interest rates have the same assumed movements (the Vasicek family of term structure models) that we have discussed throughout this chapter. Moreover, the value of company assets has the same assumed distribution as the excess return variable $Z(t)$ in the Jarrow model.

There is just one problem with using this approach to model multi-payment callable bonds on a Merton-type lattice with random interest rates and random company asset values. This problem is a serious one, and in fact, it is the key issue which led Robert Jarrow to devote his research energies to finding an alternative specification for credit risk.[9] The value of company assets in the Merton model should not be independent of cash flows on the liabilities of the company, but this kind of lattice construction implicitly assumes that payments on the company's bonds do not lower the value of company assets.

Nothing could be further from the truth. All other things being equal, each interest rate payment reduces the value of company assets by the amount of the payment (perhaps offset later with a tax deduction when taxes are due). Similarly, any full or partial prepayment on the bond will reduce the value of company assets and impact its riskiness. Robert Merton avoided dealing with this issue by restricting his model to one period and bond payments to the end of the period. Using a lattice that allows intermediate dates and payments is, in fact, a substantial departure from the original Merton formulation. To be done correctly, such a lattice approach should allow for the fact that management has the real option to issue additional liabilities at each point on the lattice where the company is not in default. This results in a 'chicken and egg' problem that is both very realistic in its description of company choices but too complex to model by any means other than a complex dynamic programming environment.

Suffice it to say that advanced lattice modeling in both the reduced form modeling framework and the Merton framework will pay big dividends in the modeling of integrated interest rate risk and credit risk.

Exercises

For purposes of the exercises that follow, assume that the parameters of the Vasicek term structure model are as given in the example above.

30.1 What would be the six-year zero-coupon bond price?

30.2 Using this zero-coupon bond price, calculate the adjusted short rates that would prevail at nodes E, F, G, H, and I on the lattice above.

30.3 What is the theoretical price of a four-year European option on a six-year zero-coupon bond with a strike price of 0.75?

30.4 What is the trinomial lattice valuation of the four-year European option?

30.5 What would the option value be if it was a four-year American option on a six-year zero-coupon bond?

30.6 What is the economic intuition behind your answer to 24.5?

30.7 What is the value of a four-year American option on a six-year bond with principal of 100, which pays \$20 interest every two years? Assume there is no interest due at time zero.

___

[9] See the introduction to van Deventer and Imai [2003] for more on Professor Jarrow's rationale for exploring other directions in credit modeling.

CHAPTER 31

Irrational Exercise of Fixed Income Options[1]

Irrationality

As we continue to progress toward the mark-to-market of the entire balance sheet of a financial institution in a way that integrates interest rate risk and credit risk, we have to deal with the reality that the vast majority (by transaction count) of financial institutions investments are extensions of credit to individuals or small businesses whose credit worthiness is inseparable from the proprietor.

One of the reasons that analysis of consumer-related financial products is so complex is because of the issue of the so-called 'irrationality' of consumers. Perhaps the most prominent example from a Wall Street perspective is the mortgage market, which we address in detail in Chapter 32. Mortgages are often prepaid when current mortgage rates are higher than the borrower's mortgage rate, and many borrowers fail to prepay even when rates have fallen far below the rate on their loan. In addition, partial prepayments are common, something that is impossible in a traditional Black-Scholes context or in the context of the fixed income options analysis we explored in Chapter 24.

As a working assumption, the hypothesis that borrowers are not very intelligent runs contrary to the assumptions behind all developments in modern financial theory over the 20 years since the Black-Scholes options formula was first published. The perception of 'irrationality' is simply a short hand description for the fact that lenders and academic researchers do not have enough data to 'see through' the individual loan or pool data to understand why the individual borrower's behavior is more rational than it appears at first glance. The authors believe even more strongly that the underlying assumption of rationality is the right one since one of them has failed to refinance his own mortgage loan, even though it must seem irrational from the bank's perspective. The bank clearly is unaware that this book is more important than

---

[1] An earlier version of this chapter appeared as Chapter 13 in van Deventer and Imai [1996].

a few yen earned from refinancing a mortgage. Once the book is done, the 'irrational' author will suddenly become rational from the bank's perspective!

The need to deal with hard-to-explain consumer behavior is essential for accurate risk management in the insurance, investment management, and banking industries. Insurance companies must deal with the reality that some traditional life insurance policy holders will cancel their policies in return for the surrender value when interest rates rise, 'putting' the policy back to the underwriter. Investment managers who suffer poor performance know that some customers of the firm will 'put' their ownership in a mutual fund back to the investment management company. Bankers who make home equity loans know that some of these loans will be 'called' by the borrower. Bankers also know that some time deposit customers will 'put' the deposit back to the bank and willingly pay an early withdrawal penalty when rates rise in order to earn more on their funds. Without dealing with the degree of irrational consumer behavior behind these products, institutions can neither price properly nor hedge their risk properly. This chapter deals explicitly with a method for doing so.

In the last section of the chapter, we explore the strong synergies between our approach to 'irrational' behavior and the credit-adjusted valuation and simulation we have been discussing in earlier chapters.

Analysis of Irrationality: Criteria for a Powerful Explanation

The irrationality problem is so all-pervasive that we deal with the problem in general terms in this chapter. This approach has two virtues. Firstly, it will help us deal with the problem from a fresh perspective, unburdened by conventional wisdom. Secondly, armed with a general solution, we can compare this general solution to the conventional wisdom and judge the relative strengths of the two approaches without prejudice. In Chapter 32, armed with the tools of this chapter, we will analyze all the traditional practices of mortgage-related products. In this chapter, however, we need to establish principles that will solve problems in insurance, investment management, and in banking. They have to apply equally well to call options, put options, and securities that are callable but have rate caps and floors as well. A few basic principles come to mind:

> *a. A general approach to irrational behavior should take advantage to as great an extent possible of the advances in finance in the last 20 years.*

All derivative pricing theory is based on the premise of no-arbitrage and rational behavior. If all consumers were totally irrational, we would not need to price the options embedded in retail finance products because the exercise of those options would be truly random and uncorrelated with economic events. Portfolio theory would allow us to argue that we can diversify away this random behavior and ignore the option all together. The reality, as we shall see in Chapter 32, however, is that consumer behavior is highly correlated with economic variables and behavior is not totally irrational. It is this mixture of rational and irrational behavior (which in fact is largely due to rational acts based on unobservable information) that makes the problem both important and difficult.

We need, then, an approach that allows us to scale the degree of irrationality to fit the particular product, company, and market at hand. We need an approach where consumer action is partially rational so we can use the first 31 chapters of this book.

> *b. History is not generally a good guide to the future, and we want to be able to derive the level of irrationality implied by observable market prices.*

Wall Street firms have spent millions of dollars examining historical data for clues to consumer behavior as reflected in historical prepayment activity. As we shall see in Chapter 32, this work has been at best partially satisfactory. For financial institutions which need to make an immediate decision about the proper hedge for a security whose market price and local rate sensitivity (i.e. the value change for small changes in interest rates) is observable, the historical approach is too slow, too inaccurate and too expensive. The parallels in the debate about the use of historical volatility versus implied volatility in the Black-Scholes options model are very strong. We want an approach that gives us the 'implied' level of irrationality. Most bankers who price retail banking products which contain embedded options come to the conclusion that most products are unprofitable if the options risk is fully hedged. Bankers implicitly recognize that consumers are partially rational and that a partial hedge is necessary. How can we use market data to calculate exactly how much rationality is embedded in a given product?

> *c. Any model of irrationality must be able to explain observable phenomenon in pools of consumer related securities: path dependent prepayment behavior, decreased interest rate sensitivity over time ('burnout'), and a lower propensity to exercise embedded options as the financial product nears its expiration.*

> *d. The model must allow for very rapid calculation time and maximum use of analytical solutions for security valuation.*

One approach that meets these criteria is the transactions cost approach, which we now discuss.

The transactions cost approach

Over the last 10 years, the rational approach to irrational behavior has steadily gained prominence among both academics (see McConnell and Singh [1994] and Stanton [1995] for recent examples) and practitioners as the best method to model consumer behavior. The rational, or transactions cost approach, holds that consumers are rational but exercise their options subject to transactions costs. These transaction costs can be both explicit financial costs (the 'points' from refinancing a mortgage or the penalty for early withdrawal of bank deposits) and more subtle costs that reflect the fact that consumers are maximizing a utility function with more arguments in it than the present value of rational action in one specific aspect of their lives. For example, someone with a life insurance policy that rationally should be canceled and re-initiated at current market pricing may have a serious disease that would cause the applicant to be rejected at the health check on the new policy. The disease is a transactions cost that at least partially blocks rational action. J. Thurston Howell III may fail to refinance the mortgage on his ski chalet in Aspen because his yacht has run aground on some deserted desert island without a Bloomberg screen to keep him abreast of the benefits of refinancing. In the authors' case, the principal amount of our bank time deposits is so small (since other investments are so superior in risk-adjusted yield) that the benefits of early withdrawal of our time deposits, while positive, are smaller than the costs of the time it takes to go to the bank and negotiate the transaction. The cost of our time is a transactions cost.

The objective of the transactions cost is to firmly divorce rational from irrational behavior. Accordingly, the transactions cost function can be any time dependent function that is not dependent on the level of interest rates. Determinants of the level of transactions costs could be any of the following:

- Time to maturity on the security;
- The level of the coupon on the security;
- The fixed dollar cost of exercising the option embedded in the security;
- The dollar opportunity cost of the time it takes to exercise the embedded option;
- The month of the year, recognizing that the transactions cost of refinancing a home in Alaska in January is higher than the cost in August;
- The date of origination of the security;
- The length of time the security has been outstanding without the embedded option being exercised.

There are an endless number of factors that can go into the transactions cost function. In short, however, as of current time t, all of these factors are non-random functions of time. We call this transactions cost function X and make it, without loss of generality, a function of the remaining time to maturity on the security:

$$\text{Transactions Cost} = X(t, T) = X(\tau)$$

We can model any degree of irrationality using this function. If the consumer is a retired Salomon Brothers partner living in Greenwich with a Bloomberg screen in his living room and a healthy bank account, $X = 0$. The consumer is totally rational. If the consumer is working hard on a book on risk management, X is infinity, the consumer is totally irrational, and no embedded options will be exercised. Any level of irrationality in between these two extremes can be modeled in the same way. We illustrate the approach for European options in the next section.

Irrational Exercise of European Options

In Chapter 24, we analyzed the value of a European option on a zero-coupon bond using Jamshidian's valuation formula. The value of an option exercisable at time T_1 on a zero-coupon bond with a maturity of T_2 was given as:

$$V(r, t, T_1, T_2, K) = P(r, t, T_2)N(h) - P(r, t, T_1)N(h - \sigma_P)$$

where:

$$h = \frac{1}{\sigma_P} \ln \left[\frac{P(r, t, T_2)}{K P(r, t, T_1)} \right] + \frac{\sigma_P}{2}$$

and:

$$\sigma_P = v_1 F_1$$

where v and F have the same definitions as in Chapters 24–29. What if the holder of this option exercises it irrationally, subject to transactions costs X?

Since it is a European option, the time-dependent nature of X is irrelevant with regard to a single European option. Only the level of X that will prevail at time T_1 matters, so we drop the time-dependent notation. We know from Jamshidian's valuation formula that the solution to the valuation of an irrationally exercised option is:

$$V(r, t, T_1, T_2, K, X) = P(r, t, T_1) \int_{-\infty}^{s^*} [P(s, T_1, T_2) - K] n(s, f_1, v_1) \, ds$$

The only difference between the rational option in Chapter 24 and the irrationally exercised option is that the holder of the irrationally exercised option exercises it only when the short rate of interest on date T_1 reaches a critical level s^* such that:

$$P(s^*, T_1, T_2) = K + X$$

The option will only be exercised if it is in the money by X dollars more than the strike price K. If X is zero, it's a rationally exercised option. The critical level of s^* is:

$$s^* = -\left[\frac{\ln(K + X) + G_{12}}{F_{12}}\right]$$

Substituting this value of s^* into the Jamshidian formulation and simplifying leads to a valuation formula for an irrationally exercised option that is nearly identical to that for a rationally exercised option, except the argument h (which we label h^* in the irrational case) differs slightly in that K is replaced by $K+X$:

$$V(r, t, T_1, T_2, K) = P(r, t, T_2)N(h^*) - P(r, t, T_1)N(h^* - \sigma_P)$$

where:

$$h^* = \frac{1}{\sigma_P}\ln\left[\frac{P(r, t, T_2)}{(K + X)P(r, t, T_1)}\right] + \frac{\sigma_P}{2}$$

When X is zero, h^* reduces to h and the valuation formula is identical. If X is infinity, h^* is minus infinity, the option will never be exercised, and the option is worthless from the perspective of the holder. We illustrate the power of this formulation with a specific example.

Valuing a Zero-Coupon Bond with an Irrationally Exercised Embedded Call Option

Consider the case of a 10-year zero-coupon bond with an embedded European call option at 0.6 after five years that is exercised irrationally. We assume the Vasicek model parameters:

$$\alpha = 0.08$$
$$\sigma = 0.015$$
$$\lambda = 0.01$$
$$\mu = 0.12$$

What is the value of this bond with the irrationally exercised embedded option? If the short-term rate of interest is 6%, the underlying 10-year zero-coupon bond is worth 0.46238. If the option is exercised subject to a 4.5% transactions cost (0.6 + 0.045), the irrationally exercised option is worth 0.03994, and the package of the underlying bond less the embedded option is worth 0.42244.

The dynamics of irrational exercise can be very complex, allowing the user to model many forms of behavior that are quite common in the real world and a few, like negative convexity, which are fairly rare. Figure 31.1 shows the complex changes in the value of this bond (with the simplest possible embedded option) at short-term interest rates of 5.5%, 6%, 6.5%, and 7% for transactions costs ranging from 4.5% to 6.5%. The combination of interest rate levels and transactions costs results in the expected smooth transition from the price of a bond with a rationally exercised option to the price of a bond with no embedded option as the transactions cost rises to a level that effectively blocks exercise. What is surprising, however, is the fact that bond prices are not necessarily monotonically decreasing as rates (as measured by the short rate *r*) rise, due to the irrationally exercised option. This is consistent with observable prices of mortgage securities which, at certain times in the recent past, have fallen as rates have fallen because even irrational options holders had their 'threshold' exceeded and began to refinance, reducing the value of the security to par.

Figure 31.1   Changes in Callable Zero-Coupon Bond Price at Different Levels of Short Rate *r* and Transactions Costs

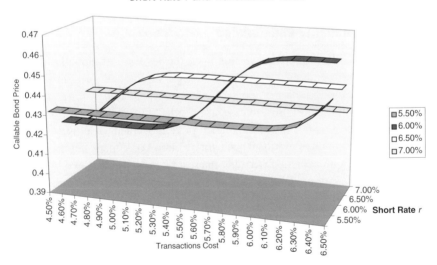

This basic approach is general and applies to all option-related securities in this book. We turn briefly to securities with embedded American options to illustrate the full generality of the approach.

The irrational exercise of American options

In Chapter 30, we reviewed the fundamentals of the pricing of American fixed income options. An American call option was valued on the premise of rational behavior throughout the life of the call, such that the holder of the call always acted in such a way as to maximize the value of the call. In the case of a callable security, the holder of the call always acts in such a way as to minimize the value of the security. Working backwards, one period from maturity, the holder of the call is assumed to prepay if there is even a one cent advantage of prepayment at par when compared to the present value of leaving the security outstanding at least one more period.

In the case of an irrationally exercised American call option, at every point (working backwards from maturity) the holder of an option to call their bond or loan will exercise that call option only if:

$$\text{Value if Prepayment Option Unexercised} > B(\tau) + X(\tau)$$

That is, exercise will take place only if the present value of the security, if the call option is left unexercised, exceeds the principal amount B by more than the transactions cost X prevailing at that instant in time. The fact that X varies over time will result in a very rich array of realistic behavior in securities modeled in this way.

Implied Irrationality and Hedging

When irrationality is modeled in this way, the level of irrationality can be implied from observable market prices just like implied volatility in the Black-Scholes model, achieving one of our primary objectives for a model of irrationality. Almost no observable security reflects the behavior of one consumer, so the best replication of the market price movement of a given security reflects a combination of irrational behavior by many consumers. Let us consider a security with value G and observable interest rate risk as measured by $rDelta$ equal to G_r. We can model this security by breaking it into two pieces, using weights of w and $1-w$. One piece consists of a rationally exercised security $V(r, t, 0)$ with zero transactions costs. The other piece consists of an irrationally exercised security $V(r, t, X)$ with transactions costs of X. We solve this equation system for the weights w and transactions cost X such that both value and interest rate risk match the observable security's actual market behavior:

$$G = wV(r, t, 0) + (1 - w)V(r, t, X)$$
$$G_r = wV_r(r, t, 0) + (1 - w)V_r(r, t, X)$$

This results in a minimal need for historical research, efficient hedging of securities which contain irrationally exercised embedded options, and very fast calculation times instead of tedious monte carlo simulation in an attempt to use a historical prepayment function or prepayment table. We turn to that topic in our next chapter. Before doing so, we explore the links between our credit risk analysis of Chapters 16–18 and prepayment analysis.

Credit Risk and Irrational Prepayment Behavior

One of the realities of consumer lending is that consumers are irrational in the three ways discussed in the example above:

- They sometimes fail to prepay when they 'should';
- They sometimes prepay when they 'shouldn't';
- They often partially prepay instead of fully prepaying as they 'should'.

In each of these cases, the word 'should' stems from an analysis of the consumer's behavior that is based only on what the lender knows—the terms of the loan. Many of these allegedly irrational acts stem from the complex interaction of the long-term creditworthiness and financial well-being of the borrower and the loan itself. We can give rational explanations for each of these types of irrational behavior.

- They sometimes fail to prepay when they 'should':
  - Case A: The price of the home may be less than the principal amount of the loan and the consumer may not have enough liquid financial assets to bridge this gap.
  - Case B: The consumer may be in financial distress and unable to qualify for a new loan.
  - Case C: The consumer may be on a one year sabbatical at the University of Tahiti.
  - Case D: The loan may be so close to maturity that the benefits of refinancing are not worth the costs of going through the process.
  - Case E: The consumer's personal wealth may now be so great that they have no intention of borrowing any more money and prepayment may simply be delayed until the consumer has enough liquid assets to prepay with cash.

There are many other similar examples we could give to further illustrate this point.

- They sometimes prepay when they 'shouldn't':
  Even in this circumstance, there are many explanations that are quite rational for this superficially irrational response, many of which again are due to the credit worthiness and net worth of the consumer:
  - Case A: The borrower may have sold the house (due to the famous trio of death, divorce, or relocation).

- Case B: The borrower may have just received very large payments from structuring special purpose vehicles for Enron Corporation; prepaying the mortgage is in fact a better risk-adjusted investment than U.S. Treasuries since the credit risk of the now very wealthy consumer is the same as the Treasury: zero. The mortgage is prepaid because it has a higher yield than Treasuries and the lender is not reflecting the borrower's credit risk correctly.
- Case C: The borrower may have been a problem borrower in the past and prepays the loan simply because the borrower can no longer tolerate a relationship with a financial institution who has pursued overly aggressive tactics to get the borrower current on the loan; this is a common refrain from consumers these days.
- They often partially prepay instead of fully prepaying as they 'should': This phenomenon is inconsistent with the 'all or nothing' implications of fixed income options explained in Chapters 24 and 30, but it is very common practice. It has a lot in common with the partial draw-downs of commercial lines of credit and with revolving charge card balances that we discuss in later chapters.
  - Case A: The consumer's credit quality has improved considerably since the mortgage was granted and the true 'market mortgage rate' for the consumer is now less than the rate on the loan, but the bank doesn't know this. The consumer signals this by prepaying in whatever amounts fit his total financial plan.
  - Case B: Market interest rates are now lower but the consumer's total financial plan suggests that occasional partial prepayments are better than refinancing the loan. There are a number of reasons why this may be the case. Most revolve around the fact that partial prepayments are less costly (with 'cost' broadly defined) to the consumer than one lump sum prepayment.

We explore the implications of these links between credit risk, interest rate risk and prepayment behavior for the Jarrow-Merton put option as a measure of integrated risk in detail using U.S. mortgage and consumer loan data in the next chapter.

Exercises

Use the term structure model parameters in the example above and consider the case of a bank deposit with three years to maturity, which pays $30 in compounded interest at maturity, which is three years away. The original term to maturity was four years. The holder of this bank deposit has the right to receive his $100 principal plus 2% interest to the point of early withdrawal.

31.1 What is the value of this put option if exercised today?

31.2 What is the value of the put option if exercised in one year? What is the value if exercised in two years?

31.3 You are in charge of asset and liability management at the bank that originated this deposit. You know with certainty that the customer faces transactions costs of $5 and that the put option is exercisable in one year. Your only possible investment is three year zero-coupon bonds. How much should you buy?

31.4 Graph the value of the three-year deposit with embedded put in problem 31.3 as a function of the short rate r and transactions cost level. Describe the rate sensitivity and transactions cost sensitivity of value.

31.5 We define a new risk parameter as *XDelta*, the derivative of the value of an irrationally exercised option-related security with respect to the level of transactions costs. Derive the value of *XDelta* for the security in 31.3.

CHAPTER 32

Mortgage-Backed Securities and Asset-Backed Securities[1]

W e are now in the 'home stretch' as we prepare for the comprehensive Jarrow-Merton put option as a measure of integrated credit and interest rate risk. Our task in this chapter is to apply the analysis of option exercise subject to transaction costs from the previous chapter to portfolios or pools of loans. The authors feel strongly that this should be done on a transaction level basis, loan by loan, rather than analyzing the 'pool' or portfolio as if that pool was a single transaction. From a computer science and financial theory perspective, there is no reason for allowing unnecessary data aggregation to obscure our analysis of the risk-adjusted return on consumer lending. We illustrate the reasons for this view during the course of the chapter and illustrate how the traditional approach to prepayment is in fact 'off track' because of attempts to value a pool of loans as if they were a single very large loan.

Introduction to the Analysis of Mortgage-Backed Securities

The valuation and analysis of mortgages, both fixed and floating rate, is perhaps the most complex analytical problem in U.S. financial markets. As mentioned above, much of this difficulty stems from the confusion between analysis of a single mortgage and analysis of a portfolio or pool of mortgages. Douglas Breeden [1991], one of the leading U.S. researchers in finance, former chief executive officer of mortgage fund manager Smith Breeden, and now Dean of the Duke University Business School, commented about the problem as follows:

> '... mortgages are viewed as far too complicated to value precisely and rigorously, even with the Black-Scholes model and the many improvements developed in the eighteen subsequent years.'

---

[1] An earlier version of this chapter appeared as Chapter 14 in van Deventer and Imai [1996].

Mortgage analysis is a process of continuous improvement, a process that will continue indefinitely as researchers approach a more complete understanding of borrower behavior in light of the complexities we outlined in the last section of Chapter 31—almost all stemming from the complex interaction of credit risk, interest rate levels and prepayment behavior. The purpose of this chapter is to take a second look at mortgage-backed securities in the light of the implications of that chapter: that the transactions cost approach promises dramatic improvements in the speed and accuracy of credit-adjusted valuation and risk analysis for consumer loans on both an individual loan level and a portfolio level. Before looking at the implications of that approach, we look first at traditional industry practice.

Prepayment speeds and the valuation of mortgages

Until fairly recently, Wall Street analysis of mortgage-backed securities relied almost exclusively on 'prepayment models' as a means of analyzing the embedded options in mortgage-backed securities. The prepayment models, in combination with monte carlo simulation, produce another number as output—the option-adjusted spread (OAS) on a mortgage-backed security. In the next few sections, we pose a number of questions and attempt to answer them:

- Do prepayment models have an options component?
- Are prepayment speeds predictable enough to use as an input for the option-adjusted valuation of mortgages?
- Is the truth about prepayment speeds obvious enough that sophisticated market participants can reach a consensus about their levels?

Most prepayment models have an objective similar to our objectives throughout this book:

1. Security valuation on a credit-adjusted and option-adjusted basis;
2. Measurement of interest rate sensitivity;
3. Accurate hedges;
4. Guidance on 'rich/cheap' analysis for security selection.

Prepayment speed models come in four basic varieties:

a. Models in which the prepayment speed is a function of time, but not rate levels. Examples are the lifetime prepayment speed models of the Public Securities Association (PSA), Conditional (or 'Constant') Prepayment Rate (CPR), and Single Monthly Mortality (SMM).
b. Tables in which different prepayment speeds are assigned depending on the remaining maturity of the mortgage, the coupon level, and the current level of interest rates. We call this the prepayment table approach.

c. Prepayment functions, which are typically derived from historical data on prepayments and include more inputs than a prepayment table to provide the accurate prepayment speed.

d. Logistic regression models, like those we used in Chapter 17, to fit default probability formulas to historical default data-bases. These logistic regression models are relatively new in prepayment analysis, but offer great promise for understanding the probability of prepayment based on historical behavior of individual borrowers. They are tested in exactly the same way as the credit model tests of Chapter 18.

Analytically, the constant prepayment speed models are the simplest. Prepayment tables, which are one step up in complexity, assume that we can accurately forecast prepayment speeds. Prepayment functions assume the future will be like the historical data set which produced the estimates used in the prepayment function. The same is true for logistic regression models to some extent. How well do these models work?

Constant prepayment speeds are a principal amortization assumption

The most important point to make about the PSA, CPR, and SMM analysis is that they have no options component at all. They represent an assumption about principal amortization and make it quite clear that the rate of principal amortization does not depend on the level of interest rates. As a result, there is no 'rational' consumer response to lower rates at all reflected in these three models. Figure 32.1 shows how principal varies on a level payment mortgage

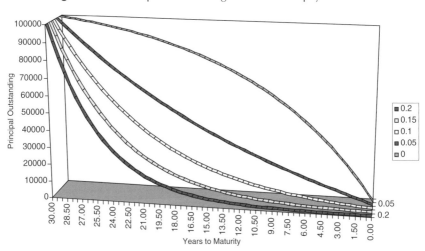

Figure 32.1 Principal Outstanding for Various Prepayment Rates

at different prepayment speeds. A higher prepayment speed lowers the level of principal outstanding.

A higher prepayment speed also has the impact of increasing cash flow on the mortgage in the early years and decreasing it in later years, effectively shortening its duration. These cash flows are not stochastic and don't depend on the level of interest rates.

Figure 32.2 Total Annualized Cash Flow (Scheduled + Unscheduled) For Various Prepayment Rates

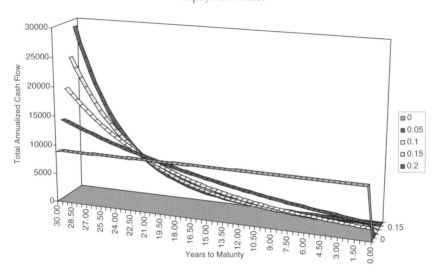

We can illustrate the derivation of prepayment formulas for a mortgage model which assumes constant, continuous payments. Most analysis of level payment mortgage loans is done on a discrete time basis, recognizing that mortgages are usually repaid in the form of equal payments paid to the lender monthly, or as in Canada, on a weekly or bi-weekly basis. The use of continuous time analysis results in simpler formulas that provide for faster computer solutions. We summarize those formulas in Appendix 1.

Fitting actual GNMA data with a single prepayment speed model
We now want to analyze the accuracy of single-speed prepayment models, regardless of whether we are using the continuous time formulas in Appendix 1 or their discrete time equivalent.

One problem is clear before we start: there is only one unknown, the prepayment speed k. If we have a Government National Mortgage Association (GNMA) mortgage-backed security whose price and interest rate risk are observable, can we match both price and risk (as measured by *rDelta* in theory or the daily price change with respect to interest rate changes using observable price data) with a single speed prepayment model? The answer is no, since we are trying to fit two equations (one equation relating the known market value with its theoretical value and a second equation which relates the known, observable amount of interest rate risk to its theoretical amount of rate risk) with only one unknown, k. Only by accident will one k value solve both equations. Still, it is interesting to see how well such a simple model works in practice.

In order to determine the relative effectiveness of the single prepayment speed model, we took 1,347 daily price quotations for a GNMA 8% mortgage-backed security. We assumed that the prepayment model was 'true', i.e. no matter what happens to interest rates the prepayment speed will stay constant over the life of the mortgage. We then compared the rate sensitivity in the real world with the prepayment model.[2] We calculated the present value of the GNMA using our model and compared to actual GNMA prices. Actual GNMA prices over the November 28 1988 to April 15 1994 sample period showed a very smooth curve with a slight bend downward on the left hand side of the graph at low rates, a plateau over a broad range of rates near a price of 105 or so, and then a decline in price as rates rise.

Figure 32.3 GNMA 8% Market Price versus 30-Year U.S. Treasury Yield, November 28 1988 to April 15 1994

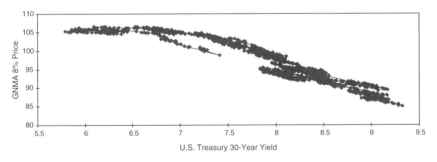

We then solved for the prepayment rate k which provided the best fit to this data over all 1,347 days and plotted predicted versus actuals for our model. At first glance, the fit was surprisingly good for a one-variable model:

When we overlaid the fitted prices versus interest rates, however, we could see very systematic mispricing in the single prepayment model.

---

[2] On each day, we took the actual 30-year U.S. government bond yield, and we assumed the credit spread was constant over the sample period (a rough first approximation).

Figure 32.4 Actual GNMA 8% Prices Plotted vs. Estimated GNMA 8% Prices Using Best Fitting Constant Prepayment Speed, November 28 1988 to April 15 1994

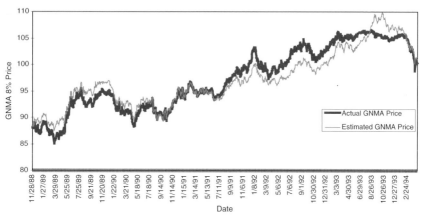

Figure 32.5 Actual GNMA 8% Prices Compared to Best Fitting Prepayment Speed Estimated Prices November 28 1988 to april 15 1994

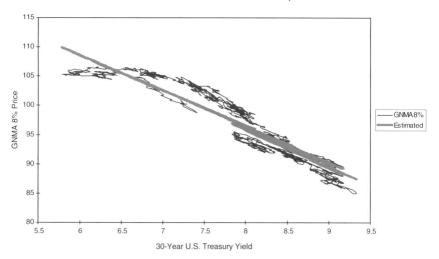

When we plot the mispricing errors, our model was consistently too high in price when rates were very low or very high, and we were too low in price in the mid-range. Our errors in the slope of the curve, the *rDelta*, were substantial except at very high rates.

Why such serious errors? Because our simple model has no option component at all and ignores the fact that some consumer borrowers are eminently sensible and rationally exercise their option to prepay. More people prepay their loans when rates are low than when they are high. Can we salvage the prepayment model approach by changing prepayment rates as interest rates change? We turn to that issue in the next section.

Figure 32.6 Errors in Pricing Using Best Fitting Prepayment Speed to Price GNMA 8% November 28 1988 to April 15 1994

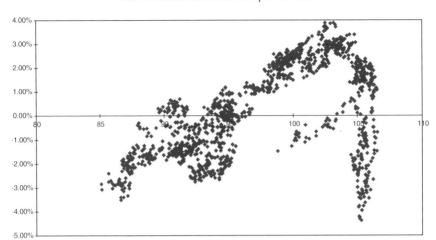

Can We Forecast Prepayment Rates?

The implications of the first section of this chapter is that the single speed approach to prepayment analysis doesn't work very well. We need to somehow do a better job of recognizing at least partially rational behavior to accurately meet our objectives:

- Correct market valuation on a credit risk and option-adjusted basis;
- Correct interest rate sensitivity analysis;
- Correct hedging.

One way many market participants seek to do this is by creating a prepayment table which specifies what prepayment rates will be at different times in different interest rate environments. Typically, a prepayment table will contain at least two dimensions (and usually more), one for each payment and another for various levels of 'refinancing advantage', the spread between the rate on the mortgage loan being analyzed and the current coupon rate on new mortgages. If there are five interest rate tiers and 360 payments, 1,800 input numbers will be required to get the three numbers we are interested in—value, *rDelta*, and the hedge amount for a given interest rate. Clearly, the prepayment table approach is expensive in terms of data input to output—a ratio of 600 numbers input for every one number output. Nonetheless, does it work?

When we ask 'does it work', we are really asking whether forecasts of prepayment speeds are accurate, since, if they are not, the prepayment table will be filled with inaccurate numbers and the output from analysis that relies on those numbers will be highly inaccurate. Douglas Breeden [1994] takes a very interesting look at Wall Street's ability to forecast prepayment speeds, and we use data from his study liberally in this section. First, Breeden shows that Wall Street typically lacks consensus on the best constant lifetime prepayment speed for a given security. Figure 32.7 shows that the estimates on a 10% FNMA mortgage-backed security maturing in 2018 ranged from 20% to 40%.

Figure 32.7   Estimates of FNMA Lifetime PSA Prepayment Rates, 12/31/92, for 10% Coupon due 2018

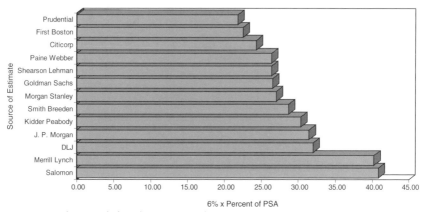

Source: D. Breeden, Journal of Fixed Income, December 1994

When we go back to our GNMA 8% data set of 1,347 numbers and solve for the prepayment rate k on each of the 1,347 days that would cause the predicted price to equal the actual price, we see that the historical prepayment rates even under the simplest of models have jumped in a way that appears almost totally random:

Figure 32.8   Perfectly Fitting Prepayment Rates for Actual GNMA 8% Prices, November 28 1988 to April 15 1994

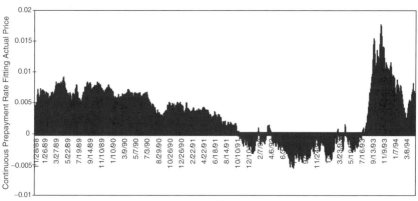

Breeden also shows that the conditional prepayment rates as a function of the coupon on the mortgage-backed security and the refinancing incentive have been very unstable and have been inconsistent with rationality in many cases. Prepayment speeds for high-coupon mortgages have often been lower than prepayment speeds for low-coupon mortgages (this phenomenon is often called 'burnout', short-hand for the fact that the most interest rate-sensitive borrowers in a pool of loans leave the pool first via refinancing, reducing the interest rate sensitivity of the pool over time). As Figure 32.9 shows, it is one thing to understand what burnout is and why it happens. It is another thing to predict the degree to which it will occur. We show how the transactions cost approach from Chapter 31 deals very effectively with this at the end of the chapter. Breeden's results show what a challenge this is:

Figure 32.9 Conditional Prepayment Rate vs. Par Coupon Level and Refinancing Incentive

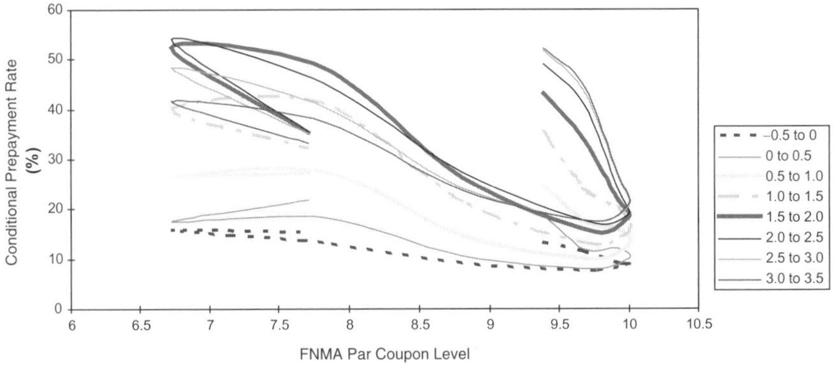

Source: Douglas Breeden, "Complexities of Hedging Mortgages," *Journal of Fixed Income*, December 1994

In fact, it is easier to guess the value of an embedded option directly than it is to guess the prepayment rates needed as inputs to a formula to calculate option values.

Option-Adjusted Spread

Given the difficulties with prepayment models in general, what are the implications for the option-adjusted spread quotations common on Wall Street? First of all, we should summarize the option-adjusted spread (OAS) procedures, for the term OAS refers more to the procedures used than it does to the true concept of the risky spread on mortgages. Typically, analysts do the following:

- They assume a prepayment function or prepayment table is true.
- They assume that Monte Carlo simulation is a good method for valuing an option, ignoring the concerns voiced in Chapter 30.

Figure 32.10 Conditional Prepayment Rates on FNMAs, Sorted by Refinancing Incentive

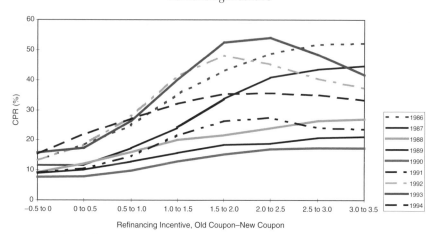

Source: Douglas Breeden, "Complexities of Hedging Mortgages," *Journal of Fixed Income*, December 1994

- They solve for the spread over a risk-free interest rate which provides a calculated value for the mortgage-backed security that matches the observable value.

In addition to the comments in Chapter 30 about the fundamental problems with the use of monte carlo simulation in the valuation of option-related securities, OAS analysis typically incorporates these errors:

a. The refinancing incentive is not measured on a matched maturity basis.

Within the prepayment table, the refinancing incentive in the current market is measured in order to choose the correct prepayment rate from the prepayment table or prepayment function. This is measured as the difference between the rate on the mortgage being analyzed and the rate on a new 30-year fixed-rate mortgage. This sounds good at first glance, but a closer look gives cause for serious concern. If there are five years remaining on the mortgage, we are comparing its five-year rate with the 30-year loan and assuming that refinancing is done on the basis of this 'apples to oranges' comparison. In a swap trading unit or an investment management firm, anyone who said '30-year bonds are better than five-year bonds because their yield is higher' would lose their job. This sort of comparison, however, is embedded in almost all OAS analysis. Why? Historical data on mortgage rates includes only rates at new issue maturities (typically 15 and 30 years in the U.S.) and the analysts had no other data to measure refinancing spread. The reason for the choice of measure is clear, but it's an important source of inaccuracy.

b. The refinancing incentive is measured on the basis of a 30-year mortgage rate which does not include a premium for the call provisions of the loan,

Within the monte carlo simulation routine, there is no capability to calculate how much the premium should be on a new mortgage that's callable compared to a hypothetical 'non-call' mortgage. Why? You have a 'chicken and egg problem'—using monte carlo and a prepayment table, we need to know what the option is worth in order to calculate what the option is worth! All of the refinancing incentives measured within the monte carlo routine are normally done assuming the mortgage is non-callable, introducing another source of error.

c. The prepayment table should be path-dependent, but it's not,

If rates start at 6%, jump to 12% for 10 years, and then fall to 4%, the prepayment function and prepayment tables will produce the same prepayment speed prediction as if rates started at 6%, fell to 3% for 10 years, and then jumped to 4%. Clearly, that should not be the case. Monte carlo is often relied upon on the rationale that prepayments are 'path-dependent'. We discuss that comment in more detail below, but it's clear monte carlo replaces a path-dependence problem in the prepayment rates themselves with a path-dependence problem in the prepayment table.

d. The OAS will match the market value of the observable security, but not its interest rate risk,

Why? For the same reason that the single prepayment speed model didn't work. We have two equations (value and rate sensitivity) we want to solve simultaneously, but only one variable (OAS) to adjust in order to do this. We can match both only by accident.

OAS is the 'plug' or balancing number that offsets all of the errors inherent in monte carlo analysis and the four problems above. It's not surprising, given the lack of consensus on Wall Street about prepayment rates, that median broker estimates of OAS show very strange patterns when plotted by coupon level. Breeden [1994] cites data for the third quarter of 1989 and the fourth quarter of 1992 which show investors could double their spread theoretical OAS by simply buying an MBS with a different coupon level, even though this discrepancy is public information widely disseminated by Wall Street firms.

The fact that this difference was not arbitraged away is due to the market's view that the OAS numbers were not accurate and that the spread differential was not real. Wall Street didn't bid up the price of the MBS with the widest reported OAS relative to the MBS with the lowest MBS. Clearly, OAS numbers are taken with a grain of salt by market participants. Gregg Patruno [1994] of Goldman, Sachs & Co. summarizes a common view by saying 'The standard measure of mortgage relative value ... OAS does not account for the complete nature of prepayment risk. Rather, it adjusts for the optionality due to interest rate fluctuations under the presumption that prepayment rates are a known, permanent function of interest rates.'[3]

The Transactions Cost Approach to Prepayments

Patruno goes on to suggest both the reason for the problems with OAS and a potential solution to the problem: 'Homeowners are willing to refinance if the financial incentive is high enough to meet their requirements. We use the measure of refinancing incentive actually considered by typical homeowners and their bankers—not an abstract interest differential or ad hoc statistical artifact, but the real dollar savings expected on an after tax basis, taking into account an appropriate mix of available mortgage rates and points.'[4] In other words, the only way to effectively model consumer prepayment behavior is to consider the rational value of the option to prepay. Patruno concludes that '...the levels of current mortgage rates and transactions costs determine what fraction of the homeowners in the distribution should be considered willing to refinance...'[5]

For these reasons, the authors believe that the transactions cost approach of Chapter 31, as analyzed by McConnell and Singh [1994] and Stanton [1995], is the only way to overcome the problems encountered in the full spectrum of prepayment and OAS analysis. How should that be done?

The answer depends on the objective. If the objective is to match *both* the value and the rate sensitivity of an observable mortgage-backed security (something OAS analysis cannot do), then the procedure is very straightforward. We use the American option version of the transactions cost approach in Chapter 31. We have two equations and only two variables that can be determined by this process. We split the mortgage-backed security into two pieces, exactly as we did in Chapter 31, and we assume that transactions costs are constant over the life of the loan.[6] We have three potential variables to solve for:

1. Transactions cost level of mortgage pool 1, which we call m_1;
2. Transactions cost level of mortgage pool 2, which we call m_2;
3. Weight w of mortgage pool 1.

---

[3] Patruno [1994], p. 53.
[4] Patruno [1994], page 47.
[5] Patruno [1994], page 47.
[6] This is for expositional purposes only. We can make the transactions cost function reflect seasonal factors, coupon on the loan, remaining life, etc.

We match value and rate risk by solving the equations:

$$\text{Value} = w\text{Value}[m_1(k_1)] + (1 - w)\text{Value}[m_2(k_1)]$$

$$\frac{\partial\text{Value}}{\partial r} = w\text{Value}_r[m_1(k_1)] + (1 - w)\text{Value}_r[m_2(k_2)]$$

for two of the three variables w, k_1, and k_2 where the ks represent the constant transactions cost of each of the two pieces of the mortgage-backed security we are trying to value. The value and *rDelta* of each of these pieces is calculated by using the trinomial lattice in Chapter 30 according to the transactions-cost-based valuation of an American option in Chapter 31. We can do the calculation in two ways:

1. Set $w = 0.5$ (or any other number) and solve for the two variables k_1 and k_2.
2. Set $k_1 = 0$ (or any other number) and solve for k_2 and w.

Implications for OAV Spread, CMOs and ARMs

The approach in the previous section is so straightforward that the power of the transactions cost approach is easy to overlook. Let us consider some of the implications:

Replace OAS with OAV spread

The primary reason for the lack of OAS consensus among Wall Street firms is that all of the assumptions being made are assumptions about the borrower. It is no wonder that consensus is impossible. Instead, we recommend the OAV (Option-adjusted value) spread. Let us consider a corporate treasurer who has to choose between issuing a seven-year non-call bond or a 10-year bond that is non-callable for seven years. He makes the decision in a straight-forward way. Firstly, he asks the rate on a comparable Treasury seven-year non-call bond and calculates his spread over Treasuries. Secondly, he calculates (since no observable Treasury is 10 years non-call seven-year bond) what the coupon would be on a 10-year non-call seven-year Treasury bond that trades at par value. His 'spread' on the 10-year non-call seven-year bond issue is the difference between his coupon and the Treasury's coupon. He issues the bond with the lowest spread.

The spread on retail-oriented securities should be measured by answering the question of spread, not by making assumptions about the borrower (since the question is unanswerable with any level of consensus). The question should be asked (in the context of a fixed-rate MBS with a 7%

coupon trading at 96 with level monthly payments and a maturity in 2017) in two parts:

1. What coupon would the U.S. Treasury pay on a callable security with level monthly payments, a maturity in 2017, and a value of 96?
2. Subtract the answer in (1) from 7. That is the OAV spread.

The odds of consensus in this calculation are much higher. It requires only the techniques of Chapter 30 applied to the U.S. Treasury. No assumptions about the consumer borrowers are necessary, and the only lack of consensus will be due to disagreements about which term structure model and lattice design to use.

The analysis can be refined still further by requiring the Treasury issue to have two components that match the two pieces of the mortgage-backed security (see the previous section) that produce matching interest rate risk and value.

CMOs and ARMs

Collateralized mortgage obligations (CMOs) and adjustable rate mortgages (ARM) can be analyzed in exactly the way we have outlined in the previous section, with McConnell and Singh providing a concrete example of that approach. ARMs, because of the path dependence of the security, are more complex, but even so, the transactions cost approach provides substantial value relative to the traditional prepayment approach. We now turn to a practical example of how the transactions cost approach can be fit to historical prepayment data in order to do forward-looking valuation and simulation on other pools of consumer loans.

Fitting the transactions cost approach to historical prepayments on asset-backed securities[7]

In this section we show how the transaction cost approach can be fitted to historical prepayments on pools of asset backed securities. In this chapter we focus on ABS issues backed by recreational vehicle loans and boat loans. This sector is particularly interesting because many market participants argue that, contrary to the mortgage market, borrowers ignore any interest rate-related prepayment opportunities. We start by asking whether this view is consistent with actual prepayment experience.

The data discussed in this section is based on public information on prepayments provided by Credit Suisse First Boston. The data covers 986 months of data on prepayments on pools of manufactured housing loans ('trailers') issued as ABS by Bank of America, 1,060 months of prepayments on manufactured

---

[7] The authors are grateful to Richard Schumacher and Joe Thomas, both formerly of Deutsche Financial Services, for helpful comments on this section.

housing loan ABS issued by Green Tree, and 602 months of prepayment experience on recreational vehicle ABS issued primarily by CIT.

The commonly used 'single prepayment speed' assumptions in the ABS market can easily be shown to be incorrect. A simple linear regression that explains prepayment rates as a function of the 10-year U.S. Treasury yield explains a significant amount of the variation in prepayment speeds:

68.5% of the Bank of America ABS prepayments;
43.3% of the Green Tree ABS prepayments;
52.3% of the CIT ABS prepayments.

The single prepayment speed approach, by definition, explains zero percent of the variation. Figure 32.11 shows the dramatic increase in prepayments as a function of interest rate levels for the Bank of America portfolio.

Figure 32.11 10-Year Treasury versus Monthly Prepayment for Bank of America

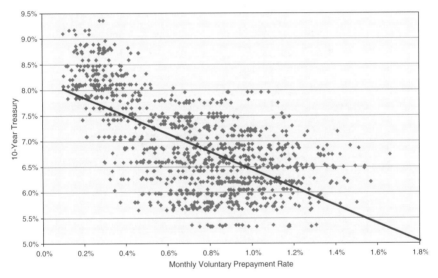

Another reality of the ABS market is the seasonality of prepayment. Prepayment rates in the ABS market fall in the winter and rise in the summer, as Figure 32.12 shows for the Bank of America manufactured housing ABS.

The impact of seasonality is even more dramatic with prepayments on the recreational vehicle ABS as shown by Figure 32.13:

Prepayment rises significantly in the spring as recreational vehicles are sold and loans prepaid, primarily due to the owners 'trading up' to new vehicles before the prime usage season in the summer.

Another factor that dramatically impacts the prepayment rates on ABS portfolios is that of aging. When seasonality, interest rates and aging are fitted to historical data and compared to the 'industry standard' prepayment

Figure 32.12 Impact of Month on Prepayment Rate, Bank of America MH

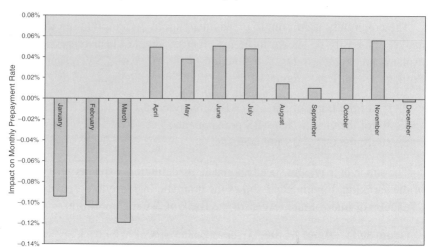

Figure 32.13 Increase in Monthly Prepayment due to Month, RV Portfolios

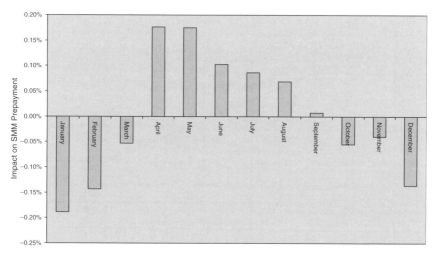

assumptions, we can see that the level of interest rate risk varies dramatically from common assumptions. Figure 32.14 shows the weighted average months to maturity at different interest rate levels on a long tranche of an asset-backed security issued by Deutsche Financial.

Even more importantly, the seasonality can be seen clearly in projected prepayment patterns at various interest rate levels for this same ABS issue when a sophisticated prepayment function is used as shown in Figure 32.15.

The pattern of prepayments at U.S. 10-year Treasury levels ranging from 3.6% to 9.6% is dramatically different from the 'industry standard' assumptions that prepayment is a function of aging alone.

Figure 32.14 Weighted Average Months to Maturity, Longest Tranche of Deutsche Financial Capital January 1998 Issue, at Various Levels of U.S 10-Year Treasury Yield

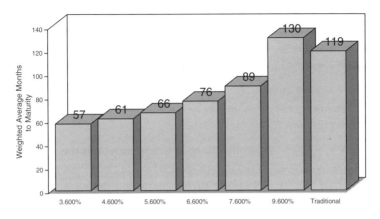

Figure 32.15 Monthly Principal Repayment and Recoveries at Different Interest Rate Levels, Longest Tranche of Deutsche Financial Capital January 1998 Issue, For Different Future of 10-Year U.S. Treasury Yield

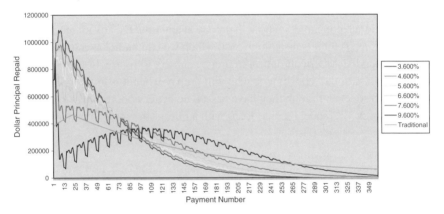

The Transactions Cost Approach

As powerfully as we have demonstrated the impact of interest rates on prepayment speeds in the ABS market, we can still do better using the transactions cost approach. Greg Patruno [1994] of Goldman, Sachs & Co. notes in the context of mortgage loans:

> *'Despite all the revolutionary changes that have occurred in the mortgage market since the first MBS prepayment data of the early 1970s, and even though the prepayment behavior of U.S. homeowners is not theoretically 'rational' by a long stretch, such behavior has been extremely consistent in key respects when viewed in terms of the real dollar incentives that homeowners actually consider in reaching their decisions.'*

'Homeowners are willing to refinance if the financial incentive is high enough to meet their requirements. We use the measure of refinancing incentive actually considered by typical homeowners and their bankers— not an abstract interest differential or ad hoc statistical artifact, but the real dollar savings expected on an after tax basis, taking into account an appropriate mix of available mortgage rates and points.

'...the levels of current mortgage rates and transaction costs determine what fraction of the homeowners in the distribution should be considered willing to refinance...'

We now implement the transactions cost approach to fit the actual prepayment rates experienced in the manufactured housing ABS issued by Bank of America from 1988 to 1991. We divide the actual prepayments into these groups:

- 'Irrational' consumers who will prepay even when they shouldn't, whom we can model as having a loan with an explicit maturity date and no embedded options. This loan has an arbitrary amortization that is invariant to changes in interest rates.
- 'Rational' consumers who will prepay at any time the advantage of doing so exceeds their transactions cost, which we can model as a loan with an embedded American option to prepay subject to transactions costs.
- 'Semi-rational' consumers, who will prepay when it is to their advantage to do so, even though they have passed up better opportunities to do so in the past. We model them as loans with a European option to prepay subject to transactions costs.

We go through these steps to make the classification of actual prepayments using the three groups above:

- Restate all monthly prepayments as a percentage of original principal, not the percentage of remaining principal. We need to do this in order to do forward looking prepayment analysis, not backward looking analysis. We want to establish a classification system that we can use looking forward on new ABS issues.
- Double check to make sure that we haven't lost any explanatory power from doing so. It turns out that interest rates still explain 65% of prepayment variation on the Bank of America portfolio when the prepayment rate is expressed as a percent of original principal, almost unchanged from the 68% we found using percentage of remaining principal.
- Classify each month into 'irrational', 'European' or 'American' categories.
- Set the amounts in each category and the relevant transactions costs for each.

After restating prepayments on this basis, prepayments as a percentage of original principal show the well-known tendency to rise as the ABS issue ages:

Figure 32.16 Prepayments as a Percent of Original Principal versus Payment Number

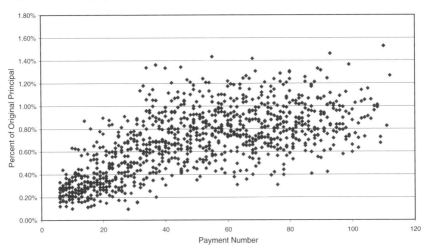

We note the following about our classification of loans by transactions cost category:

- Loans were classified on an 'all or nothing' basis, either all irrational, all European, or all American:
  - Irrational loans prepaid when there was no financial benefit to doing so;
  - American loans prepaid when the financial advantage to doing so had never been greater in the past;
  - European loans prepaid when there was a financial advantage, but there had been a bigger financial advantage.
- Some 'irrational' borrowers would have prepaid in months classified as 'European' or 'American' even if there had been no financial advantage to do so.
- Some 'European' borrowers would have prepaid in months classified as 'American' even if there had been better opportunities to prepay in the past.
- Therefore:
  - Within the American category there are both irrational and European borrowers;
  - Within the European category there are irrational borrowers.

If the transactions cost approach has validity, the breakdown of borrowers into irrational, European and American classes should be very similar for pools of loans that are the same type and which experience similar market conditions. The Bank of America manufactured housing pools are homogeneous with similar issue dates. We can see from Table 32.1 that the average percentage of loans prepaying irrationally was 2.83%, 52.94% prepaid as if they were subject to European options to prepay with transactions costs, and 8.30% prepaid as if they had American options to prepay with transactions costs. Of the total, 35.94% had not prepaid and so they could not be classified.

Table 32.1 Breakdown of Borrowers into Irrational, European, and American Classes for Loans of the Same Type

Issuer	Issue Code Analyzed	Number of Payments	Irrational	European	American	Still Outstanding	Total
Bank of America	MLMI 88 ja	112	0.48%	57.46%	8.62%	33.44%	100.00%
Bank of America	MLMI 88 pa	109	0.65%	51.61%	11.57%	36.17%	100.00%
Bank of America	MLMI 89 ca	104	0.30%	58.27%	8.55%	32.88%	100.00%
Bank of America	MLMI 89 ea	100	2.76%	49.33%	8.88%	39.03%	100.00%
Bank of America	MLMI 89 ga	98	4.88%	52.20%	9.09%	33.83%	100.00%
Bank of America	MLMI 90 a	94	0.46%	53.53%	8.22%	37.79%	100.00%
Bank of America	MLMI 90 ca	91	7.72%	54.28%	8.00%	29.99%	100.00%
Bank of America	MLMI 90 fa	88	8.39%	53.84%	7.72%	30.05%	100.00%
Bank of America	MLMI 90 ha	85	0.71%	55.34%	8.39%	35.56%	100.00%
Bank of America	MLMI 91 aa	82	4.74%	51.54%	7.46%	36.26%	100.00%
Bank of America	MLMI 91 ca	79	0.00%	44.91%	4.74%	50.34%	100.00%
Average			2.83%	52.94%	8.30%	35.94%	

In Chapters 24 and 31, we discussed how to value all of these types of options embedded in loans or bonds. All we need to know is which transactions cost levels to assign, because Table 32.1 tells us how many loans of each type are in the portfolios. We can use the average composition to evaluate the interest rate risk in new portfolios.

The data reveals some interesting insights once we have made the classification into irrational prepayments, European prepayments and American repayments. Firstly, the size of irrational prepayments seems to increase with the age of the loan. These for the most part would be people who have sold their manufactured housing unit for the standard reasons (death, divorce or relocation):

Figure 32.17 Irrational Prepayment as Percent of Original Principal

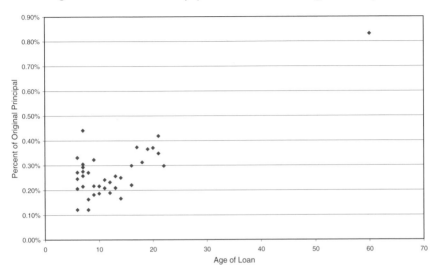

We can also show the various levels of transactions costs that were implied by the timing of the prepayment by the American options payers. If, for example, a borrower prepaid when the present value benefit of prepaying was 8% of original principal and the present value benefit had never been that great during the prior history of the loan, we would say that borrower has a transactions cost of 8% (or else he would have prepaid earlier).

Figure 32.18 Cumulative Amount of American Options by Transactions Cost

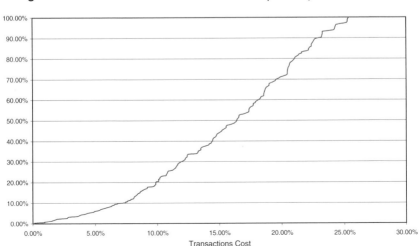

Figure 32.18 shows that the transactions costs for American prepayers in the Bank of America manufactured housing pool ranged from zero to about 26% of original principal, with a median level of about 17%. We would expect transactions costs as a percentage of principal for mortgages to be less, in part because of the larger dollar amounts involved in a home mortgage.

Figure 32.19 Cumulative Distribution of Transactions Costs for European Options

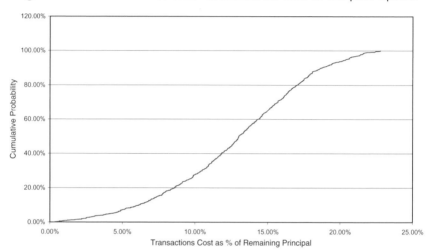

Figure 32.19 shows a similar distribution for the European prepayers. They are different from American option prepayers because the European group prepaid in a month in which the advantage of prepaying was less than it had been at some time in the past. If the borrower had an American option to repay, they would have prepaid at the point in the past where the benefit from prepaying was higher.

The levels of transactions costs found for European option-prepayers are roughly similar to those for borrowers classified as American option prepayers Figure 32.20 shows that the transactions costs implied by the behavior of the European options prepayers increased with the age of the loan.

Figure 32.21 shows that the amount of prepayment by the European option prepayers also increased with the age of the loan:

If the total amount of the original principal in a manufactured housing loan pool is going to be modeled, how should we do it, based on these insights? We start by looking at the relative sizes of the prepayment 'pieces' of principal that we classified above:

	Irrational	**European**	**American**	**Total**
Average	0.28%	0.76%	0.51%	0.69%
High	0.83%	1.53%	1.23%	1.53%
Low	0.12%	0.10%	0.10%	0.10%

Figure 32.20 European Transactions Cost by Month

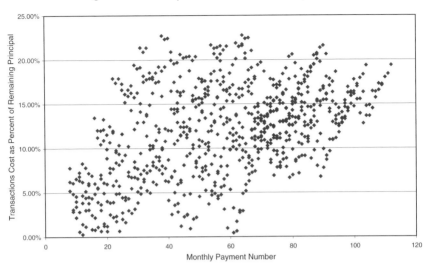

Figure 32.21 European Exercise as Percent of Original Principal, Graphed by Month of Exercise

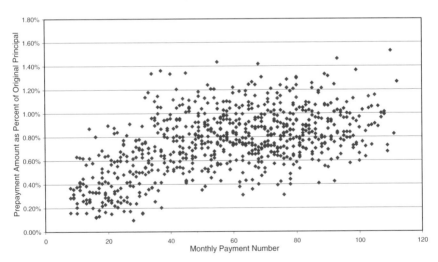

The average amount of the irrational payments was 0.28% of original principal in the pool. The average European prepayment was 0.76% of the original pool, while the average American repayment was 0.51% of the pool.

How would we break up the 100% of principal in a new pool for modeling, valuing and simulation? We note the following based on the data we have examined in this section:

- Portfolios should be modeled as a mix of loans that have no options to prepay, a European option to prepay, and an American option to prepay.

- No loan should have an amount greater than 1.5% of the original principal of the pool.
- The average should be about 0.70%.
- Irrational loans should average about 0.30%.
- Transactions costs should range from zero to 25%, increasing with exercise date.
- The size of loans in the European category should increase in size with the exercise date.
- Loan amounts in the irrational category should increase in size with the maturity date.

We also note that we can use this approach to work backwards and create a portfolio that is 100% accurate in replicating actual prepayment on the Bank of America portfolios:

- This replicating portfolio can be 100% consistent with actual experience, compared to only 65–68% with a regression-based prepayment formula.
- This replicating portfolio has built-in characteristics like:
  - 'burn-out', slowing prepayment sensitivity to rates;
  - rate path-dependent prepayment behavior;
  seasonality.
- The granularity of how finely we would model each 'piece' of the portfolio depends on our objectives:
  - If the only objective is to match observed market value, duration and convexity, we can model a loan portfolio with only three loans.
  - If we want to model 10 years of monthly prepayment performance (usually necessary only for net income simulation), we would model the loan with each of the three types (irrational, European and American) maturing in each of the 120 months, for a total of 3 x 120 = 360 instruments.
  - Maximum granularity would assign an options type at the individual loan level. For most purposes there is no reason not to do this. The logistic regression approach of the next section provides the framework to do this in an automated way.

This process of prepayment modeling gives us extremely powerful benefits over the much less accurate prepayment speed, prepayment function and prepayment table approaches. We can calculate the value of an option to prepay, even if exercised irrationally, with very high precision from observable market data. We simply imply the level of transactions costs like we imply volatility in the Black-Scholes options model. From the GNMA price data used earlier in this chapter, we observe a plateau in value at about 105% of principal. Clearly, unless the transactions costs were on average at least 5%, every mortgage in the portfolio would have prepaid and the value of the GNMA would have been 100, not 105. So implying transactions costs is extremely easy.

With the transactions costs approach, we get a much better fit to actual loan price movement than with a prepayment model. We don't have to predict future transaction costs like we would have to predict future prepayment speeds. The transactions cost approach brings real power to prepayment analysis.

Logistic Regression, Credit Risk and Prepayment

Logistic regression is another powerful tool that we are familiar with from its use in modeling default probabilities for retail, small business, and large corporations using a historical database of defaults. In a similar way, we can use logistic regression to model the probability of prepayment. With this technique we can combine variables like the following, as explanatory variables for prepayment:

- The net present value benefit of prepaying as of the current observation (which captures the interest rate benefits of prepayment);
- The age of the loan;
- The months remaining before maturity;
- The month (to capture seasonality);
- Direct transactions costs of refinancing (points, fees, etc.);
- The default probability of the borrower, as captured directly by internal models or by some kind of internal credit rating;
- Any other relevant consumer credit bureau approach.

The coefficients of this logistic regression essentially let us derive the transactions costs that we implied previously. They also automate the adjustments for seasonality that we would also have to make in the approach of the previous section.

The result is an extremely powerful integration of credit risk, interest rate risk and prepayment risk that significantly advances the accuracy of our ability to model the Jarrow-Merton put option, our integrated measure of risk for the full balance sheet.

Exercises

32.1 Using the prepayment table approach, is the analysis of mortgage backed securities path-dependent?

32.2 Assume that you use the transactions cost approach and you model the security by breaking it into 10 pieces, each of which has a different level of transactions costs reflecting the different layers of rate sensitivity among consumers. If you simulated the prepayment behavior of this transactions cost-based portfolio, would the prepayment experience be path-dependent?

32.3 Would the financial analysis required to model the portfolio in 32.2 require a technique that deals with path dependence?

32.4 Write the formula for the value of the portfolio in 32.2 assuming you have solved for the value of each piece using the techniques in Chapters 30 and 31.

32.5 Write the formula for *rDelta* of the portfolio in 32.2 assuming you know the *rDelta* of each piece from the techniques in Chapters 30 and 31.

32.6 Assume one MBS pool has been broken into three CMO tranches, the *A*, *B*, and *C* tranches. The A tranche gets all principal payments until 30% of original principal is retired. The *B* tranche gets all subsequent principal payments until another 32% of principal has been retired. The *C* tranche gets the rest. Assume you can observe in the market the value and *rDelta* of the original pool and the *A*, *B*, and *C* CMO tranches. How many pieces do you need to break each CMO tranche into using the transactions cost approach? Write down the system of equations that needs to be solved to identify the relevant transactions costs.

Appendix 1

Mortgage Prepayment Analysis in Continuous Time

For analysts who are comfortable with the continuous compounding formulas in Chapter 7 and the continuous time default intensities of credit risk models in Chapter 17, we can analyze prepayment behavior as if it were continuous as well. This avoids a lot of tedious formulas necessary in the discrete time case. We derive continuous time prepayment formulas in this section.

Let the initial principal on the loan be L^*. We assume the continuous level payment on the loan is c, and its continuous mortgage rate is y. We assume that the mortgage matures at time T and that it was originated at time zero. Its original term to maturity was $T = T - 0$ and its remaining term to maturity is $T - t = \tau$. The level payment c on the loan is the continuous constant amount such that the present value of c, discounted at the continuous mortgage yield y, exactly equals the original principal amount L^*:

$$L^* = \int_0^T ce^{-ys}\, ds = \frac{c}{y}[1 - e^{-yT}]$$

Rearranging gives the formula for c:

$$c = \frac{yL^*}{1 - e^{-yT}}$$

The remaining scheduled principal on the loan is a function of the remaining life of the loan $T - t = \tau$. We write this amount:

$$L(\tau) = \frac{c}{y} [1 - e^{-y\tau}]$$

Note that $L(0) = 0$ and $L(T) = L^*$. We can substitute the equation for c into this expression to get a formula that is independent of c for the remaining principal outstanding:

$$L(t, T) = L(\tau) = \frac{[1 - e^{-y\tau}]L^*}{1 - e^{-yT}}$$

Interest Only (IO) cash flows

The interest portion of the continuous cash flow is simply:

$$i(\tau) = yL(\tau) = c[1 - e^{-y\tau}]$$

The IO piece is the continuous yield on the mortgage y times the principal outstanding at that instant.

Principal Only (PO) cash flows

The principal only portion of cash flows is portion of the continuous cash flow c which is *not* interest:

$$p(\tau) = c - yL(\tau) = c - c[1 - e^{-y\tau}] = ce^{-y\tau}$$

Put another way, the principal portion is the negative of the instantaneous change in principal outstanding:

$$p(\tau) = -\frac{\partial L(\tau)}{\partial \tau} = ce^{-y\tau}$$

Mortgage valuation: No prepayment

The value of the mortgage with no prepayment is its simple present value:

$$\text{value} = c \int_t^T P(r, s, T) \, ds$$

In the extended Vasicek and Vasicek models, the *rDelta* or interest rate sensitivity of value with respect to changes in the short-term rate of interest is:

$$\frac{\partial \text{ value}}{\partial r} = c \int_t^T P_r(r, s, T) \, ds = c \int_t^T -\frac{1}{\alpha} \left[1 - e^{\alpha(T-s)} \right] P(r, s, T) \, ds$$

Mortgage cash flows with prepayment

Many mortgages contain the right to pay all or some of the mortgage principal outstanding early. A typical simple assumption is that the amount repaid is a constant ratio k of the principal outstanding at that time. We denote the principal outstanding on such a mortgage by M. The continuous prepayment amount is:

$$\text{prepayment} = kM(t, T) = kM(\tau)$$

If mortgages are prepaid early at the rate k, what will the continuous cash flow on the mortgage be at any given time to maturity? To answer this question, we must determine the value of principal outstanding at any given time to maturity $T - t = \tau$. We know the following about a mortgage with early prepayment:

- The continuous scheduled payment c on the mortgage will be continually reset such that:

$$c(\tau) = \frac{yM(\tau)}{1 - e^{-y\tau}}$$

- The total payment will be the continuous scheduled payment plus the early prepayment of principal:

$$\text{total payment} = c(\tau) + kM(\tau) = \frac{yM(\tau)}{1 - e^{-y\tau}} + kM(\tau)$$

- The interest portion of the continuous payment is:

$$i(\tau) = yM(\tau)$$

- The principal portion of total payment is:

$$p(\tau) = \text{total payment} - i(\tau) = \frac{yM(\tau)}{1 - e^{-y\tau}} + kM(\tau) - yM(\tau)$$

- Total principal due over the remaining life of the mortgage should equal total principal outstanding:

$$M(t, T) = \int_t^T \left[\frac{yM(s, T)}{1 - e^{-y(T-s)}} + kM(s, T) - yM(s, T) \right] ds$$

We can convert this into a partial differential equation by differentiating both sides with respect to t. This leads to the equation:

$$M_t(t, T) = -\left[\frac{y}{1 - e^{-y(T-t)}} - y + k \right] M(t, T)$$

which must be solved subject to three boundary conditions:

a. $M(0, T) = L^*$, the original principal amount on the loan;
b. $M(T, T) = 0$, zero principal remains outstanding at maturity;
c. $M(t, T) = L(t, T)$ when $k = 0$, since the loan in this case is identical to the no prepayment exampleof section 1.

The solution is:

$$M(t, T) = \left[\frac{1 - e^{-y\tau}}{1 - e^{-yT}} \right] \frac{e^{k\tau}}{e^{kT}} L^*$$

Given this solution, the total payment on the mortgage, including interest and both scheduled and unscheduled principal payments, is:

$$\text{Total Payment} = Z(\tau) = \left[\frac{y}{1 - e^{-y\tau}} + k \right] \left(\frac{1 - e^{-y\tau}}{1 - e^{-yT}} \right) \frac{e^{k\tau}}{e^{kT}} L^*$$

The value of the mortgage with early prepayment is the normal present value of these cash flows, which takes the form of an integral since payments are continuous rather than discrete:

$$\text{Value} = \int_0^\tau P(r, s) Z(s) ds$$

and rate sensitivity is:

$$r\,Delta = \frac{\partial \text{ value}}{\partial r} = \int_0^\tau P_r(r, s) Z(s) ds$$

CHAPTER 33

Non-Maturity Deposits[1]

An Introduction to Non-Maturity Deposits

In this chapter, we turn our attention to the liability side of the balance sheet of financial institutions, in particular commercial banks. This focus is critical to correct valuation of the Jarrow-Merton put option as the best comprehensive measure of integrated credit risk and interest rate risk. Why? Because we need to value a put option that includes both assets and liabilities of the financial institution, since some of the liabilities may be providing a hedge of the assets. One of the advantages of the reduced form credit modeling technology of Chapter 17 is that it can handle the complex liability structure that is typical of large financial institutions, where as the Merton model of Chapter 16 assumes a single zero-coupon bond as a liability.

The bulk of bank deposits and insurance liabilities are made up of 'securities' with explicit maturities, although they are often putable by the consumer who supplied the funds, whether they come in the form of a time deposit or life insurance policy. These liabilities can be analyzed with the techniques of Chapters 30 and 31, even if the consumer's right to put the security back to the financial institution is exercised irrationally. A substantial portion, however, of the liabilities of major banks world-wide consists of 'non-maturity deposits'. Similarly, the funds supplied to mutual fund managers of fixed income funds also have no specific maturities. This chapter is relevant to both types of liabilities, but we will refer to them as 'non-maturity deposits' within a banking industry context from here on. These deposits have no specific maturity, and individual depositors can freely add or subtract balances as they wish. The interest rate on these deposits is usually, but not always, a function of open market interest rates. Similarly, the level of deposit balances in aggregate often

---

[1] An earlier version of this chapter appeared as Chapter 15 in van Deventer and Imai [1996].

moves in sympathy with open market interest rates. With the strong trend in mark-to-market based risk management in banking, all bankers are faced with the difficult task of calculating the mark-to-market 'value' of these non-maturity deposits. This chapter provides an introduction to that difficult topic.

In September 1993, the Federal Reserve Board [1993] published proposed regulations for interest rate risk and capital adequacy. In its regulations, the Federal Reserve Board noted '…the inherent difficulties in determining the appropriate treatment of non-maturity deposits'. In this chapter, we present a number of techniques for measuring the mark-to-market value of deposits that are theoretically rigorous and yet easy to apply in practice. Most of the arguments which are applied here to the valuation of non-maturity deposits can be applied equally well to the valuation of charge card loans, where again the balance as well as the rate on the loan fluctuates in response to market rate movements. For more on both deposit and charge card valuation, see Jarrow and van Deventer [1996a, 1996b, 1998] and Janosi, Jarrow and Zullo [1998].

The 'Value' of the Deposit Franchise

When we measure the 'value' of deposits, what is it that we are trying to measure? If the bank had issued a bond to finance its assets, the 'value' of the bond is its present value—the present value of future payments that the bank must make on the security that it has issued. 'Value' is the present value of future costs.

In the case of non-maturity deposits, the 'value' of the deposit could also mean the premium that a third party would be willing to pay above the face value of the deposits to assume ownership of the bank's deposit 'franchise'.[2] In this case, 'value' means the net present value benefit of owning the deposit franchise—the value of cash provided by depositors less the present value cost of the deposit franchise.

In what follows, we use the word 'value' to refer to the present value of the cost of the deposit franchise, exactly in keeping with the analogy of the bank as bond issuer. The net present value benefit of having the deposit franchise can be calculated from the valuation formulas presented below by subtracting the 'values' we calculate from the face value of the deposit. For example, the present value cost of $100 face value of savings deposits might be $65. The net present value benefit of the deposit franchise is $100 − $65, or $35. All references to 'value' below refer to the present value of the cost of the franchise, $65.

---

[2] The average premium paid by purchasers of failed bank deposit franchises was 2.32% in 1,225 auctions run through October 28 1994 by the Resolution Trust Corporation in the U.S. The highest premium paid was 25.33%. Most of the deposits auctioned (more than 70% on average) were time deposits, which would be expected to have very low premiums.

We also assume that the deposit franchise is guaranteed by a riskless third party, which is the case in the U.S. and many other countries. This allows us to avoid dealing with the complexities of bankruptcy risk.

Some bankers prefer to focus on the value of specific non-maturity deposits owned by current clients, i.e. valuing only deposit accounts on the books of the bank today and ignoring future business. This orientation has a logical basis, because we don't value the 'franchise' of any other business line on the bank balance sheet.

There is a good reason for looking at the franchise for valuation. The pricing of non-maturity deposits is exactly the same for new customers as it is for old customers. The bank cannot control the flow of new demand deposit accounts or savings deposit accounts by changing pricing to attract new clients without immediately making the same price change on existing accounts. This is not the case for auto loans or consumer certificates of deposit or any other account on the balance sheet of the bank except for the charge card business. For this reason, we think the focus on the franchise is the right one, but we recognize that some will disagree.

Total Cash Flow of Non-Maturity Deposits

The first step in valuing non-maturity deposits is to isolate the total cash flows from the deposit franchise. Total costs consist of the following elements:

Total deposit cost cash flows in a given time period:

   = interest paid on the deposit
   + non-interest expense of servicing the deposit
   − non-interest revenue from the deposit franchise
   − net increase in deposit balances.

Many readers will be surprised to see the net increase in deposit balances subtracted from costs in the equation above. The net change in deposit balances on many deposit products is the single most important cash flow in the valuation process, and yet many analysts ignore this important determinant of value.

In the valuation of any security, total cash flow is the basic building block of valuation. For most securities, the maturity date is fixed and cash flow from "principal" stems from a pre-determined payment schedule associated with that security. In the case of the non-maturity deposit, however, the security is a perpetual one and principal is never "returned." Instead, changes in deposit balances are simply another source of cash flow. A simple example illustrates the point.

Let us consider a deposit category with balances of $100 where the sum of interest expense and processing costs is 2% of balances annually. Let's assume that this cash flow occurs at the end of every year. Let's also assume that the balances on this account grow at 2% a year, and that balances also increase in a one-time jump at the end of each year. What is the net cash flow associated with this account? On December 31 of each year, 2% of the deposit amount flows out in the form of interest expense and processing costs, and it flows back in on the same day in the form of increased deposit balances. The net cash flow from the deposit franchise is zero every year forever.

The present value cost of this deposit is zero, since there is never net cash inflow or outflow. Since the present value cost is zero, the 'net present value' or premium that would be paid to gain this deposit franchise is $100, calculated as above: the deposit balance $100 – the present value of deposit costs ($0) is $100.

This example is deceptively simple: it is consistent with common sense, and yet it will lead us to some surprising conclusions about the value of non-maturity deposits. We will analyze the value of non-maturity deposits in what follows using a series of progressively more realistic assumptions about deposit rate and balance behavior. We start by assuming that deposit balances are constant to derive a valuation formula for deposits. We then assume that interest rates are constant and balances are random. We derive deposit values for four different types of deposit variation. Finally, we provide a brief introduction to the most realistic case where both deposit balances and deposit rates are random. This is covered in more detail in Jarrow and van Deventer [1996a, 1996b, 1998] and Janosi, Jarrow and Zullo [1998].

Deposit Valuation with Constant Balances or Known Variation in Balances

In this section, we lay a foundation for random movements in deposit balance analysis by reviewing the case when deposit balances are either constant or whose future variation is known with certainty. The arguments that we make can be classified as no-arbitrage arguments in this sense—bankers are constantly comparing the cost of non-maturity deposits to other sources of funds and the present value of the non-maturity deposit is calculated by reference to these alternative sources of funds. The present value of the non-maturity deposit is the cost of replicating the cash flows of the deposit franchise from other funding sources.

Case A: Constant deposit amount with constant fixed-rate on deposits

Let us consider the case where the amount of the deposit is constant and the yield and processing costs associated with the deposit are both fixed percentages of the amount of the deposit D. In order to avoid the minutia of compounding calculations, let's assume that the interest expense and processing costs associated with the deposit franchise are paid continuously. Let the continuously paid deposit rate be y and the continuously paid processing costs be c. If both the interest and processing costs are paid continuously, the value V of the deposit is:

$$V = \frac{(y+c)D}{R_c}$$

R_c is the rate on a continuously paid consol (perpetual fixed-rate bond) consistent with the risk-free yield curve. The present value of the cost of the deposit franchise is exactly the same as the value of a perpetual bond paying the identical amount of interest. The duration of the deposit is:

$$\text{Duration} = \frac{-(\partial V/\partial R_c)}{V} = \frac{((y+c)D/R_c^2)}{V} = \frac{1}{R_c}$$

Example

The bank has a $100 non-maturity deposit that costs 4% continuously, 3% in interest and 1% in processing costs. The open market interest rate for a perpetual fixed-rate bond is 10%. The present value of the cost of the deposit is the interest cost of the deposit (4% times $100, or $4) capitalized at the 10% rate: $40 ($4/.1). The duration of the deposit is [$4/(.1)^2]/$40 = 10 years. The long duration is no surprise, since this is the equivalent of a perpetual fixed-rate bond.

Case B: Constant deposit amount with floating rate at proportional spread

There is another form of deposit that leads to simple results if the amount of the deposit is constant. We assume the rate on the deposit is a continuously paid floating rate that is a constant proportion of the short-term risk-free market rate r. For purposes of this example, we could call this short rate LIBOR.[3] We let this proportion be k. In general, the market value of a perpetual floating-rate security that continuously pays at the riskless instantaneous rate of interest is its par value.[4] Note that the cash flows on the deposit exactly equal k times the cash flows on a perpetual floater at the short-term riskless rate with a par value of kD. To avoid riskless arbitrage, this means that the value

---

[3] The discrete payment on one-month LIBOR or three-month LIBOR changes some of the formulas that follow in a minor way. We ignore this minor difference in what follows.

[4] For proof of this proposition, see Cox, Ingersoll and Ross [1980].

of the deposit on a payment date must be exactly k times the value of the perpetual floater:

$$V = kD$$

Note that the duration of the continuously paid deposit is zero since no interest rate r appears in the valuation formula.

Example

Assume that a $100 deposit account pays 60% of LIBOR forever, since the deposit is a non-maturity deposit account. The cash flows on the account $= 0.6 \times$ LIBOR $\times \$100 = $ LIBOR $\times \$60$. The cash costs of the account are identical to the cash cost of a perpetual floater with a par value of $60 which pays LIBOR. The present value cost of a perpetual bond paying LIBOR is its par value. Therefore the present value cost of the deposit must be $60. The present value does not change as rates change,[5] so the duration of the cost of the deposit is zero.

Case C: Constant deposit amount with floating rate and linear spread

If the deposit amount is constant and the deposit rate is a linear function of a floating market rate, then deposit pricing is a combination of Cases A and B. In this case, we assume the deposit rate y is a simple function of short-term rates of the form $y = a + bR_f$, where R_f is the floating market rate (such as LIBOR) and R_c is the yield on a perpetual fixed-rate bond or consol. The cash flow on this deposit can be broken into two pieces: (a) a constant payment, that can be valued as in Case 33 A assuming $y = a$, and (b) a proportional payment, with a solution as in Case 33 B using $y = bR_f$.

Once we have solved for the value of each component, the value of the total must equal the sum of each piece or arbitrage will result.

The value is:

$$V = \frac{aD}{R_c} + bD$$

The duration of the deposit is:

$$\text{Duration} = \frac{-(\partial V/\partial R_c)}{V} = \frac{(aD/R_c^2)}{V} = \frac{a}{R_c(a + bR_c)}$$

---

[5] We ignore the impact on present value of an initial coupon rate which may have already been set.

Example

The bank has a $100 non-maturity deposit which pays a rate equal to 4% plus 20% of LIBOR. These parameters of non-maturity deposit rate behavior are determined by linear regression analysis on the historical movement of deposit rates. We assume that the rate on a perpetual fixed-rate bond is 10%. The cash flows on this deposit can be broken into two pieces. The first piece is fixed—4% times $100 = $4 annually. The value of this piece is $4/.1 = $40 as in the example above. The second piece depends on the level of LIBOR. The amount paid is 20% times LIBOR times $100, which is the same as the cash flow on a $20 security (20% times $100) paying LIBOR. The value of the second piece is $20, since we assume a LIBOR floater always trades at a market value equal to par value. The sum of the fixed and floating pieces is $60, the present value cost of the deposit. The duration of this deposit is [$4/(.1)^2]/$60, or 6.67 years.

Note that this example implies a 'floor' of 4% on the deposit rate. For many periods in the U.S., this kind of result was typical. We now know from savings deposit rate behavior in Japan's low interest rate environment that these floors are really part of a lagged response of savings deposit rates to open market rate changes and that the effective floor is zero, as we discussed in Chapter 27.

Case D: Known future variation in deposit balances

Another simple case is the one where future variations in deposit balances are known with certainty, as is the interest rate and processing costs associated with deposits. The value of the deposit is simply the present value of the future known cash flows (the change in deposit amount, interest on the deposits, processing costs, etc.). We denote the present value of a dollar t years in advance as $P(t)$. The deposit value, assuming the cash flow at time t_i given by X_i, is:

$$V = \sum_{i=1}^{n} P[t_i] X_i$$

Unless this is true, there would be riskless arbitrage available, since the bank would fund itself using regular bond or time deposit issues instead of getting into the non-maturity deposit business. Using continuous time notation, the relationship between these discount factors and their continuously compounded yield to maturities y_i and maturities t_i is the same as we discussed in Chapter 7:

$$P[t_i] = e^{-y_i t_i}$$

The duration of this deposit is a direct application of Macaulay's original duration formula in continuous time terms. We assume each y_i shifts by an amount z to $y_i^* = y_i + z$. Duration[6] is:

$$\text{Duration} = \frac{-(\partial V / \partial z)}{V} = \frac{\sum\limits_{i=1}^{n} t_i P[t_i] X_i}{V}$$

Example

Let us consider a bank with $110 in deposits. We assume that the net cash outflow from the bank's deposit business (interest expense less net increase in deposit balances) follows the schedule below:

Years	Present Value Factor	Cash Flow
1	0.95	50
2	0.90	33
3	0.85	23
4	0.79	11

After year four cash flow, the deposit balance reaches zero and the bank exits from the deposit business. The present value cost of this deposit franchise is $105.4 $(0.95*50+0.9*33+0.85*23+0.79*11)$. The duration of deposit costs is 1.9.

Random deposit balances with constant interest rates

A more realistic assumption about deposits is that deposit-related cash outflows are random. One reasonable assumption along these lines is that net deposit cash flows X (interest costs + processing costs − net deposit inflow) is a random walk which drifts over time, subject to random shocks. Another possible assumption is that this random cash flow reverts to some mean or average level,

---

[6] Rate sensitivity with respect to the short-term rate of interest in a term structure model like those of Vasicek [1977] or Heath, Jarrow and Morton [1992] can be calculated as well. The exact nature of the formula would depend on the term structure model chosen. See Chapters 10–12 to review the '*rDelta*' concept.

subject to random shocks. We look at each of these assumptions and the result-ing valuations in turn, under the assumption that interest rates are constant at a level *r* for all maturities, the same assumption at the heart of the Black-Scholes option model and the Merton risky debt model discussed in Chapter 16.

Even though these assumptions sound like they will lead to complex answers, the solutions we get are surprisingly simple if we are willing to make one powerful (but realistic) simplifying assumption—that there is no risk pre-mium attached by bank shareholders to the risk of deposit balance variation. We assume that shareholders are 'risk neutral' with respect to the volatility in deposit balances. This is a good working approximation to reality if the pri-mary reason for deposit balance variation at a given bank is its battle with competing banks for market share. For example, the Federal Reserve may well target the money supply so that the aggregate growth in demand deposit bal-ances nationally is 3% annually. If this assumption is true, then individual banks will only grow faster than 3% by taking deposits from another bank; on average, demand deposits at all banks will grow by 3%. If shareholders don't like the risk of deposit balance variation, they can 'diversify away' this risk by owning, say, 1% of the stock of all banks in the U.S. In this sense, we are assuming that shareholders care only about the average expected level of deposits, not the volatility of deposit balances. This useful assumption will give answers that are both simple and realistic for many practical purposes.

Case E: The change in deposit cash outflows is normally distributed

We start by defining *X* as the net deposit cash outflows which determine the net cost of the deposit: interest expense and processing cost less deposit balance inflows. We assume that these cash flows occur continuously and that *X* changes continuously. We assume that changes in *X* are normally distributed[7]:

$$dX = \alpha\, dt + \sigma\, dz$$

dX denotes the change in net deposit cash flows *X*. Alpha is drift in net deposit cash flows. In the second term, sigma denotes the volatility of net deposit cash flows. The term *dz* is a short hand reference to the 'noise' generator which triggers jumps in deposit balances just as we used in Chapters 10–12

---

[7] This stochastic process is a random walk. Readers who would like an extremely well-written introduction to stochastic processes should refer to Shimko [1992]. His intro-duction to the subject is perhaps the most popular book on financial mathematics in the American financial services industry.

in random interest rate modeling.[8] We supplement this assumption about the variation in net deposit cash flows by the assumption above that bank shareholders are risk neutral with respect to variations in deposit cash flows.

The valuation of a security which fits these assumptions is given by Shimko [1992], with details of the calculation given Appendix 1. The value of deposits is:

$$V = \frac{X}{r} + \frac{\alpha}{r^2}$$

The duration of deposits in this case is:

$$\text{Duration} = \frac{-(\partial V/\partial r)}{V} = \frac{(X/r^2) + (2\alpha/r^3)}{V} = \frac{1}{r}\left[\frac{rX + 2\alpha}{rX + \alpha}\right]$$

These valuation formulas are surprisingly simple given the complexity of movements in deposit cash flows that we have assumed. Note that the volatility of deposit flows σ does not appear in the formula because shareholders are risk-neutral regarding deposit flows. Likewise, the absolute amount of deposits D does not appear in the valuation formula. Only the net deposit cash flows, not the accounting value of deposits D, determine the value of deposits.

Example
Net deposit franchise cash costs (X) have recently been $50 per year, consisting of $90 in interest and processing expense, less $40 annual increase in deposit balances. The change in net deposit costs (dX) is on average $10 per year (i.e. alpha is 10). The level of interest rates is 10%. The present value cost of this deposit franchise is $50/.1 + 10/(0.1)^2 = $1,500. Duration is (0.1 ∗ $50 + 2 ∗ $10)/[(0.1 ∗ $50 + $10) ∗ 0.1] or $25/($15 ∗ 0.1) = 16.7.

Case F: Net deposit cash outflows change randomly around a long-term mean level
Another possible assumption about the net deposit cost cash outflows is that they jump randomly around the same long-term average level. The volatility

---

[8] The dz term is the same standard Wiener process with mean zero and standard deviation of one that we began using in Chapters 10 and 11 in the term structure model context.

of net deposit cost cash outflows may or may not depend on the level of net deposit cash flows. We could use any number of specifications for the way that net deposit cash flows change:

$$dX = k(\mu - X)\,dt + \sigma\,dt$$

$$dX = k(\mu - X)\,dt + \sqrt{X}\sigma\,dz$$

$$dX = k(\mu - X)\,dt + X\sigma\,dz$$

In each of these three cases, k is the speed of mean reversion (the speed of the deposit 'cycles' around the long-term average level) of net deposit cash outflows X around a long-term level, μ. In the first case, the level of X doesn't affect the size of the random jumps in X. In the second and third cases, the size of the random jumps in X depend on X—the jumps are proportional to the square root of X or the level of X itself.

Shimko [1992] gives the valuation for the second case. For all three of these cases, the value of deposits is:

$$V = \frac{rX + k\mu}{r(r+k)}$$

The true duration of deposits is:

$$\text{Duration} = \frac{-(\partial V/\partial r)}{V} = \frac{(-X/(rr+k) + ((rX + k\mu)(2r+k)/(r^2(r+k)^2))}{V}$$

$$= \frac{-X}{rX + k\mu} + \frac{2r+k}{r(r+k)}$$

See Appendix 1 for the derivation.

Example

Let's assume that deposits bounce around an average level in a deposit balance cycle that lasts one year. We set $k = 1/L$ where L is the number of years that the cycle lasts. In this case both L and k are one. If the current net cash deposit outflow (interest and processing costs less deposit inflow) is at a \$10 per year annual rate, then X is 10. We assume that the long-term average level μ is 20. We assume the interest rate r is 10%. Then the mark-to-market present value of the cost of the deposit franchise is $(0.1*10 + 1*20)/(0.1*1.1) = 190.9$. Using the same assumptions, duration is 10.4.

Case G: The percentage change in deposits is normally distributed

Another reasonable assumption about deposits is that the percentage change in the amount of deposits, not the absolute change in deposit cash outflows X, jumps about randomly. A common assumption is that the percentage change in deposits is normally distributed[9]. In that case, the percentage change in the deposit balance can be written:

$$\frac{dD}{D} = \alpha \, dt + \sigma \, dz$$

Assuming that the interest rate and processing costs on the deposit are y and c respectively, the total cash cost to the owner of the deposit franchise is $(y+c)D$ less the change in deposit levels, dD. In this case, the present value of cost of the deposits is:

$$V = \frac{(y + c - \alpha)D}{r - \alpha}$$

The duration of deposits is:

$$\text{Duration} = \frac{-(\partial V / \partial r)}{V} = \frac{1}{r - \alpha}$$

See Appendix 1 for details of the derivation.

Example

Let's assume that the rate on deposits is 4% and processing costs are 2% annually. We also assume that the average annual growth rate in deposit balances α is 3%. If deposit balances are $100 and the level of interest rates r is 9%, then the calculation has the following steps. The net cash outflow on the deposits $(y+c-\alpha)D$ is $(4\% + 2\% - 3\%)100 = \$3$. This is divided by $9\% - 3\% = 6\%$, so the present value cost of the deposit is $50. The duration of the deposit is $1/(9\% - 3\%) = 16.7$ years.

---

[9] This is equivalent to assuming that the gross amount of deposits is lognormally distributed, the same assumption used for stock prices in the Black-Scholes options model and about the value of company assets in the Merton credit model in Chapter 16.

Case H: The level of deposits changes randomly around a long-term mean level

Another reasonable assumption about the absolute level of deposits is that the amount of deposits D itself changes randomly around a stable long-term level μ with deposit interest rate y and processing costs c. In that case, we can write the short hand notation for the change in deposits as:

$$dD = k(\mu - D)\,dt + \sigma\,dz$$

The valuation of deposits is again derived from calculating the present value cost of interest costs $(y+c)D$ less net deposit inflows. The present value cost in this case is:

$$V = \frac{k}{r}\left[\frac{(y+c)-r}{r+k}\right]\mu + \left[\frac{k+y+c}{r+k}\right]D$$

Duration is:

$$\text{Duration} = \frac{-(\partial V/\partial r)}{V} = \frac{Br^2 + 2Ar + kA}{Br^3 + (A+kB)r^2 + kAr}$$

where

$$A = k\mu(y+c)$$
$$B = (k+y+c)D - k\mu$$

Example

Assume the long-term average level of deposits μ is 100 and that the current level of deposits D is 80. We assume that the interest rate r is 10% and that the length of the deposit balance fluctuation cycle L is one year. Then $k = 1/L = 1$. We assume that the interest cost on the deposit y is 4% and processing costs c are 2%. Therefore the value of the deposit, using the formula above, is 40.7. The duration of the deposit is 14.3.

Case I: The valuation of deposits whose rates and balances vary with open market rates

In the first part of this chapter, we assumed that deposit balances were constant and interest rates were random. In the second part of this chapter, we assumed that interest rates were constant and deposit balances were random. Using the same basic approach as these earlier sections, we can value non-maturity deposits in the most realistic case—where deposit rates and deposit balances vary randomly in response to changes in open market interest rates. Jarrow and van Deventer [1996a, 1996b] discuss the derivation of the valuation formula for non-maturity deposits in detail and expand their approach in Jarrow and van Deventer [1998]. These more realistic valuation assumptions are critical for the correct measurement of the interest rate risk of non-maturity deposits.

There are literally an endless number of ways to specify the complex lags which link non-maturity deposit rates and balances with open market rates. Selvaggio [1996], for example, presents an elegant money-demand based relationship involving complex lags to relate deposit balances to open market interest rates. In this section, we focus on more straightforward linear relationships to illustrate the van Deventer-Jarrow approach. For readers who are interested in more complex relationships, see Jarrow and van Deventer [1998] and Janosi, Jarrow and Zullo [1998]. These relationships can be generalized in a number of ways, although some specifications have no analytical solution and have to be estimated using numerical methods.

Jarrow and van Deventer [1996a, 1996b] assume that deposit balances are a linear function of the short rate r in the Vasicek model:

$$D = a_0 + a_1 r$$

and the risk neutral short rate has the same Vasicek specification as in previous chapters:

$$dr = \alpha(\tilde{\mu} - r) \, dt + \sigma \, dz$$

Jarrow and van Deventer also assume that the deposit rate is a linear function of interest rates:

$$i = -b + nr$$

Normally, we would expect b to be positive and n to be between zero and one.[10] If b is not positive, banks will lose money on the non-maturity deposit franchise at low interest rate levels. The implications of this formulation are that the dollar interest expense on non-maturity deposits will be a quadratic

---

[10] In practical implementation, we have often found the quantity $-b$ to be positive, suggesting that at least in the short term there is an effective floor on consumer deposit rates—but the authors continue to urge readers not to assume this floor is permanent based on the Japan example.

function of the short rate r, a point to which we return later. Multiplying the balance relationship times the rate relationship gives:

$$\text{Interest Expense} = -a_0 b + (na_0 - a_1 b)r + a_1 n r^2$$

Jarrow and van Deventer show that the present value cost of the deposit franchise under these assumptions is:

$$V = D(0) - \left[a_0 b + a_1(1-n)\alpha\tilde{\mu}\right] \int_0^\tau P(t)\,dt$$

$$- \left[a_0(1-n) + a_1 b - a_1(1-n)\alpha\right](1 - P(\tau)) - a_1(1-n)[r - f(\tau)P(\tau)]$$

where $D(0)$ is the initial amount of deposits and f and P are the *tau*-maturity forward rate and zero-coupon bond price prevailing at time zero. This valuation formula is easy to apply because it involves only the parameters of the deposit balance and rate formulas and the Vasicek model parameters we have used throughout this book. The formula above assumes that the deposit franchise ends at time *tau*, but if we let *tau* reach infinity, we can rewrite the present value of deposit cost as:

$$V = H_0 V_0 + H_1 V_1 + H_2 V_2$$

where the quantities V_i represent the value of securities paying r^i on principal of \$1 in perpetuity. These 'primitive securities' have values and the weights H_i are:

$$V_0 = \int_0^\infty P(t)\,dt$$

$$V_1 = 1$$

$$V_2 = r - \alpha + \alpha\tilde{\mu} \int_0^\infty P(t)\,dt$$

$$H_0 = -a_0 b$$
$$H_1 = D(0) - [a_0(1-n) + a_1 b]$$
$$H_2 = -a_1(1-n)$$

Since these weights do not depend on r, f, or P, they are independent of the level of interest rates. Accordingly, the hedge of non-maturity deposits is one of the rare cases where we can use a 'buy and hold' hedge to manage interest rate exposure as long as we hedge with the primitive securities that pay r^i. The security paying r^0 is a perpetual bond paying $1 forever. The security paying r^1 is a perpetual floating-rate bond, and the security paying r^2 is a 'power' bond paying r to the second power.

Example

Figure 33.1 shows the valuation of $100 in non-maturity deposits when interest rates vary from a base case level of 5%. We assume that the interest rate on the deposit is 2% plus 0.4 times the level of short-term interest rates (say LIBOR). We show changes in the mark-to-market present value cost of deposits for various assumptions about the response of deposit balances to changes in LIBOR, ranging from a −$4 change for a 1% rate increase to a +$4 change for a 1% rate increase. As shown below, the valuation of deposits depends dramatically on the response of deposit balances to changes in interest rate levels.

Figure 33.1 Present Value of Cost of Non-Maturity Deposits Using Jarrow-van Deventer Approach for Various Assumptions on Changes in Deposit Balances in Response to Rate Changes

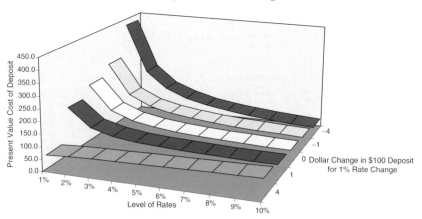

If the response of deposit balances to rates is zero, then the valuation reduces to the simple valuation in Case C. In general, a low level of market rates increases the present value cost of deposits because of the effective floor on the deposit rate of 2%. The duration, or slope of the valuation curve with respect to rates, changes fairly dramatically with the assumption about the responsiveness of deposit balances to changes in rates. For an accurate valuation of non-maturity deposits, it is essential to take this sensitivity into account.

Using the Jarrow-van Deventer Formula in Practice

The use of implied parameters in the Jarrow-van Deventer formula is essential for accurate use in practice. There are two reasons for this. The first reason is simply political—logical arguments alone cannot prove the 'truth' of deposit-pricing formulas.[11] The second reason that implied parameters are essential is that the market's view of the deposit franchise can be based on substantially different expectations about the sensitivity of rate and balance behavior than historical regression analysis would predict for the parameters a_0, a_1, b and n. Let us consider the following graph of consumer deposit rates in the U.S. There are three distinct pricing regimes—a long period of constant rates at a 5.65% level, a nearly one-to-one reduction as LIBOR fell, and then a very shallow rate of increase in the deposit rate as LIBOR returned to prior levels. Regression coefficients of the variable n, for example, could range from zero to one depending on what period was used for the regression analysis. Again, only empirical data can properly capture market expectations.

Figure 33.2 ABC Bank Savings Rate versus 3-Month Libor

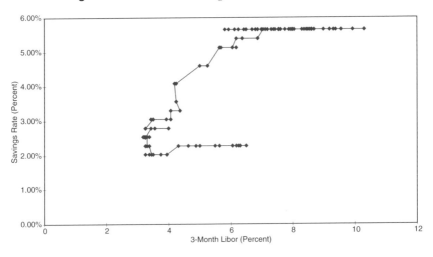

---

[11] Within almost every banking institution, there are two polarized schools of thought on the present value cost of deposits. The first school of thought says 'Deposits are putable to the bank at par at any time by consumers, therefore they are worth par and we can only invest deposit proceeds in floating-rate instruments if we want zero interest rate risk.' The other school of thought argues 'Deposits at this bank have been X or greater for 20 years, so we have a perpetual liability with principal amount X. Because of its long maturity, we can invest those funds in long-term fixed-rate assets with zero interest rate risk.' Only empirical data can resolve this kind of debate.

One set of data that is available is the auction results of deposit franchises by the Resolution Trust Corporation mentioned earlier in this chapter. Unfortunately, this data is of no value to non-American readers and its increasing age makes it less and less relevant to American banks. Moreover, the task is complicated in that the auctions were typically auctions of a mixed bag of time deposits and various non-maturity deposit categories—a large number of auctions would have to be analyzed to extract results for separate deposit categories.

Jarrow and Levin [1996] suggest a more practical approach that takes advantage of the techniques in the other chapters of this book. We want to find the assumptions which best reflect the market's view of the present value cost of the deposit franchise. We *need* to know the market's view since historical data shows management's behavior has not stayed constant and regression coefficients haven't been stable. The steps in this backtesting analysis are as follows:

1. Select the appropriate data set of peer banks for analysis (depending on the application of the analysis, this could be made up of one bank, regional peers, or a larger data set).
2. Exclude any bank whose stock price is clearly distorted by events such as mergers or other significant one-time events (such as the impact of the Procter & Gamble derivatives incident on Bankers Trust Company).
3. Select the longest relevant time frame for analysis.
4. Using the techniques highlighted in this book, mark-to-market all assets and liabilities except non-maturity deposits.
5. Calculate the implied market value of non-maturity deposits as follows:

$$\text{implied cost of non maturity deposits} =$$
$$\sum V_{\text{assets}} - \sum V_{\text{other liabilities}} - \text{stock price (number of shares)}$$

In making this calculation, we have found it very effective to use the loan loss reserve as a proxy for losses embedded in the loan portfolio.
6. Using non-linear regression analysis, solve for the coefficients a_0, a_1, b and n which best fit the historical data.

In using this method, we have reached a number of conclusions.

1. In general, it has been a very effective means of basing non-maturity deposit interest rate risk calculations on market reality, rather than arbitrary assumptions.
2. Market estimates of deposit interest rate relationships implicitly assume that banks will 'bid up' direct and indirect deposit costs if the

spread between deposit costs and open market rates gets too wide. Typically, the implied values of the parameter n are much closer to one than simple regression analysis would indicate.

3. Bankers who argue that the market isn't right on average clearly have never done the analysis we recommend.

The second conclusion is an important one that is consistent both with the authors' experience in setting bank retail deposit rates and marketing strategies and simple logic. Banks add branches, improve staff, and advertise more when the spread on retail deposits is very wide. The market knows this, even though it's not reflected in simple regressions of deposit rates on open market rates. The result means that the school of thought that argues deposits have present value costs closer to par is usually closer to being right than the school that argues deposits are a long maturity perpetuity.

There are a number of refinements that can be made to this analysis. Perhaps the most important is to recognize that banks have the option to withdraw from the retail deposit gathering business, which Bankers Trust did in the 1970s. This option keeps the market value loss on non-maturity deposits in extremely low rate environments from getting too large.

Case Study: German Three-Month Notice Savings Deposits[12]

In this section, we use the Kamakura Risk Manager enterprise wide risk management system to value and analyze the interest rate sensitivity of three-month notice savings deposits in Germany. There are 469 monthly observations on deposit balance data running from December 1959 to December 1998. There are 361 monthly observations on the deposit rate running from June 1967 to February 1999.

The valuation yield curve derived in Kamakura Risk Manager was based on April 28 1999 interest rates in Germany, including one-month, three-month, six-month, nine-month and 12 month money market rates and two-year, three-year, five-year, seven-year, 10-year, 15-year, 20-year and 30-year Deutsche Mark interest rate swap rates. The maximum smoothness forward rate smoothing technique of Chapter 8 was selected for yield curve smoothing.

The speed of mean reversion a was set at 0.01 and the interest rate volatility s in the Extended Vasicek model was set at 0.008.

Kamakura Risk Manager was used to fit the deposit interest rate regression of the Jarrow-van Deventer [1998] model to the deposit rate history.

---

[12] The authors would like to thank Robert Fiedler, formerly of Deutsche Bank, and Karin Gradischnig of Reuters for helpful comments on this section.

The regression explains deposit rate variation as a function of the lagged deposit rate, a constant, and short-term interest rate in Germany. The resulting relationship explains 98.76% in monthly variation of the three-month notice savings deposit rate, and the relationship realistically says, all other things being equal, that a 100 basis point move in short-term open market rates in Germany leads to a two basis point move in the same month in the deposit rate. Of course, the long-term equilibrium level of the deposit rate is much higher than this because of the impact of the lagged deposit rate.

The deposit balance relationship was also fitted in Kamakura Risk Manager using linear regression. The relationship explains 99.97% of the variation in deposit balances and shows quite clearly that (all other things being equal) a rise in money market rates in Germany lowers savings deposit balances—disintermediation takes place as has been found in many countries.

This excellent fit comes in spite of the impact of the unification with East Germany as we can see from Figure 33.3:

Figure 33.3 Impact of German Unification on 3-Month Notice Savings Deposit Balance in Germany

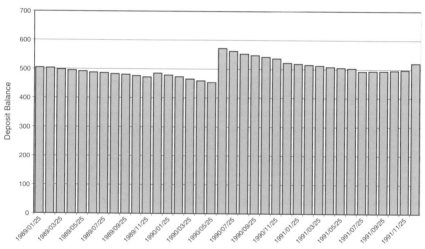

Using representative assumptions on long-term deposit balance levels, three-month notice deposits in Germany were found to have a present value cost of about 67% of their nominal amount and a negative duration of 2.29 years. This means that, all other things being equal, when interest rates rise, the present value cost of the deposits actually declines because of the reduction in balances that comes about as noted above. This is identical to the experience of the U.S. savings and loan industry during its high interest rate crisis in the late 1970s and 1980s.

Negative duration was also found for parallel shifts in the German yield curve, much the same as found by Chase Manhattan Bank in its own analysis of the effective interest rate sensitivity of non-maturity deposits in the U.S.[13]

We analyzed the Jarrow-van Deventer [1998] deposit balance formulation (which includes the lagged balance as an explanatory variable) with the Jarrow-van Deventer [1996a, 1996b] formulation, which does not have the lagged deposit balance in it.

We modeled out of sample predictive power of the two formulations by using five years of monthly data to fit the coefficients of the deposit balance forecasting equation and then predicted balances out of sample. Looking at one month out of sample performance, we can see that the lagged balance formulation is much more powerful:

Figure 33.4 One Month Out of Sample Percentage Forecasting Errors on DM 3-Month Notice Savings Deposits, 1965–1998

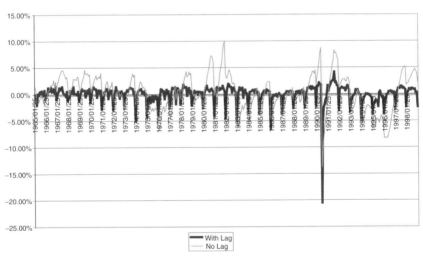

The largest forecasting error came with the unification with East Germany. The strong seasonality of Germany three-month notice deposits are clearly apparent. For longer time horizons as well, the lagged balance formulation produced forecasting errors with a much smaller standard deviation:

---

[13] Private conversation with Dr. Robert Selvaggio, formerly of Chase Manhattan Bank, and now with Ambac Financial.

Table 33.1 Standard Deviation of Percentage Forecasting Errors

Months Forward	With Lag	Without Lag
1	1.67%	3.43%
2	2.45%	3.78%
3	3.00%	4.10%
4	3.37%	4.41%
5	3.63%	4.72%
6	3.86%	5.02%
7	4.09%	5.33%
8	4.31%	5.63%
9	4.49%	5.94%
10	4.63%	6.25%
11	4.77%	6.58%
12	4.99%	6.92%

We conclude that the deposit balance formulation with the lag structure is an excellent fit and that the Jarrow-van Deventer [1998] approach applies well in the German market.

The Regulators' View

The regulatory agencies around the world clearly have a strong interest in valuation of non-maturity deposits. James O'Brien [2000] of the Board of Governors of the Federal Reserve takes a monte carlo simulation approach to the valuation of non-maturity deposits with a strong similarity to the Jarrow-van Deventer model. The National Credit Union Administration of the United States in December 2001 commissioned a study of non-maturity deposit evaluation techniques by National Economic Research Associates, with David Ellis and James Jordan [2001] as lead authors. We urge readers with a strong interest in this topic to review both papers in detail.

Credit Risk and Non-Maturity Deposits

The default probability of the financial institution offering non-maturity deposits to consumers is a critical determinant of non-maturity deposit balances and rates, but we have not included it in the comments above. This is an area that deserves a major research effort. Anecdotal evidence from the savings and loan crisis supports the observation that (even with government deposit insurance) known credit problems at an institution lead to sharp declines in deposit balances and premiums on deposit rates far above peer group levels. We revisit this issue in Chapter 40 on liquidity risk.

Exercises

For the purposes of these exercises, assume that alpha is 0.08, the long-term expected value of the risk neutral interest rate is 0.12, that the value of a security which pays $1 continuously forever is $10, and that the short rate r is 6%. Use the Jarrow-van Deventer [1996a, 1996b] deposit pricing formula to answer the following questions.

33.1 The super saver non-maturity deposit product has a current balance of $100. The rate on the deposit category follows the formula rate = 2% + 0.4 Fed funds rate.[14] Deposit balances are intermediated when rates rise, according to the formula for deposit balances D = 112 − 2 Fed funds rate. What is the current rate on the super saver account? Is the historical regression analysis on deposit balances consistent with the current account balance? If not, change the regression analysis (known in the scientific community as applying a 'fudge factor') so that there is consistency.

33.2 What is the present value cost of this deposit product?

33.3 What is the present value of profits on this deposit product?

33.4 Write down the formula for the *rDelta* of the Jarrow-van Deventer valuation formula.

33.5 What is the amount of each of three primitive securities (a consol paying $1 forever, a floater paying r forever, and a power bond paying r^2) necessary for a buy-and-hold hedge of the present value cost of the account?

33.6 How would your answers to 33.2 and 33.3 change if the coefficients measured on the deposit rate relationship were incorrect? Do a sensitivity analysis on the coefficient of 0.4, incremented from zero to one by movements of 0.1.

33.7 As a practical banker, what would you do if you were uncertain as to whether or not the value of 0.4 was accurate? Your predecessor, who was recently dismissed, couldn't answer the question and got fired for doing nothing. Assume, therefore, that 'doing nothing' is not the option you'd choose.

---

[14] Ignore any adjustment for actual/360-day interest for simplicity.

Appendix 1

Derivation of Valuation Formulas

Case E: The change in deposit cash outflows is normally distributed

The change in deposit cash outflows is X. We assume that X is a random walk, which means that changes in X are normally distributed. The changes in X are given by the formula:

$$dX = \alpha\, dt + \sigma\, dz$$

The change in the value of deposits V is given by Ito's lemma (see Shimko [1992] for an explanation of Ito's lemma):

$$
\begin{aligned}
dV &= V_X\, dX + \frac{1}{2} V_{XX}(dX)^2 + V_t \\
&= V_X[\alpha\, dt + \sigma\, dz] + \frac{1}{2} V_{XX}\sigma^2\, dt + V_t \\
&= \left[\alpha V_X + \frac{1}{2} V_{XX}\sigma^2\right] dt + V_X\sigma\, dz + V_t
\end{aligned}
$$

Since the deposits have no maturity and no time-based coefficients, the derivative with respect to time t is zero. Since investors are assumed to be risk neutral, we can analyze the value on the basis of its expected 'capital gain', noting that $E[dz] = 0$, plus its cash flow X, the change in deposits. The expected return must be equal to an equivalent amount of money invested at the short rate r to avoid arbitrage:

$$rV = \alpha V_X + \frac{1}{2} V_{XX}\sigma^2 + X$$

We must solve this equation for X. Guess $V = AX + B$. In that case the equation becomes:

$$rAX + rB = \alpha A + X$$

$$\text{so } A = \frac{1}{r}$$

$$B = \frac{\alpha A}{r} = \frac{\alpha}{r^2}$$

When X and α are both zero, the value of the deposit franchise should be zero, and it is under this valuation formula.

Case F: Net deposit cash outflows change randomly around a long-term mean level

In this case we allow the change in deposit cash outflows, X, to be described by one of three common assumptions that allow for X to move around a long-term mean μ:

$$dX = k(\mu - X)\,dt + \sigma\,dz$$

$$dX = k(\mu - X)\,dt + \sqrt{X}\sigma\,dz$$

$$dX = k(\mu - X)\,dt + X\sigma\,dz$$

The movement in the value of deposits is described by Ito's lemma:

$$dV = V_X\,dX + \frac{1}{2}V_{XX}(dX)^2 + V_t$$

By assumption, the cash outflow on the deposit is X. The expected 'capital gain' on the value of the deposit is:

$$E(dV) = V_X k(\mu - X) + \frac{1}{2}V_{XX}(dX)^2$$

where $(dX)^2$ depends on which of the three processes we have selected for X. We note that V_t is zero due to the perpetual nature of the claim and the fact that we have assumed constant coefficients for the process that describes movements in X. The solution for V comes from the partial differential equation which requires that the total return on V must equal the riskless rate times V:

$$V_X k(\mu - X) + \frac{1}{2}V_{XX}(dX)^2 + X = rV$$

We guess that the solution is of the form:

$$V = AX + B\mu$$

In that case, the partial differential equation reduces to:

$$Ak(\mu - X) + X = rAX + rB\mu$$

Solving for A and B gives:

$$A = \frac{1}{r + k}$$

$$B = \frac{k}{r(r + k)}$$

Rearranging allows us to express V as:

$$V = \frac{rX + k\mu}{r(r + k)}$$

When X and μ are both zero, the present value cost of the deposit franchise should be and is zero.

Case G: The percentage change in deposits is normally distributed

The change in deposit levels is assumed to be:

$$\frac{dD}{D} = \alpha \, dt + \sigma \, dz$$

The change in the value of deposits is given again by Ito's lemma:

$$dV = V_D \, dD + \frac{1}{2} V_{DD} \, \sigma^2 D^2 + V_t$$

The expected value of the change in value is:

$$E(dV) = V_D \alpha D + \frac{1}{2} V_{DD} \sigma^2 D^2$$

The expected net cash flow cost of deposits is the interest and processing cost of deposits less the expected change in deposit balances:

$$E[\text{cash flow}] = (y + c)D - \alpha D$$

To avoid arbitrage, the expected total cost of the deposits (interest and processing costs less deposit inflows) must be equal to the risk-free rate r times the value of deposits:

$$V_D \alpha D + \frac{1}{2} V_{DD} \sigma^2 D^2 - \alpha D + (y + c)D = rV$$

We guess a solution of the form $V = AD$. The equation above then becomes:

$$\alpha AD + (y + c - \alpha)D = r AD$$

Solving this for A leads to the solution for deposit value:

$$V = \frac{(y + c - \alpha)D}{r - \alpha}$$

When the deposit balance D is zero, the present value cost of deposits should be and is zero under this valuation formula.

Case H: The level of deposits changes randomly around a long-term mean level

The change in deposits is given by:

$$dD = k(\mu - D)\, dt + \sigma\, dz$$

As in Case F, we could have selected a number of other alternatives that allow the variation of deposits to be a function of the level of deposits. Two alternatives are:

$$dD = k(\mu - D)\, dt + \sqrt{D}\sigma\, dz$$
$$dD = k(\mu - D)\, dt + D\sigma\, dz$$

All of these alternative formulations lead to the same solution. The expected cash cost of deposits is composed of interest and processing costs less the expected change in deposit balances:

$$E[\text{cash flow}] = (y + c)D - k(\mu - D)$$

Adding this to the expected change in deposit value V leads to the valuation equation that constrains the total cost of deposits to equal the risk-free rate times V:

$$V_D k(\mu - D) + \frac{1}{2}V_{DD}(dD)^2 - k(\mu - D) + (y + c)D = r V$$

We guess a solution of the form:

$$V = AD + B\mu$$

Substituting this expression and the derivatives $V_D = A$ and $V_{DD} = 0$ and solving for A and B leads to the valuation formula for V:

$$V = \frac{k}{r}\left[\frac{(y+c)-r}{r+k}\right]\mu + \left[\frac{k+y+c}{r+k}\right]D$$

When μ and D are zero, V is zero as it should be.

CHAPTER 34

Foreign Exchange Markets: A Term Structure Model Approach[1]

Introduction to Foreign Exchange Forwards and Options

Throughout this book, we continue to progress toward our integrated measure of interest rate risk and credit risk using the Jarrow-Merton put option concept from Chapter 1. A high percentage of smaller financial institutions have the luxury of financial assets and liabilities that are almost all denominated in a single currency. In fact, due in part to the advent of the Euro, the percentage of financial institutions in this situation is rising. Nonetheless, for most of the largest financial institutions foreign currency risk is a critical element of total risk. As van Deventer and Imai [2003] showed with respect to the Korean Development Bank and many other issuers, credit risk and foreign exchange rates of the home country can move very strongly together.

The term structure model approach that we have taken in earlier chapters provides a sound foundation with which to approach foreign currency denominated securities and derivatives. The variety of foreign exchange (FX) related securities is great, but we will limit ourselves to an introductory view of the term structure model approach's implications for FX analysis. In this chapter, we concentrate solely on foreign exchange forward contracts and European options on the spot foreign exchange rate. Foreign exchange futures contracts and options on FX futures involve a combination of the techniques in this chapter and those in Chapters 24 and 25, but we leave such analysis as advanced exercises for interested readers.

One of the reasons that we introduce the impact of term structure models on FX options is that we want to minimize the degree to which common foreign exchange options models have to be extended because of pricing

---

[1] An earlier version of this chapter appeared as Chapter 17 in van Deventer and Imai [1996].

errors engendered by the model. Fitting the volatility smile is part of this extension process and was a contributor to the foreign exchange options losses at National Australia Bank that we discussed in Chapter 1. By dealing explicitly with random interest rates in both countries, we can minimize the amount of volatility smile that the model needs to fit.

Setting the Stage: Assumptions for the Domestic and Foreign Economies

We assume that the domestic market is country 1 and the foreign market is country 2. The spot rate of foreign exchange S represents the cost in country 1 currency of one unit of country 2 currency. In countries 1 and 2, we assume that the domestic bond markets behave according to the Vasicek model, and that short rates move in accordance with the mean-reverting stochastic process of that model:

$$dr_i = \alpha_i [\mu_i - r_i] dt + \sigma_i dz_i$$

Note the addition of a subscript to denote each country. In the foreign exchange market, the spot rate of foreign exchange follows a stochastic process such that the spot rate is lognormal with a drift term that can depend on other economic variables:

$$dS = \mu_s(r_1, r_2, t) dt + \sigma_s dz_s$$

The volatility of the spot foreign exchange process is assumed to be a constant. We denote the foreign exchange process parameters by the subscript s.

We further assume that the random shocks to domestic interest rates, foreign interest rates, and the spot foreign exchange rate are instantaneously correlated in accordance with the following correlation coefficients:

$$(dr_1 \, dr_2) = \rho_{12} \, \sigma_1 \, \sigma_2$$

$$(dr_1 \, dS) = \rho_{1s} \, \sigma_1 \, \sigma_s \, S$$

$$(dr_2 \, dS) = \rho_{2s} \, \sigma_2 \, \sigma_s \, S$$

This sets the analytical stage for looking at foreign exchange futures and options.

Foreign Exchange Forwards

The pricing of foreign exchange forwards can be set by an arbitrage argument that doesn't rely on any of the assumptions above. Let's assume it's time t and the observable forward price of country 2 currency at time T is a function of the spot rate S and interest rates in the two countries is $H(t, T, S, r_1, r_2)$. Let's assume we want to invest, from the perspective of our position in country 1, in country 2 currency for T years and maximize our currency 2 holdings at time T. We define $P_1 = P_1(r_1, t, T)$ as the T maturity country 1 zero-coupon bond and $P_2 = P_2(r_2, t, T)$ as the country 2 T maturity zero-coupon bond. Assume that country 1 is the U.S. and country 2 is Japan. S and H both represent the dollar cost of one yen. There are two investment strategies:

Strategy 1
1. Borrow P_1 dollars, which will become \$1 at time T.
2. Sell \$1 forward at current time t for yen deliverable at time T, which will generate yen proceeds of $1/H$.

Strategy 2
1. Borrow P_1 dollars.
2. At current time t, convert the dollars to P_1/S yen at the spot exchange rate S.
3. Invest P_1/S yen in a zero-coupon yen bond maturing at time T, resulting in time T yen proceeds of $P_1/(SP_2)$.

To avoid arbitrage, the results of these two strategies must be equal, so the forward rate H must equal:

$$H(t, T, S, r_1, r_2) = \frac{SP_2}{P_1}$$

We take advantage of this relationship to find the value of a European option on foreign exchange in the next section.

Foreign Exchange Options

Hilliard, Madura, and Tucker [1991] ('HMT') assume that bond prices in country 1 and country 2 follow the Vasicek stochastic process and that the spot rate follows a lognormal process with the form given in the previous section. Prior to the HMT work, the most popular model of foreign exchange options has been the Garman-Kohlhagen [1983] model, a variation on the Black-Scholes model which assumes that the interest rates in country 1 and country 2 are constant at levels r_1 and r_2. Garman and Kohlhagen show that the value of a European call option maturing at time T from the perspective of time t to purchase one unit of country 2's currency at a strike price of K is:

$$V(t, T, S, r_1, r_2) = Se^{-r_2\tau}N(h) - Ke^{-r_1\tau}N(h - \sigma_s\sqrt{\tau})$$

where:

$$\tau = T - t$$

and:

$$h = \frac{\ln(S/K) + \tau\left[r_1 - r_2 + (\sigma_s^2/2)\right]}{\sigma_s\sqrt{\tau}}$$

When interest rates change, the volatility used in the option calculation must change. Interest rates in both countries and their instantaneous correlation with the spot rate have an impact on the variance in the price of forward foreign exchange for delivery at time T. HMT show that the value of the call option under the stochastic interest rate case is:

$$V(t, T, S, r_1, r_2, K) = P_1(r_1, t, T)\left[H(t, T, S, r_1, r_2)N(h^*) - KN(h^* - v_h)\right]$$
$$= SP_2(r_2, t, T)N(h^*) - P_1(r_1, t, T)KN(h^* - v_h)$$

where:

$$h^* = \frac{\ln(H(t, T, S, r_1, r_2)/K) + (1/2)v_h^2}{v_h}$$

and v_h is the variance of the price of the forward foreign exchange rate H at time T from the perspective of time t.

Using our standard notation for each country for the volatility of interest rates in each country as of time T from the perspective of time t:

$$v_i^2(t, T) = \frac{\sigma_i^2}{2\alpha_i}\left[1 - e^{-2\alpha_i \tau}\right]$$

and:

$$F_i = \frac{1}{\alpha_i}\left[1 - e^{-\alpha_i \tau}\right]$$

allows us to write v_h as in HMT as follows:

$$v_h^2 = \sigma_s^2\tau + M_2 + M_5 + 2(\rho_{s1}\sigma_s M_1 - \rho_{s2}\sigma_s M_4 - \rho_{12}M_3)$$

where HMT use the notation:

$$M_1 = \frac{\sigma_1}{\alpha_1} [\tau - F_1]$$

$$M_2 = \frac{\sigma_1^2}{\alpha_1^2} [\tau - 2F_1] + \frac{v_1^2}{\alpha_1^2}$$

$$M_3 = \frac{\sigma_1 \sigma_2}{\alpha_1 \alpha_2} \left[\tau - F_1 - F_2 + \frac{1}{\alpha_1 + \alpha_2} \left(1 - e^{-(\alpha_1 + \alpha_2)\tau} \right) \right]$$

$$M_4 = \frac{\sigma_2}{\alpha_2} [\tau - F_2]$$

$$M_5 = \frac{\sigma_2^2}{\alpha_2^2} [\tau - 2F_2] + \frac{v_2^2}{\alpha_2^2}$$

Implications of a Term Structure Model-Based FX Options Formula

In an environment where the correlation between risk exposures, as popularized by the value-at-risk approach we discuss in later chapters, is a very high priority, the term structure model approach to FX option valuation provides an immense improvement over the constant interest rate-based Garman-Kohlhagen approach, despite its proven usefulness to date:

- Correlation between country 1 interest rates, country 2 interest rates and the spot rate are explicitly recognized.
- The option valuation can be stressed tested for changes in correlation, with a range of new Greeks, first derivatives with respect to these correlation parameters.
- The formula explicitly recognizes that the volatility of the spot rate at time T, the option exercise date, is directly affected by the volatility of interest rates in the two countries. The more traditional approach ignores this source of volatility.
- Interest rate-related hedges stemming from FX options and forward positions can be done using the *rDelta* approach, which we discuss in more detail in later chapters, in a way fully consistent with all other fixed income and interest rate derivative hedging. Hedges using maturities other than the maturity of the FX option can be calculated and put into place. Like its relative the Black-Scholes model, the Garman-Kohlhagen model's fixed interest rate assumption makes this impossible without some additional (and contradictory) assumptions.

All of these benefits are powerful ones, and they come with no additional cost. The term structure model approach is most probably already being utilized in other aspects of the trading floor, so bringing it to the FX desk is both desirable and probably overdue. The HMT model will bring greater accuracy in both pricing and hedging. The next section contains the evidence.

Improved Accuracy of the Stochastic Interest Rate FX Model

HMT tested a simplified version of the stochastic interest rate model, with the speed of mean reversion alpha set to zero, on 2,702 European[2] currency options from the PHLX currency options database. The authors tested out-of-sample European call options prices produced by both the stochastic interest rate model and by the constant interest rate Garman-Kohlhagen model and compared theoretical prices to actual prices from September 1987 to April 1989. Even handicapped by the assumption that alpha is zero, the model's performance was very good, as shown in Table 34.1:

Table 34.1 Comparison of Mean Absolute Pricing Errors

Stochastic Interest Rate and Constant Interest Rate Foreign Exchange Option Models

| | | Percent of Sample in Which Model Forecast was Most Accurate | |
| | Number of | FX Option Model Type | |
Currency	Obervations	Constant Rates	Stochastic Rates
Australian Dollar	1149	5.31%	94.69%
British Pound	251	8.37%	91.63%
Canadian Dollar	173	3.47%	96.53%
Deutsche Mark	76	10.53%	89.47%
Japanese Yen	83	7.23%	92.77%
Swiss Franc	970	5.26%	94.74%

Source: Hillard, Madura, and Tucker [1991]

The stochastic interest rate model substantially outperformed the constant interest rate model for every currency, with success rates ranging from 89% to 96%. Better pricing translates into better hedging, so the model offers substantial benefits in practical use. Most importantly, better pricing means

---

[2] HMT report that European currency option trading represented about 6% of the volume for American foreign currency options over the same time period.

a smaller amount of extension and a better probability of avoiding the kind of model risk problem that affected the National Australia Bank in the incident discussed in Chapter 1.

Extensions of the Stochastic Interest Rate Approach to Foreign Currency-Related Securities Pricing

The same basic approach to valuation can be taken to a wide variety of foreign currency-related securities pricing. For practical use, the extension to foreign currency futures and foreign currency futures options is essential to accurately price popular exchange-traded contracts. Since most foreign currency options that are exchange-traded are American options, numerical methods are necessary since the interim cash flow (interest payments on bonds in each country) makes early exercise of American foreign currency options a possibility. Amin and Jarrow [1991] have used the Heath, Jarrow and Morton [1992] framework to price foreign currency options, again explicitly modeling the correlation between interest rates in the two countries. Both the HMT approach and the Amin and Jarrow approach seem certain to gain increased popularity among market participants in the years ahead.

The Impact of Credit Risk on Foreign Exchange Risk Formulas

We know from the extensive evidence in van Deventer and Imai [2003] that an internationally active company has a default probability that depends on many macro-economic factors that are mutually correlated. Foreign exchanges rates and interest rates in the home country and the U.S. are almost always found to be statistically significant drivers of default probabilities.

The HMT FX option formula above, like the Garman-Kohlhagen model, implicitly assumes that our options counterparty is riskless. As J.P. Morgan discovered in 1998, it is much more likely that the default probability of the counterparty rises sharply as the amount of money owed on the FX position increases.[3] For this reason it is very important for FX rates to be explicitly modeled as drivers of default probabilities so that that the default probabilities of all international counterparties will vary properly as exchange rates move.

A failure to incorporate this critical link with credit risk will result in a substantial understatement of total risk and of the correlation between the default probabilities in broad classes of borrowers.

---

[3] See van Deventer and Imai [2003] for a discussion of this incident.

We will return to this point in Chapters 39–44 frequently as we value the Jarrow-Merton put option as a comprehensive measure of total risk—interest rate risk, credit risk and foreign exchange risk.

Exercises

Assume the following parameters in what follows:

	Country 1	**Country 2**
alpha	0.08	0.20
sigma	0.015	0.02
long-term level of r (mu)	0.09	0.13
market price of risk	0.01	0.02
rho (r_1 and r_2)	0.4	
rho (r_1 and S)	0.2	
rho (r_2 and S)	−0.5	
sigma (spot rate)	0.1	

34.1 The currency country 1 price (in domestic 'baloneys') for one unit of country 2's currency ('salamis') is 0.5, i.e. you get only 0.5 baloneys for each salami. What is the one-year forward baloney-salami exchange rate?

34.2 What is the price of a six-month European call option on the salami exchange rate at a strike price of 0.45?

34.3 How does the option price change if the correlation between country 1 interest rates and the exchange rate changes from 0.2 to 0.7?

34.4 What is the price of a six-month European put option on the salami exchange rate at a strike price of 0.45?

34.5 What Greeks should a sophisticated trader use when hedging their portfolio using the constant interest rate model? Write the formula for each Greek for a European call option.

34.6 How many securities are needed to hedge a position in the call option in 34.2?

34.7 What hedge would you recommend to a trader who is long the call option in 34.2 and doesn't want to be? Assume that the easiest hedge (closing out the position) isn't a possibility.

CHAPTER 35

The Impact of Collateral on Valuation Models

The New Capital Accord proposed by the Basel Committee on Banking Supervision[1] makes clear what bankers have known for decades—collateral can have a significant impact on mitigating the credit risk of a particular loan structure. Throughout the New Capital Accord, there are a number of adjustments to the amount of 'risk weighted assets' associated with a particular loan that depend on the nature and amount of collateral backing the loan.

In this chapter, we add collateralized transactions to our list of assets and liabilities that can be valued in a total risk management framework. Again, our objective in this effort is to be able to value the Jarrow-Merton put option on the value of the assets (and liabilities) of the firm as a measure of total integrated risk, including both interest rate risk and credit risk (and foreign exchange risk).

This chapter is an extension of Chapter 11 in van Deventer and Imai [2003], who list a number of approaches to modeling the impact of collateral on the value of a loan. We start first with a discussion of collateral in the structural model framework of Chapter 16.

Valuing the Impact of Collateral in a Structural Model Framework

As we discussed in Chapters 16–18, modeling collateralized loan structures in the Merton framework is a challenge because the assumptions of the model are very restrictive. In this section, we reject the original Merton formulation using constant interest rates as a candidate for a valuation tool. Instead our comments will focus on the random interest rates version of the Merton model proposed by Shimko, Tejima and van Deventer [1993]. This concentration on interest rates and their fluctuations is important for two reasons: random interest rates are critical to the evaluation of all fixed income

---

[1] April, 2003, available in electronic form on www.bis.org.

securities, and they usually have a very significant impact on the value of collateral as well.

As van Deventer and Imai [2003] discuss, interest rates in excess of 100% in Mexico in the mid-1990s caused as much as 50% of mortgage loans in the country to default, leaving banks as huge owners of private homes. Similarly, random interest rates and home prices are at the heart of the FDIC Loss Distribution Model, the reduced form model announced by the Federal Deposit Insurance Corporation on December 10 2003 and available on the website of the FDIC at www.fdic.gov. Van Deventer and Imai [2003] also show that home prices in three cities and interest rates are statistically significant determinants on the returns on Australian bank stock prices.

With a little imagination, we can discuss how to model the impact of collateral within a structural model framework like Shimko, Tejima and van Deventer [1993]. We do that in a series of examples.

Case A: Valuing a loan secured by collateral with known value equal to or in excess of the loan amount

Let us consider the case of a small business loan where the amount due to be paid by the company in one year is $80 and the current value of company assets is $100. Assume that the owner of the firm is independently wealthy and pledges personal assets of $80 in short-term risk-free money market assets.

What is the value of the loan? Without any mathematics, this loan is now completely riskless if the costs of collecting the collateral are zero. In reality, there are substantial costs in documenting the existence of the collateral, in documenting the right of the lender to seize the collateral, and in collecting the collateral in the event of default. Nonetheless, upon default the bank seizes both the remaining assets of the company (which will certainly be worth more than zero and less than $80) plus the $80 in risk-free money market assets. The lender is effectively heavily over collateralized.

This collateral has the same effect as a credit default swap which pays $80 in the event that the value of company assets in a year is less than $80.

Case B: Valuing a loan secured by collateral with known value less than the loan amount

A more interesting case is where the owner of the firm pledges assets worth less than the total amount due on the loan, say $30. How can we value the impact of this collateral on the value of the loan, its probability of default, and (most importantly) the loss given default and recovery rate on the loan?

Remember in both the Merton model [1974] and the Shimko, Tejima, van Deventer model [1993] of risky debt, the loss given default and the recovery rate are implicit in the model—they are not independent inputs to the model. For every single scenario for the value of company assets at the end of the one-year period, we know the loss given default and the recovery rate with certainty. If the value of company assets at the end of the year is $V(1)j$, when $V(1)$ is less than \$80 then the loss given default is $80-V(1)$ and the recovery rate as a percentage of the amount owed is $V(1)/80$.

This changes in the presence of collateral. We can write the recovery rate and loss given default as follows when $V(1)$ is less than \$80.

If $V(1)$ is greater than or equal to 50 then:

- Loss given default is zero $(\text{Max}\,(0, 80 - V(1) - 30))$
- Recovery rate is more than 100% $([\text{Min}\,(80, V(1) + 30)]/80)$.

If $V(1)$ is less than 50:

- Loss given default is $80 - V(1) - 30$
- Recovery rate is $(V(1) + 30)/80$.

The exact terms of the loan will determine if the loss given default can be negative (i.e. the lender seizes more assets than the amount of money it is owed). If we use the standard risk neutral valuation techniques (see Jarrow and Turnbull [1996] for an extensive discussion) in the Shimko, Tejima, and van Deventer framework, there is only a small change in the valuation framework for a loan with collateral that is certain. The loss in the event of default changes according to the formula above. This results in a slight 'tweak' to the STV valuation formula that increases the value of the loan without changing its probability of default. The derivation of this formula is left to advanced readers.

Case C: Valuing a loan secured by collateral with known value less than the loan amount when there are senior and subordinated loan tranches

What if the \$80 in loans to the company has a senior tranche for \$35 and a subordinated tranche for \$55 dollars and the owner has pledged \$30 in risk-free collateral?

This situation is a minor 'tweak' in the Shimko, Tejima and van Deventer [1993] version of the Merton model that affects only the loss given default for each tranche, not the probability of default. When the value of company assets in one year $V(1)$ is less than \$80, the loss given default in each scenario can be summarized as follows:

- Senior tranche: zero in all scenarios since even in the worst case the subordinated tranche absorbs \$55 in losses and gets only \$5 in collateral, with the remaining \$25 in collateral going to the senior tranche, fully offsetting senior tranche losses.

- Subordinated tranche: $\text{Max}(0, \$80 - V(1))$ – Collateral Available After Senior Tranche is Paid).

Again, the valuation formula for this case is a slight 'tweak' of the Shimko, Tejima, van Deventer [1993] risky debt formula and the expected loss given default is produced for both tranches.

Case D: Valuing a loan secured by collateral with random value

What if the collateral is a random number with an arbitrary correlation with both interest rates and the value of company assets? If the loan consists only of a senior tranche, the impact of collateral is clear. Firstly, assume interest rates are constant. Then we have effectively a security where debt holders get the larger of two assets contingent on the value of company assets $V(1)$ being less than \$80. This concept of an option on the greater of two assets has a known solution, and from that formula we can derive the expected loss given default over all scenarios for the value of company assets and the value of the collateral.

When interest rates are random, the option on the maximum of two random assets has to be generalized to the random interest rates case. Many practitioners would find this easier to do using Monte Carlo simulation of (a) interest rates, (b) the value of company assets, and (c) the value of collateral.

In any event, it is a straightforward application of the scenario generation strategies that we first mentioned in Chapters 22 and 23.

Many other Merton model applications for loan structures with collateral can either be derived analytically or simulated. They all suffer, however, from the restrictions of single period analysis. Generalizing the Merton model to allow for early hitting of the bankruptcy barrier is only a partial approximation, since payoffs on multi-payment debt should reduce the value of company assets as we discussed in Chapter 24.

An easier solution is to employ the reduced form modeling approach. We turn to that task now.

Valuing the Impact of Collateral in a Reduced Form Model Framework

The impact on collateral for multi-payment securities can be handled very neatly in the Jarrow [1999] reduced form modeling framework. In the 1999 version of Jarrow's model, the 'recovery rate' $d(t)$ is explicitly assumed to be random and can be driven by the same macro factors which are driving the default intensity $d(t)$. We can address the same kinds of examples in a reduced form modeling context that we did in the structural model context.

Case A Revisited: Valuing a loan secured by collateral with known value equal to or in excess of the loan amount

In the Jarrow model context, this example is a simple one. The availability of collateral is identical to a digital default swap that pays the known amount of collateral upon default of the borrower. The Jarrow models have an explicit formula for this digital default swap that is a function of interest rates and macro factors as reviewed in Chapter 17.

The total value of the loan to the lender is the sum of:

- the value of the loan with no collateral PLUS;
- the value of the digital default swap that pays the collateral value on default.

This structure is equally applicable to single payment or multi-payment borrowings. Since we know the value of the digital default swap, we can precisely measure the value of credit mitigation that the guarantee, or collateral, provides.

Case B Revisited: Valuing a loan secured by collateral with known value less than the loan amount

The comments from the previous section apply here as well, with no modifications.

Case C Revisited: Valuing a loan secured by collateral with known value less than the loan amount when there are senior and subordinated loan tranches

When there are senior and subordinated tranches, the key differences between the Jarrow-Turnbull assumptions [1995] and those of Duffie and Singleton [1999] and Jarrow [1999, 2001] are important. In the Jarrow-Turnbull model, the recovery rate is expressed as a percentage of principal. This means that, in the event of default, the dollar losses to the senior and subordinated debt holders are known with certainty. Both always default at the same time, so we know how collateral will be split between the senior and subordinated tranches.

The value of the collateral to the senior tranche holders in the Jarrow-Turnbull model is the value of a digital default swap that pays the senior portion of the collateral upon default. The value of the collateral to the subordinated tranche holders in the Jarrow-Turnbull model is the value of a digital default swap that pays the subordinated portion of the collateral upon default. The total value of credit mitigation in the Jarrow-Turnbull model is the sum of these two digital default swaps.

In the Duffie and Singleton [1999] and Jarrow [1999, 2001] models, the recovery rate is expressed as a percentage of the security's value just an instant before default. This is a more general formulation than the Jarrow-Turnbull structure because it allows us to consider defaultable equity options, foreign exchange forwards, credit default swaps and so on where the meaning of 'recovery rate as a percentage of principal' has a much less precise meaning. For the task at hand, however, things are slightly complicated for this set of assumptions.

Let us consider the loan above made for $80. Let us assume that it was made on a fixed coupon basis and that interest rates have risen, lowering the value of the loan in present value terms to $70. In the Jarrow and Duffie and Singleton models, if the recovery rate is assumed to be 70%, we would have a loss given default in this scenario of $70 − (0.70)70 = $21. Any collateral would be applied to reduce this loss. If, however, the loan was trading at $90 because interest rates had fallen, the loss given default would be $90−(0.70)90 = $27 and collateral would be applied to this loss.

If the amount of collateral is known with certainty, the total value of the collateral is again a digital default swap with a payoff equal to the amount of the collateral value. There is only one impact of the differing specification of the recovery rate—the split of collateral between senior and subordinated tranches becomes a function of interest rates and the timing with which default occurs (right before the maturity of the debt, the split will approach the Jarrow-Turnbull allocation to senior and subordinated tranches).

Case D Revisited: Valuing a loan secured by collateral with random value

This is the scenario that the Jarrow framework was explicitly designed for. As we mentioned in Chapter 24, the Jarrow framework can be moved to a lattice that is a function of interest rates, macro factors driving default and collateral value, and default-no default nodes. The existence of collateral has no impact on the lattice itself, only the amount of cash flow produced at each tranche. This is a straightforward exercise in computer science that produces collateral-adjusted cash flows, valuation, pricing and hedging input of extremely high quality. It allows a precise measurement of the value of credit mitigation provided by the collateral.

With this step forward toward complete valuation of the Jarrow-Merton put option, our comprehensive measure of risk, we now turn to the evaluation of revolving lines of credit.

Pricing and Valuing Revolving Credit and Other Facilities

The New Capital Accord proposed by the Basel Committee on Banking Supervision[1] outlines some of the major complexities in assessing the risk of revolving credit facilities extended to corporate clients. The Accord's ongoing reference to 'exposure at default' highlights the need to thoroughly understand what drives the balances outstanding on revolving credit facilities. Once that understanding is gained, we can proceed to valuation and simulation in order to add revolving credit facilities to the list of instruments that can be valued in our ongoing quest to price the Jarrow-Merton put option of Chapter 1 as our primary measure of comprehensive risk.

We turn to that task in this chapter.

Revolving Credits and Non-Maturity Deposit Analysis

In Chapter 33, we dealt with the risk measurement and valuation of non-maturity deposits in detail. Those instruments (and their asset side counterparty, retail charge card balances) have balances that fluctuate up and down randomly at the option of the depositor. The accounts have no explicit maturity, although the Jarrow-van Deventer methodology [1988] implicitly assumes that the deposit franchise has a finite ending date. On both the balance side and the interest rate side, the non-maturity deposit formulation of Jarrow and van Deventer [1988] explicitly incorporates open market interest rates as a major determinant of deposit balances and deposit interest rates.

Can we use this kind of analysis to value revolving credits? On the surface, there are many parallels. Deposit balances and revolving credit balances can be zero for an extended period of time and then suddenly spring into use. Similarly, other deposits will show a randomly fluctuating balance over a long period of time just like an 'evergreen' line of credit.

---

[1] April, 2003, available in electronic form on www.bis.org.

It is tempting to use the Jarrow-van Deventer methodology for non-maturity deposits if it weren't for one major assumption they make that doesn't hold in this case—they assume that the borrower of the non-maturity deposits (the bank) is riskless because of government deposit insurance. In a parallel way, they assume that the credit risk of charge card borrowers is non-zero, but known with certainty. Unfortunately, nothing could be further from the truth in the case of revolving credits.

Fluctuating credit risk and revolving credit draw-downs

The changing credit quality of a borrower, along with randomly fluctuating cash needs that are linked in part to credit quality, is at the heart of the analysis of revolving credits. Cash needs are fluctuating for various reasons:

- The fundamental business of the borrower may have highly seasonal revenues (as in retailing) but expenses that are non-seasonal.
- The fundamental business of the borrower may have very steady revenues but highly seasonal cash needs (like farming).
- Cash flows of the business are not perfectly predictable due to normal uncertainties of client payments on the asset side and payments to suppliers on the liability side.
- Scheduled payments may not occur due to operational issues (a wire transfer failure) or credit quality problems on the part of either the company or its clients.
- The deteriorating credit quality of the borrower may shut off some sources of funding that may need to be replaced with a bank line of credit.
- Conversely, improving credit quality on the part of the borrower may open up new sources of funding that decrease the need for usage on the line of credit.

All of these factors contribute greatly to the need for a special understanding of revolving lines of credit, but it is the last three factors that are most important. If the only factors driving line of credit usage were the first three factors, we could use the Jarrow-van Deventer approach to non-maturity deposit valuation in this context without hesitation.

Incorporating links between credit quality and line usage

In van Deventer and Imai [2003] there is an extensive discussion of the J.P. Morgan-SK Securities incident of 1998 where the amount of money owed to Morgan by SK Securities and the default probability of SK's special purpose vehicle borrowing the money were strongly correlated. The very nature of the revolving line of credit has this issue at its heart—one of the primary 'use of proceeds' and one of the primary motivations of line of credit usage is for 'commercial paper back up lines'. These lines are intended to provide an alternative source of funding in the event of a disruption in the commercial paper market in general, or in case the borrower for some reason is unable to issue commercial paper, presumably because of credit quality problems.

Providers of revolving lines of credit walk a fine line—they know that this change in credit quality is the primary motivator of the line and the lender guesses that the potential deterioration in credit quality will not be so severe that the lender is not fully compensated for the risk they are taking. It goes without saying that the default probabilities of all borrowers with lines of credit and the usage under the lines of credit are driven by a set of macro economic factors common to many of the borrowers.

The cash needs under the line of credit are the sum of a number of influences:

$$C(t) = C_1(t) + C_2(\lambda) + C_3(\lambda_1, \lambda_2, \ldots, \lambda_n) + Z(t)$$

Cash needs at any point in time consist of a time-dependent expected amount, which can vary seasonally, plus an amount that depends on the default intensity of the borrower λ, plus a third amount that depends on the default intensities of the major counterparties of the business, which we write $\lambda_1, \lambda_2, \ldots \lambda_n$. The final term is a random term. We don't mean to suggest any particularly functional form for these cash flow needs. In Chapters 39 and 40, we suggest precisely how these cash flow needs can be modeled and forecast.

Unfortunately, the multi-period nature of the usage on a line of credit means that the Merton model is uniquely unsuited as a framework for line of credit valuation and estimating exposure at default. Van Deventer and Imai [2003] note that the only decision points we can use in the Merton [1974] or Shimko, Tejima, van Deventer [1993] framework are at time zero or at the end of the single period assumed by the model. What we need instead is the kind of continuous time variation that is described by a function like that above or in the Jarrow-van Deventer non-maturity deposit model.

Once we specify how the cash needs of a company vary with its own default risk and the relevant macro-economic factors, we can proceed directly to valuation of the line of credit, simulation of cash needs, expected exposure at default, and the full probability distribution over time and in dollar terms of exposure of default. This analysis is completely analogous of the 'own firm' risk assessment that we explore in Chapters 39 and 40.

Is a line of credit a put option on the debt of the issuer?

Lines of credit are often thought of as a put option on the floating-rate debt of the borrower. This view is almost, but not exactly, correct. Using the analogy with the non-maturity deposit modeling of Chapter 33, part of the cash needs listed in the previous section have nothing to do with credit risk. They typically reflect the seasonality of the business. Given random interest rates and a constant default intensity of the borrower λ, this non-credit risk related cash need can be valued directly in a closed form solution using the reduced form model of Chapter 17. The second component of cash need comes from potential changes in the credit quality of the borrower's major business counterparties. In a sense, the portfolio of accounts receivable that are held by the borrower are a collection of debt instruments like those we modeled in Chapter 22 on credit risky bonds. These too have a known solution in the reduced form modeling framework.

In some cases, the credit quality of the business counterparties of the borrower affects cash flow in a more complex way than a default/no default kind of model. A rise in default probability of ABC company, for example, may lengthen the terms of payment, for example, without triggering default. These kinds of influences of the default probability of ABC company can be modeled like small portfolios of digital default swaps that are triggered, not so much by the event of default, but by the level of the default probability reaching a certain range.

The final default intensity-related component of cash needs of the company is the term $C_2(\lambda)$ in the cash need function above. This function is undoubtedly a complex non-linear function of the default intensity that reflects sources of funding like the commercial paper market. As we discuss in Chapter 40, issuers of commercial paper rated A3/P3 have dramatically less access to commercial paper than more highly rated issuers. Similarly, a much larger universe of institutions can buy investment grade bonds than can buy non-investment grade bonds. All of these factors affect the function $C_2(\lambda)$. Another factor comes into play as well. Even if the company holds relatively liquid assets, it may become obvious to other market participants that the company is in trouble if the default intensity exceeds a certain level. The famous Long-Term Capital Management incident illustrates the result—in a market that is not perfectly liquid, other market participants will lower their bid prices for the assets held by the company because they know credit problems will force the company to take any price. We return to this theme in detail in Chapter 40. In summary, the cash flows generated by the $C_2(\lambda)$ term have a nature much like that of a 'range' floater in credit derivatives terms. For a given range of default intensity, cash flows will take on a particular value. In the Jarrow model, the straightforward nature of the default intensity function gives us a good chance of a closed form valuation for this component of draws on the line of credit.

The final component of cash flow needs is the random term $Z(t)$. If we have properly included all of the macro factors driving cash flows in the other terms of the cash flow function, then we can make an argument that $Z(t)$ has mean zero and that diversification arguments with respect to the $Z(t)$ term's impact on valuation will prevail. With luck, the $Z(t)$ term will not affect valuation.

The upshot of this micro-focused discussion of the determinants of cash needs on a line of credit are that a finely detailed analysis of cash needs will allow us to do a high quality valuation and simulation of lines of credit and exposure at default. Most of what we need to do has already been discussed in other chapters in this book. What little we need to add to do a complete job on lines of credit risk analysis will be discussed in detail in Chapters 39 and 40.

We next turn to equity-linked instruments in our quest to value the Jarrow-Merton put option.

CHAPTER 37

Modeling Common Stock and Convertible Bonds on a Default-Adjusted Basis

A very large proportion of the world's financial institutions are substantial direct or indirect owners of common stock and convertible bonds. Financial institutions, via their own pension funds, often have a large exposure to equities that is overlooked in risk analysis. In addition, the direct investment in equity-related securities is large and linked in a complex way with other assets and liabilities on the balance sheet.

In Chapter 2, we mentioned the increasing concern that sophisticated investors have with the inconsistency in their management of fixed income and equity portfolios. Credit risk is typically given lots of attention on the fixed income side and ignored on the equity side. Risk analysis of a position in IBM bonds and IBM common stock is typically done in a way that recognizes the losses of default on the bonds and ignores the simultaneous impact of default on the common stock of IBM. This inconsistency should be very troubling to management, boards of directors, and regulators of the financial institutions involved.

Credit risk on the equity side has another more subtle form as well, a topic we introduced in Chapter 2. Many fund managers are judged on their performance versus an equity benchmark, such as the S&P500 index in the U.S. If a company is a 'member' of the list of 500 companies making up the index, it has to be of fairly good credit quality. If the company's default probability rises to a certain level, the odds that it is removed from the S&P500 index become very high. If the company is to be dropped, the announcement is normally made after the close of business. The stock will drop dramatically at the opening the next day, leaving the fund manager with a large loss versus the index because the weakened company is no longer in the index, but the fund manager still has the position from the previous day.

This credit risk-related loss can be substantial and has been almost completely overlooked by many financial institutions.

With this as background, we move on to a discussion of how to incorporate common stock and convertible bonds on the list of instruments that we can value as we progress toward our objective—valuing the Jarrow-Merton put option on company assets and liabilities as the comprehensive, integrated measure of interest rate, FX and credit risk.

Modeling Equities: The Traditional Fund Management Approach

For more than 40 years, it has been the fund management industry standard to model the return on a common stock as a linear combination of the return on various other factors. This approach is justified by assuming that stock prices are lognormally distributed and therefore their returns are normally distributed. A linear combination of normally distributed inputs produces the desired normal distribution. This approach dates to the original formulation of the capital asset pricing model, where the original single factor was the 'return on the market'. In this model, the return on the common stock of company J is the sum of the risk-free rate and its beta times the [return on the market less the risk-free rate] plus a random error term. For decades, there has been an enormous amount of research on correctly measuring the correlation between the returns on the common stock of company J and the return on the market. The beta is the measure of this correlation of returns.

Fund managers quickly realized that there were multiple factors driving common stock returns, some of which were macro-economic factors (like those in the reduced form credit models of Chapter 17) and some of which were company specific. The company specific factors included things like company size, its price earnings ratio, its industry sector, and so on. Many of these factors too are incorporated in the reduced form default probability models of Chapter 17. It is fairly common for a fund manager to be using a multi-factor model of common stock returns to manage 'tracking error', the amount of potential deviation between the return on the fund manager's portfolio and the return on the index.

What is wrong with this approach?

It totally ignores both the direct and indirect impact of default. Clearly, when a company has a 1% probability of bankruptcy, a normal distribution can't be an accurate portrayal of the potential distribution of returns on the common stock because there is a 1% probability that the return will be minus 100%![1]

Moreover, in the indirect risk category, there is a large drop in the common stock price that would occur if the company is dropped from the S&P index for credit risk-related or other reasons.

---

[1] We note that, even in the event of bankruptcy, in many cases common stock prices do not drop to zero in large part because of the common violation of absolute priorities of debt holders over equity holders. This is another of the many challenges facing analysts using the Merton model of risky debt from Chapter 16.

The great strength of this approach, however, is that it already incorporates many of the macro factors and company-specific factors that are related to default risk—they are just not used properly for default adjusted tracking error management.

We turn now to general assumptions about common stock price movements in the derivatives world.

Modeling Equities: The Derivatives Approach

In the derivatives world, key assumptions about the movement in equity prices also employ the lognormal assumption about stock price movements that results in normally distributed returns on common stock. As we noted in our term structure analysis of Chapters 10–12 and in Chapter 16 on the Merton model of risky debt, the analytical benefits of this assumption can be so powerful that it is worth the cost of glossing over some real world realities.

Typically, in the derivatives world, the stock price itself is used as a random factor without modeling the N macro-economic and company specific factors driving movements in the stock price. This is due in large part because the primary focus of derivatives analysts, dating from the original options model of Black and Scholes [1973], is on 'synthetic replication' of the derivative with an appropriate position in the common stock. Jarrow and Turnbull [1996] discuss the importance of this argument in detail.

It is argued that because movements in the price of the derivative can be hedged by appropriate positions in the common stock, we don't need to know the drivers of returns on the common stock.

For most of the last 30 years, equity derivatives valuation formulas have assumed away both the potential default of the counterparty on an option on common stock and the potential default of the issuer of the common stock underlying the derivative. Lately, the issue of these two potential defaults are getting a lot more attention in the literature and the real world, largely because of the insights triggered by the Jarrow-Turnbull [1995] reduced form credit model.

Modeling Equities: A Credit-Risk Adjusted Approach

The Merton [1974] model of risky debt, which we discussed in Chapter 16, is not just a model of debt prices. It is implicitly a single-factor model of equity prices where the value of a company's common stock is a function of the value of company assets. Similarly, the Shimko, Tejima and van Deventer model [1993] implies that the value of a company's common stock is a function of random interest rates and the value of company assets, which in turn can have any arbitrary correlation with interest rates. As we discussed in Chapter 18 and in detail in van Deventer and Imai [2003], tests of the consistency of these models with relative movements in common stock prices and credit spreads on bonds have proved to be disappointing. Consequently, the Merton insights have not been used by equity market participants to the extent they have been used in the debt markets.

Jarrow and Turnbull [1995] present a framework for modeling equity securities on a full credit-adjusted basis. Using a simplified assumption of a constant default intensity, they assume that stock prices are lognormally distributed and driven by random interest rates and a company specific risk factor which can have any correlation with interest rates, provide that the company does not go bankrupt. They assume that the stock price drops to zero in the event of bankruptcy. Jarrow and Turnbull show that, under these assumptions, the risk neutral drift term in the common stock's return formula has to increase by the instantaneous probability of default. This has a number of important implications for modeling not only the common stock but also options on a credit-risky company's common stock and convertible bonds, which we discuss below.

Using the Jarrow-Turnbull framework for modeling common stock returns, we can directly address all of the concerns expressed in the first sections of this chapter while preserving (in modified form) the multi-factor approach to explaining lognormally distributed returns.

Jarrow [1999] takes this approach still further and models common stock in a framework with a random default intensity driven by interest rates and macro factors as discussed in Chapter 17. A common stock pays dividends until bankruptcy, when the value of common stock goes to zero. A full exploitation of the virtues of this model look very promising, but we restrict our comments on equity derivatives on the common stock of a credit risky company to the Jarrow-Turnbull and closely related approaches.

Options on the Common Stock of a Company Which Can Go Bankrupt

Jarrow and Turnbull [1995] use their model for the common stock of a company which can go bankrupt, to value put and call options on that credit-risky common stock.

They reach a very powerful and yet intuitive conclusion. The zero-coupon bond prices in the call options formula become the zero-coupon bond prices extracted from the yield curve of the risky company (see Chapters 17 and 18 for how to do this) instead of from the risk-free yield curve. These risky zero-coupon bond prices directly reflect the default intensity of the issuer, as we discussed in Chapters 17 and 18 in the most recent Jarrow [1999, 2001] framework.

Using the Jarrow-Turnbull formula for options on common stock which can go bankrupt, we can explain much of the volatility smile issues with the constant interest rate/no default Black-Scholes options model. As many analysts have noted, equity options prices seem to be based on a probability distribution which reflects much greater downside risk than a simple lognormal distribution on stock price would imply. This is due to the risk of default (among other things) and the Jarrow-Turnbull model will improve the volatility smile problems because it deals with this increased downside risk directly.

Moreover, the Jarrow-Turnbull model can be used to imply the probability of default from equity options on a company which can go bankrupt.

Convertible Bonds of a Company Which Can Go Bankrupt

The same approach proposed by Jarrow-Turnbull [1995] can be applied to convertible bonds, which contain a complex set of options controlled by both the issuer and by the holder of the bonds. After many years of trying to model convertible bonds as a combination of the straight bond and an option on the common stock, hedge funds and other analysts have employed both structural and reduced form modeling approaches. Three recent papers by Ayache, Forsyth, and Vetzal [2003], Andersen and Buffum [2003], and Bermudez and Webber [2003] show great promise in tackling one of the most complex securities on the balance sheet of financial institutions.

Convertible bonds normally contain a call option granted to the issuer to call the bonds at a preset schedule of call prices. Separately, the holder of the convertible bonds has an option to convert the bonds normally to a preset number of common shares. This option is maintained for a prespecified number of days even if the bonds are called by the issuer to allow time for conversion. Both of these options are significantly affected by the probability of default, which is why initial approaches which ignored default led to large losses at hedge funds investing in convertible bonds.

Many of the recent papers on convertible bond valuation combine reduced form default intensities with the finite difference method of securities valuation that we discussed in earlier chapters. Andersen and Buffum [2003] note that 'While it is in principle possible to build convertible bond models using the structural approach ... the reduced-form approach is, by far, the most natural for trading applications and shall be the sole focus of this paper.'[2] At this stage it is safe to say that tremendous progress is being made on the valuation of convertible securities on a full credit-adjusted basis and they can be included in valuation of the Jarrow-Merton put option, our integrated measure of credit risk and interest rate risk.

---

[2] Andersen and Buffum, footnote 1.

CHAPTER 38

Valuing Insurance Policies and Pension Obligations

Our final chapter in individual instrument valuation and simulation is focused on insurance policies and pension obligations, since insurance companies and pension funds make up a substantial proportion of the world's financial institutions. To reiterate, our objective in reviewing valuation and simulation methodologies is to incorporate the insurance liabilities and pension liabilities in the Jarrow-Merton put option on the financial institution's assets and liabilities. We want to use a consistent methodology to calculate this comprehensive measure of integrated interest rate and credit risk.

This is particularly interesting to discuss for insurance and pension obligations because the links with what we have already covered are so strong and yet so few members of the financial community would acknowledge that that is the case. The authors hope that this chapter narrows this perception gap.

We start first with life insurance policies and then move on to pension obligations and property and casualty insurance.

Life Insurance: Mortality Rates versus Default Probabilities

The analogy between the mortality rate on a life insurance policy and the default probability on a bond of a particular issuer is strong. Figure 38.1 below shows annual mortality rates for a 50 year old male and 50 year old female:[1]

Like default or bankruptcy, mortality on a life insurance policy is a zero/one kind of event. The fundamental approach to measuring mortality risk was proposed by D.R. Cox in 1972.[2] The 'Cox process' that he developed

---

[1] Nearest birthday basis, 1990-1995 Basic Select and Ultimate Mortality Tables, Society of Actuaries, undated memorandum.

[2] "Regression Models and Life Tables", *Journal of the Royal Statistical Society*, B34, 187-220, 1972.

Figure 38.1 Annual Mortality Rate for 50-Year Old Males and Females, Nearest Birth Basis, 1990-1995 Select and Ultimate Mortality Tables

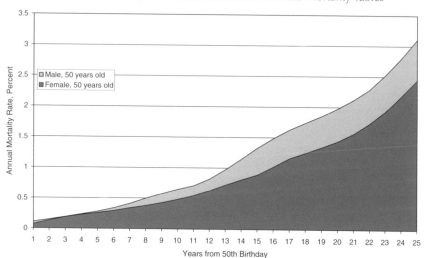

is in fact the same 'Cox process' used in reduced form modeling in the Jarrow [1999, 2001] and Duffie and Singleton [1999] credit models that we discussed in Chapter 17. The mathematics is identical. The term structure of mortality rates shown above is exactly the same as the term structure of default probabilities that we can observe in the First Interstate credit spreads provided by van Deventer and Imai [2003] or in the credit default swap market.

The other strong parallel between life insurance and credit risk is the progressive use of logistic regression to determine the probability of the event (bankruptcy or mortality) with more precision than we would get from a simple table (a transition matrix with default probability by ratings grade or a mortality table). A recent paper by Guizhou Hu[3] shows how mortality rate prediction can be improved by incorporating explanatory variables that are much more detailed than those in mortality tables (age, male or female, smoker or non-smoker); among the variables he mentions are the following:

- Systolic blood pressure;
- Total cholesterol;
- Body mass index;
- Smoker or non-smoker;
- Albumin;
- Physical activity—i.e. light, moderate or heavy;
- Income.

---

[3] "Mortality Assessment Technology: A New Tool for Life Insurance Underwriting," undated memorandum, BioSignia, Inc., Durham, North Carolina.

All of these input variables are specific to the insured, just like the accounting and stock price inputs to the Jarrow-Chava model of Chapter 17 are specific to the firm being modeled.

Cyclicality in default probabilities and mortality rates

Logistic regression can also confirm the importance of cyclicality in mortality just as it does (as required by the New Basel II Capital Accords) for default. Any Japanese banker can tell you that the mortality rate of his co-workers is much different when the Nikkei stock index is below 10,000 yen than it was when it is nearly 39,000 yen. Similarly, just as there is seasonality in the default of small businesses, there is seasonality in mortality that is logical and predictable (due to factors like weather, stresses of the school calendar year, low stress of summer vacations, and so on).

Valuing Life Insurance Policies

Life insurance policies are closely related to digital default swaps that we discussed in Chapter 23. The protection buyer on the digital default swap called a life insurance policy is (usually) the insured. The insured is also the reference name on the digital life insurance policy. The counterparty on the digital life insurance policy is the life insurance company. The amount paid on the digital life insurance policy is the policy amount. The only significant difference is the maturity—term life insurance policies, which have an explicit maturity, are almost literally identical to digital default swaps. A 'whole life' policy runs until mortality or until cancelled. Ignoring the cancellation provisions, it's like a infinite maturity digital default swap except that we know the term structure of mortality/default probabilities approaches 100% in time.

What about cancellation privileges? This is a real option of the insured that can be exercised rationally or irrationally as discussed in the prepayment context in Chapters 30–32. It is rational to cancel when (a) the mortality risk of the insured becomes lower than that implied in the current policy, allowing the insured to reinsure at a lower rate, or (b) when the insured becomes so wealthy that they no longer need insurance (they save money by not paying the insurance company costs embedded in the policy and effectively 'self insure'). 'Irrational' cancellation (like irrational prepayment) is usually for a good reason unknown to the insurance company. The financial condition of the insured, for example, may have deteriorated so much that they can't afford the premiums, even though they need the insurance.

What about investment options on a whole life policy? We know from finance theory that an option to switch from one instrument at its market price to another instrument at its market price has zero value, since there is no benefit to the options holder (if we ignore transactions costs). Many of the investment options in a life insurance policy have this nature. To the extent there is a real benefit to the holder of the insurance policy from the investment options offered, we can value them using the techniques in other chapters in this book.

One of the key benefits of life insurance to the buyer is the ability to defer taxes on the investment income of a whole life insurance policy. This tax deferral is of course a real benefit to the buyer of the insurance policy, relative to making the identical investments in the name of the insured. The value of this benefit to the buyer of the insurance policy depends on the state of the tax code now and in the future, the source and variability of income now and in the future, and the default probability of the insurance company. Clearly, valuing these tax benefits with precision is a challenge, and one that we're happy to defer to another time.

Pension obligations

Pension obligations have a very interesting mix of terms that combine part of the life insurance problem with more traditional financial instruments. One of the advantages of a pension fund in an economic sense is the on-going stream of current payments for future pension benefits from both employees and their employers. The present value of this cash inflow from any one employee, say Mr Jones, depends on three factors: the mortality probability of Mr Jones (he could be unlucky enough to pass away before leaving employment and receiving pension benefits), the probability that Mr Jones will change jobs and end up contributing to a different pension fund, and the probability of default of Mr Jones' employer. The liabilities of a pension fund, the future payments to the beneficiaries of the fund, depend on the mortality rate of the pension beneficiary, just like a life insurance policy. The difference is that the payments are made in the opposite circumstance of a life insurance policy— they are paid while the beneficiary is still living. In this sense, the future stream of pension payments are each a 'digital default' swap of sorts again, except the key probability used in valuation is the probability of no mortality prior to the payment, not the probability of bankruptcy/mortality relevant to valuing a life insurance policy.

For defined benefit pension plans, which is our focus in this section, there are normally a complex set of rules or circumstances which determine when and how pension benefits are increased over time. Similarly, even with government pension insurance, there is the probability that the pension fund defaults on its obligations to the pension beneficiaries. Both of these complexities can be dealt with using a combination of the life insurance analysis above and the techniques of other chapters. In particular, the increased use of the logistic regression technique and reduced form modeling approach allows for comprehensive credit-adjusted risk management of both the assets and liabilities of a pension fund.

Property and Casualty Insurance

Property and casualty insurance differs from life insurance in two dimensions: the term of the insurance contract is typically shorter and the events being insured are quite diverse, ranging from auto insurance to catastrophic weather-related events. Aside from events that are acts of nature, like weather and earthquakes, logistic regression again pays a powerful role in both pricing and risk management of liabilities on a property and casualty insurance contract. The price of an auto insurance policy depends on factors such as the following:

- The age of the driver;
- The sex of the driver (in some jurisdictions);
- The health of the driver (if the data is available);
- The income of the driver (again, if the data is available);
- The driving history of the driver;
- The amount of driving to be done (and the possibility that the true amount is not disclosed);
- The type of car being insured (i.e. a bus or a sports car);
- The value of the car being insured;
- The place in which the car will be stored (a deserted urban parking lot in a high crime area or a locked garage in a gated community);
- The place in which the car will be driven (i.e. downtown New York City or rural France).

In addition, it is an empirical question whether macroeconomic factors have an impact on both the probability of an insured event and the payout on the occurrence of the event. Clearly, we know from the statistics on new auto sales that new sales of cars decline in bad times so the average age of all cars being driven increases during recessions. This in turn would be expected to affect the probability of a claim and the payout on the claim. For this reason, depending on the nature of the insured event, it is often the case that macro factors drive the probability of an insurance payout just like they affect the probability of default in the reduced form credit models of Chapter 17. When this is the case, it is essential that these macro factors are incorporated in policy pricing and total balance sheet risk management or the risk of providing the policy can be dramatically underestimated. If these macro factors are relevant, they will increase the correlation in the occurrence of insured events and the fat tails of the loss distribution.

The Jarrow-Merton Put Option

In many insurance companies and pension funds, there is a sharp division between the investment or asset side of the organization and the insurance or liability side of the organization. The investment function is dominated by finance experts and the liability side is dominated by insurance experts and actuaries. This contrasts sharply with risk management at banks and securities firms where asset and liability management on a joint basis has been standard for 30 years.

Looking at the risk on only one side of the balance sheet at a time is dangerous because common macro factors drive the risk on both sides of the balance sheet. If you are looking at only half the picture, it is impossible for management, the board of directors and regulators to have an accurate view of total risk. How can we value the Jarrow-Merton put option on the assets and liabilities of the firm as a comprehensive integrated measure of interest rate and credit risk if half of the information is missing?

Fortunately, as we have seen in this chapter, the mathematics of credit risk models is taken directly from insurance expert Cox. There is literally no difference in the mathematical approach, so there are only emotional and political reasons for the long-standing divide between the actuaries and the investment side of the organization when it comes to risk management. The best practice insurance companies are solving this problem by moving actuaries to the investment side of the organization and investment managers to the insurance side of the organization. Integrated risk management teams that have both actuaries and finance experts are being established and a common view of integrated risk is widely recognized as necessary and desirable. We expect that the traditional 'walls' down the middle of insurance companies and pension funds will break down rapidly in the years ahead.

CHAPTER 39

Risk Management Objectives Revisited at the Portfolio and Company Level

In Chapter 1, we defined risk management in a practical way:

Risk management is the discipline that clearly shows management the risks and returns of every major strategic decision at both the institutional level and the transaction level. Moreover, the risk management discipline shows how to change strategy in order to bring the risk return trade-off into line with the best long and short-term interests of the institution.

In Chapter 1, we noted that this definition of risk management includes within it the overlapping and inseparable sub-disciplines such as:

- credit risk;
- market risk;
- asset and liability management;
- operational risk;
- performance measurement;
- transfer pricing.

and many other sub-disciplines. Our primary focus in this book is to show how to execute the practice of risk management in a way that is fully integrated and makes no distinction between these sub disciplines.

In Chapter 2, we told a story courtesy of Nobel prize winner Robert Merton, about the portfolio manager who asked for the cost of a put option at his current portfolio value on a strategy recommended by an equity salesman. The salesman had proposed a strategy that on average had little risk but in a few circumstances was disastrous. For that reason, such a put option would have been very expensive and the salesman, recognizing that he'd been caught red-handed, never called back.

As we noted in Chapter 2, the salesman Merton spoke about was using a tried and true technique, talking about expected returns and ignoring risk.

The portfolio manager's reply, however, reflects the highest standard of risk management theory and practice: He asked the price of a contract that insures perfectly against the risk that concerns him. Robert Jarrow, as mentioned in Chapter 2, has argued that for this reason a properly structured put option is the best comprehensive measure of integrated interest rate, foreign exchange and credit risk. In this chapter, we discuss practical implementation of this concept using the valuation techniques of Chapters 21–38.

Implementing the Jarrow-Merton Put Option as a Comprehensive Measure of Risk

'What is the hedge?' In other chapters in this book, we posed this question as the best single sentence test of risk management technology. For that reason, the Jarrow-Merton put option is a very powerful concept because the put option they propose, if properly structured, *is* the hedge.

In Chapter 3, we posed this question: 'What is the equivalent of the Merton and Jarrow put option in the interest rate risk context?' It is the value of an option to buy the entire portfolio of the financial institution's assets and liabilities at a fixed price at a specific point in time. From a pension fund perspective, a more complex string of options which guarantee the pension fund's ability to provide cash flow of $X(t)$ in each of N periods to meet obligations to pensioners would be necessary.

As we mentioned in Chapter 4, we can describe almost all common risk management risk measures using the Merton and Jarrow analysis of the put option. We gave these examples in Chapter 4 of the Jarrow-Merton put option as a practical risk management concept:

- Instead of the 10-day **value at risk** of a trading portfolio, what is the value of a 10-day put option on my current portfolio with an exercise price equal to the portfolio's current market value? The price of the put option will increase sharply with the risk of my portfolio, and the put option's price will reflect all possible losses and their probability, not just the 99th percentile loss as is traditional in value at risk analysis
- Instead of **stress testing the 12-month net income** of the financial institution to see if net income will go below $100 million for the year, what is the price of a put option in month 12 which will produce a gain in net income exactly equal to the short-fall of net income versus the $100 million target? The more interest rate risk in the balance sheet of the financial institution, the more expensive this put option will be. The put option will reflect all levels of net income shortfall and their probability, not just the shortfalls detected by specific stress tests
- Instead of the **Basel II risk-weighted capital ratio** for the bank, what is the price of the put option that insures solvency of the bank in one

year's time? This put option measures all potential losses embedded in the financial institution's balance sheet and their probability of occurrence, including both interest rate risk and credit risk, as we discuss at the end of this chapter.

- Instead of 'expected losses' on a collateralized debt obligation tranche's **B tranche**, what is the price of a put option on the value of the tranche at par at maturity? This put option reflects all losses on the tranche, not just the average loss, along with their probability of occurrence.
- Instead of 'expected losses **on the Bank Insurance Fund**' in the U.S., the Federal Deposit Insurance Corporation has valued the put option of retail bank deposits at their par value as discussed in the FDIC's loss distribution model announced on December 10 2003.

In Chapter 4, we noted that the Jarrow-Merton put option concept helps to reconcile what many regard as conflicting objectives to be managed from a risk management perspective:

- **Net interest income (or net income)**, a multi-period financial accounting-based figure that includes the influence of both instruments that the financial institution owns today and those that it will own in the future.
- **Market value of portfolio equity**, the market value of the assets a financial institution owns today less the market value of its liabilities.
- **Market-based equity ratio**, which is the ratio of the mark-to-market value of the equity of the portfolio ('market value of portfolio equity' in bank jargon) divided by the market value of assets. This is most closely related to the capital ratio formulas of the primary capital era, Basel I, and Basel II.
- **Default probability of the institution**, which is another strong candidate as a single measure of risk.

We discuss the structuring of Jarrow-Merton put options for practical risk management in a series of plain English examples for the market value of portfolio equity case. After that, we discuss how the valuation of these options can be done using the technology in the first 38 chapters of this book.

The Jarrow-Merton put option example 1: The case of deposit insurance

We start with the simplest case of the Jarrow-Merton put option, the case of bank deposit insurance. From a consumer perspective, the obligation of the Federal Deposit Insurance System to guarantee payment of principal on deposits up to $100,000 is an open-ended commitment with no explicit maturity date. From the bank's perspective, the bank's membership in the FDIC is essential from a marketing perspective as long as the fee for deposit insurance is not 'too much'. What is 'too much'? Deposit insurance premiums are 'too much' from the bank's perspective if the marginal cost of deposits with deposit insurance included is greater than the marginal cost of deposits with no insurance. Since the bank is raising deposits in amounts greater than $100,000 even if it has deposit insurance, it should be constantly aware of these marginal cost figures.

From the FDIC's perspective, its mandate to provide deposit insurance for a specified time depends on the legislative process. Similarly, its ability to change the fees for deposit insurance both overall and at the specific institution level also depends on the legislative process. For purposes of this discussion, let's assume that the FDIC's mandate to provide deposit insurance for ABC Bank is explicitly set for 10 years from today. How can we analyze this commitment by the FDIC as a put option in the Jarrow-Merton sense?

The FDIC deposit insurance cash flows for ABC works like this:

- **Event of default**: The FDIC's obligation to pay off depositors begins with the sooner of the following: (a) the inability of the bank to meet deposit withdrawal needs of any insured depositor, or (b) the default of the bank on any other instrument or (c) the determination by regulators that the bank is insolvent.

- **Payment on default**: Two sets of depositors and the FDIC potentially have cash flow affected by the default of the bank. Insured depositors are the most senior creditors and they are paid in full. Initially, they are paid by the FDIC. The FDIC then liquidates the assets of the bank. If funds are left over after fully reimbursing the FDIC for payments to uninsured depositors, then the remaining payment goes to uninsured depositors who most likely will receive only a portion of their principal amount. The FDIC incurs no loss (except perhaps in the timing sense) and the uninsured depositors suffer a 'loss given default'. If the proceeds from asset liquidation are not sufficient to fully reimburse the FDIC, then the FDIC suffers a 'loss given default' and uninsured depositors receive nothing.

- **Type of Credit Instrument**: The FDIC's obligation to pay off insured depositors is an American credit instrument with the maturity that we have assumed—10 years. The FDIC will pay whenever default occurs prior to maturity, just like on the credit derivative instruments that we discussed in Chapter 22. If the bank defaults, we assume it is permanently liquidated and the FDIC will not have a further obligation to insure its deposits in the future. This is different from some of the other Jarrow-Merton option structures, which we discuss below.

In return for the potential payment of this deposit insurance amount, the FDIC receives a stream of insurance payments from the bank at the frequencies specified by the FDIC's regulations, again just like a credit default swap.

The primary difference between the FDIC deposit insurance and the credit default swap discussed in Chapter 23 is that the nominal principal on which the payment on default is based changes over time instead of being fixed at time zero. If the insured deposits of the bank grow over time, both its FDIC insurance payments and the FDIC's payments upon default will grow over time. More likely, the insured deposits of a bank will decrease over time as the bank approaches bankruptcy, which reduces both its payments for deposit insurance and the FDIC's obligations when the bank fails.

What determines the probability of default of the bank and its timing? The answer is parallel to the discussion of collateralized debt obligations in Chapter 23—the valuation and default risk of the bank's assets have the same role in bank default that the reference collateral has in the context of the default on a CDO senior tranche.

The Jarrow-Merton put option example 2: Payment on default at the time zero market value of equity

What if the management of the bank chooses as its key risk management focus, the cost of a put option that pays the full current market value of equity today if the bank defaults at any time in the next five years?

If the bank's stock price is $10 today and there are 10 million shares outstanding, the management team wants to know the cost of an option that pays 10×10 million = $100 million upon default. The cost of this option is 10 million times the cost of a digital default swap that pays $1 upon default of the organization.

Management can set a policy limit on the maximum amount of this put option. When the cost of the put option rises, approaching its limits, the market perceives an increase in the risk of the institution. If this perception is incorrect, the bank can address it by making more complete disclosure. If the perception of increased risk is correct, then management can reduce total risk contributing to the increased probability of default by either (a) reducing interest rate risk or (b) by reducing credit risk. Management can achieve the latter by either selling credit risky assets or by putting a partial or complete credit risk hedge in place.

This kind of payoff on default is a one time only payment.

The Jarrow-Merton put option example 3: A put option on the market value of portfolio equity at zero upon default

Another very attractive put option to select as a key focus of risk management is a put option that prevents default by insuring that the market value of portfolio equity (market value of assets less market value of liabilities) upon default is never less than $X. If the value for the 'strike price' X is zero, that means that the put option will pay just enough to pay off all liabilities at par with literally nothing left over after all assets are liquidated.

If X is selected to be zero, then payment on this put option takes place only once. If X is more than zero, the institution could survive and payment could occur more than once. We deal with this issue in the next section.

What kind of events can cause the market value of portfolio of equity to become negative, resulting in default (if we did not have the put option)?

- **Credit risk**: Defaults on the bond or loan portfolio of the institution can eliminate the equity of the institution and many of the liabilities since sufficient funds will not remain to pay off the liabilities as they mature.
- **Interest rate risk**: A rise in interest rates could drive the market value of assets below the value of liabilities as happened with the savings and loan associations in the U.S. in the 1980s and 1990s. If the financial institution has originated 30-year mortgages with a principal amount of $100 that are now worth $70 and it has $90 of three-month deposits coming due, no rational depositor would leave their money at the financial institution. In this case, our put option will pay $20, the difference between the value of assets ($70) and the amount owed on deposits ($90) and the bank will be liquidated with no loss to any of the liability providers.
- **Both credit risk and interest rate risk**: Both risks could drive down asset values and trigger default.

Can this kind of option be valued? The answer is definitely yes—using the techniques of Chapters 22–24. Can this kind of option be purchased from a third party protection provider? To some extent, it is available in the market place already in the form of credit default swaps, but an institution cannot buy credit protection on itself because of the serious moral hazard (only institutions who regard this credit protection as too cheap would buy it, making all dealers reluctant to provide it). Instead, the credit protection can be replicated by incorporating the drivers of default risk across the full spectrum of bank assets, along with any interest rate risk that may be embedded in the portfolio.

The valuation of this Jarrow-Merton put option is closely related to the credit risky instruments of Chapters 22–23 and the bond option of Chapter 24.

The Jarrow-Merton put option example 4: A put option on the market value of portfolio equity at $X on demand, preventing default

What if the Jarrow-Merton put option from the previous section was exercisable by the shareholders of the financial institution whenever the market value of portfolio equity reached $X within the specified maturity of the put option?

If this put option was exercised, the ownership of the financial institution would change, but the financial institution would not fail. This is the nature of government sponsored bail outs in the U.S. and Japan where the shareholders of the financial institution receive some token payment and the institution survives, often as a nationalized financial institution.

This type of credit option can be thought of as a one time only payment, since the ownership of the institution changes hands.

This kind of option can be priced using the techniques of Chapters 22–24.

The Jarrow-Merton put option example 5: A 'put option' on the market value of portfolio equity which pays $Y whenever the market value of portfolio equity hits $X, regardless of the number of occurrences during the life of the put option

Most management teams would rather not liquidate the financial institution nor turn it over to new owners if credit risk or interest rate risk created a decline in the market value of portfolio equity to some critical level $X. Instead, management would like to be able to inject more equity, say $Y, into the institution to fight another day. If management gets in trouble again in a subsequent period (which is likely given the existence of credit cycles in which credit quality problems can persist for years), it would like to receive another payment $Y so it can go on again.

This is a credit instrument which pays $Y dollars one or more time if the market value of portfolio equity falls to $X on a specified series of dates prior to maturity of this credit instrument.

Let these dates be $T_1, T_2, \ldots, T_N$ prior to maturity at time T. If there was only one payment date, this instrument is the equivalent of a digital option on the portfolio (value of all assets less value of all liabilities), which pays $Y when the portfolio value falls to $X.

When there are N payment dates, the option potentially has more than one date on which payment is made, and the probability of a payment on date T_j depends in part upon whether payments have already been received. We have to use the techniques of Chapters 22–24 in a more comprehensive way than when there is only one potential payment date.

The Jarrow-Merton put option example 6: The case of interest rate risk

In Chapter 5, we analyzed some classic questions about interest rate risk that come from the insights of the Jarrow-Merton put option in the special case where the assets have no credit risk. Some of the interest rate risk management conclusions we reached in that chapter can be summarized again as follows:

1. Is the put option that eliminates the interest rate risk of the institution in the Jarrow-Merton sense so expensive that the financial institution can't afford to buy it? If that is the case, the interest rate risk of the institution is too large and has to be reduced by other means. The Jarrow-Merton put option can be set as either a European put option exercisable on a specific date or an American put option exercisable on many dates. In either case, we would value it using the Jamshidian approach in Chapter 24. There are many strike prices that can be used for this option—if the option is on the market value of portfolio equity (like the options above), an exercise price of zero provides only enough interest rate risk protection to liquidate the institution without loss to deposits. If the exercise price is higher, the institution will survive. We can also use 'barrier options' that allow the put option to be exercised whenever interest rate movements cause the market value of portfolio equity to hit the barrier.

2. If a change in the cash flow structure from an interest rate-related transaction smooths net income, but leaves the Jarrow-Merton put option value unchanged, then the transaction is worth doing. This has an 'information' benefit to shareholders who might otherwise misperceive the risk of the institution based on short-term changes in net income.

3. If the change in cash flow structure from an interest rate-related transaction smooths net income but leaves the bank well within the safety zone, then it is probably worth doing. In this case, the value of the Jarrow-Merton put option is zero because the fact that the bank is in the safety zone means that the probability of default is zero and the probability that the Jarrow-Merton put option will be exercised is zero.

Valuing and Simulating the Jarrow-Merton Put Option

How do we value the Jarrow-Merton put option? In some of the cases mentioned above, we already have known valuation formulas from Chapters 22–38. In most cases, however, we need to do a multi-period simulation using the risk-neutral valuation formulas now common in finance. We need to calculate the 'risk neutral' expected values of the cash flows that would be paid on the put option that we are analyzing.

We outlined the steps in this simulation in Chapter 22 in the context of a portfolio of risky bonds:

For the reduced form model, the steps are as follows:

1. Simulate the risk-free term structure as given above.
2. Choose a formula and the risk-drivers for the liquidity component of credit spread for all of the relevant asset classes as discussed in Chapter 18.
3. Choose a formula and the risk-drivers for the default intensity process in the Jarrow model as discussed in Chapter 17 for all asset classes.
4. Simulate the random values of the drivers of liquidity risk and the default intensity for M time periods over N scenarios, consistent with the risk-free term structure.
5. Calculate the default intensity and the liquidity component at each of the M time steps and N scenarios for each counterparty, from retail to small business to corporate to sovereign. Note that these will be changing randomly over time because interest rates and other factors are each of them. This is essential to capturing cyclicality in bond prices and defaults.
6. Apply the Jarrow model as we have done in Chapters 17 and 18 to get the zero-coupon bond prices for each maturity for each transaction for each counterparty.
7. Calculate the dates and cash flow amounts for the Jarrow-Merton 'put option' structure that is most relevant.
8. Calculate the put option's value by discounting by the appropriate risk-free zero-coupon bond price for each of the M time steps and N scenarios.

This is a general valuation procedure that we can apply for all instruments discussed in Chapters 22-38, but of course closed form solutions are preferred when they exist.

What's the Hedge?

Let's say management has become comfortable with one of the six sample Jarrow-Merton put options as a comprehensive measure of risk. Alternatively, one of the net income-based or Basel II-based put option structures listed at the beginning of this chapter could be made the focus of risk management. How do we address the key test of risk management technology: 'What's the hedge?'

If we have done a comprehensive job of fitting our default probability models as in Chapters 16–18 and a thorough job of fitting our interest rate models as discussed in Chapters 8–13, we can stress test the put option value that we derived in the previous section. We pick a macroeconomic risk factor to stress test. If the financial institution is a lender in the U.S., the S&P500 is a commonly used macro factor that can be proven to be a statistically significant driver of default probabilities for a large range of counterparties. We can calculate what position in S&P500 futures is needed to control changes in the Jarrow-Merton put option as a measure of risk in exactly the same way van Deventer and Imai [2003] discuss macro hedging of a portfolio of risky credits:

1. Select the base case value X for the S&P500 and all other macro factors.
2. Value the appropriate Jarrow-Merton put option using the approach of the previous section.
3. Select the stress test value Y for the S&P500 and use all of the same macro factor values as in step 1. The same monte carlo 'seed value' as Step 1 also has to be used.
4. Get the stress-tested value of the Jarrow-Merton put option.
5. The change in the Jarrow-Merton put option is the Value in Case 1 – Value in Case 2.
6. The change in the S&P500 is $X–Y$.
7. The proper hedge depends on what type of S&P500 hedging instruments are being used (futures contracts or not, maturity of futures contracts, etc.). The number of contracts to be used for the hedge is the number such that the change in the value of the futures contracts if the S&P500 moves from X to Y will exactly offset the change in the value of the Jarrow-Merton put option from its Case 1 value to its Case 2 value.

Using this approach, we always know the proper integrated hedge of interest rate risk and credit risk. Our objectives have been achieved.

Liquidity, Performance, Capital Allocation and 'Own Default' Risk

Using the Jarrow-Merton put option approach that we have built in this chapter on the foundation of Chapters 1-38, we can now definitively address key risk management issues such as these:

What is the liquidity risk of my organization?
What amount of capital should I have in the institution as a whole?
What amount of capital should I have in each business unit?
What is the performance of each business unit?

We turn to that task in the next three chapters.

CHAPTER 40

Liquidity Risk Analysis and Management[1]

I n Chapter 39, we applied the Jarrow-Merton put option concept as a comprehensive measure of integrated interest rate and credit risk. We went through a discussion of six examples of how the Jarrow-Merton concept can be applied to achieve the objectives of the risk management process that we outlined both in Chapter 1 and Chapter 39. Finally, we showed the multi-period simulation process that allows us to value the Jarrow-Merton put option, giving us a concrete measure of the dollar amount of money that would be necessary to eliminate the risk we face. We also noted in that chapter that the put option concept can be applied to risk management defined as shortfalls in net income, capital ratios or provisions for loan losses.

In this chapter, we apply the same concept to shortfalls in cash—liquidity risk—which is tightly linked with the credit risk of the institution.

We discuss liquidity risk in a step-by-step process, covering these topics:

- Types of liquidity events;
- Liquidity risk and credit risk linkages;
- Measuring liquidity risk as a 'line of credit' in the Jarrow-Merton put option sense;
- Integrating managerial behavior and market funds supply in liquidity risk measurement.

Throughout this chapter, we emphasize the fact that the Jarrow-Merton put option concept can be used to measure liquidity risk in dollar terms as well. In effect, we are going to use our knowledge of all of the financial institution's assets and liabilities to price the cost of an irrevocable line of credit to our institution that would supply any random cash needs from now until the maturity of the line of credit. In doing so, we will take advantage of our previous discussions from Chapter 36 on pricing and valuing revolving credits and exposure at default.

---

[1] The authors would like to thank Leonard Matz, Kamakura Corporation, and Robert Fiedler, formerly of Deutsche Bank, for many helpful conversations on this topic.

Types of Liquidity Events

When we talk about liquidity risk, it often seems to have a lot in common with the famous story about the group of blind men each touching a different part of the elephant, each of them believing the elephant to be a different type of animal from the others' perceptions. In order to clearly reveal the true nature of the elephant, we want to clarify the types of liquidity conditions that can come about. These are best summarized in Table 40.1 below:

Table 40.1 Types of Liquidity Conditions

	Credit Quality of the Borrower	
Market Conditions	**Risky**	**Safe**
Troubled	Asia Crisis, 1997	Bank runs and rumors
	Long-Term Capital Management, 1998	September 11 2001
	Stock Market Crisis, 1987	
	Mexico, 1995	
Normal	Security Pacific/Bank of America Merger	
	Savings & Loan Crisis	
	Barings Singapore	

Liquidity risk crises tend to revolve around a combination of borrower credit quality (risky or safe) and market conditions (troubled or normal). The Asia crisis in 1997 resulted in liquidity crises from Malaysia to Korea as a combination of very difficult market conditions in the foreign exchange and money markets with a sharp rise in the credit risk of financial institutions. This increase in credit risk was in large part directly attributable to the sharp changes in macro factors that drive default risk: foreign exchange rates and interest rates. This kind of incident fits precisely in the analytical framework that we have been using throughout this book because we have successfully linked credit risk to macroeconomic conditions. This is the central theme of the reduced form modeling techniques outlined in Chapter 17 and can be done as well in the context of the Merton model of risky debt, particularly the random interest rate version of Shimko, Tejima and van Deventer 1993. Other related incidents were the Long-Term Capital Management incident, where one troubled institution's holdings were so large that its need to sell rapidly depressed a wide array of security prices and raised the credit risk of a broad range of corporations and financial institutions.

The second type of crisis is a combination of normal market conditions and credit quality problems of a single or small number of institutions. One example is the 1992 forced acquisition of Security Pacific Corporation by Bank of America in 1992. In this case, sharp increases in credit losses in real estate at Security Pacific National Bank led regulators to cut off dividend payments to the parent company, Security Pacific Corporation. Investors were no longer willing to buy commercial paper of Security Pacific Corporation because its default risk had risen too high.

Another example of troubled institutions in what were otherwise fairly normal markets was the savings and loan crisis of the 1980s and early 1990s in the U.S. A rise in interest rates caused a sharp decline in the market value of fixed-rate home mortgages on the books of the savings and loan associations. The market value of their assets fell well below the principal amount of consumer deposits on their books. In anticipation of their failure, consumers began withdrawing their deposits in spite of the U.S. government guarantee of consumer deposits. Even if the savings and loan associations had been able to sell their mortgage holdings, they would not have had sufficient assets to meet deposit obligations. The institutions were taken over by Federal regulators and liquidated.

A final example is that of Barings, where a rogue trader in Singapore generated more than $1 billion in losses from unauthorized futures trading. The end result, due to the impaired credit quality of Barings and the liquidity problems that it generated, was the forced sale of Barings to the ING Group.

A third category of liquidity problems is a 'systemic market crisis' that isn't directly related to a troubled financial institution. Perhaps the best illustration was the impact of the September 11 2001 attack on the U.S, which caused a serious disruption in operational cash flows in the U.S. financial system. While insurance-related losses from September 11 2001 did have a concrete impact on the credit quality of many financial institutions, most institutions did not suffer an impact on their credit quality. Nonetheless, they did have a cash shortfall. Other examples are disruptions caused by power failures (for example, New York and Toronto power failure of 2003), fires (First Interstate Bancorp headquarters, in 1988), and other natural disasters.

The latter kind of crisis produces a very acute need for cash in the short-term, but the need comes from an institution that has fundamentally sound credit quality in the long-term. This is a very important distinction that we explore in the next section.

Liquidity Risk and Credit Risk Linkages

As we saw in the previous section, two of the three kinds of liquidity crises occur when the financial institution itself is troubled. The only difference between those two types of crises is in how much company the financial institution has in its troubles—it can be alone in its difficulties (Security Pacific, 1992) or it can have lots of company (Korea, 1997–1998). For that reason, we need to be more precise about the impact of a decline in credit quality of a financial institution on the willingness of other firms to lend it money.

In Chapter 36, we argued that the cash needs of a corporation are a function of a number of factors:

$$C(t) = C_1(t) + C_2(\lambda) + C_3(\lambda_1, \lambda_2, \ldots \lambda_n) + Z(t)$$

The first component of cash needs at time t $C(t)$ is a function of the time of the year, because cash demand is highly seasonal in many industries such as retailing. The second term of the total cash need is a function of the credit quality of the borrower. The third component of cash needs is a function of the credit quality of the clients of the company, because when they are having credit quality problems, they will pay on their obligations more slowly. Finally, the last term is the random component of cash flow needs.

In this section, we focus on the impact of the credit quality of the financial institution on the willingness of the market to lend money to the company. Figure 40.1 below shows a common phenomenon in the credit markets. It is the hypothetical 'supply curve' of commercial paper to a borrower at different levels of default probability of the issuer. The graph shows that the issuer can raise up to $1 billion in commercial paper for default probabilities up to about 1%, but after that the number of investors willing to supply commercial paper falls. Accordingly, the amount of money that the company can raise also declines. Clearly, the amount of commercial paper available rises and falls with overall market conditions and the single biggest determinant of availability is the default probability of the issuer.

Figure 40.1 Maximum Amount of Commercial Paper that can be Issued as Function of Default Probability

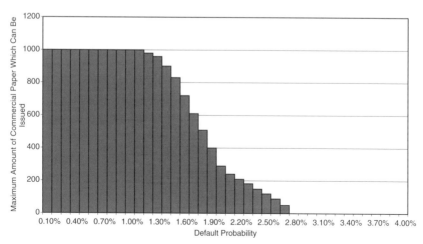

Figure 40.2 Amount of Commercial Paper Available as a Function of the CP Rate

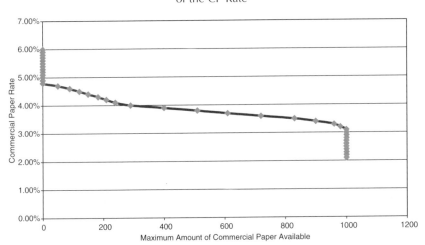

For most market observers, the effective 'default probabilities' they think about are the three or four effective short-term rates A1/P1, A2/P2, A3/P3, and 'not rated'. Supply of commercial paper is best at the highest ratings (A1/P1), it falls somewhat at A2/P2 (the mid-level rating), and then falls in a precipitous way at A3/P3. Smaller investors don't do their own credit risk analysis and have internal policies concerning what short-term (and in some cases long-term) ratings a company must have to be on the 'approved list' for purchase of the issuer's commercial paper. Larger investors are doing very aggressive credit risk analysis and are trying to maximize shareholder value on a risk-adjusted basis by purchasing the commercial paper with 'best value'. These investors are making investment decisions and 'approved amount' decisions based on a more granular view of credit risk than the three or four short-term credit ratings listed above.

We display this reducing supply of funds in Figure 40.2. This graph assumes that the risk-free one-month rate is 2.00% and the issuer's commercial paper rate is 2% plus its default probability.[2]

As the company gets riskier and bids up the rate it is willing to pay on commercial paper, the supply of funds to the company actually falls. This is the essence of a credit quality-driven liquidity crisis.

The identical phenomenon is also seen in the bond markets, where traders often talk about the huge fall in bond prices when ratings move from 'investment grade'[3] to 'non-investment grade'. This bond price decrease is very

---

[2] To keep things simple, we're assuming a 100% loss in the event of default but a similar graph could be done for any level of loss given default.

[3] BBB– or better credit ratings.

precipitous because many institutions have an automatic requirement in their investment policy to sell any bond they own with a rating below BBB–. This 'step like' fall in bond prices is the subject of massive attempts at arbitrage by the hedge fund community. For issuers, however, the meaning of this phenomenon is the same as in the commercial paper market: as the company gets in trouble, the supply of funds at all maturities will dry up at a speed that is consistent with the speed of the company's decline in quality.

We now have two problems to solve—how can companies avoid the fate of Security Pacific or the savings and loan associations? (a credit quality-induced failure with timing of failure determined by a liquidity crisis), and how can they measure the magnitude of the liquidity/credit risk they face? We turn to that in the next section.

Measuring Liquidity Risk as a 'Line of Credit' in the Jarrow-Merton Put Option Sense

How do institutions 'buy time' when they have a credit quality problem that they hope will be rectified in time? That is the essence of liquidity risk management discipline. The root cause of the problem is a credit quality problem that affects both the financial institution itself (in the case of a company-specific problem in normal market conditions like Security Pacific in 1992) and perhaps many other peer group institutions as well (such as Mexico in 1995 or Korea in 1997). If the credit problems are driven by the credit cycle, as we discussed in Chapter 17, it is logical to think that if management can assure itself three to five years to fix the problem, they are likely to be successful. If the liquidity posture of the bank is so focused on short-term financing, Figures 40.1 and 40.2 show that the bank may face a cash flow need that they can't meet and fail before the credit problem can be solved. This is what happened to Security Pacific—if they had financed the holding company with long-term floating-rate funds instead of short-term commercial paper, their potential cash need would have been postponed for long enough that the credit quality of Security Pacific could have been restored to normal levels before the cash came due.

In the example above, we showed hypothetically how the maximum amount of commercial paper that can be issued changes as default probability rises. What if a hypothetical bank holding company had $800 in on-going funding needs at a time that its default probability begins to rise due to credit quality problems in its loan portfolio. We show an hypothetical path for the bank's default probability below and its impact on funding needs over time.

As long as the bank's default probability is 1.1% or below, it can issue up to $1,000 in commercial paper[4] and its funding needs are easily met. As its default

---

[4] We assume all dollar amounts are in millions.

probability rises above 1.1%, its maximum CP availability begins to fall. Once the default probability hits 1.6%, the maximum available CP falls to $720 and the bank cannot meet its funding needs from commercial paper issuance. The funding shortfall hits $800 at a default probability of 2.8% because the bank is completely shut out of the commercial paper market for default probabilities of that level or above. If the bank can meet this funding requirement from some other source, Figure 40.3 shows that the credit quality problems will be resolved and the bank's default probability falls over time. Its access to the commercial paper market is restored, and the bank no longer has a funding shortfall.

What if the bank can't meet this $800 shortfall from another source? The answer is that the bank fails.

From a practical point of view, there are two ways that the bank can meet its funding needs in this hypothetical example.

Figure 40.3 Changes in Funding Availability and Funding Short-Fall as Function of Default Probability

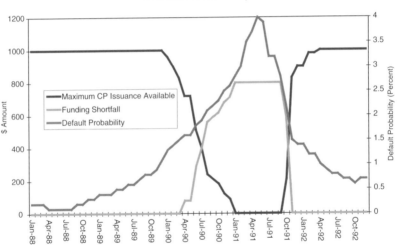

The two sources of funds to meet the $800 funding shortfall are:

- Sales of liquid assets:
  - The maturity of the funds borrowed to buy these liquid assets has to be longer than the maturity of the assets purchased or there is no net liquidity risk benefit from having the liquid assets.
- Borrowing from some other source:
  - In the case of a firm-specific crisis, this 'line of credit' can be from a peer bank in the same country and funding will still be available;
  - In the case of a market crisis that occurs at the same time as the bank's crisis, there is substantial risk that a 'line of credit' will not

be honored. For this reason, lines of credit designed to address a systemic liquidity crises should be from lenders that are highly unlikely to be subjected to such a crisis at the same time. This is another variation on the counterparty credit risk that we addressed in Chapter 23.

The bank has to secure these funds at least as fast as its own deteriorating credit quality generates increased funding needs (since it is being shut out of the commercial paper market). We need these incremental funds from March 1990 until the end of 1991 for the bank to survive the credit crisis it is facing in its own loan portfolio.

In this chapter we have mainly discussed the case in which the liquidity crisis is triggered by credit quality problems in the financial institution's portfolio, but the liquidity crisis could have been just as easily been triggered by losses from rising interest rates, as happened to many finance companies in Malaysia in 1997-1998.

What is the coherent measure of the cost of liquidity risk protection for, say, 10 years?

Again, the answer is the Jarrow-Merton put option in the context of Chapter 36 where we priced a revolving line of credit to a corporate borrower. In this case, we want the price of a 10-year irrevocable line of credit on up to $800 in borrowings with a 10-year life and a funds provider who is not in the same market as the borrower. We know this about such an irrevocable line of credit:

- It solves the liquidity crisis for 10 years and buys up to 10 years of time to solve the credit risk and/or interest rate risk problem permanently.
- If the general risk level of the financial institution is low and the funding profile of the financial institution is very long term, this line of credit will be very cheap and it is confirmation that the liquidity risk of the institution is low. In an extreme case of a financial institution where all liabilities are longer than 10 years in maturity and there are no random cash needs, the price of this line of credit will be zero, because it will never be drawn down.
- If the general risk level of the financial institution is low and the funding profile of the financial institution is very short term, the line of credit will be moderately expensive.
- If the general risk level of the financial institution is high and the funding profile of the institution is very long (all liabilities longer than 10 years), then again, the line of credit will be fairly cheap because it will not be drawn if cash needs are not random.
- If the general risk level of the financial institution is high and the funding profile of the institution is very short, then the line of credit will be very expensive because the liquidity risk of the institution is very high.

- If the general risk level of the institution gets high enough, no lender will provide quotations for the line of credit because of the same phenomenon we studied above—the supply of credit of all types falls as risk rises.

Integrating Managerial Behavior and Market Funds Supply in Liquidity Risk Measurement

How can we price the cost of a 10-year irrevocable line of credit for our own institution if we are not going to get actual market quotes to measure the degree of liquidity risk that we face? We can use exactly the same valuation and simulation techniques that we discussed in Chapter 39, but with a few important differences that revolve around building in a logical market and managerial responses to the changing interest rate risk and credit risk of the institution:

As the default probability of our financial institution rises, consumers will begin to withdraw consumer deposits. We need to specify the formula by which this will happen.

As the default probability of the financial institution rises, our access to commercial paper and bond markets will decrease or even dry up completely. We need to specify how access decreases in response to the default probability. As the default probability of the institution rises, management will begin to sell assets to meet cash needs. As these sales increase in amount and urgency, the 'transactions cost' of each sale will get larger and larger as the percent of value of the assets sold.

We value the 10-year irrevocable line of credit as a measure of liquidity risk using a process exactly like that used in Chapter 39, but we factor in a rational market and managerial response to a change in our institution's default probability:

1. Specify how our access to the commercial paper market varies with our default probability as discussed in this chapter.
2. Specify how our access to the bond market varies with our default probability as discussed in this chapter.
3. Specify how consumers will withdraw consumer deposits as our default probability rises.
4. Specify the order in which assets will be sold to meet cash needs and the transactions cost of selling those assets as a function of the asset class and the speed with which we have to sell it.
5. Simulate the risk-free term structure for N scenarios over M time.
6. Choose a formula and the risk-drivers for the liquidity component of credit spread for all of the relevant asset classes we own as discussed in Chapter 18.

7. Choose a formula and the risk-drivers for the default intensity process in the Jarrow model as discussed in Chapter 17 for all asset classes that we own.

8. Simulate the random values of the drivers of liquidity premium and the default intensity for all of our counterparties for M time periods over N scenarios, consistent with the risk-free term structure.

9. Calculate the default intensity and the liquidity component at each of the M time steps and N scenarios for each counterparty, from retail to small business to corporate to sovereign. Note that these will be changing randomly over time because interest rates and other factors are each of them. This is essential to capturing cyclicality in bond prices and defaults.

10. Apply the Jarrow model as we have done in Chapters 17 and 18 to get the zero-coupon bond prices for each maturity for each transaction for each counterparty.

11. Calculate the market value of portfolio equity for our financial institution in scenario J and time period K.

12. Calculate the probability of default for our own financial institution in scenario J and time period K (we can short cut this by using the logistic regression approach in Chapter 17 or we can be more fancy).

13. Calculate the amount of consumer deposits that we will have in scenario J and time period K based on this default probability. Do the same for commercial paper and our bond issuance capability.

14. Calculate the net needs for funds based on Steps 12 and 13.

15. Subtract from this need for funds liquid assets we can sell with no transactions costs, based on the amount of those liquid assets still remaining in time period K of scenario J.

16. The remaining funding need is X.

17. If the remaining availability on our irrevocable line if credit is more than X, we assume we draw down an additional X on the line of credit.

18. We calculate the interest rate owed on the line of credit in time period K and scenario J.

19. We simulate default/no default in period K of scenario J.

20. If we do not default, we proceed to time period $K+1$ in Scenario J.

21. If we do default, the lender on the line of credit receives our adjusted market value of portfolio assets.

22. We do this for all periods and scenarios.

23. We take the present value of these risk-adjusted, risk neutral cash flows by discounting at the risk-free yield appropriate for time period K and scenario J.

24. We calculate the value of the line of credit to the lender and the fee they need to charge us for the line of credit to be fairly priced.

This process is exactly the same process that we followed in Chapter 36 for a revolving line of credit to a corporate borrower with one major exception. Since we are evaluating the cost of a line of credit to our own institution, we have full information on every asset and every liability on the balance sheet. We know how to value each one of them, as we have demonstrated in Chapters 22–38. Therefore we can be much more precise in our calculations as the simulation process above outlines.

Determining the Optimal Liquidity Strategy

What is the optimal maturity structure of our institution's liabilities from a liquidity risk perspective? This question is easy to answer since we now have an explicit process for measuring our current liquidity risk—the cost of a 10-year irrevocable line of credit using the Jarrow-Merton put option concept.

The optimal liquidity strategy is that liability maturity structure which minimizes the cost of eliminating liquidity risk, i.e. the liability maturity structure which produces the lowest cost for the 10-year irrevocable line of credit.

Conclusion

In Chapter 39, we showed through six detailed examples how to use the Jarrow-Merton put option as a comprehensive index of the level of integrated credit risk and interest rate risk. This measure of risk is more than that—it tells us the dollar cost of eliminating the risk.

We can do the same thing with liquidity risk by pricing an irrevocable line of credit for any maturity. We used a 10-year maturity since 10 years is likely to get us all of the way through a full interest rate cycle and credit cycle, giving us time to recover from interest rate or credit risk-related losses that would have produced a liquidity crisis if we did not have (hypothetically) the irrevocable line of credit.

Next, we take the discipline and insights of the Jarrow-Merton put option measure of risk to performance measurement in order to improve on the conventional wisdom of the early chapters in this book.

CHAPTER 41

Performance Measurement:
Plus Alpha versus Transfer Pricing

In Chapters 2 and 3 of this book, we discuss in detail the common practice of performance measurement in large financial institutions. In those chapters, we made a number of points about the way in which large financial institutions manage risk:

- Commercial banks use a mix of financial accounting and market-oriented performance measurements.
- 'Transfer pricing' in commercial banks is a financial accounting-driven performance measure that has the virtue of moving interest rate risk into one central 'transfer pricing book'. The system has a 30-year history, but it mistakenly implies that each new transaction should be judged versus the average marginal risk of the bank (via the bank's marginal cost of funds) instead of the marginal risk of the asset being considered. The fact that a traditional transfer pricing system would reject the purchase of risk-free U.S. Treasuries shows this process is flawed at the transaction level, since all banks in the U.S. own at least some U.S. Treasuries.
- Fund managers, pension funds, and insurance companies almost all base performance measurement on a market price basis. A good performer is one who can generate 'plus alpha' performance over and above a predefined benchmark with equivalent risk. Banks (until recently) have almost never used this approach outside of their own fund management business.
- Banks allocate capital to judge the performance of major business units, and almost no other financial institutions do.

Our purpose in this chapter is to talk about the implications for the Jarrow-Merton put option as a comprehensive measure not only of integrated risk but as a potential guide to performance measurement. Matten [1996] presents an excellent summary of current common practice in capital allocation that will be of interest to readers who would like to supplement the material in Chapters 2 and 3 before plunging into the rest of this chapter.

Transaction Level Performance Measurement versus Portfolio Level Performance Measurement

In Chapters 2 and 3, we outlined the central rule in assessing the quality of a performance measurement system:

> *A performance measurement system which sends incorrect signals at the transaction level will be inaccurate at the portfolio level as well, since the portfolio is the sum of its individual transactions.*

In Chapters 2 and 3 and in van Deventer and Imai [2003], 'buy low/sell high' was outlined as the ultimate transaction level guide to asset and liability selection. If an asset worth 102 can be purchased at a cost of 100, we should do it. If another asset worth 101 can be purchased at a cost of 100, we should buy that too. What could be simpler than that? This basic performance measurement system has been at the heart of capitalism for thousands of years, and our objective in this chapter is to strip back some of the institutional 'baggage' of financial institutions' performance measurement systems to reveal performance as clearly as these examples.

In Chapters 22–38, we illustrated that every single type of asset and liability issued by major financial institutions can be valued precisely both before the asset or liability is added to the balance sheet and every instant thereafter. We now know enough to do the simple assessment in the previous paragraph. Are there any real or imagined complexities that may complicate the buy low/sell high transaction level performance assessment? There are only a few and we mention them briefly in this section:

Costs of origination may have both a large fixed cost component and a marginal cost component which impact our assessment of buy low/sell high.

A classic example is the consumer deposit gathering franchise of a commercial bank. On the transaction level, a 90-day consumer certificate of deposit may cost 25 basis points less than a wholesale certificate of deposit with the identical maturity. Based on this information alone, the first pass buy low/sell high decision is 'buy'—originate the retail CD. The costs of origination and servicing need to be included in the analysis for a complete answer. What if there was a $1 per month fixed cost of servicing the consumer CD that would not impact the wholesale CD? We just need to add this to the effective cost of the retail CD to have a more accurate answer. More realistically, the head of the retail banking division should be constantly re-evaluating this calculation: I can sell the building housing my River City branch for $500,000 today.

Or I can keep it, pay staff expenses of $450,000 per year, and issue a large number of consumer CDs. Which is better? This is still a buy low/sell high calculation that requires no capital allocation to do correctly. It is a question that should be continually asked. A related question is whether the 25 basis point margin on the consumer CD is the margin that produces maximum present value (and marginal revenue = marginal cost from basic economic theory is relevant here). There are other calculations that come into play that we mention below.

Future business may depend on doing current business, *with an actuarially-likely arrival of good buy low/sell high business going forward.*

The example above is a good example to illustrate another complexity in assessing performance of any business. The River City branch's existence may give us the 'real option' to do lots of retail CD business going forward. This retail business depends both on our pricing and our own default probability as we saw in the last chapter on liquidity risk. The probability of a client rolling over one profitable retail CD has characteristics that are very similar to that of the reduced form credit models we discussed in Chapter 17, the credit default swaps we discussed in Chapter 23, and the insurance policies we valued in Chapter 38. Doing a really good buy low/sell high decision analysis depends on taking these facts into account in a careful way. It has nothing to do with capital allocation—it's a straightforward net present value calculation using the analytics presented in Chapters 22 to 38.

Some costs may be shared with other products.

What if the River City branch also makes profitable small business loans (valued correctly using the technology of Chapter 22 and 23), and that there is a fixed cost of monitoring them that is in part embedded in the $450,000 staff costs of the River City branch? Again, assessing whether to close the branch or keep it and optimize pricing is a risk-adjusted present value calculation like those in Chapters 22–38—shared fixed costs simply broadens the boundaries of the calculation that has to be done and the transactions that have to be included. Capital allocation is again irrelevant. What is relevant is the available market return that has the same risk as keeping the River City branch open.

Cash might be tight

Van Deventer and Imai [2003] discuss how the buy low/sell high transaction level performance measurement strategy has to be tempered by the financial institution's ability to buy low. Chapter 38 discusses how, as a financial institution's risk rises, the supply of funds to the financial institution can fall or reach zero. At such a high level of risk, the financial institution has lost its real option to buy low/sell high. This is one of the reasons why financial institutions typically find that their optimal credit risk from a shareholder value-added perspective is consistent with a high quality credit rating in the AA to A range. This is why the buy low/sell high performance measurement test outlined above is necessary, but not sufficient, to result in the origination of an asset or liability. The financial institution's own default risk impacts its ability to exercise its option to buy low/sell high.

Transaction level versus portfolio level performance measurement

The examples above show that, even at the transaction level, portfolio considerations can be important. The decision to issue retail CDs depends on the total volume that can be done (the portfolio of CDs), not just the pricing on one CD. The decision on whether to keep or sell the branch depends on transaction level benefits of the retail CD and small business loan portfolio transactions at the branch. Finally, the decision to buy low/sell high can depend on the entire existing portfolio of assets and liabilities, since they determine the current credit risk of the institution.

Plus Alpha benchmark performance versus transfer pricing

In Chapters 2 and 3, we discussed both the financial accounting-oriented transfer pricing system used by commercial banks and the market value-based benchmark performance system used by almost every other type of financial institution. The authors believe that commercial banks would benefit from adopting the benchmark-based performance measurement approach, while being careful to avoid the pitfalls of such an approach as outlined in Chapter 2.[1]

The only trick in implementing this approach in the commercial banking arena is the need to create benchmarks. For example, as van Deventer and Imai [2003] suggest, the head of retail banking who owns the three-year auto loan portfolio should be judged by the market value of a U.S. Treasury index that replicates the exact cash flow timing and amount of each auto loan on a full option-adjusted basis. We show in Chapter 43 that this is a modest computer science effort that is already commercially available and it is merely a question of institutional will to move in this direction.

---

[1] The principal pitfall is that equity-based benchmarks like the S&P 500 have a composition that is dependent on the credit risk of the company in the benchmark. Companies are eliminated from the benchmark if their credit risk rises beyond a certain (unspoken and undisclosed) level in a way that exposes the fund manager to considerable risk even if they have the risky company in their equity portfolio with the proper weights. See Chapter 2 for more on this.

The manager of the three-year auto loan portfolio is a 'good performer' if over time the mark-to-market value of the auto loans, after expenses and after actual credit losses, is a larger number than the mark-to-market value of the artificial 'Treasury auto loan' index.

The manager of the auto loan portfolio will use transaction level analytics to decide which loans to originate and which loans to pass on. An important part of this relates directly to the reduced form modeling technology we discussed in Chapters 17 and 18:

- The **default probability** of each auto loan borrower has to be correctly assessed using state of the art logistic regression such as that discussed in the public firm default probability context in Chapter 17.
- The proper **credit spread** for the auto loan has to be assessed in light of expenses of origination and monitoring and in conjunction with the macro factors driving default. In addition, the probability of prepayment has to be taken into account as discussed in Chapters 30-32.
- Once 'break even' pricing is set for each borrower, the bank can **accept or reject the loan**. Skillful loan selection creates plus alpha performance at the portfolio level by creating value one loan at a time.

This is true buy low/sell high implementation, consistent with state of the art credit risk and interest rate risk management. A benchmark performance that is plus alpha will show management exactly how much value has been created by this business above and beyond what would have been achieved by a matched maturity investment in U.S. Treasury securities with identical payment dates, payment amounts and options characteristics. Of course the more traditional transfer pricing methodology used in commercial banking can be used to show this as well, but the transfer pricing yield curve will be the U.S. Treasury yield curve, not the marginal cost of funds yield curve of the bank. In addition, the transfer pricing rate will include a premium that reflects the prepayment option held by the auto loan borrower.

The Jarrow-Merton Put Option and Capital

In Chapters 39 and 40, we discussed the practical calculation of the Jarrow-Merton put option that is the comprehensive measure of integrated credit risk and interest rate risk that we first discussed in Chapter 2. We can relate capital and this put option using the intuition of the Merton model of risky debt from Chapter 16. We know from Chapter 16 that the value of the equity of a company under the Merton model is an option on the assets of the firm at an exercise price equal to B, the amount of debt that the company must repay at the time. The Jarrow-Merton put option is our comprehensive measure of risk of the firm. If we want to measure the Jarrow-Merton put option that guarantees that the company will never go bankrupt, we need the value of a put option on the value of company assets at an exercise price equal to the value B of the debt the company owes.[2] We can also calculate the value of this put option at any strike price above or below B. A put option with a strike price K above B is a put option that prevents the stock price from ever falling below $K–B$ when the debt matures, and the debt will be riskless and have a zero credit spread in the Merton model.

In the simple Merton model, the value of the put option is simply a function of the value of the company's assets and the amount of debt it has, because interest rates are assumed to be constant. In Shimko-Tejima-van Deventer [1993], the Merton model is generalized to include random interest rates and any degree of correlation of the value of company assets with interest rates. In this case, the Jarrow-Merton put option becomes a comprehensive measure of the amount of combined interest rate risk and credit risk (as embedded in the value of company assets V) of the company.

In Chapters 22-38, we have illustrated how we can value the assets and liabilities of any financial institution using the simulation techniques of Chapter 39. We can use this as a basis for capital allocation in a financial institution just as van Deventer and Imai [2003] use the STV model for capital allocation.

Using the Jarrow-Merton Put Option for Capital Allocation: An Introduction

As we noted in Chapters 2 and 3, most of the business units of major financial institutions have either assets only or liabilities only. They rarely have both assets and liabilities at the same time. When this is the case, there is no need to allocate capital because the benchmark performance system we discuss above can be used. Nonetheless, many financial institutions allocate capital to achieve multiple objectives:

- They want all business units, after the allocation of debt and equity, to have the same relative degree of risk.
- They then feel comfortable, using either historical market returns or financial accounting returns, in expressing performance as the ratio of historical return to allocated capital.

---

[2] The value of the put option at a strike price of B is related to the call option by put-call parity as explained in Jarrow [1996], page 79. The value of the put and the call are a function of the value of company assets V, the amount of debt B, time to maturity T and the riskless present value $P(T)$ of $1 received at time T. Put-call parity requires $Put(V,B,T) = Call(V,B,T) + P(T)B - V$. It can also be shown using the risky debt formulas from Chapter 16 that $Put(V,B,T) = P(T)B - Value\ of\ Risky\ Debt\ (V,B,T)$.

As the authors noted in Chapters 2 and 3, this approach implicitly says that 'good' business units have good returns on risk-adjusted capital and should get more emphasis. This portfolio measure of performance is thought of by many as a substitute for the buy low/sell high approach discussed in the introduction to this chapter. While the authors don't agree that this approach is valid at the transaction level (failing the necessary condition to use risk-adjusted return on capital as a tool), the authors do believe that doing this analysis carefully maximizes the probability that its implications are useful.

Van Deventer and Imai show exactly how to do this in the Shimko-Tejima-van Deventer credit model context. They follow these steps:

1. Choose the time horizon T (one year is a common choice).
2. Obtain from market sources the present value of $1 that the financial institution promises to pay at this time horizon. We call this amount D. The face amount of risky debt consistent with this is B.
3. Measure the volatility of the return on the value of company assets for each business unit.
4. Measure the correlation between interest rates and the value of company assets for each business unit.
5. Use the STV formula to imply a value of company assets V consistent with a face value amount of risky debt B for business unit J which produces a price for the business unit's risky debt $D(B,J)$ such that $1 promised to be paid at time T is exactly the same as the financial institution's zero-coupon bond price D in step 2. Since the volatility of company assets and their correlation with interest rates will be different for each business unit, the ratio of the face value of debt B to the value of company assets V will be different for each business unit.
6. Step 6 justifies lending debt to each business unit at the financial institution's marginal cost of funds since we have adjusted the zero-coupon debt price of each business unit to be the same as D, the zero-coupon bond price for the institution as a whole.
7. The capital ratio which measures how much capital is to be allocated to the business unit is $(V - D)/V$. At this amount of capital, every business unit has the same risky yield to maturity on its debt.

As van Deventer and Imai [2003] discuss, this approach justifies matched maturity transfer pricing and puts a spreadsheet-friendly formula to work in a way that integrates interest rate risk and credit risk in the simple one-period Merton-type model.[3] We can do this in a more sophisticated multi-period framework using the Jarrow-Merton put option concept.

---

[3] For more on this approach, please see Donald R. van Deventer, 'Overcoming Inadequacy', *Balance Sheet Magazine*, Summer, 1993.

Using the Jarrow-Merton Put Option Concept for Capital Allocation

In this section, we use an analogy with the STV capital allocation approach above to show how to use the Jarrow-Merton put option technology to work for capital allocation. We start with a one-period example and then generalize to a multi-period example that is consistent with the Loss Distribution Model announced by the Federal Deposit Insurance Corporation on December 10 2003.

Capital allocation for a single period

In Chapter 39, we outlined a careful process for simulating the impact of macro-economic factors on the default probabilities and legal payment obligations of all counterparties from retail borrowers to sovereigns. We will use the identical process in this section. If we set a single time horizon as relevant for capital allocation, the process works like this:

1. Choose the time horizon T (one year is a common choice).
2. Obtain from market sources the default probability for the institution. This default probability can be derived in any method with which the institution is comfortable as discussed in Chapters 16 and 17. The authors' preference is to take the default probabilities in this order of preference based on the model test results in Chapter 19 and elsewhere: first choice, default probabilities implied by credit derivatives (but they have to be adjusted from the standard five-year CDS quotation to match the financial institution's time horizon T); second choice, default probabilities implied by bond prices; third choice, Jarrow-Chava default probabilities derived from a historical default database; fourth choice, Merton default probabilities. Let us call this default probability d.
3. Obtain the business unit's current face value of debt B financing its assets V.
4. Simulate the macro factors over N scenarios as of time T.
5. Calculate the default probabilities for all counterparties.
6. Calculate N values for the value of business unit assets less the amount of debt maturing B.
7. Assume the default probability for the business unit with no Jarrow-Merton put option is d^*. We need to solve for the value of the Jarrow Merton put option which reduces d^* to the institution's own default probability d.
8. Examine the distribution of negative net worths from the simulation.
9. Determine the amount K of a digital put option payable on default such that the percentage of negative net worth scenarios after payment

of K is reduced from d^* to d. For example, if d is 1%, but 200 of the 10,000 scenarios produce negative net worth on a mark-to-market basis ($d^*=2\%$), we need to find K such that 100 of the negative scenarios would be erased. If the 100th largest loss is $72.27, then the digital option would pay $72.27 on default, reducing d^* to $1=d$.

10. Calculate the value of the Jarrow-Merton put option which pays K ($72.27) upon default (i.e. negative mark-to-market before K is paid). Let us call the value of this put option X. This is the price of portfolio insurance for a default probability of d.

11. Adjust the capital and the assets of the business unit for the value of the put option. Before the put option, the capital of the business unit was $V-B$ and its capital ratio was $(V-B)/V$. After the put option, capital will be increased by X and assets will be increased by X. Assets will be $V+X$ and capital will be $V-B+X$. The ratio of capital to assets will be $(V-B+X)/(V+X)$.

12. This process equalizes the default probabilities of every business unit at the institutional level and explicitly incorporates the risk of each individual asset or liability on the books of the business unit.

There are other choices for the terms of the pay-off on the Jarrow-Merton put option. The most obvious one is one that equalizes the 'expected loss' of each business unit. Even if default probabilities are equalized, the expected loss can differ and vice versa. This is matter for institutional strategy.

In any event, the technology for the Jarrow-Merton put option in the first 40 chapters of this book allows us to explicitly price the value of portfolio insurance (both credit risk and interest rate risk) on all assets and liabilities of each business unit so that the risk of each business unit after portfolio insurance is equalized.

Extending the Jarrow-Merton capital allocation to a multi-period framework

While most financial institutions allocate capital with a one-year time horizon in mind, the New Basel Accords point out that safety and soundness dictate that a longer time horizon may be more appropriate. The fact that the credit default swap market has crystallized around a five-year maturity is indirect confirmation that the market believes that a longer time horizon has the most value from a credit insurance policy point of view.

For this reason, it may be appropriate to analyze the Jarrow-Merton put option as a multi-period payout option that insures the survival over a longer time horizon just like the Loss Distribution Model of the FDIC (December 10 2003, available on www.fdic.gov) does.

This changes the valuation of the Jarrow-Merton put option from the previous section in only modest ways:

- Scenario simulation has to deal with reinvestment of cash flows over multiple periods for correct assessment of the probability of business unit 'default'.
- The 'default' of a business unit can happen at multiple points in time and multiple payments to the business unit may be necessary to insure survival over the entire time horizon. This is highly likely given the high correlation in defaults that we have discussed throughout this book.
- This will raise the cost of the Jarrow-Merton put option for the business unit, all other things being equal.

Conclusion

As noted in Chapters 2 and 3, backward looking measures of asset performance have minimal use as predictors of future performance. For that reason, the authors prefer forward looking measures of performance (buy low/sell high) for asset selection at both the transaction level and the portfolio level.

Nonetheless, the Jarrow-Merton put option concept can be applied neatly for capital allocation for those institutions that have the need to apply the capital allocation concept. We explicitly price the portfolio insurance (integrating credit risk and interest rate risk) for each business unit such that we equalize the (a) probability of default or (b) expected loss for each business unit. The adjusted asset totals and capital totals for each business unit reflect the incremental cost of this credit insurance, the value of the Jarrow-Merton put option.

We turn next to a related topic, the safety and soundness of our own financial institution.

Managing Institutional Default Risk and 'Safety and Soundness'

The Basel Committee on Banking Supervision has proposed New Capital Accords [2003] as a way to insure the safety and soundness of financial institutions around the world. In Chapters 39–41, we showed how modern risk management technology allows a much different approach to insuring the safety and soundness of financial institutions. In this chapter, we discuss the implications of a more modern approach to risk management for the safety and soundness of a given institution from both a shareholder value perspective and from a regulatory perspective. Along the way, we compare and contrast these implications with the approach of the Basel Committee.

Admitting the Possibility of Failure

Step 1 in using a more modern approach to risk management is for management to admit the unthinkable—that the institution they manage has a probability of failure that is not zero. It is a rare management team that can make this admission, but a failure to acknowledge this fact is to deny reality and doom the risk management exercise at the institution to 'common practice' at best.

Overwhelming evidence in the marketplace reveals that all major global financial institutions have a positive probability of failure. Rating agencies rate only a very small number of institutions in the AAA category, explicitly consigning the rest to a higher probability of failure. The credit default swap market shows the price of credit insurance on the bonds of major financial institutions every minute of every business day, and this price is definitely not zero. Finally, commercial providers of default probabilities can show concretely how the probability of failure has varied over long periods of time. Figure 42.1, provided by Kamakura Corporation, shows the short-term default probabilities of Citigroup (C) and New England regional bank FleetBoston Financial (FBF).

Figure 42.1 Short-Term Default Probabilities of Citigroup and
FleetBoston Financial

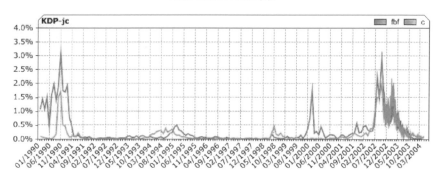

The graph shows clearly that the default probabilities of the two organizations are highly correlated and that they rise sharply at the obvious times, during the recessions in 1990–1991, 1994–1995, and during the 1999–2002 period when defaults among their retail and corporate clients were peaking. Since every counterparty of a major financial institution is looking at default probabilities on a daily basis, management cannot ignore their implications for comprehensive risk management and shareholder value.

Managing the Probability of Failure

Earlier in this book, we discussed the concept of the safety zone for interest rate risk, those interest rate risk positions where the probability of failure is zero. When we ignore credit risk, match-funding all assets except those funded by equity leaves a financial institution free to invest the equity in securities of any maturity without leaving the safety zone. Once we allow for default of the financial institution's borrowers, there is no safety zone for any financial institution that borrows money to make loans. That means management has to deal practically with a non-zero probability of failure. Just as importantly, we should note that the probability of failure has a term structure just like interest rates, as we can see in Figure 42.2, which shows the default probabilities out to five years for General Motors (GM) compared to Citigroup (C). Management needs to set a target for the amount of failure risk that creates the maximum amount of shareholder value. For most financial institutions, this means targeting a debt rating in the AA to A range. This ratings target has an equivalent target in terms of default probabilities. Unlike ratings, however, default probabilities for all maturities rise and fall during the course of the business cycle. Ratings tend to be 'through the cycle' long term ratings that are relatively insensitive to where we are in the business cycle. That is certainly not the case for the default probabilities of financial institutions, as we can see clearly from Figure 42.3 of the one-month and five-year default probabilities for

Figure 42.2 Default Probabilities out to Five Years for General Motors and Citigroup

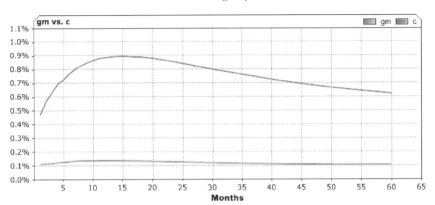

Figure 42.3 Default Probabilities of One Month and Five Years for Bank of America

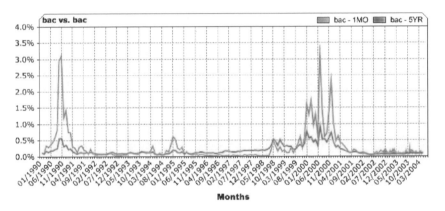

Bank of America, provided by Kamakura Corporation from its Kamakura Risk Information Services default probability database:

Both the five-year default probability for the Bank (the darker line) and the short-term one-month default probability rise considerably during the worst part of the credit cycle, but the one-month default probability responds more sharply. This is identical to the behavior of one-month and five-year interest rates during the business cycle, and the analogy is strong.

Controlling the Probability of Failure Through the Credit Cycle

What do we do next once management recognizes that its own credit quality varies over the credit cycle because of the cyclicality of the credit worthiness of its borrowers? The next step is to put a number of measurement and monitoring technologies to work regarding the credit quality of the financial institution itself. There is no reason for this not to be a daily discipline. A best practice report would include the following:

- Current credit default swap quotes on the company (if available);
- Current primary (new issue) bond credit spreads for the company;
- Current secondary market bond credit spreads for the company;
- Default probabilities for the company derived from:
  - credit derivatives prices;
  - bond prices;
  - historical default databases (the Jarrow-Chava approach of Chapter 17).

For the most technical layer of senior management, the reporting should also include:

- the cost of the Jarrow-Merton put option that would eliminate integrated credit risk and interest rate risk, as discussed in Chapter 39;
- the cost of the line of credit which would eliminate liquidity risk, as discussed in Chapter 40;
- The 'delta' of shareholder value and the Jarrow-Merton put option with respect to changes in:
  - stock price indices;
  - interest rates;
  - foreign exchange rates;
  - other relevant macro factors.

This kind of reporting discipline provides a framework for the practical action that is the ultimate measure of a risk management process—What's the hedge?

Hedging Total Risk to Maximize Shareholder Value

Once management has set a target range for the risk of failure and measured the financial institution's sensitivities to the macro-factors which cause risk, management has two complementary choices:

- Management can directly hedge the integrated risk caused by the macro factors using exchange traded derivatives and selected over the counter derivatives.
- Management can adopt a more conservative liability structure to reduce the risk of failure.

Since we know the deltas of shareholder value and the Jarrow-Merton put option with respect to the key macro factors driving risk, we can directly calculate how much hedging we need to do to put the risk of failure in the target range. The hedge ratios we derive are similar to the hedge ratios for the Merton model of risky debt which we discussed in Chapter 16. Using the technology outlined in Chapter 39, we can show the high degree of correlation between the hedging instruments and the cash instruments being hedged, as required by Financial Accounting Standard 133 in the U.S. and by International Accounting Standard 39.

Liability structure can also be managed as long as management takes action early enough when credit quality starts to deteriorate. The safest increment strategy is to issue more equity and use it to pay down short-term liabilities. This 'buys time' for any problems the institution may have to be corrected over the remainder of the business cycle. If all liabilities were paid down, obviously, the financial institution would find it almost impossible to fail.

In any event, management knows when it needs to take action and it knows which actions to take because of the risk management analysis outlined in Chapters 39 and 40. This knowledge and action orientation is good for shareholders and good for regulators.

Implications for the Basel Capital Accords

As van Deventer and Imai [2003] note, the New Basel Capital Accords are intended to improve the safety and soundness of financial institutions. The means by which this is done is the regular production of a capital ratio based on risk-weighted assets that presumably is a key predictor of potential financial institutions failure. These regulations are well intentioned and constrained by the lowest common denominator-level risk analytics that are typical of government regulations. The Basel Accords, for example, don't specifically provide for, or recommend, monte carlo simulation of risks in spite of the fact that this can be done at minimal expense in common spreadsheet software.

The Basel Accords suffer in another couple of dimensions when compared to the procedures that we have outlined in the first 41 chapters of this book:

- **Omitted variables**. The Basel Accords capital ratios effectively are a credit model which omits key explanatory variables that have been proven to be statistically important in predicting default: accounting ratios, common stock prices, macroeconomic factors, and so on.
- **No valuation framework**. The Basel Accords don't provide a consistent valuation framework that is essential to marking-to-market our current position and in simulating our potential default in the future.
- **No hedge**. The Basel Accords fail the most basic test of a risk management approach—they don't tell us the hedge we need to solve the problem.

For these reasons, the Basel Accords have to be regarded as a modest supplement to the tools of Chapters 1–41, not the core of a sophisticated risk management effort.

Simulating Our Own Probability of Default

Our greatest advantage in analyzing the risk of our own institution is a complete knowledge of all assets and liabilities we own now and a very good knowledge of what kind of assets and liabilities we are likely to own in the future. In that sense, we have an information advantage that Professor Jarrow has noted is one of the key reasons why the reduced form modeling approach is most consistent with the behavior of market participants who don't have the same information we do.

By better understanding our own risk (Chapter 39) and the timing of a credit-related liquidity event (Chapter 40), which would reveal our problems, we can take action promptly. At worst, we can take action as the market comes to similar realizations, and at best, we can avoid a problem and prevent it from becoming a public issue.

If we do not do so, we risk the needless destruction of our financial institution's franchise that has taken years or decades to build. We turn to that issue in Chapter 44, but first we turn to the information technology practices that are most likely to result in a timely, efficient and cost-effective implementation of this risk management technology.

CHAPTER 43

Information Technology Considerations

In the first 42 chapters of this book, we have reviewed all of the tools necessary to construct a fully integrated measure of interest rate and credit risk and that produces an answer to the key question 'what is the hedge?' Some of these tools have been focused on risk management strategy, such as getting used to the Jarrow-Merton put option as a comprehensive measure of risk. Other tools have been more mechanical, such as how to value an American call option embedded in a bond when the default of the issuer is a possibility. In this chapter, we focus on another set of issues that have to be faced when implementing a comprehensive risk management system—the information technology aspects of an implementation.

The authors collectively have spent 25 years in the implementation of such a system[1] in major financial institutions around the world, and our comments below reflect the world-wide best practice in that regard.

Common Practice in Risk Management Systems: Dealing with Legacy Systems

Many of the world's financial institutions face a common situation when preparing to move forward in the risk management systems area. The move forward is usually motivated not only by the New Capital Accords of the Basel Committee on Banking Supervision. Particularly in countries where there has been a recent financial crisis, managers of the most sophisticated

---

[1] All of the authors have been involved in the development of the enterprise wide risk management system Kamakura Risk Manager and the related default probabilities offered by the Kamakura Corporation. Dr van Deventer has been involved in the systems development effort since the company's founding in 1990, concentrating on the financial design of the system and micro-tasks ranging from the system's financial class libraries and the original Windows graphic user interface. Mr. Imai has headed the software development effort since 1995, and Mr. Mesler has been in charge of related default probability and data-base development since January 2002.

financial institutions now clearly realize that the common situation described in the bullet points below have left the institution unprepared for a crisis. These managers are dedicated to the comprehensive view of risk that we have described in this book because their previous failure to take this approach nearly resulted in the failure of their institution.

A common situation that senior management often faces looks like this:

- The risk management function is fragmented. Market risk, credit risk, interest rate risk and performance measurement are all handled by different groups with no central coordination at either the working level or the senior management level.
- There is at best only a partially completed enterprise wide data warehouse.
- Risk management systems have been implemented on a compartmentalized basis:
  - Vendor A provides third party default probabilities;
  - Vendor B provides credit risk loss simulation software that provides cumulative losses over a long single-period but no valuation, multiperiod simulation or hedging;
  - Vendor C provides interest rate risk management simulation and mark-to-market calculations, generally ignoring default risk;
  - Vendor D provides traditional value-at-risk calculations for market risk;
  - Vendor E provides performance measurement for each business unit, either on a benchmark basis or on a transfer pricing basis, depending on the nature of the financial institution;
  - Vendor F (often an in-house solution) provides capital allocation as a supplement to Vendor E's performance measurement data.
- These systems use different graphic user interfaces, different input database design, different financial mathematics, different reporting tools, different end-user staffs and are totally irreconcilable.

This common situation is totally wasteful, as 95% of the lines of source code in the six systems should be common. In effect, the user has bought the same system six times and then completely scrambled the picture even more with inconsistent data architecture and reporting.

Even more than the wastefulness of this situation is its danger—the systems infrastructure obscures the view of the organization's risk and return and defeats the very objectives of the risk management process that we outlined in Chapter 1. Most importantly, there is no link at all between random movements in macroeconomic factors which drive defaults and valuation for every item on the balance sheet of the financial institution. How can there be an integrated view of risk when each system is looking at a different piece of the puzzle?

A rise in interest rates will never increase default probabilities and change credit-adjusted valuation in an integrated way. The default probability vendor ignores the impact of interest rates on default probabilities. The interest rate risk system ignores default.

This architecture has extremely serious flaws that are of grave concern to many. If senior management has ended up in this situation prior to the developments in risk technology that we've outlined in this book, how can we escape this untenable situation?

It is to that task that we now turn.

Upgrading the Risk Infrastructure: The Request for Proposal Process

The first step in the process of reforming the risk infrastructure starts with a request for proposal process. In a perfect world, there would be a single risk management staff group that manages market risk, credit risk, interest rate risk and performance measurement on a fully integrated basis. There are many fine books on the subject of the organization and execution of enterprise wide risk management, so we won't detour in that direction here. We need to remain focused on the more micro-tasks of execution. Even if the staff of these groups remain separate with a different managerial reporting hierarchy for each group, a joint project team should be organized to design and implement the request for proposal process.

In order for the request for proposal process to clearly reveal the skills, strengths and liabilities of the potential vendors, it has to be both comprehensive and very detailed. This means that the project team members will have to be both relatively senior and with considerable hands on experience in each of the areas of risk we want to cover—market risk, credit risk, interest rate risk and performance measurement. A typical 'best practice' request for proposal covers all four areas with equal emphasis and has 200–1,000 very specific questions on the product functionality along the lines of the approach outlined in this book.

Prior to 1995, it was uncommon to see such integrated risk request for proposals because, frankly, the technology was still in its early stages. Now it is obvious to most market participants that the technology outlined in this book exists and has been implemented by many of the world's most successful financial institutions. For that reason, the authors estimate that 80% of the requests for proposal for risk management systems reflect this integrated approach to risk. The only area which seems to be lagging are the large American banks where the legacy of many mergers has left high walls between risk management groups of the merged banks. Even in the U.S., however, the trend toward integrated risk management is very strong and distinct.

One of the authors learned to his chagrin when he resigned from Lehman Brothers that the only profession in the world with a lower perceived integrity than investment bankers is that of software salesman. This is a sad testimony to the industry and one that the Request For Proposal process has to be explicitly designed to deal with.

The level of detail in the question of the RFP should be high for two reasons. Firstly, it will test the comprehensiveness of both the vendors' knowledge and completeness of the vendors' solutions. Secondly, it will allow for a detailed 'audit' of the vendors' solutions after the RFP responses have been gathered.

The authors believe that 'best practice' in the RFP process is for short-listed vendors (typically two or three firms) to do more than just demonstrate the product. Even a half-day demonstration can be scripted by a vendor in such a way that deficiencies in the product will remain out of view of the potential client. In addition to the demonstration, the potential client should go through every response to every question provided by the vendor and insure that the responses provided by the vendor are accurate.

Much to the authors' surprise, one very large international bank which followed this process (i.e. warning the vendors in advance), revealed that only one vendor had been truthful in their responses to the RFP.

By following this process, risk managers will both insure that they have a good understanding of the competing products and will help to root out unethical practices and unethical people from the software industry.

Most importantly, no product is perfect and no product has all features that all potential clients might want. Working with a key vendor for many years on the best future development path for the product is the very best way for a financial institution to achieve 'best practice' in integrated risk management.

Paid Pilots as Final Proof of Concept

The authors believe that once a vendor has been tentatively selected, best practice leads to a paid pilot with that vendor's system while the number two vendor waits on the sidelines. This is essentially a 'mini-installation' and insures, in as complete a fashion as possible, that the vendor's solution works as advertised. While a few vendors resist the pilot concept, the authors would not recommend purchasing any risk management system without one. They reveal the strengths and weaknesses of both the system and the management team of the vendor in short order. Since everyone in the world would be interested in a free pilot, potential clients should realize that vendors have to ration their scarce resources by charging for the pilot, with a portion of the pilot fee often credited against the ultimate purchase price of the pilot.

We strongly recommend that the key team members on the pilot from the user's perspective lead the user's installation team.

Keys to Success in Software Installation

The success rate on software installations in general is surprisingly low. The word 'surprising' is the key word here. There should be only one reason that an installation fails and that is the sad situation where the software doesn't work—this should never happen if the process above is carefully followed. As a result, the failure of an installation of software that works is truly a failure of the management process and can be avoided 100% of the time if management is diligent at both the user and the vendor level.

The key to success from the user perspective is to have a dedicated project team 100% committed to the installation as their full time job. The installation team should have a mix of business experts who represent the ultimate end-user internally and IT experts who are experts at getting the necessary input data and changing its format using standard industry tools. These tools include both data mapping and reporting of data base (both input files and output files) contents.

Turnover on this project team is the greatest risk to the success of the project, because it is quite difficult for the vendor to replace the institution-specific knowledge that is lost when someone on the user's project team resigns. This normally can come only from within the user itself.

The vendor's installation team normally has three types of experts. The first, the project manager, is a generalist whose expertise involves both clear and organized planning and reporting. The second type of expert is the excellent business user of the software from the vendor's perspective. The third type of expert is the IT expert who works closely with his peer on the user's project team.

The vendor's project team members typically come from three sources: from the vendor's staff itself, from a formal distributor of the software, or from a third party systems integrator. The authors believe that the success rate is highest if the project team on the vendor side comes either from the vendor itself or from a long-term distributor of the project. If the only relationship with the vendor is on a project basis, a third party systems integrator is in a complex position. The short-term revenue from the project is maximized by dragging out the installation, and the systems integrator suffers relatively little from the long-term reputational damage to the vendor from projects where installation was too slow, too expensive, or failed. From an end-user's perspective, the user should want an installation team very focused on how important a successful installation is to the reputation of the vendor.

When this long-term reputational perspective is properly in place, a project should never fail unless the end user for some reason doesn't staff the user side of the installation correctly.

Vendor Size: Larger Vendor or Small Vendor?

From a conceptual point of view, every head of information technology wants a AAA-rated software vendor with a 50-year history of innovation and a project team of 25-year veterans that works for minimum wage.

Unfortunately, the nature of the risk management software industry makes this dream highly unlikely to come about. As we look at the industry, a number of trends are quite clear:

- The innovation in the risk management business has consistently come from new, small firms.
- Many of these small firms have been able to accomplish only one major innovation and end-users are forced to switch vendors in order to purchase the next innovation.
- As a result, small firms which can do multiple innovations and which allow changes in risk management models in the software with just a mouse-click by the user are very highly prized.
- This increases the size of the system that must be constructed by a new entrant, 'raising the bar' and discouraging new entrants to the business.
- Large software firms generally add to their risk management products by acquisition of other firms.
- After an acquisition by a large firm, culture clashes between the large firm-small firm mentality often lead to high turnover among the most valuable staff of the acquired firm.
- In response, the large firm ceases innovation on the product and puts it into 'cash cow' mode until it dies.
- When a risk product does die because of lack of innovation, the large software firm simply buys another vendor.

How does a sophisticated potential buyer of integrated risk management software deal with these issues? The most intelligent IT experts at major financial institutions look at the stability and ability of senior management of the vendor and of the core development team. This measure of 'vendor risk' is almost flawless in indicating the chances of a successful installation and a long-term relationship, because it says a lot about the skill of the management of the vendor at all levels. It is a much better indicator of the probability of success than the size of the vendor, because firms of all sizes can score well on this measure if the firm is well-run. At a large firm, compensation schemes designed to preserve the intellectual property of a small firm that is acquired are simple to structure and execute and yet relatively few large firms have been good at it.

A couple of incidents from the recent past illustrate how risky a large software vendor can be from an end-user perspective if the low turnover strategy is not pursued:

- A major U.K. software house bought an innovative risk software firm with a 15 person development team based in Los Angeles. Shortly after the acquisition, each member of the Los Angeles development team was ordered to move to London. As attractive as London is as a place to live, 14 of the 15 team members resigned rather than relocating. This essentially destroyed the product.

- A major New York-listed software company purchased an innovative risk management firm with substantial revenue and more than 300 employees. Within a year, the CEO of the acquired firm had left and revenue in the product line fell by more than 50%.
- Another New York-listed firm acquired a company in the credit risk area with revenues of more than $50 million a year and staff of almost 200 people. Within two years, eight of the nine most senior people in the acquired company had resigned.
- A New York-listed firm in the credit risk area acquired a small but highly innovative software firm with expertise in interest rate risk management. Within one year, the CEO of the acquired firm had resigned and within two years, the acquirer notified software clients of the acquired firm that the software product of the acquired firm would no longer be supported.

From the end user perspective, assessing the maturity, longevity and commitment of the management team of the vendor is the single best way to assess the long-term risk of the vendor. As the examples above show, large size can increase risk if the managerial compensation systems are not handled skillfully.

Being a Best Practice User

Once an installation is successfully accomplished, the vendor-user relationship is just beginning. There are a number of best practices that we feel will enable end users to get the maximum benefit from an enterprise-wide software installation:

- Build mutual knowledge with the vendor through a regular exchange of visits and information. These relationships should span many levels of management, not just be concentrated at the working level.
- Encourage continued innovation by the vendor by adopting new modules as they emerge and by being an active participant in the design of expanded functionality.
- Be an active participant in the user group.
- 'Invest' in the vendor by sponsoring new functionality with financial support to speed the degree of innovation.
- Establish a test database for regular testing of new versions from the vendor and make this test database available to the vendor.
- Regularly send staff to the vendor for advanced training.

In addition to these steps, we see an increasing trend toward long-term consulting contracts between the senior management team of the vendor and the most senior end-users at major financial institutions. This kind of relationship insures that, above and beyond the day-to-day working level relationship, senior management of the financial institution is fully exploiting an enterprise wide risk management solution to achieve the objectives that we have outlined in this book.

We turn to that discussion in the next and final chapter in this book.

CHAPTER 44

Shareholder Value Creation and Destruction

R isk management is the discipline that clearly shows management the risks and returns of every major strategic decision at both the institutional level and the transaction level. Moreover, the risk management discipline shows how to change strategy in order to bring the risk return trade-off into line with the best long and short-term interests of the institution.

In Chapter 1, we began this book with the preceding definition of risk management. In the 42 chapters after that, we showed, step-by-step, how to take advantage of existing financial and information technology to achieve these objectives, complete with specifying how many questions a request for proposal should have to clearly understand risk management software vendors' capabilities.

How are the major financial institutions doing in achieving the risk management goal of showing management 'the risks and returns of every major strategic decision at both the institutional level and the transaction level'?

That is the subject of this chapter.

Shareholder Value Creation

Each of the authors works closely with major hedge funds and other institutional investors on a daily basis. Their objectives from a risk management perspective are ruthlessly simple: Given equivalent levels of risk, which bond should I go long and which bond should I go short? Day after day, if they do this skillfully, their mark-to-market returns versus their benchmark will be revealed to clients and potential clients each month. All will be able to see clearly whether the hedge funds are achieving their objectives.

Of all of the financial institutions that the authors have worked with, hedge funds have the greatest sense of urgency and the greatest link between their success in achieving best practice in risk management and their personal compensation. Their shareholder value created is manifestly clear—the excess of their management fees in excess of costs.

Among major traditional financial institutions, there are some very clear 'stars' and some rapid progress being made.

At a recent gathering of 20 senior risk managers,[1] 19 of the 20 members surveyed reported that their institution was regularly using mark-to-market technology to quantify their interest rate risk using the techniques like those we outlined in Chapters 8–13. Twenty years ago, perhaps only one or two of the institutions surveyed would have given the same answer, with the others relying primarily on the simulation of financial accrual-based net income as their primary focus for risk management effects. That focus, while clearly of interest to the CEO and Wall Street analysts, was certainly not good enough to prevent the $1 trillion collapse of the savings and loan industry from rising rates. In that sense, in the last 20 years, much progress has been made.

At the same time, the survey of the risk managers gathered at that session was striking in a 'so close but oh so far' sense. When the risk managers marked-to-market the balance sheet of their organizations, much to our surprise, most of them used only a single yield curve (usually the LIBOR curve, occasionally the risk-free curve) to calculate the market value of every obligation on this balance sheet.

Clearly, no hedge fund manager would last long by marking-to-market the present value of a Ford Motor Credit bond with present value factors from the LIBOR curve. It makes no sense in either theory or practice to use only one yield curve if your mandate is to create shareholder value on a risk-adjusted basis.

The survey response indicates that almost all of the risk managers surveyed were still 'held prisoner' in a tightly compartmentalized 'interest rate risk management' box that falls far short of the risk management definition above. Their interest was not in the mark-to-market calculation per se, but the sensitivity of the mark-to-market calculation to changes in the level of interest rates as captured by the single yield curve.

In a sense, their superiors in these major financial institutions had instructed them to perform their duties in a way in which they were getting 20% of the benefits while doing 80% of the work for a best practice risk management effort. This is the opposite of the 80/20 rule we have mentioned often in this book.

With a bit of fine-tuning of policies and procedures and with better risk management software, the institutions surveyed could have been achieving a lot more value for their shareholders using the full complement of tools and techniques in this book, not just Chapters 8–13. We can see from the examples of fund managers, hedge funds, insurance companies, banks and securities firms exactly what to do. From a senior management perspective, we need to demand the same accuracy and insights from a total balance sheet perspective that we do on the trading floor on a transaction-by-transaction basis.

---

[1] North American Asset and Liability Management Committee, Vancouver, B.C., April 28-30 2004.

Using modern integrated risk management technology in a daily production environment, management can achieve this objective at a fraction of the cost of running the disparate systems for compartmentalized risk management that we outlined in Chapter 43. Many of the world's best financial institutions have already taken this approach, and they are very successfully exploiting their peers whose risk management practices remain bogged down in the approaches used in the 1980s and early 1990s.

In the next section, we summarize what senior management of these institutions can see on a daily basis that their peers cannot yet perceive.

Daily Management Reporting of Total Risk

A state of the art set of integrated risk management reports would contain the following information on the institution's risk and shareholder value added:

- Default probabilities for the institution compared to target default probabilities:
  - Derived from historical defaults;
  - Derived from bond prices;
  - Derived from credit derivatives prices.
- Default probabilities for the five most important competitors of the institution.
- Default probabilities for the ten largest mark-to-market credit exposures of the institution.
- Sensitivity of all of these default probabilities to changes in:
  - the economy via a stock price index like the S&P500;
  - interest rates;
  - foreign exchange rates;
  - oil prices;
  - central business district building prices.
- Cost of the Jarrow-Merton put option that would eliminate all of the institution's:
  - interest rate risk;
  - liquidity risk;
  - credit risk;
  - total risk.
- Sensitivity of the Jarrow-Merton put option for each of the objectives above with respect to changes in:
  - the economy via a stock price index like the S&P500;
  - interest rates;
  - foreign exchange rates;
  - oil prices;
  - central business district building prices.

- Year-to-date shareholder valuation creation for the institution's:
  - ten largest business units;
  - ten most important product units;
  - ten most important geographical units.
- On these bases:
  - Daily mark-to-market of the relevant portfolio versus a risk-free benchmark with identical interest rate characteristics.
  - Financial accounting basis using matched maturity transfer pricing versus the appropriate yield curve (risk-free yield curve for assets, the institution's marginal cost of funds for liabilities).
- Probability of not meeting net income targets for each of the next five years.
- Probability of needing 'excessive' provisions for loan losses in each of the next five years.
- Probability of missing managerial target capital ratios in each of the next five years.
- Probability of missing regulatory capital ratios in each of the next five years.
- Probability of a ratings downgrade in each of the next five years.

Among the readers of this book, there are probably many who would like to have this information and don't have it. It is available today, and many of your competitors already have access to it. Getting this information for your own institution simply involves going through the IT process that we outlined in Chapter 43. The Federal Deposit Insurance Corporation, through its Loss Distribution Model, announced on December 10 2003 that it is already going through the process of generating information just like this for every financial institution in the U.S. with deposit insurance. If the regulators already have information like this about your institution, how can you not be looking at it as well?

Moving from Common Practice to Best Practice

In Chapters 1 and 2, the authors related how long it took for commonly accepted risk management tools of today to become accepted as 'conventional wisdom'. In the case of many management tools, this has taken two or three decades, but the pace of innovation is increasing rapidly because competition in the financial services industry is rapidly intensifying. Note that the first reduced form credit model was introduced only in 1995 (by Jarrow-Turnbull) and that the FDIC had already adopted the technology on the largest portfolio of credit insurance in the world by 2003. Black and Scholes would have been ecstatic if their options model was as widely adopted in twice that time.

Financial institutions face many barriers to innovation. As a group, the employees of financial institutions (including the authors in their prior lives) are a conservative group. Of these conservative people, risk managers tend to be super conservative. Within the group of risk managers, our colleague Leonard Matz likes to categorize the breed as being either 'place keepers' or 'bomb throwers'. Place keepers maintain the risk management discipline using existing technology with modest innovation. Bomb throwers want to make great leaps forward.

For this reason, the people involved in risk management play a critical role in the pace of innovation. For various levels of management, there are some simple ways of moving from common practice to best practice, because the regulatory agencies are moving in that direction rapidly, as the FDIC Loss Distribution Model shows. We summarize each in turn.

The senior management perspective

Senior managers in major financial institutions, should be able to readily access the daily risk reports that we outlined above—they should be demanded from staff.

For an institution with a traditional risk management structure and software infrastructure, the cost of these reports is literally negative. By gradually eliminating all of the six types of vendors discussed in Chapter 43, there will be cash left over even after an enterprise wide risk management solution has been put in place. The shareholder value created from this process will be very large but even from a short-term dollars and sense perspective it simply reduces the direct and indirect cost of risk management and provides much clearer strategic insights.

The middle management perspective

Middle managers are the key to success of every financial institution from a shareholder value-added perspective. They have both the hands on knowledge of the working level and the strategic perspective of senior management.

What if senior management is pushing to move from common practice to best practice, but the working level doesn't have the knowledge or skill set to get there? The answer is simple—replace the working level.

More likely, the working level will be interested if pushed and a change in risk vendors will provide a welcome challenge and a well-justified sense of contribution to the well-being of the organization.

What if senior management is the barrier? It is so ironic that you need a license to drive a car, but you don't need a license to be president of a major financial institution. The personality of the CEO of a financial institution has a tremendous impact on shareholder value creation and risk management best practice. How can a CEO not want to know the risk that his own institution will default? Especially if the regulators, shareholders, and rating agencies are all looking at those numbers?

With luck, a little pushing will create the interest, at least somewhere on the senior risk management committee. If not, just wait—your time will come in the senior spot and you will be able to change things quickly. Worst case, you can use cost reduction as the rationale for putting an enterprise wide risk management infrastructure in place. If the cost reduction benefits are not apparent, you are not talking to the right vendors.

The working level perspective

As the authors related early in this book, the working level has the longest wait before they can make a major impact on how the institution looks at risk-adjusted shareholder value creation and destruction. One of us tried to sell the mark-to-market risk management concept that is now standard at the major banks around the world (see the first section of this chapter) for three years at a major bank without success. When faced with that kind of barrier, what should you do as a working level staffer?

One of the most effective motivators for senior management is to prove to them that they are at risk of no longer achieving common practice in risk management, let alone best practice. Peer bank actions are the most effective of convincing people that the financial institution is being left behind. Another opportunity to effect change comes in the aftermath of a crisis in either the financial markets you operate in (say Korea after the Asia crisis), or at the institution where you work after a risk management 'incident'. Being part of the solution is very good for your career.

Many times, unfortunately, the messenger who conveys the message that a crisis is coming is not welcomed before the fact and not thanked afterwards when they prove to be right. This is a situation to be avoided at all costs.

When you find yourself employed by a financial institution that lacks the institutional will to create risk-adjusted shareholder value with the best tools available, quit! The firm is destined to be acquired or get in to trouble, so why sit around and wait for it to happen, ruining your own reputation as a risk manager?

Getting Help to Create Shareholder Value

The tools and techniques in this book are fully implemented and in place at some of the most sophisticated financial institutions around the world. The concepts are tried and true, although in some cases they are being applied in different ways from the ways they might have been used before.

Since the techniques are already at work, getting help to speed your own implementation of these ideas is as simple as sending us an e-mail at dvandeventer@kamakuraco.com. We look forward to hearing from you, and we thank you for making it all the way to the last sentence of this book.

Bibliography

Adams, Kenneth J. and Donald R. van Deventer, "Monte Carlo Simulation: The Pros and the Cons", *Balance Sheet*, Volume 2, Number 3, Autumn 1993, pp. 18–24.

Adams, Kenneth J. and Donald R. van Deventer, "Fitting Yield Curves and Forward Rate Curves with Maximum Smoothness", *Journal of Fixed Income*, 1994, pp. 52–61.

Allen, L. and A. Saunders, "A Survey of Cyclical Effects in Credit Risk Measurement Models", *Bank for International Settlements Working Paper* 126, 2003.

Altman, E., "Financial Ratios, Discriminant Analysis, and the Prediction of Corporate Bankruptcy", *Journal of Finance*, volume 23, 1968.

Altman, E., R. Haldeman, and P. Narayanan, "ZETA Analysis: A New Model to Identify Bankruptcy Risk of Corporations", *Journal of Banking and Finance*, 1977, pp. 29–55.

Andersen, Leif and Dan Buffum, "Calibration and implementation of convertible bond models", *Journal of Computational Finance*, Winter 2003.

Arnold, Ludwig, *Stochastic Differential Equations: Theory and Applications*, John Wiley & Sons, New York, 1974.

Ayache, E., P.A. Forsyth, and K. R. Vetzal, "Valuation of Convertible Bonds with Credit Risk", *Journal of Derivatives*, April 2003, pp. 9–29.

Basel Committee on Banking Supervision, "Consultative Document: The New Capital Accords", monograph, Bank for International Settlements, Basel, 2001.

Berk, J. and R. Roll, "Adjustable Rate Mortgages: Valuation", *The Journal of Real Estate Finance and Economics*, 1 June 1988, pp. 163–184.

Bermudez, Ana and Nick Webber, "An Asset Based Model of Defaultable Convertible Bonds with Endogenised Recovery", Working Paper, City University, November 26, 2003.

Black, Fischer, "The Pricing of Commodity Contracts", *Journal of Financial Economics*, March 1976, pp. 167–179.

Black, Fischer, "Interest Rates as Options", *Journal of Finance*, December 1995, pp. 1371–1376.

Black, Fischer, E. Derman, W. Toy, "A One–Factor Model of Interest Rates and Its Application to Treasury Bond Options", *Financial Analysts Journal*, 1990, pp. 33–39.

Black, Fischer and Piotr Karasinski, "Bond and Option Pricing when Short Rates are Lognormal, Capital Standards: Interest Rate Risk", *Financial Analysts Journal*,1991 pp. 52–59.

Black, Fischer and M. Scholes, "The Pricing of Options and Corporate Liabilities", *Journal of Political Economy*, May-June 1973, pp. 637–654.

Blum, M., 1974, "Failing Company Discriminant Analysis," *Journal of Accounting Research*, Spring.

Boyle, P., "Options: A Monte Carlo Approach", *Journal of Financial Economics* 4, May 1977, pp. 323–328.

Breeden, Douglas T. "Complexities of Hedging Mortgages", *Journal of Fixed Income*, December 1994, pp. 6–42.

Brennan, Michael J. and Eduardo Schwartz, "A Continuous Time Approach to the Pricing of Bonds", *Journal of Banking and Finance*, 1979, pp. 133–155.

Buono, Mark, Russell B. Gregory-Allen and Uzi Yaari, "The Efficacy of Term Structure Estimation Techniques: A Monte Carlo Study", *The Journal of Fixed Income* 1, 1992, pp. 52–59.

Caouette, John B., Altman, Edward and Narayanan, Paul, *Managing Credit Risk: The Next Great Financial Challenge*, John Wiley & Sons, New York, 1998.

Chan, K. C., G. Andrew Karolyi, Francis A. Longstaff, and Anthony B. Sanders, "An Empirical Comparison of Models of the Short Term Interest Rate", *Journal of Finance*, (July) 1992, pp. 1209–1228.

Chen, Derek H., Harry H. Huang, Rui Kan, Ashok Varikooty, and Henry N. Wang, "Modelling and Managing Credit Risk", *Asset & Liability Management: A Synthesis of New Methodologies*, RISK Publications, 1998.

Chen, Lin, *Interest Rate Dynamics, Derivatives Pricing, and Risk Management*, Springer-Verlag, Berlin, 1994.

Chen, Ren-Raw and Louis Scott, "Pricing Interest Rate Options in a Two-Factor cox-Ingersoll-Ross Model of the Term Structure", *Review of Financial Studies*, 1992, pp. 613–636.

Chen, Ren-Raw, "Exact Solutions for Futures and European Futures Options on Pure Discount Bonds", *Journal of Financial and Quantitative Analysis*, 27 (March 1992), pp. 97–108.

Cox, John C., Jonathan E. Ingersoll, Jr. and Stephen A. Ross, "An Analysis of Variable Rate Loan Contracts", *Journal of Finance*, 1980, pp. 389–403.

Cox, John C., Jonathan E. Ingersoll, and Stephen A. Ross, "The Relationship between Forward Prices and Futures Prices", *Journal of Financial Economics*, December 1981, pp. 321–346.

Cox, John C., Jonathan E. Ingersoll, Jr. and Stephen A. Ross, "A Theory of the Term Structure of Interest Rates", *Econometrica*, 1985, pp. 385–407.

Cox, John C., Stephen A. Ross and M. Rubinstein, "Option Pricing: A Simplified Approach", *Journal of Financial Economics*, 1979, pp. 229–263.

Dothan, L. Uri, "On the Term Structure of Interest Rates", *Journal of Financial Economics* 6, 1978, pp. 59–69.

Duffee, Gregory, "Estimating the Price of Default Risk", *The Review of Financial Studies*, 12 (1), 197–226, Spring 1999.

Duffie, Darrell, *Dynamic Asset Pricing Theory*, Princeton University Press, Princeton, New Jersey, 1996.

Duffie D. and K. Singleton, "Modelling Term Structures of Defaultable Bonds", *Review of Financial Studies*, Vol. 12, No. 4, 1999, pp. 197-226.

Dunn, K.B., and C. Spatt, "Private Information and Incentives: Implications for Mortgage Contract Terms and Pricing", *Journal of Real Estate Finance and Economics* 1, (April 1988), pp. 47–60.

Ellis, David M. and James V. Jordan, "The Evaluation of Credit Union Non-Maturity Deposits", National Economic Research Associates, 2001.

Falkenstein, E. and A. Boral, "RiskCalc™ for Private Companies: Moody's Default Model", Moody's Investors Service memorandum, 2000.

Federal Reserve System, *Risk-Based Capital Standards: Interest Rate Risk*, Notice of Proposed Rulemaking, Washington, D. C. September 14, 1993.

The First Boston Corporation, Handbook of Securities of the United States Government and Federal Agencies and Related Money Market Instruments, New York, 1984.

Flannagan, C.T., M.D. Herskovitz, and H.T. Loy, *Understanding and Modelling Cost of Funds ARMs Prepayments*, Mortgage-Backed Securities Research, Merrill Lynch, (February 1989).

Flesaker, Bjorn, "Testing the Heath-Jarrow-Morton/Ho-Lee Model of Interest Rate Contingent Claims Pricing", *Journal of Financial and Quantitative Analysis*, (December 1993), pp. 483–495.

Friedman, A. *Stochastic Differential Equations and Applications*, Volume 1, Academic Press, New York, 1975.

Garman, Mark B. and Steven W. Kohlhagen, "Foreign Currency Option Values", *Journal of International Money and Finance*, 1983, pp. 231–237.

Geske, Robert, "The Valuation of Compound Options", *Journal of Financial Economics*, 1979, pp. 63–81.

Green, J. and J.B. Shoven, "The Effect of Interest Rates on Mortgage Prepayments", *Journal of Money, Credit and Banking* XVIII, (February 1986).

Heath, David, Robert Jarrow and Andrew Morton, "Bond Pricing and the Term Structure of Interest Rates: A Discrete Time Approach", *Journal of Financial and Quantitative Analysis*,1990, pp. 419–440.

Heath, David, Robert Jarrow and Andrew Morton, "Bond Pricing and the Term Structure of Interest Rates: A New Methodology for Contingent Claim Valuation", *Econometrica*, 60(1), 1992, pp. 77–105.

Hildebrand, F. B., *Introduction to Numerical Analysis*, (Dover Publications Inc., New York), 1987.

Hilliard, Jimmy E., Jeff Madura, and Alan L. Tucker, "Currency Option Pricing with Stochastic Domestic and Foreign Interest Rates", *Journal of Financial and Quantitative Analysis*, 1991, pp. 139–151.

Ho, Thomas S. Y., and Sang-Bin Lee, "Term Structure Movements and Pricing Interest Rate Contingent Claims", *Journal of Finance* 41, December 1986, pp. 1011–1029.

Hosmer, D. W. and S. Lemeshow, *Applied Logistic Regression*, John Wiley & Sons, 2000.

Hull, John and Alan White, "Valuing Derivative Securities Using the Explicit Finite Difference Method", *Journal of Financial and Quantitative Analysis* 25, 1990a.

Hull, John and Alan White, "Pricing Interest-Rate Derivative Securities", *Review of Financial Studies* 3, 1990b, pp. 573–592.

Hull, John and Alan White, "One Factor Interest Rate Models and the Valuation of Interest Rate Derivative Securities", *Journal of Financial and Quantitative Analysis*, 1993, pp. 235–254.

Hull, John and Alan White, "Efficient Procedures for Valuing European and American Path-Dependent Derivatives", *Journal of Derivatives*, Vol. 1, No. 1, Fall 1993, pp. 21–31.

Hull, John and Alan White, "Numerical Procedures for Implementing Term Structure Models I: Single-Factor Models", *Journal of Derivatives*, 1994a, pp. 7–16.

Hull, John and Alan White, "Numerical Procedures for Implementing Term Structure Models II: Two-Factor Models", *Journal of Derivatives*, 1994b, pp. 37–48.

Hull, John, *Options, Futures, and other Derivative Securities*, Second edition, Prentice Hall International, 1992.

Hutchinson, D. and G. Pennacchi, "Measuring rents and Interest Rate Risk in Imperfect Financial Markets: The Case of Retail Bank Deposits", unpublished manuscript, University of Illinois, 1994.

Ingersoll Jr., Jonathan E., *Theory of Financial Decision Making*, Rowman & Littlefield, Savage, Maryland, 1987.

Ingersoll Jr., Jonathan E., Jeffrey Skelton, and Roman L. Weil, "Duration Forty Years Later", *Journal of Financial and Quantitative Analysis*, November 1978, pp. 627–648.

Jamshidian, Farshid, "An Exact Bond Option Formula", *Journal of Finance* 44, March 1989, pp. 205–209.

Jamshidian, Farshid, *Bond and Option Evaluation in the Gaussian Interest Rate Model*, Financial Strategies Group, Merrill Lynch, 1990.

Jarrow, Robert, *Modelling Fixed Income Securities and Interest Rate Options*, McGraw-Hill, New York, 1996.

Jarrow, Robert, "Technical Guide: Default Probabilities Implicit in Debt and Equity Prices", *Kamakura Corporation Technical Guide*, 1999, revised 2001.

Jarrow, Robert, "Default Parameter Estimation Using Market Prices", *Financial Analysts Journal*, September/October, 2001.

Jarrow, Robert, "Put Option Premiums and Coherent Risk Measures", *Mathematical Finance*, Vol. 12, pp. 135–142, 2002.

Jarrow, Robert, "Risky Coupon Bonds as a Portfolio of Zero-Coupon Bonds", Cornell University and Kamakura Corporation Working Paper, February 28, 2004.

Jarrow, Robert and Sudheer Chava, "A Comparison of Explicit versus Implicit Estimates of Default Probabilities", Working Paper, Cornell University, 2002b.

Jarrow, Robert and Sudheer Chava, "Bankruptcy Prediction with Industry Effects", Working Paper, Cornell University, 2002a.

Jarrow, Robert, Tibor Janoski and Ferdinando Zullo. "An Empirical Analysis of the Jarrow-van Deventer Model for Valuing Non-Maturity Deposits", *The Journal of Derivatives*, Fall 1999.

Jarrow, Robert, David Lando and Stuart Turnbull, "A Markov Model for the Term Structure of Credit Risk Spreads", *The Review of Financial Studies*, 10(2), 481–523, 1997.

Jarrow, Robert, David Lando, and Fan Yu, 2003, "Default Risk and Diversification: Theory and Applications", Working Paper, Cornell University.

Jarrow, Robert and Jonathan Levin. "The Pricing of Non-Maturity Deposits", *American Banker*, March 8, 1996.

Jarrow, Robert and Stuart Turnbull, "Pricing Derivatives on Financial Securities Subject to Credit Risk", *Journal of Finance* 50 (1), 1995, pp. 53–85.

Jarrow, Robert and Stuart Turnbull, *Derivative Securities*, South-Western College Publishing, Cincinnati, 1996.

Jarrow, Robert and Donald R. van Deventer, "Power Swaps: Disease or Cure?", *RISK* magazine, February 1996.

Jarrow, Robert and Donald R. van Deventer, "The Arbitrage-Free Valuation and Hedging of Demand Deposits and Credit Card Loans", Kamakura Corporation working paper, 1996a.

Jarrow, Robert and Donald R. van Deventer, "Integrating Interest Rate Risk and Credit Risk in ALM", *Asset & Liability Management: A Synthesis of New Methodologies*, RISK Publications, 1998.

Jarrow, Robert and Donald R. van Deventer, "Practical Use of Credit Risk Models in Loan Portfolio and Counterparty Exposure Management: An Update", *Credit Risk: Models and Management*, Second Edition, David Shimko, Editor, RISK Publications, 2004.

Jarrow, Robert, Donald R. van Deventer and Xiaoming. Wang, "A Robust Test of Merton's Structural Model for Credit Risk", *Journal of Risk*, 2002.

Jones, E. P., S. P. Mason, and E. Rosenfeld, "Contingent Claims Analysis of Corporate Capital Structure: An Empirical Investigation", *Journal of Finance* 39, 1984, pp. 611–626.

Kamakura Risk Information Services, *Credit Risk Technical Guide*, version 2.2, November 2003.

Karatzas, Ioannis and Steven E. Shreve, *Browian Motion and Stochastic Calculus*, Springer-Verlag, New York, 1991.

Kaushik I. Amin and Robert A. Jarrow, "Pricing Foreign Currency Options Under Stochastic Interest Rates", *Journal of International Money and Finance*, 1991, pp. 310–329.

Longstaff, Francis A., "A Nonlinear General Equilibrium Model of the Term Structure of Interest Rates", *Journal of Financial Economics*, 1989, pp. 195–224.

Longstaff, Francis A. and Eduardo S. Schwartz, "A Two Factor Interest Rate and Contingent Claims Valuation", *Journal of Fixed Income*, Vol. 2, No. 3, Dec. 1992, pp. 16–23.

Longstaff, Francis A. and Eduardo S. Schwartz, "Interest Rate Volatility and the Term Structure: A Two-Factor General Equilibrium Model", *Journal of Finance*, 1992, pp. 1259–1282.

Longstaff, Francis A. and Eduardo S. Schwartz, "A Simple Approach to Valuing Risky Fixed and Floating Rate Debt", *Journal of Finance* 50, 1995, pp. 789–820.

Lynch, Jr., John J and Jan H. Mayle, *Standard Securities Calculation Methods: Fixed Income Securities Formulas*, Securities Industry Association, New York, New York, 1986.

Macaulay, Frederick R., *Some Theoretical Problems Suggested by Movements of Interest Rates, Bond Yields, and Stock Prices in the United States since 1856*, New York, Columbia University Press, 1938.

Marcus, Alan J. and Israel Shaked, "The Valuation of FDIC Deposit Insurance Using Option-pricing Estimates", *Journal of Money, Credit, and Banking* 16, 1984, pp. 446–460.

Matten, Chris. *Managing Bank Capital: Capital Allocation and Performance Measurement*, Singapore, John Wiley & Sons, 1996.

McConnell, John J. and Manoj Singh, "Rational Prepayments and the Valuation of Collateralized Mortgage Obligations", *Journal of Finance* (July 1994), pp. 891–922.

McCulloch, J. Huston, "The Tax Adjusted Yield Curve", *Journal of Finance* 30, 1975, pp. 811–29.

Merton, Robert C., "An Intertemporal Capital Asset Pricing Model", *Econometrica* 41, September 1973, pp. 867–887.

Merton, Robert C., "Theory of Rational Option Pricing", *Bell Journal of Economics and Management Science* 4, 1973, pp. 141–183.

Merton, Robert C., "On the Pricing of Corporate Debt: The Risk Structure of Interest Rates", *Journal of Finance* 29, 1974, pp. 449–470.

Merton, Robert C., "An Analytic Derivation of the Cost of Deposit Insurance and Loan Guarantees: An Application of Modern Option Pricing Theory", *Journal of Banking and Finance*, 1977, pp. 3–11.

Merton, Robert C., "On the Cost of Deposit Insurance When There Are Surveillance Costs", *Journal of Business*, 1978, pp. 439–452.

Mitsubishi Finance Risk Directory 1990/1991, Researched and compiled by Risk Magazine, Ltd. London, 1990.

Modigliani, F. and M. H. Miller, "The Cost of Capital, Corporation Finance, and the Theory of Investment", *American Economic Review*, 1958, pp. 261–297.

Nielsen, L., J. Saa-Requejo and P. Santa-Clara, "Default Risk and Interest Rate Risk: The Term Structure of Default Spreads", Working Paper *INSEAD*, 1993.

O'Brien, James, Federal Reserve, non-maturity deposits, 2000.

Patruno, Gregg N., "Mortgage Prepayments: A New Model for a New Era", *Journal of Fixed Income*, December 1994, pp. 42–57.

Pearson, Neil D. and Tong-sheng Sun, "Exploiting the Conditional Density in Estimating the Term Structure: An Application to the Cox, Ingersoll and Ross Model", *Journal of Finance*,1994, pp. 1279–1304.

Pennacchi, George G., "Alternative Forms of Deposit Insurance: Pricing and Bank Incentive Issues", *Journal of Banking and Finance* 11, 1987a, pp. 291–312.

Pennacchi, George G., "A Reexamination of the Over- (or Under-) Pricing of Deposit Insurance", *Journal of Money, Credit and Banking* 19, 1987b, pp. 341–360.

Penter, P. M., *Splines and Variational Methods*, New York: John Wiley & Sons, 1989.

Quigley, J.M., "Interest Rate Variations, Mortgage Prepayments and Household Mobility", *The Review of Economics and Statistics*, LXIX November 1987, pp. 636–643.

Ramaswamy, K. and S. Sundaresan, "The Valuation of Floating Rate Instruments: Theory and Evidence", *Journal of Financial Economics* 1, December 1986, pp. 251–272.

Ranson, Brian J., *Credit Risk Management*, Sheshunoff Information Service, 2003.

Raynes, Sylvain and Ann Rutledge, *The Analysis of Structured Securities: Precise Analysis and Capital Allocation*, Oxford University Press, 2003.

Rendleman, R. and B. Bartter. "Two-State Option Pricing", *Journal of Finance*, December 1979, pp. 1093–1110.

Richard, S.F. and R. Roll, "Prepayments on Fixed-Rate Mortgage-Backed Securities", *Journal of Portfolio Management*, 15 Spring 1989, pp. 73–82.

RISK, "Easier Done than Said", *RISK*, October, 1992.

Schwartz, E. and W. Torous, "Prepayment and the Valuation of Mortgage-Backed Securities", *Journal of Finance* 44, June 1989, pp. 375–392.

Schwartz, H. R., *Numerical Methods: A Comprehensive Introduction*, 1989, (John Wiley & Sons, New York).

Selvaggio, Robert D., "Using the OAS Methodology to Value and Hedge Commercial Bank Retail Demand Deposit Premiums", in Fabozzi, F. and Konishi, A., editors, *Handbook of Asset and Liability Management*, revised edition, 1996.

Shea, Gary S., "Term Structure Estimation with Exponential Splines", *Journal of Finance* 40, 1985, pp. 319–325.

Shimko, David C., *Finance in Continuous Time: A Primer*, Kolb Publishing Company, Miami, 1992.

Shimko, David C., Naohiko Tejima, and Donald R. van Deventer, "The Pricing of Risky Debt when Interest Rates are Stochastic", *Journal of Fixed Income*, September, 1993, pp. 58 – 66.

Shumway, T., "Forecasting Bankruptcy More Accurately: A Simple Hazard Model", *Journal of Business*, volume 74, number 1, 2001.

Sobehart, J., S. Keenan and R. Stein, "Validation Methodologies for Default Risk Models", *Credit*, May 2000, pp. 51–56.

Standard & Poor's Corporation, Ratings Performance 2002: Default, Transition, Recovery and Spreads, 2002.

Stanton, Richard, "Rational Prepayments and the Valuation of Mortgage-Backed Securities", *Review of Financial Studies*, Fall 1995, pp. 677–708.

Stigum, Marcia, *Money Market Calculations,* Homewood, Illinois: Irwin, 1991.

Tavakoli, Janet M., *Collateralized Debt Obligations and Structured Finance: New Developments in Cash and Synthetic Securitization*, John Wiley & Sons, 2003.

Uyemura, Dennis and Donald R. van Deventer, *Financial Risk Management in Banking*, Chicago and Cambridge: Bankers Publishing Company, Probus Publishing Company, 1993.

van Deventer, Donald R., "The Valuation of Fixed and Floating Rate Mortgages", Kamakura Corporation research memorandum, December 1993.

van Deventer, Donald R. and Kenji Imai, *Financial Risk Analytics: A Term Structure Model Approach for Banking, Insurance, and Investment Management*, Chicago: McGraw Hill, 1996.

van Deventer, Donald R. and Kenji Imai, *Credit Risk Models and the Basel Accords*, Singapore: John Wiley & Sons, 2003.

van Deventer, Donald R. and Jaqueline Outram, "The New Capital Accord and Internal Bank Ratings", *Credit Ratings: Methodologies, Rationale and Default*, Michael K. Ong, editor, Risk Publications, 2002.

van Deventer, Donald R. and Xiaoming Wang, "Basel II and Lessons from Enron: The Consistency of the Merton Credit Model with Observable Credit Spreads and Equity Prices", Working Paper, Kamakura Corporation, 2002.

van Deventer, Donald R. and Xiaoming Wang, "Advanced Credit Model Performance Testing to Meet Basel Requirements", *The Basel Handbook: A Guide for Financial Practitioners*, Michael K. Ong, editor, Risk Publications, 2003.

van Deventer, Donald R. and Xiaoming Wang, "Measuring Predictive Capability of Credit Models Under the Basel Capital Accords: Conseco and Results from the United States, 1963–1998", Working Paper, Kamakura Corporation, 2003.

Vasicek, Oldrich A, "An Equilibrium Characterization of the Term Structure", *Journal of Financial Economics*, 1977, pp. 177–188.

Vasicek, Oldrich A. and H. Gifford Fong, "Term Structure Modeling Using Exponential Splines", *Journal of Finance* 37, 1982, pp. 339–56.

White, Alan D. and John Hull, "A Note on the Models of Hull and White for Pricing Options on the Term Structure: Response", *Journal of Fixed Income*, 1995, pp. 97–102.

Index